WOMEN'S LIVES

WOMEN'S LIVES

Kathleen J. Ferraro
Northern Arizona University

Boston   New York   San Francisco
Mexico City   Montreal   Toronto   London   Madrid   Munich   Paris
Hong Kong   Singapore   Tokyo   Cape Town   Sydney

Editor in Chief: *Karen Hanson*
Series Editorial Assistant: *Lauren Macey*
Marketing Manager: *Kelly May*
Production Supervisor: *Patty Bergin*
Manufacturing Buyer: *Debbie Rossi*
Electronic Composition: *Publishers' Design and Production Services, Inc.*
Photo Researcher: *Annie Pickert*
Cover Administrator: *Kristina Mose-Libon*

For related titles and support materials, visit our online catalog at www.ablongman.com.

Between the time website information is gathered and then published, it is not unusual for some sites to have closed. Also, the transcription of URLs can result in typographical errors. The publisher would appreciate notification where these errors occur so that they may be corrected in subsequent editions.

ISBN-13: 9780205404476
ISBN-10: 0205404472

Printed in the United States of America

10 9 8 7 6 5 4 3 2 1   HAM   11 10 09 08

Photo Credits: p. 344, Andy Kropa/Redux; p. 438, Stuart Ramson/AP Images

For Audrey Fae Zaun Ferraro

CONTENTS

PREFACE

Over the past twenty-five years that I have been teaching courses on women's lives, there have been dramatic changes in and outside of academic feminism. In the early eighties, we were excited to have our own Women's Studies programs, and classes and texts for these classes were just beginning to appear. Faculty and students were exuberant about the opportunity to focus their energies on "women" as a topic of scholarly investigation. The books and articles we used in classes were drawn from many disciplines, and there was a sense of excitement as each "malestream" canon was subjected to feminist scrutiny. Women across the spectrum of race, ethnicity, class, and sexuality have contributed to feminist scholarship from the earliest times, but in the enthusiasm of the early Women's Studies programs, the category "women" sometimes glossed over the important differences among us. Not all women's lives were incorporated sufficiently in early Women's Studies classes and the lives of privileged women were overrepresented and overgeneralized. It is a testament to the dedication and passion of Women's Studies scholars that we have struggled together to address this failure and transform curricula, research, analysis, and theory to grapple with the multiple dimensions of women's lives.

Today, Women's Studies programs are changing again to include gender in their titles and curriculum, or even to replace "women's" with "gender studies," and including masculinity as a central concern. These changes emphasize the *social processes* of developing gendered persons, institutions, and practices. This trend should not diminish the significance of the study of women's lives, but rather highlight the multidimensional complexity of our lives. This anthology focuses on women's lives within the contexts of this complexity.

I begin with an overview of the ongoing relevance of gender to people's experiences and describe the analytical perspectives that guide this book: social constructionism, intersectionality, anti-dualism, and globalization. Part One includes three pieces that elaborate the theoretical framework of these perspectives. The remaining ten parts address various aspects of women's lives, including girlhood and adolescence, economics and work, the body, violence, sexualities, mothering and the family, resistance and social change, culture and creativity, migration and globalization, and spirituality and religion. These divisions are somewhat arbitrary and overlapping as women's lives are not neatly bounded in topical categories. The contributions in each section include poetry, personal narratives, research reports, and theoretical analyses. All are written in a manner that is accessible and avoids academic jargon.

I have received patient and enthusiastic support in this project from my editors at Allyn and Bacon, Jeff Lasser, Karen Hanson, Lauren Houlihan, and Lauren Macey and from Heather Hawkins and Sarah Bylund in acquiring permissions. Holly A. Crawford provided careful copyediting. My students over the years have taught me much, alerted me to fascinating new work, and encouraged me to stay grounded in the real lives of women. I am particularly grateful to Cara Hughes and Lynnae Wenker, graduates of Northern Arizona University, for their assistance in identifying articles for this book. Many scholars, too numerous to mention, have contributed to my education on women's lives, and I am profoundly grateful for their work. My colleagues at Arizona State University and Northern Arizona University and members of the Society for the Study of Social Problems have nourished my love of feminist sociology and Women's Studies. I have also benefited from the wisdom of the activist women I have been honored to know.

Like all of my endeavors, this project has been enriched by the love and support of family and friends. I thank Kailey A. Johnson, Kyle L. Johnson, Peg Bortner, Lesley Hoyt Croft, and

Joseph Ferraro and Daniel Ferraro for all they have done for me. I am grateful to my partner, Neil Websdale, for being the perfect companion for learning about and enjoying life. Finally, my mother, Audrey Fae Zaun Ferraro, is the most influential woman in my life. This book is dedicated to her with the deepest love and admiration.

INTRODUCTION

Women in the United States appear to be breaking every gender barrier that had limited their participation in society. The proportion of women in the U.S. Congress is higher than ever before (16.1 percent in 2008), and women hold powerful positions of political authority. In 2008, Hillary Rodham Clinton was the first woman to win a major party's presidential primary for the purpose of delegate selection and fought a very tight race before conceding the nomination to Senator Barak Obama. Nancy Pelosi became the first woman Speaker of the House in 2007. Within the military, sports, and entertainment, women from all racial and ethnic backgrounds have won honors and broken records. Female scientists explore outer and inner space and the rapidly changing worlds of technology. Women have also been spotlighted for their participation in what once were considered exclusively male domains of villainy: torture, serial murder, and child sexual abuse. My students often suggest that men and women now share equally in the glory and the agony of human existence, as anyone can see from the headlines. Differences that remain, they argue, are the result of individual preferences rather than structured exclusions.

They certainly have a point. Many of the institutional barriers that restricted women's participation in society have dissolved under the united, sustained efforts of the women's liberation movement and the civil rights movement. Unlike past decades, women of all races in the United States can vote, hold political office, attend and teach at universities, become lawyers, doctors, politicians, and Supreme Court Justices, own property, serve on juries, sign contracts, and sue employers or public agencies that discriminate against them. Many women have taken advantage of these *formal rights* and are able to appreciate the multiple advantages that distinguish their lives from the more restricted lives of their foremothers.

Are my students correct, however, in arguing that gender is no longer a relevant factor in shaping people's lives in the United States? I argue that their views of a gender neutral reality overlook the micro- and macrolevel differences that continue to affect people's lives. In terms of the most basic issues in life—health, wealth, and happiness—gender still matters. This is not a simple argument, and it becomes more complex as the scholarship on women and gender expands. The complexity revolves around two major themes. First "women's lives" are shaped not only by gender but by the interplay of gender with other aspects of people's identities, particularly race, ethnicity, class, sexuality, and nation. Even while focusing on a single country, as this book does, it is impossible to examine the lives of women without considering the ways that their race, class, sexuality, and national origin intersect in the constitution of identities, experiences, and possibilities. Second, the category *women* is less stable than it was several decades ago. Today, people are aware that the sex/gender binary is a social construction that artificially separates people into social identities. Intersexuals, or people born with ambiguous sexual identities, as well as transgendered people, illustrate the fluidity of sexual identity. Where we once defined sex as biological or natural and gender as culturally constructed, we now realize that both terms depend on social and historical processes. *Women's lives*, thus, are complicated not only by the mutually constituting dimensions of identity but also by the ways that biologically based categories have been problematized. This shift in thinking is illustrated by the number of academic Women's Studies programs that have chosen to change their name to Gender Studies or to Women and Gender Studies (see http://research. umbc.edu/~korenman/wmst/programs.html for a list of women, gender and women, and gender studies programs compiled by Joan Korenman).

Gender Matters

It is therefore difficult to draw unambiguous conclusions about women's status in the world relative to men. However, it is quite clear that gender continues to influence people's access to wealth, status, and well-being at the national and global levels. Despite significant gains in rights and resources for large numbers of women, gender barriers remain that restrict the economic, educational, political, and cultural accomplishments of women as well as women's physical safety and well-being. As Margaret Anderson points out, "the persistently high rates of violence against women, the exclusionary practices directed against lesbians and gays, and the unjust impoverishment of millions of women and men remind us of the need for ongoing feminist thought and action anchored in the political-economic reality of inequality" (Anderson 2005: 452). At the same time, such an anchor allows us to explore the creative ways that women sustain and nourish themselves, their families, and their communities.

We may have reached the highest proportion of women in Congress in the history of the United States, but by the end of 2007 we ranked 71st in the world in terms of the proportion of women in the national legislature, below Afghanistan (27.7 percent), Iraq (25.5 percent), and the United Arab Emirates (22.5 percent), and below the world average of 17.7 percent (International Parliamentary Union 2008). Women remain a small fraction of what C. Wright Mills (1959: 28) called the "power elite," the "privileged stratum of the corporate rich," the "warlords, the corporation chieftains, the political directorate" (1959: 9) who are the decision makers of the society. And those women who manage to enter this stratum of power in the United States are nearly exclusively white and most often attached to men of power. Although there are almost no jobs that *legally* exclude women, the labor market in the United States is highly sex segregated, with both women and men concentrated in different occupations and industries. Occupational sex segregation accounts for much of the gender wage gap.

This gap has narrowed over the past fifty years, but even at the recent, all-time high of 77 percent of men's annual earnings, the lifetime consequences for women are stark. This statistic also disguises the ways that women's labor is underpaid relative to men's. According to a detailed analysis of gendered wages by Rose and Hartmann (2004: iii), "across the fifteen years of the study, the average prime age working woman earned only $273,592 while the average working man earned $722,693 (in 1999 dollars)." Nearly half a million dollar difference in wages over the most productive years of earning has serious consequences for wealth accumulation and long-term financial security. The proportion of women ages 18 to 64 in poverty hovers at 12.6 percent, compared to 9.6 for men; at ages 65 and over, however, 11.9 percent of women live in poverty compared to only 7 percent of men (U.S. Census Bureau 2000).

As mentioned above, these data cannot be grasped meaningfully without consideration of the impact of race, ethnicity, sexuality, nationality, immigration status, age, region, and physical ability. Of the 240 women who have served in the United States Congress, only 32 have been women of color and all but one (Carol Moseley Brown) have served in the House of Representatives (Center for American Women in Politics 2008). While the median annual earnings of white, non-Hispanic women were $28,265 in 1999, the median for Hispanic women was $21,634 (U.S. Census Bureau 2000). These abstract numbers convey some sense of the impact of race, ethnicity, and gender on women's experiences, but they cannot capture the multiple, overlapping ways in which people's everyday lives and consciousness reflect social locations defined by gender, race, ethnicity, class, and sexuality. The articles in this book offer detailed examinations of these influences across women's lives.

Historically, scholars sought to include the lives of women in the literary and scientific canon and to document the ways that sexism disadvantaged women. Although these goals are ongoing, today we also seek the unique ways that gender is

constructed and enacted in different locations as well as the ways that women resist unjust ideologies, practices, and institutions. We are interested in *how* gender influences people's lives and how women's experiences of gender vary across racial, ethnic, class, sexuality, and national locations as well as other factors, such as physical ability, age, region, religion, and immigration status.

Levels of Analysis

We can view women's lives from a variety of levels and perspectives. In this book, I have included articles that address the micro, symbolic, institutional, and social structural levels of analysis. At the microlevel, scholars examine interactional and individual meaning making. The microlevel is intimately connected to the symbolic and structural levels, but the focus is on the individual or the small group. For example, Deborah Eicher-Catt's piece on noncustodial mothering focuses on her personal experience as it is linked to cultural representations and expectations of "good mothering." Symbolic- and representational-level analyses consider how culture shapes and is shaped by women. Language and cultural representations of women provide the resources through which we understand ourselves and simultaneously challenge dominant views. DoVeanna Fulton's article on comediennes, for example, examines the "controlling images" of African American women and the ways that comediennes undermine these images through humor. Social structural analyses focus on the impact of macroforces, such as colonization, racial formation, and globalization in structuring the context of women's lives. For example, Andrea Smith situates violence against Native women within the context of colonization, genocide, and racism.

It is important to recognize all levels of analysis in understanding women's lives, as they are interconnected. Each woman faces the task of surviving, enjoying, and contributing to the world within the framework of individual, institutional, cultural, and structural influences.

The Analytical Perspectives that Guide This Book

Four analytical perspectives guided my selection of articles and are persistent themes woven throughout this book. First is the social constructionist perspective that views women's lives as a consequence of human actions rather than naturally occurring facts. Social constructionism does not *deny* biological factors, but considers the manner in which biology is given meaning in a particular context. A constructionist perspective also implies a critical rather than an absolutist stance on "normality." Human political and cultural interventions determine what is normal or good in any given social situation. Social constructionists examine and critique these interventions, rather than search for the most effective ways to implement them. So, for example, Elisabeth Sheff's analysis of polyamory is not a condemnation of sexual practices that fall outside the norm, but an exploration of monogamy and polyamory and their meanings for women. While this, and other articles included here, may contrast with some students' strongly held beliefs, the purpose of constructionist work is to analyze social meanings and build understanding and empathy for alternative points of view.

Intersectionality is the second analytical perspective guiding this book. Intersectionality means the simultaneous influence of race, class, ethnicity, gender, sexuality, and nation on people's experiences and identities and the analytical examination of this influence. This is not a matter of adding each "ism" to produce a "multicultural" whole. Intersectional analyses are based on an understanding of how power is structured and how it works in the world. There is a danger in viewing "women's lives" as individualistic examples of a range of possibilities. This view hides the ways that women's choices are shaped by forces beyond individual intentions. Intersectionality encourages us to understand the ways that women's lives are connected to what Patricia Hill Collins (2000) calls the "matrix of domination": multiple, interlocking forms of domination. From this perspective, our lives are not simply "choices" or performances, but are a struggle between social structures and human agency.

Constructionist and intersectional approaches to gender imply a third guiding analytical perspective, anti-dualism. Anti-dualism is the view that all social categories, including gender, are permeable and flexible. These categories help us to think about social experiences, but if they are portrayed in a rigid manner, without consideration of variation and change, they ultimately limit our capacity to understand. For example, the dualistic approach to masculinity and femininity disguises the many ways that men and women overlap in their behaviors and also how their gendered behaviors change over the life course. People who adhere to rigid dualisms often endorse an essentialist or naturalist view of gender; that is, dualisms contribute to the belief that women and men are naturally and inalterably different in fundamental ways. Many of the articles contained in this book emphasize the limitations of dualistic or binary categories for understanding women's lives.

Finally, I consider the influence of globalization on all aspects of women's lives. Globalization includes changing patterns of migration, labor, and communication. As Saskia Sassen (2002) explains, globalization has opened new possibilities for women in both highly skilled professional jobs and in marginalized, low-skilled, low-waged work. At the same time, globalization has deepened social inequalities and resulted in new forms of exploitation. Women in wealthy countries (often referred to as the First World) depend on the services of women migrating from impoverished countries (the Third World) to support domestic households and the consumption practices of professional workers. Globalization has also produced new "survival circuits" that illegally traffic women into the global sex industry. The demands of globalization are shifting traditional notions of gender and exacerbating the divide between privileged and marginalized women.

No single anthology can reflect adequately the breadth of the current scholarship on women's lives. In selecting work for this book, I was forced to exclude much critical, exciting work and to abbreviate the articles I included. Readers will surely find omissions on topics they find essential. I chose topics that I and my students have pursued and found of interest and sought to represent a diverse range of women's experiences in each arena. I also chose work that makes explicit links to the larger body of theoretical and empirical work on gender without the use of jargon that would hinder their accessibility to beginning students. The articles are theoretically informed but not theoretically obscure. They are a point of entry into a wealth of scholarship. I hope they arouse your curiosity and stimulate you to pursue this wealth as well as to develop your own contributions.

References

Anderson, Margaret. (2005). "Thinking About Women: A Quarter Century's View." *Gender and Society* 19(4): 437–455.

Center for American Women in Politics. (2008). "Women in the U.S. Congress 2008." National Information Bank on Women in Public Office, Eagleton Institute of Politics. Rutgers. Retrieved from http://www.cawp.rutgers.edu/Facts/Officeholders/cong.pdf March 21, 2008.

Collins, Patricia Hill. (2000). *Black Feminist Thought: Knowledge, Consciousness and the Politics of Empowerment*. 2nd ed. London: Routledge.

International Parliamentary Union. (2008). *Women in National Parliaments*. Retrieved from http://www.ipu.org/wmn-e/classif.htm. March 21, 2008.

Mills, C. Wright. (1959). *The Power Elite*. New York: Oxford University Press.

Rose, Steven J., & Heidi I. Hartmann. (2004). *Still a Man's Labor Market: The Long-Term Earnings Gap*. Washington, DC: Institute for Women's Policy Research.

Sassen, Saskia. (2002). "Global Cities and Survival Circuits." Pp. 254–274 in Barbara Ehrenreich and Arlie Russell Hochschild, eds., *Global Woman*. New York: Henry Holt & Co.

U.S. Census Bureau. (2000). *We the People: Women and Men in the United States*. Washington, DC: U.S. Census Bureau.

PART ONE

Perspectives on Women's Lives

Feminist theorizing about women's lives helps us to understand and to work toward progressive social change. Theory may seem distant from women's everyday experiences and from the urgent challenges we face. Yet theory provides tools for making sense of experience and for developing "oppositional consciousness," or a critical stance toward dominant forms of knowledge. For this section, I have chosen three pieces that are historically informed and linked to social movements. The authors articulate theoretical issues without relying on obtuse language.

Margaret Anderson, Patricia Hill Collins, and Cynthia Fuchs Epstein argue for the importance of intersectionality and against an essentialist, unitary notion of "women." Anderson clearly explains the difference between an "additive" model of difference and an intersectional model. The additive model is found in popular discourses about multiculturalism, diversity, and women's "voice." Intersectionality is not just about "including everyone" or only about gender "performance," perspectives that minimize the structural dimensions of difference. When diversity is reduced to a presentation of a plurality of individual voices, we lose sight of the specific historical and social circumstances through which experience is constituted. Most important, the operations of power are absent from the additive model of differences. As Anderson notes, "analyzing race, class, and gender must be about the hierarchies and systems of domination that permeate society" (2005: 446). Anderson also argues that not all aspects of difference can or should be treated analogously. Her emphasis on the political economy of difference, that is, the way that difference is used to structure social relations, leads her to conclude that while sexuality is a vector of power relations, it does not share the same political trajectory as race, class, and gender. Heterosexism has been a powerful influence on social relationships in the United States, and those who deviate from the heterosexual norm are still stigmatized and disadvantaged politically. Yet Anderson notes "discrimination based on sexual orientation is not the same thing as the wholesale, state-legitimated appropriation of group labor [and I would add land and natural resources] that has lain at the heart of race and class—as well as gender—relations throughout history." This is not a question of creating a hierarchy of oppressions, but of elaborating the political economy of difference.

Patricia Hill Collins illustrates the salience of race in "Learning from the Outsider Within," an article that was incorporated in her canonical book, *Black Feminist Thought*. The marginal position held by Black women affords them a unique angle of vision that challenges social and economic injustice. As "outsiders-within," the experiences of Black women have been the source of creative theoretical contributions that challenge both the *substance* and the *form* of intellectual thought. Collins elaborates three key themes in Black feminist thought: the importance of self-definition and self-valuation, the interlocking nature of oppression, and the importance of Black women's culture. Excluded from the ivory towers until very recently, Black women found alternative forms to express their intellectual contributions, such as music and poetry. The poetry of June Jordan and the music of Bessie Smith are included in this volume and exemplify the power of these alternatives. June Jordan, in particular, embodied the both/and position of a scholar and activist. She taught English and African American Studies at top universities, published 28 books of poetry and numerous essays in the progressive press, and participated in movements for racial and sexual freedom and for peace. Black women's culture, like other oppositional cultures, both reflects and helps create positive self-valuations, consciousness of oppression, and activism.

Cynthia Fuchs Epstein, in an excerpt from her 2006 presidential address to the American Sociological Association, argues that the global subordination of women to men is "the most fundamental social divide" (p. 1). She illustrates her argument with examples from throughout the world that demonstrate the continuing pattern of women's denigration and segregation. One way that this pattern is perpetuated is through the "naturalization of differences" between men and women, the belief that gender differences are innate and inevitable. This belief is contradicted by the large body of scientific evidence demonstrating the similarity of the sexes on most dimensions. Epstein's own concept of "deceptive distinctions" describes the ways that commonsense notions of gender difference ignore the *experiential* bases of most differences. She explains the persistence of women's inferior status through social mechanisms that define women as "other" to men— through kin structures, symbolic attributions of honor, clothing, time, and space. Cultural ideologies justify women's subordination on the basis of the supposed inherent gender differences and a naturalized gender hierarchy that benefits men as a group. Despite its ubiquity, Epstein emphasizes the human construction of this hierarchy and the possibilities for social change that would benefit both women and men and whole societies.

All three theorists draw our attention to the historically shifting, permeable boundaries defining gender, race, class, and sexuality. And all three insist that we attend to the material, political realities that shape people's experiences, knowledge, and social activism.

Margaret L. Andersen

Thinking about Women:
A Quarter Century's View

Early Themes: A Retrospective View

Looking back on the early themes that guided the development of the sociology of sex and gender helps us to identify lingering issues and new points for debate and questioning. By situating the field in its intellectual, social, and political history, we can understand not only how the field has developed but how it has been influenced by the context of the questions asked. Because early studies were centered on identifying the consequences of excluding women from the knowledge of the field and because the impetus at the time was to show the impact of sexism, early feminist scholarship tended to emphasize the victimization of women while also criticizing the dominant frameworks of the disciplines. Putting women into social analysis was the central concern.

In sociology, and the social sciences more generally, a major theme was to emphasize the social basis of gender roles, thus debunking the prevailing biologically determinist explanations of sex differences. And as has been well documented, in the beginning, the "sex roles" paradigm dominated most social science research (Lopata and Thorne 1978). Later, gender was conceptualized as accomplished activity, as found in the framework of "doing gender," (West and Fenstermaker 1995; West and Zimmerman 1987), as an institution (Acker 1992; Lorber 1994; Martin 2004), and as an axis of stratification (Ander-

sen and Collins 2004). I do not mean to present these different ways of conceptualizing gender as if they are phases, progressing through some theoretical hierarchy with some being more sophisticated than others. But these ideas stem from the early understanding of gender in social–cultural, not biological, terms. As a result, feminist scholars early emphasized the distinction in sex and gender, as if the line between them was clear, neat, and firm. The objective of this distinction was to focus on the social dimensions of gender. Now we have come full circle, with many pointing out that even biological differences can be interpreted as social constructions (Fausto-Sterling 1992, 2000; Lorber 1993).

A second theme pervading the early literature was contesting the presumed inevitability of institutional forms. In sociology, this theme is especially apparent in the early criticism of functionalist interpretations of the family. Feminist scholars challenged the idea, embedded in functionalism, that expressive and instrumental roles in the family were necessarily divided along lines of gender. In doing so, feminist scholars disputed the idea that some family forms were more natural than others, again asserting the fundamentally social character of major institutions—institutions that could be changed.

Third, feminist scholarship was anchored in an idea that was profound at the time—that is, to take women's lives seriously. Valuing women's lives meant that women's culture could be celebrated and studied, such as in Jessie Bernard's *The Female World* (1981). In the humanities, this meant including women's contributions to the arts and literature, but in the social sciences as

Source: Margaret L. Andersen, *Gender & Society*, Vol. 19, No. 4, August, 2005, 437–455. © 2005 by SAGE Publications. Used by permission of SAGE Publications, Inc.

well, women's lives could be studied on their own terms. Perhaps in the current context it is difficult to imagine the ridicule and sometimes contempt with which the study of women was perceived by so many in the academy and thus the need to insist that women's lives be taken seriously.

At the time, feminist studies emerged from a deep connection to the women's movement. There were different entry points for different people. For some, including me, the struggle for women's reproductive rights brought us into feminism—in a context where abortion was a criminal act and birth control was illegal for women who were not married. The path for many was through the Civil Rights Movement and activism in the New Left—thus bringing questions of race and class into feminist studies. For others, it was engagement in class-based movements, including welfare rights for poor women (an often forgotten origin of feminism). Others developed their feminism in the context of professional careers and concerns about pay equity and equal access to professional settings. Jessie Bernard, for example, demonstrated at the annual meetings of the American Sociological Association for the simple right of women to sit in the hotel bar unaccompanied by a man, and Supreme Court Justice Ruth Bader has talked about being denied access to the law library at Harvard. Perhaps for younger generations, these overt forms of discrimination are hard to imagine, but they explain why so much of the early empirical literature focused on documenting the consequences of sexism.

Because so much early academic work was based on criticism of the disciplines, feminists were asking where women fit in the dominant frameworks of different disciplinary concepts and theories. For example, inspired by the socialist feminist movement, much early feminist theory dissected women's place in the class system, trying to understand the relationship between systems of production and reproduction (Firestone 1970; Mitchell 1971). Although long ignored by Marxist theory, the centrality of gender to sys-

tems of production was a major point for early feminist theory. Feminists, especially radical feminists, also dissected the dynamics of patriarchy as a social force in its own right. Early feminists analyzed how the power of men operates—especially with regard to violence against women and control of women's sexuality—in both the public and private spheres.

The early themes guiding feminist scholarship can be summed up as conceptualizing gender in social, not biological, terms; documenting and analyzing the status of women in different social institutions; situating women's lives in the context of other forms of inequality; and asking how women resist, such as through social movements or everyday acts of rebellion (Townsend Gilkes 1980).

Persistent Themes/New Questions

In reviewing where we have been, we can see the persistent issues and current questions for feminist theory/gender studies. Although surely there are more, here I focus on three: the relationship between structure and agency; conceptualizing difference and the relationship among race, class, and gender; and theorizing sexuality, especially with regard to its intertwined relationship with race, class, and gender.

The Dialectic of Structure and Agency

Whereas early on, gender was conceptualized as a social role, there is now a more complex understanding of gender as a social reality. What is gender? There is no single answer to this question. Some posit gender as an institution, others as performance, others as structure (Acker 1992; Martin 2004; Risman 2004; West and Fenstermaker 1995; West and Zimmerman 1987). This question involves the relationship between structure and agency, and between structure and culture. Note that each of these concepts of gender—as role, as performance, as institution—tries to include the dynamic and active construction of gender that is captured by a focus on human agency. At the same time, each tries to understand the persistence of gender as a social form (and thus, the focus on structure). For example, the doing gender perspective has emphasized process and emergence, reflected in the language of gerunds that usually accompanies this literature, such as in Patricia Yancey Martin's (2003) article " 'Said and Done' versus 'Saying and Doing,' " West and Zimmerman's (1987) original formulation of the idea of "doing gender," and West and Fenstermaker's (1995) conceptualization of "doing difference."

Acker (1992) initially conceptualized institutions as gendered, and now Martin, Lorber, and others see gender itself as an institution. This new perspective has most recently been taken up by Risman (2004) in her analysis of gender as structure. She developed a conceptual framework to capture both the constraints on people's lives posed by structures that exist beyond individuals and people's internal consciousness that enables them to challenge and change gender structures. In reading her article, I am reminded of Peter Berger's (1963) earlier sexist formulation that man (*sic*) is in society and society is in man (*sic*). Now, although Risman did not state it as such, the analysis of gender as structure posits that women are in society and society is in women. Risman, like Acker, Martin, and others, tried to link the dynamic and fluid character of gender with its social structural realities. At the same time, she tried to "elevate gender to the same analytical plane as politics and economics" (2004, 431)—in other words, to make gender a social structure in its own right.

From the beginning, even within the sex roles framework, feminist scholars have recognized the fundamentally social character of gender. The newer social constructionist approach not only sees gender as socially created but interprets gender itself as constructing other forms of social relations.

Gender scholars can learn here from the scholarship on race—in particular racial formation theory (Omi and Winant 1994). Racial formation theory emphasizes the social construction of racial categories but places them squarely within the context of the political economy—namely, the role of the state in creating, defining, sustaining, and defending racial categories and the relationship of state policies and practices to the economic exploitation of racial/ethnic groups. Perhaps because gender is still frequently seen as stemming from allegedly fixed biological statuses, it is harder to see gender formation vis-à-vis anything other than families. But in tying gender mostly to the family as a social location, we may have missed ways that it is also constructed via state policy—something now becoming more clear in arguments over same sex marriage. Arguments opposing gay marriage construct traditional notions of gender vis-à-vis sexual relations, revealing a dialectical relationship between the social construction of sex and the social construction of gender—a relationship that needs additional feminist research and theorizing.

Contemporary thinking on the connection between structure and agency is strongly influenced by postmodernism and poststructuralism and, within sociology, the doing gender perspective. One of the greatest contributions of the doing gender perspective and postmodernist theory more generally is the return of human agency to gender theory. Barrie Thorne suggested that this work stems from the earlier dramaturgical metaphor in sociology but works better than the dramaturgical model because the reified noun "role" in dramaturgical analysis shifts to performance. But, she goes on to argue, "gender is more than performance and it will take much more than doing drag and mocking naturalized conceptions to transform it" (1995, 499).

The emphasis on agency also comes from trying to resist seeing women solely in terms of victimization, recognizing instead how oppressed groups have fought against oppression. Although it is important to understand how groups have resisted oppression, the emphasis on agency, such as in the doing gender perspective, tends to overstate the degree to which some people are able to resist in some structural contexts. Think of women in fundamentalist, religious cultures—not just of fundamentalist Islam, the Taliban, and Iraq, but also the Christian religious Right in the United States.

This shows the importance of including both agency and social structure in feminist analyses of gender. Without this balance, the emphasis on agency in contemporary feminist scholarship underestimates the role of power in shaping social relations. This error discounts the significance of class and race (along with other social structural forms of inequality) in shaping the experiences of different groups of women. Kennelly (2004) has recently suggested that we can integrate a focus on agency and structures of power by noting, as Foucault (2000) did, that power is exercised, not located. Analyzing power—individual, state based, and market based—is thus critical to linking structure and agency. The questions to ask in doing so are, Who exercises power? How? Under what conditions? With what effect?

In some regards, contemporary feminist theory has veered away from analyzing structures of power—sometimes because of not wanting to forget the role of individual action, internal consciousness, and the fluidity of social life, as Risman (2004) pointed out. But in emphasizing these more agentic forms of social relations, might we be forgetting what people *do to* women? The resistance to including power structures in feminist thought likely stems from the tenacity of the American belief in individualism, even among feminists. This omission may also stem from the tendency to think only within the framework of Western culture and from the position of relative privilege held by most academic feminists.

In sum, structure and agency need not be posited in opposition to each other, as is well articulated by Nancy Fraser in her recent interview with Nancy Naples (Fraser and Naples 2004). Feminist theory and research should not underestimate the constraints and power relationships that social structures generate, especially against those with the least power to negotiate their way through these structures, namely, those most oppressed by class and race and sexuality and gen-der. This leads to the second major theme in contemporary feminist scholarship: the intersectionality of gender, race, and class. These studies make clear that analyses of power, structure, and agency are central to feminist theorizing.

Race/Class/Gender: Questions of Interrelationship

Throughout the early years of the women's movement, women of color were explicitly critical of the white women's movement—a criticism that emerged into a new race/class/gender paradigm. The feminist analysis of race, class, and gender differs from traditional studies of social stratification in several regards. The first is that it is grounded in the feminist movement. Second, whereas traditional stratification studies look mostly at social class, the new paradigm of race, class, and gender sees all three simultaneously and as overlapping and intersecting—that is, as a matrix of domination (Collins 1990). Third, the new race/class/gender paradigm tends to be more interdisciplinary, stemming as it does from the full range of women's experiences and the influence of critical race studies in various disciplines. Fourth, different from stratification research, the race/class/gender paradigm begins from thinking about and learning from the experience of women of color. And finally, this new paradigm emphasized the significance of social location in framing consciousness (Andersen 1993).

In the early days, numerous scholars were thinking about the connections between and among race, class, and gender, many of whom were influenced by the Center for Research on Women at Memphis State. This work took seriously the fact that exclusionary thinking and generalizing from white women's lives results in theoretical and empirical errors. Furthermore, the race/class/gender paradigm posits that gender is manifested differently in its relationship to race, class, and sexuality. As Maxine Baca Zinn and Bonnie Thornton Dill (1996) have written, multiracial feminism emphasizes the relational and socially constructed character of gender. Gender is constructed differently in different social locations because of its relational character. But race/class/gender studies also conceptualize all three as realms of power and exploitation. Thus, gender can never be studied in isolation from race and class and related social conditions. . . .

Race, class, and gender are based on the appropriation of labor and the restriction of rights of citizenship—a point explored later in this article. Moreover, the race/class/gender paradigm does not necessarily exclude other points of social location (such as age, sexuality, nation, and region). The race/class/gender paradigm does argue for a multiple lens through which we view all women—and men, too, for that matter. Seeking metaphors to explain this complexity, Thorne has concluded that "to grasp complex relations among gender, race, class, and sexuality, we need a range of metaphors and theories honed in many sites of analysis" (1995, 499). . . .

To interrelate race, class, and gender, they should be analyzed in the context of structural changes in the world: globalization, massive redistribution of capital and wealth, growing inequality, the persistence of the color line, joblessness, homelessness, and retrenchment from the Right on all forms of feminist issues. These social structural changes have huge consequences for women depending on where they are situated—situations that are very much shaped by the social structures of race and class and gender.

This mode of thinking is not just about including everyone in our thinking nor about how we perform gender, but it is fundamentally about systems of power and domination and, to use Nancy Fraser's term, the politics of redistribution. Race, class, and gender, as Kennelly argued, are mutually constituted—that is, each influences the others. It is helpful here to distinguish two ways of thinking about the relationship between race, class, and gender: the additive model of difference and the model of interlocking forms of experience (Andersen and Collins 2004) or, as Patricia Hill Collins called it, the matrix of domination.

First, race, class, and gender are not just about diversity—as if understanding race, class, and gender is solely about a plurality of views and

experiences. This viewpoint stems from personifying voices as if people's lives were somehow detached from specific social and historical conditions. We need to overcome the silencing of various groups, but that is not enough for sociological analysis. Analyzing race, class, and gender, as Collins and I wrote, "requires analysis of existing systems of power and privilege; otherwise, understanding diversity becomes just one more privilege for those with the greatest access to education—something that has always been a mark of the elite class" (Andersen and Collins 2004, 4). In other words, analyzing race, class, and gender must be about the hierarchies and systems of domination that permeate society. This does not mean that how people act and think is unimportant. Nor does it ignore the resistance that people have put up against such systems. But it is a matter of structural and relationship thinking versus comparative and additive thinking.

Thinking comparatively centers on what can be called the analogy of "isms"—that race is like sexuality and that sexuality is like class and that homophobia is just like racism and sexism and so forth. As we will see, although such thinking reveals similar processes in all forms of oppressive social relations, making race and class and gender and other forms of oppression analogous is misleading. Thinking relationally helps you see the social structures that generate both unique group histories and the processes that link them, as well as the processes specific to the social experiences of different groups. But if you begin with a difference or additive model and just add other forms of oppression to race, class, and gender, you suggest that the analysis of one can substitute for the others—as if oppressions were equivalent or the same. As Collins and I wrote, "Ironically, this form of recognizing differences can erase the workings of power" (Andersen and Collins 2004, 5).

This error is most often made when gender scholars are thinking about gender alone—even when they add in race and class.[1] Centering more gender theorizing in scholarship on race better reveals the role of human agency in supporting and challenging these hierarchies. Evelyn Nakano Glenn (2002) articulated this in her book *Unequal Freedom*. She argued that "especially needed is a theory that neither subordinates race and gender to some broader (and presumably more primary) set of relations such as class, nor substantially flattens the complexity of these concepts" (2002, 7). In Glenn's analysis, racial, class, and gender stratification are fundamentally about labor and citizenship, as experienced in three distinct, though overlapping, realms:

1. the micro realm of interaction where norms, etiquette, and "spatial rules" orchestrate interaction (both within and across race, class, and gender boundaries);
2. the realm of representation where symbols, language, and images produce and express race/gender/class meanings; and
3. the social structural realm where power and resources are allocated along race, class, and gender lines.

Glenn's (2002) analysis puts gender and its relationship to race and class in a complex web of social relations. She clearly sees race and class and gender as relational, stating that a material analysis alone is insufficient to grasp the complexity of these social systems, none being subsumed by any others. In other words, class is not primary, and race is not derived from it. Nor is gender the primary structure—a point also argued by Kennelly (2004). To understand the interlocking relationships among race, class, and gender means incorporating an analysis of power (including state power), labor, material domination, and the formation and expression of consciousness. Such an analysis has both a material and an ideational basis. And as I will argue in the final section of this article, rather than just adding sexuality into such analyses, we need to develop an understanding of how sexuality intersects with race, class, and gender and in ways that go beyond argument by analogy or addition.

In this regard, Risman's recent argument that the "historical and current mechanisms that sup-

port gender inequality may or may not be those that are most significant for other kinds of oppression" (2004, 443) is suggestive. Race, class, gender—and sex—all have particular material, ideological, and historical specificities, and as Risman argued, "Gender must be understood within the context of the intersecting domains of inequality" (2004, 442). But Risman is wrong when she says we do not need to study them simultaneously. She wrote, "Gender research and theory can never again ignore how women's subordination differs within racial and ethnic communities or is constructed within class dynamics. Yet we should not therefore only study gender, race, and class simultaneously. . . . To focus all investigations into the complexity or subjective experience of interlocking oppressions would have us lose access to how the mechanisms for different kinds of inequality are produced" (2004, 443).

Each may have its own dynamics, but Risman stumbles in seeing race, class, and gender as "different categorical divisions" (2004, 443), overlooking that each is manifested differently in relationship to the others. For example, feminists have understood that sexuality is constructed by gender, but it is also true that gender is also constructed via sexuality. We can see this, for example, in the way that young girls construct their gender identity vis-à-vis their sexual identity, especially as encouraged by the commercial interests of the fashion, music, and popular culture industries. (Observe that thongs are marketed to very young girls!) In other words, unlike what Risman argues, gender and sexuality are not necessarily different categorical divisions; rather, they exist in a dialectical relationship, just as race and class and gender and sexuality are mutually constituted, overlapping, intersecting, and dialectically interrelated social relations. Even when studying one such form of social relations, unidimensional ways of thinking risk the error of false generalization about which early race/class/gender thinkers warned and misinterpret how each form of social relations emerges in relationship to the others.

To study the interrelationships of race, class, and gender need not mean that one is more fundamental than the others. Indeed, the whole logic of intersectional studies is that race, gender, and class are relational and reinforcing—and in emergent ways. This is what Collins and I mean by conceptualizing race, class, and gender as axes of society; it is, I think, also what Risman means in saying that all are equally fundamental. This brings us to the question of sexuality.

Sexuality

What are the implications of such an analysis for the study of sexuality and its relationship to race, class, and gender? To date the dominant framework for theorizing the relationship of sexuality to race, class, and gender has been to conceptualize sexuality as equivalent in its workings to race, class, and gender—in other words, an additive, not truly intersectional, model. Although this is a good starting point, it is not the most fruitful theoretical path to take. First, I want to be very clear about my arguments about sexuality for several reasons:

1. The question of sexuality and sexual oppression must be taken seriously as an essential form of social relations;
2. Sexuality is a system of power and privilege with serious and often damaging consequences resulting from homophobia and sexually exclusionary practices and policies; and
3. The evolving literature on sexuality is one of the most interesting and expanding fields of scholarship—one in which people, both men and women, take enormous risks for even discussing the topic.

As a form of oppression, sexuality operates in multiple ways, in multiple social sites, and with multiple consequences for all groups. Arguing that sexuality is not the same as race, class, and gender is not about ranking oppressions. And heterosexism cannot be reduced to being solely a derivative of gender. One of the major points here is that arguing by analogy (that is, that sexuality is like race,

is like gender, is like class) is not helpful to theorizing sexuality, nor theorizing about the relationship of sexuality to race, gender, and class.

The idea that sexuality is equivalent to race, class, and gender stems from thinking only in terms of a model of difference or addition, not by thinking in terms of a matrix of domination. It is not that such arguments are totally wrong; they are just incomplete. In addition, arguments making sexuality equivalent to race, class, and gender have tended to focus mostly on questions of identity and not on questions of the structural political economy, including the political economy of sexuality and its relationship to the political economies of race, gender, and class.

Conceptualizing sexuality as equivalent in its workings to race, class, and gender is well exemplified in Rosenblum and Travis's argument that "similar processes are at work when we 'see' differences of color, gender, class, and sexual orientation. The impacts of these statuses on people's lives also have important commonalities. Indeed, we will suggest that the same processes occur in the operation of other master statuses, such as disability" (2000, 2). Rosenblum and Travis proceeded to describe the parallel processes by which groups are named, labeled, and categorized because of their group status. Their work contributes much to thinking about sexuality. Specifically, they noted the importance of conceptualizing sex and disability as socially constructed, not in essentialist terms—just as we have moved from analyzing race, class, and gender in socially constructed, not essentialist, terms. Rosenblum and Travis showed other parallels in how heterosexism aggregates and dichotomizes social groups as gay/straight, just as other forms of oppression create other binary categories: Black/white, abled/disabled, male/female, and so forth. And Rosenblum and Travis pointed out that all such groups carry stigma based on their master status.

In these regards, there are significant and important parallels in how race, class, gender, sexuality, and disability (among other factors) construct identity and group experience. There are numerous other parallels we can see in how we study sexuality and race, class, and gender. The analysis of sexuality, like gender and race, has moved from a biological to a cultural framework. As with gender, sexuality is no longer theorized as natural and private. As shown in much contemporary research, sexuality, like gender, is a socially constructed identity, not one fixed by nature. Stein and Plummer (1994) attributed these changes in conceptualizing sexuality to the influence of the gay and lesbian and feminist movements, just as conceptualizing gender as a social construction flows from the women's movement. Stein and Plummer also pointed out that early sexologists were mostly concerned with classifying the etiology of homosexuality and were generally unreflective about sexuality as a social category. Such early studies thus replicated social divisions, just as early analyses of sex roles may have inadvertently emphasized gender differences and divisions, not sameness and fluidity.

The sociology of sexuality now conceptualizes sexuality as a terrain of power. Thus, we can see many parallels in studying sexuality and studying race and class and gender, but parallels do not make good theory. It is telling in Rosenblum and Travis's (2000) book that in their brief section on economy (only three articles), there is nothing on sexuality.

Many have argued for bringing the study of sexuality into the study of race, class, and gender. My purpose is not to criticize those who have been working in this field but to argue that just as we cannot add gender to the study of race or race to the study of gender or gender to the study of class, so we cannot just add sex to the study of race, class, and gender. Scholars on sexuality are all arguing that sexuality, like race, class, and gender, is an axis of social structure, but most of the work connecting race, gender, class, and sexuality deals only in the realm of ideology and representation. This work has shown how sexuality is used to support systems of racial, class, and gender privilege but does not go so far as to explicate

a political economy of sexuality and its connection to the political economy of race, class, and gender.

For instance, Lynn Weber wrote, "Race, class, gender, and sexuality are historically and geographically specific, socially constructed *systems of oppression*—they are *power relationships*" (2001, 9). She went on to say that these are not different lifestyle preferences, cultural beliefs, values, or practices: "They are power hierarchies where one group exerts control over another, securing its position of dominance in the system, and where substantial material resources . . . are at stake. . . . They are not completely independent but rather are interdependent, mutually reinforcing systems" (2001, 91). Cornel West (1993), too, analyzed how sexuality is a vehicle for supporting racial fears and racial subordination. Joane Nagel (2003) has developed a fascinating account of the ideological connections between race, ethnicity, and sexuality. Patricia Hill Collins's (2004) book *Black Sexual Politics* also adds new thinking to feminist analyses of sexuality by framing sexuality within the global and local politics of capitalism and race, gender, and homophobia. Her integration of how sexuality is commodified within popular culture is also a strong analysis of the political economy of sexuality in contemporary everyday life. . . .

One of the major differences between sexuality and relations of race, class, and gender is that sexuality has not been used as an explicit category to organize the division of labor, as have race, class, and gender. No doubt, sexuality has been a key part of the gender division of labor in the form of heterosexual households—a family structure that has historically supported and been an integral part of the system of production. Now, however, the economy seems to be able to accommodate diverse household forms, so long as workers are produced (or discarded). Heterosexual, married couples and families also have an economic advantage over other household forms (at least as best we can tell from median income data), and they enjoy numerous rights and privileges that are systematically denied gay and lesbian couples. But the appropriation and exploitation of racial/ethnic and gender labor makes race, class, and gender fundamentally different in their operation than sexuality. Although it is certainly true that discrimination is a fact in the experience of lesbian and gay workers, discrimination based on sexual orientation is not the same thing as the wholesale, state-legitimated appropriation of group labor that has lain at the heart of race and class—as well as gender—relations throughout history.

As Barbara Smith (in Gluckman and Reed 1997) argued, the nation was not founded on homophobia, but it was founded on racial stratification. This history really matters—not because sexual oppression is historically insignificant but because, as Glenn (2002) reminded us, the use of racial/ethnic groups as forced labor, cheap labor, and now labor segregated in certain segments of the workforce is deeply linked to concepts of citizenship.

Of course, issues of citizenship are a part of oppression by sexual orientation. Sexual categories are created and buttressed in law—what we might think of as sexual formation theory. Indeed, Ballard pointed out that to date there has been "no attempt as yet to tease out the implications of state action for the construction of sexuality" (1992, 103), as there has been in racial formation. Current arguments now over gay marriage would be a good place to develop such an analysis, especially as related to arguments against interracial marriage. Certainly, basic rights of citizenship have been and are denied to gays and lesbians, although to my knowledge, sexuality has never been formally used to deny sexual groups the right to vote, nor has it been used in the formal and legal definition of personhood as is historically true of African Americans and other groups. Gays and lesbians have never been formally segregated in the labor market nor denied citizenship because of the labor they provide. Gays and les-

bians, like heterosexuals, are distributed throughout the entire class structure (as best as we can tell), but as Nancy Fraser wrote, they "occupy no distributive position in the division of labor, and do not constitute an exploited class" (1997, 18). Thus, there is a political economy of sex, but it does not operate the same way as the political economy of race nor as the political economy of gender, although sexuality is clearly related to these forms of political economy through the form of heterosexual households.

Looking at sexuality through a lens of political economy also reveals other questions that have interesting race, class, and gender connections. As Seidman (2003) noted, corporate capitalism has turned sexuality into a commodity—and we should add, it does so through the dialectic of gender and sex. For instance, gays and lesbians are now perceived by corporate interests as the new consumers, thus changing some of the representations of gays and lesbians in the media and revealing how the representation of sexuality is shaped by economic relations.

The tendency in current scholarship to conceptualize sexuality primarily as an identity category obfuscates the political economy of sexuality and makes it easier to think of sexuality as like race and class and gender. There are clearly connections among sexuality, race, class, and gender, but they are not the same thing nor are they equivalent in how they are socially produced and maintained. Although much of the sexuality literature has challenged the fixedness of sexual and gender categories, we should continue to ask questions about the social structural dimensions of sexual oppression. How the political economy of sex is actually related to the political economy of race, class, and gender remains to be answered. Some of the scholarship on sex work approaches this idea, as does work looking at sexuality in a more global context, but scholarship that solely links race, class, and gender to the ideological realm, important as that is, does not answer such questions.

Conclusion

Feminist sociologists have covered amazing ground in a relatively short period of time, and we cannot underestimate the extent to which feminism has transformed thinking—in society and in our discipline. This article argues that as feminist scholarship emphasizes human agency in the shaping of social relations, it is important not to forget social structural analyses and power relations that continue to stratify society by gender, race, class, and sexuality. Theoretical arguments emphasizing the fluidity and agency of gender, race, class, and sexuality make these social factors seem inherently unstable, but they are at the same time remarkably (and frustratingly) stable over time.

Putting feminist analysis into the context of social structures reminds us of the context in which women's (and men's) lives are currently unfolding and that must be the backdrop for understanding gender. In the context of growing inequality and a significant redistribution of wealth, gender is increasingly a matter of economic justice for women, particularly when we analyze the combined effects of gender, race, and class. At the same time, the surge in conservative movements and the growth of fundamentalist religion both within and beyond the United States threatens to erode the many gains that feminism has established. Facts such as the persistently high rates of violence against women, the exclusionary practices directed against lesbians and gays, and the unjust impoverishment of millions of women and men remind us of the need for ongoing feminist thought and action anchored in the political-economic reality of inequality.

There is a long list of such unsettling facts—most of which are not about transgression and fluidity but about the continuing and persistent forms of power that oppress all women, although in different ways, in different places, and at different times. This suggests that feminist theory needs to be grounded in the connections between race, gender, sexuality, and class in the political-economic context of women's lives—a context that falls especially hard on women of color, poor women, and women not visibly attached to a heterosexual relationship. This will mean articulating feminist theory and politics within a framework of political economy that connects sexuality to race, class, and gender in more than the ideological realm.

As we review the achievements of feminist scholarship during the past quarter century, we can see an extraordinary progression from the virtual absence of thinking about women to a rich and complex body of feminist work. But our success can remind us of the need for continued vigilance—vigilance that feminism not become so established within dominant institutions that it loses the critical edge that it must have to continue locating feminist scholarship in complex interrelationships among gender, sexuality, race, and class that are reflected in the daily and diverse realities of women's lives.

Note

1. Because my work has mostly been about race, I added gender in to studying race, not the other way around, as is the case with many white feminist scholars. This remains important in how I conceptualize the relationship between gender, race, and class. I think it matters to anchor thinking in the experiences of race and class—forms of exploitation clearly linked to the appropriation of labor and the role of the state. Of course, this is true of gender as well—that is, gender inequality stems from the appropriation of women's labor and the role of the state and cultural beliefs in supporting such appropriation—but the tendency to think of gender on a smaller plane (as role, for example) makes it easier to obscure the political economy of gender relations. If you start by thinking about race, you can more easily avoid this error.

References

Acker, Joan. 1992. Gendered institutions: From sex roles to gendered institutions. *Contemporary Sociology* 21:565–69.

Andersen, Margaret L. 1993. From the editor. *Gender & Society* 7:157–61.

Andersen, Margaret L., and Patricia Hill Collins, eds. 2004. *Race, class, and gender: An anthology.* 5th ed. Belmont, CA: Wadsworth.

Baca Zinn, Maxine, and Bonnie Thornton Dill. 1996. Theorizing difference from multiracial feminism. *Feminist Studies* 22 (Summer): 321–31.

Ballard, J. A. 1992. Sexuality and the state in time of epidemic. In *Rethinking sex*, edited by R. W. Connell and G. W. Dowsett, 102–16. Philadelphia: Temple University Press.

Berger, Peter. 1963. *Invitation to sociology.* Garden City, NY: Doubleday-Anchor.

Bernard, Jessie. 1981. *The female world.* New York: Free Press.

Collins, Patricia Hill. 1990. *Black feminist thought: Knowledge, consciousness, and the politics of empowerment.* New York: Routledge.

———. 2004. *Black sexual politics: African Americans, gender, and the new racism.* New York: Routledge.

Fausto-Sterling, Anne. 1992. *Myths of gender.* 2d ed. New York: Basic Books.

———. 2000. *Sexing the body: Gender politics and the construction of sexuality.* New York: Basic Books.

Firestone, Shulamith. 1970. *The dialectic of sex: The case for feminist revolution.* New York: Morrow.

Foucault, Michel. 2000. *Power.* New York: New Press.

Fraser, Nancy. 1997. *Justice interruptus: Critical reflections on the "postsocialist" condition.* New York: Routledge.

Fraser, Nancy, and Nancy Naples. 2004. To interpret the world and to change it: An interview with Nancy Fraser. *Signs: Journal of Women in Culture and Society* 29 (Summer): 1103–24.

Glenn. Evelyn Nakano. 2002. *Unequal freedom: How race and gender shaped American citizenship and labor.* Cambridge, MA: Harvard University Press.

Gluckman, Amy, and Betsy Reed. 1997. "Where has gay liberation gone? An interview with Barbara Smith." In *Homo Economics: Capitalism, Communism, and Lesbian and Gay Life*, edited by Amy Gluckman and Betsy Reed, 195–207. New York: Routledge.

Kennelly, Ivy. 2004. The intermingling of race, class, and gender: A theoretical commencement. Unpublished manuscript, Department of Sociology, George Washington University.

Lopata, Helene Z., and Barrie Thorne. 1978. On the term "sex roles." *Signs: Journal of Women in Culture and Society* 3 (Spring): 718–21.

Lorber, Judith. 1993. Believing is seeing: Biology as ideology. *Gender & Society* 7:568–81.

———. 1994. *Paradoxes of gender.* New Haven, CT: Yale University Press.

Martin, Patricia. 2003. "Said and done" versus "saying and doing": Gendering practices, practicing gender at work. *Gender & Society* 17:342–66.

———. 2004. Gender as a social institution. *Social Forces* 82 (June): 1249–73.

Mitchell, Juliet. 1971. *Woman's estate.* New York: Pantheon.

Nagel, Joane. 2003. *Race, ethnicity, and sexuality: Intimate intersections, forbidden frontiers.* New York: Oxford University Press.

Omi, Michael, and Howard Winant. 1994. *Racial formation in the United States: From the 1960s to the 1990s.* New York: Routledge.

Risman, Barbara J. 2004. Gender as a social structure: Theory wrestling with activism. *Gender & Society* 18:429–50.

Rosenblum, Karen E., and Toni-Michelle C. Travis, eds. 2000. *The meaning of difference: American constructions of race, sex and gender, social class, and sexual orientation.* 2d ed. New York: McGraw-Hill.

Seidman, Steven. 2003. *The social construction of sexuality.* New York: Norton.

Stein, Arlene, and Ken Plummer. 1994. "I can't even think straight": Queer theory and the missing sexual revolution in sociology. *Sociological Theory* 12 (July): 178–87.

Thorne, Barrie. 1995. Symposium. *Gender & Society* 9:497–99.

Weber, Lynn. 2001. *Understanding race, class, gender, and sexuality: A conceptual framework.* New York: McGraw-Hill.

West, Candace, and Sarah Fenstermaker. 1995. Doing difference. *Gender & Society* 9:8–37.

West, Candace, and Don Zimmerman. 1987. Doing gender. *Gender & Society* 1:125–51.

West, Cornel. 1993. *Race matters.* Boston: Beacon.

Patricia Hill Collins

Learning from the Outsider Within: The Sociological Significance of Black Feminist Thought

Black women have long occupied marginal positions in academic settings. I argue that many Black female intellectuals have made creative use of their marginality—their "outsider within" status—to produce Black feminist thought that reflects a special standpoint on self, family, and society. I describe and explore the sociological significance of three characteristic themes in such thought: (1) Black women's self-definition and self-valuation; (2) the interlocking nature of oppression; and (3) the importance of Afro-American women's culture. After considering how Black women might draw upon these key themes as outsiders within to generate a distinctive standpoint on existing sociological paradigms, I conclude by suggesting that other sociologists would also benefit by placing greater trust in the creative potential of their own personal and cultural biographies.

Afro-American women have long been privy to some of the most intimate secrets of white society. Countless numbers of Black women have ridden buses to their white "families," where they not only cooked, cleaned, and executed other domestic duties, but where they also nurtured their "other" children, shrewdly offered guidance to their employers, and frequently, became honorary members of their white "families." These women have seen white elites, both actual and aspiring, from perspectives largely obscured from their Black spouses and from these groups themselves.[1]

On one level, this "insider" relationship has been satisfying to all involved. The memoirs of affluent whites often mention their love for their Black "mothers," while accounts of Black do-

Source: "Learning from the Outsider Within: The Sociological Significance of Black Feminist Thought," by Patricia Hill Collins. *Social Problems* 33(6) pp. S14–S32. © 1986 by The University of California Press. Used by permission.

mestic workers stress the sense of self-affirmation they experienced at seeing white power demystified—of knowing that it was not the intellect, talent, or humanity of their employers that supported their superior status, but largely just the advantages of racism.[2] But on another level, these same Black women knew they could never belong to their white "families." In spite of their involvement, they remained "outsiders."[3]

This "outsider within" status has provided a special standpoint on self, family, and society for Afro-American women.[4] A careful review of the emerging Black feminist literature reveals that many Black intellectuals, especially those in touch with their marginality in academic settings, tap this standpoint in producing distinctive analyses of race, class, and gender. For example, Zora Neal Hurston's 1937 novel, *Their Eyes Were Watching God*, most certainly reflects her skill at using the strengths and transcending the limitations both of her academic training and of her background in traditional Afro-American community life.[5] Black feminist historian E. Frances White (1984) suggests that Black women's ideas have been honed at the juncture between movements for racial and sexual equality, and contends that Afro-American women have been pushed by "their marginalization in both arenas" to create Black feminism. Finally, Black feminist critic Bell Hooks captures the unique standpoint that the outsider within status can generate. In describing her small-town, Kentucky childhood, she notes, "living as we did—on the edge—we developed a particular way of seeing reality. We looked both from the outside and in from the inside out . . . we understood both" (1984:vii).

In spite of the obstacles that can confront outsiders within, such individuals can benefit from this status. Simmel's (1921) essay on the sociological significance of what he called the "stranger" offers a helpful starting point for understanding the largely unexplored area of Black female outsider within status and the usefulness of the standpoint it might produce. Some of the potential benefits of outsider within status include: (1) Simmel's definition of "objectivity" as "a peculiar composition of nearness and remoteness, concern and indifference"; (2) the tendency for people to confide in a "stranger" in ways they never would with each other; and (3) the ability of the "stranger" to see patterns that may be more difficult for those immersed in the situation to see. Mannheim (1936) labels the "strangers" in academia "marginal intellectuals" and argues that the critical posture such individuals bring to academic endeavors may be essential to the creative development of academic disciplines themselves. Finally, in assessing the potentially positive qualities of social difference, specifically marginality, Lee notes, "for a time this marginality can be a most stimulating, albeit often a painful, experience. For some, it is debilitating . . . for others, it is an excitement to creativity" (1973:64).[6]

Sociologists might benefit greatly from serious consideration of the emerging, cross-disciplinary literature that I label Black feminist thought, precisely because, for many Afro-American female intellectuals, "marginality" has been an excitement to creativity. As outsiders within, Black feminist scholars may be one of many distinct groups of marginal intellectuals whose standpoints promise to enrich contemporary sociological discourse. Bringing this group—as well as others who share an outsider within status vis-a-vis sociology—into the center of analysis may reveal aspects of reality obscured by more orthodox approaches.

In the remainder of this essay, I examine the sociological significance of the Black feminist thought stimulated by Black women's outsider within status. First I outline three key themes that characterize the emerging cross-disciplinary literature that I label Black feminist thought.[7] For each theme, I summarize its content, supply examples from Black feminist and other works that illustrate its nature, and discuss its importance. . . . Finally, I discuss one general implication of this essay for social scientists: namely, the potential usefulness of identifying and using one's own standpoint in conducting research.

Three Key Themes in Black Feminist Thought

Black feminist thought consists of ideas produced by Black women that clarify a standpoint of and for Black women. Several assumptions underlie this working definition. First, the definition suggests that it is impossible to separate the structure and thematic content of thought from the historical and material conditions shaping the lives of its producers (Berger and Luckmann 1966; Mannheim 1936). Therefore, while Black feminist thought may be recorded by others, it is produced by Black women. Second, the definition assumes that Black women possess a unique standpoint on, or perspective of, their experiences and that there will be certain commonalities of perception shared by Black women as a group. Third, while living life as Black women may produce certain commonalities of outlook, the diversity of class, region, age, and sexual orientation shaping individual Black women's lives has resulted in different expressions of these common themes. Thus, universal themes included in the Black women's standpoint may be experienced and expressed differently by distinct groups of Afro-American women. Finally, the definition assumes that, while a Black women's standpoint exists, its contours may not be clear to Black women themselves. Therefore, one role for Black female intellectuals is to produce facts and theories about the Black female experience that will clarify a Black woman's standpoint for Black women. In other words, Black feminist thought contains observations and interpretations about Afro-American womanhood that describe and explain different expressions of common themes.

No one Black feminist platform exists from which one can measure the "correctness" of a particular thinker; nor should there be one. Rather, as I defined it above, there is a long and rich tradition of Black feminist thought. Much of it has been oral and has been produced by ordinary Black women in their roles as mothers, teachers, musicians, and preachers.[8] Since the civil rights and women's movements, Black women's ideas have been increasingly documented and are reaching wider audiences. The following discussion of three key themes in Black feminist thought is itself part of this emerging process of documentation and interpretation. The three themes I have chosen are not exhaustive but in my assessment they do represent the thrust of much of the existing dialogue.

The Meaning of Self-Definition and Self-Valuation

An affirmation of the importance of Black women's self-definition and self-valuation is the first key theme that pervades historical and contemporary statements of Black feminist thought. Self-definition involves challenging the political knowledge-validation process that has resulted in externally-defined, stereotypical images of Afro-American womanhood. In contrast, self-valuation stresses the content of Black women's self-definitions—namely, replacing externally-derived images with authentic Black female images.

Both Mae King's (1973) and Cheryl Gilkes' (1981) analyses of the importance of stereotypes offer useful insights for grasping the importance of Black women's self-definition. King suggests that stereotypes represent externally-defined, controlling images of Afro-American womanhood that have been central to the dehumanization of Black women and the exploitation of Black women's labor. Gilkes points out that Black women's assertiveness in resisting the multifaceted oppression they experience has been a consistent threat to the status quo. As punishment, Black women have been assaulted with a variety of externally-defined negative images designed to control assertive Black female behavior.

The value of King's and Gilkes' analyses lies in their emphasis on the function of stereotypes in controlling dominated groups. Both point out that replacing negative stereotypes with ostensibly positive ones can be equally problematic if the function of stereotypes as controlling images remains unrecognized. John Gwaltney's (1980) interview with Nancy White, a 73-year-old Black woman, suggests that ordinary Black women may also be aware of the power of these controlling images in their everyday experiences. In the following passage, Ms. White assesses the difference between the controlling images applied to Afro-American and white women as being those of degree, and not of kind:

> My mother used to say that the black woman is the white man's mule and the white woman is his dog. Now, she said that to say this: we do the heavy work and get beat whether we do it well or not. But the white woman is closer to the master and he pats them on the head and lets them sleep in the house, but he ain't gon' treat neither one like he was dealing with a person. (1980:148)

This passage suggests that while both groups are stereotyped, albeit in different ways, the function of the images is to dehumanize and control both groups. Seen in this light, it makes little sense, in the long run, for Black women to exchange one set of controlling images for another even if, in the short run, positive stereotypes bring better treatment.

The insistence on Black female self-definition reframes the entire dialogue from one of determining the technical accuracy of an image, to one stressing the power dynamics underlying the very process of definition itself. Black feminists have questioned not only what has been said about Black women, but the credibility and the intentions of those possessing the power to define. When Black women define themselves, they clearly reject the taken-for-granted assumption that those in positions granting them the authority to describe and analyze reality are entitled to do so. Regardless of the actual content of Black women's self-definitions, the act of insisting on Black female self-definition validates Black women's power as human subjects.

The related theme of Black female self-valuation pushes this entire process one step further. While Black female self-definition speaks to the power dynamics involved in the act of defining images of self and community, the theme of Black female self-valuation addresses the actual content of these self-definitions. Many of the attributes extant in Black female stereotypes are actually distorted renderings of those aspects of Black female behavior seen as most threatening to white patriarchy (Gilkes, 1981; White, 1985). For example, aggressive Afro-American women are threatening because they challenge white patriarchal definitions of femininity. To ridicule assertive women by labeling them Sapphires reflects an effort to put all women in their place. In their roles as central figures in socializing the next generation of Black adults, strong mothers are similarly threatening, because they contradict patriarchal views of family power relations. To ridicule strong Black mothers by labelling them matriarchs (Higginbotham, 1982) reflects a similar effort to control another aspect of Black female behavior that is especially threatening to the status quo.

When Black females choose to value those aspects of Afro-American womanhood that are stereotyped, ridiculed, and maligned in academic

scholarship and the popular media, they are actually questioning some of the basic ideas used to control dominated groups in general. It is one thing to counsel Afro-American women to resist the Sapphire stereotype by altering their behavior to become meek, docile, and stereotypically "feminine." It is quite another to advise Black women to embrace their assertiveness, to value their sassiness, and to continue to use these qualities to survive in and transcend the harsh environments that circumscribe so many Black women's lives. By defining and valuing assertiveness and other "unfeminine" qualities as necessary and functional attributes for Afro-American womanhood, Black women's self-valuation challenges the content of externally-defined controlling images.

This Black feminist concern—that Black women create their own standards for evaluating Afro-American womanhood and value their creations—pervades a wide range of literary and social science works. For example, Alice Walker's 1982 novel, *The Color Purple*, and Ntozake Shange's 1978 choreopoem, *For Colored Girls Who Have Considered Suicide*, are both bold statements of the necessity for Black female self-definition and self-valuation. Lena Wright Myers' (1980) work shows that Black women judge their behavior by comparing themselves to Black women facing similar situations and thus demonstrates the presence of Black female definitions of Afro-American womanhood. The recent spate of Black female historiography suggests that self-defined, self-valuating Black women have long populated the ranks of Afro-American female leaders (Giddings, 1984; Loewenberg and Bogin, 1976).

Black women's insistence on self-definition, self-valuation, and the necessity for a Black female-centered analysis is significant for two reasons. First, defining and valuing one's consciousness of one's own self-defined standpoint in the face of images that foster a self-definition as the objectified "other" is an important way of resisting the dehumanization essential to systems of domination. The status of being the "other" implies being "other than" or different from the assumed norm of white male behavior. In this model, powerful white males define themselves as subjects, the true actors, and classify people of color and women in terms of their position vis-a-vis this white male hub. Since Black women have been denied the authority to challenge these definitions, this model consists of images that define Black women as a negative other, the virtual antithesis of positive white male images. Moreover, as Brittan and Maynard (1984:199) point out, "domination always involves the objectification of the dominated; all forms of oppression imply the devaluation of the subjectivity of the oppressed."

One of the best examples of this process is described by Judith Rollins (1985). As part of her fieldwork on Black domestics, Rollins worked as a domestic for six months. She describes several incidents where her employers treated her as if she were not really present. On one occasion while she sat in the kitchen having lunch, her employers had a conversation as if she were not there. Her sense of invisibility became so great that she took out a pad of paper and began writing field notes. Even though Rollins wrote for 10 minutes, finished lunch, and returned to work, her employers showed no evidence of having seen her at all. Rollins notes,

> It was this aspect of servitude I found to be one of the strongest affronts to my dignity as a human being. . . . These gestures of ignoring my presence were not, I think, intended as insults; they were expressions of the employers' ability to annihilate the humanness and even, at times, the very existence of me, a servant and a black woman. (1985:209)

Racist and sexist ideologies both share the common feature of treating dominated groups—the "others"—as objects lacking full human subjectivity. For example, seeing Black women as obstinate mules and viewing white women as obedient dogs objectifies both groups, but in different ways. Neither is seen as fully human, and therefore both become eligible for race/gender specific modes of domination. But if Black women refuse to accept their assigned status as

the quintessential "other," then the entire rationale for such domination is challenged. In brief, abusing a mule or a dog may be easier than abusing a person who is a reflection of one's own humanness.

A second reason that Black female self-definition and self-valuation are significant concerns their value in allowing Afro-American women to reject internalized, psychological oppression (Baldwin, 1980). The potential damage of internalized control to Afro-American women's self-esteem can be great, even to the prepared. Enduring the frequent assaults of controlling images requires considerable inner strength. Nancy White, cited earlier, also points out how debilitating being treated as less than human can be if Black women are not self-defined. She notes, "Now, you know that no woman is a dog or a mule, but if folks keep making you feel that way, if you don't have a mind of your own, you can start letting them tell you what you are" (Gwaltney, 1980:152). Seen in this light, self-definition and self-valuation are not luxuries—they are necessary for Black female survival.

The Interlocking Nature of Oppression

Attention to the interlocking nature of race, gender, and class oppression is a second recurring theme in the works of Black feminists (Beale, 1970; Davis, 1981; Dill, 1983; Hooks, 1981; Lewis, 1977; Murray, 1970; Steady, 1981).[9] While different socio-historical periods may have increased the saliency of one or another type of oppression, the thesis of the linked nature of oppression has long pervaded Black feminist thought. For example, Ida Wells Barnett and Frances Ellen Watkins Harper, two prominent Black feminists of the late 1800s, both spoke out against the growing violence directed against Black men. They realized that civil rights held little meaning for Black men and women if the right to life itself went unprotected (Loewenberg and Bogin, 1976:26). Black women's absence from organized feminist movements has mistakenly been attributed to a lack of feminist consciousness. In actuality, Black feminists have possessed an ideological commitment to addressing interlocking oppression yet have been excluded from arenas that would have allowed them to do so (Davis, 1981).

As Barbara Smith points out, "the concept of the simultaneity of oppression is still the crux of a Black feminist understanding of political reality and . . . is one of the most significant ideological contributions of Black feminist thought" (1983:xxxii). This should come as no surprise since Black women should be among the first to realize that minimizing one form of oppression, while essential, may still leave them oppressed in other equally dehumanizing ways. Sojourner Truth knew this when she stated, "there is a great stir about colored men getting their rights, and not colored women theirs, you see the colored men will be masters over the women, and it will be just as bad as before" (Loewenberg and Bogin, 1976:238). To use Nancy White's metaphors, the Black woman as "mule" knows that she is perceived to be an animal. In contrast, the white woman as "dog" may be similarly dehumanized, and may think that she is an equal part of the family when, in actuality, she is a well-cared-for pet. The significant factor shaping Truth's and White's clearer view of their own subordination than that of Black men or white women is their experience at the intersection of multiple structures of domination.[10] Both Truth and White are Black, female, and poor. They therefore have a clearer view of oppression than other groups who occupy more contradictory positions vis-a-vis white male power—unlike white women, they have no illusions that their whiteness will negate female subordination, and unlike Black men, they cannot use a questionable appeal to manhood to neutralize the stigma of being Black.

The Black feminist attention to the interlocking nature of oppression is significant for two reasons. First, this viewpoint shifts the entire focus of investigation from one aimed at explicating elements of race or gender or class oppression to one whose goal is to determine what the links are among these systems. The first approach typically prioritizes one form of oppres-sion as being primary, then handles remaining types of oppression as variables within what is seen as the most important system. For example, the efforts to insert race and gender into Marxist theory exemplify this effort. In contrast, the more holistic approach implied in Black feminist thought treats the interaction among multiple systems as the object of study. Rather than adding to existing theories by inserting previously excluded variables, Black feminists aim to develop new theoretical interpretations of the interaction itself.

Black male scholars, white female scholars, and more recently, Black feminists like Bell Hooks, may have identified one critical link among interlocking systems of oppression. These groups have pointed out that certain basic ideas cross-cut multiple systems of domination. One such idea is either/or dualistic thinking, claimed by Hooks to be "the central ideological component of all systems of domination in Western society" (1984:29).

While Hooks' claim may be somewhat premature, there is growing scholarly support for her viewpoint.[11] Either/or dualistic thinking, or what I will refer to as the construct of dichotomous oppositional difference, may be a philosophical lynchpin in systems of race, class, and gender oppression. One fundamental characteristic of this construct is the categorization of people, things, and ideas in terms of their difference from one another. For example, the terms in dichotomies such as black/white, male/female, reason/emotion, fact/opinion, and subject/object gain their meaning only in *relation* to their difference from their oppositional counterparts. Another fundamental characteristic of this construct is that difference is not complementary in that the halves of the dichotomy do not enhance each other. Rather, the dichotomous halves are different and inherently opposed to one another. A third and more important characteristic is that these oppositional relationships are intrinsically unstable. Since such dualities rarely represent different but equal relationships, the inherently unstable relationship is resolved by subordinating one half of each pair to the other. Thus, whites rule Blacks, males dominate females, reason is touted as superior to emotion in ascertaining truth, facts supercede opinion in evaluating knowledge, and subjects rule objects. Dichotomous oppositional differences invariably imply relationships of superiority and inferiority, hierarchical relationships that mesh with political economies of domination and subordination.

The oppression experienced by most Black women is shaped by their subordinate status in an array of either/or dualities. Afro-American women have been assigned the inferior half of several dualities, and this placement has been central to their continued domination. For example, the allegedly emotional, passionate nature of Afro-American women has long been used as a rationale for their sexual exploitation. Similarly, denying Black women literacy—then claiming that they lack the facts for sound judgment—illustrates another case of assigning a group inferior status, then using that inferior status as proof of the group's inferiority. Finally, denying Black women agency as subjects and treating them as objectified "others" represents yet another dimension of the power that dichotomous oppositional constructs have in maintaining systems of domination.

While Afro-American women may have a vested interest in recognizing the connections among these dualities that together comprise the construct of dichotomous oppositional difference, that more women have not done so is not surprising. Either/or dualistic thinking is so pervasive that it suppresses other alternatives. As Dill points out, "the choice between identifying as black or female is a product of the patriarchal strategy of divide-and-conquer and the continued importance of class, patriarchal, and racial divisions, perpetuate such choices both within our consciousness and within the concrete realities of our daily lives" (1983:136). In spite of this difficulty, Black women experience oppression in a personal, holistic fashion and emerging Black feminist perspectives appear to be embracing an equally holistic analysis of oppression.

Second, Black feminist attention to the interlocking nature of oppression is significant in that, implicit in this view, is an alternative humanist vision of societal organization. This alternative world view is cogently expressed in the following passage from an 1893 speech delivered by the Black feminist educator, Anna Julia Cooper:

> We take our stand on the solidarity of humanity, the oneness of life, and the unnaturalness and injustice of all special favoritisms, whether of sex, race, country, or condition. . . . The colored woman feels that woman's cause is one and universal; and that . . . not till race, color, sex, and condition are seen as accidents, and not the substance of life; not till the universal title of humanity to life, liberty, and the pursuit of happiness is conceded to be inalienable to all; not till then is woman's lesson taught and woman's cause won—not the white woman's nor the black woman's nor the red woman's, but the cause of every man and of every woman who has writhed silently under a mighty wrong. (Loewenberg and Bogin, 1976:330–31)

I cite the above passage at length because it represents one of the clearest statements of the humanist vision extant in Black feminist thought.[12] Black feminists who see the simultaneity of oppression affecting Black women appear to be more sensitive to how these same oppressive systems affect Afro-American men, people of color, women, and the dominant group itself. Thus, while Black feminist activists may work on behalf of Black women, they rarely project separatist solutions to Black female oppression. Rather, the vision is one that, like Cooper's, takes its "stand on the solidarity of humanity."

The Importance of Afro-American Women's Culture

A third key theme characterizing Black feminist thought involves efforts to redefine and explain the importance of Black women's culture. In doing so, Black feminists have not only uncovered previously unexplored areas of the Black female experience, but they have also identified concrete areas of social relations where Afro-American women create and pass on self-definitions and self-valuations essential to coping with the simultaneity of oppression they experience.

In contrast to views of culture stressing the unique, ahistorical values of a particular group, Black feminist approaches have placed greater emphasis on the role of historically-specific political economies in explaining the endurance of certain cultural themes. The following definition of culture typifies the approach taken by many Black feminists. According to Mullings, culture is composed of

> the symbols and values that create the ideological frame of reference through which people attempt to deal with the circumstances in which they find themselves. Culture . . . is not composed of static, discrete traits moved from one locale to another. It is constantly changing and transformed, as new forms are created out of old ones. Thus culture . . . does not arise out of nothing: it is created and modified by material conditions. (1986a:13)

Seen in this light, Black women's culture may help provide the ideological frame of reference— namely, the symbols and values of self-definition and self-valuation—that assist Black women in seeing the circumstances shaping race, class, and gender oppression. Moreover, Mullings' definition of culture suggests that the values which accompany self-definition and self-valuation will have concrete, material expression: they will be present in social institutions like church and family, in creative expression of art, music, and dance, and, if unsuppressed, in patterns of economic and political activity. Finally, this approach to culture stresses its historically concrete nature. While common themes may link Black women's lives, these themes will be experienced differently by Black women of different classes, ages, regions, and sexual preferences as well as by Black women in different historical settings. Thus, there is no

monolithic Black women's culture—rather, there are socially-constructed Black women's cultures that collectively form Black women's culture.

The interest in redefining Black women's culture has directed attention to several unexplored areas of the Black female experience. One such area concerns the interpersonal relationships that Black women share with each other. It appears that the notion of sisterhood—generally understood to mean a supportive feeling of loyalty and attachment to other women stemming from a shared feeling of oppression—has been an important part of Black women's culture (Dill, 1983: 132). Two representative works in the emerging tradition of Black feminist research illustrate how this concept of sisterhood, while expressed differently in response to different material conditions, has been a significant feature of Black women's culture. For example, Debra Gray White (1985) documents the ways Black slave women assisted each other in childbirth, cared for each other's children, worked together in sex-segregated work units when pregnant or nursing children, and depended on one another when married to males living on distant farms. White paints a convincing portrait of Black female slave communities where sisterhood was necessary and assumed. Similarly, Gilkes' (1985) work on Black women's traditions in the Sanctified Church suggests that the sisterhood Black women found had tangible psychological and political benefits.[13]

The attention to Black women's culture has stimulated interest in a second type of interpersonal relationship: that shared by Black women with their biological children, the children in their extended families, and with the Black community's children. In reassessing Afro-American motherhood, Black feminist researchers have emphasized the connections between (1) choices available to Black mothers resulting from their placement in historically, specific political economies, (2) Black mothers' perceptions of their children's choices as compared to what mothers thought those choices should be, and

(3) actual strategies employed by Black mothers both in raising their children and in dealing with institutions that affected their children's lives. For example, Janice Hale (1980) suggests that effective Black mothers are sophisticated mediators between the competing offerings of an oppressive dominant culture and a nurturing Black value-structure. Dill's (1980) study of the childrearing goals of Black domestics stresses the goals the women in her sample had for their children and the strategies these women pursued to help their children go further than they themselves had gone. Gilkes (1980) offers yet another perspective on the power of Black motherhood by observing that many of the Black female political activists in her study became involved in community work through their role as mothers. What typically began as work on behalf of their own children evolved into work on behalf of the community's children.

Another dimension of Black women's culture that has generated considerable interest among Black feminists is the role of creative expression in shaping and sustaining Black women's self-definitions and self-valuations. In addition to documenting Black women's achievements as writers, dancers, musicians, artists, and actresses, the emerging literature also investigates why creative expression has been such an important element of Black women's culture.[14] Alice Walker's (1974) classic essay, "In Search of Our Mothers' Gardens," explains the necessity of Black women's creativity, even if in very limited spheres, in resisting objectification and asserting Black women's subjectivity as fully human beings. Illustrating Walker's thesis. Willie Mae Ford Smith, a prominent gospel singer featured in the 1984 documentary, "Say Amen Somebody," describes what singing means to her. She notes, "it's just a feeling within. You can't help yourself. . . . I feel like I can fly away. I forget I'm in the world sometimes. I just want to take off." For Mother Smith, her creativity is a sphere of freedom, one that helps her cope with and transcend daily life.

This third key theme in Black feminist thought—the focus on Black women's culture—is significant for three reasons. First, the data from Black women's culture suggest that the relationship between oppressed people's consciousness of oppression and the actions they take in dealing with oppressive structures may be far more complex than that suggested by existing social theory. Conventional social science continues to assume a fit between consciousness and activity; hence, accurate measures of human behavior are thought to produce accurate portraits of human consciousness of self and social structure (Westkott, 1979). In contrast, Black women's experiences suggest that Black women may overtly conform to the societal roles laid out for them, yet covertly oppose these roles in numerous spheres, an opposition shaped by the consciousness of being on the bottom. Black women's activities in families, churches, community institutions, and creative expression may represent more than an effort to mitigate pressures stemming from oppression. Rather, the Black female ideological frame of reference that Black women acquire through sisterhood, motherhood, and creative expression may serve the added purpose of shaping a Black female consciousness about the workings of oppression. Moreover, this consciousness is shaped not only through abstract, rational reflection, but also is developed through concrete rational action. For example, while Black mothers may develop consciousness through talking with and listening to their children, they may also shape consciousness by how they live their lives, the actions they take on behalf of their children. That these activities have been obscured from traditional social scientists should come as no surprise. Oppressed peoples may maintain hidden consciousness and may not reveal their true selves for reasons of self-protection.[15]

A second reason that the focus on Black women's culture is significant is that it points to the problematic nature of existing conceptualizations of the term "activism." While Black women's reality cannot be understood without attention to the interlocking structures of oppression that limit Black women's lives, Afro-American women's experiences suggest that possibilities for activism exist even within such multiple structures of domination. Such activism can take several forms. For Black women under extremely harsh conditions, the private decision to reject external definitions of Afro-American womanhood may itself be a form of activism. If Black women find themselves in settings where total conformity is expected, and where traditional forms of activism such as voting, participating in collective movements, and officeholding are impossible, then the individual women who in their consciousness choose to be self-defined and self-evaluating are, in fact, activists. They are retaining a grip over their definition as subjects, as full humans, and rejecting definitions of themselves as the objectified "other." For example, while Black slave women were forced to conform to the specific oppression facing them, they may have had very different assessments of themselves and slavery than did the slaveowners. In this sense, consciousness can be viewed as one potential sphere of freedom, one that may exist simultaneously with unfree, allegedly conforming behavior (Westkott, 1979). Moreover, if Black women simultaneously use all resources available to them—their roles as mothers, their participation in churches, their support of one another in Black female networks, their creative expression—to be self-defined and self-valuating and to encourage others to reject objectification, then Black women's everyday behavior itself is a form of activism. People who view themselves as fully human, as subjects, become activists, no matter how limited the sphere of their activism may be. By returning subjectivity to Black women, Black feminists return activism as well.

A third reason that the focus on Black women's culture is significant is that an analytical model exploring the relationship between oppression, consciousness, and activism is implicit in the way Black feminists have studied Black women's culture. With the exception of Dill (1983), few scholars have deliberately set out to develop such a model. However, the type of work done suggests that an implicit model paralleling that proposed by Mullings (1986a) has influenced Black feminist research.

Several features pervade emerging Black feminist approaches. First, researchers stress the interdependent relationship between the interlocking oppression that has shaped Black women's choices and Black women's actions in the context of those choices. Black feminist researchers rarely describe Black women's behavior without attention to the opportunity structures shaping their subjects' lives (Higginbotham, 1985; Ladner, 1971; Myers, 1980). Second, the question of whether oppressive structures and limited choices stimulate Black women's behavior characterized by apathy and alienation, or behavior demonstrating subjectivity and activism is seen as ultimately dependent on Black women's perceptions of their choices. In other words, Black women's consciousness—their analytical, emotional, and ethical perspective of themselves and their place in society—becomes a critical part of the relationship between the working of oppression and Black women's actions. Finally, this relationship between oppression, consciousness, and action can be seen as a dialectical one. In this model, oppressive structures create patterns of choices which are perceived in varying ways by Black women. Depending on their consciousness of themselves and their relationship to these choices, Black women may or may not develop Black-female spheres of influence where they develop and validate what will be appropriate, Black-female sanctioned responses to oppression. Black women's activism in constructing Black-female spheres of influence may, in turn, affect their perceptions of the political and economic choices offered to them by oppressive structures, influence actions actually taken, and ultimately, alter the nature of oppression they experience. . . .

Toward Synthesis: Outsiders Within Sociology

Black women are not the only outsiders within sociology. As an extreme case of outsiders moving into a community that historically excluded them, Black women's experiences highlight the tension

experienced by any group of less powerful outsiders encountering the paradigmatic thought of
a more powerful insider community. In this sense,
a variety of individuals can learn from Black
women's experiences as outsiders within: Black
men, working-class individuals, white women,
other people of color, religious and sexual minorities, and all individuals who, while from social strata that provided them with the benefits of
white male insiderism, have never felt comfortable
with its taken-for-granted assumptions.

Outsider within status is bound to generate
tension, for people who become outsiders within
are forever changed by their new status. Learning
the subject matter of sociology stimulates a reex-
amination of one's own personal and cultural
experiences; and, yet, these same experiences
paradoxically help to illuminate sociology's
anomalies. Outsiders within occupy a special
place—they become different people, and their
difference sensitizes them to patterns that may be
more difficult for established sociological insiders to see. Some outsiders within try to resolve the
tension generated by their new status by leaving
sociology and remaining sociological outsiders.
Others choose to suppress their difference by
striving to become bonafide, "thinking as usual"
sociological insiders. Both choices rob sociology
of diversity and ultimately weaken the discipline.

A third alternative is to conserve the creative
tension of outsider within status by encouraging
and institutionalizing outsider within ways of seeing. This alternative has merit not only for actual
outsiders within, but also for other sociologists as
well. The approach suggested by the experiences
of outsiders within is one where intellectuals
learn to trust their own personal and cultural biographies as significant sources of knowledge. In
contrast to approaches that require submerging
these dimensions of self in the process of becoming an allegedly unbiased, objective social scientist, outsiders within bring these ways of
knowing back into the research process. At its
best, outsider within status seems to offer its occupants a powerful balance between the strengths
of their sociological training and the offerings of
their personal and cultural experiences. Neither
is subordinated to the other. Rather, experienced
reality is used as a valid source of knowledge for
critiquing sociological facts and theories, while
sociological thought offers new ways of seeing
that experienced reality.

What many Black feminists appear to be
doing is embracing the creative potential of their
outsider within status and using it wisely. In doing
so, they move themselves and their disciplines
closer to the humanist vision implicit in their
work—namely, the freedom both to be different
and part of the solidarity of humanity.

Notes

1. In 1940/almost 60 percent of employed Afro-
American women were domestics. The 1970 census
was the first time this category of work did not contain the largest segment of the Black female labor
force. See Rollins (1985) for a discussion of Black domestic work.

2. For example, in *Of Women Born: Motherhood as
Experience and Institution*, Adrienne Rich has fond
memories of her Black "mother," a young, unstereo-
typically slim Black woman she loved. Similarly, Dill's
(1980) study of Black domestic workers reveals Black
women's sense of affirmation at knowing that they
were better mothers than their employers, and that
they frequently had to teach their employers the basics
about children and interaction in general. Even though
the Black domestic workers were officially subordinates, they gained a sense of self-worth at knowing
they were good at things that they felt mattered.

3. For example, in spite of Rich's warm memories of
her Black "mother," she had all but forgotten her until
beginning research for her book. Similarly, the Black
domestic workers in both Dill's (1980) and Rollins'
(1985) studies discussed the limitations that their subordinate roles placed on them.

4. For a discussion of the notion of a special standpoint or point of view of oppressed groups, see Hartsock (1983). See Merton's (1972) analysis of the
potential contributions of insider and outsider perspectives to sociology. For a related discussion of outsider within status, see his section, "Insiders as
'Outsiders'" (1972:29–30).

5. Hurston has been widely discussed in Black feminist literary criticism. For example, see selected essays in Walker's (1979) edited volume on Hurston.

6. By stressing the potentially positive features of outsider within status, I in no way want to deny the very real problem this social status has for large numbers of Black women. American sociology has long identified marginal status as problematic. However, my sense of the "problems" diverge from those espoused by traditional sociologists. For example, Robert Park states, "the marginal man . . . is one whom fate has condemned to live in two societies and in two, not merely different but antagonistic cultures (1950:373)." From Park's perspective, marginality and difference themselves were problems. This perspective quite rationally led to the social policy solution of assimilation, one aimed at eliminating difference, or if that didn't work, pretending it was not important. In contrast, I argue that it is the meaning attached to difference that is the problem. See Lorde (1984:114–23 and passim) for a Black feminist perspective on difference.

7. In addition to familiarizing readers with the contours of Black feminist thought, I place Black women's ideas in the center of my analysis for another reason. Black women's ideas have long been viewed as peripheral to serious intellectual endeavors. By treating Black feminist thought as central, I hope to avoid the tendency of starting with the body of thought needing the critique—in this case sociology—fitting in the dissenting ideas, and thus, in the process, reifying the very systems of thought one hopes to transform.

8. On this point, I diverge somewhat from Berger and Luckmann's (1966) definition of specialized thought. They suggest that only a limited group of individuals engages in theorizing and that "pure theory" emerges with the development of specialized legitimating theories and their administration by full-time legitimators. Using this approach, groups denied the material resources to support pure theorists cannot be capable of developing specialized theoretical knowledge. In contrast, I argue that "traditional wisdom" is a system of thought and that it reflects the material positions of its practitioners.

9. Emerging Black feminist research is demonstrating a growing awareness of the importance of including the simultaneity of oppression in studies of Black women. For example, Paula Giddings' (1984) history of Afro-American women emphasizes the role of class in shaping relations between Afro-American and white women, and among Black women themselves. Elizabeth Higginbotham's (1985) study of Black college women examines race and class barriers to Black women's college attendance. Especially noteworthy is the growing attention to Black women's labor market experiences. Studies such as those by Dill (1980), Rollins (1985), Higginbotham (1983), and Mullings (1986b) indicate a new sensitivity to the interactive nature of race, gender, and class. By studying Black women, such studies capture the interaction of race and gender. Moreover, by examining Black women's roles in capitalist development, such work taps the key variable of class.

10. The thesis that those affected by multiple systems of domination will develop a sharper view of the interlocking nature of oppression is illustrated by the prominence of Black lesbian feminists among Black feminist thinkers. For more on this, see Smith (1983), Lorde (1984), and White (1984:22–24).

11. For example, African and Afro-American scholars point to the role dualistic thinking has played in domestic racism (Asante, 1980; Baldwin, 1980; Richards 1980). Feminist scholars note the linkage of duality with conceptualizations of gender in Western cultures (Chodorow, 1978; Keller, 1983; Rosaldo, 1983). Recently, Brittan and Maynard, two British scholars, have suggested that dualistic thinking plays a major role in linking systems of racial oppression with those of sexual oppression. They note that

> there is an implicit belief in the duality of culture and nature. Men are the creators and mediators of culture—women are the manifestations of nature. The implication is that men develop culture in order to understand and control the natural world, while women being the embodiment of forces of nature, must be brought under the civilizing control of men . . . This duality of culture and nature . . . is also used to distinguish between so-called higher nations or civilizations, and those deemed to be culturally backward. . . . Non-European peoples are conceived of as being nearer to nature than Europeans. Hence, the justification . . . for slavery and colonialism. (1984: 193–94)

12. This humanist vision takes both religious and secular forms. For religious statements, see Andrews' (1986) collection of the autobiographies of three nineteenth-century, Black female evangelical preachers. For a discussion of the humanist tradition in

Afro-American religion that has contributed to this dimension of Black feminist thought, see Paris (1985). Much of contemporary Black feminist writing draws on this religious tradition, but reframes the basic vision in secular terms.

13. During a period when Black women were widely devalued by the dominant culture, Sanctified Church members addressed each other as "Saints." During the early 1900s, when basic literacy was an illusive goal for many Blacks, Black women in the Church not only stressed education as a key component of a sanctified life, but supported each other's efforts at educational excellence. In addition to these psychological supports, the Church provided Afro-American women with genuine opportunities for influence, leadership, and political clout. The important thing to remember here is that the Church was not an abstract, bureaucratic structure that ministered to Black women. Rather, the Church was a predominantly female community of individuals in which women had prominent spheres of influence.

14. Since much Black feminist thought is contained in the works of Black women writers, literary criticism by Black feminist critics provides an especially fertile source of Black women's ideas. See Tate (1983) and Christian (1985).

15. Audre Lorde (1984:114) describes this conscious hiding of one's self as follows: "In order to survive, those of us for whom oppression is as American as apple pie have always had to be watchers, to become familiar with the language and manners of the oppressor, even sometimes adopting them for some illusion of protection."

References

Asante, Molefi Kete. (1980). "International/intercultural relations." Pp. 43–58 in Molefi Kete Asante and Abdulai S. Vandi (eds.), *Contemporary Black Thought*. Beverly Hills, CA: Sage.

Baldwin, Joseph A. (1980). "The psychology of oppression." Pp. 95–110 in Molefi Kete Asante and Abdulai S. Vandi (eds.), *Contemporary Black Thought*. Beverly Hills, CA: Sage.

Beale, Frances. (1970). "Double jeopardy: To be Black and female." Pp. 90–110 in Toni Cade (ed.), *The Black Woman*. New York: Signet.

Berger, Peter L., and Thomas Luckmann. (1966). *The Social Construction of Reality*. New York: Doubleday.

Brittan, Arthur, and Mary Maynard. (1984). *Sexism, Racism and Oppression*. New York: Basil Blackwell.

Chodorow, Nancy. (1978). *The Reproduction of Mothering*. Berkeley, CA: University of California Press.

Christian, Barbara. (1985). *Black Feminist Criticism: Perspectives on Black Women Writers*. New York: Pergamon.

Davis, Angela. (1981). *Women, Race and Class*. New York: Random House.

Dill, Bonnie Thornton. (1980). "'The means to put my children through'; child-rearing goals and strategies among Black female domestic servants." Pp. 107–23 in LaFrances Rodgers-Rose (ed.), *The Black Woman*. Beverly Hills, CA: Sage.

———. (1983). "Race, class, and gender: prospects for an all-inclusive sisterhood." *Feminist Studies* 9:131–50.

Giddings, Paula. (1984). *When and Where I Enter . . . The Impact of Black Women on Race and Sex in America*. New York: William Morrow.

Gilkes, Cheryl Townsend. (1981). "From slavery to social welfare: Racism and the control of Black women." Pp. 288–300 in Amy Smerdlow and Helen Lessinger (eds.), *Class, Race, and Sex: The Dynamics of Control*. Boston: G. K. Hall.

———. (1985). "Together and in harness': Women's traditions in the sanctified church." *Signs* 10: 678–99.

Gwaltney, John Langston. (1980). *Drylongso, a Self-portrait of Black America*. New York: Vintage.

Hale, Janice. (1980). "The Black woman and child rearing." Pp. 79–88 in LaFrances Rodgers-Rose (ed.), *The Black Woman*. Beverly Hills, CA: Sage.

Hartsock, Nancy M. (1983). "The feminist standpoint: developing the ground for a specifically feminist historical materialism." Pp. 283–310 in Sandra Harding and Merrill Hintikka (eds.), *Discovering Reality*. Boston: D. Reidel.

Higginbotham, Elizabeth. (1982). "Two representative issues in contemporary sociological work on Black women." Pp. 93–98 in Gloria T. Hull, Patricia Bell Scott, and Barbara Smith (eds.), *But Some of Us Are Brave*. Old Westbury, NY: Feminist Press.

————. (1983). "Laid bare by the system: work and survival for Black and Hispanic women." Pp. 200–15 in Amy Smerdlow and Helen Lessinger (eds.), *Class, Race, and Sex: The Dynamics of Control*. Boston: G. K. Hall.

————. (1985). "Race and class barriers to Black women's college attendance." *Journal of Ethnic Studies* 13:89–107.

Hooks, Bell. (1981). *Aint' I a Woman: Black Women and Feminism*. Boston: South End Press.

————. (1984). *From Margin to Center*. Boston: South End Press.

Keller, Evelyn Fox. (1983). "Gender and science." Pp. 187–206 in Sandra Harding and Merrill Hintikka (eds.), *Discovering Reality*. Boston: D. Reidel.

King, Mae. (1973). "The politics of sexual stereotypes." *Black Scholar* 4:12–23.

Ladner, Joyce. (1971). *Tomorrow's Tomorrow: The Black Woman*. Garden City, NY: Anchor.

Lee, Alfred McClung. (1973). *Toward Humanist Sociology*. Englewood Cliffs, NJ: Prentice-Hall.

Lewis, Diane. (1977). "A response to inequality: Black women, racism and sexism." *Signs* 3:339–61.

Loewenberg, Bert James, and Ruth Bogin (eds.), (1976). *Black Women in Nineteenth-Century Life*. University Park, PA: Pennsylvania State University.

Lorde, Audre. (1984). *Sister Outsider*. Trumansburg, NY: The Crossing Press.

Mannheim, Karl. (1954) [1936]. *Ideology and Utopia: An Introduction to the Sociology of* [1936] *Knowledge*. New York: Harcourt, Brace & Co.

Merton, Robert K. (1972). "Insiders and outsiders: A chapter in the sociology of knowledge." *American Journal of Sociology* 78:9–47.

Mullings, Leith. (1986a). "Anthropological perspectives on the Afro-American family." *American Journal of Social Psychiatry* 6:11–16.

————. (1986b). "Uneven development: Class, race and gender in the United States before 1900." Pp. 41–57 in Eleanor Leacock and Helen Safa (eds.), *Women's Work, Development and the Division of Labor by Gender*. South Hadley, MA: Bergin & Garvey.

Murray, Paul. (1970). "The liberation of Black women." Pp. 87–102 in Mary Lou Thompson (ed.), *Voices of the New Feminism*. Boston: Beacon Press.

Myers, Lena Wright. (1980). *Black Women: Do They Cope Better?* Englewood Cliffs, NJ: Prentice-Hall.

Paris, Peter J. (1985). *The Social Teaching of the Black Churches*. Philadelphia: Fortress Press.

Park, Robert E. (1950). *Race and Culture*. Glencoe, IL: Free Press.

Rich, Adrienne. (1976). *Of Woman Born: Motherhood as Experience and Institution*. New York: Norton.

Richards, Dona. (1980). "European mythology; the ideology of 'progress'." Pp. 59–79 in Molefi Kete Asante and Abdulai S. Vandi (eds.), *Contemporary Black Thought*. Beverly Hills, CA: Sage.

Rollins, Judith. (1985). *Between Women, Domestics and Their Employers*. Philadelphia: Temple University Press.

Rosaldo, Michelle Z. (1983). "Moral/analytic dilemmas posed by the intersection of feminism and social science." Pp. 76–96 in Norma Hann, Robert N. Bellah, Paul Rabinow, and William Sullivan (eds.), *Social Science as Moral Inquiry*. New York: Columbia University Press.

Simmel, Georg. (1921). "The sociological significance of the 'stranger'." Pp. 322–27 in Robert E. Park and Ernest W. Burgess (eds.), *Introduction to the Science of Sociology*. Chicago: University of Chicago Press.

Smith, Barbara (ed.). (1983). *Home Girls: A Black Feminist Anthology*. New York: Kitchen Table, Women of Color Press.

Steady, Filomina Chioma. (1981). "The Black woman cross-culturally: An overview." Pp. 7–42 in Filomina Chioma Steady (ed.), *The Black Woman Cross-Culturally*. Cambridge, MA: Schenkman.

Tate, Claudia. (1983). *Black Women Writers at Work*. New York: Continuum.

Walker, Alice. (1974). "In search of our mothers' gardens." Pp. 231–43 in, *In Search of Our Mothers' Gardens*. New York: Harcourt Brace Javanovich.

Walker, Alice (ed.). (1979). *I Love Myself When I Am Laughing . . . A Zora Neal Hurston Reader*. Westbury, NY: Feminist Press.

Westkott, Marcia. (1979). "Feminist criticism of the social sciences." *Harvard Educational Review* 49:422–30.

White, Deborah Gray. (1985). *Art'n't I a Woman? Female Slaves in the Plantation South*. New York: W.W. Norton.

White, E. Frances. (1984). "Listening to the voices of Black feminism." *Radical America* 18:7–25.

Cynthia Fuchs Epstein

Great Divides: The Cultural, Cognitive, and Social Bases of the Global Subordination of Women

Female Subordination in Global Context

The "woman question" is not just one among many raised by injustice, subordination, and differentiation. It is basic. The denigration and segregation of women is a major mechanism in reinforcing male bonds, protecting the institutions that favor them, and providing the basic work required for societies to function. To ignore this great social divide is to ignore a missing link in social analysis.

I will not illustrate my thesis about the persistence of the worldwide subordination of the female sex with pictures, graphs, or charts. Instead I call on readers' imaginations to picture some of the phenomena that illustrate my thesis. Imagine most women's lifetimes of everyday drudgery in households and factories; of struggles for survival without access to decent jobs. Imagine the horror of mass rapes by armed men in ethnic conflicts, and of rapes that occur inside the home by men who regard sexual access as their right.[1] Imagine also women's isolation and confinement behind walls and veils in many societies. Some examples are harder to imagine—for example, the 100 million women missing in the world, first brought to our attention by the economist Amartya Sen (1990), who alerted us to the bizarre sex ratios in South Asia, West Asia, and China. He pointed to

Source: "Great Divides: The Cultural, Cognitive, and Social Bases of the Global Subordination of Women," by Cynthia Fuchs Epstein. *American Sociological Review*, *2007*, Vol. 72 (February: 1–22). Used by permission.

the abandonment and systematic under-nourishment of girls and women and to the poor medical care they receive in comparison to males. International human rights groups have alerted us to the selective destruction of female fetuses. It is estimated that in China and India alone, 10,000,000 females were aborted between 1978 and 1998 (Rao 2006). Also hidden are the child brides who live as servants in alien environments and who, should their husbands die, are abandoned to live in poverty and isolation. And there are the millions of girls and women lured or forced into sex work. In the Western world, only the occasional newspaper article brings to view the fact that African women face a 1 in 20 chance of dying during pregnancy (half a million die each year).[2] The persistent segregation of the workplace, in even the most sophisticated societies, in which girls and women labor in sex-labeled jobs that are tedious, mind-numbing, and highly supervised, is out of view. Unseen too are the countless beatings, slights, and defamations women and girls endure from men, including intimates, every day all over the world.

Insistence and Persistence on "Natural Differences"

These patterns are largely explained in the world as consequences stemming from natural causes or God's will. Here, I limit analysis mainly to the view of *natural causation* as the *master narrative*—the narrative that attributes role division of the sexes to biology. Some believe that early socialization cements the distinction. It is clear that strong religious beliefs in the natural subordination of women determine the role women must play in societies.

Biological explanation is the master narrative holding that men and women are naturally different and have different intelligences, physical abilities, and emotional traits. This view asserts that men are naturally suited to dominance and women are naturally submissive. The narrative holds that women's different intellect or emotional makeup is inconsistent with the capacity to work at prestigious jobs, be effective scholars, and lead others. Popularized accounts of gender difference have generated large followings.[3]

But the set of assumptions about basic differences are discredited by a body of reliable research. Although there seems to be an industry of scholarship identifying sex differences, it is important to note that scholarship showing only tiny or fluctuating differences, or none at all, is rarely picked up by the popular press. Most media reports (e.g., Brooks 2006, Tierney 2006) invariably focus on sex differences, following the lead of many journals that report tiny differences in distributions of males and females as significant findings (Epstein 1991a, 1999b). Further, the media rarely reports the fact that a good proportion of the studies showing any differences are based on small numbers of college students persuaded to engage in experiments conducted in college laboratories and not in real world situations. Or, in the case of studies indicating the hormonal relationship between men's aggression and women's presumed lack of it, a number of studies are based on the behavior of laboratory animals. Other studies compare test scores of students in college, rarely reporting variables such as the class, race, and ethnicity of the population being studied. Even in these settings, the systematic research of social scientists has proved that males and females show almost no difference or shifting minor differences in measures of cognitive abilities (Hyde 2005) and emotions.[4] And there may be more evidence for similarity than even the scholarly public has access to, because when studies find no differences, the results might

not be published in scholarly publications. The Stanford University cognitive psychologist Barbara Tversky (personal communication) notes that when she has sought to publish the results of experiments on a variety of spatial tasks that show no gender differences, journal editors have demanded that she and her collaborators take them out because they are null findings. Even so, we can conclude that under conditions of equality, girls and women perform and achieve at test levels that are the same as or similar to males—and, in many cases, they perform better.[5]

The American Psychological Association has reported officially that males and females are more alike than different when tested on most psychological variables. The APA's finding is based on Janet Hyde's 2005 analysis of 46 meta-analyses conducted recently in the United States. They conclude that gender roles and social context lead to the few differences. Further, they report that sex differences, though believed to be immutable, fluctuate with age and location.[6] Women manifest similar aggressive feelings although their expression of them is obliged to take different forms (Frodi, Macaulay, and Thome 1977). A 2006 report from the National Academy of Sciences found that after an exhaustive review of the scientific literature, including studies of brain structure and function, it could find no evidence of any significant biological factors causing the underrepresentation of women in science and mathematics.[7] Sociologists too have found women's aspirations are linked to their opportunities (Kaufman and Richardson 1982). I observe that like men, women want love, work, and recognition.

So, given similar traits, do women prefer dead-end and limited opportunity jobs; do they wish to work without pay in the home or to be always subject to the authority of men? In the past, some economists thought so. The Nobel Laureate Gary Becker (1981) proposed that women make rational choices to work in the home to free their husbands for paid labor. A number of other scholars follow the rational-choice model to explain women's poorer position in the labor force. Not only has the model proven faulty (England 1989, 1994), but history has proven such ideas wrong. The truth is that men have prevented the incursions of women into their spheres except when they needed women's labor power, such as in wartime, proving that women were indeed a reserve army of labor. As I found in my own research, when windows of opportunity presented themselves, women fought to join the paid labor force at every level, from manual craft work to the elite professions. Men resisted, seeking to preserve the boundaries of their work domains—from craft unionists to the top strata of medical, legal, and legislative practice (Chafe 1972; Epstein 1970, [1981] 1993; Frank 1980; Honey 1984; Kessler-Harris 1982; Lorber 1975, 1984; Milkman 1987; O'Farrell 1999; Rupp 1978).

Social and economic changes in other parts of the West, and in other parts of the world, provide natural field experiments to confirm this data from the United States. In the West, where women have always been employed in the unpaid, family workforce, a revolution in women's interest and participation in the paid workplace spiraled after the First World War. In the United States, from 1930 to 1970 the participation of married women ages 35 to 44 in the labor force moved from 10 percent to 46 percent and today it is 77 percent (Goldin 2006). The opening of elite colleges and universities to women students after the 1960s led progressively to their increased participation in employment in the professions and other top jobs. This was the direct result of a concerted effort to use the Civil Rights Act of 1964 to force the opening of these sectors. Ruth Bader Ginsburg and her associates in the Women's Rights Project of the ACLU fought and won important battles in the Supreme Court and Judge Constance Baker Motley, the first African American woman to become a federal judge, ruled that large law firms had to recruit women on the same basis as men to comply with the equal treatment promised by the Civil Rights Act.

Yet even as the ideology of equality became widespread and brought significant changes, the worldwide status of women remained subordi-

nate to that of men. Stable governments and a new prosperity led to something of a revolution in women's statuses in the United States and other countries in the West, notably in Canada with its new charter prohibiting discrimination. There was also an increase in women's employment in the paid labor force in the 15 countries of the European Union, including those countries that traditionally were least likely to provide jobs for women, although the statistics do not reveal the quality of the jobs (Norris 2006). And, of course, women's movements have been instrumental in making poor conditions visible. In countries of the Middle East, the East, and the Global South, women are beginning to have representation in political spheres, the professions, and commerce, although their percentage remains quite small. Women's lot rises or falls as a result of regime changes and economic changes and is always at severe risk.[8] But nowhere are substantial numbers of women in political control; nowhere do women have the opportunity to carry out national agendas giving women truly equal rights.[9]

Structural gains, accompanied by cultural gains, have been considerable in many places. Most governments have signed on to commitments to women's rights, although they are almost meaningless in many regimes that egregiously defy them in practice. And, of course, in many societies women have fewer rights than do men and find themselves worse off than they were a generation ago.[10]

In no society have women had clear access to the best jobs in the workplace, nor have they anywhere achieved economic parity with men. As Charles and Grusky (2004) document in their recent book, *Occupational Ghettos: The Worldwide Segregation of Women and Men*, sex segregation in employment persists all over the world, including in the United States and Canada. Women workers earn less than men even in the most gender-egalitarian societies. Charles and Grusky suggest that the disadvantage in employment is partly because women are clustered in "women's jobs" —jobs in the low-paid service economy or white-collar jobs that do not offer autonomy. These are typically occupational ghettos worldwide. While Charles and Grusky observe that women are crowded into the nonmanual sector, women increasingly do work in the globalized manufacturing economy—for example, in assembly line production that supplies the world with components for computers or in the clothing sweatshops in Chinatowns in the United States and around the world (Bose and Acosta-Belén 1995; Zimmerman, Litt, and Bose 2006; see also Bao 2001; Lee 1998; Salzinger 2003).

Many women in newly industrializing countries experienced a benefit from employment created by transnational corporations in the 1980s and '90s. They received income and independence from their families, but they remained in sex-segregated, low-wage work, subject to cutbacks when corporations sought cheaper labor markets. As to their suitability for heavy labor, it is common to see (as I have personally witnessed) women hauling rocks and stones in building sites in India and other places. Throughout the world, where water is a scarce commodity it is women who carry heavy buckets and vessels of water, usually on foot and over long distances, because this has been designated as a woman's job and men regard it as a disgrace to help them. Apparently, in much of the world, the guiding principle of essentialism labels as women's jobs those that are not physically easier, necessarily, but rather those that are avoided by men, pay little, and are under the supervision of men.

Of course, women have moved into some male-labeled jobs. As I noted in my book on the consequences of sex boundaries, *Deceptive Distinctions* (1988), the amazing decades of the 1970s and '80s showed that women could do work—men's work—that no one, including themselves, thought they could and they developed interests no one thought they had, and numbers of men welcomed them, or at least tolerated them.

My research shows that women may cross gender barriers into the elite professions that retain their male definition, such as medicine and law (Epstein [1981] 1993), when there is legal support giving them access to training and equal recruitment in combination with a shortage of personnel. Women made their most dramatic gains during a time of rapid economic growth in the Western world.

I first started research on women in the legal profession in the 1960s, when women constituted only 3 percent of practitioners (Epstein [1981] 1993). When I last assessed their achievements (Epstein 2001), women composed about 30 percent of practicing lawyers and about half of all law students. The same striking changes were happening in medicine (they are now almost half of all medical students [Magrane, Lang, and Alexander 2005]), and women were moving into legal and medical specialties once thought to be beyond their interests or aptitudes, such as corporate law and surgery. Yet, even with such advances they face multiple glass ceilings (Epstein et al. 1995). Only small percentages have attained high rank.[11] And it should come as no surprise that men of high rank,[12] the popular media (Belkin 2003), and right-wing commentators (Brooks 2006; Tierney 2006) insist that it is women's own choice to limit their aspirations and even to drop out of the labor force. But this has not been women's pattern. Most educated women have continuous work histories. It is true, however, that many women's ambitions to reach the very top of their professions are undermined. For one thing, they generally face male hostility when they cross conventional boundaries and perform "men's work."[13] For another, they face inhospitable environments in male-dominated work settings in which coworkers not only are wary of women's ability but visibly disapprove of their presumed neglect of their families. Women generally face unrelieved burdens of care work in the United States, with few social supports (Coser 1974; Gornick 2003; Williams 2000). And they face norms that this work demands their *personal* attention— a *female's attention*.

Even in the most egalitarian societies, a myriad of subtle prejudices and practices are used by men in gatekeeping positions to limit women's access to the better, male-labeled jobs and ladders of success, for example, partnership tracks in large law firms (Epstein et al. 1995). Alternative routes for women, "Mommy tracks" have been institutionalized—touted as a benefit—but usually result in stalled careers (Bergmann and Helburn 2002). Husbands who wish to limit their own work hours to assist working wives usually encounter severe discrimination as well. Individual men who are seen as undermining the system of male advantage find themselves disciplined and face discrimination (Epstein et al. 1999, Williams 2000). In the United States this may lead to the loss of a promotion or a job. In other places in the world, the consequences are even more dire.[14]

In the current "best of all worlds," ideologies of difference and, to use Charles Tilly's (1998) concept, "exploitation and opportunity hoarding" by men in control keep the top stratum of law and other professions virtually sex segregated. Gatekeepers today don't necessarily limit entry, as that would place them in violation of sex discrimination laws in the United States or put them in an uncomfortable position, given modern Western ideologies of equality. But powerful men move only a small percentage of the able women they hire (often hired in equal numbers with men) upward on the path toward leadership and decision making, especially in professions and occupations experiencing slow growth. Most rationalize, with the approval of conventional wisdom, that women's own decisions determine their poor potential for achieving power.

Inequality in the workplace is created and reinforced by inequality in education. Newspaper headlines reported that more women than men get B.A.s in the United States today (Lewin 2006a), "leaving men in the dust." But a report a few days later noted that the increase is due to older women going back to school, and that women's degrees are in traditional women's fields (Lewin 2006b).

But women's performance and acceptance in the world of higher education in the United States is the good news! Consider the rest of the world. In many countries girls are denied *any* education. Consider, for example, the case of Afghanistan, where the Taliban still are attempting to resume power. In July 2006, they issued warnings to parents that girls going to school may get acid thrown in their faces or be murdered (Coghlan 2006).

Consider that in Southern Asia 23.5 million girls do not attend school and in Central and West Africa virtually half of all girls are also excluded (Villalobos 2006). While poverty contributes to poor educational opportunities for boys as well as girls in many parts of the world, girls' restrictions are far greater. Some fundamentalist societies permit women to get a higher education, but this is to prepare them for work in segregated conditions where they serve other women.

The sex segregation of labor as measured by sophisticated sociologists and economists does not even acknowledge women's labor *outside* the wage-earning structure. Women and girls labor behind the walls of their homes, producing goods that provide income for their families, income they have no control over. Thus, millions of girls and women are not even counted in the labor force, although they perform essential work in the economy (Bose, Feldberg, and Sokoloff 1987).[15]

In addition, females can be regarded as a commodity themselves. They are computed as a means of barter in tribal families that give their girls (often before puberty) to men outside their tribe or clan who want wives to produce children and goods. Men also trade their daughters to men of other tribes as a form of compensation for the killing of a member of another tribe or other reasons.[16] Harmony is re-equilibrated through the bodies of females.

There is much more to report about the roles and position of women in the labor force worldwide—my life's work—but there are other spheres in which females everywhere are mired in subordinate roles. Chief among them are the family and the social and cultural structures that keep women both segregated and in a state of symbolic and actual "otherness," undermining their autonomy and dignity. Nearly everywhere, women are regarded as "others."[17]

Mechanisms Creating "Otherness"

To some extent, women are subject to the process of social speciation—a term that Kai Erikson (1996) introduced (modifying the concept of pseudospeciation offered by Erik Erikson) to refer to the fact that humans divide into various groups who regard themselves as "the foremost species" and then feel that others ought to be kept in their place by "conquest or the force of harsh custom" (Erikson 1996:52). Harsh customs and conquest certainly ensure the subordination of girls and women. I shall consider some of these below.

Kin Structures. In many societies brides are required to leave their birth homes and enter as virtual strangers into the homes of their husbands and their husbands' kin. Because of the practice of patrilocality they usually have few or no resources—human or monetary. Marrying very young, they enter these families with the lowest rank and no social supports. About one in seven girls in the developing world gets married before her 15th birthday according to the Population Council, an international research group (Bearak 2006). Local and international attempts to prevent this practice have been largely unsuccessful.[18]

In exploring the actual and symbolic segregation of women I have been inspired by the work of Mounira Charrad in her 2001 prize-winning book *States and Women's Rights: The Making of Postcolonial Tunisia, Algeria, and Morocco*. The work of Val Moghadam (2003) and Roger Friedland (2002) also informs this analysis. Writing of the relative status of women, Charrad points to the iron grip of patrilineal kin groups in North African societies. She notes how Islamic family law has legitimized the extended male-centered patrilineage that serves as the foundation of kin-based solidarities within tribal groups so that state politics and tribal politics converge. This supports the patriarchal power not only of husbands, but also of all male kin over women so that the clan

defines its boundaries through a family law that rests on the exploitation of women. Her study shows how Islamic family law (Sharia) provides a meaningful symbol of national unity in the countries of the Maghreb. This has changed in Tunisia, but it remains the case for other societies—Iraq, Saudi Arabia, Jordan, Kuwait, Afghanistan, southeastern Turkey, parts of Iran, and southern Egypt. As Moghadam (2003) points out, the gender dimension of the Afghan conflict is prototypical of other conflicts today. During periods of strife, segregation and subordination of women becomes a sign of cultural identity. We see it clearly in the ideologies of Hamas and Hezbollah, Iran, Chechnya, and other Islamic groups and societies, and in the ideologies of fundamentalist Christian and Jewish groups. Representations of women are deployed during processes of revolution and state building to preserve group boundaries within larger societies with competing ideologies, and when power is being reconstituted, linking women either to modernization and progress or to cultural rejuvenation and religious orthodoxy.

Few social scientists have paid attention to the role of kin structures and their accompanying conceptual structures in the minds of players in national and international politics, but I believe this negligence persists at our peril as we experience conflicts between kin-based collectivities in the world.

Of course, human sexuality has much to do with the cultural sex divide. The fact that men desire women sexually, and that women also desire men, means that they are destined to live together no matter what the culture and family structures in which they live. And sexuality could, and can, create equality through bonds of connection and affection. As William Goode (1959) points out in an important but perhaps forgotten paper, "The Theoretical Importance of Love," love is a universal emotion. As such it threatens social structures because the ties between men and women could be stronger than the bonds between men. Thus, everywhere the affiliations made possible by love are contained in various ways.

In societies in which marriage is embedded in a larger kin structure beyond the nuclear family, the practices and rules of domicile and the conventions around it have the potential to undermine the possibility of a truly affective marital tie, one that could integrate women in the society. A couple may face a wall of separation—apartheid in the home in separate parts of the compound or house. Or, they may be community-bound or home-bound in fundamentalist religious groups within larger secular societies such as the United States (e.g., the Jewish Satmar community in New York [where women are not permitted to drive] [Winston 2005] or some Christian fundamentalist communities where women are required to home-school their children).

I shall now focus on some other symbolic uses of sex distinctions that facilitate the subordination of women.

Honor.   Females are designated as carriers of honor in many societies. Their "virtue" is a symbolic marker of men's group boundaries. As we know from Mary Douglas (1966) and others, we can think about any social practice in terms of purity and danger. In many societies, females are the designated carriers of boundary distinctions. Their conformity to norms is regarded as the representation of the dignity of the group, while males typically have much greater latitude to engage in deviant behavior. To achieve and maintain female purity, women's behavior is closely monitored and restricted. As Friedland (2002) writes, religious nationalists direct "their attention to the bodies of women—covering, separating and regulating" (p. 396) them, in order "to masculinize the public sphere, to contain the erotic energies of heterosexuality within the family seeking to masculinize collective representations, to make the state male, a virile collective subject, the public status of women's bodies is a critical site and source for religious nationalist political mobilization" (p. 401).

The idea that girls must remain virgins until they marry or their entire family will suffer dishonor is used as a mechanism for women's segregation and subordination all over the world. It is also used as justification for the murder of many young women by male family members claiming to cleanse the girls' supposed dishonor from the family.[19] In particular, we see this at play in parts of the Middle East and among some Muslim communities in the diaspora.

When a woman strays from her prescribed roles, seeks autonomy, or is believed to have had sex with a man outside of marriage, killing her is regarded as a reasonable response by her very own relatives, often a father or brother. In Iraq, at last count, since the beginning of the present war, there have been 2,000 honor killings (Tarabay 2006), and United Nations officials estimate 5,000 worldwide (BBC 2003). In the summer of 2006, the *New York Times* reported that in Turkey, a society becoming more religiously conservative, girls regarded as errant because they moved out of the control of their parents or chose a boyfriend, thus casting dishonor on the family, are put in situations in which they are expected and pressured to commit suicide. Suicide spares a family the obligation to murder her and face prosecution (Bilefsky 2006). Elsewhere, such murders are barely noted by the police.

Female circumcision is also intended to preserve women's honor. In many areas of the African continent, girls are subjected to genital cutting as a prelude to marriage and as a technique to keep them from having pleasure during sex, which, it is reasoned, may lead them to an independent choice of mate.

Conferring on women the symbolism of sexual purity as a basis of honor contributes to their vulnerability. In today's genocidal warfare, the mass rape of women by marauding forces is not just due to the sexual availability of conquered women. Rape is used as a mechanism of degradation. If the men involved in the Bosnian and Darfur massacres regarded rape as an atrocity and a *dishonor* to their cause, it could not have been used so successfully as a tool of war. Further, we know that the Bosnian and Sudanese rape victims, like women who have been raped in Pakistan, India, and other places, are regarded as defiled and are shunned, as are the babies born of such rapes.

Clothing as a Symbolic Tool for Differentiation. The chador and veil are tools men use to symbolize and maintain women's honor. Although men, with some exceptions,[20] wear Western dress in much of the world, women's clothing is used to symbolize their cultures' confrontations with modernity, in addition to clothing's symbolic roles. Presumably worn to assure modesty and to protect women's honor, the clothing prescribed, even cultural relativists must admit, serves to restrict women's mobility. Hot and uncomfortable, women cannot perform tasks that require speed and mobility, and it prevents women from using motorbikes and bicycles, the basic means of transportation in poor societies. Distinctive clothing is not restricted to the Third World. Fundamentalist groups in Europe and the United States also mandate clothing restrictions for women.[21]

Of course, clothing is used to differentiate women and men in all societies. In the past, Western women's clothing was also restrictive (e.g., long skirts and corsets) and today, as women have moved toward greater equality, women and men are permitted to wear similar garb (such as jeans and t-shirts). Of course, fashion prescribes more sexually evocative (thus distinctive) clothing for women than it does for men.

Time and Space. How can we speak of the otherness and subordination of women without noting the power of the variables of time and space in the analysis? In every society the norms governing the use of time and space are gendered (Epstein and Kalleberg 2004). People internalize feelings about the proper use of time and space as a result of the normative structure. Worldwide, the boundaries of time and space are constructed to offer men freedom and to restrict women's choices. In most of the world, women rise earlier than do men and start food preparation; they eat at times men don't. Further, sex segregation of work in and outside the home means a couple's primary contact may be in the bedroom. If

women intrude on men's space they may violate a taboo and be punished for it. Similarly, men who enter into women's spaces do so only at designated times and places. The taboo elements undermine the possibility of easy interaction, the opportunity to forge friendships, to connect, and to create similar competencies. In the Western world, working different shifts is common (Presser 2003), which also results in segregation of men and women.

There are rules in every society, some by law and others by custom, that specify when and where women may go, and whether they can make these journeys alone or must appear with a male relative. Some segregation is to protect men from women's temptations (e.g., Saudi Arabia, Iran, the Satmar sect in Monsey, NY) and some to protect women from men's sexual advances (e.g., Mexico, Tokyo, Mumbai). But the consequence is that men overwhelmingly are allotted more space and territorialize public space.

A common variable in the time prescription for women is surveillance; women are constrained to operate within what I am calling *role zones*. In these, their time is accounted for and prescribed. They have less *free* time. In our own Western society, women note that the first thing to go when they attempt to work and have children is "free time." Free time is typically enjoyed by the powerful, and it gives them the opportunity to engage in the politics of social life. Most people who work at a subsistence level, refugees, and those who labor in jobs not protected by the authority of the dominant group, don't have free time either. Slave owners own the time of their slaves.

A Theory of Female Subordination

All of this leads me to ask a basic sociological question. Why does the subordination of women and girls persist no matter how societies change in other ways? How does half the world's population manage to hold and retain power over the other half? And what are we to make of the women who comply?

The answers lie in many of the practices I have described and they remain persuasive with a global perspective. I propose an even more basic explanation for the persistence of inequality, and often a reversion to inequality, when equality seems to be possible or near attainment. In *Deceptive Distinctions* (1988) I proposed the theory that the division of labor in society assigns women the most important survival tasks—reproduction and gathering and preparation of food. All over the world, women do much of the reproductive work, ensuring the continuity of society. They do this both in physical terms and in symbolic terms. Physically, they do so through childbirth and child care. They do much of the daily work any social group needs for survival. For example, half of the world's food, and up to 80 percent in developing countries, is produced by women (Food and Agriculture Organization of the United Nations n.d.; Women's World Summit Foundation 2006). They also prepare the food at home, work in the supermarkets, behind the counters, and on the conveyor belts that package it. In their homes and in schools, they produce most preschool and primary school education. They take care of the elderly and infirm. They socialize their children in the social skills that make interpersonal communication possible. They are the support staffs for men. This is a good deal—no, a great deal—for the men.

Controlling women's labor and behavior is a mechanism for male governance and territoriality. Men's authority is held jealously. Men legitimate their behavior through ideological and theological constructs that justify their domination. Further, social institutions reinforce this.[22]

I shall review the mechanisms:

We know about the use and threat of force (Goode 1972).[23] We know as well about the role of law and justice systems that do not accord women the same rights to protection, property, wealth, or even education enjoyed by men. We know that men control and own guns and the means of transport, and they often lock women out of membership and leadership of trade unions, political parties, religious institutions, and other powerful organizations. We know too that huge numbers of men feel justified in threatening and punishing females who deviate from male-mandated rules in public and private spaces. That's the strong-arm stuff.

But everywhere, in the West as well as in the rest of the world, women's segregation and subjugation is also done *culturally* and through *cognitive* mechanisms that reinforce existing divisions of rights and labor and award men authority over women. Internalized cultural schemas reinforce men's views that their behavior is legitimate and persuade women that their lot is just. The media highlight the idea that women and men think differently and naturally gravitate to their social roles.[24] This is more than just "pluralistic ignorance" (Merton [1948] 1963). Bourdieu ([1979] 1984) reminds us that dominated groups often contribute to their own subordination because of perceptions shaped by the conditions of their existence—the dominant system made of binary oppositions. Using Eviatar Zerubavel's (1997) term, "mindscapes" set the stage for household authorities and heads of clans, tribes, and communities to separate and segregate women in the belief that the practice is inevitable and right. Such mindscapes also persuade the females in their midst to accept the legitimacy and inevitability of their subjection, and even to defend it, as we have seen lately in some academic discourses.

The mindscapes that legitimate women's segregation are the cognitive translations of ideologies that range the spectrum from radical fundamentalism to difference feminism; all are grounded in cultural-religious or pseudoscientific views that women have different emotions, brains, aptitudes, ways of thinking, conversing, and imagining. Such mindsets are legitimated every day in conventional understandings expressed from the media, pulpits, boardrooms, and in departments of universities. Psychologists call them schemas (Brewer and Nakamura 1984)—culturally set definitions that people internalize. Gender operates as a cultural "superschema" (Roos and Gatta 2006) that shapes interaction and cues stereotypes (Ridgeway 1997). Schemas that define femaleness and maleness are basic to all societies. Schemas also define insiders and outsiders and provide definitions of justice and equality.

In popular speech, philosophical musings, cultural expressions, and the banter of everyday conversation, people tend to accept the notion of difference. They accept its inevitability and are persuaded of the legitimacy of segregation, actual or symbolic. Thus, acceptance of difference perspectives—the idea that women often have little to offer to the group, may result in rules that forbid women from speaking in the company of men (in a society governed by the Taliban) or may result in senior academics' selective deafness to the contributions of a female colleague in a university committee room.

Conclusion

In conclusion I want to reiterate certain observations:

Intrinsic qualities are attributed to women that have little or nothing to do with their actual characteristics or behavior. Because those attributions are linked to assigned roles their legitimation is an ongoing project. Changing these ideas would create possibilities for changing the status quo and threaten the social institutions in which men have the greatest stake and in which some women believe they benefit.

Is women's situation different from that of men who, by fortune, color of skin, or accident of birth also suffer from exploitation by the powerful? I am claiming *yes*, because they carry not only the hardships—sometimes relative hardships—but the ideological and cognitive overlay that defines their subordination as legitimate and normal. Sex and gender are the organizing markers in all societies. In no country, political group, or community are men defined as lesser human beings than their *female* counterparts. But almost everywhere women are so defined.

Why is this acceptable? And why does it persist?

So many resources are directed to legitimating females' lower place in society. So few men inside the power structure are interested in inviting them in. And so many women and girls accept the Orwellian notion that restriction is freedom, that suffering is pleasure, that silence is power.[25]

Of course this is not a static condition, nor, I hope, an inevitable one. Women in the Western world, and in various sectors of the rest of the world, have certainly moved upward in the continuum toward equality. Thirty-five years ago I noted how women in the legal profession in the United States were excluded from the informal networks that made inclusion and mobility possible. Now, noticeable numbers have ventured over the barriers. Similarly, there has been a large increase in the numbers of women who have entered the sciences,[26] business, medicine, and veterinary medicine (Cox and Alm 2005). This has changed relatively swiftly. Women didn't develop larger brains—nor did their reasoning jump from left brain to right brain or the reverse. Nor did they leave Venus for Mars. Rather, they learned that they could not be barred from higher education and they could get appropriate jobs when they graduated. The problem is no longer one of qualifications or entry but of promotion and inclusion into the informal networks leading to the top. But the obstacles are great.

In his review of cognitive sociological dynamics, DiMaggio (1997) reminds us of Merton's notion of "pluralistic ignorance," which is at work when people act with reference to shared collective opinions that are empirically incorrect. There would not be a firm basis for the subordinate condition of females were there not a widespread belief, rooted in folk culture, in their essential difference from males in ability and emotion. This has been proven time and time again in research in the "real" world of work and family institutions (e.g., Epstein et al. 1995) and laboratory observations (Berger, Cohen, and Zelditch 1966; Frodi et al. 1977; Ridgeway and Smith-Lovin 1999).

We know full well that there are stories and master social narratives accepted by untold millions of people that have no basis in what social scientists would regard as evidence. The best examples are the basic texts of the world's great religions. But there are also societywide beliefs of other kinds. Belief systems are powerful. And beliefs that are unprovable or proven untrue often capture the greatest number of believers. Sometimes, they are simply the best stories.

We in the social sciences have opened the gates to a better understanding of the processes by which subordinated groups suffer because the use of *categories* such as race and ethnicity rank human beings so as to subordinate, exclude, and exploit them (Tilly 1998). However, relatively few extend this insight to the category of gender or sex. The sexual divide so defines social life, and so many people in the world have a stake in upholding it, that it is the most resistant of all categories to change. Today, Hall and Lamont (forthcoming; Lamont 2005) are proposing that the most productive societies are those with porous boundaries between categories of people. Perhaps there is an important incentive in a wider understanding of this idea. Small groups of men may prosper by stifling women's potential, but prosperous nations benefit from women's full participation and productivity in societies. Societies might achieve still more if the gates were truly open.

Sociologists historically have been committed to social change to achieve greater equality in the world, in both public and private lives. But in this address I challenge our profession to take this responsibility in our scholarship and our professional lives; to observe, to reveal, and to strike down the conceptual and cultural walls that justify inequality on the basis of sex in all of society's institutions—to transgress this ever-present boundary—for the sake of knowledge and justice.

Notes

1. For more horrors see Parrot and Cummings (2006).

2. Perhaps the best known eye into this world is that of Nicholas Kristof, the *New York Times* writer, whose Op Ed articles chronicle the horrors faced by women in Africa and the inaction of Western societies to redress them (for example, the United States cut off funding to the United Nations Population Fund, an agency that has led the effort to reduce maternal deaths, because of false allegations it supports abortion) (Kristof 2006).

3. The works of John Gray (1992), the author of *Men are from Mars, Women are from Venus* and spin-off titles have sold over 30 million copies in the United States. See also Deborah Tannen's (1990) *You Just Don't Understand* on the presumed inability of men and women to understand each other on various dimensions, repudiated by the work of the linguistic scholar Elizabeth Aries (1996).

4. There has been a recent flurry over reported differences in male and female brains (cf. Brizendine 2006; Bell et al. 2006) and reports of a 3 to 4 percentage difference in IQ. The brain studies are usually based on very small samples and the IQ studies on standardized tests in which the differences reported are at the very end of large distributions that essentially confirm male/female similarities (see Epstein 1988 for a further analysis).

5. A 2006 *New York Times* report shows that women are getting more B.A.s than are men in the United States. However, in the highest income families, men age 24 and below attend college as much as, or slightly more than their sisters, according to the American Council on Education. The article also reports that women are obtaining a disproportionate number of honors at elite institutions such as Harvard, the University of Wisconsin, UCLA, and some smaller schools such as Florida Atlanta University (Lewin 2006a). A comparison of female and male math scores varies with the test given. Females score somewhat lower on the SAT-M but differences do not exist on the American College Test (ACT) or on untimed versions of the SAT-M (Bailey n.d.).

6. Girls even perform identically in math until high school when they are channeled on different tracks. In Great Britain, they do better than males, as noted

in the ASA statement contesting the remarks of then Harvard President Lawrence Summers questioning the ability of females to engage in mathematics and scientific research (American Sociological Association 2005; see also Boaler and Sengupta-Irving 2006).

7. The panel blamed environments that favor men, continuous questioning of women's abilities and commitment to an academic career, and a system that claims to reward based on merit but instead rewards traits that are socially less acceptable for women to possess (Fogg 2006).

8. Hartmann, Lovell, and Werschkul (2004) show how, in the recession of March to November 2001, there was sustained job loss for women for the first time in 40 years. The economic downturn affected women's employment, labor force participation, and wages 43 months after the start of the recession.

9. In Scandinavian countries, women have achieved the most political representation: Finland (37.5 percent of parliament seats), Norway (36.4 percent of parliament seats), Sweden (45.3 percent of parliament seats), and Denmark (38 percent of parliament seats) (U.N. Common Database 2004; Dahlerup n.d.). Of course, women in some societies still do not have the right to vote, and in a few, like Kuwait, where they have just gotten the vote, it is unclear whether they have been able to exercise it independently.

10. This is the case in Egypt, Iran, Iraq, Gaza, and Lebanon as fundamentalist groups have gained power, even in those regimes that are formally secular.

11. The current figure for women partners in large law firms (those with more than 250 lawyers) in the United States is 17 percent, although women are one-half of the recruits in these firms (National Association for Law Placement cited in O'Brien 2006; Nicholson 2006).

12. A national survey of 1,500 professors (as yet unpublished) at all kinds of institutions in the United States conducted by Neil Gross of Harvard and Solon Simmons of George Mason University shows that most professors don't agree that discrimination—intentional or otherwise—is the main reason that men hold so many more positions than do women in the sciences (Jaschik 2006).

13. In studies of jobs dominated by men that are seen as requiring traits that distinguish men as superior to women in intellect or strength, it is reported that men's pride is punctured if women perform them (see Chetkovich 1997 on firefighters; Collinson, Knights, and Collinson 1990 on managers).

14. For example, when the magazine publisher Ali Mohaqeq returned to Afghanistan in 2004 after a long exile he was imprisoned for raising questions about women's rights in the new "democracy." Afghan courts claimed his offense was to contravene the teachings of Islam by printing essays that questioned legal discrimination against women (Witte 2005).

15. Women have been unpaid workers on family farms or in small businesses, taking in boarders, and doing factory outwork (see Bose et al. 1987 for the United States; Bose and Acosta-Belén 1995 for Latin America; and Hsiung 1996 for Taiwan).

16. There are numerous references on the Web to the use of women given in marriage to another tribe or group in the reports of Amnesty International, for example in Papua New Guinea, Afghanistan, Pakistan, and Fiji.

17. The characterization of women as "other" was most notably made by Simone de Beauvoir ([1949] 1993) in her book, *The Second Sex*.

18. Struggles between human rights activists in and out of government and fundamentalist regimes have shifted upward and downward on such matters as raising the age of marriage of girls. For example, attempts by Afghanistan's King Abanullah in the 1920s to raise the age of marriage and institute education for girls enraged the patriarchal tribes who thwarted his regime. Fifty years later a socialist government enacted legislation to change family law to encourage women's employment, education, and choice of spouse. The regime failed in the early 1990s due to internal rivalries and a hostile international climate (Moghadam 2003:270) and the Taliban took power. In the early 1990s they exiled women to their homes, denied them access to education and opportunities to work for pay, and even denied them the right to look out of their windows.

19. A United Nations (2002) report found that there were legislative provisions "allowing for partial or complete defense" in the case of an honor killing in: Argentina, Bangladesh, Ecuador, Egypt, Guatemala, Iran, Israel, Jordan, Lebanon, Peru, Syria, Turkey, Venezuela, and the Palestinian National Authority (of course law does not equal practice). For example, in

Pakistan and Jordan honor killings are outlawed but they occur nevertheless.

20. In demonstrations in societies led by religious leaders, men typically wear Western style shirts and trousers although their leaders typically choose clerics' robes and turbans. Leaders of countries outside the "Western" orbit often choose distinctive dress—robes, beards, open neck shirts, and other costumes for ceremonial occasions or to make political statements.

21. Hella Winston (personal communication, September 30, 2006) told me that in the orthodox Jewish community of New Square in New York State, a recent edict by the Rabbi reminded women they were to wear modest dress, specifying that "sleeves must be to the end of the bone, and [to] not wear narrow clothing or short clothing." They were not to ride bikes or speak loudly.

22. Where religious laws govern such areas of civic life as family relations, inheritance, and punishment for crimes, for example, they invariably institutionalize women's subordinate status.

23. As one of many possible examples: when hundreds of women gathered in downtown Tehran on July 31, 2006 to protest institutionalized sex discrimination in Iran (in areas such as divorce, child custody, employment rights, age of adulthood, and court proceedings where a woman's testimony is viewed as half of a man's), 100 male and female police beat them. Reports also noted a tightening of the dress code and segregation on buses and in some public areas such as parks, sidewalks, and elevators. Another demonstration on March 8, 2006 was dispersed as police dumped garbage on the heads of participants (Stevens 2006).

24. The recent book by Louann Brizendine (2006), which asserts that the female and male brains are completely different, offering such breezy accounts as "woman is weather, constantly changing and hard to predict" and "man is mountain," has been on the top 10 on the Amazon.com book list and led to her prominent placement on ABC's 20/20 and morning talk shows. Thanks to Troy Duster for passing this on.

25. For example, a recent poll cited in the *New York Times* (June 8, 2006) indicates that a majority of women in Muslim countries do not regard themselves as unequal (Andrews 2006). Of course, this attitude is widespread throughout the world, including Western societies.

26. Comparing percentages of women attaining doctorates in the sciences from 1970–71 to 2001–2002 the increases were: Engineering .2–17.3; Physics 2.9–15.5; Computer Science 2.3–22.8; Mathematics 7.6–29.

References

American Sociological Association. 2005. "ASA Council Statement on the Causes of Gender Differences in Science and Math Career Achievement" (February 28). Retrieved September 21, 2006 (http://www2.asanet.org/footnotes/mar05/indexthree.html).

Andrews, Helena. 2006. "Muslim Women Don't See Themselves as Oppressed, Survey Finds." *New York Times*, June 7, p. A9.

Aries, Elizabeth. 1996. *Men and Women in Interaction: Reconsidering the Differences*. New York: Oxford University Press.

Bailey, Justin P. N.d. "Men are from Earth, Women are from Earth: Rethinking the Utility of the Mars/Venus Analogy." Retrieved September 28, 2006 (www.framingham.edu/joct/pdf/J.Bailey.1.pdf).

Bao, Xiaolan. 2001. *Holding Up More Than Half the Sky: Chinese Women Garment Workers in New York City, 1948–92*. Urbana, IL and Chicago, IL: University of Illinois Press.

Basow, Susan A. 1995. "Student Evaluation of College Professors: When Gender Matters." *Journal of Educational Psychology* 87:656–65.

BBC. 2003. "Speaking Out Over Jordan 'Honour Killings.'" Retrieved September 21, 2006 (http://news.bbc.co.uk/2/hi/middle_east/2802305.stm).

Bearak, Barry. 2006. "The Bride Price." *New York Times Magazine*, July 9, p. 45.

Beauvoir, Simone de. [1949] 1993. *The Second Sex*. New York: Alfred A. Knopf.

Becker, Gary. 1981. *A Treatise on the Family*. Cambridge, MA: Harvard University Press.

Belkin, Lisa. 2003. "The Opt-Out Revolution." *New York Times Magazine*, October 26, p. 42.

Bell, Emily C., Morgan C. Willson, Alan H. Wilman, Sanjay Dave, and Peter H. Silverstone. 2006. "Males and Females Differ in Brain Activation During Cognitive Tasks." *NeuroImage* 30:529–38.

Berger, Joseph, Bernard P. Cohen, and Morris Zelditch Jr. 1966. "Status Characteristics and Expectation States." Pp. 29–46 in *Sociological Theories in Progress*, vol. I, edited by Joseph Berger, Morris Zelditch Jr., and Bo Anderson. Boston, MA: Houghton Mifflin.

Bergmann, Barbara R. and Suzanne Helburn. 2002. *America's Child Care Problem: The Way Out*. New York: Palgrave, St. Martin's Press.

Bilefsky, Dan. 2006. "How to Avoid Honor Killing in Turkey? Honor Suicide." *New York Times*, July 16, section 1, p. 3.

Boaler, Jo and Tesha Sengupta-Irving. 2006. "Nature, Neglect & Nuance: Changing Accounts of Sex, Gender and Mathematics." Pp. 207–20 in *Gender and Education, International Handbook*, edited by C. Skelton and L. Smulyan. London, England: Sage.

Bose, Christine E. and Edna Acosta-Belén. 1995. *Women in the Latin American Development Process*. Philadelphia, PA: Temple University Press.

Bose, Christine E., Roslyn Feldberg, and Natalie Sokolof. 1987. *Hidden Aspects of Women's Work*. New York: Praeger.

Bourdieu, Pierre. [1979] 1984. *Distinctions: A Social Critique of the Judgment of Taste*. Cambridge, MA: Harvard University Press.

Brewer, William F. and Glenn Nakamura. 1984. "The Nature and Functions of Schemas." Pp. 119–60 in *Handbook of Social Cognition*, vol. 1, edited by R. S. Wyer and T. K. Srull. Hillsdale, NJ: Erlbaum.

Brizendine, Louann. 2006. *The Female Brain*. New York: Morgan Road Books.

Brooks, David. 2006. "The Gender Gap at School." *New York Times*, June 11, section 4, p. 12.

Chafe, William H. 1972. *The American Woman: Her Changing Social, Economic and Political Roles: 1920–1970*. Oxford, England: Oxford University Press.

Charles, Maria and David Grusky. 2004. *Occupational Ghettos: The Worldwide Segregation of Women and Men*. Stanford, CA: Stanford University Press.

Charrad, Mounira. 2001. *States and Women's Rights: The Making of Postcolonial Tunisia, Algeria, and Morocco*. Berkeley, CA: The University of California Press.

Chetkovich, Carol. 1997. *Real Heat: Gender and Race in the Urban Fire Service*. New York: Routledge.

Coghlan, Tom. 2006. "Taliban Use Beheadings and Beatings to Keep Afghanistan's Schools Closed." *The Independent*, July 11. Retrieved July 11, 2006

(http://news.independent.co.uk/world/asia/article1171369.ece).

Collinson, David L., David Knights, and Margaret Collinson. 1990. *Managing to Discriminate*. London, England: Routledge.

Connell, R. W. 1987. *Gender and Power: Society, the Person and Sexual Politics*. Stanford, CA: Stanford University Press.

Coser, Rose Laub. 1974. "Stay Home Little Sheba: On Placement, Displacement and Social Change." *Social Problems* 22:470–80.

Cox, W. Michael and Richard Alm. 2005. "Scientists are Made, Not Born." *New York Times*, February 25, p. A25.

Dahlerup, Drude. N.d. "The World of Quotas." *Women in Politics: Beyond Numbers*. International Institute for Democracy and Electoral Assistance. Retrieved September 21, 2006 (http://archive.idea.int/women/parl/ch4c.htm).

DiMaggio, Paul. 1997. "Culture and Cognition." *Annual Review of Sociology* 23:263–87.

Douglas, Mary. 1966. *Purity and Danger: An Analysis of Concepts of Pollution and Taboo*. London, England: Routledge & Keegan Paul.

England, Paula. 1989. "A Feminist Critique of Rational-Choice Theories: Implications for Sociology." *The American Sociologist* 20:14–28.

———. 1994. "Neoclassical Economists' Theories of Discrimination." Pp. 59–70 in *Equal Employment Opportunity*, edited by P. Burstein. New York: Aldine De Gruyter.

Epstein, Cynthia Fuchs. [1981] 1993. *Women in Law*. Urbana, IL: University of Illinois Press.

———. 1988. *Deceptive Distinctions*. New Haven, CT and New York: Yale University Press and Russell Sage Foundation.

———. 1991. "What's Wrong and What's Right With the Research on Gender." *Sociological Viewpoints* 5:1–14.

———. 1999. "Similarity and Difference: The Sociology of Gender Distinctions." Pp. 45–61 in *Handbook of the Sociology of Gender*, edited by J. S. Chafetz. New York: Kluwer Academic/Plenum Publishers.

———. 2001. "Women in the Legal Profession at the Turn of the Twenty-First Century: Assessing Glass Ceilings and Open Doors." *Kansas Law Review* 49: 733–60.

Epstein, Cynthia Fuchs and Arne Kalleberg, eds. 2004. *Fighting for Time: Shifting Boundaries of*

Work and Social Life. New York: Russell Sage Foundation.

Epstein, Cynthia Fuchs, Robert Sauté, Bonnie Oglensky, and Martha Gever. 1995. "Glass Ceilings and Open Doors: The Mobility of Women in Large Corporate Law Firms." *Fordham Law Review* LXIV: 291–449.

Erikson, Kai. 1996. "On Pseudospeciation and Social Speciation." Pp. 51–58 in *Genocide: War and Human Survival*, edited by C. Strozier and M. Flynn. Lanham, MD: Rowman & Littlefield.

Fogg, Piper. 2006. "Panel Blames Bias for Gender Gap." *The Chronicle*, September 29. Retrieved October 24, 2006 (http://chronicle.com/weekly/v53/i06/06a01301.htm).

Food and Agriculture Organization of the United Nations. N.d. "Gender and Food Security: Agriculture." Retrieved August 5, 2006 (http://www.fao.org/gender/en/agri-e.htm).

Frank, Marian. 1980. *The Life and Times of "Rosie the Riveter."* A study guide for the video *Rosie the Riveter*, Connie Field, director. Los Angeles, CA: Direct Cinema.

Friedland, Roger. 2002. "Money, Sex and God: The Erotic Logic of Religious Nationalism." *Sociological Theory* 20:381–425.

Frodi, Ann, Jacqueline Macaulay, and Pauline Robert Thome. 1977. "Are Women Always Less Aggressive than Men? A Review of the Experimental Literature." *Psychological Bulletin* 84: 634–60.

Goldin, Claudia. 2006. "The Quiet Revolution That Transformed Women's Employment, Education and Family." *American Economic Association Papers and Proceedings* 96:7–19.

Goode, William J. 1959. "The Theoretical Importance of Love." *American Sociological Review* 24:38–47.

———. 1972. "The Place of Force in Human Society." *American Sociological Review* 37:507–19.

Gornick, Janet. 2003. *Families that Work: Policies for Reconciling Parenthood and Employment.* New York: Russell Sage Foundation.

Gray, John. 1992. *Men are from Mars, Women are from Venus.* New York: HarperCollins.

Hall, Peter and Michele Lamont. Forthcoming. *Successful Societies* (working title).

Hartmann, Heidi, Vicky Lovell, and Misha Werschkul. 2004. "Women and the Economy: Recent Trends in Job Loss, Labor Force Participation and Wages." Briefing Paper, Institute for Women's Policy Research. IWPR Publication B235.

Honey, Maureen. 1984. *Creating Rosie the Riveter: Class, Gender and Propaganda during World War 2.* Boston, MA: University of Massachusetts Press.

Hsiung, Ping-Chun. 1996. *Living Rooms as Factories: Class, Gender and the Satellite Factory System in Taiwan.* Philadelphia, PA: Temple University Press

Hyde, Janet Shibley. 2005. "The Gender Similarities Hypothesis." *American Psychologist* 60:581–92.

Jaschik, Scott. 2006. "Bias or Interest?" *Inside Higher Ed*, September 20. Retrieved September 28 (http://insidehighered.com/layout/set/print/news/2006/09/20/women).

Kaufman, Debra R. and Barbara Richarson. 1982. *Achievement and Women: Challenging the Assumptions.* New York: The Free Press.

Kessler-Harris, Alice. 1982. *Women Have Always Worked: A Historical Overview.* Old Westbury, CT: Feminist Press.

Kristof, Nicholas. 2006. "Save My Wife." *New York Times*, September 17, opinion section, p. 15.

Lamont, Michele. 2005. "Bridging Boundaries: Inclusion as a Condition for Successful Societies." Presented at the Successful Societies Program of the Canadian Institute for Advanced Research, October, Montebello, Quebec, Canada.

Lee, Ching Kwan. 1998. *Gender and the South China Miracle: Two Worlds of Factory Women.* Berkeley, CA: University of California Press.

Lewin, Tamar. 2006a. "At Colleges, Women are Leaving Men in the Dust." *New York Times*, July 9, p. A1.

———. 2006b. "A More Nuanced Look at Men, Women and College." *New York Times*, July 12, p. B8.

Lorber, Judith. 1975. "Women and Medical Sociology: Invisible Professionals and Ubiquitous Patients." Pp. 75–105 in *Another Voice*, edited by Marcia Millman and Rosabeth Moss Kanter. Garden City, NY: Doubleday/Anchor.

———. 1984. *Women Physicians: Careers, Status, and Power.* New York: Tavistock Publications.

Magrane, Diane, Jonathan Lang, and Hershel Alexander. 2005. *Women in U.S. Academic Medicine: Statistics and Medical School Benchmarking.* Washington, DC: Association of American Medical Colleges.

Merton, Robert K. [1949] 1963. *Social Theory and Social Structure*. Glencoe, IL: The Free Press.

Milkman, Ruth. 1987. *Gender at Work: The Dynamics of Job Segregation by Sex During World War II*. Urbana, IL: University of Illinois Press.

Moghadam, Valentine. 2003. *Modernizing Women: Gender and Social Change in the Middle East*. 2d ed. London, England: Lynne Rienner.

O'Farrell, Brigid. 1999. "Women in Blue Collar and Related Occupations at the End of the Millenium." *Quarterly Review of Economics and Finance* 39:699–722.

National Women's Law Center. 2006. "New Report Analyzes What's at Stake for Women During Upcoming Supreme Court Term." Press Release. September 27. Retrieved October 2, 2006 (http://www.nwlc.org/details.cfm?id=2857&section=newsroom).

Nicholson, Lisa H. 2006. "Women and the 'New' Corporate Governance: Making In-Roads to Corporate General Counsel Positions: It's Only a Matter of Time?" *Maryland Law Review* 65:625–65.

Norris, Floyd. 2006. "A Statistic That Shortens the Distance to Europe." *New York Times*, September 30, p. C3.

Parrot, Andrew and Nina Cummings. 2006. *Forsaken Females: The Global Brutalization of Women*. Lanham, MD: Roman and Littlefield.

Presser, Harriet. 2003. *Working in a 24/7 Economy: Challenges for American Families*. New York: Russell Sage Foundation.

Rao, Kavitha. 2006. "Missing Daughters on an Indian Mother's Mind." *Women's eNews*, March 16. Retrieved October 23, 2006 (http://www.womensenews.org/article.cfm?aid=2672).

Ridgeway, Cecelia L. 1997. "Interaction and the Conservation of Gender Inequality: Considering Employment." *American Sociological Review* 62:218–35.

Ridgeway, Cecelia L. and Lynn Smith-Lovin. 1999. "The Gender System and Interaction." *Annual Review of Sociology* 25:119–216.

Roos, Patricia and Mary L. Gatta. 2006. "Gender Inquiry in the Academy." Presented at the Annual Meeting of the American Sociological Association, August 14, Montreal, Canada.

Rupp, Leila. 1978. *Mobilizing Women for War: German and American Propaganda, 1939–1945*. Princeton, NJ: Princeton University Press.

Salzinger, Leslie. 2003. *Genders in Production: Making Workers in Mexico's Global Factories*. Berkeley, CA: University of California Press.

Sen, Amartya. 1990. "More than 100 Million Women are Missing." *New York Review of Books*, 37(20). Retrieved January 25, 2006 (http://ucatlas.ucsc.edu/gender/Sen100M.html).

Stevens, Alison. 2006. "Iranian Women Protest in Shadow of Nuclear Face-off." *Women's eNews*, June 16. Retrieved September 28, 2006 (http://www.womensenews.org/article.cfm/dyn/aid/2780).

Tannen, Deborah. 1990. *You Just Don't Understand: Women and Men in Conversation*. New York: Morrow.

Tarabay, Jamie. 2006. "Activists Seek to Protect Iraqi Women from Honor Killings." *NPR Morning Edition*, May 18. Retrieved June 6, 2006 (http://www.npr.org/templates/story/story.php?storyId=5414315).

Tierney, John. 2006. "Academy of P.C. Sciences." *New York Times*, September 26, p. A23.

Tilly, Charles. 1998. *Durable Inequality*. Berkeley, CA: University of California Press.

United Nations. 2002. *Working Towards the Elimination of Crimes against Women Committed in the Name of Honor, Report of the Secretary General*. United Nations General Assembly, July 2. Retrieved October 23, 2006 (http://www.unhchr.ch/huridocda/huridoca.nsf/AllSymbols/985168F508EE799FC1256C52002AE5A9/%24File/N0246790.pdf).

U.N. Common Database. 2004. "Gender Equality: Indicator: Seats in Parliament Held by Women–2004." Retrieved September 21, 2006 (http://globalis.gvu.unu.edu/indicator.cfm?IndicatorID=63&country=IS#rowIS).

Villalobos, V. Munos. 2006. "Economic, Social and Cultural Rights: Girls' right to education." Report submitted by the Special Rapporteur on the right to education. United Nations Commission on Human Rights, Economic and Social Council. Retrieved September 28, 2006 (http://www.crin.org/docs/SR_Education_report.pdf).

Williams, Joan. 2000. *Unbending Gender: Why Family and Work Conflict and What to Do About It*. New York: Oxford University Press.

Winston, Hella. 2005. *Unchosen: The Hidden Lives of Hasidic Rebels*. Boston, MA: Beacon Press.

Witte, Griff. 2005. "Post-Taliban Free Speech Blocked by Courts, Clerics: Jailed Afghan Publisher Faces Possible Execution." *Washington Post*, December 11, p. A24.

Women's World Summit Foundation. 2006. "World Rural Women's Day: 15 October: Introduction." Retrieved September 28, 2006 (http://www.woman.ch/women/2-introduction.asp).

Zerubavel, Eviatar. 1997. *Social Mindscapes: An Invitation to Cognitive Sociology*. Cambridge, MA: Harvard University Press.

Zimmerman Mary K., Jacquelyn S. Litt, and Christine E. Bose. 2006. *Global Dimensions of Gender and Care Work*. Stanford, CA: Stanford University Press.

PART TWO

Girlhood and Adolescence

Remember what you wanted to be when you grew up? How were those dreams nurtured or frustrated by your circumstances and by those around you? The selections in this section describe some of the ways that girls' experiences are circumscribed by the structural forces of the global economy, racial stratification, immigration, domestic violence, and local gender regimes. Each selection also depicts the strategies of resistance that girls use in their struggle to develop an identity that retains their dreams and also permits their survival. From different locations within the matrix of domination, girls confront and resist pressures to relinquish their unique, spirited, and complex personhood. Nellie Wong illuminates this struggle in her poem, "When I Was Growing Up."

Over the past two decades, government and nonprofit organizations in the United States and globally have focused on the girl child. We have become more attuned to the specific gendered disadvantages faced by children and have developed educational and programmatic efforts to support girls and boys. Internationally, we know that two-thirds of the world's illiterate population is female

(UNESCO 2006). Several international human rights organizations have set goals for gender equality that include eliminating educational, health, political, and wage disparities. Although progress has been made throughout the world, the rate of progress is not adequate to stem the exponential growth in gender-based inequalities. In some countries, such as parts of sub-Saharan Africa and South and West Asia, these inequalities translate into life and death struggles for nutrition and basic health care. In others, such as the United States, the effects are more subtle and complex.

Girls today are depicted alternatively as the victims of sex discrimination and as a distinct, empowered group released from the constraints of traditional femininity (see Gonick 2006). In advanced economies, such as the United States, the negative consequences of girlhood have been analyzed in terms of "loss of voice," a "crisis in self-esteem," and sexualization. Popular books, such as the *Ophelia* series, warn parents and teachers of the vulnerability of adolescent girls and the risks posed by girls' own bodies, their schools, their peers, and the media. The American Psychological Association published a report in 2007 describing the sexualization of very young girls and girls' "self-objectification" linked to long-term mental and physical health problems (APA 2007). At the same time, the notion of Girl Power describes contemporary girlhood as exuberant, liberated, and sassy. Girl Power is variously portrayed as a commercial gimmick to sell everything from DVDs to thongs and as a younger, hipper version of feminism. As Marnina Gonick points out, however, both vulnerable and empowered images of contemporary girlhood focus on the individual girl who should be encouraged to make healthy and/or transgressive choices.

Anita Harris argues that girls today are part of a global transformation of subjectivity and citizenship that has been termed "individualization and monetarization" or "neoliberalism." This transformation draws on modernist notions about the self as autonomous and separate from social conditions. It is accelerated, however, by the advance of a transnational economic system that has reduced or eliminated many sites of civic, public participation. For many young people, female and male, citizenship in the twenty-first century is equated with consumption. The shopping mall has become the principal site of social interaction for many young women. Buy the right clothes, purse, cell phone, and car, and you are visibly a successful member of society. Markets target girls even more than boys as consumers with both capital and the desire to spend. "U.S. girls aged eight to eighteen are estimated to be worth $67 billion" (Harris 2004: 166). The struggle for identity that marks all adolescence is highly individualized and linked to consumption. You are what you buy.

Yet clearly, even within wealthier nations, many girls lack access to the money to purchase the items that signify a successful identity. Girls also rebel against the superficiality and conformity of the consumer society. L. Susan Williams, Sandra D. Alvarez, and Kevin S. Andrade Hauck describe the ways that Latina teenage transmigrants struggle with stereotypes, ineffective teachers and schools, lack of money, and family obligations. In contrast to the demeaning stereotypes held by teachers and peers, these girls are serious about their studies and have dreams of professional careers. The low expectations and deficient training of their English-as-Second-Language teachers combine with familial demands and exclusion by Anglo and Chicana peers to frustrate their desires for academic excellence and social acceptance. The girls demonstrate the "multidirectional process of both acceptance and resistance" (p. 578) through which Latinas negotiate the opportunities and challenges of their native and adopted cultures. They reject the mainstream U.S. focus on expensive clothing and jewelry and assert their identities through group, family, and cultural loyalty. This is not just an *individual* process of adjustment, but one that involves the intersection of gender, ethnicity, and immigration status in shaping the barriers and cultural resources available to young women.

Julia Hall's investigation of poor, white middle-school girls also describes structural and familial restrictions on girls' dreams. She depicts the raw edges of deindustrialization as girls in the rust belt of the United States cope with paternal abandonment, poverty, maternal alcohol and drug abuse, and domestic violence. The girls here experience adult males as dangerous and incompetent and at ages ten and eleven are determined to escape their mother's fate by becoming self-sufficient and rejecting marriage. Hall also illustrates how girls' lives are linked to globalization and the economic devastation wrought by the elimination of factory jobs in much of the United States. Despite the fear and abuse they describe, these girls are not mere victims; they are also determined advocates of their own futures. We are left to wonder how they fared through high school and young adulthood.

Susan Moon leads us through the intersections of individual biography and cultural forms as she looks back on her girlhood from the perspective of middle-age. She describes the rediscovery of her youthful tomboy self who preferred baseball cards to dolls and dungarees to dresses. Her story depicts the frustrations of girls who love the freedoms associated with boys' activities and self-presentations but are gradually goaded into more restrictive dress and pastimes by well-meaning adults. As she enters middle-age, however, Moon finds the returning "brave spirit" of her tomboy self is a welcome resource for overcoming the limitations often associated with aging.

Anita Harris closes this section by describing girl culture jammers who resist corporate culture primarily through the internet, but also through street theater, media literacy workshops, and public protests. Culture jammers reject the model of citizenship based on consumption and develop new public spheres through on-line zines and blogs. Their "virtual communities" offer an opportunity for self-expression and connection that empowers girls to also engage in more conventional political activities. In the new global markets, some girls are targeted for consumption and others for the production of commodities. Certainly this is not a new story. What is new is the ways in which girls are using communications technology to challenge the class and race inequities that are exacerbated by transnational capitalism and to create active citizenship.

References

American Psychological Association (APA), Task Force on the Sexualization of Girls. (2007). *Report of the APA Task Force on the Sexualization of Girls*. Washington, DC: American Psychological Association. Retrieved from www. apa.org/pi/wpo/sexualization.html, August 31, 2007.

Gonick, Marnina. (2006). "Between 'Girl Power' and 'Reviving Ophelia': Constituting the Neoliberal Girl Subject." *NWSA Journal* 8(2): 1–23.

UNESCO. (2006). *Strong Foundations: Early Childhood Care and Education*. Paris: UNESCO.

Nellie Wong

When I Was Growing Up

I know now that once I longed to be white.
How?   you ask.
Let me tell you the ways.

when I was growing up, people told me
I was dark and I believed my own darkness
in the mirror, in my soul, my own narrow vision.

when I was growing up, my sisters
with fair skin got praised
for their beauty and I fell
further, crushed between high walls.

when I was growing up, I read magazines
and saw movies, blonde movie stars, white skin,
sensuous lips and to be elevated, to become
a woman, a desirable woman, I began to wear
imaginary pale skin.

when I was growing up, I was proud
of my English, my grammar, my spelling,
fitting into the group of smart children,
smart Chinese children, fitting in,
belonging, getting in line.

when I was growing up and went to high school,
I discovered the rich white girls, a few yellow girls,
their imported cotton dresses, their cashmere sweaters,
their curly hair and I thought that I too should have
what these lucky girls had.

when I was growing up, I hungered
for American food, American styles
coded: *white*   and even to me, a child

Source: Nellie Wong, "When I Was Growing Up," from *The Death of the Long Steam Lady*. Copyright © 1984 by Nellie Wong. Reprinted with the permission of West End Press, Albuquerque, New Mexico.

born of Chinese parents, being Chinese
was feeling foreign, was limiting,
was unAmerican.

when I was growing up and a white man wanted
to take me out, I thought I was special,
an exotic gardenia, anxious to fit
the stereotype of an oriental chick

when I was growing up, I felt ashamed
of some yellow men, their small bones,
their frail bodies, their spitting
on the streets, their coughing,
their lying in sunless rooms
shooting themselves in the arms.

when I was growing up, people would ask
if I were Filipino, Polynesian, Portuguese.
They named all colors except white, the shell
of my soul but not my rough dark skin.

when I was growing up, I felt
dirty.   I thought that god
made white people clean
and no matter how much I bathed,
I could not change, I could not shed
my skin in the gray water.

when I was growing up, I swore
I would run away to purple mountains,
houses by the sea with nothing over
my head, with space to breathe,
uncongested with yellow people in an area
called Chinatown, in an area I later
learned was a ghetto, one of many hearts
of Asian America.

I know now that once I longed to be white.
How many more ways? you ask.
Haven't I told you enough?

ARTICLE 5

L. Susan Williams
Sandra D. Alvarez
Kevin S. Andrade Hauck

My Name Is Not María: Young Latinas Seeking Home in the Heartland

Traditional theories of immigration to the U.S. assume a unilateral movement that eventually results in the "absorption of the immigrant group into the American fold" (Gibson 1988:x). Recent studies of transnationalism introduce a more complex back-and-forth variety of migration, providing ways to explain differences among migratory subgroups. Building on segmented assimilation and transnationalism perspectives, this research addresses the maze of adjustment processes encountered by participants in this study—Latina teenagers who recently immigrated to the U.S. and attend a mid-western high school. This paper proposes an integrated model of gender and acculturation by focusing on adaptation processes. Using qualitative data gathered through group interviews, observation, and survey, the study examines how interaction is organized around gender, ethnicity, and immigrant status. The Latinas invoke ethnic identity to resist an American gender order. However, institutional structures, such as English-as-Second-Language classes, shape practices that have differential effects for girls and boys. Latinas are subject to harsher control both within families and the conformist school culture, which marks them as outsiders more than it does their male peers. These practices reveal the gendered makeup of interaction as distinct from characteristics and beliefs of the individual, and adjustment processes as segmented along structural gender lines. A gendered ethnicity and ethnic gendering reinforces the gender order, but in a way specific to local gender practices and immigrant status.

Aqui. los Americanos piensan que nosotros caminamos en burro, y que todas las chicas se llaman María. Mi nombre no es María.
(Here, Americans think that we all travel on donkeys, and that we are all called María. My name is not María).

A Latina teenager, with dreams of the future, packs her belongings for the car ride to *el Norte*. Prepared to leave extended family and commu-

Source: Williams, L. Susan, Sandra D. Alvarez, Kevin S. Andrade Hauck, *Social Problems* 49 (4) pp. 563–584, Copyright © 2002 by the University of California Press. Reprinted by Permission of the University of California Press.

nity, she tries to focus on what possibilities await her in *Los Estados Unidos*. The above excerpt, taken from group interviews, illustrates a common theme voiced by Latinas[1] in this study: They struggle for identity in America, but are plagued by American-made hurdles to successful integration. Teenage transmigrants face issues different from those of either adults or young children.

51

While we need research on boys and girls, this paper addresses the maze of challenges that face non-English speaking adolescent girls in a midwestern urban center (which we refer to as Center City), an area that has experienced only limited immigration.

The "new immigration" heralded by the passage of the Hart-Cellar Act of 1965 derives heavily from Latin America, the Caribbean, and Asia. Settlement concentrates in a handful of states (California, New York, Texas, Florida), but many regions, including the midwest, also experience significant increases. Official counts of Latinos in Center City doubled from 1990 to 2000, tripling since 1980 (Logan 2001). However, these population changes are recent, and Latinos remain a small minority in Center City—a point that differentiates the midwest from both coasts. For example, Center City Latinos constitute less than 9% of the general population, while some coastal areas maintain Latino populations of 44% (Los Angeles) and 37% (Houston). Further, the number of immigrant children in the U.S. grew 47% from 1990 to 1997 (Qin-Hilliard, Feinauer, and Quiroz 2001). One out of every five public school children in the U.S. is either an immigrant child or a child of immigrant parents; the proportion is projected to be one out of three by 2020 (Hernandez and Charney 1998). Immigrant enrollment in Center City schools recently tripled (Sanchez 2000), leaving administrations ill-equipped to cope with growing numbers of limited English proficient (LEP) speakers.

As a group, Mexicans experience several areas of disadvantage: one in four is poor (Aponte and Siles 1997), and estimates place more than 40% of Latino immigrant children in poverty (Zhou 1997). Latinos drop out of high school at an astounding rate of 46% (McMillen 1995). These disadvantages, coupled with a troubled history of relations between the U.S. and Mexico, fuel antagonism toward Mexican immigration and encourage anti-Mexican stereotypes (Guitérrez 1996), contributing to an "ethos of reception" (Suárez-Orozco and Suárez-Orozco 2001) that

shapes social relations. Negative images are readily available, and host communities, already faced with an inadequate infrastructure, are often unprepared for this unprecedented influx of immigrants.

Teenage transmigrants face an immediate paradox: A lack of English proficiency forestalls assimilation (Zhou 1997) and creates a barrier to success in America (Rumbaut 1995), but many English-as-Second-Language (ESL) classrooms, a standard response to LEP speakers, are not well suited for upper-level subject instruction. Center City relies on ESL programs to manage immigrant students but, like all regions relatively new to immigration, has had less time to fully develop such programs. For example, California schools have a much longer history of establishing programs to address needs of second language learners. Beyond other limitations of ESL programs (for example, tracking; see Gibson 1988; Valenzuela 1999), classes seriously restrict the sharing of cultural and linguistic norms with "mainstream" students. Faced with communication difficulties, limited instruction, and isolated from English-speaking peers, the LEP teenager is at high risk for dropping out of school. Young women may be at even greater risk, given that Latino families typically place higher value on education and economic success for men (Gowan and Treviño 1998; Olsen 1997). . . .

This study examines processes of acculturation, as told by young transmigrants themselves. Results are based on experiences of Spanish-speaking Latinas enrolled in ESL classes at Center City High. We incorporate a gender framework, focusing on the convergence of gender, ethnicity, and immigrant status as young Latinas adjust to a new culture. The "new gender paradigm," as anchored in feminist philosophy, stresses a gendered construction of social reality; key concepts are gender as structure and gender as interaction (Connell 1987; Ferree, Lorber, and Hess 1999; West and Zimmerman 1987), useful analytical devices for examining Latinas' adjustment processes. . . . This perspective contests conventional epistemology and transforms specific groups as subjects and "knowers"—who, in this study, are the young Latinas themselves. We identify three general observations from their accounts: social control processes often isolate immigrant girls from mainstream activities; English proficiency develops differently for girls than boys in the ESL environment; and appearance norms are strongly gendered, making cultural adjustment more difficult for girls. . . .

Transnationalism represents an emerging perspective that complicates traditional ideas of immigration: it is processual and relational, capturing a more dynamic view of migration. Studies focus on "multi-stranded social relations that link places of origin and settlement" (Orellana et al. 2001:573) and identify a variety of transmigrants such as "target earners" (who migrate temporarily to enhance family income), "sojourners" (continual and cyclical migrants), and "binationals" (who shuttle between two permanent homes), who may fill these functions because their specific gender, class, or age intersects with the structure of opportunity in a particular way (Suárez-Orozco and Suárez-Orozco 2001).

Claiming that previous theories treat children as "luggage," transnational approaches focus on children as active participants in migration, advancing their families' social and economic mobility. For example, "parachute children" are sometimes sent, often unaccompanied, to live in the U.S., taking advantage of educational opportunities. Carola and Marcelo Suárez-Orozco stress "social mirroring" in which immigrant children "craft their identities, in part, as a function of how they are viewed and received by the dominant culture" (Suárez-Orozco and Suárez-Orozco 2001:7), and Wolf (1997) identifies a transnational identity among Filipino children, in which family traditions provide positive identity, but also produce stress and alienation when they conflict with American practices. This perspective views immigrant identities as neither simple nor static, but ongoing, relational, and often contested. Teenagers, an age group already culturally de-

fined in the U.S. as experiencing conflict with parents and schools, face particular adjustment issues when they are recent immigrants as well. Since we already know that boys and girls in American schools face diverse gendered expectations about achievement, sociability, and sexuality from parents, peers, and the school system, we should particularly attend to how gender segments the experiences of immigrant adolescents.

Integrating Gender and Culture Adjustment Processes: A Model for Latina Adolescents

Gender as interaction is represented in daily practices that reinforce the gender order, such as appearance norms and acting out femininity and masculinity. Gender as structure includes lasting organizational patterns that reside within institutions such as family and school (Hess and Ferree 1987; West and Zimmerman 1987). For these Latinas, gender interconnects with race and class dynamics, often referred to as intersectionality (Hill Collins 1990; Rothenberg 1990; West and Fenstermaker 1995), and they are also influenced by their developmental position as adolescents and their status as non-English speaking immigrants. Gender traditions interact with local school organization to form a local gender regime—a "structural inventory" of local gender relations (Connell 1987)—which influences ways that adolescents enact gender. For example, local class-based ideals and practices are found to influence ways in which teenage girls "try on gender," a process in which girls experiment with various kinds of femininities (Williams 2002). Here, the local gender regime may guide Latinas' perceptions and opportunities, irrespective of their own individual orientation.

This study emphasizes *processes* of adaptation—complementing the dynamic view advanced by transnationalism—and addresses how gender affects acculturation through three processes: mechanisms of social control, development of English facility (which includes fluency, but also cultural meanings), and identity formation through appearance norms. . . .

We hope to provide a modest example of how a model of gendered acculturation can make manifest the *process* through which Latina teens negotiate pressure to assimilate. We examine the context of their transnational relations, and how two cultures shape their perceptions, expectations, and coping strategies. Two major theoretical constructs—gender as interaction and gender as structure—demonstrate how immigrant status and ethnicity affect gendering and, in turn, how gendering affects the extent of young Latinas' acculturation . . .

Gendered Social Control

A relatively subtle theme running throughout the narratives is the Latinas' experiences of double binds—instances in which they feel the pressure to fit in and to succeed, but at the same time find strong sanctions for *not* doing so. We examine situations in which such double binds reflect norms of femininity, implying gendered social control. Here, we use the term gendered social control to mean a structural constraint on acculturation: it is through these processes that a gender system operates most coercively. Control mechanisms rely on a complex relationship between interaction and structure, and we use two institutions—family and school—to illustrate contexts in which these Latinas experience gendered social control.

The Family as Gendered.   The literature suggests that Latinas, as "keepers of the culture," experience greater acculturative stress than male counterparts as they try to adapt to a new social environment. Not only may girls experience different expectations than boys (girls are more likely to help with housekeeping and care taking tasks), but the stress of migrating also creates different demands on the family. In Mexico, these girls were considered children, expected to concentrate on their studies and play. Here they need to help the family succeed, and they are without extended family and community to shield them from such demands.

RAQUEL: Now I have to watch my little sisters and brothers, but I guess it is better than having to go to work. I did that for a while, although my family did not expect it. They prefer I stay at home.

Here we see that gender is part of the segmenting structure. Migration often means that young Latinas are expected to fulfill caretaker duties previously held by mothers; now both parents more often work outside the home. Increasingly, families rely on older siblings, and for girls that means taking care of younger children and assuming household chores. All the girls mentioned significant care taking duties. Within families, the caretaker role is interpreted as a positive experience that prepares young Latinas as wives and mothers. However, for girls, this means that fewer *can* hold jobs, even if they so desire. For students who are embedded in a transnational process, the demands (and gender differences) may be even more exaggerated if they left behind one or more parents, often meaning that they must assume adult responsibilities in the host home.

Family obligations keep Latinas home, while their brothers are encouraged to work outside the home. At work, boys earn money and garner much greater opportunities to practice English language skills with co-workers and customers. They gain work experience and are better able to network for future employment. The gender structure of the family diminishes opportunities available to Latinas outside the family.

The girls accept some Mexican-focused norms, but low expectations and gendered opportunities also channel them into a resistant transnational identity. They express resistance to the historically conventional "domesticated Latina"; they want others to know that their dreams are similar to American students. They want to be artists, doctors, lawyers—in Mexico they expected to attend the university, and they cling to those aspirations. Yet, they are caught between two worlds. On the one hand, they feel a strong obligation to family and culture. At school, for a while, they escape those constraints and express high hopes for success. But there, they face other obstacles.

The School as Gendered.   The gender regime of the school incorporates stereotypes and patterns of behavior that are strongly gendered. One of the disadvantages Latinas, as *racialized* young women, face at school is the misconception that their education is a temporary stage to prepare them for marriage and the service sector labor market. They report feeling misunderstood and devalued as students.

> CAROLINA: They speak to us as though we are ignorant from rural areas, they don't try to find out about us.
>
> PILAR: Yes, we are seen as strange. [Even] people of our own race pretend to be Americanized. This is very grave. Here, the Americans look at us as though we travel on burros.
>
> ADRIANA: Really, they ask us that. The idea of us is that we are all called María. They say Hi María or Lupíta. [They all laughed.]

These comments suggest social mirroring in which the Latinas believe they are seen as illiterate children of migrant farm workers, in school because that is what the law requires. This image is far from accurate, but nevertheless remains a "stereotype threat" (Steele 1997)—a daily reminder that Latinas must manage. In fact, these urban mid-western immigrants are very different from the stereotypical picture of the migrant farm worker; many come from cities such as Juarez (3 + million) and Mexico City (30 + million). Even though these girls assume traditional caretaker duties at home, they also resist that as a singular identity and look to education to provide professional opportunities for them. Here, Adriana talks to one of the researchers about her future.

> ADRIANA: We would like better classes so that we can learn more. Things that are different.
>
> RESEARCHER: Do you feel as though you are receiving preparation to go to a university?

> ADRIANA: On the contrary, much of what we learn will not help us. I know a person has to be responsible, but it is difficult finding out what classes you need to take to graduate. As the year ends I had asked what classes I need to graduate. They finally told me, "Ooooh [with great inflection], I don't know if your classes are sufficient to give you what you need, if they will give you the credits. These [ESL] classes don't count for anything."

This particular conversation resonates strongly with the Latinas. They all join the discussion and become quite animated, describing a tremendous gap between what they need to prepare for their future goals and what they are getting. Pilar and Adriana explain:

> PILAR: You ask about your schedule and time passes, months pass, but they never do tell you. Now I know what I need *after* taking classes.

The Latinas look to the school and teachers for guidance. That failing, they try to find classes on their own, only to discover that they still lack needed requirements. These Latinas clearly take an active part in their education; yet, they are thwarted at every turn. Their frustration is partly based upon comparison to expectations in Mexico, where they believe they were provided a better education. In Mexico, several Latinas recount, they would have taken exams and be counseled regarding future goals. They are confused and disillusioned; they illustrate such sentiments in their discussion of "career day" at a nearby university:

> ELENA: When I was in Mexico, they took us to the university and told us about what programs were offered and explained all about how to apply. Here, they do not do that. They take you to see the [State U.] campus. We drove around and looked at the grass. And they bring you back.
>
> PILAR: When I asked about majors at [State U.], they said they would tell me later. But they don't.

Though such disappointments concern both boys and girls, the effects are more distilled for girls, who depend more exclusively on education to edge them toward success. Boys, on the other hand, work outside the home and envision a greater number of paths to achievement.

Another example of gendered social control comes from classroom observation. The girls report that Miss L. is more likely to use threatening language against the girls, but not the boys. One suggested that the teachers are "more fearful" of the Latino boys. Pilar reports:

PILAR: [Whenever the teacher(s) want something] they threaten with telling our father. They don't do that with the boys.

The girls interpret such actions by their teachers as discrimination and were quick to point out the instances. They added that teachers try to get more personal information from the girls, such as whom they are dating and who went to "the party." Again, Pilar comments:

PILAR: They ask us if we went to a fiesta this weekend. Then they try to get information from us or about us to use against us. Then they will try to be our friend.

CAROLINA: They don't really care about us. They care about themselves and their paycheck.

The Latinas reconcile these two types of "interest" or "caring" with cynicism. The Latinas are surprised that they are expected to provide intimate details of their lives, and they resist such control over their lives. They state indignantly that their teachers are poorly trained and clearly do not understand their students:

PILAR: I don't think these people [the teachers] treasure anything. They just think the most is graduating; they don't talk about what happens next. This is not good, you should think of your future. They say like, "graduate and marry," or this or that like that is their limit. I want more, they should bring in companies, or tell us about what we should study next.

The ESL classroom is purportedly designed to integrate immigrants educationally and socially, and to provide positive mentoring. Other research claims that valuing girls' education gives them equal footing or even an advantage over their male peers. However, the ESL environment becomes a gendered barrier for these Latinas. Clearly, instruction and resources are poor. Further, teachers, perhaps overwhelmed with high numbers of LEP students, rely upon gendered and racialized stereotypes when dealing with these girls. As a result, Latinas may be retained longer in ESL classes, leading to a cumulative disadvantage through a lack of mainstream classes, inadequate advising, and social isolation.

The Latinas' bicultural self, potentially a source of strength, becomes bifurcated: English proficiency demands denying Spanish, and familial care taking roles cut them off from jobs and sports as alternative ways of acquiring the English they want. Without money from jobs, they are less able to "look American" and neither family nor school offers them academic counseling in line with their own high educational and professional aspirations. The ESL structure seriously limits the pool of possible selves they once envisioned, and limited interaction with American students prevents a fully integrated American identity. School and family demands connect at gendered intersections to multiply their disadvantage rather than to mitigate it.

Adopting English

English competence, not the more generic "linguistic proficiency," drives the institutional motivation underlying ESL practices. The most striking finding of this study is the multitude of barriers that acutely limit Latina teens' development of English competence. The school environment interacts with gender and immigrant status to impede English adoption for these Latinas.

Though we did not directly ask about English competence, that is the first topic the girls addressed, and they define it as key to both economic and social success. The U.S. culture of reception defines Latinos as primarily immigrating for economic reasons, but does not clearly envision Latinas as economically ambitious. Education is culturally less valued for girls than for boys in Mexico, but parents who migrate may not share these norms. What girls want with and from education is, therefore, open to debate.

> MARTA: The main reason I came to this country was to learn English. I thought it would help me be successful in the future.
>
> SURVEYED LATINA: [I plan to] return to Mexico to begin the university, because I only came here for one year to learn the language, English.

While some teen immigrants accompany their families as they look for jobs, the Latinas agreed that many Mexican parents send older children to live with friends or extended family in the U.S. to learn English. The Latinas understand the economic value of English skills, and they also know that English competence is critical to adapting to American culture. They want to "fit in."

> RAQUEL: Well, it is very difficult trying to talk to the other girls in this school. We try, but . . .

These girls all agreed that English adoption is their immediate and primary goal. They believe, at least initially, that they will quickly learn English and will find encouragement from classmates. The Latinas were surprised when other students, even those of Mexican descent snubbed them:

> RACQUEL: You think that with many Mexicans in this area, they would talk to us, but they don't. They act like they don't speak Spanish or are embarrassed about speaking Spanish.
>
> ADRIANA: The Chicanos here are ignorant of their own culture. They are hesitant to speak Spanish, favoring instead to just speak English like it is better. They are jealous to be more American. They don't want to improve themselves: they just want to be more Amer-

ican. You try to speak to them in Spanish. You know, they speak Spanish, but they pretend not to.

The Latinas believe the Chicanos can speak fluent Spanish, but refuse to do so. Both boys and girls expressed dismay that "even our own race will not speak with us." Apparently, at least some Chicanos consciously dissociate from the Spanish language, which is devalued by the dominant culture. Students report being called "Mexican," as if it is a form of degradation, and are, sometimes, threatened with deportation by Chicanos. Immigrants soon recognize that no one wants to be seen as a newcomer, and that English proficiency, coupled with dissociation from Spanish, is a strong and immediately recognizable marker of acculturation. Interaction reinforces an Americanized version of language hegemony in the form of "English only" rhetoric.

Nevertheless, the Latinas come with high hopes, trusting that the school will provide necessary English instruction. They report that they are placed in ESL classrooms with minimal or no evaluation of their training and skills, but still they initially believe that they will quickly learn English. Their disappointment begins when they are given minimal instruction and elementary assignments in the ESL environment.

> ADRIANA: Every week it is the same thing, she gives us 20 words that we match with definitions.
>
> PILAR: And they repeat it and repeat it.
>
> ELENA: It is like they do not prepare for their classes. They just give us the words and make us repeat them. I think they come in and just give us the words that come to mind.

We were surprised at the low level of expectation in the ESL classroom. The Latinas all chimed in agreement about the "20-word" assignments. They would receive the word list on Monday and be done with that assignment the first day, sometimes within fifteen minutes. For the rest of the week, at least by their reports, they either had no more assignments or believed that they were on their own. We were also surprised that neither of the ESL teachers spoke Spanish and that at least one believes this is an advantage. As these young Latinas become more and more isolated, their frustration builds with each passing day.

> ADRIANA: And I told her that I am getting bored in the class. And she gave me a primer [which is for elementary school children] and said read it all and I will give you an exam.
>
> PILAR: They don't know how to teach English. And if you ask them for clarification on a word they say, "look in the dictionary." I mean if I am asking, then it is because I need guidance.

These statements attest to the Latinas frustration and disillusionment with the high school's system. They cannot be mainstreamed until they learn English: they cannot learn English while isolated in an ESL classroom that does not meet their needs. As graduation time grows closer, the Latinas realize the seriousness of their educational deficits, a pattern we did not observe with the boys. Paradoxically, the Latinas' hope of achieving status through English adoption seems to diminish with each day spent in the ESL classroom.

The boys' group also mentioned isolation and frustration in the ESL classroom, but to a much lesser extent than the girls. The girls spent much more time on the subject, were more likely to report dissatisfaction, and reported more concern for their future. The boys were much more likely to be working for pay. Elena spoke of her frustration with her overall plan of study, a common theme among the Latinas:

> ELENA: My point is, why do they give us so many classes with Miss L. if they don't count? I would rather be in normal classes than to find out later that I don't have what I need. Then I could graduate with the others.

This particular exchange went on for about 30 minutes, each Latina expressing dissatisfac-

tion. In contrast, one of the male students reported. "I just said, 'I want to be in normal classes,' and they put me [in mainstream classes]. Now I'm only in ESL two hours." Whether this was an isolated incident cannot be determined from these data, but the boys' conversation focused more on jobs and sports. One Latino explained, "Well, you learn to advocate for yourself by learning the language. Now I know more, and I can get a job." Another chimed in, "Yes, when I got here I knew nothing, and now I know you can stand up for yourself. You can get respect." The girls, on the other hand, report that the teachers will not listen to them, that "the boys have it easier" because "they can get jobs and play sports."

These girls contest limited prospects (in the classroom) and resist cultural expectations (from families); they often think of themselves as assertive, even spunky. They believe their demands are largely unheard in the ESL classroom, however, and that they experience more isolation and fewer options relative to boys. These Latinas defy cultural stereotypes that portray them as having low aspirations, content to accept gender assignments. On the contrary, they initially expect to succeed academically, finish high school, enter good American colleges, and go on to a number of professions. Clearly, these girls resist gender and ethnic expectations of Latina domesticity, crafting a gendered identity that is neither clearly Mexican nor American.

We observe gendered interaction reinforcing gender structures. The girls, more often than boys, report feeling alienated from peers. The ESL structure combines with social processes to seriously curtail Latinas' interaction with potential cultural translators. The teachers do not speak Spanish, the Chicanos refuse to do so, and the girls are contained in a classroom where they are not challenged to learn. These conditions reflect a local gender regime that deploys both ethnic and gender constraints to limit choices of these girls. The Latinas resist, but also begin adjusting aspirations away from educational and professional goals, reinforcing the gender order. The

ESL environment, initially designed to teach and to integrate, becomes an impediment to both.

Appearance Norms

Latinas in this study are in some ways "typical" teenage girls. They are concerned with outward markers that certify one as cool, attractive, and popular, reflecting a cultural emphasis on physical appearance. The Latinas want to fit in and acknowledge that looks are an important part of belonging. The process is strongly gendered and also ethnicized. Appearance was a central topic of discussion among the Latinas, but not in the boys' group, and boys find greater cultural access through sports apparel. The girls challenge heavily gendered American norms by invoking strong ethnic identification. For example, all the Latina immigrants wear long hair, styled very traditionally and with no adornment, while other girls sport a greater variety of hairstyles and accessories. Jewelry is quite distinct. Recent arrivals from Mexico wear large gold religious necklaces, styled with a cross or saint, which are patently different from others in school. However, in this section, we focus primarily on clothes as an indicator of how Latinas cope with acculturation.

The cafeteria provides a particularly disclosing setting for observing appearance norms. At lunch, one of the few times when all groups come together, differences in dress are quite noticeable. For example, the Latina immigrants wear generic brand jeans, obviously different from other girls. Their blouses are nondescript in contrast to the trendy *Hilfiger* and *FUBU* apparel that are widely popular at CCHS. A particularly obvious apparel marker is the inexpensive supermarket-brand tennis shoes that all the Latina immigrants wear. The younger researchers in our group recognized the shoes, often referred to as "bobos" (a denigrating name for cheap or duncelike), as the ultimate dress *faux pas* for teenagers. In contrast, Latino immigrants donned sports apparel, making them less distinctive from other boys in their dress code. The immigrant girls are painfully aware that they do not fit in, evidence

of how they use social mirroring to evaluate themselves and others:

PILAR: Here, they just worry about the clothes you wear and how they fit.

ADRIANA: It is difficult to talk and be like other girls in this school. They look at us as though we are so different from them because we can't afford to dress like them.

The Latinas all expressed concern about not being able to afford American clothes, and certainly part of the dilemma may be class-based. However, we noted that although the school is located in a low- to working-class neighborhood, a large proportion of non-immigrant students wear the more expensive name-brand clothing. Perhaps families who understand the cultural emphasis on clothes-as-status make sacrifices to accommodate their children. In contrast, the Latina immigrants expressed difficulty in comprehending how one could justify the cost associated with emulating dress of *Los Americanos*. Pilar and Adriana explain:

PILAR: This [snubbing] does not happen in Mexico, [where] everyone wears uniforms and is treated better.

ADRIANA: I prefer my school in Mexico. We wore uniforms and no one felt out of place. My parents cannot afford to keep buying me these clothes. (Others nodded in agreement.)

However, cost is not the only concern for the Latinas in dealing with appearance norms. They struggle to understand how to fit in, but also resist cultural norms with which they do not agree.

PILAR: Yes, the uniforms covered everything. But they also cost a lot.

ELENA: Yes, but here, after three months, you want new clothes. . . . And here, there is no respect. It should not be so important. [At home in Mexico], you could not bring tape recorders, cigarettes, no fighting; they did not have any of those things there. Those things were more serious. I would think. "Why should I smoke if I like my classes?" (Again, several nodded.)

The Latinas slip from discussion of clothes to differences in cultural values. They like to reminisce about their school in Mexico. They report that they had high hopes when they first immigrated, but their remembered life in Mexico is idyllic in comparison. They experience alienation ("no one left out of place back home") and see Center City High as not only a source of alienation, but also as encumbering success. Even though they engage in the social mirroring evident in appearance norms, they generally put it aside. For now, succeeding educationally is even more important than their clothes.

Through appearance norms, we find support for interplay between structural position, such as newcomer status, and gendered interaction. Various aspects of the acculturation process are revealed. The Latinas struggle to fit in (evidenced by their interest and chatter about clothes and popular girls), but understand that they exist on the cultural margin. They actively resist a "false self" that will, by their perception, alter their cultural identity. Perhaps their isolation in the ESL environment buffers them from negative interaction with American students, but it also leaves them with virtually no options for integrating into the social milieu of CCHS.

The three themes illustrated here—control mechanisms specific to girls, barriers to English adoption, and conflicting appearance norms—represent gendered practices combined with gendered social organization of school and family. These patterns reveal a multidirectional process of both acceptance and resistance in which Latinas shape and are shaped by social conventions from two cultures. A particular Americanized ethos of reception influences ways in which cultural elements mesh or collide.

Conclusions

The young Latina who once imagined herself finding fortune in America engages in many reflexive shifts between her native culture and a new social nebula, an experience that is at once exciting and tiresome, challenging and limiting. Young Latina transmigrants in this study engage in identity transformation that reflects a strongly gendered and racialized process. Cultural adjustment is shaped and limited by the local gender regime of Center City High, which is also racialized. We do not suggest that the experiences of these Latinas provide a commentary for larger groups of immigrant girls; rather, the study demonstrates how gender, ethnicity, and immigrant status work to vary the acculturation process.

Several control mechanisms drive the adjustment process. Gender differentiates boys from girls in the ESL classroom and in alternate paths to success such as sports and part-time employment. Racialization works through stereotype threat, separating Latinas from other groups, coloring perceptions (which sometimes become self-fulfilling) and bypassing opportunities. Immigrant status, operating both through the ESL environment and in interaction with others of Mexican descent, severely limits the Latinas' English skills, which in turn, stagnates adjustment into the host society and blocks avenues to educational and occupational success. Varied gendered mechanisms—assumed female morality, unpaid work, sex-based divisions of labor—work in concert with local structures and interaction to further entrench the gender order. These practices reveal the gendered makeup of interaction as distinct from characteristics and beliefs of the individual, and adjustment processes as segmented along structural gender lines.

This study demonstrates that gendered dynamics of adjustment processes can be observed and that they are also mediated by other culturally defined differences. Intersections of gender, ethnicity, and immigrant status are clearly observed through appearance norms. The Latinas, as transmigrants, are plainly distinguishable from mainstream students (most obvious when compared to white girls), other Chicanos (who understand and adopt American dress), and even immigrant boys (who are more likely to wear American sports apparel). These examples underscore a gendered ethnicity and ethnic gendering,[2] each line of demarcation segregating

Latinas from potentially integrating and affirming experiences.

This study represents a modest attempt to demonstrate how gendered interaction and gendered structure are mutually reinforcing. Doing gender, the interactional mainstay of gender theory, is illustrated as the girls express feminine ideals of appearance and caretaking roles. Consequences of those interactions are understood only through structural constraints of the family, which offers few choices to girls, and school organization, which tracks Latina transmigrants in a specific way. The Latinas and teachers also do gender in the classroom—through party talk, personal life, and the general non-participation in sports. But none can be fully understood outside institutional structures, such as ESL classes, which emphasize certain differences while muting others, shaping practices that differentially affect girls and boys. Latinas in this study are subject to harsher control both within families and the conformist school culture, one that marks them as outsiders more than it does their male peers.

Equally important, Latinas in this study contest the American gender order. The girls invoke ethnicity to challenge Americanized appearance norms that emphasize name-brand apparel and certain hairstyles and accessories. They also rely on a strong ethnic identity to maintain self-pride and family loyalty. In ways reminiscent of Hill Collins' (1990) portrayal of Black women, these Latinas resist the "controlling images" that *Los Americanos* perpetuate of the poor rural girl riding on a burro. They talk collectively, become indignant and angry, and even laugh at the absurdity of the image, resolving to be so much more. These examples illustrate a much more active and rebellious form of social mirroring—these girls look to American peers to consider how identity is shaped and reflected, but selectively craft a personal (and collective) identity based on their own cultural values.

Despite retaining some native ideals and customs, these young transmigrants want to belong to the American school culture. Challenges, how-

ever, loom large. Lasley Barajas and Pierce (2001) identify cultural translators—who provide information, interpretation, affirmation, and networking—as key to successful adjustment for young Latino/as. Cultural translation is virtually nonexistent for Latinas in this study; they are blocked over and over from accessing those with the greatest potential for that function—teachers, mentors, and their Chicano/a peers. Faced with isolation in the ESL classroom and limited access to English competency, the Latinas' future dims. Studies should search for evidence of potential cultural translators, and practitioners should be concerned about how subordinated groups can access those guides. Comparative work is needed to specifically identify how participation in sports may facilitate adjustment processes for girls and boys, and how access to athletics becomes gendered and racialized. High schools face unique challenges to educate and counsel recent teenage transmigrants, and athletic programs may provide an avenue for integrating and retaining non-English speaking students.

Increasingly, a socially and economically successful society depends on embracing demographic, economic, and cultural dimensions of diversity. Diversity emerges as a topic of national interest, not just because it is legislated or politically correct, but also because it is a reality. Another emerging watchword is "relational"—both gendering and ethnicized processes depend on key relationships; transnational connections are ongoing, diverse, relational. Equally important, relations are embedded in economic and political institutions. Constant reminders foretell the importance of fostering cross-border relationships, of incorporating minority and international communities. In the next two decades, immigration will account for two-thirds of national population growth, and one-fourth of all Americans will be of Hispanic origin (Hudson Institute 1997). These projections underscore the importance of identifying differences by culture of reception for various groups, and the urgency of adjusting programs and practices to better accommodate diverse groups.

Current practices fail to fully integrate talents offered by a new generation of immigrants. How does the ESL classroom described in this study represent the more general ethos of reception in America: multicultural and integrative, or ethnocentric and separatist? It is interesting to note that while American students are being encouraged, even mandated, to learn a "foreign" language (typically Spanish), Spanish-speakers in this study are coached to abandon theirs. This study calls for a more fluid, expandable conception of "immigration" experiences. In fact, as we develop increasingly diverse cross-border relationships, the term "immigrant" seems outdated. Theories should be open to perspectives that allow for multiple spheres of difference and complex patterns of cultural exchange: images of assimilation (to a "dominant" culture) versus resistance are overly simplistic. Gender theory tenets of interaction, structure, and process encourage looking at such complexity of the human experience, and placing process at the center of inquiry encourages different questions. Do cross-border travelers "try on" culture, experimenting with a variety of possible adaptation strategies? How does strategy selection take place, and to what extent are designs successful and within which contexts? How do gendered and racialized practices and ideologies in two cultures reinforce or challenge the other? Transitions remain critical to social processes. Including transnational transitions and bicultural identities becomes critical to understanding new relations of the 21st century.

Notes

1. We use the term "Latino/a" to refer to participants in this study, primarily because that is how they referred to themselves, perhaps as a strategy to demonstrate cultural commonality with other immigrant groups. We refer to students of Mexican origin who are assumed to be American citizens (primarily those who are English-speaking and appear not to be in immigrant groups) as "Chicano/a." Participants also typically refer to this (assumed) group as Chicano, while "los Americanos" seemed to sometimes mean "white" and at other times any students who were

American citizens. When referencing population statistics, "Latinos" refers to a combined group of Mexicans, Puerto Ricans, Cubans, and Dominicans; however, virtually all participants in this study are from Mexico. When specific statistics are available for Mexican immigrants, we use the term "Mexican."

2. We are particularly indebted to one of the *Social Problems* reviewers for pointing out these terms.

References

Aponte, Robert, and Marcelo E. Siles, 1997. "Winds of change: Latinos in the heartland and the nation." *Statistical Brief No. 5*, the Julian Samora Research Institute. Michigan State University, East Lansing, MI.

Connell, Robert W. 1987. *Gender and Power: Society, the Person and Sexual Politics*. Stanford, CA: Stanford University Press.

Enchautegui, María E., and Nolan J. Malone. 1997. "Female immigrants: A socio-economic portrait." *Migration World Magazine* 25:18–23.

Ferree, Myra Marx, Judith Lorber, and Beth B. Hess, eds. 1999. *Revisioning Gender*. Thousand Oaks, CA: Sage.

Gamson, William A. 1992. *Talking Politics*. New York: Cambridge University Press.

Gibson, Margaret A. 1988. *Accommodation without Assimilation: Sikh Immigrants in an American High School*. Ithaca, NY: Cornell University Press.

Gowan, Mary, and Melanie Treviño. 1998. "An examination of gender differences in Mexican-American attitudes toward family and career roles." *Sex Roles: A Journal of Research* 38:1079–1094.

Guitérrez, David G., ed. 1996. *Between Two Worlds: Mexican Immigrants in the United States*. Wilmington, DE: Scholarly Resources.

Hernandez, Donald J., and Evan Charney, eds. 1998. *From Generation to Generation: The Health and Well-Being of Children in Immigrant Families*. Washington, DC: National Academy Press.

Hess, Beth B., and Myra Marx Ferree, eds. 1987. *Analyzing Gender: A Handbook of Social Science Research*. Newbury Park, CA.: Sage.

Hill Collins, Patricia. 1990. *Black Feminist Thought: Knowledge, Consciousness, and the Politics of Empowerment*. Boston: Unwin Hyman.

Hudson Institute. 1997. *Workforce 2020: Work and Workers in the 21st Century*. Indianapolis, IN: Hudson Institute.

Lasley Barajas, Heidi, and Jennifer L. Pierce. 2001. "The significance of race and gender in school success among Latinas and Latinos in college." *Gender & Society* 15:859–878.

Logan, John R. 2001. "The new Latinos: Who they are, where they are." Lewis Mumford Center for Comparative Urban and Regional Research, University at Albany.

McMillen, Mary, 1995. *National Center for Educational Statistics: Dropout Report.* Washington, DC: Govt. Printing Office.

Olsen, Laurie, 1997. *Made in America: Immigrant Students in Our Public Schools.* New York: The New York Press.

Orellana, Marjorie Faulstich, Barrie Thorne. Anna Chee, and Wan Shun Eva Lam. 2001. "Transnational childhoods: The participation of children in processes of family migration." *Social Problems* 48:572–591.

Qin-Hillard, Desirée Baolian, Erika Felnauer, and Blanca G. Quiroz. 2001. "Introduction." *Special Issue: Immigration and Education. Harvard Educational Review* 71:v–x.

Rothenberg, Paula. 1990. "The construction, deconstruction, and reconstruction of difference." *Hypatia* 5:42–57.

Rumbaut, Rubén G. 1995. "The new Californians: Comparative research findings on the educational progress of immigrant children." In *California's Immigrant Children: Theory, Research, and Implications for Educational Policy.* Rubén G.

Rumbaut and Wayne A. Cornelius, eds., 17–69. La Jolla CA: Center for U.S.-Mexican Studies, University of California, San Diego.

———. 2000. *Assimilation, Language Acquisition, and New Immigrants, Colloquia Series.* Minneapolis: Race, Ethnicity Migration Research Center, University of Minnesota.

Sanchez, Mary, 2000. "KC language program under fire." *The Kansas City Star*, March 10, 2000.

Steele, Claude M. 1997. "A threat in the air: How stereotypes shape the intellectual identities and performance of women and African Americans." *American Psychology* 52:613–629.

Suárez-Orozco, Carola, and Marcelo M. Suárez-Orozco. 2001. *Children of Immigration*, Cambridge, MA: Harvard University Press.

West, Candace, and Sarah Fenstermaker. 1995. "Doing difference." *Gender & Society* 9:8–37

West, Candace, and Don H. Zimmerman. 1987. "Doing gender," *Gender & Society* 1:125–151.

Williams, L. Susan. 2002. "Trying on gender, gender regimes, and the process of becoming women." *Gender & Society* 16:29–52.

Wolf, Diana L. 1997. "Family secrets: Transnational struggles among children of Filipino immigrants." *Sociological Perspectives* 40:457–482.

Zhou, Min. 1997. "Growing up American: The challenge confronting immigrant children and children of immigrants." *Annual Review of Sociology* 23:63–95.

J. Hall

It Hurts to Be a Girl: Growing Up Poor, White, and Female

In this article, the author asserts that a group of poor white middle school young women in the postindustrial urban Northeast are living among high concentrations of domestic violence. Many of these females are constructing futures characterized by jobs and self-sufficiency. As their narrations indicate, such plans are fueled by the hope that by living independent lives as single career women, they will bypass the domestic violence that currently rips through their own and their mothers' lives. By not critically exploring the issue of violence against women in classrooms, the author argues that schools become implicated in the silencing and "normalizing" of abuse. This analysis is one piece of a large-scale ethnographic study in which the production of identities among poor white urban girls and boys is explored.

In this investigation, I contend that a group of poor white middle school young women in the postindustrial urban Northeast are living among high concentrations of domestic violence. I refer to this group as "Canal Town" girls.[1] These young women are envisioning lives in which, by charting a course of secondary education, they hope to procure jobs and self-sufficiency. As their narrations indicate, such plans are fueled by the hope that they will live independent lives as single career women and, therefore, will bypass the domestic violence that currently rips through their own and their mothers' lives. This research is one piece of a large-scale ethnographic study on the production of identities among poor white urban girls and boys. For more than a year, I observed and interviewed a group of 18 middle school youth in neighborhood streets, the bilingual school, and the local community center (Hall 2001).

While there are many analyses that focus on the ways in which institutions and the formation of female youth cultures contribute to inequitable futures (Finders 1996; Holland and Eisenhart 1990; McRobbie 1991; Raissiguier 1994; Smith 1988; Valli 1988; Weis 1990), none of this work picks up on the issue of violence. Fine and Weis (1998) examine this theme as it boldly emerges in data on the lives of poor and working-class adult white women and the production of identity. They found that white working-class women experience more abuse, as compared with working-class women from other cultural backgrounds, and are more apt to treat their abuse as a carefully guarded secret (Weis et al. 1997; Weis, Marusza-Hall, and Fine 1998).[2]

Informed by such work, I turn this critical lens on middle school girls. What I found is that their lives are also saturated with domestic abuse. They are not talking about it, not reporting it, and covering their bruises with clothes. They are also hiding it from others and themselves to such an extent that it is not openly dealt with at a critical level at all. Nowhere in their narrations is there any sense that males are accountable for their violent behavior.

This research is contextualized in a postindustrial economy characterized by the systematic dismantling of the basic productive capacity of a nation, a trend sharply experienced in the United States during the 1970s and 1980s. During these decades, the U.S. steel industry had already begun a process of shifting to foreign, less expensive, less regulated markets, as did other areas of manufacturing and production. As a result, smaller businesses that were dependent on industry also closed (Bluestone and Harrison 1982). No longer able economically to support its own populace, the city in this analysis currently relies on shrinking state resources. Left in the wake of global restructuring are empty factories, gutted warehouses, and people who can no longer make a decent living. Canal Town is an urban neighborhood reflecting these changes.

No longer able to find the wage-earning jobs they once enjoyed, today residents are often unemployed (Perry 1996). Many rely on food stamps and Aid to Families with Dependent Children (AFDC). The demography of Canal Town has also shifted from white to racially diverse. This change is reflected in the neighborhood school, which was transformed into a Spanish-English bilingual magnet in the late 1970s. The community center, which has traditionally been staffed by white adults, however, is almost exclusively visited by local white youth. The extent to which racism emerges in this neighborhood and the middle school, encouraged by white adults in the community center, is explored in other work (Hall 2001).

Although still socially and economically privileged by their whiteness, among most white former workers, a family wage has disappeared. The cushion of wealth that white laborers were often able to amass for their families across generations is quickly eroding. Still, there may be pockets of accumulated resources that are shared among white families in Canal Town, for example, in the form of home ownership or a pension (Fine and Weis 1998; Oliver and Shapiro 1995).

To take part in the shaping of responsive public policy, it is increasingly important for educators to understand how *poor* youth from *all* cultural backgrounds make sense of their world. Up until now, the voices of many poor adolescents have not been given room in the literature. Research that does focus on poor youth looks at rural culture (Borman, Mueninghoff, and Piazza 1988; DeYoung 1995). Yet, as economic retrenchment becomes even more invasive in the lives of urban residents who struggle to earn a living, more and more people are being forced into lives of poverty. With contemporary welfare cutbacks, the nature of life in poor families across race is arguably beginning to change. White middle school youth are at an ideal age for exploring many of these issues as they are just beginning to think seriously about the future (Everhart 1983; Finders 1996; Hall 2001).

The Canal Town girls' families have historically been working-class, most having fathers and grandfathers who worked in industry while their mothers and grandmothers stayed home. The subordination of women to men within white working-class families has been heavily investigated (Smith 1987). Others explore this subordination through the notion of the *family wage*. The family wage appeared advantageous to all family members, but in reality it supported the notion that women should receive lower wages than men or stay home (May 1987; Woodcock Tentler 1979). Although the young women in this investigation contend that the adult men around them are no longer employed in full-time labor jobs, present-day gender arrangements in the Canal Town community are linked to the ideology prevalent during the days of heavy industry. . . .

Canal Town Girls

To obtain some sense of the nine poor white sixth-, seventh-, and eighth-grade girls who participated in this research, I share information from the individual interviews pertaining to their home life. Out of the nine girls—Anne, 11; Rosie, 11; Sally, 11; Jamie, 12; Elizabeth, 12; Lisa, 12;

Katie, 13; Christina, 13; and Lisette, 13—only Jamie says she lives with both parents. Elizabeth, Anne, and Katie maintain they live with their mothers, siblings, and their mothers' steady boyfriends. The rest of the girls—Christina, Lisette, Lisa, Rosie, and Sally—report they live with their mothers, siblings, and on occasion, their mothers' different boyfriends. Only Jamie and Christina said they were in contact with their biological fathers, while the remaining girls contend they have no knowledge of their fathers' whereabouts. In terms of employment, seven of the girls state their mothers are not presently working, nor have they been in the past. Only Elizabeth says that her mother used to work as a secretary before she was born. Of the adult men who contribute to household expenses, Jamie's father holds a part-time job in the trucking industry, while Katie is the only girl to claim her mother's boyfriend earns money for their family. As Katie explains, he collects items on trash day that he sells to pawn shops. Jamie says her family receives food stamps, while all of the other girls say their families rely on food stamps and AFDC. Jamie lives in a house that her parents inherited from her grandparents, while the rest of the girls say they live in apartments.

Dream Jobs

As the Canal Town girls begin to talk about what they want their lives to look like after high school, they stress going to college and/or obtaining a good job, and only mention marriage or family after being asked. Since the girls are only in middle school, their plans for the future may not yet be specific or thought out, but the positioning of a job or career as central to the production of identity is worth noting.

> CHRISTINA: I want to be a doctor . . . I'll have to go to college for a long time . . . I don't know where I'll go [to college], hopefully around here . . . I'm not sure what type of doctor, but I'm thinking of the kind that delivers babies.

> LISETTE: I want to be a leader and not a follower . . . I want to be a teacher in [the neighborhood] because I never want to leave here . . . I want to go to [the local] community college, like my sister, learn about teaching little kids . . . I definitely want to be a teacher.

> KATIE: I want to be a scientist; I just love math . . . I want to stay [in the neighborhood]. If I live someplace else I won't be comfortable . . . I'm shy . . . I want to work with, like, chemicals, test tubes.

> LISA: I probably see myself as an educated person with a good job. The one thing I hate to see myself as is to grow up being a drunk person or a homeless person on the streets . . . I would like most of all to be an artist, you know, with my own studio . . . I'm going to start with cosmetology when I go to [the local high school] and then take it from there.

> JAMIE: I'd like to go into carpentry. I already help my dad fix stuff, like the table . . . I just want to be a carpenter. I want to go to college and also be a carpenter, which is something you don't got to go to school for; you just become one. . . . It's just what I want to be.

All of these young girls envision further education in their future, but most do not yet have a clear sense of what school they hope to attend or how long they plan to go. Christina is the only one who talks about a career that absolutely requires a four-year degree and beyond, while it is uncertain whether Lisette, Katie, Lisa, or Jamie might pursue their goals by obtaining a two- or four-year degree. Christina, Katie, and Jamie intend "nontraditional" careers in male-dominant fields, while Lisa and Katie choose those that are typically female. Lisa seems the least committed to any career and tells me she is encouraged by her guidance counselor to sign up for the female-dominated occupation, cosmetology, in high school. Any of these girls may switch ideas about careers a number of times, yet when asked about the future, all of them focus their energies on the single pursuit of furthering their schooling and landing a job. Christina says she worries about being homeless, which is likely a chronic fear among poor youth.

These white young adolescents are the daughters of presently poor adults. None of their parents continued their education beyond high school and a few did not graduate from grade 12. College, they say, is not an option that is really discussed much at home. Perhaps Lisette has the clearest idea of where she would like to go to school because she is the only white girl who I worked with who has an older sibling enrolled in an institution of higher education. Lisette's sister attends a nearby community college and studies early childhood education, a circumstance that likely influenced her little sister's plans. Interestingly, three of these white girls indicate that although they want to break out of cycles of dependence and have careers, they do not want to leave their neighborhood—whether for school or work.

The importance of a job or career is emerging within the identities of these girls, but it is too soon to say whether they will follow through on their plans for further education or training. The outlook is not promising, as all but a few of their older siblings are negotiating lives riddled with substance abuse and early pregnancies. My conversations with the principal of the area high school reveal that very few local teenagers are enrolling in any form of advanced studies.

Even though the Canal Town girls view education as important in obtaining their goals, they both accept and reject academic culture and knowledge. I observed that on a daily basis while in class, these girls copy homework, pass notes, read magazines and/or books, or, in other words, participate in the form rather than the content of schooling. Time spent in school involves passively skipping across the surface of learning.

In only a few instances did the girls actually narrate resentment toward school authority. As part of a tradition of working-class women whose personal choices have been mediated by structural constraints, the Canal Town girls, by

virtue of gender, are not part of this legacy of expressed resentment. Animosity toward institutional authority is typically male and is linked to the historical contestation between capital and workers (Everhart 1983; Weis 1990). Since white women generally labored in the private sphere or as marginalized wage workers, they did not directly engage in such struggles.

Family Planning

The Canal Town girls, like the older white working-class girls of Freeway (Weis 1990), view jobs and careers as a central part of their futures, which is in vivid contrast to working-class girls in previous studies (McRobbie 1991; Raissiguier 1994; Valli, 1988). While the Freeway girls mention the desire for marriage and family only after they are financially secure, most of the Canal Town girls, with the exception of Lisa, contend they do not wish to have husbands, homes, and families at all. Rather, the Canal Town girls claim they are looking to the life of a single career woman as a way to circumvent the abuse that they see inscribed in future families or relationships with men. It quickly becomes clear that seeking refuge from domestic violence plays a big role in constructing identities. For many of these girls, the future includes avoiding marriage and family altogether and getting a job so they can rely on themselves.

> CHRISTINA: I don't want to be married because if I was married, my husband would want a kid. I don't want to have a kid because its father may not treat us right . . . hitting and stuff. . . . There's not enough for everybody and the kid shouldn't have to suffer . . . I want to always stay in [this neighborhood] . . . live alone. . . . At least I know trouble here when I see it.

> LISETTE: I don't want to get married and be told to stay at home . . . and be someone's punching bag . . . I'll get a one-bedroom apartment and live alone and just try to be the best teacher I can be.

KATIE: I can't see myself being with a guy because they don't know how to not hit . . . that's, like, why I don't want to be married or have, like, a kid . . . I'm going to go to school and be something really good.

LISA: I guess I sort of want to be married, but I want to be free at the same time, and that's not going to happen. I won't be able to do what I want if I'm married. . . . He's got to treat me good and respect me for who I am and not for what he wants me to be, and not for what I did in the past . . . not a lot of hitting . . . I just don't know if that exists . . . I'd rather live by myself, focus on a career.

ELIZABETH: I don't know yet [if I want to marry]. With the problems that happen, you never know. A person can act nice before you marry them and then after they can be mean to you. They have all the power. They can make us do everything. My uncle is as lazy as hell. He makes my mom go to the store all the time. He makes us walk. My mom likes it, but I hate it. . . . We don't have a car, but he gets cable and my mom pays for it. He makes my mom pay for all the bills. We get our clothes from other people, but he buys his new. . . . I don't know if it's fair to have kids. If you don't put your kids first, you shouldn't bring them into the world. . . . If I get married, it will be to someone who's intelligent, willing to help, someone who doesn't drink, and someone who isn't violent . . . I don't think it exists, so I want to just get a good job and live alone.

The girls are not devising career-oriented plans simply to escape a patriarchal-dominant home. Rather, they specifically say they view a job as the ticket to a life free of abuse. By concentrating energies on the world of work instead of family, some of the Canal Town girls feel they can spare bringing children into the world, whom they feel often bear the brunt of adult problems. As Elizabeth resolves, "If I get married, it will be to someone . . . who doesn't drink, and [to] someone who isn't violent . . . I don't think it ex-

ists, so I want to just get a good job and live alone."

While the girls say they want to live as independent women in the public sphere, they are developing such identities in response to violent men. Nowhere, in more than one year of observations and interviews, did I hear these girls hold men and boys accountable for their abusive behavior. While it may be the case that they hold such a critique, the absence of any such discourse in the data is glaring, especially given the frequency and detail in which abuse was mentioned in the private space of an interview or in hushed conversations with friends.

It Hurts to Be a Girl

When these young girls are asked to describe their neighborhood, they soon begin to tell stories of women being abused at the hands of men. The women in their narrations seemingly work to conceal their abuse from authorities and ultimately end up "going back."

JAMIE: It's a pretty good place to live. . . . There's lots of auto crashes, drunk people. Lots of people go to the bars on Friday and Saturday and get blasted. They're always messing with people. Some guy is always getting kicked out of the bar for fighting. Guys are mostly fighting with their girlfriends and are getting kicked out for punching so they continue to fight in the street; I see it from my bedroom window; only the girl mostly gets beat up really bad . . . but later she was saying it was her fault.

CHRISTINA: There's lots of violence in this neighborhood. Like there's this couple that's always fighting. When the guy gets mad, he hits her. It happens upstairs in their house. She's thrown the coffee pot at him and the toaster, they [the coffeepot and toaster] landed in the street . . . I saw it while walking by. . . . The guy would show off all the time in front of his friends. One day when he was hitting her, she just punched him back and told him she wasn't going to live with him anymore. He used to hit her hard. She used to cry but she would still go out with him. She said she loved him too much to dump him. A lot of people go back.

LISETTE: It's overall a nice neighborhood. . . . There's like a lot of physical and mental abuse that goes on. Just lots of yelling. I know one mother that calls her daughter a slut. She tells her, "You're not worth anything; you're a slut" . . . There's one family where the mother's boyfriend sexually abused her little girl, and stuff like that. The girl was like seven, and like he's still with them. The mother didn't care. . . . It's like fathers and boyfriends beat on the kids. They [the mothers] don't take a stand. They don't say, "Well you know that's my daughter" or "that's my son." It's like they don't care. They think that they're just to sit down and be home . . . they just sleep all day or watch TV. Some of them drink all day and are high and spend a lot of time sleeping it off.

ROSIE: My neighborhood's quiet sometimes. It's a nice neighborhood, I guess. Sometimes it could be violent. . . . Like there was my mom's friend who came over once with bruises all over. Her boyfriend beat her up because she had a guy from downstairs come up to her house. The boyfriend got real mad and he was going to kill her because he was jealous. I didn't see the fight but I saw her. She looked like a purple people eater. . . . There's this one girl who got beat by her boyfriend. She did drugs and had another boyfriend, and the first boyfriend found out and got jealous. . . . She went back with him though. . . . Violence is pretty much common in people's lives. About 95 percent of the world is angry. They attack things or litter, abuse people, and do other bad things like rape or kill. It's just the way it is.

Even though the community is seen as "a pretty good place to live" and "overall a nice neighborhood," the girls' descriptions of residency quickly devolve into stories of violence—mostly violence directed toward women by the hands of men in both public and private spaces. As Jamie—who lives across the street from a tavern—watches out the window from her second-story flat, it is a normal occurrence for men to hit women in public sites, such as in a bar or on the street. As Christina walks through her neighborhood, she observes that violence also exists between men and women behind the closed doors of homes. Christina also notes that women often return to their abusive partners. Lisette distinguishes between different types of abuse—physical and mental—and gives examples of abuse between mothers and boyfriends, daughters and sons.[3] Rosie, it can be argued, is so desensitized to abuse that she humorously recalls how a badly beaten friend of her mother resembled a "purple people eater." In Rosie's view, "About 95 percent of the world is angry . . . it's just the way it is."

Although these girls may look at abuse differently, they all are quick to recognize violence as a defining feature of their community. Many mention that women "go back" to their abuser as if it were acceptable or normal for men to abuse women, and that it is the women's duty to negotiate their way around this violence. Again, missing in these arguments is the recognition that men are responsible for their abusive behavior. The only critique articulated is raised by Lisette, but it is directed toward neighborhood mothers whom she feels are not adequately putting their children's needs first.

Despite their young ages, the Canal Town girls have heard of abuse in a variety of different contexts and forms and, according to their narrations, women in this neighborhood do not always endure their violence in isolation. Rosie, for example, reveals that a neighbor sought refuge with her mother after a severe beating. Abuse, however, is seemingly concealed within the community—that is, complaints rarely reach a more public forum.

For girls, abuse does not just exist in public places and in the private dwellings of others. Violence also occurs in their own homes. In talking about personal experiences with abuse, they typically contextualize violence as part of the past, as "things are better now." The younger girls, though, are not consistent in packaging such events in history. For instance, Elizabeth and Sally shift from present to past in describing the abuse in their homes. Many women recall chilling vignettes of unbridled rage that pattern their upbringing.

ELIZABETH: I want my mother's boyfriend to stop drinking so much. He drinks a lot. Like a sink full of beer cans because his friends come over a lot too. They bring over cases and he usually gets drunk off a 12 pack. . . . Like every other day he will start screaming and blaming things on my sister me and my mom. My mom tells him, "No, it's not our fault." He forgets a lot too, like what he did with his money, or where he puts his pens and pencils. He starts screaming at us because he thinks we take them. The house has to be a certain way. If one thing is out of place, he'll hit us or lock us in the closet for awhile until my mom screams so much he lets us out . . . but things are better now.

SALLY: I used to think of myself as a zero, like I was nothing. I was stupid; I couldn't do anything . . . I don't anymore because we're all done with the violence in my house . . . I've tried to keep it out since I was a kid. . . . My mom and John [her mother's boyfriend] will argue over the littlest things. My mom is someone who is a violent person too. Sometimes she hits us, or he does. Then she would take a shower and we would get all dressed up, and we would all go out somewhere. After something bad would happen, she would try to make it better. She's a real fun person. . . . We're really close. We make cookies together and breakfast together.

ANNE: My mom and her boyfriend constantly fight because they drink. When I was little, I remember being in my bed. I was sleeping, only my other sisters came and woke me up because my mom and her boyfriend were fighting. We [Anne and her sisters] started crying. I was screaming. My sisters were trying to calm me down. Our door was above the staircase and you could see the front door. I just had visions of me running out the door to get help because I was so scared. My oldest sister was like nine or ten and I had to go the bathroom and we only have one and it was downstairs. She sneaked me downstairs and into the kitchen and there was glasses smashed all over, there were plants underwater, the phone cord was underwater in the kitchen sink. It was just a wreck everywhere. But most of all, there were streams of blood mixing in with the water, on the floor, on the walls.

ROSIE: I remember one Christmas my mom and my uncle were fighting. I escaped out the window to get help for my mom. We were living on the bottom floor at the time. I didn't have time to take a coat or mittens, I just grabbed my goldfish bowl . . . I think it was because I didn't want to ever go back there. I immediately ran to the [community] center but it was closed, being like three in the morning or something. So I just ran around the neighborhood and water was splashing out of my goldfish bowl, and the fish were dying, and I was freezing, and I couldn't even scream anymore.

As these narrations indicate, domestic violence patterns the lives of these girls. In a moment of desperation, Rosie seeks refuge at the community center, but it has long closed for the night. Mom can offer little salvation as she is often drunk, violent herself, or powerless as the man in her life is on an abusive rampage. As they escape into the icy night or are locked in closets, these females have little recourse from the extreme and terrifying conditions that govern their lives. In Sally's case, her mother is also violent yet is thought of as making up for that abuse by involving her daughter in family-style activities.

Sally learns, therefore, not to see or feel pain. Given these accounts, it is easy for me to conclude that the effects of domestic violence are not something that can be contained at home, and the Canal Town girls indicate that exposure to abuse profoundly shapes their behavior in other places, such as school.

ELIZABETH: About twice a month they [her mother and mother's boyfriend] fight. But not that far apart. Last time he [the boyfriend] smacked me, I had a red hand on my face. I walked around with a red hand on my face, only I wouldn't let anybody see it . . . I skipped school and the [community] center for, like, three days so no one would ask me about it . . . I hid in my closet until you could barely see it. Then when I went back to school, I stayed real quiet because I didn't want people to look at me, notice the hand on my face.

CHRISTINA: When I had a boyfriend, he [her father] got so mad at me. He told me I wasn't allowed to have a boyfriend. I didn't know that because he never told me. He said that if he ever saw him again, I would get my ass kicked. So one day he heard that Robbie [her boyfriend] walked me to school. Well, he [her father] came over that night and pulled down my pants and whipped me with his belt. I was bloody and the next day full of bruises. But I hurt more from being embarrassed to have my pants pulled down at my age. It hurt to sit all day long at school; that's all I could concentrate on. I couldn't go to the nurse because then she would find out. Nobody knew how I hurt under my clothes. I couldn't go to gym because people would find out, so I skipped. I hid in the bathroom but got picked up by the hall monitor who accused me of skipping gym to smoke. I just got so mad when I heard this, I pushed her [the hall monitor] away from me and yelled. I was out of control with anger when they were dragging me down to the principal's. I got suspended for a week and had to talk to a school psychologist for two weeks about how bad smoking is for your health.

ROSIE: My mom got money from her boyfriend for my school pictures, and when they came back, he saw them as I was getting ready for school . . . he threw them and said that I messed up my hair. But I got up an hour early that day to fix it, I remember, only my hair just flattened, not on purpose. He got real mad and picked up a lamp and threw it at her and it hit her but I tried to block it and got hit too. It fell on the floor all in pieces. She was crying because she was hurt and because he left and I was crying because I knew she would let him come back. So we were both crying picking up the glass. Then I walked to school and I didn't open up my mouth once all day because I thought I would cry if I did.

ANNE: Sometimes at school I just avoid teachers because they might feel sorry for me because they might see like bruises or something. . . . Sometimes I act bad so they won't feel sorry for me, then if they see a bruise or something they would think I deserved it. I would rather have them think that than getting the principal or nurse.

The glimpses into these lives suggest children from violent homes are learning at very young ages how to negotiate lives that are enmeshed inside a web of overwhelming circumstances. Elizabeth talks about how her mother's boyfriend blames her and her mother and sister for all that is wrong, while Rosie gets hit with a lamp while trying to protect her mom. As they devise ways to conceal their bruises, they each face their pain alone. Elizabeth skips school and seeks shelter from the world in the same closet in which she is punished by her mother's boyfriend. Christina is choked on her anger and pain and separates herself from school activity only to become embroiled in another set of problems. As Rosie quietly sits through class, her physical and mental pain renders her completely disengaged from academic and social life at school. Anne deliberately acts bad to distract teachers from focusing on her scars of abuse.

The narrations of the poor white girls in this study reflect findings in much of the existing research (Weis, Maruszo-Hall, and Fine 1998). As these girls indicate, abuse at home makes it difficult to concentrate in school, and the hurt, anger, and fear that they harbor inside often render them silent, which also corroborates these studies (Elkind 1984; Jaffe, Wolfe, and Wilson 1990). According to Afulayan (1993), some children blame themselves for the abuse and skip school to protect a parent from the abuser, while other children become ill from worry. Depression, sleep disturbances, suicidal tendencies, and low self-esteem are other symptoms exhibited among children living in violent homes (Hughes 1988; Reid, Kavanaugh, and Baldwin 1987).

All of these girls reveal they spend incredible energy on keeping their abuse a secret while in school. This is likely in response to a number of fears, including fear of public embarrassment, fear of further angering an abuser, or fear that families will be torn apart by authorities. While observing the girls at school, I noticed that some of them sustained bruises that could not be so easily hidden under long sleeves or turtlenecks. One day, for example, Christina came to school wearing an excessive amount of eye makeup, which was noticeable, considering she usually did not wear any. While talking to her outside after school, I realized this was probably an attempt to conceal a black eye, which could clearly be seen in the harsh light of day.

Interestingly, I did not hear any talk of domestic violence at school—critical or otherwise. This finding parallels the poor and working-class white women in the study of Weis et al. (1997) who also were silent about the abuse in their lives, which was similarly not interrupted by schools, the legal system, and so forth. It did not seem to me that any of the girls sought help at school from their white female peers, teachers, or anyone else in coping with abuse. Instead, in the space of the school, a code of silence surrounding domestic violence prevailed, even though the girls

articulate an awareness of others' abuse throughout the community. Not once did I hear students or teachers query others about violence, nor was abuse even mentioned as a social problem in classes in which human behavior was discussed. Even on the day that Christina came to school attempting to camouflage a bruised eye, I did not observe a teacher pull her aside to talk, nor did I hear her friends ask her if she was all right. Dragged by their families from one violent situation to the next, it is remarkable that these girls are, for the most part, able to get through the school day, go home, and come back again tomorrow.

Conclusion

The Canal Town girls are from families that had been working-class for generations. Born into the snares of a postindustrial economy, today these girls are growing up in poverty. As their narrations on work and family indicate, gender arrangements in their lives echo that of the working class in which women are subordinate to men. Embedded in this subordination is a silencing of domestic violence.

Domestic violence runs painfully deep in the lives of the Canal Town girls. These girls are socialized at an early age to conceal abuse from those outside the community who might take action. As a method of coping, they have learned to work around abuse to such an extent that by envisioning their future lives as financially independent, they hope to sidestep violence. The sting of abuse provides much of the scaffolding for how these girls wish to construct their lives, and men are seemingly not taken to task. In this tight-knit community, it often hurts to be a girl.

During an entire year of fieldwork, I never saw or heard a teacher approach a student concerning domestic violence. I also never witnessed a teacher initiate a discussion on the topic of abuse in class. Throughout the year, I had the opportunity to ask all of the teachers if they had knowledge of the extent of violence in the Canal Town community or the possibility of abuse in the lives of their students. The teachers had little to say on this topic, many indicating they had not thought much about domestic violence, although they "wouldn't be surprised."

By not responding to violence in the home, institutions that structure the lives of these girls, such as schools, arguably contribute to its concealment. The guidelines already in place in some schools, the counselors, and child abuse training for teachers do not typically address the needs of battered youth. Due to shame or punishment that awaits at home, youth do not always visit a counselor. It is often the case that teachers also are afraid to report abuse—afraid of upsetting the students, parents, and school administrators. Perhaps educators feel "unsure" about their suspicions and "wait" to see more evidence. Indeed, alerting Child Protective Services many times leads to further abuse by an angered parent. Likewise, police investigations and court appearances often prove unproductive and humiliating for women and children (Weis, Marusza-Hall, and Fine 1998).

Educators must come to the conclusion that at least some students in their classes go home to abusive situations. Teachers and policy makers, therefore, are confronted with the task of formulating more tangible responses. In English and History classes, boys and girls can often be led in critical discussions about domestic violence—as it relates to classroom material and to daily life. Through these lessons, abuse must be positioned as abnormal behavior, with social and historical roots that can be unraveled. Older kids can also be encouraged to enter internships at domestic violence shelters and hot lines, so youth can learn that abuse is wrong, it is not a personal problem, and there is some recourse (Weis, Marusza-Hall, and Fine 1998).

Educators and social scientists must additionally seek out other safe spaces in students' lives where critical conversations can take place (Fine and Weis 1998; Weis, Marusza-Hall, and Fine 1998). The Canal Town girls, for example, are regular visitors to a neighborhood community center. Places such as community centers, arts programs, and youth groups offer a location that is unbounded by state guidelines where such talk can happen. By conducting workshops in these sites by those who run domestic violence shelters, youth can be led to think critically about abuse and can come to realize they are not alone and that there is a possibility for a different way of life.

Notes

1. This name is based on the fact that during the early 1800s, this area of the city was selected as the last stop on a major canal that was constructed across the state. This opened up the city, transforming it into a formidable site for the production and transport of steel. During the past few decades, however, most of this industry has left the area.

2. Boys living in violent homes may experience more abuse than girls. This has been found to be the case because when angry, boys typically act out more than girls. Because this acting out is more apt to enrage a violent adult, boys often end up as a more primary target (Jouriles and Norwood 1995).

3. This sophisticated way of looking at abuse is likely attributed to the extremely close relationship Lisette has with Ruby, the white middle-aged activities director at the local community center, who also serves as an informal counselor to white neighborhood youth.

References

Afulayan, J. 1993. Consequences of domestic violence on elementary school education. *Child and Family Therapy* 15:55–58.

Bluestone, B., and B. Harrison. 1982. *The deindustrialization of America: Plant closings, community abandonment, and the dismantling of basic industry*. New York: Basic Books.

Borman, K., E. Mueninghoff, and S. Piazza. 1988. Urban Appalachian girls and young women: Bowing to no one. In *Class, race, and gender in American education*, edited by L. Weis. Albany: State University of New York.

DeYoung, A. 1995. *The life and death of a rural American high school: Farewell Little Kanawha*. New York: Garland.

Elkind, P. 1984. *All grown up and no place to go*. Reading, MA: Addison-Wesley.

Everhart, R. 1983. *Reading, writing and resistance: Adolescence and labor in a junior high school.* Boston: Routledge and Kegan Paul.

Finders, M. 1996. *Just girls: Hidden literacies and life in junior high.* New York: Teachers College Press.

Fine, M., and L. Weis. 1998. *The unknown city: The lives of poor and working-class young adults.* New York: Beacon.

Hall, J. 2001. *Canal Town youth: Community organization and the development of adolescent identity.* New York: State University of New York Press. In press.

Holland, D., and M. Eisenhart. 1990. *Educated in romance: Women, achievement, and college culture.* Chicago: University of Chicago Press.

Hughes, H. 1988. Psychological and behavioral correlates of family violence in child witnesses and victims. *American Journal of Orthopsychiatry* 58:77–90.

Jaffe, P., S. Wolfe, and S. Wilson. 1990. *Children of battered women.* Newbury Park, CA: Sage.

Jouriles, E., and W. Norwood. 1995. Physical aggression toward boys and girls in families characterized by the battering of women. *Journal of Family Psychology* 9:69–78.

May, M. 1987. The historical problem of the family wage: The Ford Motor Company and the five dollar day. In *Families and work*, edited by N. Gerstel and H. E. Gross. Philadelphia, PA: Temple University Press.

McRobbie, A. 1991. *Feminism and youth culture: From Jackie to just seventeen.* Boston: Unwin Hyman.

Oliver, M., and T. Shapiro. 1995. *Black wealth, white wealth: A new perspective on racial inequality.* New York: Routledge.

Perry, D. 1996. *Governance in Erie County: A foundation for understanding and action.* Buffalo: State University of New York Press.

Raissiguier, C. 1994. *Becoming women, becoming workers: Identity formation in a French vocational school.* Albany: State University of New York Press.

Reid, J., T. Kavanaugh, and J. Baldwin. 1987. Abusive parents' perception of child problem behavior: An example of paternal violence. *Journal of Abnormal Child Psychology* 15:451–66.

Smith, D. 1987. *The everyday world as problematic: A feminist sociology.* Boston: Northeastern University Press.

———. 1988. Femininity as discourse. In *Becoming feminine: The politics of popular culture*, edited by L. Roman, L. Christian-Smith, and E. Ellsworth. London: Falmer.

Valli, L. 1988. Gender identity and the technology of office education. In *Class, race, and gender in American education*, edited by L. Weis. Albany: State University of New York Press.

Weis, L. 1990. *Working class without work.* New York: Routledge.

Weis, L., M. Fine, A. Proweller, C. Bertram, and J. Marusza-Hall. 1997. I've slept in clothes long enough: Excavating the sounds of domestic violence among women in the white working class. *Urban Review* 30:43–62.

Weis, L., J. Marusza-Hall, and M. Fine. 1998. Out of the cupboard: Kids, domestic violence, and schools. *British Journal of Sociology of Education* 19:53–73.

Woodcock Tentler, L. W. 1979. *Wage earning women: Industrial work and family life in the US 1900–1930.* New York: Oxford University Press.

Susan Moon

The Tomboy Returns!

I've learned how to pass for a woman. I learned to brush my long blonde hair every day, and I wear contact lenses when I'm trying to look pretty. From time to time, I even put on a dress without being bribed. I got married, gave birth to two children, nursed them, raised them. But there's a nine-year-old inside of me who still remembers all the good climbing trees in the far-away neighborhood where I grew up, and which shrubs have the straightest twigs to make arrows out of. I've been missing her lately, needing her help, and wanting to make amends to her for the betrayals she suffered.

I'm divorced, my children have flown, and I've got nobody to make breakfast for. Menopause, that old crone, is knocking at the door. At fifty, flushed and sweating after my morning tea, I need my tomboy self again: her adventurous spirit, her brave refusal to be limited by social expectations. If I honor her, I hope she'll come forward.

In third grade at school, I was the only girl in Joel's Gang. In order to get in, you had to have a wrestling match with everybody who was already a member, but fortunately you didn't have to win. We ran around pretending to be fierce, charging through the middle of the sissy girls' hopscotch games. We practiced wrestling holds on each other and played mumbledy-peg in the forsythia bushes, where the teachers wouldn't see our jack-knives.

In those days my mother used to pay me a quarter to put on a dress, on the occasions when a dress was called for—like the visit of a relative. Otherwise I wore dungarees with a cowboy belt.

With the boys in my neighborhood—Robert and Skipper, Evan and Sammy—I played cops and robbers, and cowboys and Indians: racist, violent games which, years later, I righteously tried to keep my own children from playing. We climbed trees and rode *no hands* on our bicycles. I had cap pistols hanging on hooks on my bedroom wall. I traded baseball cards, memorized the batting averages of all the players on the Boston Braves, and played catch by the hour. I read the Hardy Boys Mysteries and *Lou Gehrig, Boy of the Sand Lots*. I started the Robin Hood Club, the Pirate Club, and the Cowboy Comic Collectors Club.

I wore boys' bathing trunks every summer, until I was eight or nine years old. I put on a girls' bathing suit, with all that frilly and deceptive packaging that poked its bones into my flat chest, only after another girl taunted me: *You think you're a boy! You think you're a boy!* I was so mad I got out of the swimming pool and hid her clothes in a closet. She went home in a wet bathing suit, and I pretended I didn't know anything about it.

But why was I in Joel's Gang, instead of playing hopscotch? It was my way of refusing to submit.

I think of my parents' body language. My mother didn't seem happy inside her skin. She moved as if trying to hide her body with her body. Other women, too, seemed to move in shuffle and shadow. But in my father's body, there was elasticity and readiness. He used to walk a lot and ride a bicycle. When my mother wanted to go somewhere, she drove a car.

Everywhere I looked, men were running the show, and women were just the helpers: the President and his wife, the school principal and his secretary, the dentist and his hygienist, the pilot and the stewardess. Though I couldn't have stated it consciously, I breathed in the knowledge that a woman's body was not a powerful place to live.

As for me, I wanted to run and jump and climb over fences, even if it meant tearing my clothes. I didn't try to pretend I was a boy, I just wanted to be ungendered, and therefore unlimited. I hated getting my hair cut, for example, and had a wild bush of hair, like a feral child. I didn't want to have to look pretty, but I liked the way I looked in my classy felt cowboy hat—a "real" one like "real" cowboys wore. Far from being a denial of my sexuality, I think my tomboyhood gave me good practice at living in my body and finding pleasure there.

My parents never objected to my bathing trunks or cowboyphilia, and my mother patiently quizzed me on baseball statistics when I asked her to. But I think it wasn't quite okay for me to be a tomboy. I looked up *tomboy* in Doctor Spock, by whose lights I was raised, but he says nothing on the subject. I think my parents must have been at a loss. Perhaps they feared that I would never agree to brush my hair my whole life long, and, by logical extension, that I would never become a wife-and-mother.

I think so because in the fourth grade, I was sent to dancing school—ballroom dancing!—years before my schoolmates had to undergo this horrible humiliation. I was taught to sit with my ankles crossed until a boy, in parallel agony no doubt, asked me to dance. I learned to do the "box step," an apt name for a spiritless movement that had nothing whatever to do with dancing. ("Step-step-right-together-step-step-left-together.")

For a brief period, I was sent on Sunday afternoons to the home of an elderly Jewish refugee from Vienna who gave me sewing lessons, an activity in which I had no interest whatever. Because I suffered from night terrors and frequent nightmares, I was taken to a child psychiatrist. He asked me mortifying questions like, "Have any of the girls in your class at school begun to menstruate?" It was rumored that one particular girl had already gotten "the curse," but I didn't see that it was any of his business, and so I answered

numbly, "I don't know." For Christmas he gave me a perfume-making kit, which I poured down the toilet in disgust.

But there were contradictory messages in my own family. On the one hand, my grandmother told me that I should brush my hair 100 strokes a day to make it shine. "On doit souffrir pour etre belle," she said, with a hint of irony in her voice. One must suffer to be beautiful. On the other hand, a photograph in a family album shows me and my two younger sisters marching around on the lawn at my grandparents' house, pretending to be soldiers, drilling, with sticks over our shoulders for rifles, wearing three-cornered newspaper hats. Grandpa, who came from a military family, was our drill sergeant. We're obviously having a great time, puffing out our childish chests.

But I always knew I wasn't a boy. One day I went into the nearby vacant lot which we kids called "the woods." I was carrying my precious hand-made bow, and I was looking for arrows. I pushed my way through a tangled arch of bushes, and there was the neighborhood bully, sitting on a stump. He was an archetypal figure, like Butch, the leader of the West Side Gang, in the *Little Lulu* comics I read so avidly. "Give me that bow or pull down your pants," he demanded. Girl that I was, trained to obedience, it never occurred to me that there were any other choices. I handed him the bow.

Not long after, the neighborhood kids gathered in my friend Sammy's back yard for a wrestling tournament. My turn came to wrestle the dreaded bully. I got him to the ground and held him down for the count of ten. I had won! Fair and square. But when I released him and we stood up, I saw that he wanted to kill me for defeating him in public. Terrified, I turned and ran, and he ran after me. I remember the rush of adrenaline which put wings on my heels. I made it safely home, locked the door behind me, and collapsed in fright. The fact that I had just wrestled him to the ground had no transfer value. As soon as the structured contest was over, I went back to being a girl who was scared of a bully.

Another time, Skipper and Evan and I were riding our bicycles around the neighborhood, and stumbled on an old Victorian carriage house. Upstairs, in the unlocked attic, we searched through boxes, and found a huge purple jewel, which we stole and buried in Skipper's back yard, 10 paces from the maple tree and 15 paces from the corner of his garage. We solemnly promised each other we'd leave it buried there forever, or at least until we grew up. Then, if one of us was in trouble, we'd dig it up, sell it, and use the money to help that person.

That night I couldn't go to sleep for feeling guilty, and finally I gave in and told my mother about the stolen jewel. The next day, she made us dig it up and take it back and apologize. Luckily, the lady who lived in the Victorian house was not too mad. She explained that the jewel was a glass doorknob. She told us to stay out of her carriage house and she gave us some cookies. Skipper and Evan were not pleased with me, cookies notwithstanding. Why did I tell? Because I was the only girl? Is that why you shouldn't let women into men's clubs?

Already, by the fifth grade, things had begun to change in ominous ways. Starting that year, girls had to wear skirts or dresses to our school. There was no rule *against* dungarees, however, so I wore both: the dress on top, the blue denim sticking out the bottom. From then on, I had to wear a dress to school. (It's hard to believe now, but when I went to Radcliffe in the sixties, we weren't allowed to wear pants to class unless it was snowing.)

In sixth grade, the ground continued to shift under my feet. I made friends with girls, some of whom, to my surprise, turned out to have things in common with me. At recess, I sometimes played jacks instead of dodge ball.

By seventh grade, my former playmates in Joel's Gang had lost interest in me. They began dating the very girls whose hopscotch games we had disrupted a few years before—girls who whispered and giggled in the bathroom, girls who wore, to my disgust, tight skirts. Try to climb a tree in a tight skirt!

And then puberty hit, like a curtain coming down. I grew breasts: tender objects that weren't there before, bodies on top of my body. They came like strangers, and I was supposed to welcome them as part of myself, even though I'd lived all thirteen years of my life without them. The left one started first, and I remember examining myself in the mirror and worrying that the right one would never catch up.

Then, when I was thirteen, I woke up one morning with dried blood on my pajama bottoms. I had imagined "the curse" would come in a red flood that would run out from under my desk and along the classroom floor. My mother gave me a pad, and explained how to attach it. Remember those horrible elastic belts with hooks in front and back? She was pleased and supportive. But I felt ashamed—I had been claimed by my tribe, marked irrevocably as a second-class citizen. I would be one of them after all. My tree-climbing days were over.

I certainly couldn't buck biology, and it never occurred to me (until much later) that I could buck the social definitions that went with it. And so I began to behave accordingly. I tried to please my teachers, to look pretty, to act polite. I grew my hair, and brushed it. At school dances I waited in silent terror that I wouldn't be asked to dance. If asked, I danced in an agony of shyness, unable to think of anything to say. In high school, by a strange twist of fate, I was invited to a formal prep school dance by Joel, of Joel's Gang. We had barely spoken to each other since the third grade. We fox-trotted together, speechless and miserable, no longer able to practice wrestling holds on each other.

All during college and into my twenties, I spurned athletic pursuits as being somehow for stupid people, especially if those people were female. Enthusiasm for physical activity had come to mean the opposite of smart, hip, and sexy. Physical exuberance was gone. I wore constricting undergarments. I hoped I wouldn't sweat, and that the wind wouldn't muss my hair. I now see *this* as my betrayal of my sex—this nice resignation, this alienation from the body called "femininity."

These days, I go to a gym, and I lift weights. I want muscles—muscles that show. I like the way they look. I like to feel strong. I like to do the bench press, to shove that big heavy bar up off my chest. If I was wrestling with the bully, I probably couldn't push him off me, but I'd sure try.

Now that I'm looking menopause in the face, I wonder if I'm coming around full circle, back to where I was before puberty. I may not wear a boy's bathing suit again, but I hope that the older I get the more I'll be able to ignore what's considered appropriate. When my body is no longer limber enough to climb trees, I hope I'll still have a limber and unladylike mind.

I've spent the last 35 years or so trying to look attractive, and more or less succeeding. The habit dies hard. But now, as a middle-aged woman, I find I am acquiring a certain transparency. Some people seem to be able to see right through me. (Can you guess which ones?) Granted, I'd rather be pretty than ugly, but the whole matter of physical beauty is becoming irrelevant—just as it was when I was nine—and in this there is some measure of relief.

For years, one of my noticeable features has been a great mass of thick blonde hair. But just a few months ago, wanting, as Yeats said, to be "loved for myself alone and not my yellow hair," I cut my hair very short, and now I own neither hairbrush nor comb. This cutting off has been both liberating and terrifying.

And it's not just a question of how I look. There's the more important matter of behavior. When I was a tomboy I started a Robin Hood club and organized cudgel tournaments. Now my creative projects may be less athletic than when I was nine, but I hope I can rediscover that brave spirit, that determination to follow my heart. When I was nine I didn't waste my time being nice. I didn't do other people's laundry, or read the manuscripts of people I hardly knew, just as a favor. My nine-year-old self thinks it would be a good idea for me to join a friend in Maine in October to photograph the blueberry barrens. Or go on retreat to a Benedictine monastery in northern California, where I can stay in a cottage made of a wine barrel and read about saints.

I'm grateful for my tomboy time, because, as my grandmother used to say, "old age is not for sissies." If I hadn't had all that practice climbing forbidden trees, I think I would more easily slip into loneliness and fear as I grow old.

The crone who's knocking at my front door is not a stranger—she's the nine-year-old girl in dungarees, her hair a glad tangle, come to guide me back to my bravest, freest self. She says I never have to brush my hair again, unless I want to. She says it's not too late to learn to play the drums.

Anita Harris

Jamming Girl Culture: Young Women and Consumer Citizenship

Well, I got my first credit card, and I was quite excited. Then I realised what it was I was excited about—oh yippee, validation in the money world, that I can be trusted to spend, spend, spend! . . . Young Adults . . . you are being welcomed into the privileged world of consumerism, and we hope you never leave! And why would you, you are SO comfortable. We just want you to spend!

—Kylie, catpounce e-zine, Australia

For young people in the twenty-first century, citizenship and participation are increasingly achieved through "validation in the money world." As the distinction between states and markets blurs, public spheres for community debate disappear, and global economic forces shape local youth experiences of rights and opportunities, citizenship for young people is being radically altered. The so-called "individualization and monetarisation of everyday life"[1] has meant that some key planks of citizenship, such as economic security and capacity for participation in civic life, are being eroded. Young people are newly obliged to create their own opportunities for livelihood, and civic engagement is difficult to operationalize in the absence of robust structures for participation. Consumption has come to stand in as a sign both of successfully secured social rights and of civic power. It is primarily as consumer citizens that youth are offered a place in contemporary social life, and it is girls above all who are held up as the exemplars of this new citizenship.

Here I look at changing modes of citizenship for young people in new times, and the ways in which young women are constructed as the ideal subjects for these new ways of enacting both social rights and participation through consumption. In the second part of the chapter I point to some examples of young women's resistance to these constructions. I suggest that some young women are developing creative strategies in response that temporarily disrupt connections between consumption and citizenship, and attempt to insert production and community-building back into youth participation.

Young People and Consumer Citizenship

Expectations of and opportunities for citizenship for youth have become increasingly complicated in the context of contemporary socioeconomic conditions. This is borne out in a number of ways. The collapse of the full-time youth job market has made economic circumstances precarious, and the new policy emphasis on education without the flow of adequate jobs for the newly skilled has seen the deferral of possibilities for an independent, financially secure life for many. The rollback of welfare has also radically redefined the role of the state in relation to youth, who are now required to make their way in a restructured economy without a social security safety net. Within the world of work for youth, competition is fierce and much stock is placed in personal effort, flexibility, and networking to secure employment. Social rights, that is, livelihoods, are no longer guaranteed, but become dependent on individual resources and capacity to create opportunities and make connections.

However, one of the most significant shifts in the construction of youth citizenship has been toward consumption. Young people's relationship to the resources in their communities, and their ability to speak out as members of these communities, are shaped through a broader reconceptualization of citizenship as consumer power.

As a consequence of the outsourcing and privatization of many of the services and utilities that were once provided, or at least monitored, by the state, community members are obliged to enter into contractual arrangements with profit-making providers to secure basic "life needs" such as electrical supply to their homes or emergency medical attention. Terms such as "customer," "client," and "consumer" have overwhelmingly taken the place of "citizen" in the areas of health, education, housing, and employment. The social rights of citizens are no longer ensured by the state, but must be negotiated on an individual level between consumer and corporation. The current generation of youth is the first to have experienced these circumstances as its only reality. It is also unique in having to negotiate this retreat of the state in a time of massive economic insecurity. Young people's capacity to enter into successful "customer relations" and make "consumer choices" among the new social rights service providers depends entirely on their economic circumstances. In other words, the new mode of enacting citizenship, that is, through empowered consumer choice, is in fact feasible only for those who have the financial capacity to take their custom elsewhere. Young people who are most vulnerable in the new economy are those least likely to be in this situation of empowered choice makers.

Citizenship is also narrowed down to this concept of consumer power in regard to active participation. Privatization and marketization have also resulted in a retraction of the public sphere. Places where people could gather to debate social issues are either disappearing or becoming corporatized. For example, Michelle Fine and Lois Weis document the ways in which community spaces have become either nonexistent or sites of surveillance.[2] For young people, the shopping mall has almost entirely replaced public spaces, such as the street or parks, and social services, such as drop-in centers, as the site for community. The commercialization of youth leisure has meant that free opportunities for assembly are far diminished. In order to participate in the new sites of community that are demarcated for youth, such as multiplex cinemas, shopping centers, and music festivals, young people must be able to pay. Further, as work diminishes as a mechanism of identity formation, self-presentation and lifestyle are becoming more important as resources for cultural capital. The global youth culture industry has been quick to respond to this situation, offering young people a vast array of products and styles to purchase as part of their identity work. Steven Miles describes this as the representation of young people as "fully-fledged citizens of a consumer society," rather than of a civil society; that is, a consumer identity operates in place of a citizenship based on secure economic and social foundations.[3] Naomi Klein notes the irony of the multinational corporations excluding some youth from the job market while generating exploitive work for others, but relying on all young people to consume their products.[4]

Girls as the New Consumer Citizens

The reinvention of youth citizenship as consumer power has been largely enacted through young women. Girls have become the emblem of this consumer citizen via a problematic knitting together of feminist and neoliberal ideology about power and opportunities, combined with some socioeconomic conditions that appear to have favored their rise in status over that of young (and older) men. All young people are expected to take increasing responsibility for their social rights, but it is young women in particular who are imagined as those best positioned to succeed in this endeavor. The so-called "feminization" of the labor market, whereby service and communication industries have expanded and manufacturing has contracted, along with a new value being placed on skills such as negotiation and close attention to presentation, is seen to have created many opportunities for young women in work. The phenomenon of feminization links success in securing social rights with success in consumption, and suggests that it is young women who are best able to make these connections. As social theorist Lisa Adkins notes, style, fashion, accessories, and presentation are the "essential preconditions for economic power."[5] Obtaining high-status work in the industries driving the new economy—lifestyle, marketing, and image—depends on consumption skills, and it is young women above all who are imagined to have this skill set. In this way, the new youth citizenship is enacted by girls, because they are apparently able to use consumption to secure their social rights.

Young women are also positioned as excellent choice makers, having taken the gains of feminism, such as increased freedoms, assertiveness, and economic independence, and applied them to the market. Their confidence and success are frequently measured by their purchasing power. In the words of one journalist, "Girl power is flexing its economic muscles" via the spending power of "single, professional, independent and confident young women."[6] Girls are imagined to have an enormous amount of control over family purchases, as well as considerable discretionary income of their own. For example, U.S. girls aged eight to eighteen are estimated to be worth $67 billion. For twelve-to-seventeen-year-old British girls, the figure is £1.3 billion, while the collective income of eleven-to-seventeen-year-old girls in Australia is AUS $4.6 billion.[7] Business magazines and market research companies report on young women's consumer patterns and habits with great excitement about the capacity and potential of this group as economic agents. Much stock is placed in girls to revitalize the economy,

both in the deindustrialized West and the Asian "tiger" economies recovering from the crisis of the late 1990s. For example, Tom Holland of the *Far Eastern Economic Review* writes that "if consumer spending is to take over from U.S. demand as the locomotive of powering Asia's economic recovery, it will be hip, young women who are driving the process."[8] Young women are thereby constructed as powerful actors in the marketplace who enact their new opportunities for independence and control by purchasing products and displaying a consumer lifestyle.

The Girl Power market not only relies on young women as its key consumer group, but sells an image of savvy girlness to them in the process. An Australian marketing manager says, "Those who wish to tap into women's purchasing power need to develop an approach that recognises this audience as media-savvy, market-educated and cashed up for a carefully considered spend."[9] Part of this "recognition" is the construction of such an image in the first place, and this has occurred primarily by drawing on the enormous discursive clout of "Girl Power." The term "Girl Power" itself has been used in innumerable advertising campaigns for products such as clothing, accessories, cosmetics, and snacks. It is also frequently used in government and nongovernment services and programs for young women that relate to health, sexuality, education, sports, business knowledge, and self-esteem. Most of these programs construct Girl Power as a personal belief system that makes girls smart and confident: to be girl-powered is to make good choices and to be empowered as an individual. These uses of Girl Power position young women as creators of their own identities and life chances, and as liberated by their participation in the consumer culture that surrounds them. They both emphasize the positive opportunities for young women to invent themselves; to become, in Ulrich Beck's words, "choice biographers."[10]

In addition to the Girl Power message of self-invention and anti-collectivism, Angela McRobbie suggests that it disconnects feminism from politics and justice, and implies that strong and empowered girls are those who have and spend money.[11] Girl Power presents itself as a discourse of young women's citizenship status and entitlements; for example, it advocates autonomy, rights, independence, and power. However, it teaches that rights and power, that is, citizenship, are best enacted through individual choices in the market.

For many young women, this conflation of power with consumption is experienced as deeply problematic. As a consequence, much of youth activism and politics has shifted to addressing this very issue of the invention of female consumer citizenship as the last word in feminist success. Next I discuss some examples of this new kind of young feminist cultural activism that challenges these attempts to position girls as powerful citizens only when they consume. I use the examples of young women involved in alternative media, such as zines and Web sites, as well as those who participate in political art and activism, such as anti-corporate globalization protest. I suggest that the efforts of these young women to "jam" consumer culture and create new public spaces for debate and community indicate important ways that consumption is being resisted and citizenship re-visioned.

Jamming Girl Culture

[In] our time, feminism is a commercial product—like the Spice Girlz, cosmopolitan feminizm. . . . And "liberated" women are a sexy and a useful product for consumption as well. . . . we have the . . . liberated sex objects and the cool fucked-up moneymakers.

(Yen, "Emancypunx" collective, Poland)

Young women such as the Polish "Emancypunx" collective are some of many who interrogate the ways "liberation" is sold to girls through the conflation of feminism and consumption. The purpose of these kinds of collectives and loose organizations is to create cultures of critique and to find other, especially anti-capitalist, sources of power and creativity for young women. In particular, they encourage girls to be active producers

of their own cultures rather than passive consumers of what is mass-manufactured for them. They suggest that although consumption is represented as a new source of power for women, real capacity to make change remains at the level of production. Vina, of the Austrian collective "Nylon," says that it is still the case that "in the field of culture, men are more likely to be seen as cultural producers, whereas women are 'only' perceived as 'consumers.'"[12] To reinsert women into culture as producers, and to resist the seduction of consumption, these girls recommend active engagement with the culture industry. Accordingly, one of the most common protest strategies utilized by these young women is the culture jam.

"Culture jamming" refers to a number of techniques that use the very material of consumer culture to undermine its messages and power. Well-known elements of commercial culture, such as slogans and icons, are interfered with so that their meanings are changed and their inherent illogic is exposed. For example, hacktivists might subtly alter text on a corporation's Web site to point out its poor labor practices, or a graffiti artist might carefully add words to a billboard to make a statement about the health consequences of using that product. The objective is to use the commercial techniques to draw people into the product and then disrupt their reading of it. As Naomi Klein argues, "For a growing number of young activists, adbusting has presented itself as the perfect tool with which to register disapproval of the multinational corporations that have so aggressively stalked them as shoppers, and so unceremoniously dumped them as workers."[13] Unlike more overt political material, such as pamphlets or protest placards, culture jams use brand advertising strategies to reinterpellate a passive, consumer-oriented audience as critical thinkers.

For example, Carly Stasko, a Canadian girl culture jammer, makes zines and stickers, writes over billboards, performs street theater and "events," and conducts media literacy workshops and high school classes on street art and social change. One of her well-known collages depicts a supermarket checkout lane filled with "Girl Power" packages, but the slogan reads: "Warning: for best results don't buy girl power. Grow your own!" She argues that these techniques enable young women to resist the passive girl consumer position, and demonstrates how disrupting mass media "instead of constantly consuming spin" constitutes a new form of feminist activism that can respond to the oppression of a mediated girl culture.[14]

Consistent with this, Canadian anti-corporate globalization "girl activists" Kimberley Fry and Cheryl Lousley argue that these kinds of strategies are necessary in an age when protest discourse and social justice agendas themselves have become appropriated and commodified. They say:

> The response among many youth, including eco-grrrls, is to target the culture industry directly. They take on Nike and other corporations whose vulnerability lies in the integrity of their brands. They take on the media conglomerates and advertising culture which sustain the exploitative, consumer economy. But rather than aim for an anti-capitalist purity, this new generation of activists play with cultural images and challenge them through a production of their own independent, consumer-free spaces.[15]

This play can, of course, be a dangerous game, since political agendas may be lost in the countercultural fun. For example, Verity Burgmann argues that these techniques are of limited value because they do not always connect with a broader political movement, and "on its own, culture jamming does not confront the power of those who produce the images parodied."[16] However, when these links are made— and for young women involved in anti-corporate globalization movements, they frequently are— the results can be powerful. These young women undermine the easy conflation of Girl Power with consumption, and at the same time campaign and protest against the corporations and practices of the global economy that separate young women

into either mindless consumers or exploited workers—and, in doing so, divide them from each other. For example, speaking of the links between the two, Vina says, "In our recent issue [of *Nylon* zine] there's an article about the global fashion industry, that creates desires based on specific images of race and gender and sells to Western consumers—those fashion items are mostly produced by women in export processing zones and sweatshops in Asia, south Europe, and Latin America."[17] A critique of and intervention into the girl market is frequently accompanied by a broader theorization and activism around the forces and conditions of global capital that create this market in the first place, and that exploit other girls far more than the Western consumers they target. Culture jamming is but one incursion that links up with many others of a more confrontational nature.

Creating New Public Spheres

> I want to support and encourage all women to be active participants in the dialogues happening in our society.
>
> (Riika, Ladybomb distribution network, Finland)

Young women involved in anti-consumer politics acknowledge that protest itself has become a more complicated experience under corporate globalization. Resistance is more easily silenced where a public sphere has diminished, and the slogans and styles of protest are frequently absorbed by the advertising industries. Possibilities for public protest as well as civic engagement are curtailed for young women who do not wish to adopt the questionable power and voice of the consumer citizen. Searching for alternative ways to speak out under these conditions has generated efforts to create new kinds of communities and new places for debate and participation. Alternative media and the Internet are central to the creation of these sites. For example, Clodagh of Ireland says, "Zines are an amazing opportunity to participate and have a say in what is going on . . . ,"[18] and an Italian girl activist, Veruska, concurs: "Zine making means people who take their own space to spread self-expression and build new bonds of communication . . . put yourself in discussion, inspiration, creativity, passion, activism."[19] The importance of generating covert modes of both self-expression and networked activism is even greater for young women in circumstances where corporate power is matched by state control. For example, Carol of the Malaysian zine *Grrrl:Rebel* says, "In countries like Malaysia and Singapore, you would get arrested if you write any articles that can be considered as threats to the government . . . . People have to be really 'underground' to run their activities . . . and this is where zines play an important role as a source of information and networking."[20] A similar concern is felt by many young women in many Western countries where "anti-terrorist" security policy has deeply affected their capacity to express critique.

Under these conditions of both corporate and state encroachment on youth political cultures, the Internet has flourished as a site where collectives and individuals can gather to share ideas, debate issues, and strategize about protest. These constitute "virtual communities" not simply because many of them exist only on the Internet, but also because they are not necessarily "real"; that is, there is no evidence of a formal social order, and membership is loose and transient. Many young women position themselves as outside their own societies and as, instead, citizens of these transnational "imagined communities"[21] precisely because they are amorphous and liminal. The communities are designed in these ways to evade the gaze of authority in order that they can accomplish political work; that is, in Riika's words, to "fight against the white supremacist capitalist patriarchy!"[22] As Veruska articulates it, "The most radical aspect [of this community] is the great underground artistic, political, literature, musical revolution we are building. . . . A community where people support each other, get inspired, collaborate together."[23] However, sometimes the capacity to construct a space for self-expression in a world that feels wholly administered can be enough. For example, Lynette,

of the Singaporean zine *There Are Not Enough Hours in the Day for All the Bitching I Have to Do!*, says that her driving force is "to create a space to escape to in this world."[24] The need for both a public forum and a haven is born of the singular interpellation of girls as consumer citizens. New media can operate as places for personal expression or political participation, but in either case they represent an urgent need on the part of young women to express themselves outside of the spaces currently available to them. This is regardless of their enduring effects as a politics, which remains an open question.

Jamming girl culture and creating new public spheres are but two ways that young female activists address the shaping of young women's "postfeminist" status around consumer citizenship. While some young women do constitute the revitalizing market for consumer products, it is many other girls who form the hidden, often informal labor force producing these goods in unregulated, outworked circumstances. The backdrop against which these new systems of consumption and production take place is the globalization of capitalism and the sharpening of class and race inequities between and among young women. Girl activists struggle with the problem that structural explanations for their differential circumstances are losing ground in the face of pervasive discourses of Girl Power, self-invention, and meritocracy. Young women's activism around consumer citizenship is therefore not limited to culture jamming or the attempted creation of new public spheres through alternative media and the Internet. Many are also involved in other kinds of political activities and movements that tackle the global political economy that has generated these limited opportunities for citizenship for young people in the first place. It is when these connections are made that the creative but often isolated techniques of the culture jammers and virtual community builders can develop solid foundations for a new girl citizen who does not merely consume commercial culture, but is an active producer and critic in her community.

Notes

1. Roberts et al. (2001).
2. Fine and Weis (2000), 1140.
3. Miles (2000), 125.
4. Klein (2001).
5. Adkins (2002), 65.
6. Lambert (2003).
7. See Barwick (2001) and Brown (2000) for U.K. figures; Nikas (1998) for Australia; and Cuneo (2002) for the United States.
8. Holland (2000), 62.
9. Quoted in Lambert (2003).
10. Beck (1992), 135.
11. McRobbie (2000).
12. Vina (2002). Thanks to Elke Zobl for her important resources at grrrlzines.net.
13. Klein (2001), 284.
14. Stasko (2001), 278.
15. Fry and Lousley (2001), 150.
16. Burgmann (2003), 306.
17. Vina (2002).
18. Clodagh (2002).
19. Veruska (2002).
20. Carol (2001).
21. Anderson (1991).
22. Riika (2002).
23. Veruska (2002).
24. Lynette (2002).

References

Adkins, Lisa. (2002). *Revisions: Gender and Sexuality in Late Modernity*. Buckingham: Open University Press.

Anderson, Benedict. (1991). *Imagined Communities: Reflections on the Origin and Spread of Nationalism*. London: Verso.

Barwick, Sandra. (2001). "Sex, Boys and Make-up: Is This What Tweenie Girls Want?" *Daily Telegraph*, February 8, p. 22.

Beck, Ulrich. (1992). *Risk Society: Towards a New Modernity*. London: Sage.

Brown, Maggie. (2000). "Give Us the Pocket Money." *The Guardian*, May 29, p. 36.

Burgmann, Verity. (2003). *Power, Profit and Protest*. Sydney: Allen and Unwin.

Carol. (2001). Quoted in Elke Zobl, "Stop Sexism with Style! *Grrrl: Rebel*. An Interview with Carol and Elise." http://grrrlzines.net/interviews/grrrlrebel.htm.

Clodagh. (2002). Quoted in Elke Zobl, "Lighting a Fire of Thought and Ideas: *Ideas Is Matches*. An Interview with Clodagh." http://grrrlzines.net/interviews/ideas.htm.

Cuneo, Alice. (2002). "Affiliation Targets Youngest Female Consumers." *AdAge*, August 27.

Fine, Michelle, and Weis, Lois. (2000). "Disappearing Acts: The State and Violence Against Women in the Twentieth Century." *Signs: Journal of Women in Culture and Society* 25 (4): 1139–1146.

Fry, Kimberley, and Lousley, Cheryl. (2001). "Green Grrrl Power." *Canadian Woman Studies: Young Women: Feminists, Activists, Grrrls* 20/21 (4/1): 148–151.

Holland, Tom. (2000). "Her Choice." *Far Eastern Economic Review* 163 (24): 62–65.

Klein, Naomi. (2001). *No Logo*. Flamingo. London: UK.

Kylie. (2001). http://catpounce.diaryland.com/credit.html.

Lambert, Catherine. (2003). "It's the Dawn of Girl Power." *Herald Sun*, April 13, Sydney.

Lynette. (2002). Quoted in Elke Zobl, "*There Are Not Enough Hours in the Day for All the Bitching I Have to Do!*: An Interview with Lynette, Singapore." http://grrrlzines.net/interviews/lynette.htm.

McRobbie, Angela. (2000). "Sweet Smell of Success? New Ways of Being Young Women." In McRobbie's *Feminism and Youth Culture*. London: Macmillan.

Miles, Steven. (2000). *Youth Lifestyles in a Changing World*. Buckingham: Open University Press.

Nikas, Catherine. (1998). "The Power of Girls." *Ragtrader*, April 3–16, pp. 20–21.

Riika. (2002). Quoted in Elke Zobl, "Challenge, Argue, Think, Define, Prove Your Points! Be Inspired and Encouraged by *Ladybomb* Distro: An Interview with Riika." http://grrrlzines.net/interviews/ladybomb.htm.

Roberts, Ken, et al. (2001). "The Monetarisation and Privatisation of Daily Life, and the Depoliticisation of Youth in Former Communist Countries." Paper presented at "Youth—Actor of Social Change?" Symposium, Council of Europe, Strasbourg, December 12–14.

Stasko, Carly. (2001). "Action Grrrls in the Dream Machine." In Allyson Mitchell, Lisa Bryn Rundle, and Lara Karaian (eds.), *Turbo Chicks: Talking Young Feminisms*. Toronto: Sumach Press.

Veruska. (2002). Quoted in Elke Zobl, "*Clit Rocket*: Queer Revolution. An Interview with Veruska Outlaw." http://grrrlzines.net/interviews/clitrocket.htm.

Vina. (2002). Quoted in Elke Zobl, "Girls, Keep on Getting the Word Out! The Austrian Zine *NYLON* Is Spreading the F-Word: An Interview with Sonja Eismann and Vina Yun from *NYLON*." http://grrrlzines.net/interviews/nylon.htm.

Yen. (2002). Quoted in Elke Zobl, "*Emancypunx*: Creating Space for Women and Making Different Perspectives Visible in Poland. An Interview with Yen." http://grrrlzines.net/interviews/emancypunx.htm.

PART THREE

Economics and Work

Women have always worked to provide the essential goods for themselves, their families, and the larger community. Based on reports by the United Nations, it is often said that women make up half of the world's population, but perform two-thirds of the world's work, receive one-tenth of the world's income and own less than 1 percent of the world's property (see Jaggar 1983). Global statistics on labor, income, and wealth may not be as accurate as local data, but these frequently referenced numbers reflect the reality that much of women's work is unpaid or underpaid and that women indeed own a much smaller share of the world's wealth than men.

In the United States, women have a complicated and ambiguous relationship with labor. For all but the wealthiest men, participation in the labor force has never been considered optional. Men's work experiences are linked to their social class, education, race, and ethnicity, but men are rarely asked, "Do you plan to continue working after you have children?" Indeed, men who do not provide financial support to their children are reviled as "deadbeat dads," and those who choose

to become full-time caregivers face social approbation. For women, social attitudes about work are more complex and linked to their traditional role within the family.

It was once considered dangerous for privileged women to work outside the home. Through the 1950s, medical, sociological and psychological experts warned of the dangers of women's work to their own health and to the health of their families. At the same time, African American women, as a group, were compelled to work for the benefit of whites under slavery and were expected to work in harsh, poorly paid conditions in the pre-Civil Rights era United States. Their labor permitted the contradictory expectation that middle- and upper-class white women should *not* work. The labor histories of women vary significantly by class, race, and ethnicity, but regardless of their position in the labor market, most women have had to balance their jobs outside their homes with the work of caring for their homes and families—what Arlie Hochschild (2003) calls the "second shift."

Women's participation in the labor force has increased dramatically since 1900. In 1900, only 20.6 percent of women worked outside the home, and only 6 percent of married women worked. By 2000, over 60 percent of women were in the paid labor force and 61 percent of married women worked (Kimmel 2004: 181). Some theorists argue that the traditional gender division of labor, with men providing income and women caring for home and children, collapsed in the last decades of the twentieth century (Thistle 2000). The traditional housewife role has been transformed by technology and by the turn to paid labor for care-giving tasks like food preparation and child care. Women continue to perform more household labor than men, but the time they spend cooking, cleaning, and doing laundry is much less than the time spent by their grandmothers on household drudgery. As we see in the article by Chisun Lee, some of this work has been transferred to immigrant women who make it possible for their employers to pursue full-time careers while their children are still young. The structural changes in the composition of the labor force have wide-ranging consequences that are still unfolding. Public policies with regard to women's work have not caught up to these changes, as we will see more fully in the section on mothering and the family.

The labor market is still segregated by gender and women still earn less than men. But both the wage and occupational gender gap narrowed in the United States over the past twenty years. Various approaches to measuring the wage gap, however, produce significantly different findings. When Stephen J. Rose and Heidi I. Hartmann measured wage differences between men and women in their prime working ages of 26 to 59 over a fifteen-year period, women earned only 38 percent of men's earnings (Rose and Hartmann, 2004: iii). This is a much larger wage gap than that found by comparing the annual, full-time, year-round income of women and men, which indicated that women earned 77 percent of men's income in 2005. Moreover, women are much more likely than men to work in low-waged sectors of the economy over a longer period of time and to have gaps in their employment. Women have begun to close the gender gap in many formerly male-dominated professions, such as the law and medicine, and in higher paid managerial positions. However, within each sector of the economy, women continue to earn less than their male peers. Even for highly educated women who do not interrupt their careers for family reasons, the glass ceiling limits women's opportunities in terms of both promotions and salaries (Blau and Kahn 2000).

The majority of working women hold jobs in the secondary sector of the labor force where wages are low, benefits are few or nonexistent, and the opportunities for advancement slim. And the intersectional influences of race, ethnicity, age, and region of the country mean that there are vast differences in wages *among* women. Within each racial category, women earn less than men; but when white male wages are compared to racial subgroups of women, white women earned 79 percent, African American women 68 percent, and Hispanic women 57 percent of white men's wages in 2003 (Eitzen and Baca Zinn 2006). There are also wide variations in the gender wage gap across regions of the United States, with women in the District of Columbia actually experiencing an increase in the gender wage gap over the past few years (Hartmann, Sorokina, and Williams 2006). And while some view the steadily decreasing wage gap as a sign of progress, others note that at least some of the decrease is due to men's worsening economic situation, and that both women and men have lost ground in terms of real, inflation-adjusted wages over the past few years (Hartmann, Sorokina, and Williams 2006).

Globalization has had different effects on women's working lives than on men's. First, women are often targeted as desirable workers in the garment and high-tech industries, valued because they are "nimble-fingered, often youthful, and deferential" (Mills 2003). Particularly in export-processing zones, the traditional gender hierarchy supported by men's waged labor has shifted due to women's increased employment opportunities. At the same time, most of the jobs on the "global assembly line" are poorly regulated in terms of health, safety, and labor standards, and women's wages are kept low. More privileged women who have entered high-wage and high-pressure professions often rely on the cheap labor of transnational migrants to sustain their homes and families. As Chisun Lee describes, women from the Philippines, the Caribbean, and South and

Central America provide care for the families of women in the United States, often using their earnings to support their own children left behind in their native countries. Within the intimate space of the home, women confront the global politics of gendered labor at a very personal level. Nannies and their employers must negotiate the resentments, distrust, and jealousy created by contrasts of privilege and dependency. The effects of globalization on women's lives are explored more fully in the section devoted to that topic.

The selections in this section focus on women's experiences of work. Aggregate data on wage differences and occupational segregation do not reveal the ways that work is simultaneously gratifying and frustrating and how women comply with and resist gender ideologies at work. Karen Brodine's poem describes not only the tedium of clerical work but also the inability of employers to buy "what actual thoughts stand behind our eyes." Women's strategies of resistance to the often dehumanizing nature of waged labor is a theme of the articles on fashion models, exotic dancers, and manual laborers. The resistance of these workers is often a form of covert rather than direct, overt protest. They both *need* their jobs to sustain themselves and *desire* their jobs as a way of expressing themselves and in preference to other jobs they define as boring and less lucrative, such as food service and clerical work. In contrast to traditional forms of labor protest, such as organizing and strikes, the women in these jobs both contest and reinforce unjust relationships among owners, workers, and customers. As Danielle Egan notes in her study of exotic dancers, resistance that fuses contestation and complicity has contradictory results; it can make dancers feel power without altering the macrolevel structures that create their frustrating and often dehumanizing work experiences. Likewise, the manual workers in Gillian Dunne's study struggled with sexist attitudes, unequal pay, and exclusion. To gain acceptance in the traditionally male jobs they wanted, they had to assertively push themselves forward and be "twice as good as the men." Ashley Mears and William Finlay's

study of fashion models describes how models use emotional labor as a coping mechanism to protect themselves from feeling like nothing but a "paper doll" who is easily dismissed and discarded. By defining their work as "acting," they are able to maintain dignity in the face of harsh criticism and objectification. These studies of women's resistance strategies at work raise questions about the viability of individual resistance in a context of diminishing labor standards and protections. If resistance stops at individual inclusion and empowerment, will unfair labor practices change? What alternatives do women have for changing sexist and abusive workplaces?

Along with the globalization of the labor force, the shape of the welfare state in the United States has shifted, with consequences for all workers. Sharon Hays's article describes the frustrations of women who are subject to the new welfare rules. The Personal Responsibility and Work Opportunity Reconciliation Act of 1996 signifies many of the contradictory attitudes of the American public to women and work. This act, known more succinctly as welfare reform, places a lifetime limit of five years on welfare receipt, requires that women work while on welfare, excludes children born while mothers are on welfare, and imposes harsh sanctions on women who fail to adhere to requirements. Many women have given up on the welfare system because it now is so difficult to negotiate caregiving responsibilities and the demands of welfare. Framed in terms of individual morality, welfare reform does not address the nation's lack of support for working mothers or the disappearance of good paying jobs from many communities. As Francis Fox Piven (1999) notes, when social welfare programs decrease benefits and link support to mandatory work, wages and conditions in the labor market also deteriorate, particularly at the low end of the occupational scale. In other words, the devolution of welfare programs affects not only the women who depend on them, but also all women and men in the labor force whose wages are framed by the lack of any alternative.

Like so many aspects of women's lives, the contemporary work scene represents exciting new possibilities and enduring obstacles, both shaped by the intersections of race, ethnicity, class, and nation in the global economy.

References

Blau, Francine D., and Lawrence M. Kahn. (2000). "Gender Differences in Pay." *Journal of Economic Perspectives* 14(4): 75–99.

Eitzen, D. Stanley, and Maxine Baca Zinn. (2006). *Social Problems*. 10th ed. Boston: Allyn and Bacon.

Hartmann, Heidi, Olga Sorokina, and Erica Williams. (2006). *The Best and Worst State Economies for Women*. Washington, DC: Institute for Women's Policy Research.

Hochschild, Arlie. (2003). *The Second Shift*. New York: Penguin.

Jaggar, Alsion M. (1983). *Feminist Politics and Human Nature*. Totowa, NJ: Rowman and Allanheld.

Kimmel, Michael S. (2004). *The Gendered Society*. 2nd ed. New York: Oxford University Press.

Mills, Mary Beth. (2003). "Gender and Inequality in the Global Labor Force." *Annual Review of Anthropology* 32: 41–62.

Piven, Frances Fox. (1999). "Welfare and Work." Pp. 83–99 in Gwendolyn Mink, ed., *Whose Welfare?* Ithaca, NY: Cornell University Press.

Rose, Stephen J., and Heidi I. Hartmann. (2004). *Still a Man's Labor Market: The Long-Term Earnings Gap*. Washington, DC: Institute for Women's Policy Research.

Thistle, Susan. (2000). "The Trouble with Modernity: Gender and the Remaking of Social Theory." *Sociological Theory* 18(2): 275–288.

Karen Brodine

Woman Sitting at the Machine, Thinking

she thinks about everything at once without making a mistake.
no one has figured out how to keep her from doing this thinking
while her hands and nerves also perform every delicate complex
function of the work. this is not automatic or deadening.
try it sometime. make your hands move quickly on the keys
fast as you can, while you are thinking about:

the layers, fossils. the idea that this machine she controls
is simply layers of human workhours frozen in steel, tangled
in tiny circuits, blinking out through lights like hot, red eyes.
the noise of the machine they all sometimes wig out to, giddy,
zinging through the shut-in space, blithering atoms;
everyone's hands paused mid-air above the keys
while Neil or Barbara solo, wrists telling every little thing,
feet blipping along, shoulders raggly.

she had always thought of money as solid, stopped.
but seeing it as moving labor, human hours, why that means
it comes back down to her hands on the keys, shoulder aching,
brain pushing words through fingers through keys, trooping
out crisp black ants on the galleys. work compressed into
instruments, slim computers, thin as mirrors, how could
numbers multiply or disappear, squeezed in sideways like that
but they could, they did, obedient and elegant, how amazing.
the woman whips out a compact, computes the cost,
her face shining back from the silver case
her fingers, sharp tacks, calling up the digits.

when she sits at the machine, rays from the cathode stream
directly into her chest. when she worked as a clerk, the rays
from the xerox angled upward, striking her under the chin.
when she waited tables the micro oven sat at stomach level.
when she typeset for Safeway, dipping her hands in processor
chemicals, her hands burned and peeled and her chest ached
from the fumes.

well we know who makes everything we use or can't use.
as the world piles itself up on the bones of the years,
so our labor gathers.

while we sell ourselves in fractions. they don't want us all
at once, but hour by hour, piece by piece. our hands mainly
and our backs. and chunks of our brains. and veiled expressions
on our faces, they buy. though they can't know what actual
thoughts stand behind our eyes.

then they toss the body out on the sidewalk at noon and at five.
then they spit the body out the door at sixty-five.

Ashley Mears
William Finlay

Not Just a Paper Doll: How Models Manage Bodily Capital and Why They Perform Emotional Labor

Modeling is a challenging occupation because employment is irregular, the physical demands are great, and competition is fierce. Success as a model requires the careful management of bodily capital and the performance of emotional labor. Drawing on participant observations and interviews with models in the Atlanta fashion industry, the authors examine how they do the former and why they do the latter. They manage their bodily capital by subjecting themselves to intense self-regulation. Models perform emotional labor to sell themselves to clients and agents, to create illusions for observers and the camera, and to find dignity in a job that is often degrading and humiliating.

> It's all about selling yourself.
>
> —Melissa, an Atlanta model, in answer to the
> question of what it takes to succeed

Modeling is an uncertain and stressful occupation. Although a handful of models achieve "superstar" status, most of them work intermittently during the course of a career that peaks in their late teens and terminates in their mid-twenties. During their brief careers, they are rejected for jobs, they are humiliated on the job, they struggle to maintain their physical appearance, and they face continual competition from younger and thinner models. It is an occupation that requires them to be passive and silent at work while paying careful attention to the management of their "bodily capital" (Wacquant 2004).

An apparent paradox of modeling, as the quotation that leads off this article indicates, is that models attach considerable importance to

Source: "Not Just a Paper Doll," Ashley Mears and William Finlay. 2005. *Journal of Contemporary Ethnography* 34(3): 317–343. Used by permission.

their performance of emotional labor (i.e., selling themselves), even though career success rests on their physical appearance. Models acknowledge that to those viewing or photographing them, they may be nothing more than "paper dolls"—pretty objects adorned with the products that others wish to sell—but they insist that to succeed as a model also takes the ability to charm agents, clients, photographers, and even, albeit indirectly, the prospective consumers of these products.

Emotional labor, as Hochschild (1983) argued more than twenty years ago, requires a worker to manage his or her own feelings to produce a desired state of mind in a customer or prospective customer. In the years since Hochschild introduced the concept, scholars have been divided in their interpretation of emotional labor. Some, including Hochschild, have seen it as a way for organizations to extend their control over workers from their bodies to their hearts and minds. Others, in contrast, have claimed that workers find emotional labor satisfying because they enjoy the sense it gives them of helping their customers or clients.

Neither of these two views of emotional labor fits the case of models, however. Models are independent contractors, not members of organizations, and they do not perform emotional labor at the direction of supervisors or employers. Models also do not interact with customers—the audience for whom their commercials and advertisements are made—so they are not comparable to other service providers whose satisfaction comes from helping their customers buy the products they represent. Nevertheless, they do find emotional labor (i.e., the management of their own feelings to create a desired facial and bodily display for those watching them) to be desirable and sometimes satisfying. Our explanation for this is that emotional labor helps them to cope with the many unpleasant aspects of modeling. Their emotional labor is a self-protection mechanism to counter the humiliation and harassment they experience at every step in the process of becoming and being a model.

In this article, we address two main questions: how models manage their physical appearance and why they perform emotional labor. We argue that models manage their bodily capital—the expectation that they be young and thin—by lying about their age and by turning their body into an object that they rigorously evaluate and monitor. We argue that they embrace emotional labor—by attempting to charm agents, clients, and photographers and by defining their work as acting—because they believe it makes it more likely that they will be hired and because it enables them to find dignity in work that mostly consists of the passive display of physical beauty. . . .

The Work of Modeling

In this section, we discuss what models do and how the labor market for models operates. Our focus is on models in the Atlanta fashion market. Although not as active as fashion capitals like New York or Miami, Florida, Atlanta is an opportune place for an aspiring young model to begin her career. It has four main modeling agencies, three of which are branches of larger national and international agencies.

Studying Models

The first author used participation observation and interviews to collect the data for this study. Having modeled in Atlanta and abroad for four years, she had access to and familiarity with the model's occupational world. She kept daily field notes during her final semester in college working as a model, totaling an average of fifteen hours of participant observation per week during the course of four months, from May through August 2002. She also conducted fifteen semistructured interviews with female Atlanta-based models in June and July 2002. Both authors conducted independent analyses of the field notes and interviews.

Only women were selected for this study for two reasons. First, modeling provides greater opportunities for women than men—the well-known supermodels are overwhelmingly female, for example. Naomi Wolf (1991) has pointed out that modeling is one of the very few occupations in which women routinely earn more than men. Second, a career as a model remains an enduring fantasy for girls, much as many boys may dream of becoming a professional athlete. Moreover, modeling is glorified in American culture as an exciting and prestigious career for young women, especially by popular culture outlets such as teenage fashion magazines (Massoni 2004).

Respondents ranged in age from sixteen to thirty-three years old. Eleven respondents were white, two black, and two of mixed racial backgrounds. They were asked questions about their careers, their earnings, their relationships with agents, clients, and other models, and what they liked and did not like about modeling. The interviews lasted one to two hours in length and were

Table 10.1   Interviewee Characteristics

Name	Age	Years as Model	Market	Annual Earnings ($)
Amanda	17	2	Local	4,000
Amelia	26	7	National	45,000
Bre	24	6	National	20,000
Bridget	17	4	Local	4,000
Cameron	19	2	National	8,000
Elizabeth	16	2	Local	5,000
Gina	28	10	National	50,000
Heather	22	7	Local	5,000
Josie	26	10	National	35,000–40,000
Kelly	18	6	Local	10,000
Kim	23	5	Local	15,000
Melissa	25	8	Local	5,000–10,000
Tara	24	2	Local	6,000
Simone	24	7	National	53,000
Sophia	33	10	National	40,000

tape-recorded. Table 10.1 provides a list of the models (all names are pseudonyms), their ages, earnings, and whether they currently work in Atlanta only or in other cities as well. The researcher invited models to participate during "bookings" or jobs that they had together. Having modeled in Atlanta for several years, the researcher was well acquainted with many of the few hundred women who work fairly regularly in this city, especially if they did fashion shows. At two of these shows, while waiting backstage for hair and makeup to be done, models were asked if they were willing to be interviewed for this project. The researcher deliberately selected models with varying years of work experience to make the sample as diverse as possible . . .

Being a Model

A model begins her career by obtaining representation with a modeling agency. There are several ways to do this. One approach for the aspiring model is to sign up for modeling schools, conventions, or competitions in the hope of meeting and impressing agency talent scouts. A second approach is to call an agency directly and to try to schedule an appointment with one of the agents. Finally, a model may be recruited into the business by an agency scout who, after spotting her in public, invites her to consider modeling. If the managers at the agency agree to represent the model, she is offered a contract. These agencies—more specifically, the "bookers" within the agencies—then arrange her "go-sees" and castings with potential clients. The agency, in turn, receives a 15 percent to 20 percent commission from the model's earnings.

A large part of any model's career is spent trying to obtain work—attending go-sees and castings. A go-see is a request from a client, such as a department store, fashion designer, or a studio that shoots for various catalogues, to see a variety of models for its upcoming jobs. A casting is an appointment to meet with a client who has asked to see particular models for an upcoming job. Castings offer a greater promise of immediate employment for a model, especially a "request casting," in which the client sees only those models under serious consideration for the job. A go-see is largely an opportunity for models to become a familiar face to clients, with the hope that this will lead to employment in the future. At a go-see or casting, the model shows her "book," or portfolio of pictures, and gives the client a composite card, which has on it a sample of her best pictures, her name, the name of her agency, and her statistics. A model's statistics include her height, dress size, bust, waist, hips, shoe size, hair color, and eye color.

Modeling is intermittent work, especially in a market such as Atlanta's. Peak season in this city is from September to December, with a second spike in demand for models in the spring months of March and April. During these periods, models may receive up to three bookings a week. In the off-season, the bookings drop to one a week or fewer for those models who do not migrate to other markets such as Miami, Dallas, and Chicago in search of employment. In Atlanta, the work itself mostly consists of low-budget catalogues, local department-store advertisements, small fashion shows, and local magazine editorials.

A model's working day depends on whether she has been hired for a photo shoot or a fashion show. For a typical photo shoot, she will pose under the direction of a photographer to display the features of clothing and products that are to be highlighted. Stylists prepare the model for the shoot—they fix her hair, apply her makeup, assemble her wardrobe, and even smooth the wrinkles in her clothes and touch up her lipstick between shots. If it is a fashion show, she will stride confidently down a runway before an audience of photographers, journalists, designers, and garment buyers. Backstage at a fashion show, dressers assist her to change clothes quickly and stylists are on hand to touch up hair and makeup.

Despite the high-profile status of modeling in American culture, most models' incomes are modest at best. According to the Occupational Outlook Handbook (U. S. Department of Labor 2002), fewer than 5,000 persons nationwide hold jobs as models and more than half of these are part-time workers. Models earned an estimated median income of $21,400 in 2002. In Atlanta, the standard hourly rate for catalogue models ranges from $100 to $150 an hour. The average annual income of the Atlanta models in this study who did not travel and were not in school was $15,000. Those who did travel to other markets earned between $40,000 and $53,000. This income is quite unpredictable. Competition from other models and fluctuations in demand for their "look" make it very difficult for models to know with any degree of certainty how much they will earn in a particular month or year. They must count on the one good job a month that will keep them afloat financially. If the job does not materialize, they have to rely on savings or what they can earn in a second job such as waiting tables.

Irregular employment is not the only financial downside to modeling. As self-employed workers, they do not get health insurance or other benefits. Some models, or their parents, may have invested thousands of dollars in start-up costs for their careers—modeling classes, photographs, hair styling, physical trainers, and transportation—with no assurance of success.

Modeling in Atlanta is neither particularly lucrative nor particularly glamorous, but young women continue to be attracted by the prospect of becoming a model. Initially, they hope to be the one who rises above all the rest to become a star or supermodel. Almost every model interviewed for this study had once aspired to be a supermodel, booking campaigns and doing runway shows in New York, Milan, and Paris and accumulating the attendant rewards of wealth and fame. Models quickly find out, however, that they are unlikely to become supermodels. There is simply too much competition, which makes the chances of any one model separating herself from the pack exceedingly slim.

Once their careers are underway and they appreciate that superstardom is probably beyond their reach, models adopt a second criterion that allows them to view their work as financially worthwhile. They turn their attention from lifetime or annual earnings to hourly pay and, more specifically, to how easy it is to earn a relatively large paycheck for a few hours of work. Annual earnings are less important than the models' realization that the effort-rewards ratio is extraordinarily favorable to them. They can earn a great deal of money by doing a job that is not difficult and that does not require any specific skills or education.

Models themselves refer to their work as "easy money." The high hourly wage is a particularly seductive feature of the business for younger models, whose only point of comparison is what they would be doing and earning as teenagers if they were not modeling. A sixteen-year-old girl who can make $500 for a few hours' work or $1,500 in a day is obviously going to be outearning her high school peers in their part-time jobs, even though she may have spent countless hours (and a considerable amount of her parents' money) in pursuit of that single day's employment. In the models' calculus, therefore, easy money trumps regular money.

Managing Bodily Capital

If a model works regularly, it means that she has learned to manage her bodily capital effectively. This consists of three processes. First, she has to figure out whether she has the right "look" (i.e., whether she has the kind of body and face that appeals to agents, clients, photographers, and art directors). Second, she has to be able to take the criticism and rejection that is a constant feature of modeling, even for models who have enjoyed considerable success. Third, she must maintain her bodily capital as she gets older and heavier.

Having the Right Look

The requirements to be a model are rigidly specific and yet indefinable. At a minimum, models need to conform to general norms of conventional attractiveness, such as symmetrical features, clear skin, and healthy teeth, as well as to the modeling industry's specific requirements for height, weight, and bodily shape. Beyond these standards, however, what makes a model's appearance right for a particualr advertising campaign or a particular client becomes somewhat variable. It depends on current fashion, the market that the advertiser has targeted, and the client's individual taste and preferences. Models, agents, and clients alike believe that it is small and subtle differences in models' physical appearance that lead to their being chosen by one client but not another. They refer to these differences as a model's "look."

The topic of their look comes up frequently when models discuss their careers because they know that this determines their employability. Models believe that client preferences are shaped by a combination of location and market. For example, Atlanta clients who advertise their products in catalogs will generally pick slightly older models with a "soft" look, also described as an "all-American girl" or a "girl-next-door" look. This look may be found in a white model or an African-American one, depending on the target market for the product. The large number of affluent African-American households in the greater Atlanta metropolitan area makes it a particularly good base for African-American models with a soft look. In contrast, it is not a good location for a model with an "edgy" or "strong" look—code for a model whose appearance is atypical and, therefore, difficult to categorize. New York designers select models with edgy looks when they want to launch a new style or trend in a fashion magazine.

Models understand, however, that the distinction between soft and edgy is a crude one. They realize that client preferences, even within a single market, are highly idiosyncratic, which means that they cannot predict with any certainty whether their look will be the one a client wants or not. They do not ever fully know what is in a client's mind's eye, and they all have stories about being inexplicably chosen or rejected for particular jobs. Amelia (twenty-six years old, seven years of modeling) described the selection process as a "game of chance":

> The art directors always have a picture of what they want in their heads. They know exactly what girl they want in their mind. They've already drawn her out. And if you don't fit her in one small shape, form, way, they don't choose you. . . . So I think it's a game of chance. You just so happen to look like the person he dreamed up in his head, or one of your pictures looks like something he dreamed up in his head.

The inherent unpredictability of the match between an art director's imagination and a model's look means that luck significantly influences whether a model will be offered this particular job by that particular client. On the other hand, her height, weight, and shape determine whether she is considered for modeling jobs in general. If she does not keep her weight and shape within the industry's narrowly defined limits, she will not be given the opportunity to find out whether her look, whether pale and blonde or dark and exotic, approximates the artistic visions of designers, photographers, and advertisers. Models have to manage their bodily capital carefully to keep it within these limits.

Taking Criticism

Rejection is guaranteed in the modeling industry because there are too many models chasing too few jobs. A model may travel for an hour to a casting, and spend another thirty minutes waiting in line, only for the client to glance her over and make an immediate decision that she is not right for the job. A model is rejected for any number of reasons. Her look may not be exactly what the client wants or the client may consider her nose too big or her bust too small. She may be too tall or her hair may be too dark or too short. Most damning of all, she may be dismissed as too fat. She may never even know why she was rejected,

but will be left to wonder, as many respondents did, "What did I do wrong?" Whatever the reason, models must harden themselves to a barrage of rejections, as Amelia (twenty-six, seven years of modeling) explained:

> I mean, you hear a hundred "no's" before you hear a "yes" with everything. So you know, everyone thinks that we have these huge egos and, in reality, it's probably quite the opposite.

Rejection is common to a number of occupations, particularly those that require occupants to persuade others to buy their products or service. Studies of life insurance salespeople (Oakes 1990), auto salespeople (Lawson 2000), and headhunters (Finlay and Coverdill 2002) have confirmed that the attempt to sell something to someone fails far more often than it succeeds. Compounding models' sense of failure, however, is the criticism, often detailed and explicit, that frequently accompanies these rejections. One occupational hazard of modeling is that everyone—clients, agents, hairstylists, photographers, makeup artists, and designers—feels entitled to make brutally pointed comments about models' physical deficiencies. Another is that this rejection is taken very personally because it challenges a model's conception of her own beauty. Disparaging remarks that could be construed as sexual harassment in most other job settings are taken as a given in the model's daily routine.

The most common criticism that models hear is that they are overweight. Of course, the average model, at five feet eleven inches and 117 pounds, is underweight relative to the average American woman who is five feet four inches and weighs 140 pounds (Smolak 1996). Yet even the thinnest of models in our sample constantly fretted about their body weight, which is consistent with Brenner and Cunningham's (1992) study of female fashion models.

Kim (twenty-three, five years of modeling) mentioned she had put on ten pounds while living in Germany. She had gone there to work but had received few modeling jobs, so she had spent the time hanging out with friends—"I drank, I ate bread, I ate cheese." She described what happened when she returned to Atlanta:

> I had a shoot the day after I came back. I went into the agency two days after that shoot. First thing I hear is, "Kim, uh, Sammy, the photographer, called. He said your ass is too big. You need to lose weight." I just burst into tears. . . . I couldn't deal with that. And then I called them back and I was like, "I'm sorry. I understand that I, I know that I gained weight. I'm very aware of that. That just, I just took that really to heart." And they were like, "you can't take this to heart, this is a business. You just need to understand. Ten pounds gone, you're working again."

Sophia (thirty-three, ten years of modeling) has a number of stories about the scrutiny to which her eating and weight have been subjected. In Milan, a booker told her not to eat fruit:

> "No fruit! People in concentration camps didn't have fruit." I swear to you. That's I think one of my all-time favorite quotes that someone in the business said to me, that people in concentration camps don't have fruit. I was like, "Well, I didn't know that I was in a concentration camp."

In New York, she had an agent who would conduct unannounced "weigh-ins" at the agency. She would take each model into the bathroom where she would weigh her and measure her waist.

Another way that models are humiliated about their weight is by being asked to try on clothes that are too small. Models have to fit into clothing, ranging from size zero to size eight, to book their jobs. Fitting into the clothes is generally not a problem in catalogue shoots because these usually come in the larger sizes (i.e., six to eight) and can be pinned on the models if the fit is not perfect. Runway shows, on the other hand, often present a challenge because these clothes have to be worn properly and because they come in far smaller sizes. As Simone (twenty-four, seven years of modeling) observed

> For runway jobs . . . they come in with their sample sizes that have been made on these really ultra skinny girls in New York, and in order to book the show you have to be able to fit in the clothes and look good in them.

If a model does not fit into them, she risks summary public dismissal from the show to the accompaniment of disparaging comments about her being "too big." Even if she is not fired, the designer's attempts to alter the clothes to fit her are likely to cause considerable embarrassment.

Fitting into clothes is an inherent problem in modeling because of the age-body relationship. Most models begin their careers when they are young, barely out of their teens in some cases, an age at which they still retain much of the shape of their skinny, prepubescent bodies. As they age, their bodies develop their mature shape and no longer fit into small sample sizes. Kelly (eighteen, six years of modeling) explained that her agents and clients had

> always known me as little size zero, fourteen-year-old, cute little girl, and all of a sudden, I was getting some curves on me and they didn't know what to do. They thought it was because I was getting fat and really it was just because I was growing up.

These models only have to look around them to see their competition—younger and thinner models who do fit into the tiny clothes. Heather (twenty-two, seven years of modeling) said,

> I know that I used to be fifteen, sixteen, and I used to be skinny-minny and I used to be the fresh face. And I'm not anymore.

Models are rejected so frequently and so quickly that it is easy for them to become disheartened, especially if they are newcomers to the business. It is hard for new models to get used to a system in which clients make instant and seemingly arbitrary decisions about which models they do want and which ones they do not want.

A model has to be able to handle rejection to succeed. First, she must accept it without becoming too discouraged. This means not taking it "personally." Although rejection is in fact deeply personal, models try to remind themselves that it is just their external appearance that is being turned down. Cameron (nineteen, two years of modeling) explained that she had to tell herself to accept rejection without considering herself a failure:

> It probably isn't just because of you. . . . You're gorgeous, but they might want a different look, and I'm not the right look right now. So you have got to say to yourself, it's not you.

As Cameron's comments suggest, models also develop self-protective rationalizations for why they were rejected. Most commonly, the explanation is bad luck or bad timing: a client wants a particular "look" that a model simply does not have. For Josie (twenty-six, ten years of modeling), this means that she is not "your average blonde bombshell." Instead, with sharp cheekbones, piercing blue eyes, and dark, choppy hair, Josie describes her look as "strong and edgy." Heather (twenty-two, seven years of modeling) said that when a client chose another model in preference to her, she simply blamed it on bad luck:

> I would just think, basically I wasn't the girl right now and they wanted something else. . . . My luck is out right now and there's nothing I can do about it. I wouldn't take it personally.

The second way in which models handle rejection is by working on their external appearance. Even though they believe that luck and timing shape careers, they are not fatalists. Instead, they spend considerable time and effort on managing their bodies to increase their chances of employment.

Taming the Body

Agencies and clients prefer models who are young and thin. If a model can conceal her true age and keep her weight down, she is more likely to book jobs. Both, with some effort, are possible. Models, of course, cannot literally prevent themselves from getting older, but they can and do lie about their age. When the first author met with agents in New York, her Atlanta agency instructed her to bump her age down from nineteen to eighteen. She lied to bookers, clients, photographers, and even to other models if they asked her age. Josie, who is twenty-six, claims to be twenty-two, and she says she has altered her date of birth in her passport to conceal her true age from agents when she works abroad.

Although age is a disqualifying factor for models, it can be circumvented, particularly if a model looks younger than she really is (this is what enables models older than twenty-five to continue working). More difficult to hide and more damaging to a model's career is weight gain. Models fear the effects of time on their figures. Simone (twenty-four, seven years of modeling) does sit-ups because she feels that her stomach is "starting to get a little bigger than it used to be." The weight gain that accompanies aging is a threat to the livelihoods of even the youngest and thinnest models—changes to their bodies may be slower than is normal for someone of their age, but they are inevitable. Amanda (seventeen, two years of modeling) has gone from a size zero to a size four during the period she has been modeling. Despite having thirty-four-inch hips and a perfectly flat stomach, younger models make her feel insecure about her body:

> You'll go to a job when there will be a younger girl who is like thirteen or fourteen or something and is really tiny and I'm like, "Oh, man, maybe I need to be skinnier."

Faced with the twin threats of demography and younger rivals, models go to considerable lengths to maintain their size and weight. Some monitor themselves and what they eat very closely. Kelly (eighteen, six years of modeling) keeps a tape measure on her kitchen table, which she uses daily to check her waist and thighs. She is working with a personal trainer to reduce her hips to thirty-six inches, as instructed by her agents. Since the age of fourteen, Elizabeth (sixteen, two years of modeling) has been trying to lose weight. She had even tried the Slim Fast diet ("That about killed me!" she said) but now counts her caloric intake to make sure she does not exceed 1,200 calories in a day. Amelia (twenty-six, seven years of modeling), after first declaring her aversion to dieting, admitted that she would diet during the fall bathing-suit season:

> I'm just like every other girl and I want to drop three pounds before the show. I'm only eating salad for a week because, you know, I want to fit in that swimsuit.

In addition to dieting, models exercise rigorously and lift weights.

The effect of these pressures has been to make models the permanent overseers of their own bodies who continually compare themselves to an industry standard that becomes increasingly difficult for them to maintain. Furthermore, models have to do this on their own, unlike boxers who are monitored by trainers to ensure that they are managing their bodily capital correctly (Wacquant 2004). At most, a model might be told by an agent to keep her hips down to a certain size or to lose a few pounds, but little, if any, guidance is provided as to how to do this. Instead, models must internalize the expectations of agents, clients, and designers to become the harshest critics of their own bodies. It is striking how readily they disparage their own physical appearance by comparing it to what they consider to be normal—the ideal of the perfect thin body. This self-objectification leads them to one conclusion: they

are abnormal or deviant because they are not thin enough.

It first occurred to Kelly (eighteen, six years of modeling) that her body was deviant when she was in Milan:

> Going to a casting and seeing these tiny, little girls who are a size zero and they are like fifteen . . . but they are just so skinny and they're going, "Oh, I am fat, I have to lose weight.". . . So it just makes me feel like a cow.

Heather (twenty-two, seven years of modeling) said that castings caused her considerable self-doubt because of the comparisons she drew between herself and her younger rivals:

> I feel like I'm the biggest girl there. You know, you walk in there and it's like these itty, bitty girls walking around like toothpicks.

Finally, Cameron (nineteen, two years of modeling), who is five-feet ten-and-a-half inches tall and 112 pounds, feels like she will never be thin enough, despite having lost 33 pounds since beginning her modeling career:

> No matter how skinny you are, you always think you can be skinnier, and there's other people that are going to be skinnier than you. And I don't know, you always worry about your legs are too big, your arms are too flabby, your gut is too flabby. . . . You are all the time looking at your body and criticizing yourself. You always think that you have to be perfect or more perfect than the next girl that comes along. . . . You walk into a casting with a hundred beautiful girls and you kind of say to yourself, "I look like shit compared to these beautiful girls."

Strippers and exotic dancers are also conscious of how they compare to others in their occupations, but their efforts are directed toward transforming their bodies through technology in addition to taming them. For example, Wesely argues that the various body technologies that strippers use to make themselves attractive to customers—including breast implants, dying of their hair, nose jobs, chin surgery, and liposuction—represent an attempt to "further the doll-like image of the female body while hiding the realities of biology" (2003, 654). The available technology is too crude, however, to transform models' bodies into a physical state that would meet the stringent facial and bodily standards of the fashion industry (aside from the near impossibility of making someone taller). Models depend on their genetic predisposition to tallness and thinness, which is then cultivated and maintained through exercise and dieting.

Doing Emotional Labor

Turning her body into an object to be criticized and worked on is one way in which a model can increase her chances of getting a job. Another is by using her personality or charm to woo agents and clients—to engage in emotional labor. Wooing agents and clients is not the only reason for their emotional labor, however. They also do it because the work of modeling requires the creation of illusions and because emotional labor allows them to resist the stereotype of being just a pretty face and a slim body.

Winning Clients: Turning on the Charm

Models engage in "strategic friendliness" (Pierce 1995) toward agents, bookers, clients, and photographers. Pierce defines strategic friendliness as a form of emotional manipulation of another person, using friendliness, politeness, and tact, to achieve a desired outcome (1995, 72). In the case of models, this behavior takes a couple of forms. One is the deference that they display toward those who control access to castings and jobs— agents, bookers, and clients—to secure employment. Deference can mean "schmoozing" and "sucking up" with her agents, as Bre (twenty-four, six years of modeling) explained:

> You have to say, really politely, "look, son-of-a-bitch, I want some work." And you have to go

in and smile all the time and hug them and kiss them.

It can mean bringing her agents gifts, like the bottles of wine Kelly (eighteen, six years of modeling) brought back from modeling in Milan. It can mean a model's following her agent's advice about her appearance; this includes not only, as always, weight and shape, but also clothes, makeup, and hairstyle. Finally, it can mean joking and flattering clients, just as sales workers do (e.g., Dorsey 1994; Leidner 1993; Wood 2000). Gina (twenty-eight, ten years of modeling), who is one of the most successful models in our sample, described how she adapted her behavior to her client's personality:

> You have to be really outgoing when you see the clients. If the client has requested to see you, then you already know that they like your pictures. They just want to see what your personality is like, if they are like going to mix with you, if you are going to be a good representation to them. Whenever I go in, I try to be really, really outgoing or, if the client is kind of like laid-back, like try to match whatever their personality is. And that seems to be working so far.

Josie (twenty-eight, ten years of modeling) said that she felt that to book a job, she needed "to bullshit a little." When asked to explain what she meant by this, she said,

> You know, like having a chat or making a joke or using a little bit of my sense of humor to, like I said, feel out the client or the personalities.

A number of models explicitly compared themselves to sales workers. Melissa (twenty-five, eight years of modeling) said that when she did a show she always tried to talk to the designer: "It's all about selling yourself." Tara (twenty-four, two years of modeling) said that going to castings and go-sees was like selling products door to door: "it is almost like being a salesperson but you are marketing yourself." She added that no matter how frustrated she might be about being rejected or about any other difficulties she might be experiencing, she had to put on a bright, cheerful face each time she walked into a go-see.

Models employ a second type of strategic friendliness once they are on the job. They are enthusiastic and affable—displaying what they refer to as "personality" or "energy"—to make clients, photographers, and others with whom they are working feel at ease. This is similar to the way in which flight attendants allay the concerns of airline passengers (Hochschild 1983), trial lawyers ingratiate themselves with witnesses (Pierce 1995), waitresses solicit tips from diners (Paules 1996), and personal trainers motivate clients to work out (Maguire 2001).

Although on-the-job friendliness might appear to have little to do with success or failure in modeling, in contrast to the other occupations identified above, models insist that it is in fact crucial. First, it makes clients want to hire them and photographers want to shoot them—no one likes to work with a "dud." Heather (twenty-two, seven years of modeling) pointed out that some of the castings resemble "cattle calls," so a model has to find some way of standing out. Her advice was to be personable:

> Have a personality, go in there and don't just be a model, don't just be a face, you know.

Second, friendliness translates into better work. Models believe that personality or energy, even if it is faked, will be revealed in their performance. Amelia (twenty-six, seven years of modeling) said,

> If you have energy, you can give that energy to the camera. That makes good pictures.

Creating Illusions: Faking It

The performance that models give on the job involves more than just being friendly to everyone. Models have to act, that is, express in their faces and bodies the feelings that the client and pho-

tographer want to associate with the particular product that is being modeled. These feelings may be quite different from a model's true feelings, particularly if the acting requires her to assume a difficult or uncomfortable position.

Models frequently experience physical discomfort at work. One reason for it is that they are expected to pose in awkward positions or wear clothes that are unsuited to the weather, such as modeling bathing suits when the temperature is close to freezing. Another reason for discomfort is that models may be told not to sit down so as to avoid wrinkling the clothes, which means that they may have to stand for the entire day. Discomfort may also result from a model's having to squeeze into clothes that do not fit properly or from having to change rapidly from one outfit to another, with little or no privacy and a dresser constantly tugging at her clothes and body.

No matter how uncomfortable a model may be, it is crucial for the job (and her career) that she accept the discomfort and mask her true feelings—at least while she is working. Her face should reflect the illusion the client and photographer want to create, not what the model is actually enduring or thinking. As Amelia (twenty-six, seven years of modeling) said,

> We grin and bear it, and we're on our feet for fifteen hours, doing a shoot in an uncomfortable position, and you learn to just focus on other things, and think about the picture and also think about getting hired again.

Josie (twenty-six, ten years of modeling) similarly emphasized the link between a model's performance of emotional labor and her career. She described how she consciously reminded herself to put on a good show:

> Okay, it's thirty degrees outside and I'm here in a bikini and it hurts all over my body, but I've got to get fucking paid.

This kind of acting is also found among waitresses (Paules 1996) and strippers (Murphy

2003), where it is used both to please customers and to manipulate them into providing more generous tips.

Models, like waitresses and strippers, put on a performance so that they will get paid—in their case, the rewards come if they make good photographs and get rehired. But they do it for more than material reasons—it is a personally satisfying form of emotional labor. The satisfaction comes from their sense of being active in a job in which passivity is expected and from being able to create a level of dignity for themselves in a work environment in which they are often degraded. We consider each of these points in turn.

Models reject objectification—constantly being measured, scrutinized, and evaluated—by defining their work as acting. By emphasizing the importance of performance, models are in effect asserting that their true merit lies in their theatrical talent. For example, they suggest that when they put on clothes and walk on a runway, it is the equivalent of an actor taking a role on the stage. They use terms like "adrenaline," "high energy," and a "drug" to describe their feelings about their performance. Like actors on a stage, models know that when they are on a runway or in front of a camera, they are the center of attention—they are the stars of the show. Josie (twenty-six, ten years of modeling) observed,

> Getting to play dress up and look completely different every time you do a show or every time you do a shoot . . . is so much fun, it can be really, really wonderful. You are the center of attention, of course, there you are, on stage, everybody is watching you. So, yeah, just the attention and that's pretty much it.

Similarly, Amelia (twenty-six, seven years of modeling) said,

> Modeling gives me a certain satisfaction that is like no other. I mean, you get this adrenaline rush when you're on a runway, it's an amazing feeling. Just like being on a stage. You're performing, and you're able to put on this mask

and this performance and it gives you a great adrenaline rush.

Cameron (nineteen, two years of modeling) echoed Josie's and Amelia's comments:

> You have to kind of go into character. I mean, modeling is like acting, you know, you kind of like, you are putting on a show, putting on the clothes and do whatever you have to do to make whatever you are doing look good.

Kim (twenty-three, five years of modeling) talked about the pleasure that being photographed could bring:

> Sometimes you just get tired of that world, that pretty world that you're supposed to be involved in. It's not so pretty, and you're just like, "Urrrgh!" But then when you're having a great day, and you're on this awesome shoot with this awesome photographer and hair stylist and you're all having fun, and you're making beautiful pictures. You're just like, "This does not get any better." You know, I'm so lucky to be able to do this.

Models enthusiastically perform the emotional labor involved in acting because it allows them to claim a share of the spotlight from the clothes that are the ultimate object of attention. It is enjoyable. Doing emotional labor is not only pleasant, however. It provides dignity as well, by reminding them that they are more than just paper dolls to be dressed up or objects to be weighed and measured. It allows them to define modeling as a job that takes effort, energy, and intelligence, as Amelia (twenty-six, seven years of modeling) explained:

> Everybody thinks that we're just paper dolls, you know, and that's unfortunate because there's a lot of girls that I've met throughout the years that are very bright. They have college degrees or don't have college degrees, but they chose a path that may have been a little "offbeat" according to the real world, but you

know, there's vast opportunities in modeling just as there is in any other field. And it is a job, and it is hard work, as you know, but it's not this glamour thing that everybody perceives it be. . . . I think that in order to be successful at it you have to have a really good head on your shoulders. As much as these people think that we don't have brains, in order to make it you have to. Because if you can't take the mental anguish of hearing these things about you on the outside, you can't take them on the inside. Like I said, when you're being told and bashed that you're too fat, you don't fit in these clothes—you know, there are people in the business that are not so wonderful. And, you know, you have to have a good head on your shoulders to be able to just keep going and keep working at it.

Amelia's comments suggest that a model who remains outwardly composed in the face of criticism and rejection is performing emotional labor also. She is engaging in a face-saving "cultural performance," to use a term employed by Sass (2000) and Williams (2003), the effect of which is to maintain her pride and strengthen her resolve to continue working.

The significance of models' emotional labor, therefore, is that it realizes twin goals: the manipulation of others and the assertion of their own worth. Previous studies of emotional labor have largely focused on the relationship between emotional labor and the control of employees and clients (e.g., Hochschild 1983; Leidner 1993; Pierce 1995). Models are similarly manipulative, but they also use emotional labor to establish that they are doing meaningful work. Emotional labor for models is the counterpoint to working in an industry in which bodily capital is valued so highly. It signals their unwillingness to be taken at face value alone.

Conclusions

Emotional labor, although most commonly associated with sales and service-providing jobs, is by no means limited to them (Mann 1999). We have shown that models, ostensibly hired just for their appearance, in fact perform a substantial amount of emotional labor. The emotional labor of models differs, however, in at least three significant respects from that of other workers.

First, as we have noted, models might be expected to have little need to do emotional labor because their selection into the occupation depends so heavily on their bodily capital. In their case, this assumption is unwarranted—they have to manage their bodily capital and do emotional labor to be successful. Second, models have to learn how to perform emotional labor and manage bodily capital without being explicitly told how to do either of these. Their emotional labor is not scripted or in other ways performed under the authority of managers or supervisors; similarly, models receive little guidance in managing their bodily capital, in contrast to athletes, who usually do this under the supervision of trainers and a coaching staff. Third, models do emotional labor for two purposes: to manipulate others and to resist objectification. Models, often demeaned by those who hire them as brainless beauties whose only talent is for making the products of others look good, welcome emotional labor because it allows them to feel that they are performers whose work requires effort and has value. . . .

References

Brenner, Jennifer B., and Joseph G. Cunningham. 1992. Gender differences in eating attitudes, body concept, and self-esteem among models. *Sex Roles* 27:413–37.

Dorsey, David. 1994. *The force*. New York: Random House.

Finlay, William, and James E. Coverdill. 2002. *Headhunters: Matchmaking in the labor market*. Ithaca. NY: Cornell University Press.

Hochschild, Arlie Russell. 1983. *The managed heart: Commercialization of human feeling*. Berkeley: University of California Press.

Lawson, Helene M. 2000. *Ladies on the lot: Women, car sales, and the pursuit of the American dream*. Lanham, MD: Rowman and Littlefield.

Leidner, Robin. 1993. *Fast food, fast talk: Service work and the routinization of everyday life*. Berkeley: University of California Press.

Maguire, Jennifer Smith. 2001. Fit and flexible: The fitness industry, personal trainers and emotional service labor. *Sociology of Sport Journal* 18:379–402.

Mann, Sandi. 1999. Emotion at work: To what extent are we expressing, suppressing, or faking it? *European Journal of Work and Organizational Psychology* 8:347–69.

Massoni, Kelley. 2004. Modeling work: Occupational messages in *Seventeen* magazine. *Gender and Society* 18:47–65.

Murphy, Alexandra G. 2003. The dialectical gaze: Exploring the subject-object tension in the performances of women who strip. *Journal of Contemporary Ethnography* 32:305–35.

Oakes, Guy. 1990. *The soul of the salesman: The moral ethos of personal sales*. Atlantic Highlands. NJ: Humanities Press International.

Paules, Greta Foff. 1996. Resisting the symbolism of service among waitresses. In *Working in the service society*, edited by Cameron Lynne Macdonald and Carmen Sirianni, 264–90. Philadelphia: Temple University Press.

Pierce, Jennifer L. 1995. *Gender trials: Emotional lives in contemporary law firms*. Berkeley: University of California Press.

Sass, James S. 2000. Emotional labor as cultural performance: The communication of caregiving in a nonprofit nursing home. *Western Journal of Communication* 64:330–58.

Smolak, Linda. 1996. *The development of psychopathology of eating disorders*. New York: Lawrence Erlbaum.

U. S. Department of Labor. 2002. *Occupational outlook handbook*. Available at http://stats.bls.gov/oco-home.htm.

Wacquant, Loic. 2004. *Body and soul: Notebooks of an apprentice boxer*. New York: Oxford University Press.

Wesely, Jennifer K. 2003. Exotic dancing and the negotiation of identity. *Journal of Contemporary Ethnography* 32:643–69.

Williams, Claire. 2003. Sky service: The demands of emotional labour in the airline industry. *Gender, Work, and Organization* 10:513–50.

Wolf, Naomi. 1991. *The beauty myth: How images of beauty are used against women*. New York: William Morrow.

Wood, Elizabeth Anne. 2000. Working in the fantasy factory: The attention hypothesis and the enacting of masculine power in strip clubs. *Journal of Contemporary Ethnography* 29:5–31.

Chisun Lee

The Heart of the Work: Professionals Navigating a Personal World

It was billed as the kind of routine function where constituents complain and politicians nod. But by the end of the three-hour town hall, hardly a speaker had kept from breaking down, and one City Council aide, clad in suit and tie, choked into the microphone, "I can't even explain to you how I feel right now, how disturbed and troubled."

To the surprise even of organizers, the April 6 event, showcasing a household workers' rights bill pending in the council, crescendoed into a sort of group catharsis. Some of the nannies and housekeepers who testified whispered through tears. Others sobbed. The moderator, clutching a tissue, announced at one point, "If anyone wants to share something, come up here. I mean, this is nakedness."

The facts by themselves were not horrifying. No one mentioned physical violence or hazards of the extent some industrial workers face. A live-in housekeeper said she lacked privacy where she slept and was not allowed to use a fan because of the electrical expense. One woman described working more than 10 hours a day for under a dollar an hour. Another said she guessed her current salary of $250 a week was better than her previous $250 a month, but then she was unable to go on and abruptly left the floor.

What gripped listeners more than the detail was the depth of emotion. It seemed there was something about cuddling people's babies and making their beds that sharpened the usual stings

of a crummy job into arrows. Indeed, as the women spoke, it became clear that domestic labor involves an intimacy that sets it apart. The private setting and personal nature of the job not only create a climate for exploitation, but also enable indignities not found in other, more public kinds of work.

There was the woman, for instance, who worked as a nanny on Park Avenue for "a decent wage," private living quarters, and a food allowance. "On a scale of one to 10, my working conditions were an eight," she said. Yet she told of a pattern of put-downs that culminated on her birthday: "My employer forgot to give me my lunch break. I got a bagel from her bread keeper. She screamed at me for eating her bagel." Pause. "I loved the boys. But the humiliation . . ."

A domestic and the people she works for can grow very close, says Upper West Side employer Suzanne Levine. A woman whose real name Levine asks be changed to Annie cooked and cleaned for her family and cared for her two children for nearly 20 years.

"We went to all her children's weddings. She came to all our family things, knew all our family secrets. She mothered us, she was very important to us. She was absolutely wonderful," says Levine. Annie, mother of three and about 10 years Levine's senior, knew more about child care than her boss. The children were "so lucky to have her," says Levine. She laughs, "When I came home, everything would fall apart."

Some workers also speak of that kind of familiarity. Family events and troubles are shared, advice exchanged in both directions. Employers might offer a special gift—a typewriter, for instance, for a worker's child starting college—or aid navigating legal labyrinths like the INS.

But the tightest bond inevitably forms between a caregiver and her charge. Nanny Carla Vincent cares for the 17-month-old twins of a family she lives with here, to support her own daughter who visits from Trinidad in the summers. "All the love I have for her, I pour into my employers' kids," she says. "It is exactly the same feeling; you really do feel like they're your own. You defend them the same. I have yet to meet a nanny who can separate her feelings from the child."

Says another, "You are with a child from infancy to when you have taught her how to look up and down before crossing the road. They turn into little people, and you're building their self-esteem, preparing them for the next adventurous time in their lives. You're just not there for the next stage."

It is rare for a worker to stick with one employer as long as Annie did with Levine, a seeming testament to their closeness. When tending to a family's most personal needs, for 20 years no less, caring goes with the job. Even the most astute employer, however, can fail to see the labor in the love.

"As a feminist with an overweening sense of sisterhood, I think it's possible I imposed too much intimacy with somebody who was just trying to do her job," says Levine, who was the editor of *Ms.* magazine from 1972 to 1987. "[Annie] was always aware that I was her employer. It was always a big surprise to me, when that turned out to be at the heart of a problem, because I thought we were so beyond that."

Levine recalls, "Annie would come on vacation with us. I thought she was glad to come. On the other hand, that meant she was on duty for five or six days around the clock. I always felt bad about that. I know a lot of people do. I don't know how you deal with that."

Levine declined to put the *Voice* in touch with Annie, who she said was in her seventies and in poor health. But other household workers invariably say, no matter how warm the friendship,

when push comes to shove, they are employees. "We're not equals," says one, "we're working."

Five days a week, Annie arrived before 8 a.m. and usually worked until 6 p.m., says Levine, who is married to an entertainment lawyer. With regular raises, Annie retired several years ago earning about $20,000, or less than $8 an hour.

"That's the work of several people, but not enough pay for one," says one domestic told about Annie. Yet even lower wages are common. In 2000, half of family child care providers surveyed nationwide earned under $4.82 an hour and typically worked 55 hours a week, according to an analysis of federal data by the nonprofit Center for the Child Care Workforce in Washington, D.C. Housekeepers, considered to be less skilled, usually earn less than caregivers, although those roles, as in Annie's case, can overlap. Wages in New York are higher than elsewhere, but so is the cost of living, and a large number of the workers here are presumed to be undocumented and earning substandard pay.

This low-wage work is done almost entirely by women, and largely by women of color. The D.C. center reports that 98 percent of child care providers are female, and they are often of racial minorities and mothers themselves. Industry experts believe more women in New York may work in households than in any other field.

No doubt many an at-home mom could confirm what scholars contend: The paltry pay reflects society's longstanding failure to value domestic labor as taxing or income-worthy. That lack of recognition has everything to do with the work's intimate quality. Not only does caretaking continue to be seen, post-feminist movement, as a natural and therefore effortless talent of women, but there are shades of slavery in demands for employee devotion that exceed compensation. Chicago-Kent College of Law professor Peggie Smith has painstakingly researched how government denials of rights to household workers were based on sexist or racist arguments. Until 1974, domestics were not entitled to the federal minimum wage, and they are still excluded from laws like the one that protects union activity.

Handicapped by history, workers are also burdened by the unreasonable emotional demands of some employers, says Carol Bandini, a psychoanalyst and co-author of *Child Care for Love or Money?*, a guide based on 85 interviews with local families and caregivers. "We take for granted what women do. We all want to be taken care of, to be cared for. But we don't want to pay for it, we want it to be given out of affection," she says. An employer's longing for a wife-mother-servant figure, someone duty-bound to nurture, can doom an employee seeking fair return for her labor.

Especially when children and genuine caring are involved, workers say, complaining about salary or duties can seem coldly mercenary or just plain awkward. Says nanny Vincent, "A lot of the nannies, they love the kids, and that's why they put up with bad pay, with parents being rude. We're only human. The parents take advantage of that."

Nannies who do speak up may encounter another daunting assumption—that caring for employers' children is a priceless joy. Says Bandini, "It's one of the reasons they're low-paid. The parent feels envious of the caregiver—'Why should I give them so much money for the pleasure of being with my child?'" If that envy grows extreme, a worker could actually be fired for getting too close to her charge, Bandini says. "If she does a good job, she's damned. If she doesn't, she's damned. It's difficult to live inside a paradox."

Some domestics live inside a different paradox, where what they do is viewed not so much as work as payment on a personal debt. In a profession so closely associated with family or old-fashioned servant roles, the worker in this case is something of a poor maiden aunt. Levine, the former *Ms.* editor, acknowledges her domestic Annie's position "was certainly a low-salary job. She would be here sometimes long hours." But before she was hired, Annie had been cleaning several homes a week for far less than the $20,000 she ultimately made, says Levine. "I think she

would say what happened was, we liberated her from the worst years of her life."

Without input from Annie, it is impossible to be sure, although her long tenure suggests she was satisfied. However, Mary Romero, herself a former housekeeper and now professor at Arizona State University, takes a dimmer view. "Employers always want to cast themselves as caring for the less fortunate," she says. "There's real resistance to thinking that whatever they pay results in a standard of living for the workers."

In the upcoming revision of her book *Maid in the U.S.A.*, Romero shares her own degrading experiences and denounces people like Linda Chavez, who was, ironically, George W. Bush's pick for labor secretary until it was revealed she was harboring an undocumented Guatemalan woman. Chavez defended the arrangement as charity, claiming she donated shelter and pocket money and the Guatemalan thanked her by doing chores. Romero doesn't buy that, and Chavez withdrew amid criticism from others who didn't, either. "This is the only occupation I've ever heard of where the employer will give an employee their old clothes and expect gratitude for it," fumes Romero.

Advocates say the labor-as-a-favor guise is common here, and so some women, especially immigrants without legal status or English skills, work for next to nothing. A Brooklyn Haitian organization reports getting calls from people offering to board a woman if she would work for free. Says Romero, "It's a throwback to feudalism and slavery."

Such patronizing attitudes toward caretakers have more troubling ramifications still when the employee belongs to an ethnic group already subject to prejudice. It is no wonder that domestic work carries such stigma. Erline Brown, a nanny, says, "I have been out with the kids, and I have had people call me names for the work that I do." A Barbadian Brit with braids, she says she's been told, "You're an Aunt Jemima." Employer Levine says balancing her employee's status relative to the family, "because Annie was white . . . was easier." But in many cases, relations with household workers are, for better or worse, children's first en-counters with American racial dynamics.

The association of inferiority with race is not just metaphor. Housework was for many decades the only field where most African American women could get hired. As other areas opened to them and to the European immigrants who also did the work, women from the Caribbean, Asia, and Latin America replaced them. There were in-voluntary migrants, too: A State Department an-alyst reported in 1999 that over 45,000 women and children, nearly all from the third world, were trafficked into the U.S. each year, most for sex work but many for domestic labor in top destina-tions like New York. In less overt forms of coer-cion, employers might confiscate passports or threaten to call the INS on an undocumented worker.

Moreover, racism in hiring leaves the most back-breaking, low-paid work to minorities, says Julia Wrigley, a City University of New York so-ciologist, drawing from over 150 interviews with families and employees. "Women of color are often assigned very stigmatized tasks, like clean-ing up after dogs or providing table service to their employers," she says, while white women are more likely to be hired strictly for child care.

But domestics can't sue based on discrimi-nation. Most relevant laws exempt household and other small employers. Law professor Smith says these exemptions were created when employers argued that in intimate settings, conflicts could be more personal than professional.

The emotional testimonies of workers at the April 6 town hall showed that intimacy has a con-siderable dark side. The personal interaction that might make a good job more enjoyable could make a bad one humiliating. The women could have made no better case for legislating labor rights. As Councilmember Christine Quinn, a leading sponsor of the workers' rights bill, said, "A domestic worker quite literally could never see anybody but the employer for days on end. There are probably many more good employers than bad, but the job of government is to make sure everybody is protected."

A formal structure is better even for the best employers, says Jean Kunhardt, co-director of the Soho Parenting Center. "I tend to see [parents] who are so guilt-ridden, they overcompensate by cooking meals for their nannies, paying for col-lege courses. I often say, 'This is an employer-employee relationship. You're not adopting somebody in the family.' "

And perhaps worst for both sides, in the ab-sence of decent standards there is frequent turnover. The D.C. child care organization found annual rates among caregivers nationwide hover-ing at between 30 and 40 percent. Not surpris-ingly, its research showed that fair wages based on merit helped retain experienced workers.

"This is a valuable service we're providing," says nanny Brown, "and it's a pleasurable job." One housekeeper, who says others see her job as pure drudgery, finds "satisfaction in creating beauty out of chaos." But, wonders Brown, "why should we stay in a job with no benefits, where our employers sometimes don't even acknowledge us when we say good morning? The industry is losing the crème de la crème of professionals. When we're seen as doing a real job, we'll stay."

Andrea Townsend[*]

Woman

In this world a woman is not a woman
She is hands
She is a short breath of stale air
She is lungs raked by flyaway fibers
And a raw nose and eyes dripping from glue fumes

A woman is not a woman in a world like this
She is numbers on clothing, 50% cotton, 50% polyester . . . .
A word in someone else's language

A woman cannot be a woman
It's against regulations
Only when the late night supervisors overstep their boundaries
Then she is a woman for a moment, in his eyes
Beneath his rough hands,
Never under her own

These hands bleed,
So that people can love their children in the "American" way
Curl them up with a plush toy in a warm home
While her children curl up with the night

A woman is not a woman
She is hours of labor
Hours of sitting,
Her back bent like a willow in a windstorm

In every second, minute, hour, day—she becomes the whir of machinery
Years go by and she is a sound,
A breath,
A thrumming pattern
A needle charging across fabric, a suspended heartbeat

Source: "Woman" by Andrea Townsend first appeared in *Rethinking Globalization: Teaching for Equity and Justice*, edited by Bill Bigelow and Bob Peterson. Milwaukee: Rethinking Schools, 2002. Used by permission.

[*] Andrea Townsend was an 11th grade student at Franklin High School in Portland, Oregon when she wrote this poem.

Then, all at once and slowly,
a whisper rises through the stale air, the dim light,
Cuts through the ceaseless mechanical droning
And a hand slows its perpetual motion,
Stretches slowly across the space between the machine and the woman

Down the rows of workbenches,
one by one, these hands close over one another
Become clenched fists
Remind themselves that they are not just hands,
They are women

Gillian Dunne

Lesbians in Manual Jobs

Gillian Dunne interviewed sixty lesbian women in England about their work experiences and used their narratives to develop a theory of sexuality linked to economics. This excerpt from her book, Lesbian Lifestyles: Women's Work and the Politics of Sexuality *(Macmillan, 1966), focuses on women who choose traditionally male occupations.*

Respondents' Experience in Male-Dominated Manual Occupations

On examination of the sample's work histories, at least fifteen had some experience of male-dominated manual work. These were unconventional women because they had expanded their occupational choices to include working-class jobs which their fathers and brothers, rather than their mothers and sisters, might have considered. Within these occupations, respondents' movement up the hierarchies was often slow and plagued by difficulties, but most found the experience rewarding, both intrinsically and extrinsically. The armed forces were viewed by some respondents as a useful entry point to traditional male occupations.

The Armed Forces

In all, five respondents, including two Black women, entered the armed forces, while many others spoke of having had the desire to do so. The armed forces provided four respondents with the opportunity to develop 'male' technical and/or craft skills, and a fifth to gain a nursing qualification. They were particularly appealing to women from less privileged social backgrounds, who did not have the opportunity to stay on at

school to study 'A' levels. Given the limited job opportunities they felt were available to them, entering the forces clearly represented a career with prospects for advancement and job security. Furthermore, it was seen to offer a chance to travel and an opportunity to keep up their sporting interests. Thelma explains her reasons for entering the forces. She has spent most of her working life in male-dominated occupations, using the skills that she had developed while in the forces:

> [*Were there any other aspects that appealed about going into the Forces?*] The security, the availability of travel, also the different types of sports that you could do. I would never have been able to have afforded to learn [these sports] . . . The girls were doing the same sports as the boys . . . I could do everything that a man could do. [*Why did you go for driving in the Forces?*] To be able to learn the mechanics of a car. I would have liked to have been a fully fledged mechanic, but they didn't actually have mechanics in the [Women's Corps]. Doing this I was affiliated to the Mechanics Corps and could go and learn from the boys, and I learnt as much as the mechanics did. I had the ability, when I came out, to maintain my own car. (43*I*)

As with women interviewed in Faderman's (1992: 150) detailed history of twentieth-century lesbian life in America, the military appealed to respondents for a range of important reasons. These respondents tended to be fairly ambitious and achievement-oriented and they all wanted to learn a trade. Further, most wished to develop more technical and mechanical skills, and the forces were perceived as being a more 'equal opportunities' environment where occupational gender boundaries were more blurred. They could perform jobs that were physically demanding, which were freer from the constraints of physical confinement that they associated with clerical and factory work. Verity expresses these sentiments:

> I don't want to be a typist, that's the last thing, that's another reason why I joined the forces. I didn't want to go into an office, I didn't want to be a clerk, secretary, etc. . . . I wanted to be out and about, I wanted to do something different, I didn't want to do what the girls did. I am not saying I wanted to do what the boys wanted, or did . . . The driving suited me down to the ground: I was outside, I was learning something, I was doing something different, I wasn't doing what all the girls used to do, and I excelled in it . . . The forces, they do try their best to make you one of the team; you have the same rank as the blokes. If you have a bloke soldier to give him orders, you have to give him orders whether you are female or male, and I take orders from males or females, and they have to accept what a woman tells them. (29*M*)

Respondents who were keen on entering the forces had usually been questioning their sexuality. They saw the forces as providing an environment where they might come into contact with lesbians and clarify the possibilities. All the respondents who had been in the forces spoke of the existence of tightly knit lesbian networks. In some cases exposure to this community raised questions in the minds of respondents regarding their own sexuality; lesbianism could be seen as a feasible option. Furthermore, this community was always reported as being highly achievement-oriented and career-minded. Wendy is typical of the rest in her description of her lesbian colleagues' approaches to their jobs:

> The gay girls were certainly the stronger . . . and wanted to get on more than the straights . . . Not

physical strength, it's as people, they were always the harder workers. Why they were doing it or what they were doing it for I don't know, but certainly . . . the girls that had the boyfriends didn't want to work the longer hours anyway, because they wanted to meet their boyfriends at night. Whereas the gay girls—I wouldn't say they didn't want to meet their women—put their work first somehow. There was no extra money, you got paid the same as someone that didn't want to do it. I just used to love the job, so I didn't mind how many hours I did anyway. (34*M*)

The tendency to put career first seemed to affect their approaches to relationships. As marriage was never an option for them, frequent postings meant that long-term relationships were hard to maintain. Consequently, relationships were described as being entered on the understanding that they would probably be short-lived.

Lesbians, however, appear to hold a very ambiguous position in the forces. One respondent remarked that the Women's Corps would probably be unable to function without the competent input of the lesbians, yet the level of official homophobia was particularly high.[1] Purges were commonplace and respondents lived under the continual threat of exposure. Ali originally intended joining the Military Police. However, her experience of their behavior towards lesbians made her reconsider:

> When I got in and saw how the military operated I thought no way [am I going to join the Military Police]. They were just a bunch of animals. I couldn't relate to that; the women were as bad as the men. They would have your bunk ripped apart, the mattresses off, looking for letters . . . Because being gay is illegal in the army and they used to have these purges . . . What would happen is, the young girls coming in would get frightened of what was going on [high level of lesbian visibility] and freak, and would hand in a list of names to whoever, to the CO even, and they would have to act on it, and there would be this purge, and all the names on the list were investigated. The young girls coming in were very dangerous one way

or another, which is why I kept really low-key about things. (*35M*)

One respondent fell victim of a purge and was discharged. This had serious repercussions, as she lost her opportunity to train in medicine. Furthermore, the knowledge that the forces are intolerant of homosexuality deterred some respondents who would have really liked to join up. For these respondents fear of building a career and then being exposed as a lesbian influenced their decision against entry. Moreover, I was unable to interview any serving military women, as those who had been approached were worried about the possibility of being identified.

The four women who developed more 'male' mechanical and technical skills in the forces utilized them when they re-entered civilian life. One entered higher education to develop her technical skills further, and the others entered driving or motor-trade occupations. Several remarked that they found civilian life, in terms of employment opportunities, far more gender-segregated than was their experience in the forces. They also commented on the difficulty in reaching the relatively high levels of pay and perks which they had experienced in the forces.

Making a Career in Male-Dominated Manual Occupations

Three respondents were currently employed in traditionally 'male' manual occupations at the point of interview. A further four had moved up from male-dominated manual occupations to low-level management. All these seven women were from intermediate or manual backgrounds. Interestingly, these women tended to be older: their median age was thirty-six, and two women were in their forties. In the case of the older women, their earlier unconventional employment choices were very much perceived as being made in the context of an extreme polarity between women's and men's work. For them, women's work offered little in the way of job security, pay or prospects; in contrast, men's work represented the possibility of developing skills and establishing a career.

Occupations which involved driving were popular with many of the fifteen respondents who had had some experience of male manual occupations. . . . Some had previously been in factory and shop work, which they found highly regimented; they spoke of disliking the constant surveillance of supervisors and of having to clock in and clock out. In contrast, driving occupations represented greater freedom and the ability to exercise greater control. They enjoyed being able to organize their daily work routines, setting their own pace, and being out and about. Tamsin explains why she chose to enter a job in transport. She enjoys this work, although she sometimes has to put up with the sexist attitudes of male co-workers:

It's been a very successful move for me. There are other women that do driving and they have a very good work record . . . The customers we deal with always ask for us back. [*How have you found the job as a woman?*] It's quite interesting; you get these blokes: 'Here you go, we have a woman trying to do a man's job,' that sort of attitude thrown at you. That's not what I am trying to do. I'm trying to earn a decent wage, that's all. I don't want to be a secretary, so I want to be a driver instead . . . They [men] do find it quite a novelty, really, especially [with me being] in the big trucks, because they do find that quite hard. (*29M*)

Others found the sexist hostility from male co-workers more enduring. Their experience highlights the important role played by sexist male workplace culture in 'policing' the boundaries of traditionally male occupations.[2] In the case of some respondents, their interest in particular occupations was dampened by the sexism and homophobia that prevailed. Consequently, they were propelled out of jobs that they found challenging into jobs where the working environment was more pleasant. This was the case for Christine, who went to work backstage in a theatre in the Midlands. She was involved in carpentry and painting. Although she loved the actual job, she found having to defend herself from the sexist attitudes of her male co-workers too great a strain. She left the job after a year and is now self-employed:

> I found it very hard going because of the sexism involved. It was very sexist, and I thought all theatres would be like that. It was also very homophobic. It's a total double standard, a lot of homosexuality in the theatre, but the sort of butch attitude with the people who shifted the scenery was quite horrible. . . .

Many of the respondents in male-dominated areas of employment found that male co-workers were initially hostile to new female co-workers. However, those respondents who have remained in such occupations found that, once they had proved themselves competent, they seemed to have good working relationships with their colleagues.

Respondents who have made long-term careers in male manual occupations usually worked themselves up to low-level management. Typically, they started their careers in driving or garage work. However, initial entry into male occupations had been fairly difficult for respondents as school leavers. Lenora talks of the sexist attitudes of an employer in her first job interview after leaving school. She had seen an advertisement for an apprenticeship with a sign-writing company and thought it would be a good craft to learn:

> They advertised for an apprentice. I got an interview—don't know why they bothered to interview me—and then got told, 'We're looking for a lad.' They had no intention of employing me. I told them I wasn't going to rush off and marry—I couldn't' say, 'Look, pal, I'm queer!' What can you say? (38)

Very unequal treatment in gaining access to training in male craft skills was common for respondents now in their late thirties and forties. They saw themselves as early pioneers in their chosen occupations. Three were semi-skilled mechanics, none had trained formally on apprenticeship schemes. They learnt their skills on the

job, picking up information from their male colleagues. Lenora . . . eventually learnt her trade, after working in a garage as a petrol pump attendant . . .

. . . For several respondents, entry into male occupations was facilitated by fathers. Carol's father helped establish her in a career in mechanical parts:

> I followed in my father's footsteps [into the motor trade]—selling parts, everything to do with looking after parts, selling them, ordering them. . . .

However, achieving equal pay proved much more difficult for her:

> [The job isn't well paid] until you start getting up through the ranks. It took me about ten years to rise up and command a decent wage, but then that wasn't the same as the men were getting. . . .

Fighting against this kind of discrimination was common amongst respondents in male-dominated occupations. Jackie talks of the problem of being taken seriously by employers. She had been delivering parts for a company. She had an interest in mechanics, was ambitious and wanted to move into a better paid, more demanding job. She spent any free time at work with the parts store-man learning the trade. A chance came up to join the sales team:

> [I] ended up mainly in the stores, because I knew a bit about cars and parts; . . . knew more than the storeman did . . . There again I came up against the male bit. We had about five reps on the road, selling the parts. If one was off sick or on holiday I got his job to go and do his round, and I was as good as he was on that . . . I said to the manager, thinking on promotion lines, 'If one of the reps leaves, do I get a chance of his job if I work hard and prove I can do it?' They said, 'No, no chance! It's always men that are reps.' I thought, no, I am not going to be a toerag just because I am female. (39)

Jackie left this company; she later achieved a management position in transport, and eventually did well enough to set up her own business.

Like Jackie, respondents usually persevered until they were taken seriously by their bosses. Jessy managed to move up from 'male' manual work to a management position in a garage:

It was very difficult to get into the actual management position. [My company] was a very old-fashioned firm and there weren't any women in management positions. The manager went on holiday and I used to cover for him . . . No one [else] wanted to cover; no one wanted to know about [it]. It was a very difficult [area of work] to get into. It's a hell of a responsibility. They said no, so someone said, 'What about [Jessy]' and they said, 'She's a woman!' They said it really wouldn't hurt covering, and I covered. I got quite good at it and I did enjoy it. (34)

It was not until she became frustrated with her manual job, and decided to leave, that she was seriously considered for promotion. Her employers were unwilling to let her go, she refused to stay unless she was given a permanent management position and finally they agreed to give her the job. . . .

Promotion for these women came as the result of this actively putting themselves forward. They had not been considered 'natural' promotion candidates by their bosses, and attention had to be drawn to their merits. It seemed that they often had the support and encouragement of male co-workers who had perhaps greater awareness of their individual competences . . .

Respondents in male occupations tended to enjoy their work. It provided variety and challenge. They also recognised that they had to be very good at their jobs to earn the respect of the men that they worked with. They knew that, if they made mistakes, this would be understood in gender terms by their male co-workers. Consequently, they were very aware of the need to work doubly hard to earn the respect of male colleagues. As one respondent put it, 'You have to be twice as good as the men.'

Notes

1. For a very entertaining discussion of the central role played by lesbians in the military see Faderman (1992: chapters 5–6) and Miller (1995). For information on brutal and underhand tactics used in catching lesbians see Faderman (1992).

2. See, for example, Adkins (1995), Cockburn (1991) and Stanko (1998) for a discussion of the implications of the sexual harassment of women by men in maintaining gender separation.

References

Adkins, L. (1995) *Gendered Work: Sexuality, Family and the Labour Market*. Buckingham: Open University Press.

Cockburn, C. (1991) *In the Way of Women: Men's Resistance to Sex Equality in Organizations*. Basingstoke: Macmillan.

Faderman, L. (1992) *Odd Girls and Twilight Lovers: a History of Lesbian Life in Twentieth-century America*. London: Penguin.

Miller, N. (1995) *Out of the Past: Gay and Lesbian History from 1869 to the Present*. London: Vintage.

Stanko, E. (1988) 'Keeping women in and out of line: sexual harassment and occupational segregation', in S. Walby (ed.) *Gender Separation at Work*. Milton Keynes: Open University Press.

Sharon Hays

Off the Rolls: The Ground-Level Results of Welfare Reform

It's hard to date it precisely, but I think my severe case of cognitive dissonance set in on a summer evening in 1999. As part of my research on welfare reform, I'd spent the afternoon playing on the floor with Sammy, the four-year-old son of a welfare recipient. I was struck by his intelligence and creativity and imagined that if his mom were middle-class, she'd soon be having him tested and charting the gifted and talented programs he'd attend.

But Sammy's mom, Celia, had other things on her mind. Cradling her infant daughter, she told me that she had been recently diagnosed with cancer. Her doctor wanted her to start treatments immediately. Although she'd been working at a local Fotomart for three months, the welfare office still helped her with the costs of child care—costs she couldn't otherwise manage on her $6 per hour pay. When she asked her boss about flexible hours to manage the cancer treatments, he told her she was just too easily replaced. She'd also checked with her welfare caseworkers; they told her that if she lost her job she'd have to quickly find another or risk being cut off the welfare rolls. I talked to her about the Social Security Disability program, even though I knew that she had only a slim chance of getting help there. Celia had an eighth-grade education, no financial assets, few job skills, and no extended family members with sufficient resources to see her through. And she needed those cancer treatments now.

Source: "Off the Rolls: The Ground-Level Results of Welfare Reform," by Sharon Hays. *Dissent* magazine 50 (4): 48–53, Fall 2003. Used by permission.

Under the old welfare system, she could have simply returned to full welfare benefits. Yet, knowing what I did from my research into the worlds of low-wage work, welfare, and disability, I was sure there was now virtually nowhere for her to turn, save all those local charities that were already incredibly overburdened. I didn't have the heart to tell her.

When I went home that night, the local television news was interviewing a smiling former welfare mother recently employed at a supermarket chain. It was a story of redemption—the triumph of individual willpower and American know-how—and the newscaster cheerfully pronounced it a marker of the "success" of welfare reform. That's when the dissonance set in. I've been suffering from it ever since.

From one point of view, it makes perfect sense that so many have celebrated the results of the 1996 Personal Responsibility Act. The welfare rolls have been cut by more than half—from twelve million recipients in 1996 to five million today. Among those who have left welfare, the majority (60 percent to 65 percent) are employed. Add to this the fact that public opinion polls show that almost no one liked the old system of welfare and most people (including most welfare recipients) agree that the principles behind reform—independence, self-sufficiency, strong families, a concern for the common good—are worthy ideals.

The problem is that there is a wide gap between the more worthy goals behind reform and the ground-level realities I found in the welfare office. There is also a tremendous amount of diversity hidden in those large-scale statistical accountings of the results of reform—and much of it is a great deal more disheartening than it first appears. After three years of ethnographic research inside two (distant and distinct) welfare offices, after interviewing more than 50 caseworkers and about 130 welfare mothers, and after five years of poring over policy reports on reform, it is clear to me that the majority of the nation's most desperately poor citizens are in worse shape now than they would have been had the Personal Responsibility Act never been passed.

Between Success and Failure

Political speeches, policy reports, and the popular media all cite the declining rolls and the employment of former recipients as the central evidence of the success of welfare reform. By these standards, Celia and her children would count as a success.

Of course there are genuine success stories. Take Sally. With a good job at the phone company, medical benefits, sick leave and vacation leave, a nine-to-five schedule, possibilities for advancement, and enough income to place her and her two kids above the poverty line, she was better off than she'd ever been on welfare benefits or in any of the (many) low-wage, no-benefit jobs she'd had in the past. And there was no question that the supportive services that came with reform had helped her to achieve that success. She got her job through a welfare-sponsored training program offered by the phone company. Welfare caseworkers had helped her out with clothing for work, bus vouchers, and a child care subsidy that got her through the training. "I think welfare's better now," she told me. "They've got programs there to help you. They're actually giving you an opportunity. I'm working and I feel like I can make it on my own."

Monique was also helped by reform. A messy divorce with an abusive (and stalker) husband had cost her her job as a nursing assistant.

With two young sons to worry about, she sought help from the welfare office. Fortunately, she lived in one of the few states with a welfare policy that exempted domestic-violence victims from the immediate demand to find work. Using special funds made available by reform, welfare caseworkers not only provided her with a welfare check, but also helped her to manage car repairs and the down payment on an apartment. Once she and her children were settled, her boss planned to hire her again. If Monique could remain hidden from her ex-husband, things would work out just fine. Like Sally, she was grateful for the help she'd received from the welfare office.

About one-half of the welfare mothers I met experienced at least temporary successes like these. Yet under the terms of reform, the long-term outlook for the majority is not so positive. And in many cases it is difficult to distinguish the successes from the failures.

Proponents of reform would mark Andrea, for instance, as "successful." When I met her, she was earning $5.75 an hour, working thirty-five hours a week at a Sunbelt City convenience store. After paying rent, utility bills, and food costs for her family of three, she was left with $50 a month to cover the costs of child care, transportation, clothing, medical bills, laundry, school costs, furniture, appliances, and cleaning supplies. Just four months off the welfare rolls, Andrea was already in trouble. Her phone had been turned off the month before, and she was unsure how she'd pay this month's rent. Her oldest daughter was asking for new school clothes, her youngest had a birthday coming soon, and Andrea couldn't take her mind off the upcoming winter utility bills. If she were single, she told me, she would manage somehow. But with children to worry about, she knew she couldn't make it much longer.

National-level accountings of reform would also place Teresa and her three children in the plus column. When I met her, she had a temporary (three-month) job at a collection agency. Thanks to public housing and the time-limited child care subsidy offered by the welfare office, she was making ends meet. Teresa was smart and capable, but had only a high school diploma and almost no work experience. She'd spent most of her adult life outside the mainstream economy— first married to a drug dealer, then working as a street-level prostitute, and finally, drug free, on welfare. As much as Teresa thought she was doing better than ever and spoke of how happy she was to be getting dressed up every morning and going out to work, she was still concerned about the future. The child care costs for her three kids would amount to nearly three-quarters of her paycheck if she had to cover them herself. And her job, like that child care subsidy, was only temporary. Given her résumé, I wondered just what career ladder she might find to offer her sufficient income and stability to stay off the welfare rolls and successfully juggle her duties as both primary caregiver and sole breadwinner for those three kids.

The cycle of work and welfare implied by these cases is the most common pattern among the welfare-level poor. It is a cycle of moving from welfare to low-wage jobs to mounting debts and problems with child care, husbands, boyfriends, employers, landlords, overdue utility bills, broken-down cars, inadequate public transportation, unstable living arrangements, job layoffs, sick children, disabled parents, and the innumerable everyday contingencies of low-income life—any and all of which can lead a poor family back to the welfare office to repeat the cycle again. Most of the people caught up in this cycle face a number of social disadvantages from the start. Welfare recipients are overwhelmingly mothers (90 percent), they are disproportionately non-white (38 percent are black, 25 percent Latino, and 30 percent white), nearly half are without high-school diplomas (47 percent), the majority have experience in only unskilled jobs, about half suffer from physical or mental health disabilities, almost as many have a history of domestic violence, and all have children to care for. At the same time, most welfare recipients have work experience (83 percent), and most want to work. This was true long before welfare reform. Yet

given their circumstances, and given the structure of low-wage work, it is not surprising that many have found it difficult to achieve long-term financial and familial stability.

Of those who have left the rolls since reform, a full 40 percent are without work or welfare at any given time. Of the 60 percent who do have jobs, their average wage is approximately $7 per hour. But most former recipients do not find full-time or year-round work, leaving their average annual wage estimated at just over $10,000 a year. Following this same pattern, about three-quarters of the families who left welfare are in jobs without medical insurance, retirement benefits, sick days, or vacation leave; and one-quarter work night or evening shifts. It is true that their average annual wages amount to more income than welfare, food stamps, and Medicaid combined. Yet, as Kathryn Edin and Laura Lein demonstrated in *Making Ends Meet*, taking into account the additional costs associated with employment (such as child care, transportation, clothing), working poor families like these actually suffer more material hardship than their counterparts on welfare.

The reality behind the declining welfare rolls is millions of former welfare families moving in and out of low-wage jobs. Some achieve success, most do not. Approximately one-third have found themselves back on welfare at least once since reform. Overall, two-thirds of those who have left welfare are either unemployed or working for wages that do not lift their families out of poverty. And there are still millions of families on welfare, coming in anew, coming back again, or as yet unable to find a way off the rolls.

The Personal Responsibility Act itself produced two primary changes in the lives of the working/welfare poor. On the one hand, welfare reform offered sufficient positive employment supports to allow poor families to leave welfare more quickly, and in some cases it offered just the boost that was needed to allow those families to achieve genuine long-term financial stability. On the other hand, welfare reform instituted a system of rules, punishments, and time limits that has effectively pressured the poor to steer clear of the welfare office.

A central result of welfare reform, in other words, is that a large proportion of desperately poor mothers and children are now too discouraged, too angry, too ashamed, or too exhausted to go to the welfare office. Nationwide, as the welfare rolls were declining by more than half, the rate of dire (welfare-level) poverty declined by only 15 percent. To put it another way; whereas the vast majority of desperately poor families received welfare support prior to reform (84 percent), today less than half of them do. Why are all these mothers and children now avoiding welfare? To make sense of this part of the story, one needs to understand the complicated changes that have taken place inside welfare offices across the nation. I can here offer only a glimpse.

Punishment and the Push to Work

Upon arrival at the Arbordale welfare office, the first thing one sees is a large red sign, two feet high, twelve feet long, inquiring, "HOW MANY MONTHS DO YOU HAVE LEFT?" This message is driven home by caseworkers' incessant reminders of the "ticking clock," in the ubiquity of employment brochures and job postings, and, above all, by a carefully sequenced set of demanding rules and regulations.

The pressure is intense. It includes the job search that all new clients must start immediately (forty verifiable job contacts in thirty days), the "job readiness" and "lifeskills" workshops they are required to attend, the (time-consuming and difficult) child support enforcement process in which they must agree to participate, and the constant monitoring of their eligibility for welfare and their progress toward employment. Welfare mothers who are not employed within a specified period (thirty days in Arbordale, forty-five in Sunbelt City), are required to enroll in full-time training programs or take full-time unpaid workfare placements until they can find a job. Throughout, these working, training, and job-searching wel-

fare mothers are expected to find somewhere to place their children. Although welfare recipients are all technically eligible for federal child care subsidies, only about one-third receive them. With only a $350 welfare check (the average monthly benefit for a family of three), child care arrangements can be very difficult to manage.

In Sunbelt City the pressure to get off the welfare rolls is introduced even more directly and forcefully. As is true in about half the states nationwide, Sunbelt City has a "diversionary" program designed to keep poor mothers and children from applying for welfare in the first place. Before they even begin the application process, potential welfare clients are required to attend the diversion workshop. The three workshops I went to all focused on the importance of "self sufficiency," the demanding nature of welfare requirements, and the advantages of work—and left most of the poor mothers in attendance weary and confused.

For those who persisted through the application process, their compliance to the rules of reform was assured not just by the long-term threat of time limits, but by the more immediate threat of sanctions. Any welfare mother who fails to follow through with her job search, workfare placement, training program, child support proceedings, reporting requirements, or the myriad of other regulations of the welfare office is sanctioned. To be sanctioned means that all or part of a family's welfare benefits are cut, while the "clock" keeps ticking toward that lifetime limit. National statistics suggest that about one-quarter of welfare recipients lose their benefits as a result of sanctions.

Inside the welfare offices of Arbordale and Sunbelt City many of the women I met became so disheartened that they simply gave up and left the rolls. This included women who made it through some portion of the job search, or the employment workshops, or even took a workfare placement, but just couldn't manage the pressure. Some were sanctioned, others left on their own. Connected to these, but harder to count, were all those poor mothers who gave up before they got started. Eligibility workers in Arbordale estimated that as many as one-quarter of those who started the application process did not complete it. Caseworkers in Sunbelt City guessed that about one-third of the mothers who attended their diversion workshops were ("successfully") diverted from applying for benefits. In Arbordale, about one-quarter gave up before completing the application process.

Sarah was one example of a "diverted" potential welfare client. She was the full-time caregiver for her grandchild on a lung machine, her terminally ill father, and her own two young children. She'd been managing with the help of her father's Social Security checks and her boyfriend's help. But her boyfriend had left her, and medical bills were eating up all her father's income. Sarah discovered at her initial Arbordale welfare interview that in order to receive benefits she would need to begin a job search immediately. Because no one else was available to care for her father or grandchild, she said, it just didn't make sense for her to get a job. I met her as she conveyed this story to her friends in the Arbordale waiting room, fluctuating between tones of anger and sadness. "I have to swallow my pride, and come in here, and these people just don't want to help you no more," she told us. Leaving the office, she vowed never to return. As was true of so many others, it was unclear to me what she would do.

Sonya was one example of the many sanctioned welfare clients I met, though her case was more dramatic than most. She was so quiet and shy that I wondered if anyone would notice how she'd been affected by reform. Twenty years old, with a tenth-grade education and two children, she'd been on welfare most of the time since she gave birth to her oldest son at age thirteen. She'd had only one job in her lifetime, and that lasted for just four months. In the hours I spent with her, it became clear to me that she suffered from serious mental health problems—matching clinical definitions of depression and obsessive-compulsive disorder. She rarely left her apartment and lived in fear that she would catch a cold, or pneumonia, or worse. When I commented on her spotlessly clean and carefully decorated apartment, she told me that she completely rearranged it at least once a month and sometimes once a week. I watched her feed lunch to her son: every can, jar, plate, and utensil in her kitchen was precisely ordered, and she was unable to continue our conversation until all the dishes were washed and dried and the counters disinfected, twice, for good measure. When we talked about the possibilities for employment, she explained that she found it necessary to take four showers a day, and worried that she couldn't handle this with a full-time job, especially, she said, since buses don't always run on schedule. In responding to my question about the men in her life she let me know, quietly, that her father had sexually abused her as a child. (She did not volunteer and I did not ask if her pregnancy at age twelve was the result of that abuse.) Sonya had been sanctioned for failing to carry out her job search. Without welfare income, she had no idea what she would do. I worried, a lot, about how she and her kids would get by.

Kendra might be included among those who found themselves too ashamed, discouraged, or exhausted to return to the welfare office when she needed help. One of the first welfare clients I met, Kendra was much loved by the caseworkers who knew her. She was sweet, quietly charming, and deeply earnest. Twenty-six years old, with two daughters aged six and eight, she had a history of working only part-time, on and off, in unskilled jobs. She'd finally landed a secure and meaningful job, she thought, working at a homeless shelter run by the Salvation Army. Even though it was the night shift and the pay was low, she felt good about helping out the homeless, and was grateful for the mentoring and support she'd received from the welfare office. She still didn't make enough money to get by without child care help and an income supplement from welfare, but was hoping for a raise, studying for her high school equivalency exam, and thinking about taking a second job. She was cheerful when last I saw her. Six months later her caseworkers told me how quickly Kendra's life had unraveled. In a heated argument, one of Kendra's brothers had shot and killed her other brother. One brother was dead, the other on his way to prison. Kendra fell apart emotionally, lost her job, and left the welfare rolls. Two caseworkers spent a day off trying to find her (an extremely rare undertaking), but no one knew where she had gone.

All these women and their children have contributed to the decline of the welfare rolls. They are a central basis for the celebration of reform. They are also a central basis for my case of cognitive dissonance.

The Costs

In focusing on the hardships wrought by reform, I do not mean to suggest that the successes of welfare reform are trivial or inconsequential. Those successes matter. I also don't mean to imply that all welfare mothers are saints and victims. They aren't. But there are many other issues at stake in the reform of welfare.

Reading the daily news these days, one can't help but notice that the topic of poverty has lost its prominence, especially relative to the early days of reform. One reason for this neglect, it seems to me, has been the highly effective campaign pronouncing the triumph of the Personal Responsibility Act. Like all the information that was invisible in popular accounts of the invasion of Iraq, the ground-level hardship and human costs of reform are largely hidden from view. Yet the price tag on welfare reform is real.

By 2002, the National Governors' Association found itself begging Congress not to follow through on plans to increase the pressure on welfare offices and welfare recipients across the nation—the costs, they explained, would be far too high for already stretched state budgets to bear. The U.S. Conference of Mayors found itself pleading with the Bush administration for more financial help to manage the rising populations

of the hungry and homeless in American cities. Food banks were running short on food, homeless shelters were closing their doors to new customers, and local charities were raising their eligibility requirements to contend with rising numbers of people in need. The Medicaid system was in crisis, and large numbers of poor families were no longer receiving the food stamps for which they were eligible. Half of the families who left welfare had no money to buy food; one-third have had to cut the size of meals, and nearly half have had trouble paying their rent or utility bills.

In the meantime, only a fraction of welfare families have actually hit their federal lifetime limits on welfare benefits: just 120,000 welfare mothers and children had reached their limits by 2001. Given the work/welfare cycling process, and given that many families can survive at least temporarily on below-poverty wages and pieced-together alternative resources, it will take many more years for the full impact of reform to emerge. But, over the long haul, we can expect to see rising rates of hunger, homelessness, drug abuse, and crime. More children will wind up in foster care, in substandard child care, or left to fend for themselves. More disabled family members will be left without caregivers. Mental health facilities and domestic violence shelters will also feel the impact of this law, as will all the poor men who are called upon to provide additional support for their children.

Of course, this story is not apocalyptic. The poor will manage as they have always managed, magically and mysteriously, to make do on far less than poverty-level income. Many of the most desperate among them will simply disappear, off the radar screen, off to places unknown.

In any case, assessing the results of welfare reform is not just a question of its impact on the poor. It is also a question of what this law says about our collective willingness to support the nation's most disadvantaged and about the extent to which welfare reform actually lives up to the more worthy goals it purports to champion.

R. Danielle Egan

Resistance under the Black Light: Exploring the Use of Music in Two Exotic Dance Clubs

This article examines how exotic dancers strategically use music in two exotic dance clubs in the New England area. Music functioned as a form of resistance for dancers in three ways: as a direct form of protest against owners, as a covert strategy of reappropriation, and as an overt expression of discontent in their interactions with regular customers. I also analyze the ways in which "buying against" gender inequality, through the use of music, falls short as a form of protest. For example, dancers often unwittingly fetishized the racial politics undergirding the genre of music. This research is informed by four years of ethnographic research in the New England area.

When one walks into an exotic dance club, it is not uncommon to be bombarded by the music and lighting prior to ever seeing a woman on-stage. Music serves as an important component in the overall production of a dancer's erotic repertoire and her sensual performance.[1] More than simply background noise, music influences dancers' experiences. Helping women craft particular workplace personas, musical choice can provide a degree of freedom and extend a form of creative license in the workplace. Music choice may also offer dancers a lyrical form of protest in their jobs, one that is considered less offensive, and thus less threatening, than other more overt tactics workers may use to dispute particular forms of inequality in the workplace. The strategic use of music aids dancers in their interactions with management and their clientele.

Expressing the dissatisfaction many women dancers feel over inequitable gender relations at work, music helps them engage in practices of resistance (both in the open and behind the scenes) in exotic dance clubs (for more information on other forms of workplace resistance, see Egan 2003, 2004, 2006; Egan, Frank, and Johnson 2006; Barton 2002; Montemurro 2001; Ronai-Rambo 1998, 1999). Highlighting concrete examples of how dancers dispute inequality in the workplace, I examine how music both promotes empowerment for women dancers and falls short as a form of protest. The questions guiding this inquiry are as follows: What are the benefits and limits of using music as a form of gendered resistance in exotic dance clubs? What are the differing ways in which music signifies protest at the clubs? To this end, I examine the predominant ways music gets employed in the club: as an expression of discontent in dancers' relations with management, as a direct or indirect challenge to inequitable situations with regular customers (men who come to the club at least once a week, form an emotional attachment to a particular exotic dancer, and spend large amounts of money in tips or gifts in-kind), and as a covert strategy of reappropriation. I further examine the limits of utilizing music in the clubs. Exploring the use of music by exotic dancers further complicates the literature on resistance by highlighting the polyvalent manner in which discontent is made manifest among women workers. For example, dancers reflexively incorporated music as a form of gendered protest, while often fetishizing the politics of race that undergird the music many of them employed in the clubs—hip-hop and rap.

Exotic dance is an ever-growing and highly lucrative legal subset of the overall sex industry. Between 1987 and 2000, the number of exotic dance clubs in the United States doubled (Egan 2006). For example, Rick's Cabaret International was publicly traded on NASDAQ in the late 1990s (Flint 1996, A1) and showed revenues of $15 million in 2003 and $16 million in 2004 (http://www.ricks.com; http://www.hoovers.com). Moreover, Spearmint Rhino, a multinational four-star gentleman's club, boasts of having "6000 entertainers" working in the United States, the United Kingdom, Europe, and Australia (http://www.spearmintrhino.com). Given the pervasiveness of this genre of the adult service industry, it seems particularly crucial to understand how dancers negotiate this form of work. To this end, exploring specific strategies of covert and not-so-covert resistance within a seemingly exploitative context is imperative.

Resistance, Oppositional Culture, and Everyday Life

Employing oppositional cultural products as a form of social unrest offers marginalized populations tools to express their dissatisfaction, anger, and alienation from dominant cultural norms (Foucault 1981; Hechter 1978, Herman and Musolf 1998; Scott 1990; Mitchell and Feagin 1995). Dick Hebdige's (1979) work highlights how British youth utilized clothes, music, and other cultural items as signifiers of unrest to grate against the strictures of hegemonic culture. Ultimately, dissatisfied with the lack of social-structural change

emerging from such forms of protest, Hebdige questions the macro-level effectiveness of this mode of discontent.

Conversely, Haenfler (2004) and Leblanc (1999) theorize that female punks and straight-edge youth move beyond "signifying unrest" through clothing and music. Youth in both movements "demonstrated that subcultures use many methods of resistance, both personal and political" actively constructing an "oppositional consciousness" ignored by earlier critiques focusing solely on macro-level resistance (Haenfler 2004, 428). Mitchell and Feagin (1995) argue that in the United States, African Americans, Latinos, and Native Americans have successfully employed music and visual art to create an oppositional culture to mitigate against "the effects of oppression and reaffirm that which is distinct from the majority culture" (p. 68). As Stuckey (1987) and Scott (1990) illuminate, the use of music as a form of protest and as a strategy of survival emerged for African Americans during slavery when music acted as a medium to send covert messages that were unnoticed by white slave owners (Stuckey 1987; Scott 1990). The tradition remains of using music as a vital form of oppositional culture and resistance within African American communities in the form of hip-hop and rap (Baker 1993; Costello and Foster Wallace 1990; Cross 1993; Dimitriadis 2001; Martinez 1997; Pratt 1990; Rose 1994; Smitherman 1997; Stapleton 1998). As Tricia Rose (1994) argues, hip-hop and rap often operate as a form of political locution that can create situations where individuals "mock those in power, express rage, and produce fantasies of subversion . . . (that) quite often serve as the cultural glue that fosters communal resistance" (p. 100).

Consumption as a Form of Social Protest

Fiske (1989) further complicates macro-level theories of resistance by shedding light on the relational quality of resistance through practices previously assumed to be passive, such as consumption. Far from static, the meanings individuals make of particular consumer objects can transgress a producer's intention. As such, consumption is a dynamic process where individuals struggle over meaning and render visible the contradictory and inequitable milieus within which they find themselves (Fiske 1989). Kates and Belk (2001) shed light on how gays and lesbians challenge homophobia through the consumption of gay- and lesbian-pride paraphernalia and "inflect their consumption practices with more libratory meanings in relation to the dominant heteropatriarchy" (p. 402). Through their consumptive practices, gays and lesbians also took part in "Meta" consumer resistance to "ponder the complexity of contradictions and predicaments" of buying against homophobia (p. 416).

Extending these theories to highlight the complexity of consuming to protest, I fuse previous insights gained from micro-level theories of resistance with Marx's theory of the commodity fetish. Utilizing both theories illuminates how music produced by others helps to create and hinder expressions of discontent. Marx (1906/1971) argues that commodities come to possess magical qualities and that the labor involved in the production of commodities becomes erased in the process of consumption. Taking Marx's theory of fetishism seriously shows how individuals might employ consumer objects as tools of protest and forget the means of production that went into the construction of such objects. I argue that dancers at times fetishize the means of the political production (challenging racism and white privilege) of the very songs they are using to demonstrate their anger. To this end, the use of music as a mode of resistance becomes more complicated than previously assumed. Music in the clubs does not operate as a static message; rather, it is read and reread in a variety of ways by dancers who are consuming it and using it in their strategies of protest within the clubs. This should not demean or mitigate how dancers challenge gendered inequality in the clubs; rather, it shows the complex terrain in which discontent is negotiated within

exceedingly complex networks of gendered, raced, and classed forms of power. . . .

The Clubs

Glitters is the only remaining exotic dance club in a former urban red-light district in a New England city and features "all nude" stage acts. Due to legal restrictions imposed by the state, dancers are not allowed to have physical contacts with customers while disrobed. Glitters is a lower-tier hustle club, attracting predominately white, working- to middle-class, male customers and showcasing mainly white dancers. Dancers earn the majority of their wages onstage and through the sale of alcohol. Glitters also grants dancers a larger degree of aesthetic license in terms of dress, size (women ranged from size two to size twelve), and body modification (tattoos, piercing, and scarification).

Conversely, Flame is a middle-tier suburban club, which offers seminude and fully nude services in the form of stage shows and lap dancing. Dancers earn the majority of their income from their time onstage, performing lap dances, and during time spent in the Champagne Room. Lap dances cost 20 dollars per song if a dancer is topless and 40 dollars if a dancer is nude. Time spent in the Champagne Room costs between 75 and 250 dollars depending on the amount of private time a customer wants to buy with a dancer. Flame caters to a predominantly white, suburbanite, male clientele and employs predominately white dancers. Flame has strict aesthetic requirements in terms of weight (dancers were fired if they went above a size eight), dress (i.e., dancers were not allowed to wear high-cut jean shorts, a.k.a. Daisy Dukes), and body modification (dancers were actively discouraged against tattoos and piercing and were fired if such practices became extreme). Due to the race and class of both the dancers and the customers, this analysis is inherently partial. Therefore, these findings are not representative of all exotic dance clubs but rather illuminate two particular ethnographic scenes.

Creative License, Club Rules, and Resistance

Exotic dancers, like other service-industry workers, are subject to standardization and increasing infringements by owners and management on individualized expressions of freedom in the work place (Egan 2004; Egan, Frank, and Johnson 2006; Frank 2002). As Hausbeck and Brent (2002) argue, the sex industry is facing increasing managerial intervention in the attempt to "McDonaldize" what is offered both aesthetically and servicewise. I would argue that limiting music choice is also an example of such intervention. Sex-radical feminists illuminate how power in the sex industry rarely operates in a binary fashion (Barton 2002; Chapkis 1997; Egan 2003, 2004, 2006; Egan, Frank, and Johnson 2006; Frank 1998, 2002; Liepe-Levinson 2002; Montemurro 2001; Murphy 2003; Ronai-Rambo 1998, 1999). Dancers' reactions to such standardization renders visible the unique ways laborers actively challenge attempts to control creative license and freedom in the workplace.

At Glitters, dancers played their own music (there were no deejays), but their CDs had to be approved by management. Conversely, at Flame, dancers were required to pay the deejay a 15 dollar "play fee" per shift. In addition to their mandatory play fees, dancers often "tipped" the deejays 10 to 20 dollars to ensure that their music would be played. During my research, the owner of Flame tried to impinge on the dancer's choice of music by stating that dancers could only play "top-forty hits" in the club; to do otherwise would result in a 20 dollar fine. "Flame is a classy place," the owner argued, "and our customers don't want to hear rap, hip-hop or heavy metal" (Egan 2004, 2006). The owner feared that dancers, through their use of music, would drive away the customers and, hence, the owner's profit. I would argue, however, that the owner was also put off by the messages found in the music, particularly the attacks on white, middle-class culture found in certain types of rap music. In his discussion of

Flame as "classy," the owner set boundaries between rap, which signified something for him that was unclassy—race, poverty, and political unrest—and the hegemonic order he attempted to enforce in the club: a predominately white audience who would secure his profit.

Dancers were, of course, also concerned about profit (as the money from customers made up the entirety of their salary), but they also felt that for artistic and aesthetic reasons, maintaining their control over music selection was imperative. When I asked Marie, a dancer of several years, about the owner's regulations on the music, she stated,

> Look, there are so many other rules on what parts of our bodies we can and cannot touch, on how much we have to tip out, you know the bull shit, but I am not going to dance to fucking Britney Spears to make Gary happy. My music is what helps me here. It's mine. So I am just going to play what I want and face the fees.

Echoing Marie's sentiments, dancers were unwilling to give up control over their music selection. Dancers decided to protest the owner's decision in two ways. First, they used their regular customers by asking them to request the music they wanted when onstage. Second, they played the music they wanted and faced the fines.

The Customer Is Always Right

Dancers at both clubs enlisted regulars' help in their struggles over music selection. Since the "customer was always right" and the club existed to serve them, the owner could not complain (Egan 2004, 2006). In this way, dancers created an alliance between themselves and their regulars to challenge the rules set up by the owners and management. Regulars often referred to Glitters and Flame as places where "men could be men"—a feeling the owners worked to insure. This was particularly true with regulars, who due to the level of profit generated, were personally greeted by owners who wanted to make them feel "special" (Egan 2004, 2006; Frank 2002). When dancers used their regulars as a way to take money out of the owners' pockets (in the form of fees), the dancers subverted the male bonding upon which the club is predicated (Egan 2004). Hope, a dancer at Glitters, discussed her relationships with regulars and music in this way:

> When I really love a certain song I tell a regular that it's "our song." That way if the owner or managers give me any shit . . . I just tell my regular that the manager won't let me play our song and he tells the manager that he wants to hear it. I mean I can't like say to a regular that something totally hard core is our song. But I can play some hip hop that otherwise would be banned.

Hope's strategy highlights how music can create allegiances between dancers and regulars by infusing particular songs with romantic sentiment. By attaching the sentiment of "our song" to a particular song, Hope is able to tap into her regulars' feelings of romantic interest while also subverting managerial rules.

Trena used a similar strategy with her regular Henry:

> TRENA: Henry helps whenever I want to play my music. He knows it's important to me and he feels protective so he helps out. There are also songs that have special meaning for him . . . like the song that was playing when he first saw me onstage.
>
> DANIELLE: What song was that?
>
> TRENA: "California Love" by Tupac. I mean what is the manager going to say when a regular asks for a song . . . the customer is always right. Right?
>
> DANIELLE: Yep.

Trena utilized Henry's status as a customer and his feelings of protection and romance to help guarantee her creative freedom at work. Later in the interview, Trena discussed that she often "played helpless" with her regulars so that they felt "more manly" and compelled to help her. In her use of romance and helplessness,

Trena drew on traditional gender roles to help her protest inequitable work conditions.

Regulars' feeling of attachment and care secured their loyalty to dancers and trumped male bonding between owners and customers. Through the use of regulars, dancers challenged the owners' rules by showing that the very group they were fearful of losing was requesting Rage Against the Machine, Tupac Shakur, and PJ Harvey.

Playing It Anyway

The second strategy dancers used to protest the owner's rule on "classy" music was to play the music they wanted regardless of the rules. For several weeks after the decision was made at Flame to limit music choice, dancers expressed their anger in the dressing room with one another. Lelia, a small-framed and particularly boisterous dancer, said, "We should all play what we want and refuse to pay the fines—they can't fire all of us. Without us who is going to come into this place?" After this discussion, dancers tipped the deejays extra to play the music they brought and paid the fine demanded by the owner. During my time as a dancer-researcher, the discussions over music were, by and large, the only venue where dancers discussed the possibility of collective labor action. Within a month of witnessing both of these strategies, the owner of Flame gave up and let dancers play whatever they wanted.

Walking into Glitters one evening, I watched Gina dance seductive moves to the Smashing Pumpkins's song "Bullet with Butterfly Wings":

> Now I'm naked nothing but an animal But can you fake it for just one more show And what do you want I want to change And what have you got When you feel the same Even though I know I suppose I'll show All my cool and cold like old Job *Despite all my rage I am still just a rat in a cage Despite all my rage I am still just a rat in a cage.* (Emphasis added)

Somewhat surprised that she would dance to a song like this in a strip club, I watched as customers tipped and the manager signaled to Gina to see him after the set. After Gina returned to the main floor, I asked her if she received a fine for playing her music. She laughed and said,

> That was my second set. I played Marilyn Manson during my first. I am having a fucking shitty night and I am pissed. I don't care if I have to pay or not. I am sick of being told what to do!

Gina directly challenged her manager's rules not to play "that kind of music" and paid the fines. Dancers at Glitters rarely took such direct action, and it was usually the result of a "larger issue" (a bad financial night, the loss of a regular, or a fight with the boss). The management never fired dancers for these actions, but when dancers chose to play banned music, they paid a fine of 10 dollars per song. At Glitters and Flame, dancers, through their struggles over creative freedom, attempted to create more hospitable work spaces for themselves and their interactions with management. In so doing, dancers actively challenged the attempts owners made to control the space of the club and women's erotic performance therein. As Beth Montemurro (2001) and Wesely (2003) highlight, in a work context where women can feel powerless, access to strategies for empowerment become important for dancers' overall sense of self.

Reappropriation and Erotic Performance

Serenity, an experienced and particularly savvy dancer (she was one of the top moneymakers in the club), portrayed a demure and "high-class" persona in the club.[2] She often danced to songs such as "Cherish," by Madonna, and "What a Man," by En Vogue. Both songs foreground feminine love and the importance of a good man. The lyrics state, "What a man, what a man, what a mighty, mighty good man. Yes he is." At the same time, Serenity clearly viewed this music as a form of lyrical protest:

> The women I dance to are strong women. Nobody gives Madonna shit. So although these

songs are kind of gushy.... I think they are by strong women who kick ass. And so I feel like a kick ass woman. Plus it's about the cake [money] right? I need to make it and I want them to give it to me.... I wanna make them pay to play so I need to make them think they are getting more. If they think that I really want to cherish the love we share together then they are more likely to stick around.

Serenity used the dominant tropes (monogamy, loyalty, love, and affection) found within these love songs and reappropriated them to mean something altogether different (power and covert resistance). She was able to cultivate feelings of strength in relation to music, which seldom offer overt messages of female power. It is through her "play" of meanings that she reframed the artists' intentions for her own use (power in her interactions with customers). Serenity performed dominant femininity while extending beyond its limitations.

Hope, a dancer at Glitters, discussed reinscription this way:

> When I am at home I like rap, hip-hop, and hard core, but here I am the college student [Hope was a student at an Ivy League University] and for some reason a lot of men associate college students with sorority girls. You would think my tattoo [she had a large women's symbol tattooed on her back] would give it away, but it's not who you are, it's how you act. So I play along and dance to all this pop crap. Sometimes I just laugh because I could not be farther from Britney Spears, but I always want to shake her hand because I have made a shit load of money from her crappy music. Her music helps with the act—it's like a mask.

Similarly, Marie stated that her music "always helps me . . . play a part to make money and you know, create the act. I need my regulars to believe certain things and that's what I do and my music is a part of it." Music functions as a highly important aspect of setting the erotic and economic contexts of interactions between dancers and regulars as well as helping to forge agency within interactions. Marie, Hope, and Serenity took music that portrayed hegemony in one way or another and reappropriated it by using dominant cultural norms of femininity against itself.

All three in their various uses of music not only portrayed an image of loyalty and feminine submission, which perpetuated dominant stories of femininity, but also covertly challenged each one. This is not to say that dancers do not, at times, feel care and even attraction toward customers that could be exemplified through music choice (Egan 2003, 2006; Frank 1998, 2002; Liepe-Levinson 2002; Ronai-Rambo 1992, 1998, 1999). Rather, it is to say that most often, dancers view their time onstage as work, not courting (Frank 1998, 2002; Ronai-Rambo and Ellis 1989; Murphy 2003; Wood 2000). Dancers constructed these images to serve their performance of eroticism that provided their livelihood. Within exotic dance clubs, expressions of discontent are complex because dancers must rely on customers for their income. Consequently, the forms of resistance used by dancers were often covert. In their use of music, dancers embodied a mode of covert protest that created a space of female empowerment in the clubs.

Unlike other forms of more overt protest, such as drag or Guerilla Theater, dancers used covert forms to continue working within this context while disputing their position within it (Egan 2003, 2006). If dancers were to directly challenge their customers, they would either get fired or lose a large amount, if not all, of their income. It is this strategy of covert protest that enabled dancers to excessively perform their position as both virgin and whore, to use this position as a site of resistance. Dancers were able to use their position as an object of desire to construct a space for themselves that was anything but passive. Not unlike other marginalized populations located within exploitative relations, dancers used forms of resistance that allowed them to negotiate an otherwise oppressive structure (Negron-Muntaner and Grosfoguel 1997; Bhabha 1994).

Letting Tupac Do It for Me

Music with counterhegemonic messages created more overt modes of resistance within Flame and Glitters. For example, one night, during my first few months of fieldwork at Glitters, a dancer named Margarita was onstage dancing and lip-synching,

> All hell can't stop us now All hell can't stop us now All hell can't stop us now All hell can't stop us now.

It was a fairly slow night in the club, and in the middle of the song, she yelled out, "Look you assholes I am not up here for fun." Stunned, three men went to the stage to tip (possibly due to some combination of embarrassment and obedience) as she mouthed the words of the song to them. Margarita, who self-fashioned herself as "a spicy Latina" showed her anger, frustration, and rage onstage.[3] Her striptease seemed closer to the feminist performance art of Karen Findley than to the erotic titillation of exotic dance. Later, during our conversation, Margarita told me,

> I was just sick of not making money and of feeling powerless so I said fuck it. If I am not going to make money at least I am going to show what I feel. It's a fucking trip though I made more onstage with Rage Against the Machine than I did with anything else.

Margarita's resistance was manifested through her music. By lip-synching that she "won't do what you tell [her] to do," she created a space where she could express her emotions. Although dancers' resistance was rarely as overt as Margarita's (i.e., yelling at customers and telling them "fuck you" through her lip-synching), strategies of overt resistance were not uncommon in either club.

Dancers' use of this type of music happened, most often, when they got "sick and tired" of a particular situation within the club. Feelings of powerlessness, for example, often emerged when dancers felt that their control over their work was threatened (i.e., a slow night, exploited by the owner, or disrespected by a customer's comment).[4] Amid feelings of frustration, dancers attempted to regain a sense of control over their work life while onstage. Consequently, music selection was pivotal. Tammy, a dancer at Glitters, illuminated this point:

> TAMMY: Look Danielle you know . . . you have done this shit . . .
>
> DANIELLE: Umm hmm.
>
> TAMMY: Where you have to scream or cry. So you just put your favorite fuck you song on and it helps. It's not like I can tell a room full of customers, "Fuck you!" or tell the managers "You're stupid and I hate your ass," so I just get up there and let Tupac do it for me.

In Tammy's discussion of letting "Tupac do it for [her]," she expressed a common theme dancers used with music: letting the artist express what they cannot. Tammy used Tupac's lyrical protests in a new way—to express her discontent.

Marie, a dancer at Flame, also employed rap narratives when "venting" her frustrations:

> MARIE: I love rap because Missy Misdemeanor Elliot can say the shit I can't say. You know what I mean? She can tell people to fuck off, that she kicks ass and that she won't take their shit . . . it's easier for her.
>
> DANIELLE: Why?
>
> MARIE: Because she's getting paid to say what she is saying and we would probably lose a lot of money if we said what we wanted to say when we're having a bad night.

Marie, like Tammy, felt that the music she used helped her say the "shit [she] can't say."

Moreover, Jenny, a dancer at Flame, talked about rap in this way:

> I love hard core rap. It just like tells everybody to fuck off so it's perfect 'cause there are nights where I just want to tell everybody to fuck off. When I am really pissed it works for me. I mean if using rap meant I made no money I

wouldn't do it because I need to support myself, sometimes I make less using rap and sometimes I don't.

By employing these narratives of resistance, Marie, Jenny, and Tammy felt power in a context where they could not voice opposition without penalty. Their fear is not unfounded; direct opposition can result in the loss of income or of their job. Rap and the messages found therein were, by far, the most commonly used narratives by dancers in the club. I am not trying to romanticize or unproblematically celebrate rap music's subversive possibilities.[5] Rather, I have tried to show how rap served as a particularly useful vehicle of subversion for women in the club when they were feeling powerless and how, more generally, music functioned as one of many tools dancers had at their disposal to resist inequitable situations. Similarly, I do not want to argue that dancers' reappropriation of this form of music is wholly unproblematic either.

Fetishization, Gender, and Whiteness

In their reappropriation of the lyrical discontent found in rap for gendered purposes, dancers often fetishized the political motivations underlying its production—to protest racism and white privilege. As a result, the consumption of music by dancers in their attempt to buy against gendered inequality obscured racial politics and the systems of production used to create the songs used in the clubs. Challenge and complicity fused, highlighting how reflexivity in one domain, gender, does not guarantee insights into other areas of inequality (Hill-Collins 1990; hooks 1992; Williams 1991). In this regard, dancers were guilty of "eating the other" (hooks 1992)—of consuming and appropriating an aspect of African American culture while fetishizing the material conditions within which it was produced.

Adding further to the complexity of the situation, some of the lyrics of the rap music used were not particularly positive in their representations of women and, at times, were overtly misogynist. Simultaneously located within systems of racial privilege, gendered inequality, and economic uncertainty, dancers were constantly negotiating the intersections of biography, social structures, and subversion. In such a complex cultural milieu, subversion often looks like bricolage where individuals use whatever means at hand to create the tools necessary to handle a situation rooted in structures of inequality, which they are both reinforcing and contesting (Geertz 1983; Levi-Strauss 1966).

Conclusion: Resistance, Change, and Effectivity

Music provided a medium for dancers to express their discontent over workplace inequality and gendered interactions in the clubs. The strategic use of music made dancers feel "powerful," "strong," and "like [they] have a say" and allowed them to tell "the customers and owners to fuck off." While taking these feelings seriously, I want to explore the structural effects of such activities and the extent to which the strategic use of music transformed the practices of the clubs.

In dancers' use of covert strategies, concerns over macro-level problems were placed on the back burner. Given the fact that such modes of protest are meant to go unnoticed by customers and management, it should come as no surprise that dancers' covert expressions of discontent aid individual dancers instead of redressing larger structural issues. For example, through the reappropriation of music that had overtly hegemonic messages of romance, like En Vogue's song "What a Man," dancers created a particular persona that gave them access to profit while offering the distance necessary to "protect" themselves in their interactions. Within such forms of protest, structural problems continue unabated and resistance remains squarely located at the micro level. This should not imply that such methods lack positive benefits—they help dancers—but their effects do not pierce the broader social-cultural sit-

uation of the workplace of both Flame and Glitters. However, I would argue that most overt forms did have larger effects as witnessed by the social control imparted by the owners in response to such strategies.

In their use of rap and other more overtly political music, dancers created a "disruptive" situation wherein owners responded and attempted to severely limit music selection. By drawing on narratives of protest found within rap music, which took as its target the very clientele the club sought and valued—white, middle- to upper-middle-class men—dancers illuminated and rendered visible the hegemony of the club. In so doing, dancers protested the authority that came with masculinity—particularly the owners and the managers—who usually had the power to define the ambiance and gendered hierarchy within the walls of the clubs (Egan 2006; Liepe-Levinson 2002). Through their use of music, dancers challenged the gendered relations upon which the clubs were predicated—that dancers were fantasy girls who existed to fulfill men's fantasies. Such expressions of protest registered more seriously with the owners and managers who operated as agents of social control than with the regulars who conceptualized themselves as "protectors" of the dancers. It is my contention that owners may have been more sensitive to the narratives found within the music because their interactions were based on profit, whereas interactions between dancers and regulars were based on desire and romance (Egan 2003, 2006).

Dancers reacted in both covert and overt manners to challenge interventions into their individual expression at work and organized to secure their creative freedom. These strategies caused owners to reverse their decisions, giving dancers a victory and a sense of autonomy. These forms of resistance had a direct effect on their workplace. Unfortunately, this sense of agency did not carry over into more exploitative workplace practices such as high work fees, scheduling fees, or other ways owners extracted cash from dancers. When I asked dancers about this, many replied, like Serenity, "I would love to tell them to fuck off on fees, but there is no way they aren't going to make us pay and I need this money." What becomes evident here is that the hegemony of gendered relations offers more opportunities to challenge the status quo than the hegemony of capitalist work relations. This illuminates how individuals in their negotiations of resistance may be, in part, embedded in certain hegemonic ideologies while actively protesting others.

By examining the complex and nuanced ways dancers used music within the clubs, we can gain a sense of how individuals both challenge and are complicit with the inequitable social contexts within which they find themselves. People are rarely passive victims or liberated agents but instead are most often squarely situated at the liminal space in between these extremes (Law 1997, 2000). Avery Gordon (1997), in her discussion of "complex personhood," argues that

> complex personhood means that people (albeit in specific forms whose specificity is sometimes everything) remember and forget, are beset by contradiction, and recognize and misrecognize themselves and others. Complex personhood means that people suffer graciously and selfishly too, get stuck in the symptoms of their troubles, and also transform themselves. (p. 4)

Dancers were complex people in every sense of the term—they were subject to and subverted dense networks of raced, classed, and gendered forms of power in ways that were both hegemonic and counterhegemonic.

Exploring how women embody Gordon's theory of complex personhood allows us to begin to envision how resistance operates in the materiality of everyday life. It further illuminates how discontent can function in the seemingly mundane aspects of people's lives, which mean far more than we may have anticipated. Moreover, in examining how individuals express their discontent, we may be able to create a more complex sociological analysis of how commodities (in this case, music), power, and resistance oftentimes collide in ways that cannot be predicted at the

outset. Finally, it may provide a better picture of the multiple subject positions that individuals occupy and how it is within those locations that subversion and complicity get enacted in various ways, thereby providing an interesting point of departure for further theories of power and agency.

Notes

1. Whether exotic dancing qualifies as "dancing" is open to debate. For more on the legal struggles surrounding exotic dance as a valid form of dance, see Hanna (1998).

2. *High class* is a term many dancers used in their descriptions of themselves. The definition of the term was rarely elaborated but was in contradistinction to the term *trashy*, which was often described as women who dress in cheap outfits or do not wear jewelry or have nice things. Helena, a self-described high-class dancer, said that she wanted to look like she was going to an opera or a prom with her customers. She felt that she could be taken out for dinner at a four-star restaurant in any of her outfits.

3. Margarita's description is a purposeful persona, and she uses language, music, and other behavior to play off of men's desire to "eat the other" to make money (hooks 1992). For more on Margarita, see Egan (2003).

4. Dancers define *slow nights* as nights when they make very little money. Because dancers must pay the club to work, a slow night can be devastating, as a dancer may have to pay out more money than she has actually made on her shift. For more on the labor dynamics of exotic dance clubs, see Barton (2002) and Funari (1997).

5. Rap music, in its resistance against dominant race and class structures in the United States, creates narratives of resistance and gives voice to marginal groups that are most often silenced in our culture (Rose 1994; Martinez 1997; Stapleton 1998). In this way, rap functions as a public discourse of dissent that seeks to fissure the hegemony of white, middle-class culture. However, even strategies of resistance are oftentimes, at least in part, complicit with the systems they critique. As James Scott (1990) argues, we can never get completely outside that which we critique. Rap both subverts hegemony and is a site of

commodification. Its distribution is often subject to the whims of large production companies and, thus, is never truly "free" in its expression.

References

Baker, H.A. 1993. *Black studies, rap and the academy*. Chicago: University of Chicago Press.

Barton, B. 2002. Dancing on the mobius strip: Challenging the sex war paradigm. *Gender & Society* 16(5): 585–602.

Bhabha, H. 1994. *The location of culture*. New York: Routledge.

Chapkis, W. 1997. *Live sex acts: Women performing erotic labor*. New York: Routledge.

Costello, M., and D. Foster Wallace. 1990. *Signifying rappers: Rape, race and the urban present*. New York: Ecco Press.

Cross, B. 1993. *It's not about salary: Rap, race and resistance in Los Angeles*. New York: Verso.

Dimitriadis. G. 2001. *Performing identity/performing culture: Hip hop as text, pedagogy and lived practice*. New York: Peter Lang.

Egan, R.D. 2003. I'll be your fantasy girl if you'll be my money man: Desire, fantasy and power in an exotic dance club. *Journal of the Psychoanalysis of Culture and Society* 8(1): 109–20.

———. 2004. Eyeing the scene: The uses and (re)uses of surveillance cameras in an exotic dance club. *Critical Sociology* 30(2): 299–320.

———. 2006. *Dancing for dollars and paying for love: The relationships between dancers and their regular customers*. New York: Palgrave Macmillan.

Egan, R. D., K. Frank, and M. L. Johnson. 2006. *Flesh for fantasy: Producing and consuming exotic dance*. San Francisco: Thunders Mouth Press.

Fiske, J. 1989. *Reading the popular*. London: Routledge.

Flint, A. 1996. Skin trade spreading across US: High tech fuels boom for $10 billion dollar industry. *Boston Globe*, December 1, A1–A4.

Foucault, M. 1981. *The history of sexuality Vol. 1: An introduction*. New York: Vintage.

Frank. K. 1998. The production of identity and the negotiation of intimacy in a gentleman's club. *Sexualities* 1(2): 175–201.

———. 2002. *G-Strings and sympathy: Strip club regulars and male desire*. Durham, NC: Duke University Press.

Funari, V. 1997. Naked, naughty and nasty: Peep show reflections. In *Whores and other feminists*. ed. J. Nagle, 19–35. New York: Routledge.

Geertz, C. 1983. *Local knowledge*. New York: Basic Books.

Gordon, A. 1997. *Ghostly matters: Haunting and the sociological imagination*. Minneapolis: University of Minnesota Press.

Haenfler, R. 2004. Rethinking subcultural resistance: Core. . . values of the straight edge movement. *Journal of Contemporary Ethnography* 33(4): 406–36.

Hanna, J.L. 1998. Undressing the First Amendment and corsetting the striptease dancer. *Drama Review* 42:38–69.

Hausbeck, K., and B. Brent. 2002. McDonaldization of the sex industry? The Business of sex. In *McDonaldization: The reader,* ed. G. Ritzer, 91–107. Thousand Oaks, CA: Pine Forge Press.

Hebdige, D. 1979. *Subculture: The meaning of style*. London: Methuen.

Hechter, M. 1978. Group formation and the cultural division of labor. *American Journal of Sociology* 84:293–318.

Herman, N. J., and G. R. Musolf. 1998. Resistance among ex-psychiatric patients: Expressive and instrumental rituals. *Journal of Contemporary Ethnography* 26(4):426–49.

Hill-Collins, P. 1990. *Black feminist thought: Knowledge, consciousness, and the politics of empowerment*. London: HarperCollins.

hooks, b. 1992. *Black looks: Race and representation*. Boston: South End Press.

Kates, S., and R. W. Belk. 2001. The meanings of lesbian and gay pride day: Resistance through consumption and resistance to consumption. *Journal of Contemporary Ethnography* 30(4): 392–429.

Law, L. 1997. Dancing on the bar: Sex, money and the uneasy politics of third space. In *Geographies of resistance*, ed. S. Pile and M. Keith. London: Routledge.

———. 2000. *Sex work in Southeast Asia: The place of desire in a time of AIDS*. New York: Routledge.

Leblanc, L. 1999. *Pretty in punk: Girls' gender resistance in a boys' subculture*. New Brunswick, NJ: Rutgers University Press.

Liepe-Levinson, K. 2002. *Strip show: Performances of gender and desire*. New York: Routledge.

Martinez, T. 1997. Popular culture as oppositional culture: Rap as resistance. *Sociological Perspectives* 40(2): 265–86.

Marx, K. 1906/1971. *Capital*. Vol. 1. New York: Modern Library.

Mitchell, B. L., and J. R. Feagin. 1995. America's racial-ethnic cultures: Opposition within a mythical melting pot. In *Toward the multicultural university*, ed. B. Bowser, T. Jones, and G. A. Young, 35–52. Westport. CT: Praeger.

Montemurro, B. 2001. Strippers and screamers: The emergence of social control in a noninstitutionalized institution. *Journal of Contemporary Ethnography* 30(3): 275–304.

Murphy, A. 2003. The dialectical gaze: Exploring subject-object tension in the performances of women who strip. *Journal of Contemporary Ethnography* 32(3): 305–35.

Negron-Muntaner. F., and R. Grosfoguel, eds. 1997. *Puerto Rican jam: Rethinking colonialism and nationalism*. Minneapolis: University of Minnesota Press.

Pratt, R. 1990. *Rhythm and resistance: The political uses of American popular music*. Washington, DC: Smithsonian Institutional Press.

Ronai-Rambo. C. 1992. The reflexive self through narrative: A night in the life of an erotic dancer/researcher. In *Investigating subjectivity: Research on lived experience*, ed. C. Ellis and M. G. Flaherty, 112–32. Thousand Oaks, CA: Sage.

———. 1998. Sketching with Derrida: An ethnography of a researcher/dancer. *Qualitative Inquiry* 4(3): 405–20.

———. 1999. The next night sous rature: Wrestling with Derrida's mimesis. *Qualitative Inquiry* 5(1): 1–13.

Ronai-Rambo, C., and C. Ellis. 1989. Turn-on's for money: Interactional strategies of the table dancer. *Journal of Contemporary Ethnography* 18(2): 271–98.

Rose, T. 1994. *Black noise: Rap music and black culture in contemporary America*. Hanover, NH: Wesleyan University Press.

Scott, J. 1990. *Domination and the arts of resistance*. New Haven, CT: Yale University Press.

Smitherman, G. 1997. The chain remains the same: Communicative practices in the hip hop nation. *Journal of Black Studies* 28(1): 3–25.

Stapleton, K. R. 1998. From the margins to mainstream: The political power of hip hop. *Media, Culture and Society* 20:219–34.

Stuckey, S. 1987. *Slave culture*. New York: Oxford University Press.

Wesely, J. 2003. Where am I going to stop? Exotic dancing, fluid body boundaries, and effects on identity. *Deviant Behavior* 24:483–503.

Williams, P.J. 1991. *The alchemy of race and rights: A diary of a law professor*. Cambridge, MA: Harvard University Press.

Wood, E. A. 2000. Working in the fantasy factory: The attention hypothesis and the enacting of masculine power in strip clubs. *Journal of Contemporary Ethnography* 29(1):5–31.

PART FOUR

Women and the Body

Women's bodies have been worshiped, idealized, desired, and revered. They have also been feared, restricted, punished, abused, and treated as a defective version of men's bodies. Our biological bodies are a foundation for our being in the world. But the social and cultural meaning of our bodies is a human accomplishment. What we consider "normal" and beautiful, the relationship of women's bodies to political rights, and perceptions of aging and reproduction are shaped by the politics of embodiment. Every semester my students write about their bodies, and most women and men express dissatisfaction—most commonly with their weight. However, there are always students who take pride in their body's abilities and in their unique piercings and tattoos. Women celebrate and enjoy their bodies while acknowledging their insecurities.

This section focuses on three major topics regarding women and the body: aesthetics, the social construction of normal and pathological bodies, and the role of technology in shaping women's views of their bodies and health. A great deal has been written about women's bodily dissatisfactions and the harmful consequences of un-realistic body ideals. We know that eating disorders are common among women and girls and are more prevalent in the United States than in other countries. Deborah Carr addresses bodily aesthetics and investigates how women employ technology to accomplish the ideal version of femininity, which is always shifting out of reach. Cosmetic surgeries that were once considered extreme are now commonplace, with 11.5 million surgical and nonsurgical procedures performed in the United States in 2005, a four-fold increase since 1997 at a cost of more than $12 billion. The most common nonsurgical procedure was botox injections, and the most common surgical procedure was liposuction. Women had 91 percent of these procedures (American Society for Aesthetic Plastic Surgery 2005). Cosmetic procedures also reflect racist aesthetics, with women of color undergoing surgery that shapes their features to appear more "white." Comparing ourselves to other women, to fashion images, and to our younger selves, we employ technology as a resource for approximating unrealistic body ideals, a process that can repeat endlessly.

Yet we also know that many young women are rejecting the dominant model of femininity and developing their own standards of beauty. Christine Braunberger, for example, describes "monster beauty," women's creation of new body aesthetics that incorporate both resistance to hegemonic standards and a desire for beauty and adornment. Braunberger focuses on the monster beauty of tattoos as a source of pleasure and rebellion against cultural norms of femininity. Tracing the history of tattoos, she links P. T. Barnum's freak shows to his development of the beauty contest. The display of tattooed women as "freaks" helped define the boundaries of normality, and the beauty contest encouraged women to compare themselves to a dominant standard and to compete against one another. Today, tattoos are a way for women to "subvert proscribed physicality and broaden our sense of bodily aesthetics with monster beauty."

Women's bodies are also evaluated on the basis of a medically defined "normality." Women who deviate from this norm, in terms of mental or physical health, or both, often face social stigma, regulation, and rejection. Lori Ann Dotson, Jennifer Stinson, and LeeAnn Christian interviewed women with developmental disabilities about their experiences with health care, sexuality, and reproductive rights. They found that these women were often treated as asexual beings and denied information about their own bodies. Noting high rates of sexual abuse as well as the history of forced sterilization of women with developmental disabilities, they argue that failure to provide specialized education and services puts women at risk and denies their sexual subjectivity.

April Herndon discusses fat embodiment and physical disabilities as a "problem within social contexts, social expectations and built environments, not within individuals." She joins feminist disability scholars who argue that the "impairment" model of disability treats people as deficient rather than different. For example, deaf culture employs a shared language, American Sign Language, rather than the spoken word. Deaf people do not view their language or culture as deficient and do not necessarily believe that medical interventions, such as cochlear implants, are desirable. Herndon suggests that fat people and disabled people are both viewed through a "medicalized rubric" that interprets their bodies as defective. The medicalized rubric discounts the social and political context of disability. Fat phobia prevents women from challenging the medicalized rubric and exploring their shared political interests. Fat people are excluded from the Amer-

icans with Disabilities Act, and their bodies are assumed to reflect lax moral habits, such as overeating and lack of exercise. For Herndon, social attitudes that pathologize differently shaped and abled bodies legitimate oppressive standards of "normality" and make it difficult for groups to form alliances in the struggle for social justice.

Women's aging, menopause, and childbirth have also been medicalized and defined negatively as problems. Sarah Blustain discusses the ways that advanced technology has ironically made childbirth a dangerous experience directed by physicians rather than birthing mothers. According to Blustain, "the U.S. spends more per capita than any other developed nation on maternity care . . . (but) the World Health Organization ranks the U.S. thirtieth out of 33 developed countries in preventing maternal mortality, and 32nd in preventing neonatal mortality." Blustain outlines the arguments in several recent books on American births that critique the "active management" of even normal births. Almost 30 percent of births in the United States were by caesarian section in 2005, which is a rate double that recommended by the World Health Organization. Technology can improve maternal and neonatal health, but when it is used routinely to decrease medical liability, women's safety declines.

Finally, Heather Dillaway explodes the idea that menopause is traumatic and sad for women. Her interviews with 45 postmenopausal women found just the opposite. Women are happy to move to a phase of life where they do not have to worry about contraception or menstruation. In fact, the general consensus was that middle-age was the best time of their lives. Dillaway hypothesizes that this generation of baby-boomer women is the first to have access to birth control technology that gave them the ability to determine the end of their childbearing years prior to menopause. Thus, menopause no longer marks the end of reproductive capacity, but the beginning of freedom from reproductive duties.

Our bodies have benefited from technology in many ways—birth control, immunizations, improved medical procedures, and early identification of diseases. It is the social context, however, that determines whether technological advances reinforce beliefs that some bodies are defective or encourage an environment where all bodies are able to enact their full, unique potential.

Reference

American Society for Aesthetic Plastic Surgery. (2005). 2005 ASAPS News Release. Retrieved from http://www.cosmeticplasticsurgerystatistics.com/statistics.html October 5, 2007.

Deborah Carr

Body Work

Forty years ago, baby boomers vowed not to trust anyone over 30. Today, they don't want to look older than 30. The same youth culture that once inspired a generation to tune in and drop out is now compelling them to nip, tuck, lift, and separate. An estimated 11.5 million cosmetic procedures were done in the United States in 2005, a fourfold increase since 1997. Cosmetic surgeries account for about 20 percent of all procedures, while the remaining 80 percent are "nonsurgical" touch-ups such as Botox injections and microdermabrasion. All told, Americans spent more than $12 billion on cosmetic procedures in 2005.

How exactly are Americans reconstructing themselves? The top five cosmetic surgeries in 2005 were liposuction, breast augmentation, eyelid surgery, nose reshaping, and tummy tucks, according to data from the American Society of Plastic Surgeons (ASPS). [See Figure 16.1] The explosion in cosmetic procedures over the past 14 years may be even more dramatic than the ASPS data suggest, however. The society documents only procedures done by its members. The actual number may be anywhere from two to five times higher, as more and more procedures are done by physicians from other specialties. Using this more expansive count, there were an estimated 3.3 million Botox shots, 455,000 liposuctions, 170,000 tummy tucks, and 200,000 nose jobs in 2005.

Media images of "metrosexual" men notwithstanding, cosmetic surgery is women's territory. Although the raw number of procedures done to men has also skyrocketed over the past decade, women have consistently accounted for 85 to 90 percent of patients. And while middle-class white women are still the most likely to go under the knife, growing numbers of black, Asian, and Hispanic women are reshaping their faces and bodies into what many would deem a "white" ideal: a proportional hourglass figure, button nose, and round eyes. Black women are having their noses narrowed and their breasts reduced, while Asian women are redoing their eyelids and increasing their bust lines.

Experts point to three forces driving the makeover mania. First, an unprecedented 60 percent of Americans are now overweight or obese. The quick fix of a tummy tuck or liposuction may be preferable to a lifetime of dieting and Pilates. Second, baby boomers—the 75 million babies born between 1946 and 1964—are now middle-aged. Aging is inevitably accompanied by slower metabolism and loss of skin elasticity. Even those older women who proudly embrace their crow's feet and forehead creases as badges of experience and wisdom cannot escape daily media images glorifying youthful beauty. A competitive (and arguably ageist) workplace and perhaps a more cutthroat dating market for older women may make cosmetic surgery seem like a necessary evil to those vying for a promotion or a date.

Finally, "having work done" has been normalized in recent years. TV shows like *Nip/Tuck* and *Extreme Makeover* carry the message that everyone is doing it. With Restylane injections and chemical peels now available at the neighborhood day spa, cosmetic procedures no longer seem so invasive or extreme. Some observers

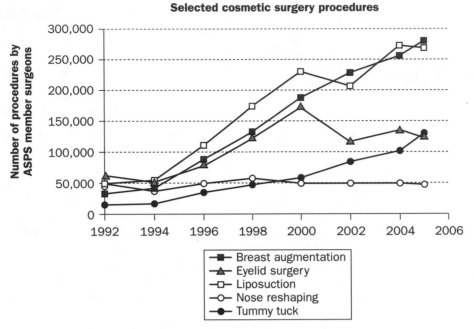

Selected cosmetic surgery procedures

■ **FIGURE 16.1**   Selected Cosmetic Surgery Procedures

Source: American Society of Plastic Surgeons (2006).

liken nonsurgical procedures to a "gateway" drug. Nervous customers dip their feet into the pool with a quick Botox shot in the forehead or a collagen injection in their lips. After this first foray, they may progress to the "harder" stuff, like a full-blown facelift or liposuction.

Advocates say that a lift here or stitch there makes men and women feel better about themselves. Yet critics point out that anywhere from 25 to 50 percent of patients become repeat customers, and that many will never be satisfied in their elusive quest for eternal youth and beauty.

Christine Braunberger

Revolting Bodies:
The Monster Beauty of Tattooed Women

This is an essay about bodies in revolt. Tattooed women complicate recent body theory by staging an aesthetic revolution in "feminine" beauty. My research combines elements of participant observation, oral history, archival research, and the use of secondary sources in order to trace the motives of, and cultural responses to, tattooed women. This essay will proceed through several competitive venues, from the nineteenth century to the present, where the meaning of tattoos for women, and the concomitant authority over women's bodies, has been challenged: from beauty salons to courtrooms, high society to the working class, freak shows to tattoo contests, soft porn to novels. By demonstrating the ruptures that have occurred at various points of conflicts between and among these sites, I will show how aspects of what I am calling monster beauty have developed. I will argue that we read the risks women have taken in becoming tattooed in terms of a revolutionary aesthetic for women.

A woman who works at my favorite bookstore recently told me about her boyfriend's reaction to the large intricate tattoos adorning her shoulders. "He said they make him think of prostitutes and biker chicks. I've never even been on a motorcycle. So I said, 'but this is me. You know me.' But he says he needs time to get over the connection." My bookseller's struggle with the disjunctive identification occasioned by her tattoos is not unusual. Tattooed women register on many people's radar screens for the first time either as circus side-show acts, "the tattooed lady," hippies, prostitutes, or "biker chicks." The rebellious politics and performances of these "types" of women seem easily identifiable: they are physically transgressive, rootless, loose, troublemakers. Less discernible has been the discomfort caused by their

Source: Braunberger, Christine. "Revolting Bodies: The Monster Beauty of Tattooed Women." *NWSA Journal* 12:2 (2000), 1–3, 9–23. © The National Women's Studies Association Journal. Reprinted with permission of The John Hopkins University Press.

speaking bodies that exceed the protocols of simple body language. As symbols demanding to be read, tattoos on women produce anxieties of misrecognition. Masculine tattoo connotations—brave, heroic, macho—slip off the skin of women. The stories behind sailors' tattoos are not women's stories. In a culture built on women's silence and bent on maintaining silence as a primary part of the relationship between women's bodies and cultural writing, the rules have been simple. The written body may only speak from a patriarchal script that tries to limit women's voices and bodies to supporting roles and scenery. So on a woman's body any tattoo becomes the symbol of bodily excess. When a woman's body is a sex object, a tattooed woman's body is a lascivious sex object; when a woman's body is nature, a tattooed woman's body is primitive; when a woman's body is spectacle, a tattooed woman's body is a show. It would seem that whatever manifold meanings women attach to their tattoos are culturally written over to simply and only punctuate meanings already attached to their bodies within a larger cultural domain.

Whatever women have wanted to demonstrate with their tattoos—a rejection of those supporting roles, perhaps, or an embrace of the heroics those roles require—their tattoos have been always already culturally remarked to hold them at stable symbolic borders. But does the choice to become tattooed denote only scripted excess, or are there other remainders here as well? While we may seem culturally well-equipped to read women's skin, feminists know that women aren't necessarily interested in simply maintaining and punctuating their roles as the workhorses of the culture's symbolic, inhabiting the overdetermined constituent in gendered pairings: *mother* to father, *wife* to husband, *desirable* to desiring, *victim* to perpetrator, and also as *nature* to culture, *emotion* to logic, and *beauty* to beast. Language and power make and re-make us into entities that both breathe and have representative meaning. And while we may know this intellectually, where we really feel it is in our guts. The body has become a site for commentary and resistance to these scripts.

This essay is about women writing bodies in a culture of smothering inscriptions. It is about women who change their skin, who deliberately transform themselves through and against the cultural imaginary of what their transformations mean. Tattoos complicate the current interest in the skin and body as field for self-expression, a trend discussed by such theorists as Kathy Davis in regard to plastic surgery (1995, 1997); Susan Bordo in regard to dieting and weight control (1993, 1997); Anne Balsamo in regard to body building (1996); and Naomi Wolf in regard to cosmetics (1991).[1] Unlike plastic surgery and diets that speak, in simple and complex ways, about desires for normalcy, beauty, and control, tattoos in American culture are not "normal."

Tattoos also complicate the two distinct positions feminist theory has negotiated in order to speak the written body. Broadly stated, we either follow Judith Butler (1990, 1993) in intellectual play with our symbolizing selves, becoming ob-scure Madonnas forever in a game of dress-up, or agitate with Andrea Dworkin (1974, 1991) to get the make-up off. At the moment, feminism seems polarized in these two modes, more inclined to address theories of performance in academic realms, and sexual objectification in political realms.[2] Alternatively, I find myself returning to Sandra Bartky's call for a "revolutionary feminist aesthetic," which would both support narcissistic gratification and seek to eradicate "introjected representatives of agencies hostile to the self" (1990, 42–4). Women need to be able to make the double move of decolonizing the "fashion-beauty complex" from our minds, while allowing for the joy and exploration in the body play of masquerade and performance. Interweaving the now-familiar arguments that have followed the work of Butler and Dworkin creates a new politics of the performative, a third term that addresses the need for aesthetics and anger. Language for this third term is beginning to develop when performance artist Joanna Frueh speaks of "monster beauty" and critic Mary Russo writes of "monstrification," creating new possibilities for body aesthetics on the limitations of former definitions (Frueh 1994, Russo 1994).[3] Materialization of this third term comes to life in women's tattooed bodies.

In the following pages I will show how the monster beauty of tattooed women has developed through larger struggles over the author(ity) of women's bodies. By tracing the "primitive" excitement of tattooed society women and the "criminal" agency of tattooed working-class women to the ambiguous stages of freak shows and tattoo contests, I believe we can make some sense of the impulse toward bodily transformation that runs counter to cultural acceptability. In addition to analyzing tattoo artifacts, I will recount relevant material from my participant observation and oral history work that I conducted primarily in the Chicago area from June 1998–March 1999. My primary argument is that tattoo provides one access point for revolutionary aesthetics for women. This is not to say that everyone would or should get tattoos, or to confer some awesome power to being tattooed. Instead,

I want to encourage the development of a tattoo aesthetic for women as a way to configure radical difference in rewarding, self-confirming ways. . . .

Freak Shows, Beauty Pageants, and Tattoo Contests

> Lydia, oh Lydia,
> Say, have you met Lydia?
> Lydia the tattooed lady . . .
> On her back is the Battle of Waterloo
> Beside it the Wreck of the Hesperus too,
> And proudly above waves the Red, White, and Blue."
>
> —Groucho Marx song,
>   "Lydia the Tattooed Lady" (1939)

In the United States the staging of women's bodies in freak shows, tattoo contests, and beauty pageants all grew up on the same carnival stage that P.T. Barnum had dedicated to the monstrous, the beautiful, and their hybrids. Although physical contests enjoy a global ubiquity, Americans can credit Barnum with the Western version of these. Barnum was staging contests for children and pets to extend his side-show business, when, in 1854, he suggested that women take the stage so that their beauty may be judged (it may be noted this is six years after Lucretia Mott and Elizabeth Cady Stanton took another stage at Seneca Falls, but this is not the place to explore that connection). Women refused to participate in Barnum's scheme, so their daguerreotypes were used instead, and thus began the public warming to this form of scrutinized beauty, later picked up by eager newspapers. This shift in playing fields, from the stage to the newspaper, made it possible for beauty contests to contribute to the shift in the general public's perception of women as commodity images without women directly participating. It also encouraged women to take those stages and accept scrutiny. By 1880 a Miss U.S. contest was in existence, and by 1920 Miss America, both designed to publicize resort areas (Cohen et al. 1996, 2–5).

Concurrent with the first Miss U.S. contests was the arrival of tattooed women on sideshow stages. Beginning in 1882 with Nora Hildebrandt, a handful of women became heavily tattooed so that they could travel with circuses and carnival sideshows. Their appeal superseded that of tattooed men for the titillation they engendered in their audiences; not only were "tattooed women" publicly displaying themselves with fewer clothes than women in any other line, but the stories describing how they became tattooed typically consisted of tattoo rape (Mifflin 1997, 18–25; Parry 1971, 64–8). Each woman was kidnapped and forcibly tattooed by savages, often cast as American Indians. Their stories were the new captivity narratives, granddaughters in spirit to Mary Rowlandson—whose seventeenth-century autobiography became the prototypical captivity narrative—and from show to show and woman to woman, these stories varied little. For Nora Hildebrandt, whose father had the first tattoo shop in America, the story was necessarily somewhat different. In her version she and her father were kidnapped by Sitting Bull, who, along with his tribe, forced father to tattoo daughter. Every day for a year, so the story goes, she was tied to a tree until she was tattooed from head to toe (Mifflin 18).

For several reasons deprivation of agency was always the crucial element in these stories. On one level, these were the narratives on which America was built. Annette Kolodny identifies captivity narratives as the "single narrative form indigenous to the New World," filling the popular imagination with "the victim's recounting of unwilling captivity" (1984, 6). Like the captivity narratives of the seventeenth and eighteenth centuries, in which savage interlopers preyed on "delicate pioneer women," the (fictive) fact of savage mistreatment catered to prevailing fantasies that supported colonial and genocidal efforts. Tattooing would be cast as torture, thus making any tattooed man that much more brave, the poor tattooed woman on stage that much more pathetic, and the savage that much more savage. Most importantly, the female body was a spectacle of admonition against women having/taking too much physical freedom.

The forced incest allusion in Hildenbrandt's story was a fitting addition to the traditional captivity narrative, America's first form of pornography. Captivity narratives invigorated excitement over the unknown, encouraging the press onward. Writing incest and kidnapping together on a woman's body was a powerful combination for protecting some boundaries and eradicating others. Not only could the Indians steal women, but their whims included the theft of civilizing propriety as well. Such concepts were to find their expression through a young Sigmund Freud in the next decades. In *Civilization and Its Discontents* he writes that the taboo against incest is necessitated by "the progress of civilization" (1961, 51). It was this line that Irene Woodward capitalized on in her 1880s tale of father/daughter tattoo; postcards she sold read "In spite of the pain the girl [daughter] was delighted and coaxed her father to continue" (qtd. Mifflin 1997, 20). One hardly needs Freud's curiously inverted reading of little girls wanting their fathers sexually to understand how well this story sold.

More broadly, tattooed women had to fashion responses to the impact of Cesare Lombroso, one of the first "criminal anthropologists" who, in the 1880s, was an outspoken critic of tattoos. In developing his "scientific" theory of criminality, Lombroso studied 7,000 tattooed people over a 13-year period. He concluded that tattooed people were "instinctive criminals," something which they demonstrated by tapping into this "most characteristic trait of primitive man" (Scutt and Gotsch 1974, 109). Lombroso's work vindicated all those disgusted or otherwise put off by tattoos, but for the sideshow stage his work was useful because it provided scientific backing for tales of savagery, criminality, and decadence (Bogden 1988, 251). When Lombroso focused specifically on tattooed women, he found that their criminality manifested most often in prostitution. Reasoning in circles, he concluded that the more "degraded" the prostitute, the more likely she was to have tattoos (Lombroso 1958, 116–20). Tattooed women were thus in the position of either representing criminality, which in terms of tattooed bodies meant prostitutes, or its victims. While their tattooed bodies hinted at prostitution, hinted that they were "bad girls," their stories renounced ownership of their tattoos—and bodies—reinscribing them as "good girls." In her study of *fin de siécle* prostitution, Shannon Bell argues that the pathologizing efforts by Lombroso and his ilk could never eradicate the ambiguity between these two positions (1994, 40–3). For tattooed women, then, playing the role of victim created the most viable mix of good and bad.

In contrast to their stories of victimization, women who made their livings off their tattoos had more independence, money, and opportunities for travel than were otherwise available to women, save through precious few vocations. In effect, their tattoos and the tales they told of them spoke one reality while they experienced quite another. Such doubling is often the role of those who embody a society's boundaries, and as Bahktin has taught us, carnivals are a place where we may witness and/or experience excesses and transgressions that remind us of where our "real" boundaries are. In other words, the (patriarchal) culture that marks women with purity and a "connection to nature," and then values them/us for those projected marks is bolstered by evidence that women can be marked impure also; efforts to protect purity can be that much more rigid when hints that it isn't natural seep through, as in a freak show tent. . . .

There is a reckless kind of freedom in horrifying others, in making one's body into the seductive and scary and strange combination that is monster beauty. Tattooed women could revel in their freakiness, enjoy the act of display, and delight in the tease of their tales. But such pleasures rarely last. With the advent of electric tattooing, tattoos became more plentiful and less exotic. By the late 1920s there was a glut in the business of being a tattooed attraction, and women had to capitalize on the sexual side of their work (Bogden 1988, 253). In order to have a viable career, the stories told by tattooed women

necessarily grew more lurid, tainted with economic desperation. Enter Betty Broadbent.
Broadbent had run away to join the circus in
1927, and by 1939 was a Ringling Brothers and
Barnum and Bailey "youngest tattooed woman"
sideshow (Mifflin 1997, 30). While working the
sideshow at the 1939 World's Fair, Broadbent
also participated in a beauty pageant there. Perhaps she simply intended to pull a publicity stunt,
but her actions were also a commentary on the
politics of beauty and the ownership of women's
bodies. Through her smiles and tattoos of the
Madonna and Charles Lindbergh that she wore,
she was demanding a revision of feminine beauty.
Broadbent didn't have a prayer of winning, of
course, but her challenge to the ideal feminine
beauty of the beauty contest existed on several
levels. Her face and body were conventionally
beautiful according to the standards of the time,
but her skin was monstrous. The transgressive
agency she manifested in her body alterations
were what drove people to see freak shows, which
was how she made her living; now she was asking
to be judged based on her adherence to cultural
ideals. Eliding the gap between beauty pageant
and freak show, she was, in that moment of contest participation, two Barnum acts in one.

Beauty pageant ethnographers (gathered in
the 1996 volume, *Beauty Queens*) agree that "these
contests showcase values, concepts and behavior
that exist at the center of a group's sense of itself
and exhibit values of morality, gender, and
place," but also can constitute ritual spaces in
which these same values are challenged (Cohen et
al. 1996, 2). Here I am casting Broadbent as a
forerunner to the women who participated in the
watershed 1968 protest of the Miss America
Pageant. Often cited as the beginning of feminism's second wave (and erroneously the infamous site of bra burning), the demonstrators
galvanized watching women by reinterpreting
beauty pageant contestants as pieces of meat.
Ironic for this equation, they carried posters of a
naked woman, on whose body were drawn lines
delineating various butcher cuts labeled "ribs,"
"chuck," "loin," "round," etc., and they crowned

a sheep as Miss America. The media reading of
this event attempted to turn the protesters into
monsters, as Susan Douglas summarizes:

> [I]t equated the women's movement with exhi-
> bitionism and narcissism, as if women who
> unstrapped their breasts were unleashing their
> sexuality in a way that was unseemly, laugh-
> able, and politically inconsequential, yet dan-
> gerous . . . the media, with a wink, hinted that
> these women's motives were not at all political
> but rather personal: to be trendy, to attract men.
> (1994, 160)

Operating on social margins, the tattooed
woman and the protester are both read as excessively sexual while the pageant contestants on
center stage operate within acceptable sexual parameters. At the same time, for the protesters it is
those in the beauty pageant who are excessively
sexualized. Not only does this paradox signal a
marked difference between the female and male
gaze, it fixes that difference through the bodies
that look back. The tattooed women who mark
themselves as alien, as freaks, cannot be contained by their fictive autobiographies of victimization. They look at their audience with a tacit
demand that it recognize itself as their other: pale,
quotidian, bland, normal. In the world of the
freak show, a challenging gaze may have reduced
the bravery of hecklers, but more importantly
such looks doubled the probable challenge experienced by audience members. For their part, the
pageant contestants are as willful as the media in
avoiding any possibility of alienation—their
looks are full of hope that they will be judged
worthy by their viewers.

The multiple determinations of these gazes
created a space for women to follow Broadbent's
lead in being both sexual subjects who welcome
certain gazes and at the same time challenge
them through marks that continue to have multiple readings. Still, little happened for tattooed
women in the years between Broadbent's
pageant participation and the wholehearted embrace of the freak in the countercultural praxis of
the 1970s. An excerpt from a 1967 article in the

soft-porn magazine, *Night and Day*, entitled "Tattooed Teasers: A Threat to American Womanhood" illustrates:

> Before you become too alarmed about this threat to American womanhood, we should point out that the blue scourge hasn't yet reached our hallowed shores in any significant strength. But the threat is definitely in the air. If we did it to our cars, we might easily do it to our women. (16)

Whatever this "threat" is, the writer clearly expects the reader to implicitly understand it. Perhaps the threat isn't clearly articulated because it isn't clearly understood. Tattooing, here, is something men do to women, akin to detailing their cars, an analogy the article opens on. It seems that the implied male audience potentially can control this threat, which threatens them by way of threatening "their" women. Encroaching from foreign origins, the danger is of national scope, an impurity on its way to conquer American women. Accompanying the article are several photos of tattoos lurking dangerously in the skin of smiling Australian women.

The real danger was that women might identify with the tattooed Aussies, a possibility largely dormant until identifying with otherness became an important political move, to "freak out" was the early call of 1960s social movements (Russo 1994, 75–7). Hundreds lined up for Janis Joplin's heart tattoo after her death, and countercultural identification focused on the "freak," a term popularized in the language of rock. The liner notes to Frank Zappa and the Mothers of Invention's first album *Freak Out!* (1966) capture the spirit:

> On a personal level, *Freaking Out* is a process whereby an individual casts off outmoded and restricting standards of thinking, dress and social etiquette in order to express CREATIVELY his [sic] relationship to his immediate environment and the social structure as a whole. . . . We would like everyone who HEARS this music to join us . . . become a member of *The United Mutations* . . . FREAK OUT!

By the 1970s freaks were everywhere, and particularly for women the call to mutation, to radical fundamental change, could be answered with a commitment-demonstrating tattoo. By militantly re-marking their bodies and embracing alternative bodily aesthetics, the spirit of carnival sideshows' tattooed women was revived and embellished.

From the 1970s into the 1990s, the obvious femininity of the most popular images—butterflies, flowers, and hearts—equated the feminine with the natural and seemed to annul the contestation of the tattoo. These two contradictory meanings of the possessed and liberated body functioned simultaneously, meaning that for some bodies the feminine was celebrated through these images (without, I might add, anyone perceiving a need to interrogate them). For others the omnipresent rose floated next to the man's name who "possessed" that woman's body. Twenty-plus years of "Property of . . ." tattoos mark an extended backlash to feminist possibilities, and continue to factor in the lives of gang women. While these tattoos signify membership and mark a sense of community, of "belonging," their larger purpose is to demand a sacrifice of autonomous subjectivity.

On stage this entanglement of intentions and bodily ownership plays out in the tattoo contest: a mutant progeny, one part beauty contest, one part freak show. There is little to no money in winning, but tattoo contests have flourished since their inception at tattoo conventions in the early-1970s. Conventions began as a place for tattooists to find some professional camaraderie, share information, and show off their work, but are now prime locations for tattoo aficionados to connect with artists. Today scores of conventions are held in the United States and around the world, with a hierarchy established following regional, national, and international lines. . . . These events are tattoo safe-havens where social rules governing bodies change, and an exhibitionist melancholy to share one's tattoo can be eased. People are free to stare; strangers touch each other as they admire tattoos, they tug clothing away; most wear little to begin with. On the contest stage, women and men display themselves in relative proportion to their presence at the convention (there are more men on stage because there are more men off stage), but their desire to do so manifests in radically different, clearly gendered ways.

At several of these conventions, I've watched two different kinds of competitions happening during tattoo contests. For male bodies the tattooist is represented, and the tattooed men on stage act as proud but often only grudgingly willing hosts. They shuffle on stage, eyes fixed on the floor, shoulders frequently hunched. For a female participant it is never clear whether the judges give more weight to her tattoo or her body, but it is clear that her body's desirability is part of the competition. High heels and swimsuits comprise the typical ensemble, but however they are clad, the women are not embarrassed to take the stage the way their male counterparts are. Acknowledging this disparity, Mifflin quotes veteran tattoo competitor Stephanie Farinelli about a loss at a prior competition, "I felt that I was not feminine-looking enough and scantily-clad enough to win. I got a wardrobe change, went on a diet, and won first place the following year" (1997, 162). At first it seems that these different kinds of exhibition are simple enactments of cultural expectations that associate voyeurism with men and exhibitionism with women. Farinelli altered her body in order to display herself to her best advantage within the codes she understood were important for her performance, those of the beauty pageant. The men, meanwhile, display their discomfort along with their bodies because this is their expected stance. As Kaja Silverman notes, the exhibitionism at the heart of men's spectator sports is a functional equivalent of the more thoroughly interrogated woman-as-spectacle, only with codes men have come to understand and embody (1994, 185).

Between the stage and the convention floor, the competition for ascendancy of bodily codes collapses. For both genders, tattoo conventions promise—and deliver—relief from the alienation they have written upon their bodies. However, the safe boundary space of the convention, which values tattoo above all, is disrupted by the act of staging bodies. Even here at this permeable limit of body aesthetics, women are expected to maintain their bodies within larger social codes of size and shape. The stage re-establishes the importance of these codes, as if a normalizing discourse were inherent in its geography.

By seeking to be judged, contestants straddle an undecided boundary, in part because this other space of the tattoo contest isn't other at all, but more of the same. A story like Farinelli's presents some possible insight into why women bother in terms of the monster who is afraid of frightening others. Farinelli's tattoo is a necklace of a stunningly colorful variety of thickly veined penises. Judges and audience members might interpret her tattoos as trophies or marks of castration fantasies. Farinelli does what she thinks is necessary to put her fellow tattoo enthusiasts at their ease through gestures that recuperate non-threatening female spectacle. Hers is an obvious example, but less overt tattoo imagery can be read as threatening, too. William Gibson articulates this threat in his description of a character and her tattoo in *Idoru* (1996):

> . . . Kathy Torrance. Palest of pale blonds. A pallor bordering on translucence, certain angles of light suggesting not blood but some fluid the shade of summer straw. On her left thigh the absolute indigo imprint of something twisted and multibarbed, an expensive savage pictoglyph. Visible each Friday when she made it her habit to wear shorts to work. . . . The tattoo looked like something from another planet, a sign or message burned in from the depths of space. (5–6)

A radical otherness from "the depths of space" displaces the otherness of Kathy's inner space. She is frightful, but because of some agent ultimately outside her, something written on her body *á la* Kafka, rather than by a paid artist and by her own choice. Coupled with this other-wordly reading is the juxtaposition of "expensive" while also "savage." Framed in this way, Kathy becomes the postmodern realization of a society woman's fad from 100 years ago, off-putting but inert. Such interpretations do not succeed in taking her bodily power away from her, however. Her tattoo still seems like a weapon, "twisted and multibarbed," forever at hand for an attack. The "depths of space" from which her tattoo has come may indeed be inner space, a sign burned outward, a warning glyph only recognized when her conservative clothes are shed. Casual Fridays can reveal so much more than skin.

Thus far, I have described tattooed women in a culturally familiar sense: scary, hyper-sexualized, freaky, threatening, excessive, and slippery to read, in other words monstrous. Exploring the machinations of the tattooed body as a cultural artifact begins to explain the transgressive opportunities women have found in tattoos: working class women at the turn-of-the-century defied the convention of quiet, pale beauty with colorful tattoos; tattooed women in carnivals used their tattoos as passkeys to travel; . . . hippies of the 1970s find peaceful militancy in tattooing. Despite this history of monster beauty, part of the tattoo's radical undecidability means that women assume a tremendous risk by refusing the cultural claim on their/our bodies to be decidedly not freaky. Limits placed on the value of difference not only mean "don't get a tattoo," but also drive women to starvation diets and cosmetic surgery. Women who get tattoos as a way to defy this proprietorship must face the other women still trapped by its spell.

To illustrate this point: for her 60th birthday, North Dakota lawyer Elaine Schieve had a small tattoo of a Nile River goddess tattooed on her right ankle. The figure is approximately two inches high; a female form holding a small sphere above her head, the whole image cast in swirls of light blue. Elaine is reluctant to philosophize about her choice of image, much less her choice to be tattooed, though she does note that it is bound up in the difficult transformation from "a head-turning beauty to another old lady" coupled with the "liberation of menopause." Contem-

plating her tattoo after one year, she remarked, "I like it every time I see it. But I know it could be used to label me as a flake and would be almost unanswerable." Recognizing that the risk of being interpreted in terms of a negative symbolic, as "a flake," could be professionally damaging, that the tattoo could be used as proof of some deficit of character, she nonetheless had it placed in a visible spot (1998).

Expecting a positive response, Elaine shared her tattoo with friends. Female friends, many of them professional women like herself who are all-too-well acquainted with the continuing struggles to be taken seriously by their male colleagues, asked first what her husband thought and went on to comment on what their husbands would think if they were to get a tattoo. They did not ask if it hurt (the most common first question), they did not ask if she was pleased (a common second question), nor did they ask how much it cost, how long it took, why she chose the image, or how she planned on negotiating the public space of her ankle in court or at depositions. In murder mysteries, the murderer is the one who doesn't ask how the crime was committed. In the mysteries of tattoo, the proprietorship of the body goes to the one whose approval is sought. By their questions, these women demonstrated that on some level they do not think that Elaine owns her body, nor do they seem to think that they own theirs. Theirs is a common response, though for Elaine, a woman-oriented woman who has been a life-long feminist and tries to surround herself with like-minded women, the reaction was shocking.

Discussing her similar experience, novelist Kathy Acker suggests that many women have reacted negatively to her tattoos because of the "bad girl" stigma: "[W]hat women have done is internalize this bad girl/good girl distinction, and out of fear say, 'I've got to be a good girl; I'm not going to be a bad girl.' So they're the ones who really get down on the bad girls" (1991, 179). This dichotomy returns us to the Butler/Dworkin to-perform-or-not-to-perform split. Policing the "bad" body is a familiar maneuver for women who have learned they can just barely contain the evidence of such indiscretions as aging, childbirth, and eating. Through creams, cosmetic surgery, and diets one may perform her, but there really is no good girl. Acker's detractors seem unaware that bodies have a world of things to say beyond whether one is good or bad.

It may be that women interested in tattooing will find inspiration in those artists, like Acker, who do "body art," Amelia Jones's catch-all term for performance and other forms of art that focus on the body (1998). Several women artists, novelists and painters, singers and sculptors, have gotten tattoos as part of their artistic experiments with the speaking body. Across the knuckles of one hand, singer Diamanda Galas has spelled out H-I-V-+, an homage to a brother who died of AIDS, and a political act demonstrating humanity's interconnected implications of HIV and AIDS, or as Galas says, we are all HIV positive (Galas 1991, 12). On performance artist Valie Export's left leg, a rendering of a garter belt clip acts as a "historical antique" reminding her of "obsolete" definitions of women (Export 1991, 193).

I have argued that the history of tattooed women as freaks provides a touchstone for many tattooed women in the West. The boundary position of the tattooed freak is a chosen one, a refusal to submit to the cultural inscriptions written on women's bodies. This act of transgression does not reverse the insidiousness of cultural inscriptions, however. Rather, by speaking one's bodily ownership, tattooed women risk further reinscription by the Others who are troubled by their tattoos. What tattooed women's bodies do, by writing back to the larger culture through their tattoos, is subvert proscribed physicality and broaden our sense of body aesthetics with monster beauty.

Note

1. See, for instance, Greer (1999); Zita (1998); and such anthologies as Conboy, Medina, and Stanbury (1997); and Price and Shildrick (1999).

2. Those following Butler include Grosz (1994 and 1995); Jones (1998); and within the frame of queer theory such work as Case, Bret, and Foster, eds. (1995). Those taking what I am calling the Dworkin tack include Bordo (1993 and 1997); Wolf (1991); and such recent work on cosmetic surgery as Haiken (1997); and Davis (1995).

3. The term "monstrification" was coined by John Ruskin in relation to architectural practices of marking the borders of buildings with gargoyles. Following Russo, I am expanding the concept to include bodies who alter themselves to thus mark the borders of culture. I move between the terms "monster" and "freak" in this essay with the understanding that "monster" was the preferred term during the seventeenth and eighteenth centuries until the dawn of teratology inaugurated the "freak." See Thomson (1996).

References

Acker, Kathy. 1991. "Interview by Andrea Juno and V. Vale." In *Angry Women*, eds. Andrea Juno and V. Vale, 177–85. San Francisco: Re/Search Publications.

Balsamo, Anne. 1996. *Technologies of the Gendered Body: Reading Cyborg Women.* Durham, NC: Duke University Press.

Bartky, Sandra Lee. 1990. *Femininity and Domination.* New York: Routledge.

Bell, Shannon. 1994. *Reading, Writing, and Rewriting the Prostitute Body.* Bloomington: Indiana University Press.

Bogdan, Robert. 1988. *Freak Show.* Chicago, IL: University of Chicago Press.

Bordo, Susan. 1993. *The Unbearable Weight: Feminism, Western Culture, and the Body.* New York: Routledge.

———. 1997. *Twilight Zones: The Hidden Life of Cultural Images from Plato to O.J.* Berkeley: University of California Press.

Butler, Judith. 1993. *Bodies that Matter.* New York: Routledge.

———. 1990. *Gender Trouble: Feminism and the Subversion of Identity.* New York: Routledge.

Case, Sue-Ellen, Philip Bret, and Susan Leigh Foster, eds. 1995. *Cruising the Performative: Interventions into the Representation of Ethnicity, Nationality, and Sexuality.* Bloomington: Indiana University Press.

Cohen, Colleen Ballerino, Richard Wilk, and Beverly Stoeltje, eds. 1996. *Beauty Queens on the Global Stage.* New York: Routledge.

Conboy, Katie, Nadia Medina, and Sarah Stanbury, eds. 1997. *Writing on the Body: Female Embodiment and Feminist Theory.* New York: Columbia University Press.

Davis, Kathy. 1995. *Reshaping the Female Body: The Dilemma of Plastic Surgery.* London: Routledge.

———. 1997. "'My Body is My Art': Cosmetic Surgery as Feminist Utopia?" In *Embodied Practices,* ed. Kathy Davis. London: Sage.

Douglas, Susan. 1994. *Where the Girls Are: Growing Up Female with the Mass Media.* New York: Times Books.

Dworkin, Andrea. 1974. *Woman Hating.* New York: Dutton.

———. 1991. *Pornography: Men Possessing Women.* New York: Dutton.

Export, Valie. 1991. Interview by Andrea Juno and V. Vale. In *Angry Women,* eds. Andrea Juno and V. Vale, 186–93. San Francisco: Re/Search Publications.

Freud, Sigmund. (1930) 1961. *Civilization and Its Discontents.* Ed. and trans. James Strachey. New York: Norton.

Frueh, Joanna. 1994. "The Erotic as Social Security." *Art Journal* 53(Spring):1: 66–72.

Galas, Diamanda. 1991. Interview by Andrea Juno and V. Vale. In *Angry Women,* eds. Andrea Juno and V. Vale, 6–22. San Francisco: Re/Search Publications.

Gibson, William. 1996. *Idoru.* New York: Berkley Books.

Greer, Germaine. 1999. *The Whole Woman.* New York: Knopf.

Grosz, Elizabeth. 1995. *Space, Time, and Perversion: Essays on the Politics of Bodies.* New York: Routledge.

———. 1994. *Volatile Bodies: Toward a Corporeal Feminism.* Bloomington: Indiana University Press.

Haiken, Elizabeth. 1997. *Venus Envy: A History of Cosmetic Surgery.* New York: Routledge.

Jones, Amelia. 1998. *Body Art: Performing the Subject.* Minneapolis: University of Minnesota Press.

Kolodny, Annette. 1984. *The Land Before Her: Fantasy and Experience of the American Frontiers, 1630–1860.* Chapel Hill: University of North Carolina Press.

Lombroso, Cesare, with William Ferrero. 1958. *Female Offender.* New York: Philosophical Library.

Mifflin, Margot. 1997. *Bodies of Subversion: A Secret History of Women and Tattoo.* New York: Juno Books.

"New Yorkers Adopt a Startling French Fad." 1897. *New York World,* 23 August, 36.

Parry, Albert. (1933) 1971. *Tattoo: Secrets of a Strange Art.* New York: Macmillan.

Price, Janet, and Margit Shildrick, eds. 1999. *Feminist Theory and the Body: A Reader.* New York: Routledge.

Russo, Mary. 1994. *The Female Grotesque: Risk, Excess, Modernity.* New York: Routledge.

Schieve, Elaine. 1998. Interviews by author. Lafayette, IN. February 1998.

Scutt, R.W.B., and Christopher Gotch. 1974. *Art, Sex, and Symbol: The Mystery of Tattooing.* New York: Cornwall Books.

Silverman, Kaja. 1994. "Fragments of a Fashionable Discourse." In *On Fashion,* eds. Shari Benstock and Suzanne Ferriss, 183–96. New Brunswick, NJ: Rutgers University Press.

Steward, Samuel. 1990. *Bad Boys and Tough Tattoos: A Social History of the Tattoo with Gangs, Sailors, and Street-Corner Punks 1950–1965.* New York: Harrington Park.

"Tattooed Teasers: A Threat to American Womanhood." 1976. *Night and Day* (February): 14–8.

Thomson, Rosemarie Garland. 1996. "From Wonder to Horror—A Genealogy of Freak Discourse in Modernity." In her *Freakery,* 1–19. New York: New York University Press.

Wolf, Naomi. 1991. *The Beauty Myth.* New York: Anchor Books.

Zappa, Frank. (1966) 1995. Liner notes to *Freak Out!.* Ryko.

Zita, Jacqueline. 1998. *Body Talk: Philosophical Reflections on Sex and Gender.* New York: Columbia University Press.

Lori Ann Dotson
Jennifer Stinson
LeeAnn Christian

"People Tell Me I Can't Have Sex": Women with Disabilities Share Their Personal Perspectives on Health Care, Sexuality, and Reproductive Rights

In the past decade, increasing attention has been given to women with developmental disabilities and their unique needs regarding sexuality (Williams & Nind, 1999). Historically, women with developmental disabilities have been an invisible group. They have been segregated in institutions and denied their identities as women, mothers, and sexual beings. While many positive changes have occurred, women with developmental disabilities still face conflicting stereotypes, which portray them as either asexual, childlike and dependent, or oversexed, undiscriminating and "easy" (Olney & Kuper, 1998; Tilley, 1998; Williams & Nind, 1999). These stereotypes are harmful because they lead either to the belief that a woman's sexual expression can be ignored or that it must be suppressed.

While many barriers continue to exist for the sexual expression of women with developmental disabilities, it is encouraging that they are being increasingly recognized and discussed. However, studies are most often presented from the perspectives of service providers, parents and advocates. First-hand accounts and opinions from

Source: "People Tell Me I Can't Have Sex: Women with Disabilities Share Their Personal Perspectives on Health Care." Lori Ann Dotson, Jennifer Stinson, and LeeAnn Christian, 2003. *Women and Therapy* 26(3/4):195–209. Used by permission of The Haworth Press.

women with developmental disabilities are largely absent from the literature. In an innovative study, British researcher McCarthy (1998) interviewed several women with developmental disabilities, asking questions about their feelings towards their bodies, health and reproduction and how much control they had over choices concerning their bodies. Her findings indicated that women had a lot to say about their experiences when given the opportunity. Many expressed dissatisfaction with their bodies, did not regard their bodies as a source of pleasure and felt they had little control over important choices in their lives, such as what type of contraception to use, if any. McCarthy's study (1998) demonstrated a need to set aside theories and assumptions and listen to the actual experiences of women with developmental disabilities.

Gynecological health care is an essential component of both general health maintenance and sexuality. Yet, gynecological exams can pose various problems for many women with developmental disabilities. Doctors might be unfamiliar with the cognitive needs of women with developmental disabilities and might not explain things in language that is easy to understand (Welner, 1997). They also might address questions and give information to accompanying parents or caregivers instead of speaking directly to their patients.

153

Doctors can be insensitive to the anxiety that many women feel when subjected to a Pap smear. This invasive procedure is anxiety producing for many women without disabilities. Women with developmental disabilities might experience heightened anxiety if they do not know what to expect, are not treated with respect and understanding by their doctors, or if they have histories of sexual abuse (Welner, 1997). Women with developmental disabilities face a much higher risk of sexual abuse than women without disabilities. It has been estimated that as many as 70% of women with developmental disabilities have experienced some form of sexual abuse in their lifetimes (Petersilia, 2000). Traumatic memories of abuse can be evoked during the gynecological exam causing many women to avoid the exam altogether, thus putting themselves at higher risk for undiagnosed health problems. As a result, some women with developmental disabilities experience so much anxiety that they require sedation in order to get a Pap smear. Unfortunately, this can be a costly procedure. It might be difficult for women to obtain adequate insurance coverage for health care services (Welner, 1997).

Breast exams are another important component of the complete gynecological exam. To aid in the early detection of cancerous lumps, women need to learn to do breast self-exams each month. As indicated by a lack of inclusion in the literature, many women with developmental disabilities do not receive adequate education about breast self-exams due to the same barriers that limit access to routine Pap smears. This procedure can be explained in language they do not understand or it might be overlooked with the assumption that they will not understand or lack the skills to learn or perform the monthly procedure.

Sex remains an uncomfortable topic to directly discuss in both disability and mainstream culture. Literature on this topic predominantly focuses on the attitudes of parents and support staff and how negative attitudes may contribute to poor supports for sexual expression. There also have been many studies on the high rate of sexual abuse for women with developmental disabilities

and the difficulty of detecting and reporting abuse (Olney & Kuper, 1998; Petersilia, 2000; Schaller & Feiberg, 2000). Studies of this nature are invaluable in examining shortcomings and seeking solutions for better service provision. However, it is unclear how women with developmental disabilities perceive these problems.

Furthermore, homosexuality, and sexual acts such as anal intercourse and oral sex are often ignored or mentioned only superficially in the literature (Williams & Nind, 1999). Studies of the attitudes of service providers indicate that these activities continue to be met with discomfort or disapproval from support staff (Scotti, Slack, Bowman, & Morris, 1996; Wolfe, 1997). Masturbation is another topic that may elicit negative responses from staff and parents or even be defined as a "problem behavior." Yet, it is likely that many women experience confusion and frustration related to orgasmic difficulty and would benefit from education and masturbation training. Ultimately, it remains unknown whether women with developmental disabilities feel limited in their means of sexual expression or whether they are even aware of a range of human sexual behaviors.

Women with developmental disabilities are commonly regarded as dependent, incapable of raising children and incapable of making appropriate choices regarding reproduction (Waxman, 1994). Thousands of women were involuntarily sterilized during the Eugenics Movements of the late nineteenth and early twentieth centuries in an effort to quell their sexuality and prevent the passing of "disabled" genes to offspring (Kempton & Kahn, 1991; Olney & Kuper, 1998; Wolfe & Blanchett, 2000). While involuntary sterilization is no longer legal, surgical sterilization is still presented as a viable option to minors and adult women with developmental disabilities and is legally performed on consenting patients (Nelson et al., 1999).

It has been suggested that contraceptive agents, such as birth control pills and Depo-Provera injections, are routinely dispensed with little or no explanation given to the women using them (McCarthy, 1998; Waxman, 1994). As with other issues of gynecological care, doctors might not use clear language to describe why and how contraceptives are used, what side effects to expect or present options for alternative forms of contraception. Parents and caregivers also can fail to provide adequate education regarding birth control. Thus, women with developmental disabilities might lack important information about using contraception and can even be unaware that they are using it (McCarthy, 1998; Waxman, 1994). This serves to perpetuate a lack of control over reproductive choices just as forced sterilization did in the past. Women also might be at higher risk of contracting sexually transmitted diseases if they do not receive education about specific forms of birth control, such as condoms, which prevent the transmission of bodily fluids (Welner, 1997). Furthermore, studies indicate that women who are unable to have children because of sterilization or birth control use might be at higher risk for sexual abuse if perpetrators know their actions will not be detected through pregnancy (McCarthy, 1998).

What do women with developmental disabilities think about having children? What are the ramifications of being denied this option? The present study was designed to assess women's level of knowledge, their access to resources and their feelings of control over choices concerning their bodies. Additionally, this study sought to examine the impact that disability has on sexuality from the women who experience it. It is imperative that we begin listening to the voices of women with developmental disabilities, not only to witness their experiences, but to begin meeting their needs.

Method

Participants

Eight women with developmental disabilities served as participants in this study. Their average age was 35 years old with a range of 32 to 40 years old. Seven of the participants were European American, and one participant was Latina.

Few participants received psychotropic medications for challenging behaviors such as aggression, self-injurious behavior, and property destruction, but half (50%) received psychotropic medications for mental health problems. All participants received supported living, supported employment or behavior management day services from a human services agency in California.

Instruments

A Health and Sexuality Interview was developed to determine the women's knowledge and perceptions about their gynecological care, sexual activity, and reproductive decisions. The 103-item interview contained "yes/no" questions (e.g., "Do you know what a gynecologist is?"), as well as open-ended questions (e.g., "What does it mean to you when I say that someone is sexually active?"). Additionally, the interview contained several short statements such as, "My gynecologist talks to my staff person or parent during my exam" and "My gynecologist explains what is going to happen in ways that I can understand," that were endorsed as either "never true," "sometimes true," or "always true" by the respondent. Demographic information, such as age and services received, was collected during the interview and was verified through a review of case records. Ethnicity, diagnoses, and medication regimes were gathered from the records review. To the extent possible, other information gathered during the interview process also was verified through records review and/or support staff interview (e.g., doctor's name, last appointment, who made the appointments). The instrument was developed from a variety of sources (Matikka & Vesala, 1997; McCarthy, 1996, 1998; Welner, 1997; Williams & Nind, 2000) and is available from the first author. . . .

Results and Discussion

The results of the health care portion of the interview indicated that only three of the eight participants had been to the gynecologist in the previous year. One woman said she had never been, and four women said they had gone a long time ago. Additionally, the participants' staff could not provide the dates of their last exams, further indicating that reproductive health is a low priority for caregivers. Of those women who had been to the gynecologist, all indicated their doctors were friendly, but most reported that their doctors sometimes explained things in ways they couldn't understand. Only one woman had been both told about and instructed on conducting breast self-exams. She indicated, however, that she didn't really understand how to give herself a breast exam, and thus, did not do it regularly. One woman reported that she didn't know whom she could talk to if she had a problem or question about her body or her health.

In the portion of the interview designed to elicit responses about sex, many of the participants gave incomplete or incorrect answers to the question, "What does it mean to you when I say someone is sexually active." Responses included "interested in sex," "bad," "sick," "have sex every day with different partners," and "kissing." One participant reported that she didn't know the answer, and another requested that the question be skipped. Five of the women reported that they had had sex, or were currently sexually active. The participants learned about sex from a variety of places, including family members, school, and support staff. However, one participant reported that "nobody" has taught her about sex. Seven of the eight participants positively endorsed the statement "I have sexual feelings toward men." However, all of the women responded "never true" to questions about having sex with women or wanting to have sex with women, despite collateral information to the contrary. While most participants indicated that they had varying levels of control regarding their sexuality and reproductive health decisions, one participant indicated that she did not have control over the choice of whether or not to have sex. She reported that staff controlled these decisions. Four women said they knew how to make themselves feel good by masturbating, although one expressed extreme shame about this topic. Two women indicated

that they did not know how to make themselves feel good by masturbating. One woman said she had never masturbated and one passed on the question.

In regards to contraception and birth control, only one woman had never heard of birth control, and six of the women report they are currently using or have used contraception in the past. Six of the eight participants could describe what a sexually transmitted disease was and give examples. Half of the participants were unsure about whether or not they could become pregnant. Seven women reported that they had not been pregnant in the past, and one woman was unsure. Half of the participants reported that they'd like to become mothers someday.

What follows are the stories of the eight women we interviewed. To help understand or clarify some of their responses to the interview questions, collateral information from their support staff also is included. The women's names have been changed to protect their privacy.

Sara is a 35-year-old European American woman diagnosed with mild mental retardation and depressive disorder. As a woman who had lived and worked in a variety of places throughout her life, Sara was often perceived as "streetwise" and capable of advocating for herself within the social service system that provided her support. As reported by her support staff, Sara regularly voiced how important it was to her to be in control of her life at all times. She was known as an open person who frequently shared her sexual experiences with her closest support staff as a way of expressing that she did indeed have control of her life and could make her own choices. As such, it was not surprising to learn that Sara made her own doctor's appointments, went to the doctor without the support of a paid staff, and was knowledgeable about the purpose of Pap smears and clinical breast exams as well as about sexually transmitted diseases, birth control, and contraception. In fact, she astutely reported that she had to get Pap smears twice a year because her pap smears results frequently had been abnormal in the past. Not surprisingly, a repeated theme throughout Sara's interview was control. For example, when asked whether she felt that she had control over whether or not she had sex or used birth control or contraception, Sara emphatically insisted, "No one can control me. I don't like it." However, Sara's responses to questions regarding same-sex relationships were surprising based on her usual candidness. When asked whether she had sexual feelings towards women, had ever had sex with women, or was interested in having sex with women, she became agitated and said, "I'm not gay!" Outside the interview situation, Sara openly talked about the sexual relationship she and her female roommate shared as well as the relationship she had with her current boyfriend. Her later concern for who would have access to the answers she had given during the interview might explain her unwillingness to truthfully share her sexual experiences. Moreover, it seemed that Sara was adamantly denying a possible attraction to women because she had been told it was not appropriate or acceptable behavior. When asked about reproductive issues, Sara explained that she did not currently use birth control nor did she use barrier methods to prevent sexually transmitted diseases because her boyfriend was "fixed." It was interesting that she so faithfully got Pap smears twice a year and was knowledgeable about STDs, yet so naïve about the potential risks she was exposing herself to in this area. The most poignant moment of the interview came during a discussion of childbearing. When asked whether she thought her disability affected her sexuality, she icily replied, "No," but when asked if she might like to have a child one day, she quickly said, "No, because of my mental illness."

Mary is a 32-year-old European American woman diagnosed with moderate mental retardation, cerebral palsy, and a seizure disorder. The impression one got during Mary's interview was that she was embarrassed by and yet intrigued with the interview questions. She visibly struggled with embarrassment at the directness of some of the questions, but seemed to want to answer them. Perhaps after a lifetime of constant

supervision by paid staff or family members, Mary finally saw an opportunity to share her feelings about an area that was not often openly discussed. With regard to her health care, Mary was unable to name the doctor who did her gynecological exams and reported that her caregiver made her doctor's appointments. Mary said her doctor was more likely to talk to her caregiver during her gynecological exam than directly to her. She also said her doctor sometimes used words that she didn't understand. Considering the sheltered life Mary has led in her family's home and then in a group home providing 24-hour support, Mary's lack of sexual activity was predictable. She said she had never been sexually active nor had anyone ever taught her about sex. Interestingly, Mary reported that she never had sexual feelings towards men or women, and was not interested in having sex with men nor women, but answered "So-so" when asked if she was satisfied with her level of sexual activity. She did report that she was always able to make herself feel good sexually by masturbating. Notably, when asked who did or would have control over the choice of whether or not she had sex, Mary said her boyfriend would control those choices. (One wonders where this perception comes from for a woman who has never had a sexual relationship.) Mary's lack of sexual experiences did not seem to thwart her knowledge about birth control or sexually transmitted diseases. Although her knowledge was not sophisticated, she at minimum knew that women took birth control pills so they wouldn't have a baby and that AIDS was a sexually transmitted disease. As anticipated based on her other answers, Mary had never used birth control or contraception. Mary did not know whether she was physically able to become pregnant, but her caregiver reported that she was able. When asked whether she thought her disability affected her sexuality, Mary seemed surprised and disturbed by this question and adamantly answered, "No." Poignantly, when asked if she would like to have children some day, she first said no, but under her breath said, "In my dreams." When asked what she meant by that, she said she actually would like having children, but that it was just a dream because people told her she never could.

Martha is a 33-year-old Latina woman diagnosed with mild mental retardation. She receives round the clock supportive employment and living services. Martha reported that she has a gynecologist, but is unsure when she last saw him. Her staff confirmed that it had been over a year since her last check-up, but could not provide a date. Martha reported that her gynecologist sometimes asks about her health and her body, and sometimes explains things in language she understands. She reported that she had never been informed about how to conduct a breast self exam (BSE), and was unaware of reasons for conducting a BSE, or for going to the gynecologist more than once a year. She defined being sexually active as being "bad" and "sick." When asked if she was happy about her level of sexual activity, Martha indicated that she was happy she didn't do "that thing." This theme continued throughout her interview, indicating that using birth control is "bad—not good." Further, she reported that she does not masturbate. Martha has a boyfriend, who is also developmentally disabled, and who receives twenty-four hour daily supportive services. Martha did not mention her boyfriend during the interview.

Crystal is a 39-year-old European American woman diagnosed with mild mental retardation, schizophrenia, and anxiety disorder. She receives in-home supporting living services a few hours a day. She is currently employed. Crystal identified her gynecologist by name, and reported that she is responsible for making appointments with her doctor. She reported that her doctor sometimes speaks in language she doesn't understand. She identified pregnancy as a reason that a woman should go to a gynecologist more than once a year. Crystal reported that she might have been pregnant in the past but was unsure, and stated that the doctor told her she "might have been because of having sex." Her support staff reported that Crystal last visited her gynecologist one and a half years ago for abnormal periods and be-

cause she was lactating. Crystal identified sexually active as meaning "hav[ing] sex with another person." Further, she identified herself as sexually active, and reported that she currently has one male sexual partner. Crystal is taking birth control pills and reported that she feels that she is in control of whether or not she takes them. However, she reported that she felt her doctor controlled what type of birth control she takes, and reported that she had not been informed about the potential risks and or side effects of the birth control pills she is taking. She reported that she has not used contraception to protect her from sexually transmitted diseases (STD). Crystal identified two sexually transmitted diseases when asked to list the ones she'd heard of. She did not, however, identify herpes, a sexually transmitted disease for which she is currently being treated.

Susie is a 40-year-old European American woman diagnosed with mild mental retardation and depression. She is currently employed, and receives minimal supportive living and supportive employment services, for a total of four hours of supportive services daily. Additionally, Susie sees a psychologist every other week to address her symptoms of depression. She identified her gynecologist by name, and reported that her last exam was eight months ago. She reported that her gynecologist is friendly, but doesn't always explain things in a language that she can understand, and reports that he doesn't notice if she's uncomfortable. Susie reported that she's been sexually active in the past, but is "waiting" to have sex with her current boyfriend. When asked if she felt her disability affected her sex life, she reported that she has never had an orgasm with a man, and expressed that she felt that men are "not patient." She reported that she knows how to make herself feel good sexually by masturbating but expressed a lot of concern about views other people have about masturbating. She reported that she had attended a class which included sex education information, and felt that she could utilize her staff, doctor or psychologist if she needed more information. Susie reported that her mother decided when she was nineteen or twenty that her tubes should be tied. Susie skipped the question which inquired about her desire to have a child. She reported that it's a "hard responsibility to have a kid."

Carol is a 38-year-old European American woman diagnosed with mild mental retardation, a seizure disorder, and hemiplegia. She is currently employed and receives supportive employment services ten hours a week, and supportive living services forty-two hours a week. She reported that her mother has a gynecologist but was unsure of whether or not she had one. She reported that she had never had a Pap smear, and that she "gathers it's painful." Reporting further, "[I] can't tolerate pain—[they] stick all that crap up inside you." Carol was unaware if she is at risk for breast cancer, had difficulty identifying any special risks for women in regard to their reproductive health. She reported that she had never been sexually active, and was happy about her current level of sexual activity "because you don't know where it's [sexual activity] going to lead." Carol requested to pass on the question regarding whether or not she knew how to please herself sexually by masturbating. Carol reported that she cannot have children because of "all the medication taken over the years." When asked if she desired having a child, she responded simply, "I can't for medical reasons." When asked if her disability affects her sex life, Carol indicated that her disability "slows me down in a lot of ways."

Jill is a 34-year-old European American woman with a diagnosis of mild mental retardation. She is currently employed and receives supportive living services 12 hours a week, and supportive employment services 14 hours a week. She identified her gynecologist by name, but could not remember when she last had a gynecological visit. She had difficulty identifying the reasons for gynecological check-ups and reported that she had neither been told nor instructed about how to do a breast self-exam. She reported that she had had one sexual partner in the last year. She reported that her mother introduced the concept of birth control to her, and described contraception as a way to "help protect to not have

any kids." She reported that a side effect to taking contraception is that one "feel[s] sad—when you miss a pill you have to go through everything." Jill reported that she had never been pregnant and doesn't want to become a parent. She reported that she was unaware of whether of not she could get pregnant. However, she was aware of the status of her boyfriend, and indicated that he was sterile.

Rhonda is a 33-year-old European American woman diagnosed with Asperger's syndrome, and severe/recurrent major depressive disorder. She is employed and receives supportive living services nine hours a week, and supportive employment services twenty hours a week. Rhonda identified her gynecologist by name, and reported that she makes her own appointments. Rhonda's last visit was one month prior to the interview. When asked why she goes to the gynecologist she replied, "I go to the gynecologist once a year. I have to make sure I don't have anything wrong with my reproductive system." She reported that her gynecologist always uses words that she understands, and that he explains things to her. She reported that if a woman has an abnormal Pap smear, or a yeast infection, she may need to go to the gynecologist more than once a year. She reported that she had been told about breast self-exams but never taught to perform one. She reports that she got information from other sources and learned how to do breast exams on her own. It is particularly disappointing that Rhoda was not taught this skill by her gynecologist since she is very interested in her physical health and has a history of good follow-through regarding health-related behaviors. Rhonda reported that she is happy with her level of sexual activity and reported "I feel like I'm in control of my life." She identified several sexually transmitted diseases and was informed about how they're transmitted. She included herpes, a sexually transmitted disease for which she is being treated. Rhonda reported that she previously took birth control pills, and identified several side effects that resulted. She reported that she feels comfortable asking her staff and her doctor about contraception and reproduction issues. She also indicated that she utilizes the Internet for health related information. Rhonda reported that she'd like to have a child someday "but not now." She reported that she can get pregnant because she doesn't have her "tubes tied off." She reported "I vowed never to have them tied off."

Conclusions

In response to the invaluable personal information each woman in this study provided, we felt a strong need to make a relevant, reciprocal gesture. Thus, all participants were offered the chance to participate in a "Special Touch" Breast Self-Exam (BSE) Class sponsored by the Community Education Center of a local hospital. Two of the participants from this study were able to attend the class. Two of the woman declined to participate in the BSE class, and the remaining four women expressed interest in attending, but could not due to scheduling conflicts. An instructor that often volunteered at the Community Education Center taught the class. She was trained as a Special Touch BSE Instructor by the American Cancer Society. The instructor adapted the class for the women in the following ways: (1) the class time was lengthened from 1.5 hr to 2 hr; (2) information provided through lecture was minimized; (3) one-to-one instructor attention was maximized by a limited class size and (4) time spent in practicing with a breast model was increased.

Classes such as this one are a good first step in addressing the health needs of women with developmental disabilities. Additionally, same-sex and co-ed psycho-educational groups on other health, reproduction, and sexuality related topics would likely benefit women with developmental disabilities. Topics could include: friendship, intimacy, masturbation, non-conventional and safe-sex practices, co-habitation, sexual side-effects to medications, sexual exploitation, as well as social and protective skills and assertiveness training. Support staff and family members would also likely benefit from the availability of social support groups. Additionally, women with develop-

mental disabilities should be included in the development and oversight of all programs and policies that impact their lives.

The lack of similar research in this area necessitates much trial and error in conducting this type of study. In hindsight, this interview included some language and formatting that was difficult for the participants to understand. For instance, asking participants to respond "never true," "sometimes true," or "always true" to negatively worded statements (e.g., "my gynecologist does not notice if I am uncomfortable") was universally problematic. This indicates a need to refine this interview tool for future use. An additional limitation was that the present research design excludes woman with lower cognitive abilities and verbal skills. Women with more severe disabilities are routinely absent from sexuality research studies due to a lack of appropriate tools and research designs. Unfortunately, these might be the women whose needs and experiences are least understood and most requiring of attention through research. It is imperative that future studies make efforts to include women with more severe disabilities. This might include utilizing sign language, photos, role-plays, naturalistic observation or possibly developing interactive computer programs as communication devices.

The invisibility of the special needs of women with developmental disabilities in research about sexuality is almost as insidious as the invisibility of people with developmental disabilities in other areas of research, as well as their general lack of representation in main-stream culture. Although we are aware that our inclusion of collateral information can be viewed as paternalistic, we have included it in the hopes that it may enrich others' awareness that women with disabilities, like those without, must make difficult decisions about self-disclosure, based on experienced and perceived biases. It is our hope that research such as this can begin to remove barriers to sexual expression, and challenge biases as they relate to gender, disability and sexuality. Further, this study aims to extend a budding dialogue regarding the importance of first person narratives, especially as it relates to the stories of people who have been previously denied a voice.

References

Kempton, W., & Kahn, E. (1991). Sexuality and people with intellectual disabilities: A historical perspective. *Sexuality and Disability, 9*, 93–111.

Matikka, L. M. & Vesala, H. T. (1997). Acquiescence in quality-of-life interviews with adults who have mental retardation. *Mental Retardation, 35* (2), 75–82.

McCarthy, M. (1996). The sexual support needs of people with learning disabilities: A profile of those referred for sex education. *Sexuality and Disability, 14* (4), 165–278.

McCarthy, M. (1998). Whose body is it anyway? Pressures and control for women with learning disabilities. *Disability & Society, 13*, 557–569.

Nelson, R. M., Botkin, J. R., Levetown, M., Moseley, K. L., Truman, J. T., & Wilfond, B. S. (1999). Sterilization of minors with developmental disabilities. *Pediatrics, 104*, 337–340.

Olney, M. F., & Kuper, E. V. (1998). The situation of women with developmental disabilities: Implications for practitioners in supported employment. *Journal of Applied Rehabilitation Counseling, 29*, 3–11.

Petersilia, J. (2000). Invisible victims. *Human Rights, 27*, 9–12.

Schaller, J. & Fieberg, J. (2000). Issues of abuse for women with disabilities and implications for rehabilitation counseling. *Journal of Applied Rehabilitation Counseling, 29* (2), 9–19.

Scotti, J. R., Slack, B. S., Bowman, R. A., & Morris, T. L. (1996). College student attitudes concerning the sexuality of persons with mental retardation: Development of perceptions of sexuality scale. *Sexuality and Disability, 14* (4), 249–263.

Tilley, C. M. (1998). Health care for women with developmental disabilities: Literature review and theory. *Sexuality and Disability, 16* (2), 87–102.

Waxman, B. F. (1994). Up against eugenics: Disabled women's challenge to receive reproductive health services. *Sexuality and Disability, 12* (2), 155–170.

Welner, S. L. (1997). Gynecologic care and sexuality issues for women with disabilities. *Sexuality and Disability, 15* (1), 33–40.

Williams, L., & Nind, M. (1999). Insiders or outsiders: Normalisation and women with learning difficulties. *Disability & Society, 14*, 659–668.

Wolfe, P. S. (1997). The influence of personal values on issues of sexuality and disability. *Sexuality and Disability, 15*, 69–90.

Wolfe, P. S., & Blanchett, W. J. (2000). Moving beyond denial, suppression and fear to embracing the sexuality of people with disabilities. *TASH Newsletter, 26(5)*, 5–7.

April Herndon

Disparate But Disabled:
Fat Embodiment and Disability Studies

This paper explores questions of fat embodiment and how tensions between and among biologically based descriptions of fatness and disability feature in the lives of women. In tracing the medicalization of fatness and disability and exploring important shared experiences of fat women and disabled people, this paper dislodges both fatness and disability from biological moorings and examines them within cultural and political contexts. In particular, the experiences of oppression and pathology are analyzed to expose the commonalities between what might initially appear to be disparate groups. By illustrating why medicalized rubrics cannot usefully account for the stigma associated with fat and/or disabled embodiments, this paper seeks to set the stage for a feminist disability studies that recognizes disability as a diverse social category and meaningfully incorporates fat embodiments.

At a recent conference on race, a prominent but controversial white male academic presented a paper on buckshot skull studies, noting comparisons between Caucasian and African skulls. Well-known for his race/ist scholarship, this scholar concluded that such studies represent facts that cannot be ignored, implying that racism, at least on some levels, can be biologically and scientifically justified. During the discussion of his paper, I posed a question about feminist standpoint epistemology, his obvious belief in science as purely objective, and his recalcitrance to situate himself, as a white male, within the context of his own study and scientific epistemology. After replying with the tiresome argument that only scientists can criticize science and stating that feminist standpoint epistemologists needed

to build a rocket that made it to the moon before he would take their criticisms seriously, he continued to argue for pure objectivity, stating he could "show me studies that empirically prove women's hips are wider than men's."

Unpacking his choice of example exposes the liability I faced as a woman of size in a culture that values thinness. First, his example reminded me of my body size (while I was standing in the front of a crowded room) lest I forget that I am a large woman violating the ideal figure of womanhood. While I often out myself as a fat woman, the politics of this situation certainly erased my ability to define myself and articulate my own identity in meaningful ways.[1]

Second, this scholar's comment drew attention to the fact that I am a large **woman** and have sinned not once but twice. Thus, he hailed me on two different but conjoined levels of subjectivity. His emphasis on gender distinctions and his marking of me as both a woman and as fat with large hips served to elicit shame on two levels. First, I should be ashamed because a powerful,

Source: Herndon, April. "Disparate But Disabled: Fat Embodiment and Disability Studies." *National Women's Studies Association Journal* 14:3 (2002), 120–130, 132–137. © NWSA Journal. Reprinted with permission of The John Hopkins University Press.

older, academic male marked me as an undesirable woman by gesturing to the breadth of my hips, assuming I would be invested in what he as an established male academic thought of my hips (or perhaps all women's hips). In this sense, his comment reflects both patriarchal power and heteronormativity. Finally, pointing out body size publicly can injure the psyche enough to impose silence. The cultural script reads that once called out on being fat, a woman re-assumes her proper place and remains quiet.

Perhaps the final observation to be gleaned from such condescension and marginalization is an obvious inability to understand the complex relationship between empirically proven data, the influence of questions on resulting data, and the relevance accorded data. Yes, it might be true that women's hips, on average, are larger than men's. This observation alone, however, is not particularly problematic. The problem is that the questions posed about fatness, within both medical and socio-cultural realms, indicate a profound bias. Like inquiries launched to find the causes of homosexuality, the search for medical and/or psychological origins of fatness reveals the place of fatness, fat embodiment, and fat people within current epistemological rubrics. The issue is how this information is used to support social decisions; in the case of the aforementioned scholar, it can be argued that his deployment of the empirical fact of the size of women's hips publicly pathologized and discredited a fat woman.

Physically discernible "imperfections" such as fatness manifest as further evidence of women's pathologies. Particularly unfortunate is the evocation and acceptance of these pathologies without investigation of political commitments spurning such studies onward. Initiating inquiries from the lives of fat women raises hosts of questions about how it is that fatness features in the lives of women and whether or not fatness is best understood within the context of disability studies. What consequences emerge when women, already facing sexual discrimination, are also large? How do discussions about socially and/or physically disabled bodies both echo and expand

feminism's long battle over natural and socially-constructed bodies? Can examining the contours of fat embodiment and medical models of fatness help us better understand how we can usefully frame such inquiries? How does gender feature in these struggles and why might examining the specific construction of the female body in conjunction with disability be particularly revealing? This paper will explore these questions and others by mapping the terrain of feminism, disability studies, and fatness alongside mainstream medical paradigms most often used to describe fatness. By exposing and illustrating why these medical rubrics cannot usefully account for the stigma associated with fat embodiment, this paper seeks to set the stage for political commitments that recognize disability as a diverse social category that can meaningfully incorporate fat embodiments.

Why Disability Studies?

Within the language of the *Americans with Disabilities Act of 1990 (ADA)*, an impairment is defined as "[any] physiological disorder, condition, cosmetic disfigurement, or anatomical loss affecting one or more of the following systems: neurological, musculoskeletal, special sense organs, respiratory (including speech organs), cardiovascular, reproductive, digestive, genito-urinary, hemic and lymphatic, skin and endocrine" (Solovay 2000, 135). Following disability scholars such as Simi Linton and Susan Wendell, I aim to dislodge disability from its origins in impairments and medicalized physical conditions. This is not to suggest that physical impairments are unimportant; certainly there is physical suffering endured by many. Rather I am interested in how such impairments feature in people's lives and divulge cultural values about bodies and normativity.

Similarly, Wendell encourages readers to defamiliarize the most common notions about disability by looking for social and environmental factors. She writes:

> One of the most crucial factors in the deconstruction of disability is the change of perspective

that causes us to look in the environment for the source of the problem and the solutions. It is perhaps easiest to change perspective by thinking about how people who have some bodily difference that does not impair any of their physical functions, such as being unusually large, are disabled by the built environment—by seats that are too small . . . doors and aisles that are too narrow . . . the unavailability or expense of clothing that fits. (1996, 46)

Examining the terrain of disability from the perspective that problems inhere, not within particular individuals, but rather within social contexts, social expectations, and built environments allows us to map disability as a socially-constructed phenomenon rather than a physical trait.

For both Wendell and Linton, disability studies must move beyond the study of physical impairments and toward a study of group politics. In other words, the distinction between impairments and disabilities must be understood as both theoretically and epistemologically important. In Linton's germinal text *Claiming Disability* (1998), she maintains the distinction between impairment and disability in order to articulate and theorize differentiations between medical and cultural, individual and group. Thus, she characterizes impairments as related more closely to medicalized individuals while disability refers to disabled people as a culturally recognized and defined group. Linton argues that "we should . . . utilize the term *disability studies* solely for investigations of disability as a social, cultural, and political phenomenon" (149). Thus, while understanding that there are fat people who suffer impairments due to size, I choose to focus on disability studies in terms of Linton's use of the concept. While physical impairments surely cause personal struggles, the treatment of fat/disabled people as social pariahs must be addressed first and foremost. The reliance upon biological truths about bodies, as I will discuss and argue more intensely later in the paper, serves only to further pathologize individuals. I will use feminist theory and disability studies to criticize cul-

turally embedded values about fat people as a group.

Resistance to seeing fatness as a disability and fat people as a politicized group situates itself within medical epistemological frameworks that focus mostly on the biology of individuals. In a striking comparison between the politics of the supposed biological categories of race and disability, Wendell states that "the belief that 'the disabled' is a biological category is like the belief that 'Black' is a biological category in that it masks the social functions and injustices that underlie the assignment of people to these groups" (1996, 24). Echoing the problems with individualization and medicalization, Sondra Solovay writes that the battle between those who choose to see weight as a disability and those who discredit any attempt to do so stems from the belief that weight constitutes a problem with an impaired individual (2000, 135). For weight in particular, dominant definitions of impairment and disability are entangled in cultural debates about medicalization, group and individual autonomy, cultural decisions and consequences of pathologizing certain bodies, demanding corrective action on the part of individual people rather than collective social action.

Yet another resistance to thinking of fatness as a disability is the fact that fatness is not specifically named in the *ADA*. If we stop to consider the numerous policies written to protect one group then later extended to others, it becomes painfully obvious that there is inherent *fatphobia* in the very decision to deny weight explicitly. Sexual harassment policies, for example, were originally aimed at protecting women from unwanted sexual attention and harassment proffered by men. However, recent cases have, rightfully, moved beyond the original purpose and dated language of such policies to protect men who are sexually harassed by same sex colleagues. Thus, interpretations of sexual harassment policies acknowledge dynamic cultural shifts. Similarly, those interpreting the *ADA* and state legislation passed for similar purposes have also remained open to considering newly proposed forms of disability. When members of the medical community began to cite scientific studies suggesting that alcoholism was a disease, in the sense that those suffering from it shared similar physical traits and characteristics, courts adopted similar views. As a result, alcoholism, although not explicitly named under the *ADA* as a disabling condition, is often legally recognized as a disability. Thus, courts clearly do engage in considering shifting paradigms of disability—but often not where fatness is concerned. There is far more at stake in locking out obese individuals than merely being true to the original nomenclature or intention of anti-discrimination legislation; closing the door on disability claims is far more about the pervasive and perverse *fatphobia* of our culture.

The frequent dismissal of fatness as a disability lodges itself in an intense cultural fear of frivolous *ADA* claims and what it might mean to accommodate larger bodies. *The Simpsons*, a television sitcom, provided a classic episode that exemplifies this fear. Entitled "King Size Homer," the episode consisted of Homer, one of the lead characters, getting another wacky idea to escape work; he decided to purposefully gain enough weight so he would be able to work at home. His goal weight, which he eventually exceeded, was 316 pounds. To surpass this weight, Homer stuffed his face with hamburgers, ice cream, and in the end, Play-Doh. At his desired weight, Homer was depicted as a muumuu-wearing fat man who loafed all day and changed television channels with a broomstick (1995). Recounting familiar narratives of fatness as a voluntary condition resulting from poor eating habits and sedentary lifestyle and of disabled people as dangerous to the American purse because accommodation must be suffered by the public writ large, the episode stripped the issues down to elemental fears of Otherness. "King Size Homer" underscored the role of volition in dominant understandings of both fatness and disability.

Sadly, the fear of frivolous claims is not restricted to media satire or speculation. The most serious consequences of the panic generated by disability claims are "negative decisions . . .

based on unfounded fears" (Solovay 2000, 36). The Department of Justice itself is also concerned, and attempting to allay the public's fears. On the *ADA* website, the section entitled "Myths and Facts About the *Americans with Disabilities Act*" addresses questions concerning weight and the *ADA*, facts and myths about the frivolity of *ADA* cases, and abuse of legislation by those with "emotional problems" (1990). In essence, the facts and myths included on the site address people's fears about the government being bamboozled into providing accommodations for those who are undeserving, such as fat people who are "eating up" more than their share of funds. Discussions of weight and disability seem perpetually freighted with issues of choice and frivolity.

Medical Constructions of Fatness

In addition to fears of frivolous claims, many people fear that accepting fatness as a disability, and thus as a protected category under the *ADA*, condones fatness at a time when obesity is considered a public health crisis of epidemic proportions. The medicalization presents fatness as a disease epidemic and strips away humanity, focusing solely on a medical condition, and ignoring the people involved. While a majority of people in the United States believe that fat is unhealthy, immoral, and often downright disgusting, medical opinions on weight are actually quite mixed. Even well-respected members of the medical community are beginning to understand that such assertions display a woefully fatphobic and misguided understanding of obesity that damages fat people in very tangible ways.

For example, 1 January 1998, Dr. Jerome Kassirer and Dr. Marcia Angell published an editorial in *The New England Journal of Medicine* that succinctly stated the reasons why any New Year's resolution to lose weight was doomed. Citing the well-known fact that 95 percent of diets fail, Kassirer and Angell ask that the medical community stop pushing for weight loss. In addressing the issue of "health" so often used to justify fatphobia, they write: "Given the enormous social pressure to lose weight, one might suppose there is clear and overwhelming evidence of the risks of obesity and the benefits of weight loss. Unfortunately, the data linking overweight and death, as well as the data showing the beneficial effects of weight loss, are limited, fragmentary, and often ambiguous" (1998, 52). Thus, there is very little compelling evidence that losing weight equals a step toward health or that losing weight is even really possible for the vast majority of folks, putting claims about volition and the possible consequences of the epidemic of obesity to rest.

Despite the efforts of doctors such as Kassirer and Angell, misinformation continues to circulate, further confusing the American public about fatness. In 1993, the *Journal of the American Medical Association* published a brief statement entitled "Actual Causes of Death in the United States." This short piece contained the statement that 300,000 people had died in the previous year due to factors such as poor eating habits and sedentary lifestyle (2208). Weight was never specifically mentioned. In the following months, however, weight was all that was mentioned. Exhibiting the power of fatphobia—even where supposedly objective medicine is concerned—this information suddenly appeared in other sources, but subsequent citations failed to indicate that sedentary lifestyle and poor eating habits contributed to these 300,000 deaths; instead, obesity was cited as the cause of these deaths, conflating poor eating habits and sedentary lifestyles with a particular embodiment.[2]

My own experience with doctors resonates with these examples of fatphobia and the overwhelming cultural narratives of fatness, which are constructions fueled far more by the drive toward normative bodies than by solid medical evidence. I have many times been reminded that—despite the fact that my blood pressure, cholesterol, and pulse are within acceptable ranges—I am unhealthy, for no other reason than my weight. Although it is difficult to find scientific studies that suggest fatness is in and of itself the catalyst behind diseases such as atherosclerosis or high blood pressure, it seems that many medical prac-

titioners feel quite comfortable telling patients that regardless of any other aspect of their lifestyle or health, they are ill. The doctors who have confronted me have offered a litany of possible impairments they see in my future, ranging from heart disease to arthritis in my knees.

These hypothetical corporeal futures are based in stereotypes of people of size, laying bare the stigma associated with larger-than-average bodies. A careful and complete review of scientific studies does not, as many assume, reveal direct ties between fatness and the diseases we so closely associate with it.[3] Steeped in both the creation and reflection of popular narratives about fatness, many medical accounts (despite confounding scientific evidence) dramatize negative aspects of obesity, further stigmatizing fat people. It is this stigma, these cultural narratives about fatness, the black cloud of misunderstanding and hatred that heavily hangs around the shoulders of people of size (our albatross if you will), that medicalized accounts and those focusing on impairments alone fail to address. Medical narratives of fatness and the language of impairment often cannot usefully address alternative accounts offered by those embodied as fat and/or disabled. Alternative accounts, especially those that resist popular accounts of suffering and self-hatred, disrupt expectations of what it means to be fat and/or disabled. Linton writes, "We [disabled people] further confound expectations when we have the temerity to emerge as forthright and resourceful people, nothing like the self-loathing, docile, bitter, or insentient fictional versions of ourselves the public is more used to" (1998, 3). As Wendell explains in *The Rejected Body*, the stigma associated with certain bodies and abilities can sometimes be as disabling as physical impairments themselves: "the distinction between the biological reality of a disability and the social construction of a disability cannot be made sharply, because the biological and the social are interactive in creating disability" (1996, 35). Further, Wendell states, "being identified as disabled also carries a significant stigma in most societies and usually forces the person so identified to deal with stereotypes and unrealistic attitudes and expectations that are projected on to her/him as a member of a stigmatized group" (12). When medical narratives of disability maintain such firm footing within cultural imaginations, little room is left for political self-definition.

Group Identity? The Cases of Deaf Culture and Fatness

Although medicine's analysis of weight works under the assumption that it is the individual's responsibility to control her body, it is also clear that medicine finds little room for individual analyses of fat people as individuals. Instead, almost anyone considered obese by medical standards will be given the same list of possible conditions and complications. Having previously argued that fat people are not usually treated as individuals, even (or especially) during medical exams, I would like to move on to examining the contours of what guaranteeing Fat people group status might entail.[4] Historically, civil rights legislation has been informed by the belief that certain groups have been oppressed via social structures such as racism, sexism, and nationalism; however, fat people remain largely unprotected by such legislation. In addition to fears about frivolous claims, the belief that fat people do not constitute a cohesive social group hinders progress toward protection. Yet, many of the criteria for politicized group identities are met by fat folks because they inhabit a similar stigmatized social location.

In character with medical narratives previously discussed, "the obese" are often referred to as a group, particularly when they are accused of emptying our national health care budget and driving up insurance rates for healthy Americans (Gaesser 1996, 60; Albrecht and Pories 1999, 149). Psychoanalysis is another branch of medicine that refers to "the obese" and "the disabled" as groups. One particularly interesting study, supposedly conducted to better understand "the morbidly obese patient," states that "depression is the hallmark of the obese" and that many of us are very "angry people" (Fox, Taylor, and Jones

2000, 479).[5] Familiar with such strategies, Linton notes a trend in psychological and psychoanalytical studies of disabled people of casting personality traits as pathologies related to embodiments (1998, 99). Thus, the stigma and pathology surrounding both fat and disabled people are conceived around the notion that both are cohesive groups. Unfortunately, the group *fat* is often evoked for the purposes of pathology rather than activism.

There are many other shared experiences among fat people, despite our diversity. First, we are constantly told to change our bodies, regardless of how we might feel about such proposals. Second, we are repeatedly told to lose weight even though mounting evidence shows weight loss as a false panacea. Third, our bodies are held up as public spectacles on a daily basis. Pitted against one another, particularly in the case of women, we are often represented as warning signs for those who are currently thin as well as those who are already heavy. Watching *The Jerry Springer Show* on any given day provides ample evidence of many women's ability to chastise other women about weight. Thin women castigate fat women, and women who are themselves large play the game of "at least I'm not that fat." Despite conflict and differentiation within the group, these experiences remain similar across such lines, suggesting that Fat is a shared political identity. Regarding Fat as a viable political identity might encourage protection for fat people as a class. However, resistance to such proposals is quite strong. Why? What specifically makes the proposition of acknowledging fat persons as a group so threatening? How are notions of individual responsibility and "choice" implicated here?

As disparate as the identities Fat and Deaf might seem, critically reading recent debates about deafness and what is now being referred to as "elective disability" is especially helpful in thinking through these questions. As a quick review, both Fat and Deaf people are often considered morally blameworthy when they choose not to adopt recommended treatment. Similarly, both fatness and deafness are routinely recognized as medical conditions but seldom as the counter-hegemonic identities of Fat and Deaf, especially within the contexts of law and medicine. These are only a few of the comparisons we should examine if our goal is to better understand the current criteria and narratives necessary for qualifying for civil rights protection. Doing so enables us to better understand both Fat and Deaf identities as well as the political commitments and values that underpin the representations of both as mutable, curable conditions.

Beginning with current debates between those who believe cochlear implants can and should be used to cure deafness and those who believe these implants are pieces of genocidal quackery, a careful analysis of fatness and deafness reveals similar strategies for eliminating both physiological traits despite the fact that medical interventions produce neither thin nor hearing people. While cochlear implants are touted as cures for deafness, members of Deaf culture fight to be recognized as a legitimate social group, a group that should not be forced to assimilate into a mainstream hearing culture. As Bonnie Poitras Tucker explains in "Deaf Culture, Cochlear Implants, and Elective Disability," Deaf culture is based on several practices believed to create cultural autonomy:

> The theory of Deaf culture is primarily premised on a shared language—American Sign Language (ASL). Individuals who communicate via ASL clearly *do* speak a different language. . . . in addition, some members of the Deaf cultural community claim to be part of a separate culture as a result of attending segregated . . . schools for Deaf children, or as a result of their participation in Deaf clubs or wholly Deaf environments in which they socialize or work. (1998, 6–7)

Additionally, most individuals who identify as members of Deaf culture take great pride in their deafness (7). Those inside and outside Deaf culture, who both acknowledge and wish to support this culture and pride, refuse to view Deaf

people as flawed individuals who should be "cured."

Despite protestations, support for mandatory cochlear implants and demands for responsible self-correction are intensifying. Is it the responsibility of the Deaf to assimilate? First, we must elaborate on what assimilation entails when achieved via cochlear technology. Proponents of cochlear implants, such as Tucker, describe the technology as "a surgically implanted device that is capable of restoring hearing and speech understanding to many individuals who are severely or profoundly deaf" (1998, 6). Supporters of cochlear implants often view the surgical insertions of the devices as Deaf culture's responsibility to larger society, especially when deafness is discovered in children.

Furthermore, cochlear implant advocates consider Deaf individuals as impaired *individuals*, failing to consider Deaf as a legitimate cultural group identity. From this perspective, the presence of a "cure," and Deaf people's refusal of it, amounts to choosing disability, which of course angers both advocates of cochlear technology and people who worry about frivolous disability claims for supposedly volitional conditions. While I'm not making an argument for Fat culture, I want to suggest, as Rosemarie Garland Thomson has suggested that "the shared experience of stigmatization creates commonality" (1997, 15). Similarly, Harlan Lane, Robert Hoffmeister, and Ben Bahan maintain that because many Deaf people grow up in hearing homes, physically and culturally distanced from one another, common experiences, such as time spent in schools for the Deaf, are more generative of the "DEAF-WORLD" than "any single locale" (1996, 124–5). Hence, the experiences and status of being Fat and being Deaf are what bind individuals in these groups together, and the groups Fat and Deaf are then bound together by their struggles against mainstream culture's treatment of people thought to have abnormal embodiments.

Many opponents of cochlear implants are concerned about both the possible coercive power involved with this technology and its questionable success rate. Some members of the Deaf culture might persuasively argue that there is no "choice" of disability because cochlear implants simply do not create hearing people. For example, Robert A. Crouch, who is a staunch opponent of cochlear implants, believes that there are serious limitations to cochlear technology. The author of the section on cochlear implants included at *Healthlibrary.com* writes that as a result of Crouch's work we must reconsider the "miracle" of technology. S/he writes: "We need to recognize the limitations of cochlear implants. A recent study found that after five years of hard work, patients with such implants were able to correct [sic] pronounce just 70% of vowel sounds" ("Cochlear Implants" 2001).

Likewise, bariatric surgeries, which often reduce stomach capacity to around two tablespoons and bypass sections of bowel, are encouraged despite questionable outcomes.[6] The National Association to Advance Fat Acceptance (NAAFA) maintains a staunch position against such surgeries: "the National Association to Advance Fat Acceptance condemns gastrointestinal surgeries for weight loss under any circumstances" ("NAAFA Policy: Weight Loss Surgery" 2002). NAAFA opposes these surgeries due to a lack of follow-up studies, the performance of new surgeries without adequate testing, and a host of surgical complications, including death. Most similar to cochlear implants, however, is the fact that weight loss surgeries simply do not produce thin people. NAAFA states, "Currently, the most frequently performed procedure, vertical banded gastroplasty, results in weight loss of about 20% within 18–24 months. Because weight regain is common within two to five years after operation, doctors plan 'staged surgery'." In spite of the limited success and serious complications accompanying weight loss surgery, the IRS currently offers tax deductions for those who pay for their own bariatric surgeries ("A Taxpayer's Guide" 2000). In sum, both fatness and deafness continue to be represented as mutable and ideally curable despite the mixed outcomes of medical technologies designed for carrying out the task.

When Fat and Deaf people are not recognized as disabled, fatness and deafness are depoliticized. For Fat people who are often already isolated from both mainstream culture and other disabled people, non-recognition further breaks down group bonds, isolates us as discrete individuals, and severely hinders the forming of politically conscious Fat politics. Linton states, "the material that binds us [disabled people] is the art of finding one another, of identifying and naming disability in a world reluctant to discuss it" (1998, 5). This "art" can be severely hindered by the isolation of disabled people into discrete individuals who are thought to share no common experiences due to the diverse nature of impairments. The experiences of Fat and Deaf people reveal commonalities between seemingly disparate groups of people and can form the basis for new and perhaps previously untapped political alliances.

Weight, Feminism, and Disability

Flipping through the pages of the morning paper or perusing magazines while standing in checkout lanes, women are constantly reminded that to be overweight, and especially to be obese, is not only a medical emergency but also an affront to dominant aesthetic values of female embodiment, both of which constitute ripe ground for further discrimination of women. Hence, the social positioning of fat women demands careful and thoughtful analysis within the framework of disability studies. As legal scholar Sondra Solovay argues, young women and girls are much more likely to fall prey to the self-deprecation of "internalizing anti-fat discourses" (2000, 36). In short, already socially disadvantaged by nature of female embodiment, fat women find themselves in a difficult position that requires an analysis of fatness as a central component in shaping their lives. . . .

For many women, and/or feminist scholars, fat is particularly scary and threatening, often evoking contradictory desires and troubling realizations. Fat tests the boundaries between individual desires for certain embodiments and larger feminist goals of resisting corporeal ultimatums precisely because so many women and/or feminists struggle with their own physical identities.[7] The complexities surrounding fatness, women's bodies, and the possibilities of fatness as a transitory and fluid embodiment also work on another level. In addition to possibly negating the identity of women for whom fatness is not a transitory condition, the notion of fatness as fluid is dangerous and threatening because it serves as a reminder that our bodies are dynamic rather than fixed. Thus, the female body, already thought to be flawed, is at risk of being further pathologized by fatness. As Margrit Shildrick points out in *Leaky Bodies and Boundaries*, "the body is a fabrication that mimics material fixity" (1997, 13). Our bodies are forever in the process of undeclared construction, and once we dislodge fatness from biology and begin to think of who is categorized as fat as a social decision (in the same way that categorizing who is disabled is a social decision) what once appeared as solid categories surface as fluid boundaries.

In my experience, even the most enlightened friends and colleagues tend to be fatphobic, partly because biologically-based cultural narratives are so pervasive and because, in some sense, the boundaries of who is fat and who is not are recognized as contextual. Any woman who has walked down a street to hear the word (and insult in this case) "fat" hurled from a passing car understands that no particular female embodiment provides safe haven from such comments. Part of the power of "fat," when used as an insult, is lodged in the very fact that no standard definition exists. There are, of course, the weight charts referred to in medical accounts, but culturally "fat" can mark any woman, referencing body size in general, a jiggle of a thigh, or the slight swell of a tummy. As Solovay reminds us, negative associations with fatness are far ranging and difficult to pin down to any one body type: "all gradations of fat, even slight to moderate, have been regarded by government agencies and popular culture as mutable, volitional, and dangerous conditions that are synonymous with physical and moral

shortcomings" (2000, 151). Thus, the lack of firm cultural definitions of fatness exposes all women to the danger of discrimination.

Fatness and disability also remind us that bodies are subjected to changing socio-cultural contexts as well as physiological changes. While always casting Fat as a transitory identity is problematic, the physical conditions of both fatness and disability can be usefully understood as fluid. Recognizing this fluidity moves away from ideas of inherently flawed individuals and toward accounts of dynamically situated bodies and identities. For many women, there are times in their lives when they gain weight and/or become disabled. Regardless of whether either is permanent or temporary, the existence of these possibilities removes bodies from solid ground and acknowledges once again that bodies are unstable. As Susan Bordo notes in *Unbearable Weight*, femininity is both empowering and disempowering, an argument clearly played out in the fear of fatness and/or disability (1993). The approximation of ideal femininity can offer social capital to women, albeit social capital that is, as Bordo points out, ultimately disempowering. The prospect of having one's body read as a text about slovenly behavior, inherent flaws, and abnormality—all narratives associated with fat people and disabled people in general—robs many women of what they think of as a significant source of power. With "normal" and "ideal" always defined by what is pathologized and classed as abnormal, the possibility of the slippage between these categories and the contingent power involved can prove divisive to women as a social group.

Revolutionary Fatness

In *Fat? So! Because You Don't Have to Apologize for Your Size*, Fat activist Marilyn Wann succinctly describes the position in which feminist scholars dedicated to fully understanding the lives of all women find themselves: "once you become aware of the system, it's your choice, your responsibility, to choose how you will relate to it" (1998, 33). Wann's statement provides direction for Fat women in particular and disabled people in general, as well as political theorists who attempt to illuminate marginalized identities. The "system" Wann speaks about works to silence Fat women and their status as disabled, but scholarship that initiates inquiries from the lives of Fat women—not as biologically categorized by weight and impairments but as socially situated—can break this silence in profound ways.

I am the Fat woman pointed out during academic conferences. I am the graduate student who is disabled by seats in auditoriums that don't accommodate my body. I am the woman Susan Powter swears can and should be thin, and I am the tragic woman over whom Richard Simmons sheds tears. I am also the Fat woman whose identity and narration of fat embodiment resists fatness's cultural moorings in sadness and despair but whose story is seldom represented. Unfortunately, representations of disabled people most often focus on pain and suffering: "Particularly noteworthy for its absence is the voice that speaks not of shame, pain, and loss but of life, delight, struggle, and purposeful action" (Linton 1998, 113). Representations of women, and especially representations of women characterized as fat and/or disabled by popular media, often focus on pain and suffering rather than the possibilities of such embodiments. One such possibility rests in demystifying fatness and disability, making it possible for fat women; disabled men and women; non-fat, nondisabled men and women; and those living at multiple conjunctions of these identities to work together around shared goals rather than pitting themselves against one another in struggles for power. While Fat and Deaf people may seem so disparate that political alliances would be strained, the shared goal of social justice and commonality of experiences has the potential to bind these diverse groups to one another in meaningful ways.

Nomy Lamm in her essay "It's a Big Fat Revolution" shares her frustration with what she sees as a refusal to deal with fatness and fat oppression as a political issue: "maybe we should be demystifying fat and dealing with fat politics as a whole. And I don't mean maybe, I mean it's a necessity"

(1995, 91). Lamm's urgency stems from what she sees as a general lack of scholarship that deals with fatness and women in a productive way. Rather than side-barring discussions of fatness within scholarship, the lives of Fat women should be catalysts for analyses of fatphobia and oppression. When scholars initiate thinking from the lives of Fat women, it becomes apparent that body size does matter. Fat women's social location affords them a view of fatphobia and weightism from which feminist scholars can learn a great deal. Subjected to medicalization and stigmatization, fat women's bodies must also be represented as sites of power, entitlement, and freedom rather than loci of fear, misunderstanding, and pity. Situating fatness and Fat women within the context of disability studies and feminist standpoint epistemology can proffer resistant accounts of marginalized embodiments and identities.

Notes

1. The concept of "outing" one's self as a Fat woman is discussed by both Marilyn Wann (1998) and Eve Kosofsky Sedgwick (1990). Both authors understand that although fatness is very visible, it is often ignored, both by fat people themselves and by thin people, because it can be difficult to discuss. Additionally, the concept of "coming out" as a Fat woman resists the idea that "I am just like everyone else" or desires to be so by directly confronting people with my weight and my difference and deviance from the standard body.

2. Here I am greatly indebted to Dr. Jon Robison. During the summer of 1998, I took a summer class with Jon, which turned out to be germinal to my work. Jon's refusal to settle for the easy explanations of obesity and his desire to offer socially just accounts of fatness that took into account both medical and cultural narratives were both inspiring and informational. It was during Jon's class that I first heard about the misquotation of this particular statistic.

3. For a comprehensive review of scientific studies, I recommend Glen Gaesser's *Big Fat Lies* (1996).

4. During this paper, I use *Fat* to indicate a politicized identity similar to *Deaf* when expressed as a cultural and political identity that moves away from impairments and medical conditions and toward a politics of

embodiment. At times, I also use *fat* and *fatness*, usually when speaking about the medicalized understandings of these terms. Finally, I use *obesity* and *obese*, terms that are rightfully controversial, when speaking within the framework of medicine where those are the terms of choice.

5. The trend of characterizing the "obese" as psychologically damaged is rampant throughout texts encouraging bariatric surgeries. Two examples of such texts are Norman B. Ackerman's *Fat No More* (1999) and Michelle Boasten's *Weight Loss Surgery* (2001).

6. In addition to the Ackerman and Boasten texts, Carnie Wilson's autobiographical text *Gut Feelings* (1998) offers a particularly honest account of the process involved in such surgeries. Although Wilson's account is an endorsement of such procedures, it presents bariatric surgeries as both painful and problematic procedures. The NAAFA website also contains detailed descriptions of various procedures housed under the general heading of bariatric surgeries.

7. I also struggle with ambiguous desires where my embodiment is concerned. Some days I feel wonderful and other days I wonder why I don't just go on a diet. Acknowledging and working through these disparate feelings and the contradictions between my personal feelings and my political commitments is an integral part of my scholarship and my lived experience as a Fat woman. Duncan Woodhead, a colleague from the history department here at Michigan State University, tells me that I am in "full possession of my fatness." For me, being in "full possession of my fatness" means dealing with these contradictory feelings and political commitments. Thus, my intent is not to chastise women who find fatness problematic but rather to suggest that these are issues that must be recognized and engaged.

References

"A Taxpayer's Guide on IRS Policy to Deduct Weight Control Treatment." 2000. American Obesity Association Home Page. Retrieved 28 May 2001, from www.obesity.org/taxguide.

Ackerman, Norman B. 1999. *Fat No More: The Answer for the Dangerously Overweight.* Amherst, NY: Prometheus Books.

"Actual Causes of Death in the United States." 1993. *Journal of the American Medical Association* 270(18):2208.

Albrecht, Robert J., and Walter J. Pories. 1999. "Surgical Intervention for the Severely Obese." *Balliere's Clinical Endocrinology and Metabolism* 13(1): 149–72.

Americans with Disabilities Act. U.S. Public Law 101–336. 101st Cong., 2nd sess., 26 July 1990.

Boasten, Michelle. 2001. *Weight Loss Surgery: Understanding and Overcoming Morbid Obesity.* Akron, OH: FBE Service Network and Network Publishing.

Bordo, Susan. 1993. *Unbearable Weight: Feminism, Western Culture, and the Body.* Berkeley: University of California Press.

"Cochlear Implants." 2001. Healthlibrary.com. Retrieved 28 May 2001, from www.healthlibrary.com/reading/ethics.

Fox, Katherine M., Susan L. Taylor, and Judy E. Jones. 2000. "Understanding the Bariatric Surgical Patient: A Demographic, Lifestyle and Psychological Profile." *Obesity Surgery* 10:477–81.

Gaesser, Glenn A. 1996. *Big Fat Lies: The Truth About Your Weight and Your Health.* New York: Fawcett Columbine.

Kassirer, David, and Marcia Angell. 1998. "Losing Weight: An Ill-Fated New Year's Resolution." *NEJM* 338(1):52–4.

"King Size Homer." 1995. *The Simpsons.* Retrieved 28 May 2001, from www.thesimpsons.com.

Lamm, Nomy. 1995. "It's a Big Fat Revolution." In *Listen Up: Voices from the Next Generation*, ed. Barbara Findlen, 85–94. Seattle, WA: Seal Press.

Lane, Harlan, Robert Hoffmeister, and Ben Bahan. 1996. *A Journey into the Deaf-World.* San Diego, CA: Dawnsign Press.

Linton, Simi. 1998. *Claiming Disability: Knowledge and Identity.* New York: New York University Press.

"Myths and Facts About the *Americans with Disabilities Act.*" 1990. U.S. Department of Justice Home Page. Retrieved 28 May 2001, from www.usdoj.gov.

"NAAFA Policy: Weight Loss Surgery." 2002. National Association to Advance Fat Acceptance Online. Retrieved 28 May 2001, from www.naafa.org.

Sedgwick, Eve Kosofsky. 1990. *Epistemology of the Closet.* Berkeley: University of California Press.

Shildrick, Margrit. 1997. *Leaky Bodies and Boundaries: Feminism, Postmodernism and (Bio)Ethics.* New York: Routledge.

Solovay, Sondra. 2000. *Tipping the Scales of Justice: Fighting Weight-Based Discrimination.* Amherst, NY: Prometheus Books.

Thomson, Rosemarie Garland. 1997. *Extraordinary Bodies: Figuring Physical Disability in American Culture and Literature.* New York: Columbia University Press.

Tucker, Bonnie Poitras. 1998. "Deaf Culture, Cochlear Implants, and Elective Disability." *The Hastings Center Report* 28(4):6–14.

Wann, Marilyn. 1998. *Fat So! Because You Don't Have to Apologize for Your Size.* Berkeley, CA: Ten Speed Press.

Wendell, Susan. 1996. *The Rejected Body: Feminist Philosophical Reflections on Disability.* New York: Routledge.

Wilson, Carnie, with Mick Kleber. 1998. *Gut Feelings: From Fear and Despair to Health and Hope.* Carlsbad, CA: Hay House, Inc.

Sarah Blustain

Modern Childbirth: Failure to Progress

In spring 2005, a study of 5,000 planned home births in North America, one of the most comprehensive of its kind, found that women who had such births needed fewer interventions than those who had hospital births, and that the home births were as safe as the hospital births. The following spring, Great Britain's secretary of health announced that by 2009 all low-risk British women would be given the option of a home birth. Then, in November 2006, the American College of Obstetricians and Gynecologists struck back. ACOG, the lobbying organization for the obstetric profession, announced,

> The development of well-designed research studies of sufficient size, prepared *in consultation with obstetric departments* and approved by institutional review boards, might clarify the comparative safety of births in different settings. Until the results of such studies are convincing, ACOG strongly opposes out-of-hospital births [emphasis added].

Of course ACOG opposes out-of-hospital births! This is what American obstetrics is all about. Its first priority is not healthy birth per se, but *obstetric* birth. Two new books—*Pushed*, by Jennifer Block, and *Born in the USA*, by Marsden Wagner—tell us just what goes wrong when birth is controlled by obstetricians. In their view—based on evidence and science, albeit *not* in con-

Source: "Modern Childbirth: Failure to Progress," by Sarah Blustain. This article first appeared in the July/August 2007 issue of *Women's Review of Books*. Used by permission.

sultation with obstetric departments—that's just about everything.

Wagner and Block come from different worlds. Wagner was formerly the director of Women's and Children's Health at the World Health Organization (WHO). He has experience as a medical doctor, an epidemiologist, and a scientist. While he is sympathetic to obstetricians, who he recognizes are stretched thin and unable to fully attend the unpredictable and often lengthy process of normal birth, he calls himself a "whistleblower." He offers a scathing attack on professional standards of care, suggesting they are abusive at worst, and based on nonscience that mainly serves doctors' interests at best.

Block was an editor at *Ms.* magazine, and her book covers, in extraordinarily readable terms, much of the same scientific ground that Wagner's does. As a reporter, however, her strength is in getting doctors and nurses—some self-satisfied and some repentant—to confess that obstetric care is corrupt to its very core. No woman who is pregnant, has been pregnant, or plans to be pregnant should set foot inside the office of her ob/gyn before reading these books.

Here are two central facts about American birth: first, the US spends more per capita than any other developed nation on maternity care. Second, the World Health Organization ranks the US thirtieth out of 33 developed countries in preventing maternal mortality, and 32nd in preventing neonatal mortality. Our country is not doing well by mothers and babies.

Block, a wry and pointed writer, starts her narrative with a history of the Blonsky, a machine that received a patent in 1965. It was to spin a laboring woman around at a force of seven Gs (astronauts experience three Gs on liftoff), creating enough force "to push aside the constricting vaginal walls, to overcome the friction of the uteral and vaginal surfaces and to counteract the atmospheric pressure opposing the emergence of the child." The baby was to be sucked out and land in a basket, which was to trigger an automatic shutoff. Lucky for all of us, the machine was never built, but, writes Block, the Blonsky "is eerily similar to how most American women give birth."

Both these books describe, in splendid detail, the myriad interventions of "active management"—the practices perpetrated upon even a healthy woman planning the most unremarkable of births. Although these practices may help in critical situations, they are more likely to cause harm than good in a normal birth. For example, active management includes the induction of labor in as many as forty percent of all American births, even though this leads to longer and more painful labors and "ups a woman's chance of a [cesarean] section by two to three times," according to Block. Wagner warns that doctors (with ACOG's approval) use the ulcer drug Cytotec for induction, despite the manufacturer's pleas and evidence that it has caused maternal death by hyperstimulating the uterus until it ruptures. Active management also includes speeding up a woman's labor with the use of Pitocin in perhaps a majority of American hospital births today. According to Block, "a recent ACOG survey found that in 43 percent of malpractice suits involving neurologically impaired babies, Pitocin was to blame." And it includes routine electronic fetal monitoring, used in 93 percent of hospital births even though studies show that its only effect is to increase the c-section rate. The list goes on.

The quintessential intervention is the cesarean section, which is how nearly thirty percent of American women delivered their babies last year. WHO says that when a population has a c-section rate of higher than fifteen percent, the risks to the mother and baby outweigh the benefits—and a WHO study found that "the main cause of maternal deaths in industrialized countries is complications from anesthesia and cesarean section," Block reports. She cites another study published last year, of 100,000 births, which found that "the rate of 'severe maternal morbidity and mortality'—infection requiring rehospitalization, hemorrhage, blood transfusion, hysterectomy, admission to intensive care, and death—rose in proportion to the rate of cesarean section." As for the baby, other research has found that "preterm birth and infant death rose significantly when cesarean rates exceeded between 10 and 20 percent," and that "low-risk babies born by cesarean were nearly three times more likely to die within the first month of life than those born vaginally." Nonetheless, ACOG not only rejects the fifteen percent target, but even continues to support the idea of elective c-section. Indeed, the doctor appointed head of ACOG in 2000, W. Benson Harer, has written treatises on "prophylactic elective cesareans" for preventing later incontinence—even though there has been no evidence that c-sections help at all.

So what is the purpose of all this intervention? In the most damning sections of these books, it becomes clear that there are several, none of which have anything to do with helping women.

The first is convenience. The Centers for Disease Control and Prevention (CDC) has noted what it calls the "weekend birth deficit." As Block reports, Kathleen Rice Simpson, a professor of nursing at St. Louis University School of Nursing, found that doctors were "most concerned with increasing the oxytocin [Pitocin] rate to "keep labor on track' and 'get her delivered.' . . . [One physician] remarked, 'When I hear I've got a nurse who will go up on the Pit, I know it's going to be a good day.' " Ethical? Given the risks of induction, probably not. Yet in 1999, ACOG reversed its policy on labor induction, sanctioning it for "social" or "logistic" reasons.

The second reason for the interventions is "standard of care" protocols, which doctors decide upon through trial and error. Both books include infuriating narratives about the sloppy and nonscientific research that led to today's hospital protocols, including the demand that labor "must progress at a minimum speed and occur within a maximum duration" or be labeled "failure to progress." As Block tells it, failure to progress is responsible for one-third of all c-sections. But as both books show, failure to progress in fact means failure to progress on the doctor's schedule. More and more women are having problems not because they are unhealthy but because doctors have redefined normal. In another egregious example of arbitrary standards, Wagner cites a 1999 ACOG recommendation against vaginal birth after cesarean (VBAC). The rate of uterine rupture among VBACing women had been increasing "at an alarming rate, . . . almost certainly related to the fact that the percentage of births in which powerful drugs, such as Cytotec, were used to induce labor had doubled," he writes. But instead of banning induction among VBACing mothers, ACOG banned VBAC itself, a decision that alone has led to a stunning increase in the c-section rate in this country.

The third is doctors' fear of litigation and, related to that, rising malpractice insurance costs. Doctors are practicing "defensive" medicine—to women's detriment. Electronic fetal monitoring and c-sections have become "a kind of insurance against litigation," Wagner writes. In one of the many stunning admissions that Block has elicited from her sources, one doctor said,

> The risks are maternal, and maternal risks are much smaller to us as obstetricians. There's no doubt in my mind that there's more maternal morbidity with a cesarean. But a hole in the bladder, a post-operative infection—that's not going to ruin their lives. A bad baby is going to ruin our lives.

Another doctor told Block,

> To be blunt, you don't get sued when you do a cesarean. . . . You get sued when there's a damaged baby. . . . And that causes doctors to say, "Well, it's got to look like I've tried my best. And trying my best would be to deliver the baby." So you explain to the mother that the fluid's a little low.

What's most nefarious about these justifications is that doctors lie to women in order to scare them into consenting. They play what one midwife Block interviews calls the "big baby card," the "dying placenta card," the "convenience card," the "exploding uterus card," and the ubiquitous "dead baby card." Yet they do not routinely tell women of the risks of the interventions. Indeed, the standards of care are so inconsistent that ACOG opposes VBAC but offers no objection to amniocentesis, even though the risk of miscarriage after an amnio is one in 200—"the same as the risk of uterine rupture in a VBAC," writes Block. Informed consent, these books make clear, is a fantasy.

There is, however, an alternative. In an amazing narrative, Block describes the experiences of one hospital in Florida after Hurricane Charley knocked out power in 2004. The labor-and-delivery nurse she interviews, who later quit in disgust, describes the scene: no woman was admitted unless she was in active labor. The hospital suspended induction. "Women were delivering within hours of arriving, even first-time mothers, without any Pitocin," the nurse told Block. "We had no cases of fetal distress during labor and no respiratory distress of neonates following delivery. . . . We had an incredibly low cesarean rate. Amazingly, the babies were mostly evenly distributed between day and night shifts"—the weekend birth deficit vanished. "[B]asically, they did better than if they had been induced. We thought, 'wow, this is amazing!'"

As evidence is increasingly showing, the people who best enable normal births are midwives. Obstetricians, after all, are surgeons, and many never witness a natural, normal birth in their training. Midwives, in contrast, are women who know that one of the best answers to pain is sitting in a warm tub, who know how to manually palpate a woman's belly to find the baby's weight and position, and who know how to help a woman handle labor in ways that facilitate birth.

One of the most moving sections of *Pushed* comes as Block introduces us to two homebirth midwives: Linda, who practices in an undisclosed state; and Cynthia Caillagh, of Virginia, who attended some 2,500 births before a bad outcome drove her out of practice. (The family of her client, who later died, didn't think Caillagh was responsible, but the state tried her anyway.) Block shows Linda attending births, providing a wonderful, woman-focused counterpoint to the medical births she's dissected in earlier chapters. She frames her discussion in terms of women's power and women's rights but is not didactic, instead relying on the midwives' words to make her point. Says Caillagh of her clients, "At no time did I own their health or the information they were gathering. . . . The choices were theirs."

But midwifery in the US is up against some powerful forces—mainly, again, obstetricians and ACOG. Doctors throughout American history have worked to discredit midwives—labeling them dirty, uneducated, and unskilled—and to drive them out of business. Today certified nurse-midwives who practice in hospitals report having their hands tied by doctors and hospital protocol. Direct-entry midwives, who are not nurses and attend home births, and who are illegal in eleven states and the District of Columbia, are persecuted by doctors, who use any opportunity to convince the state to prosecute them into court. As Block reports, at ACOG's 2006 conference, the group gave out bumper stickers that read, "Home Deliveries Are for Pizza."

Block asks, "Do women have the right to give birth with whom, where, and in the manner in which they choose? And if so, is that right being upheld?" Other related questions come to mind: Is it ethical to allow women to give birth at home, as does every state, but to make it illegal or intimidating for her to be attended by a direct-entry midwife? Should doctors and courts decide what risks are acceptable for a birthing woman—based on nonscientific data? Even if their data were scientific, would they have the right to make a woman's decisions for her? May a hospital compel electronic fetal monitoring if a woman re-

fuses? May a doctor drop a patient out of fear of liability, if she refuses a c-section against medical advice?

Many of these complaints are not new, and much of the research showing the dangers of hospital birth dates from the 1970s and 1980s, as women and women's health advocates realized that hospitals were following protocols that were more useful to the hospital than they were to women. We've all heard stories from women who birthed in the 1950s and 1960s, strapped to beds, drugged into twilight sleep.

What arose from the new, liberated women's consciousness, though, was a concept of birthing that only *appeared* to be woman-centered. Hospital birthing rooms now have flowery wallpaper. The equipment is hidden behind pleasant drapes. And it is trendy for a pregnant woman to create a "birth plan" document, written in consultation with her doctor, to communicate her wishes to the hospital staff during her labor. For instance, she may specify that she wants to wear her own clothes, to give birth without drugs, and to be free to walk around. But the truth is that most women are still required to give birth on their backs with their feet in stirrups—the least efficient way to push a baby out. As for the birth plan? "It's an illusion," Judith Lothian, author of *The Official Lamaze Guide*, tells Block. "[I]t does women a disservice because they really do think that they have choice, and then they don't."

The prospects for change under our current health care system are grim. Wagner believes universal healthcare may help. He also encourages families who feel their rights have been abused to litigate against their doctors. For her part, Block ends with a challenge to today's organized feminists to bring birthing under the umbrella of "choice," quoting childbirth educator Erica Lyon, who says, "I think this is the last leap for the feminist movement. This is the last issue for women in terms of actual ownership of our bodies."

Is it possible for change to come from women themselves? It would take a revolution. These books deal only peripherally with one of the most problematic issues: what do you do when women freely choose, or think they freely choose, medical procedures that increase their risk and that of their children? If women believe their obstetricians are their best advocates, how do you convince them to think skeptically? Indeed, ACOG has tried to spin "patient choice" of cesarean section as a major issue. But as Block points out, a woman often "chooses" surgical birth after her doctor has handed her one or several of the risk "cards." Until women take birth into their own hands, until they realize that doctors are not necessarily women's advocates, until they seek out the evidence, which is in these books but not in doctor's offices, about the normalcy of birth and the dangers of interventions, they are going to continue to believe that birth is a crisis about which only one person—the obstetrician—knows best.

If ever there was a book that gave credence to this concern, it is Tina Cassidy's *Birth*. She writes, "for the vast majority of us over the years, the 'best' care has often meant isolating babies in nurseries, receiving an unnecessary episiotomy, or having a breast dipped in iodine before every feeding. . . . If only we'd known how skeptical we should have been. And should still be."

Cassidy herself knows of what she speaks: she describes her own birthing experience, in which her baby was not in the optimal position during labor and got "stuck."

> I asked to have a midwife come and offer suggestions to move my labor along, but the har-

ried staff said she was unavailable. I asked them to shut off the epidural (yes, I had succumbed the fifth time the nurse asked me if I wanted one), so that I could try other labor positions. They obliged but only, I think, because they were annoyed and knew the pain would be so severe I wouldn't care what happened next. . . . My son's heart rate was fine, but things had dragged on too long, as far as the staff was concerned. The doctor insisted upon an emergency c-section . . . throughout which I vomited and shook violently.

And yet Cassidy concludes that even knowing what she knows, "I doubt there's much I would have changed." She says, "Women will forever give birth in many different ways—either by design or through forces out of our control. As for the latter, we can only hope to be pleasantly surprised." Oh how these final words infuriate me. Yes, she says, the emperor has no clothes—but my, what an interesting outfit he's wearing.

At the core of these books are two issues: women's right to make their own medical choices, and their right not to have their health compromised by the demands of the American medical system. These issues deserve much more than the amused shrug that Cassidy gives them. Despite our birth plans and natural birthing classes, American women are still giving birth in a patriarchal system that puts the needs of the hospital, the doctor, and the profession well above the safety of women.

A R T I C L E   2 1

Heather E. Dillaway

Menopause Is the "Good Old": Women's Thoughts about Reproductive Aging

Recent feminist research suggests that individual women find menopause an inconsequential or positive experience overall. While recent aging scholarship also documents that contemporary individuals often define aging neutrally or positively, menopause may not resemble other aging processes in meaning and experience. The author argues that menopause, or reproductive aging, may be unique because of its reproductive and aging contexts. Data in this article are based on interviews with 45 middle-class, heterosexual, menopausal women in a midwestern state in 2001. Interviewees propose that, upon menopause, they do not feel old. They explain these feelings by describing their widespread use of contraceptive technologies, greater enjoyment of sexual activity upon menopause, and parallels between menopause and menarche. As women in this sample place menopause within the context of previous reproductive experiences and compare it to other aging processes, they suggest that reproductive aging represents a "good old."

Menopause is part of the general process of aging (Gannon 1999). It is also a reproductive process experienced specifically by women, along with menarche and menstruation, most contraceptive practices, conception, pregnancy, childbirth, and breast-feeding. Similar to other aging and reproductive processes, menopause has been constructed by clinical communities and popular culture as a solely biological or physiological event and a negative period of loss (Barbre 1998; Ferguson and Parry 1998; Martin 1992). Recent feminist research suggests, however, that individual women find menopause an inconsequential or positive experience overall (Gannon and Ekstrom 1993; Winterich 2003; Winterich and Umberson 1999). While recent aging scholarship also documents that contemporary individuals often define aging neutrally or positively (Cremin 1992;

Furman 1997; Laz 2003), menopause may not resemble other aging processes in meaning and experience (Gannon 1999). That is, menopause can be distinguished from other aging processes when we look at particular social contexts of women's lives. I argue that menopause is understood more fully within the context of women's previous reproductive experiences, comparisons of menopause with other aging processes, and structural and ideological shifts that shape the meanings of reproduction and aging.

Previous literature neglects explorations of the reproductive and aging contexts that may encourage particular definitions or experiences of menopause. This article describes how a sample of middle-class, heterosexual women discusses menopause as a reproductive and aging process and examines how menopause is distinct from other aging processes. An analysis of unexplored social contexts allows us to see why my interviewees might define menopause as a "good old." . . .

Source: Heather E. Dillaway, *Gender & Society* Vol. 19, No. 3, June 2005, 398–417. © 2005 SAGE Publications, Inc. Used by permission of SAGE Publications, Inc.

Findings

Findings analyzed here are related to the reproductive and aging contexts of menopause, emphasizing the importance of structural and ideological shifts. First, I present data illustrating women's long-term use of contraceptive technologies and discuss how this contraceptive behavior makes menopause an insignificant marker in some women's lives, because menopause no longer represents a symbolic end of fertility. Second, I show data suggesting that women can enjoy their sexuality more fully upon/after reproductive aging, as they feel free from the gendered burdens of contraceptive use and monthly menstruation. Third, I present women's ideas about the connections between menopause and menarche or girlhood, and how the similarities between these life stages contradict the notion that women are aging upon menopause. Fourth, I discuss how menopause is considered a "good old" compared to other aging processes and argue that women define menopause as a reproductive experience first and only an aging experience second.

Do Menopausal Women Feel Old?

Experientially, aging and menopause seemed like distinct and separate processes to women in my sample, thus most did not feel old upon reproductive aging. Thirty-six women said they did not feel old at the time of the interview. Nine women did report feeling old, but they were no different from the other women in terms of their race, stage of menopause, or chronological age. Seven of these women said they felt old because of menopause, although none of these women cited menopause as the main reason for feeling old. Other family situations (e.g., "my daughter just turned 30"), and personal or family health problems were cited as the primary reasons why the latter women felt old.

Even when they recognized that their chronological age might place them in a life stage that others define as "old," most interviewees suggested that the idea that menopause would make

them feel old ran contrary to their own views. "I could swear if I don't look in the mirror, I feel that I'm really still only 35 years old. It's just when I sit down and think about it, it's like 'Okay. I'm going to be 60 this year. That's moving right along.' But I don't really feel old. And menopause certainly didn't make me feel old at 52. . . . I was just moving along in my life" (Francine, white).

In this case, Francine demonstrates a disconnect between how "old" she feels and how "old" her chronological age "should" make her feel. Comments such as "I don't feel like I'm 55" were widespread in my interviews. Similar to other recent research on age identities (Cremin 1992; Featherstone and Hepworth 1991; Kaufman and Elder 2002; Laz 2003), interviewees reported feeling "the same as I did when I was [younger chronologically]." They felt young rather than old. In addition, the fact that Francine started menopause did not make her feel old. This was true for 38 respondents.

Contraceptive Technology Creates Distinctions Between Menopause and Feeling Old

Virtually all interviewees (44) reported ending their reproductive years artificially through the use of contraceptive technology or medical intervention before the onset of reproductive aging; therefore, menopause does not represent the end of fertility for women in my sample. For many interviewees, the end of fertility or reproductive capacity came when they took conscious action to rid themselves of the possibility of biological motherhood. Some women and their partners made the decision to have a tubal ligation (6) or a vasectomy (8) early in their reproductive lives, usually in their late 20s to mid-30s. Most interviewees (also or instead) used reversible contraceptive technologies as a way to control their reproductive capacity. Of the 37 women who reported using reversible contraceptive methods, 31 reported using the birth control pill at some point in their lives, and many others reported using intra-uterine devices (IUDs), barrier methods such as diaphragms, and condoms. About half (22) reported using more than one method in protecting against conception; if they reported only one method, it was most often the birth control pill. While I did not ask specifically about abortions, three women also mentioned having abortions.

A key to understanding why women might not feel old upon menopause or why menopause did not signify an end to fertility is that most interviewees and their partners actively avoided reproduction long before the onset of reproductive aging. Rather than reproductive capacity being determined by menarche and menopause, most women and their partners confined it to a much shorter period of time and spent most of their reproductive lives contracepting. Of the 40 women who were biological mothers, 37 birthed their last child more than 10 years before the interview. Ten women birthed their youngest child more than 26 years before the interview. The mean age of women's youngest children was 19.5 years; the median was 17.5 years.

The abilities of women in my sample to confine reproductive capacity to a finite time and avoid motherhood for an average of 19.5 years must be put within a particular social context. The generation of women I interviewed is the first to have full access to the birth control pill and other contraceptive technologies, which the women in my sample expected to and did use. Interviewees saw fertility rather than reproductive aging as a problem; they impatiently waited for reproductive aging to arrive. Many noted the bother and inconvenience of menstruation and what it signified in the context of long-term contraceptive use.

> Enough is enough. I think people should go through menopause early. . . . I had my tubes tied when I was 35. So that I knew, you know, from the time I was 35 until 52 I could still have sex and not get pregnant. So [menopause] meant nothing to me. I knew I wasn't having any more kids. That's why I had my tubes tied. . . . And I've been having [sex] all those years. And I was on the pill for 10 years before that so I never had an issue with that. I had my two kids and I wasn't having any more. (Jenna, white)

> In all sincerity, it just never occurred to me [to mourn] the loss of [reproductive capacity]. I mean, final for me was a tubal that I had when my 22-year-old son was born. . . . That was just another phase of my life, you know. I guess I just don't think about [menopause] a whole lot. (Lenora, African American)

A third woman, whose youngest child was 16 and who had spent all the years since that birth on the pill, said, "I've been looking forward to menopause the day I knew I had my last baby" (Mary, white). It was difficult for many interviewees to fathom feeling a loss upon menopause because they purposefully lost or ended their reproductive capacity many years ago.

Out of 45 women, only 4 specifically connected menopause to a loss of reproductive capacity and mourned this loss. These were not the youngest interviewees; 1 woman was in her early 40s, but the other 3 were in their late 50s. All 4 were white and were already biological mothers. Three women had undergone tubal ligations after their children were born, their youngest child being 13. Entrance into menopause may have triggered ambivalence for these women because all were in new relationships. In these cases, however, choices to end reproduction artificially were final, and women's decisions came long before menopause began. All 3 women knew this. The 4th woman prioritized her career and delayed childbearing until age 35, only to begin perimenopause three years later. She was only able to birth two children before the onset of menopause. This woman's experience was dissimilar from others'; as mentioned earlier, all the other women made a decision prior to menopause to avoid biological motherhood.

While an explicit comparison with previous generations is impossible due to a lack of data, my sample of women may experience menopause differently from their mothers and grandmothers who could not make such a final and/or early choice about reproduction.[1] Because easy access to contraceptive technologies is fairly new, the lack of a direct link between menopause and the end of reproductive capacity also may be fairly new.

Menopausal Women Desire and Enjoy Sex

Many women were very interested in sex and introduced the topic themselves during interviews. While women are supposed to be uninterested in sex (Brumberg 1997; Winterich 2003) and menopause has been characterized as the end of sexual desire (Gannon 1999; Wilbush 1993; Winterich 2003), many interviewees reported feeling "sexier" and more "womanly" than before. Cindy, an African American woman, explained, "I look in the mirror and I say, 'My, you've gotten sexier since you've gotten here [i.e., to this stage of life]. (laugh) More sexy and more good looking.'"

In more than half (26) of my interviews, lengthy discussions of women's excitement over sex and the prospect of not having to use contraception anymore arose.[2] The logistics of using contraception for many years (if they had not opted for surgical methods) discouraged women in my sample from having as much sex as they desired. While the availability of contraceptive technology brought reproductive freedom in theory, menopause brought freedom in practice; this is illustrated in their discussions of sex. Menopause released interviewees from the gendered burdens of contracepting (as well as menstruation) and, consequently, allowed them to enjoy sex more than they ever had.

Even when interviewees discussed menopause's detrimental effects on sexual intercourse (e.g., vaginal dryness or a perceived lack of sexual desire at certain times), they also talked about desiring and anticipating sex. Winterich (2003) reports similar data. Many also talked about feeling more confident sexually and/or having more sexual energy than before. Patricia, a white woman, illustrates her continued (if not increased) interest in sex.

> I am much more open than I used to be sexually [because I] don't give a shit anymore. Sorry! (laugh) It's like once you get over 50, who cares? You know? I mean it's like I've lived all my life for everybody else, right? So that part of it is really good. The part I have problems with is reaching orgasm. It used to be a whole lot easier.

> [*HD: And do you think that's because of menopause?*] . . . You know, I don't know, but I enjoy it more than I ever did. [*HD: Do you think it's because you know you can't get pregnant, or do you think it's for other reasons?*] That part plus . . . I just reached a time where it was just like, this is really silly . . . to have all these inhibitions and worrying about this and worrying about that. You know? . . . I think that was freedom. . . . These days people hit menopause and . . . they have half their lives still to lead at least. You'd be surprised how many young guys are interested in older women, too. You know? So . . . it's kind of funny because . . . I guess I never thought about that when I was young. (laugh)

Patricia, although characterizing herself as older, suggests she is more "open" and enjoys sex more now despite some minor physical difficulties, her age, or her menopausal life stage. This enjoyment is due to a new confidence in sex brought on by her conviction that she still has half her life to lead and a reduction in her "worrying" about sexual activity.

Similarly, Mary, a white woman, discussed how she was more interested in sex after she did not have to worry about contracepting or the threat of pregnancy: "It's kind of coming to the end of an era. Well, . . . or you're opening some new doors. I'd be apt to say, 'Hell, you can have sex all the time without doing anything! You can do what ever you want to!'" Another told me that her husband has trouble "keeping up" with her sexual desire, but "he is just happy. (laugh) Not having to [contracept] makes it a lot easier for heaven's sake . . . no faltering. . . . Yeah, oh yeah. He wouldn't have anything to complain about . . . just freedom. [I'm] a wild woman (laugh)" (Lenora, African American). Interviewees frequently discussed their sexual selves this way, highlighting that sex after menopause is exciting because it is easier and less worrisome.

Conditions such as vaginal dryness or a weak sex drive were an issue for some interviewees, temporarily hindering their abilities to have or enjoy frequent sexual activity. Instead of becoming uninterested in sex or stopping sexual intercourse, however, these women visited doctors and invested in alternative herbal remedies to alleviate sexual discomfort or fluctuating desire. The important theme in women's conversations is that they do not feel too old to engage in sexual activity, again denying any link between menopause and feeling or being old. Regardless of current impediments to sexual activity (e.g., relationship problems or physical problems), interviewees define themselves as sexual beings and "too young to not have a good sex life" (Elise, white).

"I Feel Like a Teenager Again!" Parallels Between Menopause and Menarche

Ten women described menopause as "similar to puberty" or to "when you first get your period." Women created this analogy because they could not control their bodies as much as they could in previous years. Menopause therefore seemed similar to the experience of first getting periods, with episodes of menstrual irregularity, hormone fluctuations, changing skin conditions, weight gain, and the like. Women disregarded a general chronology of age and feeling old and, alternatively, thought about menopause in the context of earlier reproductive experiences and feeling young. At the onset of menopause, interviewees were more cognizant of what had happened in their lives prior to that point (i.e., reproductive experiences) than what would happen to them in the future (i.e., other aging processes). Janet, a white woman, said she "felt like a teenager again, quite frankly." Others made similar comments.

> I think menopause is exactly like puberty, but we make a big deal and say how hard it is for teenagers to get through [puberty], and then we don't make a big deal of it on the other end, when it's exactly the same thing. I feel like a teenager now just like I did when I was, really, because now I'm more confident, I have more energy, I'm excited about life, and it's exactly the way I felt when I was little. (Natalie, African American)
>
> [When perimenopause began] sometimes I'd get my period after three weeks, sometimes it

would be three months. . . . it was sort of like back to being 14 again. [Gloria, white]

Not only do these women report feeling like teens again, they also report some of the thoughts teenagers have. For instance, previous research on the baby boom generation suggests that girls often are glad to get their periods for the first time because then they are similar to, and can converse with, their friends (Brumberg 1997, 51). If they are not menstruating, they are "left behind," "undeveloped" compared with their peers. Peer networks become important at menarche because they provide a benchmark for judging one's own experience. Judy, a white woman, illustrates the same phenomenon upon menopause. "I knew [menopause] was going to happen, and I was really rather excited when [the doctor] told me that I was starting that, you know. [*HD: And what was the most exciting part?*] . . . Just knowing that I was towards the end, I guess, the beginning of the end. . . . It was just a new phase of my life, and it was something that I could relate to my friends with and, you know, you could talk over and . . . it wasn't anything negative at all."

Rather than linking menopause with feeling old, interviewees made sense of menopause by thinking about it in the context of other reproductive processes that they and their peers experienced. Morell (2003) and Lysack and Seipke (2002) note that comparing one's own conditions to those of peers is not uncommon among aging women, but Brumberg (1997) proposes that the "tolerance for menstrual talk" among women took hold when the baby boomers were in adolescence. Thus, comparison of one's menopausal experiences with friends' (instead of just with family members') may be a fairly new phenomenon.

Relating it to their own previous reproductive experiences and others' experiences, interviewees saw themselves entering a third plateau of experience or phase of life: the first being before menarche, the second being the years between menarche and menopause (i.e., potential childbearing years), and the third being menopausal and/or beyond. Women thought of their life stage in terms of continuity of experience rather than heading toward an end stage. This is not unlike the findings that other research reports on age identities (Cremin 1992; Kaufman and Elder 2002; Laz 2003; Twigg 2004). Yet, when interviewees talk about reproductive aging, they make specific connections between menopause and previous reproductive experiences, and a discussion of this context has been absent from the literature on menopause and aging. If we think about menopause the way Cindy, an African American woman, does in the following quote, it is understandable why my interviewees did not feel old.

> When it starts, there is a certain cycle, and then when it stops, it is another point in a woman's life. It doesn't mean you are not a woman anymore, this is [just] another point in a woman's life. . . . We do say the[y are] little girls and they are turning to women. And maybe we should be careful about that, 'cause [my words] suggest that when you are not [menstruating] you are not a woman, and I didn't realize that until just now when we were talking. [*HD: So would you compare the whole process to puberty?*] Oh yes, it is the same thing . . . because when you think about it, maybe . . . you get to be a girl again. You know what I mean? You can look at it like that. . . . You get to be a girl again. I mean, you don't have to worry about that stuff. (laughs) Gees, you know. . . . you can really have the time of your life, I'm thinking.

Because of the similarity between menarche (i.e., the transition between "girl" and "woman") and menopause, menopause is the transition back to being a "girl again." In fact, Cindy implies that there are only two life stages (girl and woman) and that one reverts back to the better stage upon menopause. Being a "girl again" means one is no longer concerned with reproductive capacity and the gendered burdens (e.g., contraception, menstruation, the threat of pregnancy) related to it. Behind Cindy's reference to girlhood is a wish to be carefree and worry-free. To be carefree, as a woman, one must be released from reproductive burdens. Because Cindy already experienced a

nonreproductive phase as a "girl," she uses this as a reference point for the freedoms gained via reproductive aging.

Pamela, a white woman, also explains, "You no longer have to take care of kids or have kids and it's kind of like it was when you didn't have kids, you are free." Interviewees replay an earlier life stage and enjoy it more this time because they understand its worth after experiencing reproductive burdens. This idea contradicts equations of menopause and feeling old. While aging research suggests aging individuals do not feel old anymore, the idea that this feeling relates to gender-specific experiences or that feelings of youthfulness are brought on by women's comparison of menopause with previous reproductive experiences is a new finding.

Menopause Is the "Good Old"

According to interviewees, menstruation is an expendable and unnecessary bodily process. The loss of biological reproductive capacity remained distinct from other forms of aging specifically because most women wanted to be rid of menstrual cycles and contraceptive routines. Most women in my sample therefore described menopause in positive terms while discussing other aging processes in negative terms. Valerie, a white woman, described, "There is a bad old and a good old." She declared that if menopause had to be characterized as an aging process, it represented the "good old." I asked Valerie to explain further.

> The bad old is ill health, not being able to take care of yourself, and the good old is a wonderful lifetime of memories and things that you've done and activities, um, and being able to do them . . . [*HD: What kind of activities?*] Well, living a full life, continuing to work until you don't want to, being able to travel and to be active, outdoor things if that's what you would like. . . . Being able to be comfortable with yourself, sitting and reading a book if that's what you want, doing what you're choosing to do. Not what someone chooses to do for you. [And] the work, the work world is going to go

on for a lot of years for our generation. . . . I think a lot of people do end up working either full- or part-time for a number of extra years beyond [when] our parents probably worked. And being able to do that, having the freedom to do it. That's good old. (laughs)

For Valerie, menopause enhanced freedom, choice, and ability, while other aging processes signified restriction, lack of choice, and the loss of ability. Conceptualized this way, menopause becomes the opposite of other aging experiences.

Similarly, when I asked women what came to mind when they thought about aging, they reported conditions that their 70- to 90-year-old parents had. Almost everyone in my sample was worried about Alzheimer's, cancer, or physical disabilities they might experience in the future (Cremin 1992; Kaufman and Elder 2002). Maureen, a white woman, worried about the possibility of acquiring Alzheimer's like her father; in the context of her father's ailments, Maureen's menopause experiences seemed trivial. If interviewees were worried about their current aging conditions, their worries concerned bodily changes like the loss of eyesight.

There [are] other things that have changed about my body that I've associated more [with aging] and that I've had more trouble with. Like my eyes. I mean, I never [wore] glasses, I mean, . . . I fought it like, you know, (laughing), I mean, there was like no way! And I kept thinking when my eyes first went, you know, I thought, "Oh, this is just temporary." (laughing) You know? And I've been having like lower back problems and stuff like that, and that's made me feel . . . or noticing that you don't recover like you used to. You know, those are the things that I've actually associated with getting old. . . . Because . . . it's more of a loss of a function that I would like to have rather than this other function that I'm ready to let go of. [June, white]

For June, losing her eyesight and having to buy glasses, or having lower back pain and not being able to recover from that pain, was much more traumatic than menopause. In fact, she celebrated menopause with her mother (even throwing a "menopause party" for herself and her friends) because it was the loss of a bodily process that she was "ready to let go of." Almost all of the women I interviewed thought other aging processes could influence them more than menopause. Getting bifocals—a relatively minor problem in the larger scheme of bodily problems and health conditions—seemed more negative to many women than menopause at the time of the interview. The difference revolved around whether or not women felt they were losing a necessary bodily capacity or not. Laz (2003) cites similar findings when she describes how individuals typically deny feeling old until they "embody" aging and experience severe physical ailments (see also Cremin 1992; Lysack and Seipke 2002).

Furthermore, while menopause was overwhelmingly defined as a positive transition by my interviewees, women's worries about menopause as an aging condition centered on osteoporosis, breast cancer, and heart disease, all concerns brought on by the wealth of media attention to these problems. Also because medical discourse on HRT currently focuses on the long-term health risks for women brought on by their "loss" of hormones upon menopause (Murtagh and Hepworth 2003), many interviewees defined these potential future health conditions as more problematic than current ones. Some women reported taking HRT specifically to avoid heart disease, and others decided against HRT specifically to avoid breast cancer. Many exercised and took calcium supplements to avoid osteoporosis or at least knew they should. The health conditions they tried to prevent, however, were also those that would eventually affect their physical bodies, mobility, and longevity. Because a menopausal life stage had not yet brought on these physical conditions, reproductive aging did not currently represent limitations, ailments, or the embodiment of aging; to the contrary, it represented a gendered freedom for women in my sample.

In addition, women I interviewed insinuated that being fertile or "reproductive" held them back from what they wanted to do or be. Early radical feminists hypothesized that when and if women could be freed of biological reproduction, they would experience personal liberation and, ultimately, a better life (Firestone 1970). Silver (2003) also hints that particular aging processes may induce a degendering of women's lives. Likewise, when I asked, "How would you describe your life after reaching menopause?" interviewees suggested that menopause ushered in a gendered freedom long awaited and deserved.

> This is the second half of your life, and this is the freedom part. This is the best part of your life. That's how I look at it. (Patricia, white)
>
> Menopause [is] wonderful. It's like years ago, taking off your bra! No more Tampax! (Brenda, white)
>
> It's change. It's going to another phase in your life. It's probably like that thing that becomes a butterfly. The butterfly is really the best stage because it's free. It can explore the world, and do more things without restrictions . . . You don't have to worry about periods. You're more confident. You're more energetic. . . . It's almost like you're getting a second chance at life. For most women, by the time they get to that stage, they're even better off financially. A lot of the stress, like childrearing, is gone. So it's more freeing. It's a good state, I think. (Natalie, African American)

The language used by these women is wholly positive. Reading these quotes, one might think that menopause is the best experience women ever had. The negative side to menopause should not be overlooked; menopause did bring forth many problematic symptoms, somewhat uncontrollable bodies, and regular doctor's visits for some interviewees. Yet weighing their perception and knowledge of other aging processes versus the gendered freedoms gained via menopause,[3] interviewees can neither equate reproductive aging with other aging processes nor with feeling old. My finding that menopause has positive meaning for interviewees specifically because of its reproductive and aging contexts offers a new lens for thinking about menopause.

Summary and Conclusions

Findings in this article highlight the importance of reproductive and aging contexts for understanding menopause. Having access to contraceptive and birth control technology, women in my sample finalized their reproduction long before menopause. Thus, reproductive aging no longer represents a symbolic end to reproductive capacity; more often it represents an end to contraceptive use and menstruation. Interviewees reported enjoying sex more than ever before because they could engage in this activity without the hassles of contraception and menstruation. Also, because women's menopausal experiences were reminiscent of menarche and a previous life stage, they felt younger rather than older upon this transition. Differentiating it from other forms of aging, interviewees said menopause was the "good old," whereas other aging processes were "bad." Reproductive aging ushered positive changes in their lives. They also suggested that menopause is a reproductive experience first and only an aging experience second.

Women in my sample may be the first to voice distinctions between menopause and other forms of aging because of contemporary structural and ideological changes affecting women's reproductive and aging experiences in recent years. Increased longevity, the fact that baby boomers are engaging in "youthful" activities into midlife, and the availability of contraceptive technology throughout their lives may affect how this particular generation of women experiences reproductive aging. My interviewees identified with ideas about the uniqueness of their generation and experiences of reproductive aging; without prompting, 17 women specifically explained that the baby boomers or "1960s generation" is different in attitude and behavior. I call for feminist scholars to explore the uniqueness of contemporary menopause and baby boom women more fully.

My study is one of the largest qualitative projects to date on the meanings and experiences of menopause in the United States. Nonetheless, my sample has limitations. First, my research is based on a snowball sample, so I cannot generalize my results to any group of menopausal women. Second, women in my sample are middle-class. Other scholars note class differences in women's health experiences (e.g., Brumberg 1997; Ruzek, Olesen, and Clarke 1997); thus, interviewees may be different from menopausal women of other class locations in their attitudes and experiences. For instance, because middle-class women have greater access to birth control during their lifetimes than working-class women, middle-class women might view menopause as freedom from contraceptive burdens, while working-class women might view menopause as freedom from the threat of pregnancy. Thus, the reproductive freedom gained from menopause may vary with social class. In addition, while I present interviewees' race locations to illustrate potential commonalities across women in my sample, commonalities as well as differences by race must be explored further with a more diverse sample of menopausal women. Reproductive aging experiences may be affected by other social locations as well, such as sexuality (Winterich 2003), national origin (Lock 1993), marital status, or disability. Future studies must explore women's social locations as important contexts for reproductive aging.

This study contributes to the feminist literature on menopause in several ways. First, I highlight the necessity of analyzing two social contexts simultaneously. Simply put, menopause cannot be understood as a unique aging process unless we look at its gendered, reproductive contexts. Second, in focusing on reproductive and aging contexts, I remedy two key oversights in the feminist scholarship on menopause. For the most part, we have left (1) the study of aging to aging scholars and (2) the study of reproductive contexts for menopause to medical science. By doing so, we have allowed menopause to be equated with other aging processes and ignored potentially positive connections between women's attitudes on menopause and their earlier reproductive experiences. An analysis of reproductive and aging contexts allows us to truly document the gendered meanings and experiences of men-

opause and other reproductive processes and explore the gendered connections among women's past, present, and future life stages. Third, contemporary menopausal women are experiencing reproductive aging alongside important structural and ideological shifts that must be studied in their own right. We have yet to understand the full social impact of increased longevity, the availability and use of contraceptive technologies, and the changing meanings of activities like sex; I attempt to show how the impact of these shifts can be realized through discussions with contemporary menopausal women. Exploring the social contexts of menopause is a complicated task, but I hope this article illustrates how we can push the boundaries of feminist analyses further than we already have.

Notes

1. Of course, individual women have shown agency in controlling their own fertility throughout history and often before technology existed. I am merely suggesting that with the contemporary availability of contraceptive technology, entire *groups* of women can easily expect to, and do, control fertility. I thank an anonymous reviewer for encouraging me to clarify this point.

2. The remaining 19 women were similar to the women who discussed sex. The presence/absence of sex talk depended on interviewing circumstances more than anything else. For example, sometimes interview locations (e.g., a coffee shop versus a private home) curtailed these conversations. Other interviews were cut short because of time constraints, and discussions about sex usually occurred late in interviews.

3. Natalie's quote suggests that middle age also brings other gendered freedoms for some women, specifically greater financial stability and children's exit from the home (although Natalie still had children in her home). I choose to analyze reproductive freedoms, but future research should explore other freedoms that may emerge for women in midlife.

References

Barbre, Joy W. 1998. Meno-boomers and moral guardians: An exploration of the cultural construction of menopause. In *The politics of women's bodies*, edited by R. Weitz. New York: Oxford University Press.

Brumberg, Joan Jacobs. 1997. *The body project: An intimate history of American girls.* New York: Random House.

Cremin, Mary C. 1992. Feeling old versus being old: Views of troubled aging. *Social Science & Medicine* 34 (12): 1305–15.

Fausto-Sterling, Anne. 1992. *Myths of gender.* 2nd ed. New York: Basic Books.

Featherstone, M., and M. Hepworth. 1991. The mask of ageing and the postmodern life course. In *The body: Social process and cultural theory*, edited by M. Featherstone, M. Hepworth, and B. Turner. London: Sage.

Ferguson, S., and C. Parry. 1998. Rewriting menopause: Challenging the medical paradigm to reflect menopausal women's experiences. *Frontiers* 19(1): 20–41.

Furman, Frida Kerner. 1997. *Facing the mirror: Older women and beauty shop culture.* New York: Routledge.

Gannon, Linda R. 1999. *Women and aging: Transcending the myths.* New York: Routledge.

Gannon, L., and B. Ekstrom. 1993. Attitudes toward menopause: The influence of sociocultural paradigms. *Psychology of Women Quarterly* 17:275–88.

Kaufman, G., and G. Elder Jr. 2002. Revisiting age identity: A research note. *Journal of Aging Studies* 16:169–76.

Laz, Cheryl. 2003. Age embodied. *Journal of Aging Studies* 17:503–19.

Lock, Margaret. 1993. *Encounters with aging: Mythologies of menopause in Japan and North America.* Berkeley: University of California Press.

Lysack, C., and H. Seipke. 2002. Communicating the occupational self: A qualitative study of oldest-old American women. *Scandinavian Journal of Occupational Therapy* 9:130–39.

Martin, Emily. 1992. *The woman in the body: A cultural analysis of reproduction.* 2nd ed. Boston: Beacon.

Morell, Carolyn M. 2003. Empowerment and long-living women: Return to the rejected body. *Journal of Aging Studies* 17(1): 69–85.

Ruzek, Sheryl, Virginia Olesen, and Adele Clarke, eds. 1997. *Women's health: Complexities and differences.* Columbus: Ohio State University Press.

Twigg, Julia. 2004. The body, gender, and age: Feminist insights in social gerontology. *Journal of Aging Studies* 18 (1): 59–73.

Wilbush, Joel. 1993. The climacteric kaleidoscope: Questions and speculations. *Maturitas* 16:157–62.

Winterich, Julie, 2003. Sex, menopause, and culture: Sexual orientation and the meaning of menopause for women's sex lives. *Gender & Society* 17(4): 627–42.

Winterich, J., and D. Umberson. 1999. How women experience menopause: The importance of social context. *Journal of Women & Aging* 11(4): 57–73.

Zita, Jacquelyn. 1997. The premenstrual syndrome: "Dis-easing" the female cycle. In *Feminism and science*, edited by N. Tuana. Bloomington: Indiana University Press.

PART FIVE

Violence

One of the most prevalent and persistent gender differences is the propensity to engage in violence. Across cultures and time periods, males as a group are much more likely than females to perpetrate violent acts against each other and against women. People who believe that men and women are naturally *essentially* different often point to gender differences in aggression and violence to support their position. This is true of some cultural feminists who view women as inherently superior to men and more oriented toward harmony, peace, and justice. It is also true of some people on the conservative right who believe that innate gender differences dictate separate spheres of activity; men are designed for war and leadership, women for domesticity. Some scholars argue that this difference is based in biology, that is, in genetic structures and hormones. There is evidence, for example, that testosterone is linked to aggression in animals and humans. However, there is also research demonstrating that the links between testosterone and aggression are mediated by the social environment. Hormones do not dictate behavior; there is a relationship between the body's responses to the environment, the production of hormones, and the cultural and social con-

text of behavior (Fausto-Sterling 2000; Kimmel 2008). It goes against common experience to suggest that there is no connection between biology and behavior. But like all other aspects of human existence, the gendered nature of violence is the outcome of a complicated interaction among bodies, biographies, and context. Essentialist arguments on either side of the political spectrum reinforce the idea that biology is destiny and change is therefore undesirable and ultimately impossible.

People usually associate the term *violence* with face-to-face interpersonal acts, such as assault, rape, and murder. However, even the most severe interpersonal violence depends on social context for its meaning. For instance, up until the 1980s, in the United States, men could not formally commit the criminal act of rape on their wives since legal statutes exempted wives as victims (Bergen 2000). Unfortunately, individual perpetrators and legal actors still have difficulty distinguishing consent from coercion, particularly in cases of acquaintance, date, and marital rape. Internalizing a partner's claims to legitimate or even unlimited sexual access, many women are hesitant to name their experiences "rape" (Ferraro 2006; Finkelhor and Yllo 1987). Historical transformations in norms surrounding violence, contextual factors (such as self-defense), and individual and situational factors all influence the evaluation of behavior. When we move to the more ethereal realm of emotional or psychological abuse, the

189

definition of violence becomes even more elusive. Most women who experience intimate partner violence find that emotional abuse causes more long-lasting damage than minor physical abuse. However, nonphysical violence is much more dependent on subjective evaluations and is almost impossible to prove to outsiders and legal actors.

Gender is also linked to more collective and distal forms of violence, such as war, genocide, environmental destruction and pollution, and corporate crime. Men have been the architects and actors for many of these events that have caused such horrific suffering. Women have also participated as active agents in collective violence, often solidifying masculinist values and goals in the process. Men and women are also victimized by these more distal forms of violence in uniquely gendered ways. In war, men are more likely to experience the trauma of taking the lives of others and watching the pain and death of comrades. Women are more often the targets of sexualized violence, the caretakers of the wounded, and the grieving survivors of lost family and friends. Women also represent the symbolic terrain on which men fight to protect national values. Yet on the issue of violence, we once again must consider the ways that gender intersects with other aspects of identity. In the military, for example, it is most often young, low-income men and women who are on the front lines. Today in the United States, young people of color are overrepresented in the volunteer armed forces. As Andrea Smith (Cherokee) points out in her article, "Not an Indian Tradition," American Indian people have borne the brunt of the carcinogens produced by uranium mining, military testing, and toxic wastes. She rightly points out that this is a continuation of centuries of sexualized violence against Native peoples, since women's reproductive capacities are directly harmed by these carcinogenic by-products of militarism.

Smith points out that Susan Brownmiller's early feminist statement on male violence reflects a tendency to view male violence and female victimization as a homogeneous phenomenon without history or politics. The idea that "Rape is nothing more or less than a conscious process of intimidation by which all men keep all women in a state of fear" obscures the ways that sexual violence and racism have been part and parcel of the colonial imagination. Sexual violence was perpetrated against American Indian women as part of a campaign of genocide; African American men were falsely accused of raping white women to justify lynching, and again, to support the racist exclusion and domination of an 'internal enemy.' Reading the historical record conveyed in Smith's article, it is clear that neither "all men" nor "all women" have the same relationship to rape. People experience rape within the matrix of domination that includes colonialism as well as hierarchies of power based on gender, race, class, and sexuality.

Cathy Winkler brings us to the very personal, visceral level by telling her own story of surviving rape. This is, of course, also a political narrative of the vulnerability to rape of strong, accomplished women of all ages, races, classes, sexual orientations, and physical abilities. While we need to recognize the unique experiences of women, we should not forget the commonalities. It is important that women tell their stories of rape so that their suffering is visible and understood by other women and by men who want to end rape. Winkler wants people to understand that she experienced rape as "social murder"; rapists try to define women socially, psychologically, mentally, and sexually. Survivors recall this as a "social murder" and continue to relive their terror over many months, sometimes years. One of the devastating consequences of rape is the survivor's ongoing feelings of responsibility, of being in the "wrong place." Rapists, especially acquaintance rapists, often try to instill these feelings in victims. June Jordan's poetry about her own rape ("Poem about My Rights") poignantly links that rape with the colonizing rape of nations' resources and sovereignty. And she powerfully rejects any rationalization of violence that invokes the *victim's* behavior and neglects the humanity and right to existence of all people. We need both theoretical analyses and personal accounts to communicate the experience of rape and to develop effective strategies to end violence against women.

My article addresses the "blurred boundaries" between women's victimization and offending. I argue that some of our strategies for ending violence have contributed to the "criminalization of victimization," in Meda Chesney-Lind's terms. Although some women are physically violent without experiencing prior victimization, the majority of women and girls incarcerated as violent offenders are also victims of violent abuse. The women I met over many years of serving as an expert witness on battering do not fit into the categories we have developed for describing and working against domestic violence. None were comfortable with the term "battered woman." They were not helpless; many continued to love the men who abused them, and they were all offenders as well as victims. As many other authors in this book have argued, women's lives overlap the categorical boundaries that define "normality." When we focus on enforcement of these boundaries and lose sight of women's lived experience, we inevitably exclude and often punish women.

Meda Chesney-Lind and Joanne Belknap also describe the ways that the victimization of girls is linked to their arrest and detention. They challenge the recurrent theme of girls' and women's increasing violence that circulates through the scholarly and popular press. The lurid, high profile cases of girls' violence that capture media attention belie the more mundane facts that both boys' and girls' violence *decreased* during the 1990s and that girls are still far less likely to engage in violent crime than boys. Chesney-Lind and Belknap describe policy changes, including relabeling, rediscovery, and up-criming, that explain apparent increases in girls' violence through changes in the ways that identical behaviors are categorized. For example, many minor forms of violence, such as throwing cookies, are now labeled assaults as part of the zero tolerance policies of the 1980s and 1990s. They also emphasize that the get-tough policies of the last two decades have had a much greater effect on African American and

Latina girls than on whites. Once again, in terms of official sanctions and public perceptions, gender is not the only factor affecting experience.

PJ McGann describes her encounter with a female motorist who nearly ran her over in a crosswalk, then yelled at her "you look like a man besides!" McGann locates this experience within the contradictory cultural representations of variant sexualities. People are murdered brutally solely on the basis of their gender identity, and these murders are often depicted as sad but predictable reactions to the dominant sexual order. At the same time, the popular media now incorporate a range of sexual and gender identities in a manner that suggests normalization and acceptance. Certainly, there has been progress in social acceptance of gender variance. Yet McGann's experience of symbolic and physical violence in reaction to her queer identity reflects the continuing cultural investment in a binary model of gender.

Finally, Cynthia Enloe reminds us that wherever violence occurs, we must examine the organizational configuration of gender. Lynndie England symbolized for many the fact that women are just as capable of inflicting torture as men. Pictures of England laughing and pointing at a pile of naked male prisoners at Abu Ghraib demonstrated to the world that U.S. military personnel were violating the Geneva Conventions. They also demonstrated that women participated in these war crimes. Like many other highly publicized cases of violence, however, official investigations and discussions of these crimes did not address gender. Enloe argues that the feminist concept of climate should have helped clarify the dynamics of masculinity and femininity at Abu Ghraib. She states that by asking "Has this organization become masculinized in ways that privilege certain forms of masculinity, feminize its opposition, and trivialize most forms of femininity?" investigations could move beyond the theory of "bad apples" to an analysis that would take gender seriously and develop organizational and policy-based transformations to address torture. She returns us to issues raised by Smith. That is, it is impossible to end violence against women without confronting and challenging the larger purposes and politics of gendered and sexualized violence.

References

Bergen, Raquel Kennedy. (2000). "Rape Laws and Spousal Exemptions." Pp. 223–25, in N. H. Rafter, ed. *Encylopedia of Women and Crime.* Phoenix, AZ: Oryx Press.

Fausto-Sterling, Anne. (2000). *Sexing the Body.* New York: Basic Books.

Ferraro, Kathleen J. (2006). *Neither Angels nor Demons: Women, Crime, and Victimization.* Boston: Northeastern University Press.

Finkelhor, David and Kersti Yllo. (1987). *License to Rape.* New York: Free Press.

Kimmel, Michael S. (2008). *The Gendered Society.* 3rd ed. New York: Oxford University Press.

June Jordan

Poem about My Rights

Even tonight and I need to take a walk and clear
my head about this poem about why I can't
go out without changing my clothes my shoes
my body posture my gender identity my age
my status as a woman alone in the evening/
alone on the streets/alone not being the point/
the point being that I can't do what I want
to do with my own body because I am the wrong
sex the wrong age the wrong skin and
suppose it was not here in the city but down on the beach/
or far into the woods and I wanted to go
there by myself thinking about God/or thinking
about children or thinking about the world/all of it
disclosed by the stars and the silence:
I could not go and I could not think and I could not
stay there
alone
as I need to be
alone because I can't do what I want to do with my own
body and
who in the hell set things up
like this
and in France they say if the guy penetrates
but does not ejaculate then he did not rape me
and if after stabbing him if after screams if
after begging the bastard and if even after smashing
a hammer to his head if even after that if he
and his buddies fuck me after that
then I consented and there was
no rape because finally you understand finally
they fucked me over because I was wrong I was
wrong again to be me being me where I was/wrong
to be who I am
which is exactly like South Africa

penetrating into Namibia penetrating into
Angola and does that mean I mean how do you know if
Pretoria ejaculates what will the evidence look like the
proof of the monster jackboot ejaculation on Blackland
and if
after Namibia and if after Angola and if after Zimbabwe
and if after all of my kinsmen and women resist even to
self-immolation of the villages and if after that
we lose nevertheless what will the big boys say will they
claim my consent:
Do You Follow Me: We are the wrong people of
the wrong skin on the wrong continent and what
in the hell is everybody being reasonable about
and according to the *Times* this week
back in 1966 the C.I.A. decided that they had this problem
and the problem was a man named Nkrumah so they
killed him and before that it was Patrice Lumumba
and before that it was my father on the campus
of my Ivy League school and my father afraid
to walk into the cafeteria because he said he
was wrong the wrong age the wrong skin the wrong
gender identity and he was paying my tuition and
before that
it was my father saying I was wrong saying that
I should have been a boy because he wanted one/a
boy and that I should have been lighter skinned and
that I should have had straighter hair and that
I should not be so boy crazy but instead I should
just be one/a boy and before that
it was my mother pleading plastic surgery for
my nose and braces for my teeth and telling me
to let the books loose to let them loose in other
words
I am very familiar with the problems of the C.I.A.
and the problems of South Africa and the problems
of Exxon Corporation and the problems of white
America in general and the problems of the teachers
and the preachers and the F.B.I. and the social
workers and my particular Mom and Dad/I am very
familiar with the problems because the problems
turn out to be
me
I am the history of rape
I am the history of the rejection of who I am
I am the history of the terrorized incarceration of
my self

I am the history of battery assault and limitless
armies against whatever I want to do with my mind
and my body and my soul and
whether it's about walking out at night
or whether it's about the love that I feel or
whether it's about the sanctity of my vagina or
the sanctity of my national boundaries
or the sanctity of my leaders or the sanctity
of each and every desire
that I know from my personal and idiosyncratic
and indisputably single and singular heart
I have been raped
be-
cause I have been wrong the wrong sex the wrong age
the wrong skin the wrong nose the wrong hair the
wrong need the wrong dream the wrong geographic
the wrong sartorial I
I have been the meaning of rape
I have been the problem everyone seeks to
eliminate by forced
penetration with or without the evidence of slime and/
but let this be unmistakable this poem
is not consent I do not consent
to my mother to my father to the teachers to
the F.B.I. to South Africa to Bedford-Stuy
to Park Avenue to American Airlines to the hardon
idlers on the corners to the sneaky creeps in
cars
I am not wrong: Wrong is not my name
My name is my own my own my own
and I can't tell you who the hell set things up like this
but I can tell you that from now on my resistance
my simple and daily and nightly self-determination
may very well cost you your life

Andrea Smith

Not an Indian Tradition: The Sexual Colonization of Native Peoples

This paper analyzes the connections between sexual violence and colonialism in the lives and histories of Native peoples in the United States. This paper argues that sexual violence does not simply just occur within the process of colonialism, but that colonialism is itself structured by the logic of sexual violence. Furthermore, this logic of sexual violence continues to structure U. S. policies toward Native peoples today. Consequently, anti-sexual violence and anti-colonial struggles cannot be separated.

[Rape] is nothing more or less than a conscious process of intimidation by which all men keep all women in a state of fear

—Susan Brownmiller, *Against Our Will*

Rape as "nothing more or less" than a tool of patriarchal control undergirds the philosophy of the white-dominated anti-violence against women movement. Anti-violence activists generally understand rape solely as gender violence. This philosophy has been critiqued by many women of color, including critical racist theorist Kimberle Crenshaw, for its lack of attention to racism and classism. Crenshaw analyzes how male-dominated conceptions of race and white-dominated conceptions of gender stand in the way of a clear understanding of violence against women of color. It is inadequate, she argues, to investigate the oppression of women of color by examining race and gender oppressions separately and then putting the two analyses together because the overlap of racism and sexism transforms the dynamics of both. Instead, Crenshaw advocates replacing the "additive" approach with an "intersectional" approach that accounts for the overlap.

"The problem is not simply that both discourses fail women of color by not acknowledging the "additional" issue of race or of patriarchy, but rather, that the discourses are often inadequate even to the discrete tasks of articulating the full dimensions of racism and sexism" (1996, 360).

Despite her intersectional approach, however, Crenshaw falls short of describing how a politics of intersectionality might fundamentally shift how we analyze sexual/domestic violence. If sexual violence is not simply a tool of patriarchy, but is also a tool of colonialism and racism, then entire communities of color are the victims of sexual violence. As Neferti Tadiar argues, colonial relationships are themselves gendered and sexualized. "[T]he economies and political relations of nations are libidinally configured, that is, they are grasped and effected in terms of sexuality. This global and regional fantasy is not, however, only metaphorical, but real insofar as it grasps a system of political and economic practices already at work among these nations." Within this context, according to Tadiar, "the question to be asked . . . is, Who is getting off on

Source: "Not an Indian Tradition: The Sexual Colonization of Native Peoples," by Andrea Smith. *Hypatia* 18(2): 70–85. Used by permission of Indiana University Press.

this? Who is getting screwed and by whom?" (1993, 183). Haunani Kay Trask draws similar analysis about U. S.-Hawai'i relationships, which she frames in terms of "cultural prostitution":

> "Prostitution" in this context refers to the entire institution which defines a woman (and by extension the "female") as an object of degraded and victimized sexual value for use and exchange through the medium of money . . . My purpose is not to exact detail or fashion a model but to convey the utter degradation of our culture and our people under corporate tourism by employing "prostitution" as an analytical category . . . The point, of course, is that everything in Hawai'i can be yours, that is, you the tourist, the non-native, the visitor. The place, the people, the culture, even our identity as a "Native" people is for sale. Thus, Hawai'i, like a lovely woman, is there for the taking. (1993, 194)

Within the context of colonization of Native nations, sexual violence does not affect Indian men and women in the same way. However, when a Native woman suffers abuse, this abuse is not just an attack on her identity as a woman, but on her identity as Native. The issues of colonial, race, and gender oppression cannot be separated. This explains why, in my experience as a rape crisis counselor, every Native survivor I ever counseled said to me at one point, "I wish I was no longer Indian." Women of color do not just face quantitatively more issues when they suffer violence (that is, less media attention, language barriers, lack of support in the judicial system, etc.) but their experience is qualitatively different from that of white women.

Historical Context

Ann Stoler argues that racism, far from being a reaction to crisis in which racial others are scapegoated for social ills, is a permanent part of the social fabric. "[R]acism is not an effect but a tactic in the internal fission of society into binary opposition, a means of creating 'biologized' internal enemies, against whom society must defend itself" (1997, 59). She notes that in the modern state, the constant purification and elimination of racialized enemies within that state ensures the growth of the national body. "Racism does not merely arise in moments of crisis, in sporadic cleansings. It is internal to the biopolitical state, woven into the web of the social body, threaded through its fabric" (1997, 59).

Similarly, Kate Shanley notes that Native peoples are a permanent "present absence" in the U.S. colonial imagination, an "absence" that reinforces at every turn the conviction that Native peoples are indeed vanishing and that the conquest of Native lands is justified. Ella Shoat and Robert Stam describe this absence as "an ambivalently repressive mechanism [that] dispels the anxiety in the face of the Indian, whose very presence is a reminder of the initially precarious grounding of the American nation-state itself . . . In a temporal paradox, living Indians were induced to 'play dead,' as it were, in order to perform a narrative of manifest destiny in which their role, ultimately, was to disappear" (1994, 118–19). This "absence" is effected through the metaphorical transformation of Native bodies into a pollution of which the colonial body must purify itself. As white Californians described in the 1860s, Native people were "the dirtiest lot of human beings on earth." They wear "filthy rags, with their persons unwashed, hair uncombed and swarming with vermin" (Rawls 1984, 195). The following 1885 Proctor & Gamble ad for Ivory Soap also illustrates this equation between Indian bodies and dirt:

> We were once factious, fierce and wild,
> In peaceful arts unreconciled
> Our blankets smeared with grease and stains
> From buffalo meat and settlers' veins.
> Through summer's dust and heat content
> From moon to moon unwashed we went,
> But IVORY SOAP came like a ray
> Of light across our darkened way
> And now we're civil, kind and good
> And keep the laws as people should,
> We wear our linen, lawn and lace

As well as folks with paler face
And now I take, where'er we go
This cake of IVORY SOAP to show
What civilized my squaw and me
And made us clean and fair to see.
    (Lopez n.d., 119)

In the colonial imagination, Native bodies are also immanently polluted with sexual sin. Alexander Whitaker, a minister in Virginia, wrote in 1613: "They live naked in bodie, as if their shame of their sinne deserved no covering: Their names are as naked as their bodie: They esteem it a virtue to lie, deceive and steale as their master the divell teacheth them" (Berkhofer 1978, 19). Furthermore, according to Bernardino de Minaya: "Their [the Indians'] marriages are not a sacrament but a sacrilege. They are idolatrous, libidinous, and commit sodomy. Their chief desire is to eat, drink, worship heathen idols, and commit bestial obscenities" (cited in Stannard 1992, 211).

Stoler's analysis of racism in which Native peoples are likened to a pollution that threatens U. S. security is indicated in the comments of one doctor in his attempt to rationalize the mass sterilization of Native women in the 1970s: "People pollute, and too many people crowded too close together cause many of our social and economic problems. These in turn are aggravated by involuntary and irresponsible parenthood . . . We also have obligations to the society of which we are part. The welfare mess, as it has been called, cries out for solutions, one of which is fertility control" (Oklahoma 1989, 11). Herbert Aptheker describes the logical consequences of this sterilization movement: "The ultimate logic of this is crematoria; people are themselves constituting the pollution and inferior people in particular, then crematoria become really vast sewerage projects. Only so may one understand those who attend the ovens and concocted and conducted the entire enterprise; those "wasted"—to use U.S. army jargon reserved for colonial hostilities—are not really, not fully people" (1987, 144).

Because Indian bodies are "dirty," they are considered sexually violable and "rapable." That is, in patriarchal thinking, only a body that is "pure" can be violated. The rape of bodies that are considered inherently impure or dirty simply does not count. For instance, prostitutes have almost an impossible time being believed if they are raped because the dominant society considers the prostitute's body undeserving of integrity and violable at all times. Similarly, the history of mutilation of Indian bodies, both living and dead, makes it clear to Indian people that they are not entitled to bodily integrity, as these examples suggest:

> I saw the body of White Antelope with the privates cut off, and I heard a soldier say he was going to make a tobacco-pouch out of them. (cited in Wrone and Nelson 1982, 113)

> Each of the braves was shot down and scalped by the wild volunteers, who out with their knives and cutting two parallel gashes down their backs, would strip the skin from the quivering flesh to make razor straps of. (cited in Wrone and Nelson 1982, 90)

> One more dexterous than the rest, proceeded to flay the chief's [Tecumseh's] body; then, cutting the skin in narrow strips . . . at once, a supply of razor-straps for the more "ferocious" of his brethren. (cited in Wrone and Nelson 1982, 82)

> Andrew Jackson . . . supervised the mutilation of 800 or so Creek Indian corpses—the bodies of men, women and children that he and his men massacred—cutting off their noses to count and preserve a record of the dead, slicing long strips of flesh from their bodies to tan and turn into bridle reins. (Stannard 1992, 121)

Echoing this mentality was Governor Thompson, who stated in 1990 that he would not close down an open Indian burial mound in Dickson, Illinois, because of his argument that he was as much Indian as are current Indians, and consequently, he had as much right as they to determine the fate of Indian remains.[1] He felt free to appropriate the identity of "Native," and thus felt justified in claiming ownership over both Native identity and Native bodies. The Chicago press similarly attempted to challenge the identity of the Indian people who protested Thompson's decision by stating that these protestors were either only "part" Indian or were only claiming to be Indian (Hermann 1990).[2] The message conveyed by the Illinois state government is that to be Indian in this society is to be on constant display for white consumers, in life or in death. And in fact, Indian identity itself is under the control of the colonizer, subject to eradication at any time. As Aime Cesaire puts it, "colonization = 'thingification'" (1972, 21).

As Stoler explains this process of racialized colonization: "[T]he more 'degenerates' and 'abnormals' [in this case Native peoples] are eliminated, the lives of those who speak will be stronger, more vigorous, and improved. The enemies are not political adversaries, but those identified as external and internal threats to the population. Racism is the condition that makes it acceptable to put [certain people] to death in a society of normalization" (1997, 85).

Tadiar's description of colonial relationships as an enactment of the "prevailing mode of heterosexual relations" is useful because it underscores the extent to which U. S. colonizers view the subjugation of women of the Native nations as critical to the success of the economic, cultural, and political colonization (1993, 186). Stoler notes that the imperial discourses on sexuality "cast white women as the bearers of more racist imperial order" (1997, 35). By extension, Native women as bearers of a counter-imperial order pose a supreme threat to the imperial order. Symbolic and literal control over their bodies is important in the war against Native people, as these examples attest:

> When I was in the boat I captured a beautiful Carib women . . . I conceived desire to take pleasure . . . I took a rope and thrashed her well, for which she raised such unheard

screams that you would not have believed your ears. Finally we came to an agreement in such a manner that I can tell you that she seemed to have been brought up in a school of harlots. (Sale 1990, 140)

> Two of the best looking of the squaws were lying in such a position, and from the appearance of the genital organs and of their wounds, there can be no doubt that they were first ravished and then shot dead. Nearly all of the dead were mutilated. (Wrone and Nelson 1982, 123)

> One woman, big with child, rushed into the church, clasping the alter and crying for mercy for herself and unborn babe. She was followed, and fell pierced with a dozen lances . . . the child was torn alive from the yet palpitating body of its mother, first plunged into the holy water to be baptized, and immediately its brains were dashed out against a wall. (Wrone and Nelson 1982, 97)

> The Christians attacked them with buffets and beatings . . . Then they behaved with such temerity and shamelessness that the most powerful ruler of the island had to see his own wife raped by a Christian officer. (Las Casas 1992, 33)

> I heard one man say that he had cut a woman's private parts out, and had them for exhibition on a stick. I heard another man say that he had cut the fingers off of an Indian, to get the rings off his hand. I also heard of numerous instances in which men had cut out the private parts of females, and stretched them over their saddle-bows and some of them over their hats. (Sand Creek 1973, 129–30)

American Horse said of the massacre at Wounded Knee:

> The fact of the killing of the women, and more especially the killing of the young boys and girls who are to go to make up the future strength of the Indian people is the saddest part of the whole affair and we feel it very sorely. (Stannard 1992, 127)

Colonization and the Normality of Patriarchy

Native women are threatening to the project of genocide in many ways. Hazel Carby notes that in the Afro-American context, white men justified the lynching of black men as a means of protecting white women from the supposed predations of black men. "White men used their ownership of the body of the white female as a terrain on which to lynch the black male. White women felt that their caste was their protection and that their interests lay with the power that ultimately confined them" (Carby 1996, 309). The racist violence, then, used by white men against black men simultaneously strengthened patriarchal relationships within white society as white men were pictured as the protectors of white women. Similarly, the colonization of Native women as well is part of the project of strengthening white male ownership of white women.

Karen Warren sheds light on how the colonization of Native women strengthens patriarchy within white society. She argues that patriarchal society is a dysfunctional system that mirrors the dysfunctional nuclear family. That is, when there is severe abuse in the family, the abuse continues because the family members regard it as "normal." Only when a victim of abuse has contact with less abusive families may she come to see that her abuse is not "normal." Similarly, Warren argues, patriarchal society is a dysfunctional system based on domination and violence. "Dysfunctional systems are often maintained through systematic denial, a failure or inability to see the reality of a situation. This denial need not be conscious, intentional, or malicious; it only needs to be pervasive to be effective" (1993, 125).

Europe at the time of Columbus's misadventures was just such a completely dysfunctional system wracked with violence, mass poverty, disease, and war. Hundreds of thousands of Jews were killed in the Inquisition, and their confiscated property was used to fund Columbus's voyages. David Stannard states: "Violence, of course, was everywhere . . . in Milan in 1476 a man was torn to pieces by an enraged mob and his dismembered limbs were eaten by his tormenters. In Paris and Lyon, Huguenots [sic] were killed and butchered, and their various body parts were sold openly in the streets. Other eruptions of bizarre torture, murder, and ritual cannibalism were not uncommon" (1992, 61; see also Sale 1990, 28–37).

European societies were thoroughly misogynistic. Europe's hatred for women was most fully manifest in the witch hunts. In many English towns, as many as a third of the population were accused of witchcraft (Stannard 1992, 61). Women were the particular targets of these witch hunts (Barstow 1994, 21). The women targeted for destruction were those most independent from patriarchal authority; single women, widows, and women healers (Ehrenreich and English 1979, 35–39).

By contrast, Native societies were relatively more peaceful and egalitarian. Their egalitarian nature poses a threat to the ability of white men to continue their ownership of white women because they belie patriarchy's defense of itself as "normal." And in fact, the nature of Native societies did not escape the notice of the colonizers. It was a scandal in the colonies that a number of white people chose to live among Indian people while virtually no Indians voluntarily chose to live among the colonists. According to J. Hector St. John de Crevecoeur, "Thousands of Europeans are Indians, and we have no example of even one of these Aborigines having from choice become Europeans!" (Stannard 1992, 104). As William Apess (Pequot) once stated in the 1800s: "Where, in the records of Indian barbarity, can we point to a violated female?" (O'Connell 1992, 64). Brigadier General James Clinton of the Continental Army said to his soldiers as they were sent off to destroy the Iroquois nation in 1779: "Bad as the savages are, they never violate the chastity of any women, their prisoners" (cited in Wrone and Nelson 1982, 17). As Shoat and Stam argue, the real purpose behind this colonial terror "was not to force the indigenes to become Europeans, but to keep Europeans from becoming indigenes" (1994, 72).

The high status of women in Native societies did not escape the notice of white women either. White women often looked to the Native societies as models of equality from which the white society should base itself, often to the dismay of white men. Even in war, European women were often surprised to find that they went unmolested by their Indian captors. Mary Rowlandson said of her experience: "I have been in the midst of roaring Lions, and Savage Bears, that feared neither God, nor Man, nor the Devil . . . and yet not one of them ever offered the least abuse of unchastity to me in word or action" (Rowlandson 1974, 108–109). Between 1675 and 1763, almost 40 percent of women who were taken captive by Native people in New England chose to remain with their captors (Namias 1993, 25).[3] In 1899, Mrs. Teall wrote an editorial in the *Syracuse Herald-Journal* discussing the status of women in Iroquois society:

> They had one custom the white men are not ready, even yet, to accept. The women of the Iroquois had a public and influential position. They had a council of their own . . . which had the initiative in the discussion; subjects presented by them being settled in the councils of the chiefs and elders; in this latter council the women had an orator of their own (often of their own sex) to present and speak for them. There are sometimes female chiefs . . . The wife owned all the property . . . The family was hers; descent was counted through mother. (Lopez n.d., 101)

In response to her editorial, a man who signs himself as "Student" replies:

> Women among the Iroquois, Mrs. Teall says . . . had a council of their own, and orators and chiefs. Why does she not add what follows in explanation of why such deference was paid to women, that "in the torture of prisoners women were thought more skilful and subtle than the men" and the men of the inquisition were outdone in the refinement of cruelty practiced upon their victims by these savages. It is true also that succession was through women,

not the men, in Iroquois tribes, but the explanation is that it was generally a difficult guess to tell the fatherhood of children . . . The Indian maiden never learned to blush . . . The Indians, about whom so much rhetoric has been wasted, were a savage, merciless lot who would never have developed themselves nearer to civilization than they were found by missionaries and traders . . . Their love was to butcher and burn, to roast their victims and eat them, to lie and rob, to live in filth, men, women, children, dogs and fleas crowded together. (Lopez n.d., 103)

Thus, as Warren argues, the dysfunctionality of patriarchal white society can only be maintained if it seems like the only option. The relatively egalitarian nature of Native societies belies patriarchy's claims to normality, and thus it is imperative for a patriarchal society to thrive to destroy egalitarian societies that present other ways of living. The demonization of Native women, then, is part of white men's desires to maintain control over white women.

Sexual Violence and Reproductive Health

Native women are also threatening because of their ability to reproduce the next generation of peoples who can resist colonization. While the bodies of both Indian men and women have been marked by sexual violence, Ines Hernandez-Avila notes that the bodies of Native women have been particularly targeted for abuse because of their capacity to give birth. "It is because of a Native American woman's sex that she is hunted down and slaughtered, in fact, singled out, because she has the potential through childbirth to assure the continuance of the people" (Hernandez-Avila 1993, 386). David Stannard points out that control over women's reproductive abilities and destruction of women and children are essential in destroying a people. If the women of a nation are not disproportionately killed, then that nation's population will not be severely affected. He says that Native women and children were targeted for wholesale killing in order to destroy the Indian nations (1992, 121). This is why colonizers such as Andrew Jackson recommended that troops systematically kill Indian women and children after massacres in order to complete extermination.

This practice of controlling Native women's ability to reproduce continues in new forms. The General Accounting Office released a study in November 1976 indicating that Native women were being sterilized without informed consent. Dr. Connie Uri (Cherokee/Choctaw) conducted further investigations leading her to estimate that 25 percent of all Native women of childbearing age had been sterilized without their informed consent, with sterilization rates as high as 80 percent on some reservations (Jarvis n.d.; Dillingham 1977a; Dillingham 1977b; Oklahoma 1989).

While the institution of informed consent policies has somewhat curbed the abuse of sterilization, it has reappeared in the form of dangerous contraceptives such as Norplant and Depo-Provera. These are both extremely risky forms of long-acting hormonal contraceptives that have been pushed on Indian women.[4] Depo-Provera, a known carcinogen which has been condemned as an inappropriate form of birth control by several national women's health organizations, was routinely used on Indian women through Indian Health Services (IHS) before it was approved by the FDA in 1992. It was particularly used for Indian women with disabilities. The reason given: hygienics. Depo- Provera prevents Native women with disabilities from having their periods, keeping them "cleaner" for their caretakers. Once again, Native women's bodies are viewed as inherently dirty, in need of cleansing and purification. The Phoenix IHS policy in the 1980s, according to Raymond Jannet, was, "We use it to stop their periods. There is nothing else that will do it. To have to change a pad on someone developmentally disabled, you've got major problems. The fact they become infertile while on it is a side benefit." Jannet argues that Depo Provera helps girls with emotions related to their periods. "Depo Provera turned them back into their sweet, poor handicapped selves. I take some pride in being a pioneer in that regard." But, he said, while he has no problems using the drug on Indian women, "I will not be going out and using it on attractive 16–year-old girls who one day hope to be mothers" (Masterson and Guthrie 1986).

The colonization of Native women's bodies continues today. In the 1980s, when I served as a non-violent witness in the non-violent witness program for the Chippewa spearfishers being harassed by white racist mobs, one persecutor carried a sign saying "Save a fish; spear a pregnant squaw." During the 1990 Mohawk crisis in the town of Oka, a white mob surrounded the ambulance of a Native woman attempting to leave the Mohawk reservation because she was hemorrhaging after having given birth. She was forced to "spread her legs" to prove she had given birth. The police at the scene refused to intervene. An Indian man wearing jeans was arrested for "wearing a disguise," he was brutally beaten, and his testicles were crushed. Two women from Chicago Women of All Red Nations (the organization I belong to) went to Oka to videotape the crisis. They were arrested and held in custody for eleven hours without being charged, and were told that they could not go to the bathroom unless the male police officers could watch. The walls of the place where they were held were covered with pornographic magazines.

This colonial desire to subjugate Indian women's bodies was quite apparent when, in 1982, Stuart Kasten marketed a new video game, "Custer's Revenge," in which players get points each time they, in the form of Custer, rape an Indian woman. The slogan of the game is "When you score, you score." He describes the game as "a fun sequence where the woman is enjoying a sexual act willingly." According to the promotional material:

> You are General Custer. Your dander's up, your pistol's wavin'. You've hog-tied a ravishing Indian maiden and have a chance to rewrite history and even up an old score. Now, the

Indian maiden's hands may be tied, but she's not about to take it lying down, by George! Help is on the way. If you're to get revenge you'll have to rise to the challenge, dodge a tribe of flying arrows and protect your flanks against some downright mean and prickly cactus. But if you can stand pat and last past the strings and arrows—You can stand last. Remember? Revenge is sweet.[5]

Sexual Violence, Land, and Environmental Racism

The connection between the colonization of the bodies of Native peoples, particularly those of Native women, is not simply metaphorical. Many feminist theorists have argued for a connection between patriarchy's disregard for nature, for women, and for indigenous peoples. It is the same colonial/patriarchal mind that seeks to control the sexuality of women and indigenous peoples that also seeks to control nature (Merchant 1980; Caputi 1993; Ruether 1975). As Shoat and Stam explain, "Colonized people are projected as body rather than mind, much as the colonized world was seen as raw material rather than as mental activity and manufacture" (1994, 138).

Certainly, even today, colonizers justify the theft of Native lands on the grounds that Native peoples did not or do not properly control or subdue nature. For instance, among the Christian Right, John Eidsmoe contends that Christians never stole Indian land. He argues that since Native people did not privatize land, and since their communities had not been "established by God," then Europeans had a right to seize the land from them. And furthermore, while Christianity may have been forced on Native people, "millions of people are in heaven today as a result" (Eidsmoe 1992, 133, 140). As Pat Robertson states:

These tribes are . . . in an arrested state of social development. They are not less valuable as human beings because of that, but they offer scant wisdom or learning or philosophical vision that can be instructive to a society that can feed the entire population of the earth in a single harvest and send spacecraft to the moon . . . Except for our crimes, our wars and our frantic pace of life, what we have is superior to the ways of primitive peoples . . . Which life do you think people would prefer: freedom in an enlightened Christian civilization or the suffering of subsistence living and superstition in a jungle? You choose. (Robertson 1993, 153)

Immanuel Wallerstein argues that "racism is meant to keep people inside the work system [at a state of marginalization], not eject them from it" (1991, 34). In the case of Native peoples, however, who have an unemployment rate on many reservations as high as 90 percent, the intent of racism is to exclude them. Because the majority of the energy resources in this country are on Indian lands, the continued existence of Indian people is a threat to capitalist operations. Thus, the connection between the colonization of Native bodies and Native lands is not simply metaphorical but is rooted in material realities.

One way in which capitalism has succeeded in continuing its unrelenting assault against the environment is that certain populations become deemed as "surplus" populations and hence either worthy repositories of environmental waste or scapegoats of environmental crisis in need of population control. Samir Amin describes this process as "apartheid," where "sacrifices imposed on some do not carry the same weight as the benefits obtained by others" (1977, 142). Those peoples who have already been rendered dirty, impure, and hence expendable are then forced to face the most immediate consequences of environmental destruction. Unfortunately for colonizers, it is not so easy to contain environmental degradation to those populations deemed expendable.

It is not an accident that 100 percent of uranium production takes place on or near Indian land (La Duke 1993, 99). Nor is it a coincidence that Native reservations are often targeted for toxic waste dumps. To date, over 50 reservations have been targeted for waste dumps (Beasely 1991, 40). Military and nuclear testing also takes place almost exclusively on Native lands. For instance, there have already been at least 650 nuclear explosions on Western Shoshone land at the Nevada test site. Fifty percent of these underground tests have leaked radiation into the atmosphere (Taliman 1991). Native peoples, the expendable ones, are situated to suffer the brunt of environmental destruction so that colonizers can continue to be in denial about the fact that they will also eventually be affected. As Aime Cesaire notes, the processes of colonization are not containable; ultimately everyone is impacted: "Colonial activity, colonial enterprise, colonial conquest, which is based on contempt for the native and justified by the contempt, inevitably tends to change him who undertakes it; that the colonizer . . . tends objectively to transform himself into an animal. It is this result, this boomerang effect of colonization, that I want to point out" (1972, 20).

A case in point is the current plan to relocate all nuclear wastes into a permanent high-level nuclear waste repository in Yucca mountain on Shoshone land, for a cost of $3.25 billion. Yucca Mountain is located on an active volcanic zone where kiloton bombs are exploded nearby, thus increasing the risks of radioactive leakage (Taliman 1991). In addition, if this plan is approved, the proposed repository on Yucca mountain would receive nuclear wastes throughout the United States. Only five states would not be affected by the transportation of high-level radioactive wastes. With up to 4,000 shipments of radioactive waste crossing the United States annually, trucking industry statistics reveal that up to fifty accidents per year could occur during the thirty-year period during which nuclear waste would stream to Yucca Mountain (Taliman 1991).

Katsi Cook, Mohawk midwife, argues that this attack upon nature is yet another attack on Native women's bodies because the effects of toxic and radiation poisoning are most apparent in their effect on women's reproductive systems.[6] In the areas where there is uranium mining, such as in Four Corners and the Black Hills, Indian people face skyrocketing rates of cancer, miscarriages, and birth defects. Children growing up in Four Corners are developing ovarian and testicular cancers at fifteen times the national average (Taliman 1992). Meanwhile, Indian women on Pine Ridge experience a miscarriage rate six times higher than the national average (Harden 1980, 15). And on the Akwesasne Mohawk reserve, one of the most polluted areas in the country, the PCBs, DDT, Mirex and HCBs that are dumped into their waters are eventually stored in women's breast milk (Contaminated 1994, 11). Through the rape of earth, Native women's bodies are raped once again.

As long as Native people continue to live on the lands rich in energy resources that government or corporate interests want, the sexual colonization of Native people will continue. Native bodies will continue to be depicted as expendable and inherently violable as long as they continue to stand in the way of the theft of Native lands. The United States is indeed engaged in a "permanent social war" against the Native bodies, particularly Native women's bodies, which threaten its legitimacy (Stoler 1997, 69). Colonizers evidently recognize the wisdom of the Cheyenne saying, "A Nation is not conquered until the hearts of the women [and their bodies as well] are on the ground."

Notes

1. Press conference, Chicago, Illinois, August 17, 1990.

2. As a result of the organizing efforts of Native people in Illinois, the site was eventually closed, but the remains were not reburied when the next governor took office.

3. I am not arguing that the non-patriarchal nature of Native societies is the only reason white women may have chosen to live with their captors, but that it is a possible explanation for why many chose to stay.

4. For a description of the hazards of Depo-Provera, see Minkin, who concludes that "the continued use of Depo-Provera for birth control is unjustified and unethical" (n.d.). Depo-Provera, a known carcinogen

that has been condemned as an inappropriate form of birth control by several national women's health organizations, was routinely used on Indian women through Indian Health Services (IHS) before it was approved by the FDA in 1992 (Masterson and Guthrie, n.d.). There are no studies on the long-term effects of Norplant, and the side-effects (constant bleeding, sometimes for over ninety days, tumors, kidney problems, strokes, heart attacks, sterility) are so extreme that approximately thirty percent of women on Norplant want it taken out in the first year, with the majority requesting to have it taken out within two years, even though it is supposed to remain implanted in a woman's arm for five years (Hanania-Freeman 1993, 20). To date, over 2,300 women have joined a class action suit against Norplant, who are suffering from 125 side effects relating to Norplant (Plant 1994, 46). For a statement on Depo-Provera from the National Black Women's Health Project, National Latina Health Organization, the Native American Women's Health Education Resource Center, the National Women's Health Network, and Women's Economic Agenda Project, contact NAWHERC, PO Box 572, Lake Andes, South Dakota 57356–0572.

5. Promotional material from Public Relations: Mahoney/Wasserman & Associates, Los Angeles, Calif., n.d.

6. Lecture at Indigenous Women's Network conference at White Earth reservation, September 17, 1994.

References

Amin, Samir. 1977. *Imperialism and unequal development*. New York: Monthly Review Press.

Aptheker, Herbert. 1987. *Racism, imperialism, and peace: Selected essays by Herbert Aptheker*, ed. Marvin J. Berlowitz and Carol E. Morgan. Minneapolis: MEP Press.

Asetoyer, Charon, and Lin Krust. 1993. Study of the use of Depo-Provera and Norplant by the Indian Health Services. Lake Andes: Native American Women's Health Education Resource Center.

Barstow, Anne. 1994. *Witchcraze*. New York: Dover.

Beasely, Conger. 1991. Dances with garbage. *E Magazine*, 40.

Bellanger, Pat. 1982. Native American women, forced sterilization, and the family. In *Every woman has a story*, ed. Gayla Wadnizak Ellis. Minneapolis: Midwest Villages and Voices.

Berkhofer, Robert. 1978. *The white man's Indian*. New York: Vintage.

Brownmiller, Susan. 1986. *Against our will*. Toronto: Bantam Books.

Caputi, Jane. 1993. *Gossips, gorgons and crones*. Santa Fe: Bear Publishing.

Carby, Hazel. 1986. On the threshold of women's era: lynching, empire, and sexuality in black feminist theory. In *Race, writing, and difference*, ed. Henry Louis Gates Jr. Chicago: University of Chicago Press.

Cesaire, Aime. 1972. *Discourse on colonialism*. New York: Monthly Review Press.

Crenshaw, Kimberle. 1996. The intersection of race and gender. In *Critical Race Theory*, ed. Kimberle Crenshaw, Neil Gotanda, Gary Peller, and Kendall Thomas. New York: New Press.

Contaminated Milk in Mohawk Women. 1994. *Sojourner* (April): 11.

Deer InWater, Jessie. 1992. The war against nuclear waste disposal. *Sojourner* 15.

Dillingham, Brint. 1977a. Indian women and IHS sterilization practices. *American Indian Journal* (July): 27–28.

———. 1977b. Sterilization of Native Americans. *American Indian Journal* (July): 16–19.

Drinnon, Richard. 1980. *Facing west*. New York: Schocken Books.

Ehrenreich, Barbara, and Deirdre English. 1979. *For her own good*. Garden City: Anchor.

Eidsmoe, John. 1992. *Columbus and Cortez: Conquerors for Christ*. Green Forest, Ark.: New Leaf Press.

Hanania-Freeman, Debra. 1993. Norplant: Freedom of choice or a plan for genocide? *EIR* 18:23.

Harden, Lakota. 1980. Black Hills PAHA sapa report. Rapid City.

Hermann, Andrea, and Maureen O'Donnell. 1990. Indians rap Thompson over burial site display. *Chicago Sun Times*, 17 August.

Hernandez-Avila, Ines. 1993. In praise of insubordination, or what makes a good woman go bad? In *Transforming a rape culture*, ed. Emilie Buchwald, Pamela R. Fletcher, and Martha Roth. Minneapolis: Milkweed.

Jarvis, Gayle Mark. n.d. The theft of life. WARN Report, 13–16.

LaDuke, Winona. 1993. A society based on conquest cannot be sustained. In *Toxic Struggles*, ed. Richard Hofrichter. Philadelphia: New Society Publishers.

Las Casas, Bartolome de. 1992. *Devastation of the Indies*. Baltimore: John Hopkins University Press.

Lopez, Andre. n.d. *Pagans in our midst*. Mohawk Nation: Awkesasne Notes.

Masterson, Mike, and Patricia Guthrie. 1986. Taking the shot. *Arizona Republic*.

Merchant, Carolyn. 1980. *Death of nature*. San Francisco: Harper & Row.

Minkin, Stephen. n.d. Depo-Provera: A critical analysis. San Francisco: Institute for Food and Development.

Namias, June. 1993. *White captives*. Chapel Hill: University of North Carolina Press.

O'Connell, Barry, ed. 1992. *On our own ground: The complete writings of William Apess, a Pequot*. Amherst: University of Massachusetts.

Oklahoma: sterilization of women charged to I.H.S. 1989. *Akwesasne Notes* (mid winter):11–12.

Plant, Katherine. 1994. Mandatory Norplant is not the answer. *Chicago Sun Times*, 2 November.

Rawls, James. 1984. *Indians of California: The changing image*. Norman: University of Oklahoma Press.

Robertson, Pat. 1993. *The turning tide*. Dallas: Word Books.

Rowlandson, Mary. 1974. *A narrative of the captivity and removes of Mrs. Mary Rowlandson*. Fairfield, Wash.: Ye Galleon Press.

Ruether, Rosemary Radford. 1975. *New woman, new earth*. Minneapolis: Seabury Press.

Sale, Kirpatrick. 1990. *The conquest of paradise*. New York: Plume.

Sand Creek massacre: A documentary history. 1973. Introduction by John Carroll. New York: Sol Lewis.

Sanders, Ronald. 1978. *Lost tribes and promised lands*. Boston: Little, Brown and Company.

Shoat, Ella, and Robert Stam. 1994. *Unthinking eurocentricism*. London: Routledge.

Stannard, David. 1992. *American holocaust*. Oxford: Oxford University Press.

Stoler, Ann. 1997. *Race and the education of desire*. Chapel Hill: Duke University Press.

Tadiar, Neferti. 1993. Sexual economies of the Asia-Pacific. In *What's in a rim? Critical perspectives on the Pacific region idea,* ed. Arif Dirlik. Boulder: Westview Press.

Taliman, Valerie. 1991. Tribes speak out on toxic assault. *Lakota Times*, Rapid City, 18 December.

———. 1992. Toxic waste of Indian lives. *Covert Action* 17 (spring): 16–22.

Trask, Haunani-Kay. 1993. *From a native daughter: Colonialism and sovereignty in Hawai'i*. Monroe, Maine: Common Courage Press.

Up front. 1982. *Perspectives: A Civil Rights Quarterly* 14 (fall): 10.

Wallerstein, Immanuel. 1991. The ideological tensions of capitalism: universalism versus racism and sexism. In *Race, nation, class*, ed. Etienne Balibar and Immanuel Wallerstein. London: Verso.

Warren, Karen. 1993. A feminist philosophical perspective on ecofeminist spiritualities. In *Ecofeminism and the sacred*, ed. Carol Adams. New York: Continuum.

Wrone, David, and Russel Nelson, eds. 1982. *Who's the savage?* Malabar, Fla.: Robert Krieger Publishing.

A R T I C L E   2 4

Cathy Winkler

Rape as Social Murder

Definitions of Rape

Rape is a horrifying crime, but what is the meaning of this horrifying act of rape? For twenty years, researchers have investigated the attacks, the attackers, the survivors,[1] and the personal and institutional ramifications on the victim-survivors. In general, definitions of rape point out that rape is a loss of control or power. Legal definitions of rape stress the use or threat to use force. Metzger notes that rape is depersonalization (1976:406). Burgess and Holmstrom (1974b) and Millett (1971) define rape as violence, MacKinnon stresses rape as sex without consent (1982:532), and Sheffield (1987) emphasizes rape as terror. Weis and Borges point out that 'rape is a total attack against the whole person, affecting the victim's physical, psychological and social identity' (1973:72). Some emphasize that the attack of rape is not just against the person but is targeted at the sexuality of the individual: Barry takes this perspective and explains 'where there is any attempt to separate the sexual experience from the total person, the first act of objectification is perversion' (1979:266). Researchers then explain that rape is a depersonalization, a terror, a perverse objectification. Their definitions of rape reveal crucial and integral parts of what is rape, and on these ideas, I would like to build my perspective.

In order to explain my position, I analyse a rape attack. In this instance, I want to use the words and actions of the rapist who attacked me along with the effects of rape trauma that I expe-

Source: "Rape as Social Murder," by Cathy Winkler. *Anthropology Today* 7(3) (2005): 7–8. Used by permission of Blackwell Publishing.

rienced in order to demonstrate the meaning of rape. The use of this attack for data enables me to have an investigator-victim perspective[2] not otherwise conceivable.

I argue that the rapist tried to completely define himself into my existence. In general, rapists' attempt to define their existence over and above the existence of their victims is an attempt to define victims out of existence. Rapists overrule not only the words and actions of their victims but also attack victims' definition of their body and their sexual self. Rapists' threats extend beyond superficial retorts and mentally and psychologically invade victims' being and self-definition.

Case Study

The attack began when the rapist awakened me. His body stood over my body, with his arms and shoulders raised in an assault position. Not only did he have me cornered but he blocked the one exit. His physical force began by grabbing my clothes with the intent to tear them off. At the onset, he wrenched my wrist and forced my body over his by grabbing the back of my head, and inserting his penis into my mouth. His control of my body varied from pushing his penis into my vagina to his forcing me to lick his penis and anus, with continual variations of these as pleased him over a three and half hour period.[3] For the supposed act of sex, he held my body, moving it back and forth with his arms and legs while he simultaneously banged his body onto and inside of mine in the supposed mimic movements of sexual intercourse. He amused himself with my body: in fact, he masturbated inside me. His intermittent actions of bruising me from clenching my arms to pounding his body on my vaginal area to squeezing my nipples implanted his body on my body externally and internally. His sweat drenched down from his face and fell over my forehead and cheeks, drops of which I could not turn away from. To leave his imprint in terms of body fluids on me, he licked me with his tongue, salivating on my face, breasts, and genital area. His arms constantly pushed my face away in order to prevent my eyes from memorizing his face and to control my vision. When I initially failed to respond to his orders, he beat me numerous times. His fists to my face made me realize that his[4] attack of rape was my escape and only hope from physical death. By his actions, the rapist had given me a choice: to suffer his attack or to face my physical death. Of the two, I chose[5] to live through and survive after the rape attack.

The definition of his body on mine extended to his definition of himself throughout my home, from thrown items to cigarettes ground into the wood floor. He tore out the phones and took my car keys. In other words, his relocation of my material items and his cutting off of my communication and transportation temporarily imprisoned me.

My bodily reactions throughout the attack shocked even myself. The first feeling was nausea which remained throughout the ordeal. The dryness of my mouth made my tongue feel like sandpaper as he forced me to sodomize him countless times.

The most gripping bodily response was smell. As the attack began, the room filled with the odours of urine and bowel movements: these lasted for hours. The reality of the smells convinced me to tell the police of these as part of the rapist's crimes. Yet when I returned with the detectives to my home—now the scene of the crime—the room was vacant of such evidence. His terror transformed my environment into a room filled with excretion. The disgusting forms of these imagined smells reflected my feelings of horror.

The rapist's endeavours to define his life over mine were also clear by his words. As he ma-

noeuvred the movements of my body in regard to his wants, he interpreted the situation. He announced what and why an action had happened. He sexually invaded me in every orifice, and after he pushed his penis into my anus, he announced: 'Oh, you like that.' He wanted to decide my wants and likes sexually. Further data on his sexual definition of me was his image of pleasure on his face as he repeatedly inserted his penis into my vagina, and as such, he announced what he thought should be my feelings: 'I know 'I know I'm your boyfriend. You like it.' None of these statements needed a response from me. His words were to be declarations of my ideas.

As frequently noted in the literature, power is an issue of rape. Unlike negotiated power though, rapists demand an autocratic, monarch-like power. At the beginning of the attack, he said: 'I'm here and I'm going to get what I came for.' In other words, no obstacle was to stand in the way of his wishes. His power to control his entrance into any abode again was an announcement of his rambo-like power: 'I can break into any place. No house can keep me out.' While the truth of such points may be in question, nevertheless the intentions of the rapist were clear.

In many cases of power, the issue is that people demand control without evidence of their right or without a basis for their force. The rapist too took that approach: he wanted power even if his backup force was imaginary. He stated: 'I've got a knife in my back pocket.' While I wondered why a person makes threats in such cases without visible evidence, I did not want to know whether or not his material force was imaginary or real. Moreover, his power was not in a material object, but his power was, and he knew this, that I could not test the visibility of the evidence. To challenge him would have ended my existence. One must understand that, in this case, not challenging the rapist was a mechanism of self-defence.

Rapists impose guilt upon their victims. During his conversation, the rapist justified his actions by attempting to implant these feelings of guilt in order to hamper me from reporting the crime, and from learning to live beyond the attack. He tried to turn my resistance to his actions into feelings of guilt by mismatching his actions and his statements of the situation. His first words after clubbing me with his fists were: 'You made me beat you up.' He reiterated this line many times throughout the attack: 'It's your fault. I didn't want to hurt you.' The rapist wanted to control me after the attack, and in this regard, guilt was his method of control.

Many of the rapist's responses were schizophrenic, contradictory statements, and sometimes one after the other. At one point, he made the emphatic statement: 'You liked it,' and then he immediately followed with the matter-of-fact contradiction: 'I'm a rapist. I know that I raped you.' Another set of schizophrenic statements began with the definition of himself as omnipotent: 'I watched you for three weeks. I was going to get you' and 'I can break into any place.' Later, his savage acts seemed to transform him also, and in this aspect, into denial of my vulnerability: 'Use this type of locks on the windows, and you'll be safe.' At one point when he was glorifying himself, he announced that he had five girlfriends that he could visit any time, and later when I said that his girlfriends must like him sexually—and this kindness was another one of my methods of self-defence—he announced that 'They're just five holes.'

Rapists play mind games with their victims. This attacker, who acknowledged that he raped me, also acted as a protector toward me. 'You don't have to leave [the neighborhood]. I'm not coming back. You can stay [here]. I'll take care of that.' As the bruised colours on my face along with my swollen head became apparent, the rapist responded in a gentle and believable manner: 'Do you want me to take you to the hospital?' One wonders about the logic of a rapist: he blamed me for the beating, and then acted as my protector and caretaker by offering to drive me to a hospital. Yet he caused the damnation to my body.

My self-defence was rape-defined, and the attack had made self-defence a necessity. From my conversation, the rapist had noted several of my characteristics: 'You're a smart one. You'll go to the police. I'm not going back there for this.' His fear of a police investigation was a fear of me reporting the crime. First, to make myself a valued and alive commodity to him, I treated him like a respected human being, the essence of goodness, of manliness, and of sensibility, and I praised him as a man of handsome beauty, and one loved by women for his lustful prowess. He dictated my freedom by forcing me to verbalize a beauty in the repulsiveness that I was experiencing. Second, while I did not believe this, I convinced him that a police report was vacuous: his features, even with a moustache, were indistinguishable from many men in the neighbourhood. Third, my body had to physically decease. The less I reacted the more pleasure he personified. My demonstration of complete subjugation, even to whims of his forcing me to lick his anus and his penis, resulted in his facial displays of immense ecstasy. His face gave the appearance of a drug-like high while attacking me. My escape was his obliteration of my freedom.

My ability to control my body and its movements was non-existent. The one control that I had and that I held onto was my mind. Yet this too was in jeopardy. Every thought was a rejection and fight against his schizophrenic statements and his mental games along with those distorted actions. Since my thoughts were my only means for sanity, in my mind I shouted at myself not to believe him; silently I screamed that he was guilty, and secretly I fought for my sanity. No time existed for me to think about anything other than about the rapist and his attack.

Rape Trauma: Context and Meaning

To understand the rapist's attempts during the attack to take control over my body and mind is insufficient to completely explain the meaning of rape. One must further investigate the trauma. This area likewise holds evidence of the rapist's intent and impact. Rapists bury land-mines in the bodies of their victims, and these emotional explosions—such as confusion, nausea, night-mares, tremors, depression, shakiness—form the 'rape trauma syndrome.'[6] I argue that the types of trauma result in an experiential feeling[7] of partial and temporary mind-body separation[8]—usually unrecognizable and unseen by others.[9]

Rapists' terror is an attempt to split our bodies from our minds.[10] In effect, rapists are partially successful. Because of this feeling of a split between the mind and body, which in a healthy situation act in unison, the body's response to that terror and shock is trauma, and more importantly, the raped body's trauma becomes a means for the survivor to analyse the terror that rapists force inside us. In a trauma-like fashion, the body—superseding the mind's protective barriers—announces to the raped person a context which is of potential or immediate danger. Trauma reactions by the raped person's body, I argue, contain meanings such as protective trauma and reclamation trauma but these are not of primary concern to this argument.

In summary form, I will present some of the data on the rapist's land-mines of horror that exploded inside me months after the attack. For myself, what I call 'rapist-identified trauma' surfaced when I was in the presence of the rapist on the street; visually, I could not recognize him.[11] Instead my body by means of trauma reenacted the terror that he had placed there. At the time of the attack, he was the rapist—a face I saw and knew then, but on the street he visually appeared to me like a stranger. When 'the stranger' came within six to nine feet of my personal boundaries, my body relived again his terror to warn me of his dangerous presence. My body felt the rapist's presence while my mind could not visually identify him. Not only had he invaded my body with his repulsion, but he had invaded me mentally. My inability to visually identify him—note that my ability in visual identification has always been a characteristic in which I pride myself—demonstrated further how he had tampered with my mind.

In another instance, trauma exploded like a bombshell. In the calm and comfort of my place,

alone and without others' presence, this trauma erupted in a volcanic-like blast: my mouth screamed, and my body evacuated its contents. In the newspaper account that I was reading at the time, another rapist's words—which paralleled the meaning of the words that the rapist had said to me—made my body realize that my life had been a fraction away from extermination during the attack. My body's explosion revealed my confrontation with death.

Discussion

I want to argue that we need a more poignant definition of rape, one that concisely duplicates rapists' acts. The data here demonstrate that the rapist tried to control my being bodily through my movements. Verbally he dictated the conversation or lack of. In regards to my identity, he penetrated my existence, physically tearing me up and battering my body. His bodily control over me was an attempt to bodily disfigure me. Mentally he tried to infiltrate my existence from his impact upon my olfactory responses to my visual difficulty in identification of him.

His rape attack left me with two choices: not to report the crime and live with the knowledge that he would continue inflicting his hell on other women—a hell that I am now familiar with, or, to spend years[12] as I have in the court system trying to stop his attacks. Even this paper must be interpreted not just as a person speaking out against a crime we hate, but a description of a crime against my body and my being which in its public pronouncement contains an embarrassing horror that I felt and that I now feel again as you read this.

Rapists attempt to socially, psychologically, mentally and sexually define their victims. Their torture and terror are their efforts to brand us. As Barry notes, '[rapists are] *out of control'* (1979:254, author's emphasis). While they are successful in scorching our beings, thankfully they are not always successful in taking over ourselves, hence the word 'rape survivor'. Whether their attempts contain the threat of physical death or not, I argue that the rapist's attempts are those of social murder. Without our abilities to think and feel ourselves as we choose, then our existence becomes like a body on life support. During an attack, victims have confronted social death, and grappled with it to save themselves.

As my student/friend/informant, Renata McMullen[13] pointed out, 'violation is a death in itself' (personal communication: 1990), and she further stresses that even without physical battering, her body felt battered as if the date rapist had physically beaten her up. Likewise, George Scott[14] remembers the feelings of humiliation when two rapists attacked him: 'Humiliation is psychological battery that feels like physical battery' (personal communication: 1991).

Rape is the experience of social death. Rapists want to socially exterminate us. Victims' fear of death is not an imaginary experience. Our fears are a result of rapists' intentions. I argue for such a definition of rape as social murder, not just from my hate of the act, but to explain the meaning of rape. If we don't understand these acts of horror, and if we cannot succinctly define them as they really exist and are experienced, then people in this culture from jurors to our family members will continue to support rapists and their act of horror.

Postscript

I assume that this might have been a difficult paper for you to read, and I don't want to leave people in such a state. Therefore, I have two hopefully amusing anecdotes to help the readers release built-up tension from the reading of this article and to demonstrate that survivors like myself are still human beings with their own sense of humour.

Anthropologists are becoming more and more careful with their presentation of data cross-culturally because unlike the informants of fifty years ago, today's informants have access to our writings and sometimes have doctoral degrees. A sinking feeling comes over us when an informant would like to comment on our research in their community. But in my area of research on the rape-attack, I actually wish the rapist would speak up and say: 'Excuse me, Dr. Winkler, but you misquoted one of my lines from the attack.' Unfortunately, rapists' silence about their attacks lasts an indeterminable period of time.

On another level and in response to today's computer dependency, it is amazing how many of the words used in this paper are not in the computer spell check.

Notes

1. My use of the terms 'victim', 'survivor', and 'victim-survivor' varies with the meaning of the context. If a context is inescapable for the person, such as in rape, the person is a victim. If a context is a bombardment against the person, but exiting that context is possible, I use the term 'victim-survivor'. And, if a context allows a person freedom to act and speak as they choose, such as the editors of ANTHROPOLOGY TODAY have encouraged me, then I use the word 'survivor'.

2. My term 'investigator-victim' opens up avenues of study—fortunately and unfortunately—not easily attainable by non-victims. This perspective allows me to bridge the gap between objective and subjective approaches, and hopefully, integrate my analysis with the impact of the data. This term parallels the meaning behind DuBois' concept 'double consciousness' (1961).

3. While the length of time provided an extensive amount of data, the feelings of terror, horror, and the rest described in this paper on rape are no different if the attacker raped the person for five minutes, ten minutes, or more. Before the attack on the body began, I felt the hell of terror which the rapist initiated with his presence, and thus my feelings of shock and horror remained largely unaltered throughout the rest of the attack.

4. In order to change the 'blame-the-victim' perspective, alteration of phrases and word choices is important. In regards to the attack, I note that it was *his* attack and *his* rape, not mine, emphasizing that I did not participate in the rape by choice. Also, I avoid such a passive phrase as 'I was raped', and instead state that 'he raped me', or 'the attacker raped me'.

5. Victims make choices and decisions during the rape attack even though these decisions are choices

between different types of terror. This realization helps the victim live as a survivor.

6. Burgess and Holmstrom (1974a, 1974b) were the first ones to define and describe the 'rape trauma syndrome'. Yet not until 1990 did New York state accept rape trauma syndrome as part of the crime of rape. Moreover, little information on rape trauma exists cross-culturally.

7. I have written further on this perspective of mine in the articles 'The Meaning of Rape Trauma', and 'The Contexts of Rape Trauma'. These are works-in-progress.

8. Blacking (1978) argues that the body and mind work in unison, but his work does not centre on situations of trauma.

9. Examples of this extreme experiential split are cases in which rapists trigger episodes of manic depression in people with this condition.

10. Incest victims likewise note this feeling of a split between the mind and body by what they term 'out-of-body experiences'. Many rape victims have noted that during the attack they step outside of their body and mentally watch the attack.

11. Each time I have seen the rapist he appears to me as a different person. As a result, I have five unmatched images of him in my mind: the attack context, a police photograph, street encounter, arraignment hearing, and pre-trial motions.

12. The attack occurred in September 1987. While the rapist was found within the following months, legal action is still ongoing.

13. Renata and I recognize that the identification of rape with our name is no shame.

14. Because of a sense of privacy, George Scott prefers to use a pseudonym.

References

Barry, Kathleen. 1979. *Female Sexual Slavery.* NY: New York U. P.

Blacking, John. 1978. *The Anthropology of the Body.* NY: Academic P.

Burgess, Ann Wolbert, and Lynda Lyttle Holmstrom. 1974a. Rape Trauma Syndrome. *Am. J. of Psychiatry* 131:981–6.

———1974b. *Rape: Victims of Crisis.* Bowie, MD: Prentice-Hall.

DuBois, W.E.B. 1961. *The Philadelphia Negro.* Greenwich, CT: Faucet.

MacKinnon, Catharine A. 1982. Feminism, Marxism, Method, and the State: An Agenda for Theory. *Signs* 7(3):515–44.

Metzger, Deena. 1976. It is Always the Woman Who is Raped. *Am. J. of Psychiatry* 133(4):405–8.

Millett, Kate. 1971. *The Prostitution Papers: A Candid Dialogue.* NY: Basic.

Sheffield, Carole J. 1987. 'Sexual Terrorism: The Social Control of Women'. In *Analyzing Gender: A Handbook of Social Science Research.* Beth B. Hess and Myra M. Ferree, eds. Newbury Park: Sage.

Weis, Kurt, and Sandra S. Borges. 1973. Victimology and Rape: The Case of the Legitimate Victim. *Issues in Criminology 8:71–115.*

Kathleen J. Ferraro

Blurred Boundaries and the Complexities of Experience

The social movement to end violence against women has challenged many of the conventional binary categories defining social realities. What was once viewed as a private matter is now considered a social problem. Violence that was accepted as "moderate chastisement" in the nineteenth century is now a crime, both legally and in popular opinion.[1] As these categories have shifted, the boundaries circumscribing "normal" and "acceptable" behavior have been modified. The ways in which these categories are defined not only *prescribe* behaviors, but also help to *constitute* what people take for granted as true and real.

Our efforts to describe experiences of intimate partner violence have helped to create new vocabularies. Like many aspects of women's experience, there was no specific language to capture the forms of violence in intimate relationships prior to the emergence of the anti-violence against women movement in the mid-1970s in Western Europe and the United States.[2] It is difficult to think about experience when there is no language to describe it, or when the language available is inconsistent with one's experience.[3] In terms of women's experiences of male violence, scholars and activists developed the terms "sexual harassment," "stalking," "domestic violence," "femicide," "marital rape," and "intimate partner violence," thus helping to shift public views of behaviors and experiences that had al-ways occurred but were absent in discourse and policy.

Women's experiences of male violence have formed the basis for activism and scholarship. As the movement to combat violence against women has progressed, the diversity of women's experiences has become more apparent. Without a political analysis of these experiences, it is possible to develop knowledge that replicates existing power hierarchies. Activism in the absence of theory is dangerous. A growing number of activists are documenting the problems that have emerged as a result of policies that developed with the encouragement of many people in the anti-violence against women movement.[4] For example, improvements in police and court responses to battering were one of an array of needs identified by activists in the early 1970s. By 1990, however, the criminal processing system became the primary focus of activism and funding.[5] Women's needs for housing, health care, income, transportation, education, and childcare were submerged in the focus on treating domestic violence as a crime.[6] The criminal control model excludes the needs of many and is directly punitive to significant numbers of women.

In this chapter, I examine the ways that knowledge, power, and experience operate in the lives of women who are both victimized by intimate partner violence and who commit crimes of their own. These women occupy two social locations that are ordinarily viewed as dichotomous and mutually exclusive: victim and offender. But this artificial dichotomy represents only one of the ways that the lives of women spill over the boundaries of popular and legal discourse.

Source: Kathleen Ferraro, *Neither Angels nor Demons: Women, Crime, and Victimization*, pp. 10–45. © 2006 by Northeastern University Press. Reprinted by permission of University Press of New England, Hanover, NH.

Women's experiences with intimate violence and crime do not fit neatly into legal or social science categories. The categorical boundaries between victimization and offending, physical assault and emotional abuse, fear and love, past and present, truth and lies, woman and child, self and other blur together in the lived experience of everyday life. These categories are all socially constructed, both shaping and being shaped by broad historical and cultural trends, individual experience, social policies, and legal decision making. The specific content of categories varies across cultures and time, changing with shifts in economies, technologies, resources, and ideologies. Some change is gradual and relatively consensual, such as shifts in the definition of "childhood" that occurred in Western Europe between the seventeenth and twentieth centuries.[7] Other change is more conflictual and violent, such as changes in the social acceptability of same-sex intimate partners. Both accommodation of change and reinforcement of tradition occur, often simultaneously, as people negotiate the categorical boundaries of everyday life.

The Language of Intimate Partner Violence

The language that we have adopted to think about violence and abuse in intimate relationships focuses our perceptions of what gets included, what it means, and what actions we should take.[8] As the boundaries of acceptable interpersonal behavior in intimate relationships have shifted, the techniques of social control have expanded. A new vocabulary has emerged that creates expectations and assigns responsibility. The terms "domestic violence," "intimate partner violence," "battered woman," and "batterer" are all recent additions to popular language in the United States, dating from the 1970s.

The social construction of "intimate partner violence" is an example of how categories are constructed and reinforced, then treated as if they were naturally occurring phenomena that existed prior to human processes.[9] Both individual behavior and the harm it causes exist apart from social constructions of their meaning. But the processes of identifying those behaviors and harms, labeling them, and prescribing interventions are social constructions. It is possible to forget and hide the social aspect of these processes and to view the human behaviors as facts; sociologists call this process "reification."[10] Many of the categories related to intimate partner violence have become reifications of people's lived experiences. According to popular conceptions, battered women have low self-esteem, are passive and weak, and perhaps have "learned helplessness."[11] Such women are deserving of sympathy and support, but may also be disparaged for poor choices and submissive acceptance of violence. Women who do not conform to these expectations of a "real" battered woman have a difficult time convincing people that they have been battered and that their partner's abuse terrified them and caused them to be complicit in criminal acts.[12] When women who are battered become labeled as criminal offenders, they face the struggle of translating their experiences into language that transcends the conventional categories of intimate partner violence. This struggle is both internal and external. Women must confront the categories of thought that they and the people with responsibility for helping or punishing them share about intimate partner violence.

The new language of intimate partner violence developed through an interaction between individual women seeking help, grassroots activists, institutional actors, scholars, and politicians. From the beginning of the anti-violence movement, the varying political and ideological commitments of these groups resulted in struggles over appropriate language. The best-documented struggles surrounded the issue of gender neutrality.[13] Feminists argued that gender-neutral language, such as "family violence" or "spouse abuse," failed to signal the critical role of patriarchy and male dominance in perpetuating violence. They used the terms "woman battering," "wife abuse," or "violence against women" in preference to language that left the sex of perpetrators and victims in question. People also raised concerns about focusing on "marital" violence, since many cases involved intimate partners who were not married. The term "domestic violence" gained prominence by the 1980s, and in the late 1990s, the language of "intimate partner violence" emerged as a corrective to the image of battering as a phenomenon limited to co-residing couples and heterosexuals. This current preferred language focuses on the sexual and emotional link between abusers and abused persons and is inclusive of same-sex partners, dating partners, and former partners.

The terms "battering," "batterer," and "battered woman" have also been problematic. This language emphasizes the physical aspects of violence. It tends to reinforce the view that intimate partner violence is nothing more than physical assault directed at a spouse or intimate partner. The context of intimidation, degradation, isolation, cruelty, and threats is obscured when language focuses on physical violence. Yet this is the language that dominates domestic violence discourse. Michael P. Johnson has developed an analysis differentiating between intimate partner violence that does not involve coercive control (situational couple violence) and violence that is one technique in a repertoire of control strategies (intimate partner terrorism).[14] This important distinction, however, has not yet altered the pervasive tendency to view intimate partner abuse as a single, homogeneous phenomenon.

Knowledge of intimate partner violence depends on language that is saturated with judgments. The social meaning of "violence" changes over time and across cultures. For example, the use of physical punishment in order to control the behavior of wives was both legal and socially acceptable during the nineteenth century in the United States and England.[15] Women were defined as the morally inferior wards of their husbands, who were thus given authority to control them. The same behavior in the twenty-first century is grounds for arrest and prosecution. The behavior is the same, but the social definition and response have changed.

The anti-violence against women movement has focused primarily on physical violence as opposed to the symbolic and emotional violence that women deem much more damaging. When we speak of "intimate partner violence," in legal, social science, and lay terms, people distinguish between "hitting, kicking, and beating up," and making derogatory comments, ignoring a loved one's need for attention and respect, or engaging in emotionally frightening or damaging behavior. Men who physically beat their wives are subject to legal interventions, even if those interventions are light and sporadic. Men who denigrate their wives' appearance, performance and abilities; flaunt marital infidelity; monitor and control their wives' actions; and scare them with aggressive driving, angry verbal outbursts, or other frightening behaviors are rarely subject to criminal sanctions. Women who eventually seek help almost always say that emotionally abusive behaviors hurt more and are more difficult to repair than actual physical assaults.[16] When I interview women about their experiences, they spend much more time talking about the ways in which their partners hurt and terrified them emotionally than about physical violence. As Beth expressed it, "The physical abuse doesn't hurt. It doesn't. I don't feel pain anymore. It's the emotional shit that he'd do to me." But these nonphysical assaults are separated from bodily harm in the dominant discourses on intimate partner violence.

The broader paradigm of understanding associated with the modernist project shapes the language used to describe intimate partner violence.[17] Within this paradigm, there is faith in the capacity of social scientists to adopt the methods of natural scientists to accurately and objectively define and measure the behavior of humans. Scientific observers can produce valid, objective knowledge of society by adherence to the scientific method. The social facts produced by scientists are also viewed as relatively stable, fixed truths that mean the same thing to different people in a diverse range of settings and the same thing to the same person across various circumstances and times. For example, there is an assumption that when people indicate they were "beat up" by an intimate partner they are all describing the same type of experience and could all be categorized or "coded" in the same way. Other aspects of their identities, such as their childhood experiences of physical abuse, could be coded as easily and correlated with this category and then used in causal models attempting to explain intimate partner violence. Most social scientists and some natural scientists have challenged and revised these epistemological assumptions about our social lives that were components of the positivist paradigm. However, a great deal of social science continues to reflect their influence.[18]

In the realm of intimate partner violence, modernist assumptions about the clarity and fixity of social categories have implications for research and policy. Prevalence and incidence studies, for example, define intimate partner violence in a way that permits accurate counting of cases and of "variables" that can then be correlated with both victimization and perpetration. The Conflict Tactics Scale (CTS), developed by Murray Straus and Richard Gelles, is the most common tool used to measure intimate partner violence. The CTS and revised CTS2 list behaviors used to resolve conflicts, ranging from "discussed the issue calmly" to "used a knife or gun"; people are asked which behaviors they have used in their relationships.[19] A line is drawn between verbal and physical aggression and between minor and severe violence to determine instances of violence.[20] It is necessary to operationalize intimate partner violence through links to specific actions in order to measure it. The data produced through these studies have been essential to raising public awareness and garnering support. Astoundingly, in the 1970s many people believed that intimate partner violence was rare; the surveys that documented violence in a significant proportion of relationships challenged this belief successfully.[21] But the success of the research has consequences for perceptions of intimate partner violence. The process of operationalization transforms amorphous, complex human experiences

into codeable categories that take on a life of their own.[22] The definition of violence and the variables associated with it create what we accept as knowledge. That is, the actions of scholars and activists do not simply *describe* the facts of intimate partner violence; they *create* those facts by deciding what counts and what does not count as the truth of intimate partner violence. I do not mean that there is no physical and psychological suffering within intimate relationships apart from this definitional process. I do mean that the messy, complicated, shifting meanings of suffering undergo a transformation as they are forced into the categories consistent with the new truth of intimate partner violence.

The Battered Woman

One example of the way in which language, or discourse, shapes knowledge is the way the term "battered woman" has influenced individual women's and the general public's opinion about the experience of violence within an intimate relationship. This term developed during the early 1970s when the contemporary battered women's movement took shape and was meant to describe women who were physically assaulted by their current and former intimate partners. The development of language that identified violence in intimate relationships and the gendered nature of this violence was important in challenging the complacency that surrounded violence in the home. In 1970 there were no shelters for battered women, policies instructed police officers *not* to arrest men for assaulting their wives, and social scientists were silent on the topic.[23] A review of articles in the *Journal of Marriage and the Family* did not locate a single article on marital violence between 1939 and 1969.[24] Language that identified women's experiences was empowering; it also contributed to cultural understandings that have not been helpful for all women.

The term "battered woman" focuses on victimization and suggests an *identity* as victim rather than a set of experiences.[25] The victim identity is stigmatized in a culture that stresses individual responsibility, strength, and assertiveness. Disdain for those who overemphasize their victimization is reflected in the popular phrase "get over it" and in the media's attention to "victim feminism" and feminist "whining."[26] Popular pundits argue that the nation has succumbed to a culture of victimization that shifts personal responsibility onto external forces and undermines the moral fabric of the country.[27] Cultural imagery of victims of abuse portrays women victims as mentally ill (say, suffering post traumatic stress disorder), damaged, and helpless.[28] "Ideal victims" are also meek and distraught, innocent of provoking their victimization, and possessing a body that symbolizes these qualities. Young, white, middle-class, attractive (but not overtly sexy) women embody cultural notions of deserving victims.[29] Cultural expectations and evaluations of female victims may distance women from accepting a self-definition as victim.

Few women actually view themselves as totally pure and innocent prior to victimization—or permanently damaged and defective after. If involvement with the criminal processing system forces them to consider their experiences as "battering," they are drawn into a process of remembering and self-definition that reflects cultural constructions of victims as defective. The women I interviewed struggled with remembering events in their relationships, as well as with issues of responsibility, blame, and pathology. Women's narratives often reflected cultural stereotypes that something was wrong with *them* because they were abused by their partners.

Mona's narrative exemplifies the difficulty of forcing experience into narrow legal categories, as well as her own resistance to the label "battered woman." Mona was a twenty-five-year-old, working-class Italian-American woman who grew up in New York City. She was feisty and funny, and our interview was filled with both laughter and tears. Mona's account of her marriage included many descriptions of emotional and financial abuse as well as physical assault. Her husband was a methamphetamine addict and dealer who moved in with his 18-year-old girlfriend during

the first year of his marriage to Mona. Both women became pregnant with daughters at about the same time. He moved back and forth between households, but did not pay the bills. Mona and her daughter lived without electricity or hot water. He had choked her on several occasions, thrown her against walls and across rooms, punched her in the face, and pistol whipped her. After she moved in with her parents for protection, he stalked her, and police found a shrine with her picture surrounded by machetes in his room. Her husband accidentally shot and paralyzed her father while attempting to shoot Mona, but she could not "picture" herself as battered. After the shooting, he was released on low bail and continued to stalk and harass Mona. She went to his apartment to tell him to leave her alone, and he again assaulted her, repeatedly hitting her in the face. Mona escaped to her car where she had a loaded handgun and shot her husband. He sustained minor injuries, but Mona was charged with attempted murder. She explained her reaction at the scene:

MONA: The detective said, "How many times were you battered before?" I said, "Does this matter to you?" I didn't know they were considering me battered. He said, "Yes," that mattered. I said, "Well, I guess I was battered before." He said, "When?" I said, "I don't know." He was kind've telling me it was going to help the case, but I didn't know what to tell him. I didn't think I was really what they call . . . They put me down as a battered woman. I didn't know who they were referring to. I said, "Who's battered?" I asked one of the cops there. They said, "You're the battered victim." I was like, "I'm battered?" I couldn't imagine.

KATHLEEN: You couldn't think of yourself that way?

MONA: No, never was I a battered woman. That sounds . . . I still really wouldn't consider myself really "battered." Maybe "mentally tortured" or "married a bad man" but "battered" is so . . . like a picture of a coma or I don't know what picture. I just never pictured *me*. Like Farrah Fawcett in *The Burning Bed*, she's battered. She looks battered.

At the scene described above, Mona's face was severely cut and bleeding from being hit by her husband. A detective tried to elicit information from her that would help explain why she took violent, defensive action. His efforts to document prior abuse in a legalistic fashion, however, did not make sense to Mona who rejected the label "battered woman." For Mona, the "picture" of a battered woman was the image she held in her own mind about what constituted a "real battered woman." She focused on what could be seen, and the "picture of a coma" or the terrified, thin, blond, white victim portrayed by Farrah Fawcett was incompatible with her own self-image as a strong, self-sufficient woman with a good sense of humor. Despite the extreme emotional and physical violence she endured, and the shooting of her father, she did not think of herself as battered.

Mona was a small woman—about 100 pounds—who went to her violent, drug-dealing husband's apartment with a loaded gun in the car. Why would a woman who was terrified of a man deliberately seek him out? This question was raised about a number of women I interviewed who had been severely abused yet continued to have contact with their male partners after separation. The men that women seek out are not strangers, but are men they have loved, shared their lives with, and who are the fathers of their children. Even the most extreme abusers are only violent a small portion of all of the time they spend with their partners. Women may be afraid of their abusive partners, but continue to perceive them as part of their intimate circle. Past experience of abuse, however, will lead women to take precautions, such as carrying a weapon. This is not the action of someone who is completely "helpless," as the concept of "learned helplessness" implies. It is the action of someone who is afraid but still believes the person they married or shared an intimate relationship with is someone

they *can* talk to, or *must* talk to. Mona's decision to visit her husband reflected her continuing view of herself as someone who could resolve her own problems and protect herself. The detective's label of "battered victim" did not fit with her own self-image.

None of the women I have interviewed described themselves as battered women, and none of them focused on physical assaults. Many forgot to mention violent incidents that were documented in police or medical records. While some people have noted the possibility that women will *exaggerate* experiences of abuse in order to gain a more lenient response from the courts, my experience and that of others has been that women routinely *minimize* physical abuse.[30] Minimization is one strategy for surviving in a violent relationship.[31] It is also a common aspect of the difficulties of remembering the trauma of abuse.

Another reason that women were reluctant to define themselves as battered was lingering hope that their relationships would improve. Some women said they still loved their violent partners, and others expressed a desire to preserve positive memories of the "good parts" of their relationships.

Boundaries between Good Parts and Bad Parts

For most women (not all), the abuse was also mingled with positive experiences. This combination of abuse and nonabuse did *not* follow a routine pattern, such as that described in Lenore Walker's "cycle of violence" model. Walker describes battering relationships as following a cycle of tension building, acute battering, and loving contrition, also called the "honeymoon" phase.[32] Women did not describe such a *cycle*, and very few women indicated that their partners apologized for the battering, or even acknowledged that they did it. Instead, there were "good parts" to the relationship that women wanted to preserve. The term "battered woman" seemed inappropriate as a self-descriptor because it focused a woman's identity on the bad parts. Dorothy, who killed her husband said, "I miss him, you know, the good parts, you know, I think about. I always want to remember the good parts . . . mostly it was bad, but there was some good parts. And that's the one I like to remember."

For most women, these "good parts" were the companionship and love they shared with their partners. It was disturbing and confusing to them that they continued to hold these feelings despite their partners' violence and abuse. They judged themselves: "I still do love him, sometimes I think I'm crazy, after all the things that I went through, all the pain" (Crystal). And they suspected that others judged them as well, "I think sometimes that people think I shouldn't love him, but I do, not like I used to, but I do" (Jane). Despite these judgments, women recounted the "good parts," and wanted me to understand that their partners were not "all bad." Teresita described how she felt about her boyfriend when they first fell in love:

> I fell in love with him. He was like the world. He did everything to make me happy. What I'm saying is, like, he was like my friend, but then my boyfriend. Something like you need in a relationship, like a friend and a boyfriend. It was like he was the world, he was like the king. You know. Primo this, Primo that, . . . Oh yes, Primo. It was like that good for awhile, until then he started beating me. And he didn't started beating me, it's been about a year after I had the twins.

Teresita struggled with ambivalent feelings of love and hate toward Primo after the death of her baby due to neglect, the crime for which both she and Primo were charged.

Dianne also expressed ongoing feelings of love toward her abusive husband who she was charged with killing during a violent confrontation. She felt tremendous loss over his death; as she tried to describe their relationship, she was overwhelmed with sadness:

> We were pretty close (*crying*). He was my best friend, you could say. He liked to go to the

horse races, he liked to gamble. We used to go to Laughlin a lot, and to the ponies, he liked ponies, of course I did too. Then he taught me how to golf, and that was fun. He was into sports, he loved sports, which is great too, 'cuz I love football, and so did he, we watched football together and stuff, on Sunday, nobody worked, just laid around, ate ice cream, naked, and watched movies and stuff. . . . I seen more in him than anybody else did (*crying hard*)— everybody else thought he was a bad person.

Dianne's sorrow over the loss of her best friend and her ability to see "more in him than anybody else," are aspects of "battered women who kill" that are rarely addressed in media or academic accounts.[33] It is difficult for people to reconcile high levels of control, violence, and degradation with friendship and love, and it also is hard for women who experience these contradictions to understand their partner's behavior and their own reactions. Because violence was unpredictable and inexplicable, women found the mixture of the good and bad parts of their relationships particularly distressing. Nicole used the term "struggling relationship" to describe the mixture of love and fear she felt toward her partner: "I wanted to get away from him even then, but then he would treat me real nice, and then I was just so much in love with him. I thought I was. And so everything would be okay, and it was a whole, kind've a struggling relationship all the way through. I would wanna leave, and then I wouldn't wanna leave, and then everything would be okay, and I was just so much in love with him."

Although psychological labels have been applied to this ambivalence, such as the battered woman syndrome and traumatic bonding, these labels suggest that women's emotions are pathological or deviant. Women frequently share these public interpretations and express the sentiment that "something's wrong" with them. Mona, who did not think she was a "battered woman," explained that she did not want to try to remember all the abuse she experienced, even though it would help explain her violent actions. She thought the abuse indicated that something was wrong with *her*.

> MONA: I just don't want to have to remember and then realize who I was with, because *there's something wrong. There's something wrong with me.*
>
> KATHLEEN: Why do you think that?
>
> MONA: Because you just don't stay with a person who does that to you. You just don't.

Women sometimes asked me if there was something wrong with them. They searched for understanding of their ambivalent feelings and reactions to violence. The sense of being "in love" with a man who is also terrifying and cruel creates a struggle. In retrospect, women judged their love and commitment as pathological, misguided, or naïve. Romantic scripts of being in love do not include ambivalence, and certainly exclude terror. Women desired relationships that conformed to these romantic scripts, and men provided some confirmation that this was possible. Having fun together, feeling uniquely understood and connected to another person, and sharing sexual intimacy were "good parts" that endorsed women's feelings of love and commitment. The "Jekyll-Hyde" phenomenon described by so many women challenged their love and commitment and contributed to their personal sense of pathology. These women judged themselves harshly, feeling they *should* have known better, been able to get out, or rejected the "good parts" that sustained their commitment to their relationships. Their self judgments—despite their own experiences of death threats, severe violence, stalking, and the ineffectiveness of outside interventions—mirrored social prejudices that women can "just leave" violent relationships. "Leaving" not only means confronting his threats but also relinquishing homes, financial security, and in some cases, child custody.

Not all women described this struggle. For some, fear and terror dominated their relationships and they no longer (if they ever had) felt there were any "good parts."[34] The designation of psychological labels is an artificial attempt to impose order and consistency on experiences that are an on-going struggle "all the way through." Good and bad are not clear, binary categories that alternate in predictable cycles. Rather, they are confusing components of relationships that are meaningful in ways difficult to explain or understand.

Boundaries between "Normal" and Abusive Sexuality

The definition of "normal" sexuality is also a political process that varies over time and location. Perceptions of normality in sexual behavior exhibit tremendous variation. Within the context of an abusive relationship, definitions of normal sexuality depend on a struggle between women's emotional and bodily reactions, what they believe is expected of them, and men's desires for sex. Women who had experienced childhood sexual abuse found the negotiation of sexuality in abusive relationships particularly problematic.

Few women volunteered information about sexual abuse without being asked. Obviously, feelings of shame and embarrassment restricted spontaneous recollections of sexual violence, but some women did not define unwanted sex as abuse. Ronnie, for example, thought that her displeasure at her husband's practice of having sex with her while she slept was a consequence of her own disordered sexuality. She thought there was something wrong with her because she did not like this practice. Forced to perform oral sex on her father as a child and raped by a stranger as she walked to school at age fourteen, Ronnie viewed her dislike of sex while sleeping as a response to these earlier assaults. She was very surprised when I told her that this was not a normal practice between husbands and wives, and that many people would define it as rape.[35]

Many women said that they became repulsed by sex in their relationships because the violence and emotional abuse destroyed the pleasure they initially felt with their partners. They would acquiesce to sex in order to placate their partners and avoid arguments or violence.[36] Angie said, "I don't even like sex," and only participated in sex to comply with her boyfriend's demands and avoid a fight. Danielle said that her husband told her he had affairs with other women because she was frigid. But she viewed her lack of interest in sex as a result of his abusive and neglectful behavior:

> He said I was frigid. How can I not be frigid? And I would tell him, "You don't even show me any affection, except when you wanna' sleep with me at night, and then I'm everything?" I'm sorry, I can't just "Oh, okay." I need to feel love, and it got to the point it was sad because I knew when I had to have sex with him that night 'cuz he'd come home and he'd kiss me. And it was like my clue, and it would just, after a while it just would turn my stomach.

While some women just gave in to their partner's sexual requests, other women were forced to participate in painful or degrading acts. Forced sodomy was mentioned by five of forty-five women—a particularly painful memory for women who did discuss it, that always resulted in silence and weeping. Other forms of sexual violence committed by abusers included putting objects inside women's vaginas, punching women on their vaginas and breasts, making videotapes of sexual activity and threatening to sell it or show it to others, asking women to have sex with other men, raping a woman while she was handcuffed to a motorcycle, urinating on a woman, selling a woman to a fellow gang member, making sexually explicit, degrading comments in front of women's children, forcing fellatio for hours at a time, and, in one case, raping a woman while fondling their eleven-year-old daughter. One woman reported that she was forced to perform fellatio on her partner for ten hours. When she was questioned about the accuracy of this memory, she said, "Well, it *seemed* like ten hours!"

Twelve women reported sexual abuse while they were children or teenagers, ten by adult men and two by adult women. As far as the women knew, only two of the people who sexually abused or assaulted them throughout their lives were incarcerated as a result. Both of these men had abused other females, both young girls. These women's stories substantiate the arguments offered by Chesney-Lind, Bortner and Williams, and Gaardner and Belknap that the criminal processing system often fails to protect young women and girls from sexual victimization, but holds them accountable when their own behavior results in harm to others.[37]

Another pattern described by several women was men's insistence on having sex with them following a beating. Women were angry and upset that men thought they could use them sexually after beating them, and initially tried to stop them. Eventually, they gave in because they believed there was nothing they could do to stop them. Teresita described this pattern with her boyfriend, Primo:

> You know, so it's, like, after he got done beating me it was sex time. Yep, it was like that all the time. I mean there would be times where I wouldn't let him, and he'll say that if I didn't give it up, he'll just take it from me. You know and I'll tell him that's rape. You know what I'm sayin'? And he's like, "It's not rape, you're my baby's momma, how is that rape?" You know I'm like, "If you say no, it's rape, Primo." He'll be like "No, like I said, I'll just take it from you, you're my baby's momma, I can have sex whenever I want it." You know, so it's just like I mean, I look at him with disgust. There will be times where I got to the point where I'm like I didn't want to fight with him anymore, where I just let him do what he wanted. I'll just lay there with tears comin' out of my eyes and you would think that he would stop, but he didn't.

Primo's belief that he "can have sex whenever" he wants it violates the basic boundary between consensual and coercive sexuality. His patriarchal attitude that Teresita owed him unlimited sexual access because she had given birth to his child had been traditionally supported by legislation that excluded marital rape from criminal statutes. This legislation only began to change in the 1980s; in many states, marital rape is still a less serious offense with more stringent evidentiary requirements.[38]

Beth also reported that following beatings, her partner Matt would insist on having sex with her. She told him that it was impossible for her to feel sexual desire for him after he assaulted her, but he forced himself on her. She tried to avoid him, but he usually prevailed:

> That night Matt raped me. I don't care what anybody says, if you don't consent to sex, it's rape. He did not own me. He had no right to take me. He would wake up in the morning and he would just take me. I would not consent to him. Or he would get up and I wouldn't get up until he was gone. He'd turn up everything in the house. He'd turn up the TV, turn up the stereo, slam the door, anything to get me up and I wouldn't get up. I was afraid to move. He'd walk out and he'd go, "I know you're awake bitch." I wouldn't get up until I'd hear the truck start. Then I would get up and son-of-a-bitch if he wouldn't come back in the door.

Unlike Ronnie, Teresita and Beth were clear in their own minds that they were being raped. But they were unable to prevent it on their own, and never reported it to the police. For Teresita, prior efforts to obtain police assistance produced nothing but anger in Primo and, like other women, she did not know how she would support their five children without him. Beth's continuing love of Matt and belief that she could help him overcome his addictions deterred her from calling the police.

Negotiating Resistance and Compliance to Men's Commands

These relationships demonstrate complicated patterns of repression and resistance. Men lashed out with physical and psychological violence when women transgressed their always shifting expectations for service, obedience, and loyalty. Some of these expectations reflect cultural no-

tions of gendered behavior. For example, service of food and drink to men by women is a pattern in many cultures. The linkage of women and food service is also influenced by class, with upper-class people expecting hired help to perform this job. For all of the women in this study, male partners expected to be served food and drink.

Women attempted to fulfill these expectations, even when they rejected most other aspects of conventional femininity. For example, Sarah was a "biker chick," an exotic dancer who was involved with a series of men who belonged to an outlaw motorcycle gang. Sarah found straight society and law-abiding men boring. She resisted gendered expectations for women's sexual modesty and sobriety yet she complied with the subservient role of servant to the biker gang. She prided herself on adhering to the men's demands for "respect" and rationalized being beaten for not being strong enough. After her third lover died, this one from an overdose, she earned the reputation of a "black widow" and was shunned by the biker community:

> I blamed myself for it. I coulda' done this, I coulda' done that, if I'da' been a little bit stronger, you know, he didn't beat me that bad, I deserved it, I'd get drunk and talk back, or I didn't show the respect that I should have, to his brothers. It's a big respect thing with those bikers. I would sit at a poker table for twelve hours. I'd sit one chair behind where everybody sat. Anytime anybody pulled a cigarette out, the cigarette was lit. I knew when there was this much left in a beer can, and it was replaced, you know. I was a trained dog.

Phyllis did not view her husband's demands as legitimate, but her resistance to them resulted in severe physical punishment. She described how he made her take off her clothes and feed him while she was naked as a way of degrading her:

> I don't know what he was on, but he got it in his head that I would leave him, and when he come back, he took off alla my clothes and

threw 'em out the window, so I couldn't leave him, and he was tellin' me (*crying*) to feed him and everything, and so, and I didn't know if they [his friends] were gonna' walk in any moment, I'm still naked, but I opened up a can of soup and brought it to him, and he wanted me to feed it to him, he was just trying to degrade me, and I started to feed it to him and after a couple of bites, I thought, fuck this, and I threw the hot soup in his face and I took off runnin', naked and everything, and I ran outside and he chased me down and he caught me, of course, and he brought me back in and he started chokin' me, and I wasn't gonna' let him choke me out again, he'd done it so many times, and so I started pullin' his hands away from me and he got mad because I'm too little to be overpowering him, you know, so I was actually that scared, so he stomped me (*crying hard*). My temples were swollen out and bruised. I had a boot print on the back of my neck, on my chest, and my arms.

Phyllis did not acquiesce to her husband's demands, but she was physically unable to protect herself. If his friends had not returned and called 9-1-1, he might have killed her. She lost consciousness and was hospitalized for two days.

Other women spoke of "just accepting it," deciding not to resist, trying to comply with demands, and not questioning men's authority. Crystal explained how her husband spoke to her when she returned from an errand for him to the neighbors:

He said, "Did you get fucked by him before he gave the pump to you?" I didn't talk to him. Usually when he starts sayin' those things, I don't bother him. If I say something, I'm gonna' get a punch in the face or a kick. So I just told him to hurry up and pump up the tire, breakfast is on the table for you. He said, "It better not be cold." It seemed like he wanted everything perfect. He would, if the food was cold, just throw the whole plate at me, and I would stand there with food comin' down my face, and he would say, like, "EAT IT!" and I would do that, 'cuz he's standin' right there, and if I don't do that, I would get a beating. I

tried cheering him up, calling him "hon," "please don't say that," in Navajo.

Several women described having plates of food thrown at their faces when the food did not meet the arbitrary, shifting criteria set by their partners. Not only does throwing food or drink at a woman cause physical harm and degradation, but also it demonstrates disdain for the acts of nurturance and love involved in the preparation and service of food. Her offering is rejected, and she is forced to clean up the mess.

The physical violence involved in throwing a drink or a plate of food at a woman cannot be separated from the psychic violence she experiences. Repeated experiences of these random acts of violence led women to decide not to challenge their partner's authority, or, in some cases, to speak at all. Jane described how she decided to conform her talk to her husband's desires: "There's been times when we'd be sitting there having a conversation about anything, and maybe I didn't agree with him, and he'd haul off and smack me one. I got so I didn't express my opinion, I found out how he felt about it, and that's what I'd say. It was just easier." Dorothy described how she pretended to be asleep while riding in the car so that she would not be accused of flirting:

Wherever you go, you know, you can't even go around the corner and you'll be accused of something. And then you can't even look at somebody walkin' down the street or road, and he'll get mad at you, tell you "Get your goddam eyeballs back in your eyes." You know, stuff like that, so, wherever I used to go, I used to just go to sleep. Once we start goin' down the street, I'll just lay back and close my eyes, and sleep, or just pretend to sleep, half the time, until we get to where we're going.

These strategies helped women prevent violence, but simultaneously constricted their freedom and confidence. When women acquiesced and spoke or behaved as they believed men wanted them to, violence could be deferred. Their acquiescence, however, was never a permanent solution: Their partners inevitably became enraged and accused them of imagined infidelities, imperfections, and disobedience. Although women tried to negotiate resistance and compliance, they could not control how their partners interpreted their actions. Women thought they were adhering to men's rules, but men attributed meanings that were beyond women's intentions. Dianne described her inability to understand why her husband always thought she was cheating on him:

> He was always accusin' me of messin' around with somebody else, like all the time, I mean, I couldn't even look at men, if I was drivin' down the road, and just happened to glance over, thought I'd recognized somebody, "Who the hell was that? One of your boyfriends?" He was just, if I was five minutes late from work, I was screwin' somebody, and that just drove me crazy. It seemed like the harder I tried, the worse he'd get. Why is that? I never understood it.

The physical and psychological impact of these acts reinforces larger patterns of male dominance that have shaped intimate relationships for centuries. The expectations for service, combined with punishment for real or imagined transgressions, draw individual men and women into recreating historical axes of domination. When men assault women for not showing proper respect, serving pasta shells instead of spaghetti, or being a little slow delivering a drink, they are establishing control over an individual woman. Criticizing women's eye movements, suspecting infidelity if they only *looked* at someone walking down the street, reinforced the belief that the women were their sexual property. As sexual property, they had no right to look at other men, and certainly not to talk to or spend time with other men. By punishing women's transgressions of the rules they set, men are performing masculinity in a manner that reinscribes patriarchy. When women acquiesce to men's demands and decide to "just accept it," they may avoid some

abuse, but they also participate in upholding male privilege. When they directly challenged a demand, as Phyllis did above, they were punished with severe violence. As women adapt to the threat of violence, they become accustomed to ignoring their own moral compass and obeying commands. Commands may eventually involve women in committing illegal or immoral acts, rather than being victimized.

It is interesting that women's accounts so rarely linked violent outbursts to arguments or conflicts, as the primary quantitative scale for measuring intimate partner violence, the Conflict Tactics Scale, relies on questions about methods used to resolve conflicts.[39] For most women, for most instances of violence, there was no conflict being resolved. The violence directed against them could more aptly be termed an "intimidation tactic." That is, violence was used to reinforce a man's position of authority with regard to a woman's conduct and to demonstrate the punishment that would accompany disobedience. For example, Katy, who was prosecuted for buying her boyfriend's drugs, explained that his unprovoked attacks helped establish his sense of superiority: "I never could understand why he'd hit me, I could never figure it out, or why he flipped out the way he did, I really couldn't and that's so dumb. He didn't have a reason. That's why he never stated a reason, he just wanted to beat up on somebody to make himself feel, I don't know what, to reinforce his own, who knows what, it's sick."

Despite the arbitrary nature of men's violence, women still tried to make sense of what happened by examining their own behavior, particularly when they felt others were hurt as a consequence of their inability to control their partner's violence.

Why?

> The closer home got, seems like I could just feel that pain, and that chill goin' through my body. And I remember I kept telling him, "Hon, why, please don't hurt me when we get home. Please,

what did I do?" I kept begging him, I said, "Why? why?" I don't know what was goin' through his head. He didn't try to talk, he kept on being mad (Crystal).

In trying to make sense of their experiences, women often said they thought about why their partners abused them. No women said they *deserved* the abuse, but some did think if they had tried harder to meet men's demands, then they could have controlled the violence. They learned men's rules and what things would trigger violence. Most women also said that there were violent incidents that they could not predict or explain. They struggled to understand what they did that apparently made their partners so angry, violent, and cruel. Simultaneously, they described the arbitrariness of the abuse and the accusations. Kim Lane Scheppele makes the case that women participate in "stories of self-blame and complicity" in cases of sexualized violence because they recognize that a woman's "own story of abuse requires, as a matter of cultural legibility, a prominent role for herself as the reason for the abuser's conduct and also a knowing judgment of what such a role would mean about herself in the eyes of others."[40] Developing stories of self-blame also helps women restore a sense of control over their lives: If I don't do "X," that caused me to be hurt, then I won't get hurt again.[41] When I asked women what led to the abuse, what preceded a violent incident, most said they had no idea. Finding the words to express their experiences was also difficult. For example, Danielle, convicted of first-degree conspiracy to commit the murder of her husband, explained:

DANIELLE: That's what I started calling 'em, just an episode. I didn't know how else to label it because it was like turning on a light switch. It would start and it would be over. And I'm just sittin' there, like, I don't even know what happened! And, so, they were episodes.

KATHLEEN: And what did he do in the episodes?

DANIELLE: That's when he'd become— *violent!* Like I said, it would be like a light switch. He'd come in, everything'd be fine, and he'd say, "Can you get me somethin' to drink?" "Yeah, okay," I'd get up and walk in the kitchen, get somethin' to drink, and in that amount of time, come back, "Here you go," and he'd throw it in my face. What'd I do? *I mean what did I do?* [her emphasis] I didn't get it fast enough, I guess. I mean, it got to the point I didn't even question what I did anymore. I just accepted it. I would just accept it.

Danielle used the term "episode" to describe her husband's outbursts because they seemed to begin and end arbitrarily and be unconnected from anything she did. The unpredictability of her husband's violence was reflected in many women's accounts. Women described being awakened by being hit, being hit for an innocuous statement, for accidentally looking at a man walking down the street, or for getting a phone call from someone who dialed the wrong number. Women relayed these apparent catalysts for men's violence in order to explain that they could not predict or control it. But they also frequently offered possible explanations: "maybe I didn't get it fast enough," "maybe I didn't cook right for him," "I have to blame his mother and his sisters a lot, 'cuz his mother was a prostitute." These techniques for rationalizing their partner's abuse helped them to think about their situations as at least partially explicable rather than completely random.[42]

Although men's use of physical violence, accusations of infidelity, and emotional abuse seemed unjustified, uncontrollable, and inexplicable, women did not want to think of their partners as complete monsters, or themselves as *only* victims. They searched for reasons to explain what happened, why their partners were so cruel, and why they stayed. As Dorothy, charged with the stabbing death of her husband, said, "You get so scared, he threatens all the time, you don't know when you're gonna' be hit, or when you're gonna' be kicked. I probably had my bad points too. Maybe I irritated him, maybe I didn't cook right for him, or somethin'." The label "battered woman" did not help women understand their situations, and the term's focus on physical violence was at odds with their memories. Organizing their narratives to focus on abuse as part of their criminal defense was difficult because the abuse was "so much" intertwined with daily expressions of disdain, mistrust, and threats of punishment.

Unruly Women

The binary opposition of angels and demons is replicated in the opposition of "real" battered women and women engaged in "mutual combat," and other "unfeminine" conduct, such as drug abuse, prostitution, and other forms of criminality. "Real battered women" are portrayed as being overcome by their partner's violence and abuse. Sympathy is reserved for such women who must also adhere to feminine prescriptions for good mothering, sexual fidelity, and sobriety. Women who fight back, do not protect their children from their partner's abuse, have affairs, or abuse drugs or alcohol—unruly women—do not fit comfortably within the cultural construct of the battered woman, and are likely to have a difficult time accessing the resources that have been developed for battered women. Women of color and immigrant women are particularly disadvantaged in this regard.[43]

The notion of "the battered woman" has been useful in some contexts, such as criminal trials, to assist in describing the effects of being terrorized by an intimate partner. Simultaneously, the creation of this category has contributed to the dilution of complexity and diversity in the experiences of women and added to the view that scientific expertise is able to determine the truth of women's lives. Women who are strong and resistant to male dominance and prescribed domesticity are not easily recognized as belonging to this category of pathetic victims, this "picture of a coma." The development of a category of "battered women" to describe women's experiences reflects dominant, conventional notions of femininity that reinforce those notions and draws boundaries around certain kinds of women who conform to these notions. While racist conceptions of femininity complicate this categorization, the narrowness and contradictions within expectations for "pure victims" exclude most women, particularly those who participate in violent crimes.

The tenuous boundaries between victimization and offender, love and fear, and self and other described here challenge the knowledge that has developed in the field of intimate partner violence. Much of that knowledge is incompatible with the ways that women experience their lives and the desires they have for love and safety. What women who have experienced intimate partner violence and who also commit violent crimes say about their lives does not represent the "truth" that should replace previous ideas. It does represent a more complicated and situated knowledge that can complement and revise the rather rigid categories and analyses that have come to dominate public policy and scholarly research in the area of intimate partner violence.

Notes

1. Dobash and Dobash, 1979; Ferraro, 1989a; 1996.

2. Pleck, 1987, p. 4.

3. Spender, 1980, explains the ways that man-made language shapes our ways of thinking and endorses the myth of male superiority.

4. INCITE! Women of Color Against Violence was organized in 2000 by women who viewed the mainstream anti-violence against women movement as a depoliticized movement that did not recognize the experiences of women of color or the connections between violence against women, racism, colonialism, militarism, the prison industrial complex, and transnational capitalism. The 2005 conference theme was "Stopping the War on Women of Color." Visit their web site for information: http://www.incite-national.org/about/index.html.

5. Ferraro, 1996.

6. Websdale and Johnson, 1997, demonstrated that providing women with these basic resources was the most effective way of reducing violence in their lives.

7. See Ariès, 1962.

8. Rebecca Emerson Dobash makes this point in her response essay, 2003.

9. Quinney, 1970.

10. Lucáks, 1972.

11. Walker, 1979.

12. Elizabeth M. Schneider (2000) makes a similar point in Chapter 4.

13. Yllo and Bograd, 1988.

14. Johnson and Leone, 2005; Johnson and Ferraro, 2000.

15. Dobash and Dobash, 1979; Pleck, 1987.

16. Ferraro, 1979, 1983.

17. The "modernist project" is "a belief in the possibilities opened up by modernity involving a commitment to social progress through a rational and reasoned engagement with the world." See Bilton et al., 1997, p. 18.

18. For a discussion of epistemological debates and sociological methods, see Alcoff and Potter, 1992; Longino, 2002; Denzin and Lincoln, 2005, especially Chapter 8.

19. The revised version of the CTS expands the items to include emotionally abusive behaviors and some physically violent behaviors excluded from the original version, as well as measures of the consequences of behaviors. It is available on line at: http://pubpages.unh.edu/~mas2/test%20form-CTS.htm. Some adaptations of the CTS do not frame the survey in terms of resolving conflicts, recognizing that much intimate partner violence is not a response to a specific conflict. See Johnson and Sacco, 1995.

20. Straus, 1979; Straus, Gelles, and Steinmetz, 1980. The Conflict Tactics Scale has been the subject of a great deal of research and debate. It has been revised since its original formulation, but remains tethered to assumptions that it is possible to objectively bracket and measure intimate partner violence. See Ferraro, 2000.

21. When I worked with a group of people to open a shelter in 1978 in Scottsdale, Arizona, behavioral health funding officials told us they did not think wife beating occurred frequently enough to justify public funding. We used national statistics to help make our case. In 2005, there were 41 shelters in Arizona and, in 2004, 16,000 women and children had been turned away.

22. For example, the survey data generated by Straus and Gelles have been twisted to support fathers' rights and men's rights groups that argue that women are as abusive as men in relationships. See Gelles, n.d. Gelles has consistently argued that this is an invalid interpretation of their data because serious injuries and death are much more likely to be inflicted on women by men.

23. Martin, 1976.

24. O'Brien, 1971.

25. Ferraro, 1983.

26. Schneider, op. cit., Chapter 5; Renzetti, 1999.

27. Sykes, 1992; Dershowitz, 2000.

28. O'Dell, 1997.

29. Benedict, 1992; Lamb, 1999; Madriz, 1997.

30. Schechter, 1982.

31. Ferraro, 1997.

32. Walker, 1979.

33. Barnett and LaViolette, 1993, review some of the work that analyzes women's love of their abusive partners.

34. See Ferraro, 1997.

35. In several instances, I violated the neutrality expected of researchers by telling women that men's behavior was not "normal." As one of the few, or only, people they had told about their experiences, I felt it was important to help shift their self-blame by saying that most people would not agree with their partner's definitions of "normality."

36. See Rosen, 2004, for a discussion of this phenomenon among adolescent mothers.

37. Chesney-Lind, 2004; Bortner and Williams, 1997; Gaarder and Belknap, 2002; Belknap, Holsinger, and Dunn, 1997.

38. Bergen, 2000.

39. Ferraro, 2000.

40. Scheppele, 1992, p. 144.

41. Scheppele, 1992, p. 143 and Scheppele and Bart, 1983, p. 79.

42. Ferraro and Johnson, 1983.

43. See Smith, 2005a, 2005b; Richie, 1996, 2000; Ritchie, 2005; Dasgupta, 2002.

References

Alcoff, Linda, and Elizabeth Potter. 1992. *Feminist Epistemologies*. New York: Routledge.

Ariès, Phillippe. 1962. *Centuries of Childhood: A Social History of Family Life*. Trans. R. Baldock. New York: Knopf.

Barnett, Ola W., and Alyce D. LaViolette. 1993. *It Could Happen to Anyone: Why Battered Women Stay*. Newbury Park, CA: Sage.

Belknap, Joanne, Kristi Holsinger, and Melissa Dunn. 1997. "Understanding Incarcerated Girls: The Results of a Focus Group Study," *Prison Journal* 77(4):381–404.

Benedict, Helen. 1992. *Virgin or Vamp: How the Press Covers Sex Crimes*. New York: Oxford.

Bergen, Raquel Kennedy. 2000. "Rape Laws and Spousal Exemptions." Pp. 223–25 in N. H. Rafter, *Encyclopedia of Women and Crime*. Phoenix, AZ: Oryx.

Bilton, Tony, Kevin Bonnett, Pip Jones, David Skinner, Michelle Stanworth, and Andrew Webster. 1997. *Introductory Sociology*. 3rd ed. London: Macmillan.

Bortner, M. A., and Linda M. Williams. 1997. *Youth in Prison: We the People of Unit Four*. New York: Routledge.

Chesney-Lind, Meda. 2004. *Girls and Violence: Is the Gender Gap Closing?* Harrisburg, PA: VA Wnet Applied Research Forum.

Dasgupta, Shamita Das. 2002. "A Framework for Understanding Women's Use of Nonlethal Violence in Intimate Heterosexual Relationships," *Violence Against Women* 8(11):1364–89.

Denzin, Norman K., and Yvonna S. Lincoln. 2005. *Sage Handbook of Qualitative Research*. 3rd ed. Thousand Oaks, CA: Sage.

Dershowitz, Alan M. 1994. *The Abuse Excuse*. New York: Little Brown.

Dobash, R. Emerson. 2003. "Domestic Violence: Arrest, Prosecution and Reducing Violence," *Criminology and Public Policy* 2(2):313–318.

Dobash, R. Emerson, and Russell P. Dobash. 1979. *Violence Against Wives*. New York: Free Press.

Ferraro, Kathleen J. 1979. "Physical and Emotional Battering: Aspects of Managing Hurt," *California Sociologist* 2(2):134–149.

———. 1983. "The Rationalization Process: How Battered Women Stay," *Victimology* (34): 203–214.

———. 1989. "The Legal Response to Battering in the U.S." Pp. 155–184 in M. Hanmer, J. Radford, and E. Stanko, eds., *Women, Policing and Male Violence: International Perspectives*. London: Routledge.

———. 1996. "The Dance of Dependency: A Genealogy of Domestic Violence Discourse," *Hypatia* 11(4):77–91.

———. 1997. "Battered Women: Strategies for Survival," In A. Carderelli, ed., *Violence Between Intimate Partners: Patterns Causes and Effects*. Boston: Allyn and Bacon. Pp. 124–140.

———. 2000. "Woman Battering: More Than a Family Problem." Pp. 135–53 in L. Goodstein and C. Renzetti, eds., *Women, Crime and Justice: Contemporary Perspectives*. New York: Roxbury.

Ferraro, Kathleen J., and John M. Johnson. 1983. "How Women Experience Battering: The Process of Victimization," *Social Problems* 30(3): 325–39.

Gaarder, Emily, and Joanne Belknap. 2002. "Tenuous Borders: Girls Transferred to Adult Court," *Criminology* 40(3):481–517.

Gelles, Richard J. n.d. *Domestic Violence: Not an Even Playing Field*. http://thesafetyzone.org/everyone/gelles.html. *Accessed September 25, 2005.*

Johnson, Holly, and Vincent Sacco. 1995. "Researching Violence Against Women: Statistics Canada National Survey," *Canadian Journal of Criminology* 37(3): 281–304.

Johnson, Michael P., and Kathleen J. Ferraro. 2000. "Research on Domestic Violence in the 1990s: Making Distinctions," *Journal of Marriage and the Family* 62: 948–968.

Johnson, Michael P., and Janel M. Leone. 2005. "The Differential Effects of Intimate Terrorism and Situational Couple Violence," *Journal of Family Issues* 26(3):322–349.

Lamb, Sharon. 1999. "Constructing the Victim: Popular Images and Lasting Labels." Pp. 108–138 in S. Lamb, ed., *New Versions of Victims*. New York: New York University.

Longino, Helen E. 2002. *The Fate of Knowledge*. Princeton, NJ: Princeton University.

Lukács, Georg. 1972. *History and Class Consciousness*. Cambridge, MA: MIT Press.

Madriz, Esther. 1997. *Nothing Bad Happens to Good Girls*. Berkeley: University of California.

Martin, Del. 1976. *Battered Wives*. San Francisco: Glide.

O'Brien, John. 1971. "Violence in Divorce-Prone Families," *Journal of Marriage and the Family* 33: 692–698.

O'Dell, Lindsay. 1997. "Child Sexual Abuse and the Academic Construction of Symptomatologies," *Feminism and Psychology* 7(3): 334–39.

Pleck, Elizabeth. 1987. *Domestic Tyranny*. New York: Oxford.

Quinney, Richard. 1970. *The Social Reality of Crime*. Boston: Little Brown.

Renzetti, Claire. 1999. "The Challenge to Feminism Posed by Women's Use of Violence in Intimate Relationships." Pp. 42–56 in S. Lamb, ed., *New Versions of Victims: Feminists Struggle with the Concept*. New York: New York University.

Richie, Beth. 1996. *Compelled to Crime: The Gender Entrapment of Black, Battered Women*. New York: Routledge.

———. 2000. "A Black Feminist Reflection on the Anti-Violence Movement," *Signs* 25(4):1134–38.

Ritchie, Andrea. 2005. "Police Violence Against Women of Color in the Context of Domestic Violence." Paper presented at the annual meetings of the Society for the Study of Social Problems, Philadelphia, PA, August 12–14.

Rosen, Daniel. 2004. "'I Just let Him Have His Way,'" *Violence Against Women* 10(1):6–28.

Schechter, Susan. 1982. *Women and Male Violence*. Boston: South End.

Scheppele, Kim Lane. 1992. "Just the Facts, Ma'am: Sexualized Violence, Evidentiary Habits, and the Revision of Truth," *New York Law School Law Review* 37(1–2): 123–72.

Scheppele, Kim Lane, and Pauline Bart. 1983. "Through Women's Eyes: Defining Danger in the Wake of Sexual Assault," *Journal of Social Issues* 39(2): 63–80.

Schneider, Elizabeth M. 2000. *Battered Women and Feminist Lawmaking*. New Haven, CT: Yale University.

Smith, Andrea. 2005a. *Conquest: Sexual Violence and American Indian Genocide*. Boston: South End.

———. 2005b. "The Anti-Violence Movement as an Alibi for the State in American Culture." Paper presented at the annual meeting of the Society for the Study of Social Problems, Philadelphia, August 12–14.

Spender, Dale. 1980. *Man-Made Language*. London: Routledge & Kegan-Paul.

Straus, Murray A. 1979. "Measuring Intrafamily Conflict and Violence: The Conflict Tactics (CT) Scales," *Journal of Marriage and the Family* 41(1):75–89.

Straus, Murray A., Richard J. Gelles, and Suzanne K. Steinmetz. 1980. *Behind Closed Doors: Violence in the American Family*. Garden City, NY: Anchor/Doubleday.

Sykes, Charles. 1992. *A Nation of Victims*. New York: St. Martin's.

Walker, Lenore. 1979. *The Battered Woman*. New York: Harper and Row.

Websdale, Neil S., and Byron Johnson. 1997. "Reducing Woman Battering: The Role of Structural Approaches," *Social Justice* 24(1): 54–81.

Yllo, Kersti, and Michel Bograd. 1988. *Feminist Perspectives on Wife Abuse*. Beverly Hills, CA: Sage.

ARTICLE 26

Meda Chesney-Lind
Joanne Belknap

Trends in Delinquent Girls' Aggression and Violent Behavior: A Review of the Evidence

Introduction

Girls in the juvenile justice system were once "dubbed" the "forgotten few" (Bergsmann, 1989). That construction of female delinquency has rapidly faded as increases in girls' arrests have dramatically outstripped those of boys for most of the last decade. Girls now account for 28 percent of juvenile arrests up from 23 percent at the beginning of the last decade (Federal Bureau of Investigation, 1991, 2001), and attention is being drawn to the fact that their arrests for nontraditional, even violent, offenses are among those showing the greatest increases. These shifts and changes all bring into sharp focus the need to better understand the dynamics involved in female delinquency and the need to tailor responses to the unique circumstances of girls growing up in the new millennium.

This chapter provides a critical examination of these trends in female juvenile delinquency with a specific focus on current research examining trends in girls' aggression and violence. We examine national trends, and then we take a closer look at self-report data, which amplify the trends seen in the more global arrest and incarceration data. The findings emphasize the importance of examining how girls' violence and aggression is measured and framed. Whether it is

by criminologists or journalists, the authors conclude the girls' violence and aggression has been misrepresented too often in both research forums and the media.

Patterns in Girls' Delinquency: Are Girls Really Closing the Gender Gap in Violence?

Between 1991 and 2000 in the United States, girls' arrests increased 25.3 percent while arrests of boys actually decreased by 3.2 percent (Federal Bureau of Investigation, 2001: 221). Concomitant with these arrest increases are increases in girls' referrals to juvenile courts; between 1987 and 1996, the number of delinquency cases involving girls increased by 76 percent compared to a 42 percent increase for males (Stahl, 1999). Arrests of girls for serious violent offenses increased by 27.9 percent between 1991 and 2000; arrests of girls for "other assaults" increased by even more: 77.9 percent (Federal Bureau of Investigation, 2001: 221). The Office of Juvenile Justice and Delinquency Prevention (1999) found that the female violent crime rate for 1997 was 103 percent above the 1981 rate, compared to 27 percent for males. This prompted them to assert that "increasing juvenile female arrests and the involvement of girls in at-risk and delinquent behavior has been a pervasive trend across the United States" (p. 2). Discussions of girls' gang behavior and, more recently, girls' violence have also been extremely prevalent in the media (see Chesney-Lind, 1999 for a review).

Trends in Girls' Violence. With reference to what might be called girls' "nontraditional" delinquency, it must be recognized that girls' capacity for aggression and violence has historically been ignored, trivialized, or denied. For this reason, self-report data, particularly from the seventies, showed higher involvement of girls in assaultive behavior than official statistics from that period would indicate.[1]

More recent self-report data of youthful involvement in violent offenses fail to show the dramatic changes found in official statistics during either the eighties or the nineties. Consider data collected by the Centers for Disease Control over the last decade. The CDC has been monitoring youthful behavior in a national sample of school-aged youth in a number of domains (including violence) at regular intervals since 1991 in a biennial survey entitled the Youth Risk Behavior Survey. A quick look at data collected over the nineties reveals that while 34.4 percent of girls surveyed in 1991 said that they had been in a physical fight in the last year, by 1999 that figure had dropped to 27.3 percent or a 21 percent decrease in girls' fighting; boys' violence also decreased during the same period but only slightly—from 44.0 percent to 42.5 percent (a 3.4 percent drop) (Brener, Simon, Krug, & Lowry, 1999:443; Centers for Disease Control, 1994–2000). Similarly, the rate of girls who reported carrying weapons and carrying guns also declined substantially. A logistic analysis of these trends (for the years 1991–1997) published in the *Journal of the American Medical Association* concluded that "while analyses revealed a significant linear decrease in physical fighting for both male and female students the B [beta] for females was larger, suggesting they had a steeper decline" (Brener et al., 1999:444).

Earlier, a matched sample of "high-risk" youth (aged 13–17) surveyed in the 1977 National Youth Study and the more recent 1989 Denver Youth Survey also revealed significant *decreases* in girls' involvement in felony assaults, minor assaults, and hard drugs, and no change in a wide range of other delinquent behaviors—including felony theft, minor theft, and index delinquency

(Huizinga, 1997). Finally, there are the trends in girls' lethal violence. While girls' arrests for all forms of assault have been skyrocketing in the nineties, girls' arrests for robbery fell by 45.3 percent and murder by 1.4 percent between 1991 and 2000. If girls were in fact closing the gap between their behavior and that of boys, would not one expect to see the same effect across all the violent offenses (including the *most* violent offense)? That simply is not happening.

Further support of this notion comes from recent research on girls' violence in San Francisco (Males & Shorter, 2001). Scholars' analyses of vital statistics maintained by health officials (rather than arrest data) conclude that there has been a 63 percent drop in San Francisco teen-girl fatalities between the 1960s and the 1990s, and they also report that hospital injury data show that girls are dramatically under-represented among those reporting injury (including assaults) (girls are 3.7 percent of the population but were only 0.9 percent of those seeking treatment for violent injuries) (Males & Shorter, 2001:1–2). They conclude: Compared to her counterpart of the baby boom generation growing up in the 1960s and 1970s, a San Francisco teenage girl today is 50 percent less likely to be murdered, 60 percent less likely to suffer a fatal accident, 75 percent less likely to commit suicide, 45 percent less likely to die by a gun, 55 percent less likely to become a mother, 60 percent less likely to commit murder, and 40 percent less likely to be arrested for property crimes (Males & Shorter, 2001:1).

Data from Canada indicate the same pattern. A recent report on delinquent girls incarcerated in British Columbia concludes that "despite isolated incidents of violence, the majority of offending by female youth in custody is relatively minor" (Corrado, Odgers, & Cohen, 2000). Even a study of girls tried and convicted as adults in the United States found the majority of the girls had relatively minor offenses (Gaarder & Belknap, 2002).

In short, other measures of girls' violent crime that are less susceptible to changes in policing practices fail to reflect the trends shown in the arrest data. Having said that, there is still a need to understand the gender dynamics in girls' and boys' aggression and violence: a topic the next section covers in more detail. Moreover, once these are fully understood, it is clear that they interface with the various societal changes in the framing of girls' aggression that have occurred in the past decades.

What's in a Name: Enforcement Practices and Arrest Data

If the levels of girls' physical aggression, or violence, has not changed, what explains the dramatic increases in female arrest, particularly in arrests of girls for "other assaults"? Relabeling of behaviors that were once categorized as status offenses (noncriminal offenses like "runaway" and "person in need of supervision") into violent offenses cannot be ruled out in explanations of arrest rate shifts, nor can changes in police practices with reference to domestic violence. A review of the over two thousand cases of girls referred to Maryland's juvenile justice system for "person-to-person" offenses revealed that virtually all of these offenses (97.9 percent) involved "assault." A further examination of these records revealed that about half were "family-centered" and involved such activities as "a girl hitting her mother and her mother subsequently pressing charges" (Mayer, 1994).

More recently, Acoca's study of nearly 1,000 delinquent girls' files from four California counties found that while a "high percentage" of these girls were charged with "person offenses," a majority of these involved assault. Further, "a close reading of the case files of girls charged with assault revealed that most of these charges were the result of nonserious, mutual combat situations with parents." Acoca details cases that she regards as typical including: "father lunged at her while she was calling the police about a domestic dispute. She (girl) hit him." Finally, she reports that some cases were quite trivial in nature including a girl arrested "for throwing cookies at her mother" (Acoca, 1999: 7–8). In a Colorado study, a girl reported that she was arrested for "as-

sault" for throwing her Barbie doll at her mother (Belknap, Winter, & Cady, 2001).

In essence, when exploring the dramatic increases in the arrests of girls for "other assault," it is likely that changes in enforcement practices have dramatically narrowed the gender gap. As noted in the above examples, a clear contribution has come from increasing arrests of girls and women for domestic violence. A recent California study found that the female share of these arrests increased from 6 percent in 1988 to 16.5 percent in 1998 (Bureau of Criminal Information and Analysis, 1999). African American girls and women had arrest rates roughly three times those of white girls and women in 1998: 149.6 compared to 46.4 (Bureau of Criminal Information and Analysis, 1999).

Relabeling of girls' arguments with parents from status offenses (like "incorrigible" or "person in need of supervision") to assault is a form of "bootstrapping" that has been particularly pronounced in the official delinquency of African American girls (Robinson, 1990; Bartollas, 1993). This practice also facilitates the incarceration of girls in detention facilities and training schools—something that would not be possible if the girl were arrested for noncriminal status offenses. Similarly, some parents admit to using detention as a "time out" from conflict with their daughters, including some mothers who would rather have their daughters in detention than at home with the mothers and their boyfriends, when it is often the mothers' boyfriends who caused the girls' running away (Lederman & Brown, 2000).

"Up-criming" cannot be ruled out in terms of the increases seen in arrests of youth for schoolyard fights and other instances of bullying that were ignored or handled internally by schools and parents. Such an explanation is particularly salient as increasing numbers of schools adopt "zero tolerance" policies for physical aggression and/or weapon carrying. It has long been known that arrests of youth for minor or "other" assaults can range from schoolyard tussles to relatively serious, but not life-threatening assaults (Steffensmeier & Steffensmeier, 1980).

Currie (1998) adds to this the fact that these "simple assaults without injury" are often "attempted" or "threatened" or "not completed." At a time when official concern about youth violence is almost unparalleled and school principals are increasingly likely to call police onto their campuses, it should come as no surprise that youthful arrests in this area are up. It is noteworthy that this unparalleled police involvement on secondary school campuses is largely due to "Columbine" and other school shootings and "massacres" perpetrated almost exclusively by boys (see Steinem, 2001).

The possibility of up-criming of minor forms of youthful violence is supported by research on the dynamics of juvenile robbery in Honolulu (another violent offense where girls' arrests showed sharp increases in the mid-nineties). In the last decade, Hawaii, like the rest of the nation, had seen an increase in the arrests of youth for serious crimes of violence[2] coupled with a recent decline. In Hawaii, violent crime (murder, rape, robbery, and aggravated assault) arrests increased 60 percent from 1987 to 1996 coupled with an 8.6 percent decline between 1996 and 1997 (Department of the Attorney General, 1996, 1997). Most of the change can be attributed to increases in the number of youth arrested for two offenses: aggravated assault and robbery. Between 1994 and 1996, for example, the number of youth arrested for robbery doubled in Honolulu.

These increases prompted a study of the actual dimensions of juvenile robbery in Honolulu (see Chesney-Lind & Paramore, 2001). In this study, police files from two time periods (1991 and 1997) that focused on robbery incidents resulting in arrest were identified. According to these data, in 1991, the vast majority of those arrested for robbery in Honolulu were male—114 (95 percent) versus 6 (5 percent) female. However, a shift occurred in 1997—83.3 percent were males. Thus, the proportion of robbery arrests involving girls more than tripled, between 1991 and 1997.

Taken alone, these numeric increases, along with anecdotal information are precisely why the "surge" in girls' violence has been made. How-

ever, in this study, we were able to carefully characterize each of these "robberies" during the two time periods. Essentially, the data suggested that no major shift in the pattern of juvenile robbery occurred between 1991 and 1997 in Honolulu. Rather it appears that less serious offenses, including a number committed by girls, are being swept into the system perhaps as a result of changes in school policy and parental attitudes (many of the robberies occurred as youth were going to and from school). Consistent with this explanation are the following observable patterns in our data: During the two time periods under review, the age of offenders shifts downward, as does the value of items taken. In 1991, the median value of the items stolen was $10.00; by 1997, the median value had dropped to $1.25. Most significantly, the proportion of adult victims declines sharply while the number of juvenile victims increases. Finally, while more of the robberies involved weapons in 1997, those weapons were less likely to be firearms and the incidents were less likely to result in injury to the victim. In short, the data suggest that the problem of juvenile robbery in the City and County of Honolulu is largely characterized by slightly older youth bullying and "hi-jacking" younger youth for small amounts of cash and occasionally jewelry and that arrests of youth for these forms of robbery accounted for virtually all of the increase observed.

In a slightly different study of gender differences in youthful violence, when 444 incarcerated delinquent youth in Ohio were recently asked to report on an anonymous survey the offenses involved in their current incarceration, there were major gender differences (Holsinger, Belknap, & Sutherland, 1999). Although girls and boys reported similar rates for having burglary as an offense (one-fifth of both), girls (one-third) were more likely than boys (one-fifth) to report an assault as an offense, and far more likely to report a property crime as an offense (53 percent of girls and 31 percent of boys). Boys (16 percent) were twice as likely as girls (8 percent) to be incarcerated for an offense involving drugs, almost five times as likely to be incarcerated for a sex offense (5 percent of girls, and 24 percent of boys), and more than twice as likely to report robbery as an offense that resulted in their current incarceration (7 percent of girls and 16 percent of boys). There were no significant gender differences in the youths' reports of whether they were in for a violent offense; about half of both sexes reported violent offenses as leading to their current incarceration (Holsinger et al., 1999).

An examination of these youths' self-reported offenses of the charges leading to their current incarcerations implies that the girls and boys are similar in the severity of their levels of offending overall. Yet, the girls received significantly shorter sentences (mean = 12 months for girls, mean = 16 months for boys) (Holsinger et al., 1999). It is useful to examine some of the qualitative data in order to speculate why this may be the case. Focus groups with delinquent girls in this same state found reports of girls' attempts to protect themselves incriminating (Belknap, Dunn, & Holsinger, 1997). For example, when asked why she was incarcerated, one girl told a story of her otherwise "clean" delinquent record until she carried a knife to school. She had repeatedly told school authorities that an older boy in the school was following her as she walked to and from school and that she was afraid of him. The school refused to look into it, but when the girl put a knife in her sock in order to protect herself getting to and from school, the school's "no tolerance" code for weapons was triggered. This girl reported extreme frustration regarding the school's tolerance of the boy stalking and sexually harassing her, but no tolerance for her attempts to protect herself when the school failed to assure her safety.

Gender Matters in Girls' Aggression and Violence

The psychological literature on aggression, which considers forms of aggression other than physical aggression (or violence), is also relevant here. Taken together, this literature generally reflects that, while boys and men are more likely to be physically aggressive, differences begin to even out when verbal aggression is considered (yelling, insulting, teasing) (Bjokqvist & Niemela, 1992). Further, girls in adolescence may be more likely than boys to use "indirect aggression," such as gossip, telling bad or false stories, telling secrets (Bjokqvist, Osterman, & Kaukiainen, 1992). When this broad definition of "aggression" is utilized, only about 5 percent of the variance in aggression is explained by gender (Bjokqvist & Niemela, 1992).

Does relational aggression occur more frequently with girls and boys? Research addressing this question has been mixed (see Okamoto & Chesney-Lind, 2002). Crick and Grotpeter (1995), consistent with Bjokqvist and Niemla (1992), found that girls in their sample of third- through sixth-grade students were significantly more relationally aggressive than were boys. They found that these youth were significantly more disliked and lonelier than nonrelationally aggressive peers. Other research, however, has found no difference in the frequency of relational aggression between boys and girls (e.g., Gropper & Froschl, 2000; Tiet, Wasserman, Loeber, McReynolds, & Miller, 2001). In these studies, however, researchers coded observations of aggression, while in the Crick and Grotpeter (1995) study, peer nomination was used as the data collection procedure. This suggests that manifestations of relational aggression may be difficult to detect by adult observers, and may need to be identified by members of the youth peer group. Because of the relatively indirect nature of behaviors related to relational aggression, Crick and Grotpeter (1995) state that "it might be difficult for those outside the peer group to reliably observe and evaluate [this form of aggression] in naturalistic settings" (p. 712).

Why is relational aggression important for those concerned about girls in the juvenile justice system? First, it is likely that girls in delinquency prevention and intervention programs have considerable problems with relational aggression, since it has been shown to be related to internalizing problems, peer rejection, and depression

(Crick et al., 1998:126–127). Second, while girls' aggressive behavior often remains relational in nature, overt manifestations of aggression are often preceded by relational aggression. This phenomenon is evident in both the school and group home settings for girls. Often, the rationale for a physical fight is, "She's talking behind my back," or "She's after my boyfriend." By addressing the relational aspect of aggression early and often, practitioners working with youth are in essence conducting overt violence prevention. The significance of this process extends to boys as well. The massacre at Columbine High School, for example, might have been prevented if the relational aggression associated with the ostracism and ridicule extended to Eric Harris and Dylan Klebold by their peers were addressed. In other words, relational aggression, while seemingly insignificant, can lead to serious consequences if left unaddressed by youth practitioners.

Those who study aggression in young children and young adults also note that girls' aggression is usually within the home or "intrafemale" and, thus, likely to be less often reported to authorities (Bjokqvist & Niemela, 1992). The fact that scholars as well as the general public have largely ignored these forms of aggression also means that there is substantial room for girls' aggression to be "discovered" at a time when concern about youthful violence is heightened.

Finally, girls' behavior, including violence, needs to be put in its patriarchal context. In her analysis of self-reported violence in girls in Canada, Artz (1998) has done precisely that, and the results were striking. First, she noted that violent girls reported significantly greater rates of victimization and abuse than their nonviolent counterparts, and that girls who were violent reported great fear of sexual assault, especially from their boyfriends. Specifically, 20 percent of violent girls stated they were physically abused at home compared to 10 percent of violent males, and 6.3 percent of nonviolent girls. Patterns for sexual abuse were even starker; roughly one out of four violent girls had been sexually abused

compared to one in ten of nonviolent girls (Artz, 1998). Follow-up interviews with a small group of violent girls found that they had learned at home that "might makes right" and engaged in "horizontal violence" directed at other powerless girls (often with boys as the audience). Certainly, these findings provide little ammunition for those who would contend that the "new" violent girl is a product of any form of "emancipation."

Detailed comparisons drawn from supplemental homicide reports from unpublished FBI data also hint at the central, rather than peripheral way in which gender has colored and differentiated even the most serious of girls' and boys' violence. In a study of these FBI data on the characteristics of girls' and boys' homicides between 1984 and 1993, Loper and Cornell (1996) found that girls accounted for "proportionately fewer homicides in 1993 (6 percent) than in 1984 (14 percent)" (p. 324). They found that, in comparison to boys' homicides, girls who killed were more likely to use a knife than a gun and to murder someone as a result of conflict (rather than in the commission of a crime). Girls were also more likely than boys to murder family members (32 percent) and very young victims (24 percent of their victims were under the age of three compared to 1 percent of the boy's victims). When involved in a peer homicide, girls were more likely than boys to have killed as a result of an interpersonal conflict and were more likely to kill alone, while boys were more likely to kill with an accomplice. Loper and Cornell concluded that "the stereotype of girls becoming gun-toting robbers was not supported. The dramatic increase in gun-related homicides … applies to boys but not girls" (p. 332).

In conclusion, what needs to be understood about girls' delinquency, particularly from a programmatic and policy standpoint is that gender provides an important and complex context within which violence is enacted. For girls who enter the juvenile justice system, including girls with a history of violence and aggression, there is a clear link between victimization, trauma, and delinquency. The other major theme that must be addressed is the fact that most often this trauma produces not violent offenses but rather what have long been regarded as "trivial" or unimportant offenses like running away from home.

Simply stated, the current trends in juvenile justice suggest that social control of girls is once again on the criminal justice agenda—this century it is justified by their purported "violence" just as in the past century it was justified by their sexuality. (See Corrado et al., 2000, for a similar pattern in Canada.)

Girls' Troubles and Trauma— Nonaggressive Offenses and Violent Victimizations

While the media has focused attention on girls' violent, nontraditional delinquency, most of girls' delinquency is not of that sort at all. However, understanding these offenses is also important in exploring girls' aggression and violence, since these are the behaviors that are currently being relabeled as "person offenses."

Examining the types of offenses for which girls have historically been arrested, it is clear that most are arrested for the less serious criminal acts and status offenses (noncriminal offenses for which only youth can be taken into custody such as "running away from home" or "curfew violation"). Even today, despite the increases in girls' arrests for violent offenses, roughly half of girls' arrests were for either larceny theft (21.5 percent) much of which, particularly for girls, is shoplifting (Shelden & Horvath, 1986) or status offenses (21.8 percent). Boys' arrests were far more dispersed (Federal Bureau of Investigation, 2001:221).

Status Offenses. Status offenses have long played a significant role among the offenses that bring girls into the juvenile justice system. They accounted for about a quarter of all girls' arrests in 2000, but only 10 percent of boys' arrests—figures that remained relatively stable during the last decade. In 2000, over half (58.9 percent) of those arrested for one status offense—running away

from home—were girls (Federal Bureau of Investigation, 2000:221). Running away from home and prostitution remain the only two arrest categories where more girls than boys are arrested.

The passage of the Juvenile Justice and Delinquency Prevention Act in 1974, which, among other things, encouraged jurisdictions to divert and deinstitutionalize youth charged with status offenses, did result in a slight decrease in these arrests. As an example, the last decade did show a 16.3 percent drop in arrests of girls for runaway (although ironically, the decrease for boys was sharper—20.2 percent). However, some of the leveling off of these arrest numbers is likely explained by the relabeling of these offenses as person offenses. Parents increasingly seek to do this, since police will often refuse to arrest and detain youth charged only with status offenses because of the de-institutionalization mandates. Such is not the case with person offenses, particularly "domestic violence," which in some states, like Florida, *requires* detention.

Similarly, abolishing status offenses and the implementation of the fair-procedure 1982 *Young Offenders Act (YOA)* in Canada is reported by some to have not changed or improved the treatment of delinquent girls (Corrado et al., 2000; Duffy, 1996; Reitsma-Street, 1999). "Since the inception of the YOA, the use of custodial dispositions for young females has not decreased as expected," particularly for minor offenses (Corrado et al., 2000).

Why are girls more likely to be arrested than boys for running away from home? There are no simple answers to this question. Studies of actual delinquency (not simply arrests) show that girls and boys run away from home in about equal numbers. As an example, Canter (1982) found in a National Youth Survey that there was no evidence of greater female involvement, compared to males, in any category of delinquent behavior. Indeed, in this sample, males were significantly more likely than females to report status offenses. There is some evidence to suggest that parents and police may be responding differently to the same behavior. Parents may be calling the police when their daughters do not come home, and police may be more likely to arrest a female than a male runaway youth.

Finally, research on the characteristics of girls in the CYA system reveals that while these girls cannot be incarcerated in the Youth Authority for status offenses, nearly half (45 percent) had been charged with status offenses prior to their incarceration in the CYA for more serious offenses (Bloom & Campbell, 1998). Focus groups with program staff working in a variety of settings in California also indicated that these individuals felt that girls in that state were chiefly involved in the juvenile justice system for offenses such as "petty theft, shoplifting, assault and battery, drug violations, gang activity and truancy, lying to a police officer, and running away" (Bloom & Campbell, 1998).

Sexual and Physical Abuse. Research illustrates the differences in the reasons that boys and girls have for running away. Girls are, for example, much more likely than boys to be the victims of child sexual abuse with some experts estimating that roughly 70 percent of the victims of child sexual abuse are girls (Finkelhor & Baron, 1986). Not surprisingly, the evidence also suggests a link between this problem and girls' delinquency—particularly running away from home.

Studies of girls on the streets or in court populations depict high rates of both sexual and physical abuse. [A study of a runaway shelter in Toronto found, for example, that 73 percent of the female runaways and 38 percent of the males had been sexually abused. This same study found that sexually abused female runaways were more likely than their non-abused counterparts to engage in delinquent or criminal activities such as substance abuse, petty theft, and prostitution. No such pattern was found among the male runaways (McCormack, Janus, & Burgess, 1986).] A similar study of 372 homeless and runaway youth in Seattle living on the street and in shelters reported that girls (30 percent) were twice as likely as boys (15 percent) to report sexual abuse histories, and that "extreme violence" was higher among the girls' than the boys' sexual abuse re-

ports (Tyler et al., 2001). Girls were significantly more likely than boys to report being victimized in their homes as well as on the street after they ran away. Furthermore, the more sexual abuse the youth experienced at home, the more likely he or she was to run away at a younger age. This is particularly important given research that finds for both boys and girls that an early age of delinquency onset is related to more serious delinquency past age 14 (Piquero & Chung, 2001). The Seattle study also found that the runaway girls were more likely than the runaway boys to report both selling sex and being sexually victimized on the street (Tyler et al., 2001). This is consistent with Schaffner's (1998) contention that the "solutions" to girls' sexual victimization (such as running away from home to escape sexual abuse) are often sexually troubling situations.

Detailed studies of youth entering the juvenile justice system in Florida have compared the "constellations of problems" presented by girls and boys entering detention (Dembo, Williams, & Schmeidler, 1993; Dembo et al., 1995). These researchers have found that female youth were more likely than male youth to have abuse histories and contact with the juvenile justice system for status offenses, while male youth had higher rates of involvement with various delinquent offenses. Further research on a larger cohort of youth (N = 2104) admitted to an assessment center in Tampa concluded that "girls' problem behavior commonly relates to an abusive and traumatizing home life, whereas boys' law violating behavior reflects their involvement in a delinquent life style" (Dembo et al., 1995:21).

More recent research confirms Dembo's insights; Cauffman, Feldman, Waterman, and Steiner (1998) studied the backgrounds of 96 girls in the custody of the California Youth Authority and compared these results with those garnered from a comparison sample of male youth (N = 93) held by CYA. In this comparison, Cauffman et al. found that while boys were more likely to be traumatized as observers of violence, "girls were more likely to be traumatized as direct victims" (more than half the girls were the victims of either sexual or physical abuse). Perhaps as a result, girls were significantly more likely than boys to be currently suffering from posttraumatic stress disorder; the levels of PTSD found in this population were "significantly higher than among the general adolescent female population" (65 percent compared to 11 percent), (Cauffman et al., 1998). Interestingly, about two-thirds of the girls in this sample were serving time for a violent offense (murder, assault, robbery), and 43 percent of the girls identified as gang members (Cauffman et al., 1998).

A study of 444 incarcerated youth in Ohio found that for every measure of experienced or witnessed violence, girls reported significantly higher rates. Given that the boys' reported rates were still alarmingly high, this is particularly troubling. The most extreme gender differences were for sexual abuse, followed by physical abuse by nonfamily members. Two-thirds of the boys and three-fourths of the girls reported physical abuse from a family member, while two-thirds of girls and one-third of boys reported physical abuse by a nonfamily member. Three-fifths of girls and almost one-fifth of boys reported sexual abuse histories (Holsinger et al., 1999).

In short, while these offenses appear trivial, girls who exhibit these behaviors have problems (usually as a result of exposure to sexual and physical victimization) that are profound. All the more ironic is the fact that if current trends continue, more and more of these girls will find themselves arrested, detained, and labeled as "violent" themselves when they seek to escape violent situations.

Conclusions

Girls' aggression and violence has long been ignored, trivialized, and minimized. This denial not only permits the occasional "discovery" of "bad girls," particularly by the media, but it also means that minor changes in enforcement practices can make it appear that girls' behavior has changed, when in actuality, that is not the case.

Specifically, we suggest that the "closing gender gap" in youthful violence and aggression is largely a myth. Rather, it appears that changes in arrest data over time are likely the product of changes in the behavior of parents, school officials, and law enforcement. One of these shifts is the relabeling of behaviors that were once subsumed under status offenses as crimes of violence (often so that the parents can get their daughter arrested and detained). For example, youth who hit a parent were once charged as CHINS (Children in Need of Supervision) or PINS (Persons in Need of Supervision). Today these girls are likely to be charged with "assault." In addition to this "relabeling," the popularity of "zero tolerance policies" on and around school campuses has meant the minor forms of youth on youth violence that were once handled internally are increasingly criminalized.

This chapter also emphasizes the need to avoid both denial and demonization of girls' violence, and to seek to understand the context which produces girls' aggressive behavior. How is it that girls and boys use aggression differently? How do those who label the behavior as criminal decide to do so? Finally, despite dramatic changes in girls' arrests for "violent" offenses, most girls are still arrested for nonaggressive and drug offenses. Even those girls arrested for "violent" offenses are likely quite different from their violent male counterparts and far more like the "traditional" girl delinquent than many assumed.

Endnotes

1. As an example, Canter (1976) reported a male versus female, self-reported delinquency ratio of 3.5:1 for serious assault and 3.4:1 for minor assault. At that time, arrest statistics showed much greater male participation in aggravated assault (5.6:1) and simple assault (3.8:1) (Federal Bureau of Investigation, 1980). Currently, arrest statistics show a 3.3:1 ratio for "aggravated assault" and a 2.2:1 ratio for "other assaults" (Federal Bureau of Investigation, 1999).

2. In this report, "serious crimes of violence" will refer to the Federal Bureau of Investigation's index of-

fenses, which are used to measure violent crime: murder, forcible rape, aggravated assault, and robbery.

References

Acoca, L. (1999). Investing in girls: A 21st century challenge. *Juvenile Justice, 6*(1), 3–13.

American Bar Association and the National Bar Association. (2001). *Justice by Gender: The Lack of Appropriate Prevention, Diversion and Treatment Alternatives for Girls in the Justice System*, 47 pp. Washington, DC: Author.

Artz, S. (1998). *Sex, power and the violent school girl*. Toronto: Trifolium Books.

Bartollas, C. (1993). Little girls grown up: The perils of institutionalization. In C. Culliver (Ed.), *Female criminality: The state of the art* (pp. 469–482). New York: Garland Press.

Belknap, J., Dunn, M., & Holsinger, K. (1997). *Moving toward juvenile justice and youth-serving systems that address the distinct experience of the adolescent female*. Gender Specific Work Group Report to the Governor. Office of Criminal Justice Services, Columbus, OH. February, 36 pp.

Belknap, J., Winter, E., & Cady, B. (2001). *Assessing the needs of committed delinquent and pre-adjudicated girls in Colorado: A focus group study*. A Report to the Colorado Division of Youth Corrections, Denver, CO, 36 pp.

Bergsmann, I. R. (1989). The forgotten few: Juvenile female offenders. *Federal Probation, LIII*(1), 73–78.

Bjokqvist, K., & Niemela, P. (1992). New trends in the study of female aggression. In K. Bjokqvist & P. Niemela (Eds.), *Of mice and women: Aspects of female aggression* (pp. 1–16). San Diego: Academic Press.

Bjokqvist K., Osterman K., & Kaukiainen, A. (1992). The development of direct and indirect aggressive strategies in males and females. In K. Bjokqvist & P. Niemela (Eds.), *Of mice and women: Aspects of female aggression* (pp. 51–64). San Diego: Academic Press.

Bloom, B., & Campbell, R. (1998). Literature and policy review. In B. Owen & B. Bloom (Eds.), *Modeling gender-specific services in juvenile justice: Policy and program recommendations*. Sacramento: Office of Criminal Justice Planning.

Brener, N. D., Simon, T. R., Krug, E. G., & Lowry, R. (1999). Recent trends in violence-related behaviors among high school students in the United States. *Journal of the American Medical Association, 282*, 330–446.

Bureau of Criminal Information and Analysis. (1999). *Report on arrests for domestic violence in California, 1998*. Sacramento: State of California, Criminal Justice Statistics Center.

Canter, R. J. (1982). Sex differences in self-report delinquency. *Criminology, 20*, 373–393.

Cauffman, E., Feldman, S. S., Waterman, J., & Steiner, H. (1998). Posttraumatic stress disorder among female juvenile offenders. *Journal of the American Academy of Child and Adolescent Psychiatry, 31*, 1209–1216.

Centers for Disease Control. (1992). *Youth Risk Behavior Surveillance—United States, 1991*. CDC Surveillance Summaries. U.S. Department of Health and Human Services. Atlanta: Centers for Disease Control.

Centers for Disease Control. (1994). *Youth Risk Behavior Surveillance—United States, 1993*. CDC Surveillance Summaries. U.S. Department of Health and Human Services. Atlanta: Centers for Disease Control.

Centers for Disease Control. (1996). *Youth Risk Behavior Surveillance—United States, 1995*. CDC Surveillance Summaries. U.S. Department of Health and Human Services. Atlanta: Centers for Disease Control.

Centers for Disease Control. (1998). *Youth Risk Behavior Surveillance—United States, 1998*. CDC Surveillance Summaries. U.S. Department of Health and Human Services. Atlanta: Centers for Disease Control.

Centers for Disease Control. (2000). *Youth Risk Behavior Surveillance—United States, 1999*. CDC Surveillance Summaries. U.S. Department of Health and Human Services. Atlanta: Centers for Disease Control.

Chesney-Lind, M. (1999). Media misogyny: Demonizing 'violent' girls and women. In J. Ferrel & N. Websdale (Eds.), *Making trouble: Cultural representations of crime, deviance, and control* (pp. 115–141). New York: Aldine.

Chesney-Lind, M., and Paramore, V. (2001). Are girls getting more violent?: Exploring juvenile robbery trends. *Journal of Contemporary Criminal Justice, 17*, 142–166.

Corrado, R. R., Odgers, C., & Cohen, I. M. (2000). The incarceration of female young offenders: Protection for whom? *Canadian Journal of Criminology, 2*, 189–207.

Crick, N. R., & Grotpeter, J. K. (1995). Relational aggression, gender, and social-psychological adjustment. *Child Development, 66*, 710–722.

Crick, N. R., Werner, N. E., Casas, J. F., O'Brien, K. M., Nelson, D. A., Grotpeter, J. K., and Markon, K. (1998). Childhood aggression and gender: A new look at an old problem. In D. Bernstein (Ed.), *Gender and Motivation* (pp. 75–141). Lincoln, NE: University of Nebraska Press.

Currie, E. (1998). *Crime and punishment in America.* New York: Metropolitan Books.

Dembo, R., Sue, S. C., Borden, P., & Manning, D. (1995). *Gender differences in service needs among youths entering a juvenile assessment center: A replication study.* Paper presented at the Annual Meeting of the Society of Social Problems. Washington, DC.

Dembo, R., Williams, L., and Schmeidler, J. (1993). Gender differences in mental health service needs among youths entering a juvenile detention center. *Journal of Prison and Jail Health, 12*, 73–101.

Department of the Attorney General, State of Hawaii. 1996. *Crime in Hawaii: A Review of Uniform Crime Reports, 1996.* Honolulu, HI.

Department of the Attorney General, State of Hawaii. 1997. *Crime in Hawaii: A Review of Uniform Crime Reports, 1997.* Honolulu, HI.

Duffy, Ann. (1996). Bad girls in hard times: Canadian female juvenile offenders. In G. O'Bireck (Ed.), *Not a Kid Anymore.* Scarborough: Nelson Canada Publishing.

Federal Bureau of Investigation. (1991). *Crime in the United States 1990.* Washington, DC: Government Printing Office.

Federal Bureau of Investigation. (2001). *Crime in the United States 2000.* Washington, DC: Government Printing Office.

Finkelhor, D., & Baron, L. (1986). Risk factors for child sexual abuse. *Journal of Interpersonal Violence, 1*, 43–71.

Freitas, K., & Chesney-Lind, M. (2001, August/September). Difference doesn't mean difficult: Workers talk about working with girls. *Women, Girls, & Criminal Justice*, 65–78.

Gaarder, E., & Belknap, J. (2002). Tenuous borders: Girls transferred to adult court. *Criminology, 40*, 481–517.

Gropper, N., & Froschl, M. (2000). The role of gender in young children's teasing and bullying behavior. *Equity & Excellence in Education, 33*(1), 48–56.

Hirsch, B. J., Roffman, J. G., Deutsch, N. L., Flynn, C. A., Loder, T. L., & Pagano, M. E. (2000). Inner-city youth development organizations: Strengthening programs for adolescent girls. *Journal of Early Adolescence, 20*, 210–230.

Holsinger, K., Belknap, J., & Sutherland, J. L. (1999). *Assessing the Gender Specific Program and Service Needs for Adolescent Females in the Juvenile Justice System.* A Report to the Office of Criminal Justice Services, Columbus, OH.

Huizinga, D. (1997). *Over-time changes in delinquency and drug use: The 1970's to the 1990's.* Unpublished report, Office of Juvenile Justice and Delinquency Prevention.

Lederman, C. S., & Brown, E. N. (2000). Entangled in the shadows: Girls in the juvenile justice system. *Buffalo Law Review, 48*, 909–925.

Loper, A. B., & Cornell, D. G. (1996). Homicide by girls. *Journal of Child and Family Studies, 5*, 321–333.

Males, M., & Shorter, A. (2001). *To Cage and Serve.* Unpublished Manuscript.

Mayer, J. (1994). *Girls in the Maryland juvenile justice system: Findings of the female population taskforce.* Presentation to the Gender Specific Services Training Group, Minneapolis, MN.

McCormack, A., Janus, M. D., & Burgess, A. W. (1986). Runaway youths and sexual victimization: Gender differences in an adolescent runaway population. *Child Abuse and Neglect, 10*, 387–395.

Office of Juvenile Justice and Delinquency Prevention. (1998). *What About Girls? Females in the Juvenile Justice System (flyer).* Washington, DC: Department of Justice.

Okamoto, S., & Chesney-Lind, M. (2002, October/November). Girls and relational aggression: Beyond the "mean girl" hype. *Women, Girls, & Criminal Justice*, 81–90.

Okamoto, S. K. (2002). The challenges of male practitioners working with female youth clients. *Child and Youth Care Forum, 31*(4), 257–268.

Piquero, A. R., & Chung, H. L. (2001). On the relationships between gender, early onset, and the seriousness of offending. *Journal of Criminal Justice, 29,* 189–206.

Reitsma-Street, M. (1999). Justice for Canadian girls: A 1990's update. *Canadian Journal of Criminology, 41,* 335–364.

Robinson, R. (1990). *Violations of girlhood: A qualitative study of female delinquents and children in need of services in Massachusetts.* Unpublished doctoral dissertation, Brandeis University.

Schaffner, L. (1998). Female juvenile delinquency: Sexual solutions, gender bias, and juvenile justice. *Hastings Women's Law Journal, 9,* 1–25.

Schaffner, L., Shorter, A. D., Shick, S., & Frappier, N. S. (1996). *Out of sight, out of mind: The plight of girls in the San Francisco juvenile justice system.* San Francisco: Center for Juvenile and Criminal Justice.

Shelden, R., & Horvath, J. (1986). Processing offenders in a juvenile court: A comparison of male and female offenders. Paper presented at the annual meeting of the Western Society of Criminology. Newport Beach, CA.

Sherman, F. (1999). What's in a name? Runaway girls pose challenges for the justice system. *Women, Girls and Criminal Justice, 1,* 19–20, 26.

Snyder, H. N., & Sickmund, M. (1999). *Juvenile offenders and victims: 1999 national report.* Washington, DC: Office of Juvenile Justice and Delinquency Prevention.

Stahl, A. L. (1999). *Delinquency cases in juvenile courts, 1996.* (OJJDP Fact Sheet No. 109. Washington DC: U.S. Government Printing Office.

Stahl, A. L. (2001). *Delinquency cases in juvenile courts, 1998.* OJJDP Fact Sheet, No. 31. August. Washington, DC: U.S. Government Printing Office.

Steffensmeier, D. J., & Steffensmeier, R. H. (1980). Trends in female delinquency: An examination of arrest, juvenile court, self-report, and field data. *Criminology, 18,* 62–85.

Steinem, G. (2001). Supremacy crimes. In L. Richardson, V. Taylor, and N. Whittier (Eds.), *Feminist Frontiers* (pp. 462–464). Boston: McGraw Hill.

Tyler, K. A., Hoyt, D. R., Whitbeck, L. B., & Cauce, A. M. (2001). The impact of childhood sexual abuse on later sexual victimization among runaway youth. *Journal of Research on Adolescence, 11,* 151–176.

U.S. Department of Health and Human Services, Public Health Service, Centers for Disease Control and Prevention, National Center for Health Statistics. *National Health Interview Survey—Youth Risk Behavior Survey, 1993, 1995, 1997,* and *1999.*

PJ McGann

Getting It Straight

Every now and then my sometimes tenuous toe-hold in shared reality slips. Like now, for instance. I mean, it's one thing to chant the mantra that social orders *contain* contradictions; it's another to have them served up so conspicuously, so relentlessly, that I'm not sure if they're real or if they're Memorex. You decide.

In local news: the "most recent" beating of a differently gendered person, and the most recent developments in the most recent "gay murders". In national news: the most recent sentencing of the perpetrator of the not most recent homo-hating/fearing murder. Also in national news, GM extends benefits to same-sex domestic partners, and the State of Vermont prepares to make history.

My head-spin problems are many. To begin, the "most recent" language—arguably accurate given the recurrence of such incidents—suggests a sort of commonplace acceptance, as if acknowledging the taken-for-granted Truth that yes, *of course*, gender different people and those perceived to be gay will be beaten and/or murdered. That is just the way the world *is*. Which is, of course, the problem since, repugnant as it is, such "everyday" violence accurately reflects prevailing relations of sex, gender, race, and class (and enforces them, *to boot*). Boys, afterall, will be boys.

Trouble is, now some of the girls will be boys, too—and I don't mean the boy-girls or the girly-boys, the drag kings or the drag queens, the fairies, the gender benders and gender

Source: "Getting It Straight," by PJ McGann. *Sexual Contact: Newsletter of the Sexual Behavior, Politics, and Communities Division*, December, 2000. Used by permission.

*&^#@!ers, the weirdoes, the trannies, or even the hermaphrodites with or without attitude. Here I refer to women such as Dr. Laura and/or the "lady" who commented recently on my sartorial sensibilities.

Returning to my Boston condo from an early morning dog walk, I crossed Beacon Street and was nearly run over. I caught my breath and noted these facts: I was in the cross-walk; the light for oncoming traffic was red; and the fashion critic driver was speeding. Ever so succintly I noted some of these facts aloud: "Red light, damnit!"

"What's it to you!?" she screamed in reply.

Normally (!) I ignore such things, but the idiocy of her retort—exacerbated, perhaps, by the fact that I hadn't yet had my coffee—caught me off-guard. Before I knew it I replied. "Well, it matters to me since *I'm* walking here and *you* nearly ran me down!" (I *so* wanted to add "Well, duh!" but somehow thought better of it.)

She countered: "You should be more careful about who you *%$#@ with!"

Pause. Although I suspected her remark was no neighborly safer sex reminder, I decided to let it go—and I might actually have done so had her car not suddenly lurched forward, stopping a mere eight inches from my leg. I froze; the deer in headlights thing, I guess. I turned, looked at her, stunned in part by the swiftness of the escalation, in part weary of such public abuse, another part strangely sanguine; it was, after all, how such things *normally* go … I stood thus for a moment or so, pondering whether or not what was happening was happening, decided it was, and again attempted to continue on my way. I was, however, apparently quite menacing.

"AND YOU LOOK LIKE A MAN BE-SIDES!!"

Jarred from my decaffeinated haze I countered, "Well, *you* must find *me* attractive then!" A witty retort, no doubt. But strategically stupid—at least if the idea is to avoid being bashed, which it was. Luckily—I'd like to say for her, what with my "menace" and all, but then again, she had the car, I the tennis shoes—the light turned green, the cars behind her honked, and she was off.

Later, sipping coffee at last, I caught the tail end of an NPR editorial essay proclaiming Vermont's impending legalization of gay and lesbian "civil unions" a "bell weather of our times." Apparently, times have changed: "homosexuals" and those perceived as such are now "mostly accepted by the American people." What a relief! For a minute there I thought that that woman had tried to run me down, and that the group of boys who earlier in the week aggressively yelled "FAGGOT!" at me (a head-spinner itself, no matter how many times I hear it) had meant to do me harm. Dopey me!

These and similar events were on my mind this week when amidst the current hullabaloo of the growing acceptability of the "homosexual lifestyle" (custom window treatments and Versace bed linens?) I came across a 1998 newsclipping. Rita Hester, a trans-woman who lived only a few miles from me, had been stabbed multiple times and left for dead on the floor of her apartment. Glancing through the articles, I experienced again the horror I first felt when I learned of the crime. This time though, I also grew nauseous: the bulk of the coverage concerned whether Rita was or was not a man, which pronoun to use in reference to Rita, whether Rita was a transexual or a transvestite, whether or not Rita was gay, and whether or not her family "accepted" her. Recognition of the pain felt by Rita's family and friends was mostly absent, as was outrage—or even concern—that a murderer was at large. Not to mention analysis of or commentary on the gratuitous brutality of Rita's vicious murder: as is often the case in anti-queer hate violence

the multiple stab wounds were over and above what was "necessary" to kill her.

Rewind now, to a few hours earlier the same day and a delightful ad for some electronic something or other. The ad's straight man (!) asks "What's it like to be a supermodel, Ru?" "Well," Ru Paul says, "I have meetings with *all* kinds of people, *all* the time. But *now* I can take care of all that at home—*in bed*!" "Now, Ru—" the obviously uncomfortable yet titillated man begins, but is cut off by Ru's product pitch. As the segment ends, the straight man returns, and jokes with Ru (in a culturally respectful manner, no doubt), "Fabulous darling!" Since I mostly avoid commercial radio, I didn't know the spot was but one in a popular and well-received threesome of ads. (ahem)

So. Let me get this straight: we murder differently-gendered people in one instant, then exclaim our affection for them in the next? And then, before you can swish your hips, snap your fingers, and drop your best "Go girl!", we plunk down millions to see *Boys Don't Cry*?

* * *

Yesterday morning I took my coffee outside to sit on the steps of the jazz-era condo building in the sun. I watched a squirrel and tried to ignore the commotion in the street, some man yelling something about some "asshole driver." But when the ruckus grew louder I looked up—and saw a large white man crossing the street toward my car. I admit confusion; in some weird obverse Boston parking universe mine was now the only car left on the street, parked there some fifteen hours or so earlier in what seemed to be the only spot left in the neighborhood.

When he reached my car the man pushed down hard on the trunk and the bumper, repeatedly, violently, bouncing the back end up and down—an attempt, I suppose, to damage my shock or strut? (As if!) Just as suddenly, he stopped, turned, crossed the street, bickering about the "insensitive asshole" all the while. He reached past his companions into their truck, returned to my car and left me a little something under the wiper. He walked again toward the trunk, kicked my tire, and noted with obvious disgust: "*And* it's a *&%$#!@ing queer!" (A comment inspired, I presume, by a small rainbow sticker?)

So, let me get this straight: three of them, one of me? "And the day hasn't even begun?" I said to myself. I sipped in silence, telling myself it was the smart thing to do, my sitting there on the stoop pretending I didn't hear, pretending it wasn't my car. But shame welled-up inside, and my previously sweet coffee suddenly sipped bitter.

I thought of that guy, and the others before him, while falling asleep on the eve of Vermont's triumph. I thought of the positive changes the law might bring. I thought about how as some institutional relations of power begin to shift, practices of micro-enforcement seem to intensify—or is it that we just notice them more in the newly lit space of the contradiction? I thought, too, that whether or not gay "marriage" is politically savvy, the beginning of the end to the openly anti-gay sentiments that re-emerged in the Reagan-Bush era, and/or another manifestation of a normalizing dynamic that may further marginalize those already marginal, the law represents "progress." I

thought that even if "merely" symbolic, the symbol matters. Indeed, the Civil Union law has some folks up in arms (not all of 'em straight), others joining them (not all of 'em queer). With these thoughts and others I drifted to sleep, eager for Saturday's morning promise: a new day, fresh coffee, Scott Simon's wit, and Weekend Edition's senior news analyst's insightful commentary on Vermont's history-making day. Funny, isn't it? How one little mass media nod can render one (temporarily) visible and thus reaffirm one's existence if not one's right to simply be? Thus we scan the headlines, we surf the channels, we listen intently for some evidence of Us in their midsts ("we are everywhere," afterall).

As it turned out, I awoke to hear somebody other than Scott Simon (where is he, anyway?) announce that two lesbians were "married" in Vermont just after midnight—and neither the world nor The American Family ended. As it also turned out, though, I was, sadly, out of cream. As for that supposed stalwart of liberalism, Daniel Shore, and Vermont's historic day? Not even a peep. Just like the half-n-half, nowhere to be seen.

And here I sit, contradictions abound, coffee long gone, *still* unable to think straight.

Cynthia Enloe

Wielding Masculinity inside Abu Ghraib: Making Feminist Sense of an American Military Scandal

In April, 2004, a year after the US government launched its massive military invasion of Iraq, a series of shocking photographs of American soldiers abusing Iraqi prisoners began appearing on television news programs and the front pages of newspapers around the world. American male and female soldiers serving as prison guards in a prison called Abu Ghraib were shown deliberately humiliating and torturing scores of Iraqi men held in detention and under interrogation. The American soldiers were smiling broadly. They appeared to be taking enormous pleasure in humiliating their Iraqi charges.

Most people who saw these photographs—people in Seattle and Seoul, Miami and Madrid, Bangkok and Boston—can still describe the scenes. An American male soldier standing self-satisfied with his arms crossed and wearing surgical blue rubber gloves, while in front of him, an American woman soldier, smiling at the camera, is leaning on top of a pile of naked Iraqi men forced to contort themselves into a human pyramid. An American woman soldier, again smiling, holding a male Iraqi prisoner on a leash. An American woman soldier pointing to a naked Iraqi man's genitals, apparently treating them as a joke. American male soldiers intimidating naked Iraqi male prisoners with snarling guard dogs. An Iraqi male prisoner standing alone on a box, his

Source: "Wielding Masculinity inside Abu Ghraib: Making Feminist Sense of an American Military Scandal," by Cynthia Enloe. *Asian Journal of Women's Studies* 10(3): 89–102. © 2004. Used by permission of the author.

head hooded, electrical wires attached to different parts of his body. An Iraqi male prisoner forced to wear women's underwear. Not pictured, but substantiated, were Iraqi men forced to masturbate and to simulate oral sex with each other, as well as an Iraqi woman prisoner coerced by several American male soldiers into kissing them (Hersh, 2004a).

What does a feminist curiosity reveal about the causes and the implications of the American abuses of Iraqi prisoners at Abu Ghraib? Few of the US government's official investigators or the mainstream news commentators used feminist insights to make sense of what went on in the prison. The result, I think, is that we have not really gotten to the bottom of the Abu Ghraib story. One place to start employing a feminist set of tools is to explain why one American woman military guard in particular captured the attention of so many media editors and ordinary viewers and readers: the twenty-one year old enlisted army reservist Lynndie England.

What proved shocking to the millions of viewers of the prison clandestine photos were several things. First, the Abu Ghraib scenes suggested there existed a gaping chasm between, on the one hand, the US Bush administration's claim that its military invasion and overthrow of the brutal Saddam Hussein regime would bring a civilizing sort of "freedom" to the Iraqi people and, on the other hand, the seemingly barbaric treatment that American soldiers were willfully meting out to Iraqis held in captivity without trial. Second, it was shocking to witness such blatant abuse of imprisoned detainees by soldiers representing a government that had signed both the international Geneva Conventions against mistreatment of wartime combatants and the UN Convention Against Torture, as well as having passed its own anti-torture laws.

Yet there was a third source of shock that prompted scores of early media commentaries and intense conversations among ordinary viewers: seeing women engage in torture. Of the seven American soldiers, all low-ranking Army Reserve military police guards, whom the Pentagon court-martialed, three were women. Somehow, the American male soldier, the man in the blue surgical gloves (his name was Charles Graner), was not shocking to most viewers and so did not inspire much private consternation and or a stream of op-ed columns. Women, by conventional contrast, were expected to appear in wartime as mothers and wives of soldiers, occasionally as military nurses and truck mechanics, or most often as the victims of the wartime violence. Women were not—according to the conventional presumption—supposed to be the wielders of violence, certainly not the perpetrators of torture. When those deeply gendered presumptions were turned upside down, many people felt a sense of shock. "This is awful; how could this have happened?"

Private First Class Lynndie England, the young woman military guard photographed holding the man on a leash, thus became the source of intense public curiosity. The news photographers could not restrain themselves two months later, in early August, 2004, from showing England in her army camouflaged maternity uniform when she appeared at Fort Bragg for her pre-trial hearing. She had become pregnant as a result of her sexual liaison with another enlisted reservist while on duty in Abu Ghraib. Her sexual partner was Charles Graner. Yet Charles Graner's name was scarcely mentioned. He apparently was doing what men are expected to do in wartime: have sex and wield violence. The public's curiosity and its lack of curiosity thus matched its pattern of shock. All three were conventionally gendered.

Using a feminist investigatory approach, one should find this lack of public and media curiosity about Charles Graner just as revealing as the public's and media's absorbing fascination with Lynndie England.

Responding to the torrent of Abu Ghraib stories coming out of Iraq during the spring and summer of 2004, President George W. Bush and his Secretary of Defense, Donald Rumsfeld, tried to reassure the public that the graphically abusive behavior inside the prison was not representative of America, nor did it reflect the Bush administration's own foreign policies. Rather, the Abu Ghraib abuses were the work of "rogue" soldiers, a "few bad apples." The "bad apple" explanation always goes like this: the institution is working fine, its values are appropriate, its internal dynamics are of a sort that sustain positive values and respectful, productive behavior. Thus, according to the "bad apple" explanation, nothing needs to be reassessed or reformed in the way the organization works; all that needs to happen to stop the abuse is to prosecute and remove those few individuals who refused to play by the established rules. Sometimes this may be true. Some listeners to the Bush administration's "bad apple" explanation, however, weren't reassured. They wondered if the Abu Ghraib abuses were not produced by just a few bad apples found in a solid, reliable barrel, but, instead, were produced by an essentially "bad barrel." They also wondered whether this "barrel" embraced not only the Abu Ghraib prison, but the larger US military, intelligence and civilian command structures (Hersh, 2004b; Hersh, 2004c; Human Rights Watch, 2004).

What makes a "barrel" go bad? That is, what turns an organization, an institution, or a whole system into one that at least ignores, perhaps even fosters abusive behavior by the individuals operating inside it? This question is relevant for every workplace, every political system, every international alliance. Here too, feminists have been working hard over the past three decades to develop a curiosity and a set of analytical tools with which we can all answer this important question. So many of us today live much of our lives within complex organizations, large and small—work places, local and national governments, health care systems, criminal justice systems, international organizations. Feminist researchers have revealed that virtually all organizations are gendered: that is, all organizations are shaped by the ideas about, and daily practices of masculinities and femininities (Bunster-Burotto, 1985; Ehrenreich, 2004; Enloe, 2000; Whitworth, 2004). Ignoring the workings of gender, feminist investigators have found, makes it impossible for us to explain accurately what makes any organization "tick." That failure makes it impossible for us to hold an organization accountable. Yet most of the hundred-page long official reports into the Abu Ghraib abuse scandal were written by people who ignored these feminist lessons. They acted as if the dynamics of masculinity and femininity among low-level police and high level policy-makers made no difference. That assumption is very risky.

A series of US Senate hearings, along with a string of Defense Department investigations tried to explain what went wrong in Abu Ghraib and why. The most authoritative of the Defense Department reports were the "Taguba Report," the "Fay/Jones Report" (both named after generals who headed these investigations) and the "Schlesinger Report" (named after a civilian former Secretary of Defense who chaired this investigatory team) (Human Rights Watch, 2004; Jehl, 2004; Lewis and Schmitt, 2004; Schmitt, 2004; Taguba, 2004). In addition, the CIA was conducting its own investigation, since its officials were deeply involved in interrogating—and often hiding in secret prisons—captured Afghans and Iraqis. Moreover, there were several human rights groups and journalists publishing their own findings during 2004. Together, they offered a host of valuable clues as to why this institutional "barrel" had gone bad. First was the discovery that lawyers inside the Defense and Justice Departments, as well as the White House, acting on instructions from their civilian superiors, produced interpretations of the Geneva Conventions and US law that deliberately shrank the definitions of "torture" down so far that American military and CIA per-

sonnel could order and conduct interrogations of Iraqis and Afghans in detention using techniques that otherwise would have been deemed violations of US and international law.

Second, investigators found that an American general, Geoffrey Miller, commander of the US prison at Guantanamo Bay, Cuba, was sent by Secretary Rumsfeld to Iraq in September, 2003, where he recommended that American commanders overseeing military prison operations in Iraq start employing the aggressive interrogation practices that were being used on Afghan and Arab male prisoners at Guantanamo. Somewhat surprisingly, General Miller later was named by the Pentagon to head the Abu Ghraib prison in the wake of the scandal. Third, investigators discovered that the intense, persistent pressure imposed on the military intelligence personnel by the Defense Department to generate information about who was launching insurgent assaults on the US occupying forces encouraged those military intelligence officers to put their own pressures on the military police guarding prisoners to "soften up" the men in their cell blocks, thus undercutting the military police men's and women's own chain of command (which led up to a female army general, Janice Karpinski, who claimed that her authority over her military police personnel had been undermined by intrusive military intelligence officers). This policy change, investigators concluded, dangerously blurred the valuable line between military policing and military interrogating. A fourth finding was that non-military personnel, including CIA operatives and outside contractors hired by the CIA and the Pentagon, were involved in the Abu Ghraib military interrogations in ways that may have fostered an assumption that the legal limitations on employing excessive force could be treated cavalierly: We're under threat, this is urgent, who can be bothered with the Geneva Conventions or legal niceties?

Did it matter where the women were inside the prison and up and down the larger American military and intelligence hierarchies—as low level police reservists, as a captain in the military intelligence unit, as a general advising the chief

US commander in Iraq? Investigators apparently didn't ask. Did it matter what exactly Charles Graner's and the other male military policemen's daily relationships were to their female colleagues, who were in a numerical minority in the military police unit, in the military interrogation unit and in the CIA unit all stationed together at Abu Ghraib? The official investigators seemed not to think that asking this question would yield any insights. Was it significant that so many of the abuses perpetrated on the Iraqi prisoners were deliberately sexualized? Was hooding a male prisoner the same (in motivation and in result) as forcing him to simulate oral sex? No one seemed to judge these questions to be pertinent. Was it at all relevant that Charles Graner, the older and apparently most influential of the low-ranking guards charged, had been accused of physical intimidation by his former wife? No questions asked, no answers forthcoming. Among all the lawyers in the Defense and Justice Departments and in the White House who were ordered to draft guidelines to permit the US government's officials to sidestep the Geneva Conventions outlawing torture, were there any subtle pressures imposed on them to appear "manly" in a time of war? This question too seems to have been left on the investigative teams' shelves to gather dust.

Since the mid-1970s, feminists have been crafting skills to explain when and why organizations become arenas for sexist abuse. One of the great contributions of the work done by the "Second Wave" of the international women's movement has been to throw light on what breeds sex discrimination and sexual harassment inside organizations otherwise as dissimilar as a factory, a stock brokerage, a legislature, a university, a student movement, and a military (Bowers, 2004; Kwon, 1999; Ogasawara, 1998; Stockford, 2004; Whitworth, 2004). All of the Abu Ghraib reports' authors talked about a "climate," an "environment," or a "culture," having been created inside Abu Ghraib that fostered abusive acts. The conditions inside Abu Ghraib were portrayed as a climate of "confusion," of "chaos." It was feminists who gave us this innovative concept of organizational climate.

When trying to figure out why in some organizations women employees were subjected to sexist jokes, unwanted advances, and retribution for not going along with the jokes or not accepting those advances, feminist lawyers, advocates and scholars began to look beyond the formal policies and the written work rules. They explored something more amorphous but just as, maybe even more potent: that set of unofficial presumptions that shapes workplace interactions between men and men, and men and women. They followed the breadcrumbs to the casual, informal interactions between people up and down the organization's ladder. They investigated who drinks with whom after work, who sends sexist jokes to whom over office email, who pins up which sorts of pictures of women in their lockers or next to the coffee machine. And they looked into what those people in authority did not do. They discovered that inaction is a form of action: "turning a blind eye" is itself a form of action. Inaction sends out signals to everyone in the organization about what is condoned. Feminists labeled these webs of presumptions, informal interactions, and deliberate inaction an organization's "climate." As feminists argued successfully in court, it is not sufficient for a stock brokerage or a college to include anti-sexual harassment guidelines in their official handbooks; employers have to take explicit steps to create a workplace climate in which women would be treated with fairness and respect.

By 2004, this feminist explanatory concept—organizational "climate"—had become so accepted by so many analysts that their debt to feminists had been forgotten. Generals Taguba, Jones and Fay, as well as former Defense Secretary Schlesinger, may never have taken a Women's Studies course, but when they were assigned the job of investigating Abu Ghraib they were drawing on the ideas and investigatory skills crafted for them by feminists.

However, more worrisome than their failure to acknowledge their intellectual and political debts was those journalists' and government investigators' ignoring the feminist lessons that went hand in hand with the concept of "climate." The first lesson: to make sense of any organization, we always must dig deep into the group's dominant presumptions about femininity and masculinity. The second lesson: we need to take seriously the experiences of women as they try to adapt to, or sometimes resist those dominant gendered presumptions—not because all women are angels, but because paying close attention to women's ideas and actions will shed light on why men with power act the way they do.

It is not as if the potency of ideas about masculinity and femininity had been totally absent from the US military's thinking. Between 1991 and 2004, there had been a string of military scandals that had compelled even those American senior officials who preferred to look the other way to face sexism straight on. The first stemmed from the September, 1991, gathering of American navy aircraft carrier pilots at a Hilton hotel in Las Vegas. Male pilots (all officers), fresh from their victory in the first Gulf War, lined a hotel corridor and physically assaulted every woman who stepped off the elevator. They made the "mistake" of assaulting a woman navy helicopter pilot who was serving as an aide to an admiral. Within months members of Congress and the media were telling the public about "Tailhook"—why it happened, who tried to cover it up (Office of the Inspector General, 2003). Close on the heels of the Navy's "Tailhook" scandal came the Army's Aberdeen training base sexual harassment scandal, followed by other revelations of military gay bashing, sexual harassment and rapes by American male military personnel of their American female colleagues (Enloe, 1993; 2000).

Then in September, 1995, the rape of a local school girl by two American male marines and a sailor in Okinawa sparked public demonstrations, new Okinawan women's organizing and more US Congressional investigations. At the start of the twenty-first century American media began to notice the patterns of international trafficking in

Eastern European and Filipina women around American bases in South Korea, prompting official embarrassment in Washington (an embarrassment which had not been demonstrated earlier when American base commanders turned a classic "blind eye" toward a prostitution industry financed by their own male soldiers because it employed "just" local South Korean women). And in 2003, three new American military sexism scandals caught Washington policy-makers' attention: four American male soldiers returning from combat missions in Afghanistan murdered their female partners at Fort Bragg, North Carolina; a pattern of sexual harassment and rape by male cadets of female cadets—and superiors' refusal to treat these acts seriously—as revealed at the US Air Force Academy; and testimonies by at least sixty American women soldiers returning from tours of duty in Kuwait and Iraq described how they had been sexually assaulted by their male colleagues there—with, once again, senior officers choosing inaction, advising the American women soldiers to "get over it" (Jargon, 2003; Lutz and Elliston, 2004; The Miles Foundation, 2004; Moffeit and Herder, 2004).

So it should have come as no surprise to American senior uniformed and civilian policy makers seeking to make sense of the abuses perpetrated in Abu Ghraib that a culture of sexism had come to permeate many sectors of US military life. If they had thought about what they had all learned in the last thirteen years—from Tailhook, Aberdeen, Fort Bragg, Okinawa, South Korea and the US Air Force Academy—they should have put the workings of masculinity and femininity at the top of their investigatory agendas. They should have made feminist curiosity one of their own principal tools. Perhaps Tillie Fowler did suggest to her colleagues that they think about these military sexual scandals when they began to delve into Abu Ghraib. A former Republican Congresswoman from Florida, Tillie Fowler, had been a principal investigator on the team that looked into the rapes (and their cover-ups) at the US Air Force Academy. Because of her leadership in that role Fowler was appointed to the commission headed by James Schlesinger investigating Abu Ghraib. Did she raise this comparison between the Air Force Academy case and Abu Ghraib? Did her male colleagues take her suggestion seriously?

Perhaps eventually the investigators did not make use of the feminist lessons and tools because they imagined that the lessons of Tailhook, the Air Force Academy and Okinawa were relevant only when all the perpetrators of sexualized abuse are men and all the victims are women. The presence of Lynndie England and the other women in Abu Ghraib's military police unit, they might have assumed, made the feminist tools sharpened in these earlier gendered military scandals inappropriate for their explorations. But the lesson of Tailhook, Okinawa and the most recent military scandals was not that the politics of masculinity and femininity matter only when men are the perpetrators and women are the victims. Instead, the deeper lesson of all these other military scandals is that we must always ask: Has this organization (or this system of interlocking organizations) become masculinized in ways that privilege certain forms of masculinity, feminize its opposition and trivialize most forms of femininity?

With this core gender question in mind, we might uncover significant dynamics operating in Abu Ghraib and in the American military and civilian organizations that were supposed to be supervising the prison's personnel. First, American military police and their military and CIA intelligence colleagues might have been guided by their own masculinized fears of humiliation when they forced Iraqi men to go naked for days, to wear women's underwear and to masturbate in front of each other and American women guards. That is, belief in an allegedly "exotic," frail Iraqi masculinity, fraught with fears of nakedness and homosexuality, might not have been the chief motivator for the American police and intelligence personnel; it may have been their own home-grown American sense of masculinity's fragility—how easily manliness can be feminized—that prompted them to craft these prison humiliations. In this distorted masculinized scenario, the presence of women serving as military police might have proved especially useful. Choreographing the women guards' feminized roles so that they could act as ridiculing feminized spectators of male prisoners might have been imagined to intensify the masculinized demoralization. Dominant men trying to utilize at least some women to act in ways that undermine the masculinized self-esteem of rival men is not new.

What about the American women soldiers themselves? In the US military of 2004 women comprised 15 percent of active duty personnel, 17 percent of all Reserves and National Guard (and a surprising 24 percent of the Army Reserves alone). From the very time these particular young women joined this military police unit, they, like their fellow male recruits, probably sought to fit into the group. If the reserve military police unit's evolving culture—perhaps fostered by their superiors for the sake of "morale" and "unit cohesion"—was one that privileged a certain form of masculinized humor, racism and bravado, each woman would have had to decide how to deal with that. At least some of the women reservist recruits might have decided to join in, play the roles assigned to them in order to gain the hoped-for reward of male acceptance. The facts that the Abu Ghraib prison was grossly understaffed during the fall or 2003 (too few guards for spiraling numbers of Iraqi detainees), that it was isolated from other military operations, and that its residents endured daily and nightly mortar attacks, would only serve to intensify the pressures on each soldier to gain acceptance from those unit members who seemed to represent the group's dominant masculinized culture. And Lynndie England's entering into a sexual liaison with Charles Graner? We need to treat this as more than merely a "lack of discipline." We need to ask what were the cause and effect dynamics between their sexual behaviors and the abuses of prisoners and staging of the photographs. Feminists have taught us never to brush off sexual relations as if they have nothing to do with organizational and political practices.

Then there is the masculinization of the military interrogators' organizational cultures, the masculinization of the CIA's field operatives and the workings of ideas about "manliness" shaping the entire US political system. Many men and women—as lawyers, as generals, as Cabinet officers, as elected officials—knew full well that aggressive interrogation techniques violated both the spirit and the language of the Geneva Conventions, the UN Convention Against Torture and the US federal law against torture. Yet during the months of waging wars in Afghanistan and Iraq most of these men and women kept silent. Feminists have taught us always to be curious about silence. Thus we need to ask: Did any of the American men involved in interrogations keep silent because they were afraid of being labeled "soft," or "weak," thereby jeopardizing their status as "manly" men. We need also to discover if any of the women who knew better kept silent because they were afraid that they would be labeled "feminine," thus risking being deemed by their colleagues untrustworthy, political outsiders.

We are not going to get to the bottom of the tortures perpetrated by Americans at Abu Ghraib unless we make use of a feminist curiosity and unless we revisit the feminist lessons derived from the scandals of Tailhook, Fort Bragg, Annapolis, Okinawa and the Air Force Academy. Those tools and lessons might shed a harsh light on an entire American military institutional culture and maybe even the climate of contemporary American political life. That institutional culture and that political climate together have profound implications not only for Americans. They are being held up as models to emulate in Korea, Japan, the Philippines, Afghanistan and Iraq. That, in turn, means that the insights offered by feminist analysts from those societies who have such intimate experiences with this US institutional culture and this political climate are likely to teach Americans a lot about themselves.

References

Bowers, Simon (2004), "Merrill Lynch Accused of 'Institutional Sexism,'" The Guardian, (London), June 12.

Bunster-Burotto, Ximena (1985), "Surviving beyond Fear: Women and Torture in Latin America," Women and Change in Latin America, eds. June Nash and Helen Safa, South Hadley, MA: Bergin and Garvey Publishers: 297–325.

Enloe, Cynthia (1993), The Morning After: Sexual Politics at the End of the Cold War, Berkeley: University of California Press.

——— (2000), Maneuvers: The International Politics of Militarizing Women's Lives, Berkeley and London: University of California Press.

Ehrenreich, Barbara (2004), "All Together Now," Op. Ed., New York Times, July 15.

Hersh, Seymour (2004a), "Annals of National Security: Torture at Abu Ghraib," The New Yorker, May 10: 42–47.

——— (2004b), "Annals of National Security: Chain of Command," The New Yorker, May 17: 38–43.

——— (2004c), "Annals of National Security: The Gray Zone," The New Yorker, May 24: 38–44.

Human Rights Watch (2004), The Road to Abu Ghraib, New York: Author.

Jargon, Julie (2003), "The War Within," Westword, January.

Jehl, Douglas (2004), "Some Abu Ghraib Abuses are Traced to Afghanistan," The New York Times, August 26.

Kwon, Insook (1999), "Militarization in My Heart," unpublished PhD Dissertation, Women's Studies Program, Clark University, Worcester, MA, USA.

Lewis, Neil A. and Eric Schmitt (2004), "Lawyers Decided Bans on Torture Didn't Bind Bush," New York Times, June 8.

Lutz, Catherine and Jori Elliston (2004), "Domestic Terror," Interventions: Activists and Academics Respond to Violence, eds. Elizabeth Castelli and Janet Jackson, New York: Palgrave.

The Miles Foundation (2004), "Brownback/Fitz Amendment to S. 2400," email correspondence, June 14, from Milesfdn@aol.com.

Moffeit, Miles and Amy Herder (2004), "Betrayal in the Ranks," The Denver Post, May, Available on the Web at: http://www.denverpost.com.

Office of the Inspector General (2003), The Tailhook
    Report, US Department of Defense, New York:
    St. Martin's Press.
Ogasawara, Yuko (1998), Office Ladies and Salaried
    Men: Power, Gender and Work in Japanese
    Companies, Berkeley and London: University of
    California Press.
Schmitt, Eric (2004), "Abuse Panel Says Rules on In-
    mates Need Overhaul," The New York Times,
    August 25.

Stockford, Marjorie A. (2004), The Bellwomen: The
    Story of the Landmark AT&T Sex Discrimina-
    tion Case, New Brunswick, NJ: Rutgers Univer-
    sity Press.
Taguba, Antonio (2004), "Investigation of the 800th
    Military Police Brigade," Washington, DC: US
    Department of Defense, April.
Whitworth, Sandra (2004), Men, Militarism and UN
    Peacekeeping: A Gendered Analysis, Boulder,
    CO: Lynne Rienner Publishers.

PART SIX

Sexualities

Women have contested the meanings and politics of sexuality throughout each wave of feminist activism in the United States. Sexuality generates passionate feelings on both sides of the structure/agency continuum. On the one hand, sexuality has been viewed as an arena of victimization and objectification. Sexuality appears as a limiting, harmful structure when defined as an institution that objectifies and denigrates women for the pleasure of men. Prostitution, pornography, and sexual coercion are at the extreme end of this continuum, but some feminists have theorized that heterosexuality itself is foundational to women's subordination. Andrea Dworkin and Catherine MacKinnon are often identified with this position and described as "anti-sex" feminists. In Dworkin's book *Intercourse*, and MacKinnon's *Feminism Unmodified*, these scholars articulate the connections between male dominance and heterosexual practices. Their work in developing theoretical analyses of the role of sexuality in maintaining patriarchy and in crafting anti-pornography legislation became part of the "sex wars" that characterized feminist discussions of sex in the 1980s.

Many feminists opposed the censorship approach to sexuality embodied in Dworkin and MacKinnon's works. Ellen Willis, Pat Califia, and Ann Snitow, among others, argued that sexuality was a realm of pleasure and that feminist attempts to define "good" sex were as oppressive as patriarchal definitions of women's sexuality. They encouraged women to explore their sexual desires and use their self-defined pleasure as a source of energy and power. These so-called "pro-sex" arguments emphasize women's agency as sexual subjects over women's victimization as sexual objects of male desire.

Women's sexual landscape in the new century reflects transformations in technology, the economy, and interpersonal relationships. Some of the sex wars debates of the 1980s echo in the controversies over prostitution and media portrayals of women's sexuality. For example, some women argue that prostitution is a form of work that should be legalized and regulated like other jobs. Others view prostitution as violence against women. Similarly, some women are opposed to all forms of pornography while others find many forms of pornography pleasurable and liberating. Yet in general, feminism is in a "sex positive" phase that embraces women's agency in crafting sexual subjectivity. Sexual subjectivity means a person's capacity to know and express sexual desire in the context of pleasure and safety; it contrasts with sexual objectification in which a person's sexuality is defined by the needs and desires of others without regard for their own pleasure and safety. We are now in the third generation of women who have access to reliable contraception and legal abortion. This generation of women has sex at a younger age with more partners and is far less likely than their grandmothers to link sexual activity with childbearing and marriage. Women's full-scale entry into the paid labor force has given women more freedom to live independently and make sexual choices based on desire rather than economic dependence on a male. The shifts in social conceptions of the self have also encouraged both women and men to focus on personal fulfillment to a much greater extent than prior generations when sexuality was more tightly interwoven with kinship obligations. As baby boomers pass middle age, sexuality among older people has become more widely discussed, valued, and assisted through pharmaceutical interventions. Although the gender divide in sexual attitudes, behaviors, and desires remains, women in the twenty-first century are closing that gap and embracing sexuality as a joyful aspect of life from their teens through their retirement years.

This section opens with the classic article by Audre Lorde, "Uses of the Erotic: The Erotic as Power." In this essay Lorde describes the erotic as "the nurturer or nursemaid of all our deepest knowledge." She argues that our erotic energy has been perverted, trivialized, and confined to narrow, socially approved forms of sexual contact. Although sexuality is a powerful expression of the erotic, it is only one expression. By channeling erotic power into conventional models of approved sexuality, women are denied knowledge of their deep capacity for joy and connection with others. In Western European cultures, sexuality is usually viewed as separate from, often in opposition to, spirituality. Lorde describes the ways that being in touch with the erotic within empowers women to be true to themselves and to work for genuine social change. Lorde challenges the boundaries between spirituality, sexuality, and self-validation and encourages women to develop a sexual subjectivity that "feels right" to them.

Lorde's essay is inspiring, but Alex Jabs portrays the painful realities of being a lesbian in a family that rejects her sexuality. Jabs draws courage from people who embrace their own and others' sexuality and is determined to be honest with herself and her family. It is still the case, however, that many women (and men) feel that a central aspect of their identities is rejected by the people they love, as well as by their faith communities.

Shere Hite reviews the work of Alfred C. Kinsey and his colleagues and compares it to her own study of female sexuality. Kinsey's work expanded people's understanding of human sexuality by decoupling sex from reproduction and encouraging a diverse view of the forms of sexuality. He and his colleagues documented the wide variety of sexual behaviors in animals, including same sex genital contact, prolonged mutual grooming, and other forms of non-coital sex play. Animal behaviors do *not* confirm the priority of heterosexual coitus as the *natural* form of sexuality. Rather, they suggest that human preoccupation with coitus as the "real" sex act is restrictive and rather prudish. However, Kinsey's analysis perpetuated the belief that orgasms achieved through coitus, for both women and men, were the most normal and desirable form of sexual pleasure. Hite's research confirms and elaborates on the finding that Kinsey chose to downplay; that is, most women do not reach orgasm through coitus and find external clitoral stimulation a much more reliable method of achieving orgasm. This, Hite emphasizes, means that external clitoral stimulation is the *normal* way for women to reach orgasm. This fact is well established in the scientific literature, but Kinsey and other sex researchers concluded that women who did not orgasm during intercourse were "defective, flawed, or 'dysfunctional,' psychologically abnormal." Sex researchers' and popular notions about the primacy of intercourse are cleverly captured by Hite's question: "Why is the beginning of intercourse almost always described as 'vaginal penetration' and not 'penile covering'?" Her work underscores the prevalence of a phallocentric discourse of sexuality and the gap between this discourse and women's experiences.

Elisabeth Sheff describes a group of women who have applied Lorde's advice to their search for a sexuality that is compatible with their desires and identities. For the women in Sheff's research, heterosexual monogamy is restrictive and unsatisfactory. Sheff interviewed women engaged in polyamory, and she also participated in the polyamorous community for seven years. "Polyamory is a form of relationship in which people have multiple romantic, sexual, and/or affective partners. It differs from swinging in its emphasis on long-term, emotionally intimate relationships and from adultery with its focus on honesty and (ideally) full disclosure of the network of sexual relationships to all who participate or are affected by them" (Sheff 2005: 252–3). Women engaged in polyamory reject dualistic sexual roles and often refuse labels of sexual orientation, such as hetero, homo, or bisexual. Their experiences of polyamory contain elements of creative empowerment as well as more traditional relationship dynamics and social stigma for the violation of sexual mores. Sheff emphasizes that women's ability to challenge conventional morality hinges on racial and class privilege, with the majority of her sample possessing both forms of privilege. Women of color and those with tenuous occupational status face greater material consequences as a result of stigmatization of their sexual choices and feel less free to express those choices publicly. Despite the incomplete success of polyamorous women in crafting sexual subjectivity, Sheff concludes that their attempts are progressive interventions in developing new, gynocentric models of sexuality.

These essays on sexuality may make you uncomfortable, may validate your own search for sexual subjectivity, or both. Irrespective of their resonance with your personal experience, they illuminate areas of ignorance and conflict about our embodied and social sexualities and the fluidity of the categories circumscribing our sexual pleasures.

Reference

Sheff, Elisabeth. (2005). "Polyamorous Women, Sexual Subjectivity and Power." *Journal of Contemporary Ethnography* 34(3): 251–83.

Audre Lorde

Uses of the Erotic: The Erotic as Power

There are many kinds of power, used and unused, acknowledged or otherwise. The erotic is a resource within each of us that lies in a deeply female and spiritual plane, firmly rooted in the power of our unexpressed or unrecognized feeling. In order to perpetuate itself, every oppression must corrupt or distort those various sources of power within the culture of the oppressed that can provide energy for change. For women, this has meant a suppression of the erotic as a considered source of power and information within our lives.

We have been taught to suspect this resource, vilified, abused, and devalued within western society. On the one hand, the superficially erotic has been encouraged as a sign of female inferiority; on the other hand, women have been made to suffer and to feel both contemptible and suspect by virtue of its existence.

It is a short step from there to the false belief that only by the suppression of the erotic within our lives and consciousness can women be truly strong. But that strength is illusory, for it is fashioned within the context of male models of power.

As women, we have come to distrust that power which rises from our deepest and nonrational knowledge. We have been warned against it all our lives by the male world, which values this depth of feeling enough to keep women around in order to exercise it in the service of men, but which fears this same depth too much to examine the possibilities of it within themselves. So women are maintained at a distant/inferior position to be psychically milked, much the same

way ants maintain colonies of aphids to provide a life-giving substance for their masters.

But the erotic offers a well of replenishing and provocative force to the woman who does not fear its revelation, nor succumb to the belief that sensation is enough.

The erotic has often been misnamed by men and used against women. It has been made into the confused, the trivial, the psychotic, the plasticized sensation. For this reason, we have often turned away from the exploration and consideration of the erotic as a source of power and information, confusing it with its opposite, the pornographic. But pornography is a direct denial of the power of the erotic, for it represents the suppression of true feeling. Pornography emphasizes sensation without feeling.

The erotic is a measure between the beginnings of our sense of self and the chaos of our strongest feelings. It is an internal sense of satisfaction to which, once we have experienced it, we know we can aspire. For having experienced the fullness of this depth of feeling and recognizing its power, in honor and self-respect we can require no less of ourselves.

It is never easy to demand the most from ourselves, from our lives, from our work. To encourage excellence is to go beyond the encouraged mediocrity of our society is to encourage excellence. But giving in to the fear of feeling and working to capacity is a luxury only the unintentional can afford, and the unintentional are those who do not wish to guide their own destinies.

This internal requirement toward excellence which we learn from the erotic must not be misconstrued as demanding the impossible from ourselves nor from others. Such a demand incapacitates everyone in the process. For the erotic is not a question only of what we do; it is a question of how acutely and fully we can feel in the doing. Once we know the extent to which we are capable of feeling that sense of satisfaction and completion, we can then observe which of our various life endeavors bring us closest to that fullness.

The aim of each thing which we do is to make our lives and the lives of our children richer and more possible. Within the celebration of the erotic in all our endeavors, my work becomes a conscious decision—a longed-for bed which I enter gratefully and from which I rise up empowered.

Of course, women so empowered are dangerous. So we are taught to separate the erotic demand from most vital areas of our lives other than sex. And the lack of concern for the erotic root and satisfactions of our work is felt in our disaffection from so much of what we do. For instance, how often do we truly love our work even at its most difficult?

The principal horror of any system which defines the good in terms of profit rather than in terms of human need, or which defines human need to the exclusion of the psychic and emotional components of that need—the principal horror of such a system is that it robs our work of its erotic value, its erotic power and life appeal and fulfillment. Such a system reduces work to a travesty of necessities, a duty by which we earn bread or oblivion for ourselves and those we love. But this is tantamount to blinding a painter and then telling her to improve her work, and to enjoy the act of painting. It is not only next to impossible, it is also profoundly cruel.

As women, we need to examine the ways in which our world can be truly different. I am speaking here of the necessity for reassessing the quality of all the aspects of our lives and of our work, and of how we move toward and through them.

The very word *erotic* comes from the Greek word *eros*, the personification of love in all its aspects—born of Chaos, and personifying creative power and harmony. When I speak of the erotic, then, I speak of it as an assertion of the lifeforce of women; of that creative energy empowered, the knowledge and use of which we are now reclaiming in our language, our history, our dancing, our loving, our work, our lives.

There are frequent attempts to equate pornography and eroticism, two diametrically opposed uses of the sexual. Because of these attempts, it has become fashionable to separate the spiritual (psychic and emotional) from the political, to see them as contradictory or antithetical. "What do you mean, a poetic revolutionary, a meditating gunrunner?" In the same way, we have attempted to separate the spiritual and the erotic, thereby reducing the spiritual to a world of flattened affect, a world of the ascetic who aspires to feel nothing. But nothing is farther from the truth. For the ascetic position is one of the highest fear, the gravest immobility. The severe abstinence of the ascetic becomes the ruling obsession. And it is one not of self-discipline but of self-abnegation.

The dichotomy between the spiritual and the political is also false, resulting from an incomplete attention to our erotic knowledge. For the bridge which connects them is formed by the erotic—the sensual—those physical, emotional, and psychic expressions of what is deepest and strongest and richest within each of us, being shared: the passions of love, in its deepest meanings.

Beyond the superficial, the considered phrase, "It feels right to me," acknowledges the strength of the erotic into a true knowledge, for what that means is the first and most powerful guiding light toward any understanding. And understanding is a handmaiden which can only wait upon, or clarify, that knowledge, deeply born. The erotic is the nurturer or nursemaid of all our deepest knowledge.

The erotic functions for me in several ways, and the first is in providing the power which comes from sharing deeply any pursuit with another person. The sharing of joy, whether physical, emotional, psychic, or intellectual, forms a bridge between the sharers which can be the basis for understanding much of what is not shared between them, and lessens the threat of their difference.

Another important way in which the erotic connection functions is the open and fearless underlining of my capacity for joy. In the way my body stretches to music and opens into response, hearkening to its deepest rhythms, so every level upon which I sense also opens to the erotically satisfying experience, whether it is dancing, building a bookcase, writing a poem, examining an idea.

That self-connection shared is a measure of the joy which I know myself to be capable of feeling, a reminder of my capacity for feeling. And that deep and irreplaceable knowledge of my capacity for joy comes to demand from all of my life that it be lived within the knowledge that such satisfaction is possible, and does not have to be called *marriage*, nor *god*, nor *an afterlife*.

This is one reason why the erotic is so feared, and so often relegated to the bedroom alone, when it is recognized at all. For once we begin to feel deeply all the aspects of our lives, we begin to demand from ourselves and from our life-pursuits that they feel in accordance with that joy which we know ourselves to be capable of. Our erotic knowledge empowers us, becomes a lens through which we scrutinize all aspects of our existence, forcing us to evaluate those aspects honestly in terms of their relative meaning within our lives. And this is a grave responsibility, projected from within each of us, not to settle for the convenient, the shoddy, the conventionally expected, nor the merely safe.

During World War II, we bought sealed plastic packets of white, uncolored margarine, with a tiny, intense pellet of yellow coloring perched like a topaz just inside the clear skin of the bag. We would leave the margarine out for a while to soften, and then we would pinch the little pellet to break it inside the bag, releasing the rich yellowness into the soft pale mass of margarine. Then taking it carefully between our fingers, we would knead it gently back and forth, over and over, until the color had spread throughout the whole pound bag of margarine, thoroughly coloring it.

I find the erotic such a kernel within myself. When released from its intense and constrained pellet, it flows through and colors my life with a kind of energy that heightens and sensitizes and strengthens all my experience.

We have been raised to fear the *yes* within ourselves, our deepest cravings. But, once recognized, those which do not enhance our future lose their power and can be altered. The fear of our desires keeps them suspect and indiscriminately powerful, for to suppress any truth is to give it strength beyond endurance. The fear that we cannot grow beyond whatever distortions we may find within ourselves keeps us docile and loyal and obedient, externally defined, and leads us to accept many facets of our oppression as women.

When we live outside ourselves, and by that I mean on external directives only rather than from our internal knowledge and needs, when we live away from those erotic guides from within ourselves, then our lives are limited by external and alien forms, and we conform to the needs of a structure that is not based on human need, let alone an individual's. But when we begin to live from within outward, in touch with the power of the erotic within ourselves, and allowing that power to inform and illuminate our actions upon the world around us, then we begin to be responsible to ourselves in the deepest sense. For as we begin to recognize our deepest feelings, we begin to give up, of necessity, being satisfied with suffering and self-negation, and with the numbness which so often seems like their only alternative in our society. Our acts against oppression become integral with self, motivated and empowered from within.

In touch with the erotic, I become less willing to accept powerlessness, or those other supplied states of being which are not native to me, such as resignation, despair, self-effacement, depression, self-denial.

And yes, there is a hierarchy. There is a difference between painting a back fence and writing a poem, but only one of quantity. And there is, for me, no difference between writing a good poem and moving into sunlight against the body of a woman I love.

This brings me to the last consideration of the erotic. To share the power of each other's feelings is different from using another's feelings as we would use a kleenex. When we look the other way from our experience, erotic or otherwise, we use rather than share the feelings of those others who participate in the experience with us. And use without consent of the used is abuse.

In order to be utilized, our erotic feelings must be recognized. The need for sharing deep feeling is a human need. But within the european-american tradition, this need is satisfied by certain proscribed erotic comings-together. These occasions are almost always characterized by a simultaneous looking away, a pretense of calling them something else, whether a religion, a fit, mob violence, or even playing doctor. And this misnaming of the need and the deed give rise to that distortion which results in pornography and obscenity—the abuse of feeling.

When we look away from the importance of the erotic in the development and sustenance of our power, or when we look away from ourselves as we satisfy our erotic needs in concert with others, we use each other as objects of satisfaction rather than share our joy in the satisfying, rather than make connection with our similarities and our differences. To refuse to be conscious of what we are feeling at any time, however comfortable that might seem, is to deny a large part of the experience, and to allow ourselves to be reduced to the pornographic, the abused, and the absurd.

The erotic cannot be felt secondhand. As a Black lesbian feminist, I have a particular feeling, knowledge, and understanding for those sisters with whom I have danced hard, played, or even fought. This deep participation has often been the forerunner for joint concerted actions not possible before.

But this erotic charge is not easily shared by women who continue to operate under an exclusively european-american male tradition. I know it was not available to me when I was trying to adapt my consciousness to this mode of living and sensation.

Only now, I find more and more women-identified women brave enough to risk sharing the erotic's electrical charge without having to look away, and without distorting the enormously powerful and creative nature of that exchange. Recognizing the power of the erotic within our lives can give us the energy to pursue genuine change within our world, rather than merely settling for a shift of characters in the same weary drama.

For not only do we touch our most profoundly creative source, but we do that which is female and self-affirming in the face of a racist, patriarchal, and anti-erotic society.

Alex Jabs

Outspoken

I have come out as a lesbian to my parents three times. The first two times I scrambled to deny it all when they reacted negatively, blaming it on a moment of weakness.

But between my freshman and sophomore years of college I met a girl who inspired me to embrace my love, and I courageously came out to everyone, parents included, again. And this time I stayed out. It's not that I had been unsure of who I was before; it's just that in high school my Republican family was my core foundation and affected everything I did. It was really tough to know that in their eyes I was never going to be the same.

I'm now a senior in college, and to this day my family rarely discusses my sexuality unless it is used as a source of anger or resentment. My parents skirt any topic dealing with my relationships future or present, and my sexuality is rarely recognized as an orientation but instead a preference. It is extremely hard, coming from a dedicated Catholic family, knowing that my church and my own family will never accept my sexuality.

Don't get me wrong—my parents are wonderful people who think they have only my happiness in mind. They say they don't want me to have to live a life full of discrimination and judgment. Why would any parents wish that on their child? But at the same time, they refuse to respect that my sexual orientation is something I can't control. They see it as a choice. My parents ask why I "won't even try to change" and why I "have to be so in-your-face gay if it's not a choice."

They often attack me for my "college-brainwashed" way of thinking. My political activism scares them. Their daughter, who once rallied for abstinence-only and pro-life causes, now marches in Take Back the Night rallies and proudly wears rainbow ribbons. My opinions haven't changed, but my priorities have.

My parents are stubborn. After many attempts to convert their conservative ideas, I've been told through tears and red faces that I will never be "accepted" as queer in the family. This is heartbreaking to me, and each time it gets harder to hear.

But they are my parents, and even though it hurts, I believe it would hurt me more not to have them in my life. Despite their conservative and unbending views toward homosexuality, I know they only want what's best for me. I know that they love me; I just wish they could love all of me.

Source: "Outspoken," by Alex Jabs. *Advocate,* 9/12/2006, Issue 970, p. 30. Used by permission.

Shere Hite

Sexual Behavior in the Human Female

I would like to write a bit here about my agreements and disagreements with *Sexual Behavior in the Human Female*.

Much, if not most, of the Kinsey-Pomeroy-Martin-Gebhard work is visionary. First, the book encourages diversity in sexuality. While it has been implied that petting is "immature" or "for the woman," something teenagers do when they aren't able to "go all the way," the fact is that petting has been a major form of sexuality throughout time and is prevalent also in the animal kingdom. As the Kinsey volume points out, "*Among most species of mammals there is, in actuality, a great deal of sex play which never leads to coitus. Most mammals, when sexually aroused, crowd together and nuzzle and explore with their noses, mouths, and feet over each other's bodies. They make lip-to-lip contacts and tongue-to-tongue contacts, and use their mouths to manipulate every part of the companion's body, including the genitalia. . . . The student of mammalian mating behavior, interested in ob animal stocks, sometimes may have to wait through hours and days of sex play before he has an opportunity to observe actual coitus, if, indeed, the animals do not finally separate without ever attempting a genital union.*" If people try to suppress their desire to "play around" and focus only on coitus, they are the poorer for this.

Since most forms of sexuality other than intercourse were declared illegal in the United States and elsewhere for centuries—and remain illegal in many places today including oral sex—people's erotic energies have been narrowed in focus, channeled into the single direction of "the act" sanctioned by church and state. Yet the full

spectrum of physical contact is exhibited by other mammals—and "their mental health has not been questioned," unlike the questioning that women have endured when they did not reach orgasm during coitus or asked for additional clitoral stimulation for orgasm, or simply wanted more "foreplay." (Sigmund Freud in the twentieth century questioned women's mental health, as many psychiatrists do today, if they do not have orgasm during coitus or require "additional stimulation" or prefer "making out.") Indeed, as the Kinsey volume explains, intercourse is not the main focus of other mammals' sexual relations—and recent primate research shows that it may not be the way female primates have orgasm, either—but only one activity out of many. Animals spend more time on mutual grooming than they do on specifically sexual contact, including the chinchilla, rabbit, porcupine, squirrel, ferret, horse, cow, elephant, dog, monkey, chimpanzee, and others, according to the Kinsey volume.

Although we assume that sexual feelings are provided "by nature" to insure reproduction, and that therefore intercourse should be the basic form of our sexuality—even though women's physical desires are often strongest when women are not in a fertile part of their cycle (for example, during menstruation) so they cannot become pregnant—in fact other forms of sexuality ("foreplay") are just as basic, perhaps masturbation is more basic since chimpanzees brought up in isolation have no idea how to have intercourse, but do masturbate more or less from birth. Yet with the reductionist idea that "the sex drive" is for reproduction only, women were expected to find their greatest pleasures and orgasms in coitus, just as men are supposed to do. Never mind if the facts (when women had orgasms) just didn't fit!

Source: "Sexual Behavior in the Human Female," by Shere Hite. *Sexuality & Culture*, Winter 2006, Vol. 10, No. 1, pp. 49–62. Used by permission of Springer.

In my 1976 book, *The Hite Report: A Nation-wide Study of Female Sexuality*—the editors concocted the name, "The Hite Report," undoubtedly influenced by the title "The Kinsey Report," wording used so often even though it was not the proper title of the book—I conclude, "There is no reason why we should not create as many different degrees and kinds of sex as we want—whether or not they lead to orgasm, and whether or not they are genital. If the definition of sexual pleasure is sustaining desire and building arousal higher and higher—not ending it—many possibilities for physical pleasure and exciting another person open up. The truth is that "sex" is bigger than orgasm, and involves any kind of deep physical intimacy one shares with another person."

A second point I found fascinating in "The Kinsey Report" is the explanation that sex was very different in the archaic past; in fact it was even part of religious services (!)—erotic statues outside Indian Hindu temples seem to validate this point, archaic cultures having been more interconnected than we imagined. This further demonstrates that today's version of sex is limited and prudish. As the Kinsey book reads, "*it is generally accepted by Bible scholars that the earliest Jewish tribes mentioned in the Old Testament accepted cunnilingus and homosexuality as a valid part of life and physical relations, as did the societies around them—which were not, for the most part, totally patriarchal. In fact, prior to the seventh century B.C.,[1] [various] sexual activities were associated with Jewish religious rites, just as in the surrounding cultures . . . as the small and struggling Jewish tribes sought to build and consolidate their strength and their patriarchal social order and to bind all loyalty to one male god, Yahweh, all forms of sexuality except the one necessary for reproduction were banned by religious code. The Holiness Code, established at the time of their return from the Babylonian exile, sought to fence out the surrounding cultures and set up rules for separating off the Chosen People of God. It was then that non-heterosexual, non-reproductive sexual acts were condemned as the way of the Canaanite, the way of the pagan. But these activities were proscribed as an indication of allegiance*

to another culture, an adjunct to idolatry—not as 'immoral'. . . ." That volume continues, "*Judeo-Christian codes still specifically condemn all sexual activity that does not have reproduction as its ultimate aim. Our civil law is largely derived from these codes, and the laws of most states condemn non-coital forms of sexuality (in and out of marriage) as punishable misdemeanors or crimes. Thus, intercourse has been institutionalized in our culture as the only permissible form of sexual activity.*"

The third concept which I found profoundly important and visionary is the "homosexual-heterosexual" scale, the idea that there are no "homosexual people" only "homosexual acts" (although this is spelled out in the "male report" more than in the "female report"): in other words, the book asserts that we each have a spectrum of behaviors and feelings that vary from 1 to 5 in terms of desires for activities that are "gay" or "straight," that no one is completely gay or straight: activities are "gay or straight," but people are not. The study points out that sexual orientation can change during a lifetime, or change several times; that what is called "gender identity" is not so cut and dried as statistics imply; there are not two discrete groups, one heterosexual and one homosexual: "The living world is a continuum in each and every one of its aspects," and homosexuality and heterosexuality are only the extreme types sitting at the poles of "a rich and varied continuum." The terms "lesbian," "homosexual," and "heterosexual" should be used as adjectives, not nouns: "*People are not properly described as homosexuals, lesbians, or heterosexuals; rather, activities are properly described as homosexual, lesbian, or heterosexual. In other words, it is really only possible to say how many persons have had, at any particular time, a given type of relationship, and that is how the figures in this study should be viewed.*"

As Kinsey and co-authors Pomeroy, Martin, and Gebhard further explain: "*The general condemnation of homosexuality in our particular culture apparently traces to a series of historical circumstances which had little to do with the protection of the individual or the preservation of the social organization of the day. In Hittite, Chaldean, and early Jewish codes there were no over-all condemnations of such activity, although there were penalties for homosexual activities between persons of particular social status or blood relationships, or homosexual relationships under other particular circumstances, especially when force was involved. The more general condemnation of all homosexual relationships (especially male) originated in Jewish history in about the seventh century B.C., upon the return from the Babylonian exile. Both mouth-genital contacts and homosexual activities had previously been associated with the Jewish religious service, as they had been with the religious services of most of the other peoples of that part of Asia, just as they have been in many other cultures elsewhere in the world. In the wave of nationalism which was then developing among the Jewish people, there was an attempt to disidentify themselves with their neighbors by breaking with many of the customs they had previously shared with them. Many of the Talmudic condemnations were based on the fact that such activities represented the way of the Canaanite, the way of the Chaldean, the way of the pagan, and were originally condemned as a form of idolatry rather than a sexual crime. Throughout the Middle Ages homosexuality was associated with heresy. The reform in the custom (the mores) soon, however, became a matter of morals, and finally a question for action under criminal law."*

Kinsey, who was originally a biologist, reminds us that mammals as well as other animals routinely have lesbian and homosexual relationships: *"The impression that infra-human mammals more or less confine themselves to heterosexual activities is a distortion of the fact which appears to have originated in a man-made philosophy, rather than in specific observations of mammalian behavior. Biologists and psychologists who have accepted the doctrine that the only natural function of sex is reproduction have simply ignored the existence of sexual activity which is not reproductive. They have assumed that heterosexual responses are a part of an animal's innate, 'instinctive' equipment, and that all other types of sexual activity represent 'perversions' of the 'normal instincts.' Such interpretations are, however, mystical. They do not originate in our knowledge of the physiology of sexual response, and can be maintained only if*

one assumes that sexual function is in some fashion divorced from the physiologic processes which control other functions of the animal body. It may be true that heterosexual contacts outnumber homosexual contacts in most species of mammals, but it would be hard to demonstrate that this depends upon the 'normality' of heterosexual responses, and the 'abnormality' of homosexual responses." The book mentions specifically that lesbian contacts have been observed in such widely separated species as mice, hamsters, guinea pigs, rabbits, porcupines, marten, rats, cattle, antelope, goats, horses, pigs, lions, sheep, monkeys, and chimpanzees. And adds, *"Every farmer who has raised cattle knows . . . that cows quite regularly mount cows."*

A final point: Was one of the four co-authors of this book a closet "feminist"? The volume makes an interesting point on the then widely believed subject of "blue balls": *"There is a popular opinion that the testes are the sources of the semen which the male ejaculates. The testes are supposed to become swollen with accumulated secretions between the times of sexual activity, and periodic ejaculation is supposed to be necessary in order to relieve these pressures. Many males claim that their testes ache if they do not find regular sources of outlet, and throughout the history of erotic literature and in some psychoanalytic literature the satisfactions of orgasm are considered to depend upon the release of pressures in the 'glands'— meaning the testes. Most of these opinions are, however, quite unfounded. The prostate, seminal vesicles, and Cowper's are the only glands which contribute any quantity of material to the semen, and they are the only structures which accumulate secretions which could create pressures that would need to be relieved. Although there is some evidence that the testes may secrete a bit of liquid when the male is erotically aroused, the amount of their secretion is too small to create any pressure. The testes may seem to hurt when there is unrelieved erotic arousal (the so-called stoneache of the vernacular), but the pain probably comes from the muscular tensions in the perineal area, and possibly from the tensions in the sperm ducts, especially at the lower ends (the epididymis) where they are wrapped about the testes. Such aches are usually relieved in orgasm because the muscular tensions are relieved—but not because of the release of any pressures which have accumulated in the testes. Exactly similar pains may develop in the groins of the female when sexual arousal is prolonged for some time before there is any release in orgasm.*"

In other words, if a man's desire for intercourse is not shared by a woman, there is no reason why she must "accommodate him"; masturbation will provide him with an equally strong orgasm, although the psychological satisfaction may not be the same. There is no physically demanding male sex drive that forces men to pressure women into intercourse, as *The Hite Report* pointed out, thus women need no longer be intimidated by these arguments; a woman's body is her own. As one woman answered my research question when asked, "Have you ever been afraid to say 'no'?," "No! This is my body, my breasts and my cunt—they are my territory and if anyone, even my husband, tries to take what I do not wish to give, it's WAR, baby."

The portion of the "Kinsey" volume that is disappointing to me is the overall depiction of female sexuality, which is set in a culture-bound framework. The Kinsey authors fail, it seems, to understand female orgasm—though why they should not have understood it is a mystery, since their work explains so well the historical development (cited above) of our culture's definition of sex. Didn't they see that sex seen as "the act" enables men to reach orgasm more easily than women? The sections on female orgasm focus on whether or not women are able to have orgasm during coitus, separate by chapter the results for married women, then attempt to conclude that those women (why doesn't the same difference apply to men?) who have been married longer are more likely to have orgasm during coitus. Masters and Johnson, working 20 years later, also seemed to share this coital framework and were disappointed to find that women generally remained "dysfunctional" even after "treatment." Masters and Johnson, although stating that they believe clitoral stimulation is important for women's orgasms, also believe a "normal" woman should get enough "indirect" clitoral stimulation from simple intercourse (coitus) to

lead to orgasm.[2,3] To use manual stimulation for orgasm would mean that a woman is "dysfunctional" and needs "treatment." *The Hite Report on Female Sexuality*, which showed that intercourse alone does not stimulate most women to orgasm, called attention to the duo's lack of solid laboratory proof as to exactly how the physical motion of coitus ("thrusting") could cause clitoral stimulation.

The Kinsey group's views are disappointing, in that—although there is reference to how much easier it is for women to reach orgasm via masturbation than coitus—there is no detailed description of female masturbation that could have been used to contrast the stimulation to orgasm that women use themselves during masturbation with the stimulation available to them during coitus or "normal sex." Were the four authors blind to this important point, or was there some dispute among them about how to treat the topic—or were all four simply less interested in female sexuality or even unconsciously intimidated by the enormity of the issue's implications?

Pomeroy commented on my work in 1982, emphasizing that it has the best data on female masturbation and orgasm to be found anywhere (1982 speech to SSSS annual meeting). *The Hite Report* documents female masturbation in detail, it seems a vital source of information: since women reach orgasm easily via self-stimulation, and since no one teaches women how to do it, is an essential source of direct information about the types of stimulation women need in order to reach orgasm; this is why the first chapter of *The Hite Report* is devoted to these testimonies and my analysis. I was surprised that the authors of the Kinsey book did not pose more questions to themselves and readers about these facts, nor draw the conclusion that the reason most women do not easily reach orgasm during coitus is because coitus offers such different stimuli than they experience during masturbation—a different part of the body is touched. Yet the four men's ideas about female sexuality were an advance over Freud's, who up until that time was considered the primary reference point on the topic, despite his lack of research! The Kinsey writers could have availed themselves of several important studies done by women during the early twentieth century, such as Katherine B. Davis' *Factors in the Sex Life of Twenty-Two Hundred Women* (published in 1929), H. L. Dickinson and Laura Beam's *A Thousand Marriages* (published in 1932), or Leah Schaefer's doctoral thesis done under Professor Margaret Mead, the famous anthropologist ("Experiences and Reactions of a Group of 30 Women as Told to a Female Psychotherapist," 1946). Had any of them read Simone de Beauvoir's groundbreaking, internationally famous best-selling book *The Second Sex*, published around that time?

Why didn't Kinsey go into this subject more thoroughly, since it had been "common knowledge" for so long that "women have a problem" having orgasms during "sex"—coitus—and that women could orgasm much more easily from clitoral stimulation or masturbation? The majority of the women in Kinsey's study masturbated to orgasm within four minutes, similar to the women in the Hite Report study. It is, obviously, only during inadequate or secondary stimulation like intercourse that women take "longer" or need prolonged "foreplay" more than men. Yet this idea has remained fixed: women "take longer to orgasm than men," because women are more "psychologically delicate" (nonsense). In private correspondence, however, it is said that Kinsey did discuss the matter of female orgasm, and that he believed clitoral stimulation by hand or mouth to be by far the easiest way for women to orgasm. In other words, "Although the problem had been known for some time, it was not until research was done for *The Hite Report on Female Sexuality*, and given a culturally related analysis, that the ideological misunderstanding of female sexuality was made clear, on the basis of scientific evidence," as Dr. William Granzig, Professor and Dean of Clinical Sexology at Maimonides University, has put it.

The major disagreement I have with the Kinsey study is its portrayal of female orgasm and therefore of women. Why did the Kinsey group

stick to old views of female sexuality, when they were so intelligent, well informed and inventive in other ways? Later research for *The Hite Report* showed that most women, however much they like coitus, need specific stimulation of their exterior clitoral area in order to reach orgasm. Looking objectively at women, one could see that if they could orgasm easily during one form of stimulation but not another, this did not mean there was "something wrong with them," it meant (using scientific standards) that having orgasm in that way was normal for the human female. Indeed, research for *The Hite Report* focused on asking women themselves to describe when they most often orgasm, from which stimulation, and how they felt about it. While society has long known that it is easier for women to orgasm during self-stimulation (masturbation) than coitus—and that masturbation is clitoral and exterior, not vaginal—its most frequent reaction has been to blame women, call them "dysfunctional," as if their bodies' feelings are wrong. A more objective view would be to simply accept the way women's bodies are built.

In fact, much previous research into female sexuality had been less than "scientific," replicating a hidden bias: rather than taking the information that most women can orgasm more easily during masturbation or clitoral area stimulation than coitus, concluding that therefore this is "normal" if the majority find it so (as would be done if examining rocks or weather), Kinsey's study and other studies started with the assumption that women "should" orgasm during coitus, concluding that if they did not, there must be something wrong with them—thus finding that the majority of women were defective, flawed, or "dysfunctional," psychologically abnormal. (Do you remember the word "frigid"?) Research was often geared to finding the cause of this "defect."

In the twentieth century, though both Freud and Kinsey knew that women could orgasm more easily with exterior clitoral stimulation than "vaginal penetration," both failed to draw the logical conclusion; instead of seeing that society was oppressing women, they expected women to change—Freud believed women should grow up to "adjust" and become mature, while Kinsey thought that when a woman had been married longer, and had had more sexual experience, she would achieve this result. On the basis of the testimony of over 3,000 women, *The Hite Report* demonstrates that most women can orgasm easily during clitoral or pubic area stimulation (either by themselves or another person, by hand or mouth), while only one-third can orgasm easily during the "act" of "penetration" or intercourse with "no hands." [Why is the beginning of intercourse almost always described as "vaginal penetration" and not "penile covering"?] For most women, the stimulation during masturbation and coitus is different; there is rarely penetration of the vagina during masturbation.

Finally, to compare Kinsey and Hite methodology, how did the Kinsey group do their research? Is the criticism justified? I cannot discuss this without also explaining my own methodology, since the two share the similarity of having tried to capture people's statements on a topic considered deeply private and even "shameful." Here I will let one of Kinsey's co-authors, Wardell Pomeroy, have the final word, as taken from his 1982 speech to SSSS: *"Because I am used to and involved with a taxonomic, statistical approach in understanding human sexuality, I was originally disturbed by Hite's approach, which is quite different. I changed my mind after reading the Female Report as well as the Male Report and now believe that focusing on understanding behavior, feelings, and attitudes adds an important dimension to the overall understanding of human sexuality which cannot be obtained in other ways. I quibble with Shere Hite about the advantage of a questionnaire versus a face-to-face interview—obviously I would because my Kinsey technique has been one thing and hers has been another. I really believe that for what we set out to do we were both right. It seems to me that for some things a direct interview is helpful, and in other cases, and in this case, it could not have been done in that way and needed a questionnaire approach . . . I believe The Hite Reports are very valuable pieces of work . . . there are five groups of people who need to read these books: women who have sexual problems; women who don't have sexual problems; males with sexual problems; males without sexual problems—and therapists with or without sexual problems."*

Kinsey's survey method was to select people who statistically approximate those ranges found in the general population (as to age, marital status, etc.) and use them as control groups. The four Kinsey researchers were aiming to conduct a large-scale survey of sexuality seeking representative accuracy, questioning people from as many walks of life, backgrounds, and economic levels, etc., as possible to try to approximate a representative selection. *The Hite Report on Female Sexuality* used the same basic approach (even though the aim was to do a "study" not a "survey"), working to include as wide a cross-section of the population as possible, then checking this against U.S. population statistics to ensure that the study would be as broad-based or "scientific" (i.e., representative) as possible. However, Hite Report research used an anonymous essay-type questionnaire rather than direct conversations, endeavoring to give women answering more privacy. Although there have been assertions made that the women who answered may not have been "typical" (that is, "normal women"), in fact, when the statistics are studied and compared with the U.S. population, it is clear that they are quite similar. The same accusations were made of the Kinsey study—that his research was flawed because the people participating couldn't be "normal," etc.; such accusations usually hide another agenda, that of saying that the results are displeasing.

The Hite Report on Female Sexuality contained two significant differences in methodology from the Kinsey reports, thought important to improve the study. First, whereas Kinsey and his (male) associates interviewed women face to face and knew the complete names and addresses of those they interviewed, *The Hite Report on Female Sexuality* used an anonymous essay-type questionnaire, believing that women would feel freer to talk about themselves in detail if they were offered the protection of complete privacy and anonymity.[4] In fact, many women who responded said that they had been able to write about things that they would never have been able to tell someone face to face, especially a stranger. The second significant difference (after that of the overall framework of the work's design and the questions on which it was based) is that *The Hite Report on Female Sexuality* presented not only statistical findings, but also offered many direct quotations from the replies to illustrate its findings, thus giving participants and readers direct access to each other.

This was an innovation in social-science methodology which was often misunderstood. Its purpose was to avoid, insofar as possible, setting up rigid new "norms" which might seem to be telling women what they should feel, and instead, to give women a chance to re-examine and re-evaluate their lives, deciding for themselves how they felt, what they agreed and disagreed with. In other words, the Hite Report methodology was conceived as providing a large forum in which women could speak out freely—giving everyone reading those replies the chance to decide for themselves how they felt about the answers. The methodology was seen as a process, both for the individual woman answering the questionnaire, and for the person reading what the 3,019 women had written—a process of rethinking, self-discovery, and getting acquainted with many other women in a way that had never before been possible, "an anonymous and powerful communication from the women who answered to all the women of the world."

Despite our vast differences on the theme of female orgasm, I owe a great debt to the Kinsey researchers, who clearly shaped and improved the world that I and others inherited. I am grateful to the four men who worked as they did to compile such a study, and sorry that Kinsey did not live to see the way his influence is continuing today.

Notes

1. Although according to the *Jews: Biography of a People* by Judd Teller, it was the sixth century B.C., not the seventh, and recent Israeli archaeological discoveries continue to update these dates.

2. Masters, W.H., & Johnson, V.E. (1966). *Human sexual response*. Boston: Little Brown.

3. Masters, W.H. & Johnson, V.E. (1970). *Human sexual inadequacy*. Boston: Little Brown.

4. Although some opinion polling and market research claims to be using anonymity as one of its primary elements, this is not quite correct. In such research, while it does not divulge the names or identities of the participants to the general public or to the company for whom the research is undertaken, the people asking the questions or observing do themselves know the names and identities of the persons involved, and usually their home telephone numbers. Under such circumstances, how could anyone easily disclose, for example, the frequency of their masturbation or whether they are having an extramarital affair? For this reason, research for Hite Reports was made "blind," that is, people were asked to send in their replies unsigned so they would have no such fears.

Elisabeth Sheff

Polyamorous Women, Sexual Subjectivity and Power

In the shifting gendered and sexual social landscape of the early twenty-first century, multiple-partner relationships remain eroticized and undertheorized. Pornographic films (Roof 1991; Swedberg 1989) and magazines (Jenefsky and Miller 1998) frequently present images of multiple-partner sex, most often of multiple women or a man with several women. Rather than challenging gendered and sexual roles or enlarging women's sexual sphere, these scenes actually reinforce heteronormativity (Jenefsky and Miller 1998). These highly sexualized images fail to capture the lived experiences of the people, especially the women, who actually engage in multiple partner relationships. Feminist theorists have criticized such androcentric images of women's sexuality (Dworkin 1979; MacKinnon 1986) and have argued instead for an agentic female sexual subjectivity (Martin 1996; Tolman 2002).

Polyamory is a form of relationship in which people have multiple romantic, sexual, and/or affective partners. It differs from swinging in its emphasis on long-term, emotionally intimate relationships and from adultery with its focus on honesty and (ideally) full disclosure of the network of sexual relationships to all who participate in or are affected by them. Both men and women have access to additional partners in polyamorous relationships, distinguishing them from polygamy. Very little sociological research has examined polyamory, and the scant extant

scholarship (R. Rubin 2001) mentions it only in passing and provides no in-depth analysis of participants' experiences.

The study of polyamory is essential to forming a more complete understanding of women's sexual subjectivity and power. My analysis provides empirical evidence that suggests new complexities associated with multiple-partner relationships and expands sociological understanding of women's sexuality by investigating a previously unexamined area of sexual subjectivity. To explore polyamorous women's potential to enlarge the concept of sexual subjectivity through engagement in nontraditional relationships and their attempts to reject sexual objectification, I analyzed data based on seven years of participant observation and in-depth interviews.[1] I conclude this article by suggesting possible avenues for future research, particularly an examination of women involved in same-sex multiple-partner relationships, longitudinal research that investigates shifting power relationships as women age, and more thorough interaction with polyamorous men.

Literature Review

While social theorists have examined multiple-partner relationships in the context of bisexuality (Hutchins and Kaahumani 1991; Rust 1993, Weinberg, Williams, and Pryor 1994), homosexuality (Connell 1995; Yip 1997), open marriage (Constantine and Constantine 1973; Smith and Smith 1974), adultery (Jones 1997; Michael et al. 1994), and swinging (Bartell 1971; Fang 1976; Jenks 1998), these discussions have focused on variations within a conventional sexual framework. Analysis

Source: "Polyamorous Women, Sexual Subjectivity and Power," by Elisabeth Sheff. *Journal of Contemporary Ethnography* 34(3): 251–283. © 2005. Used by permission.

indicates that swingers maintain conservative attitudes regarding gender roles (Henshel 1973), heterosexuality (Bartell 1971), and politics (Jenks 1998; Gould 1999). Although there are several self-help books written for people attempting polyamorous relationships (Anapol 1997; Easton and Liszt 1997; Nearing 1992; West 1996) and polyamory has received some (largely negative) attention in the popular press (Cloud 1999; Kurtz 2003), there has been virtually no scholarly work of any depth on the topic. Addition of polyamory to the catalog of women's sexual identities augments contemporary sociological research by acknowledging an alternate form of sexuality that offers women expanded horizons of choice.

The polyamorous women in my sample engage in multifaceted and sometimes contradictory relationships with sexual subjectivity. Tolman (2002, 5–6) terms sexual subjectivity, "a person's experience of herself as a sexual being, who feels entitled to sexual pleasure and sexual safety, who makes active sexual choices, and who has an identity as a sexual being. Sexual desire is at the heart of sexual subjectivity."

Martin (1996, 10) asserts, "Sexual subjectivity is a necessary component of agency and thus of self-esteem. That is, one's sexuality affects her/his ability to act in the world, and to feel like she/he can will things and make them happen." Sexual subjectivity for girls and women contrasts heterocentric, patriarchal objectification in which female sexuality is commodified or colonized in the service and convenience of men (Dworkin 1979; MacKinnon 1986; Ramazanoglu and Holland 1993; L. Rubin 1990a; see also L. Rubin 1990b).

Sexual subjectivity is integrally linked with power—the power to appropriate sexuality, relational power, and social power connected to defining versions of sexuality outside rigidly controlled norms as deviant (Ramazanoglu and Holland 1993; Tannenbaum 1999). Women with no access to their own sexual subjectivity have bodies that Tolman (2002) terms "silent," disempowered by being spoken for and defined by masculine ideas and desires. In the sexualized social landscape of contemporary Western culture, even (or especially) lesbians and bisexual women are defined by masculine terms (Lorde 1984; Rust 1993).

Some women refuse the mandates of androcentric versions of sexuality and redefine themselves as sexual agents. Crawley and Broad (2004, 68) discuss the shift in the authority of storytelling from doctors and psychologists to "the everyday person" who becomes the agent in her own construction of a sexual and political self through "self-storying as activism." The bisexual women (and men) who participated in Weinberg, Williams, and Pryor's (2001) longitudinal study created lasting images of themselves as bisexual by concentrating on their feelings of attraction to both sexes rather than sexual behaviors. "As the bisexuals aged, rather than focusing on the nature of their current sexual lives as the important dimension, more of them turned to their history of sexual feelings—their having sustained a dual attraction over such a long time," which allowed participants to carve out a "more expansive identity" (Weinberg, Williams, and Pryor 2001, 202). While some respondents in Shalet, Hunt, and Joe-Laidler's (2003) examination of women in gangs occupied "respectable" roles in which male gang members defined and controlled their sexuality, others refused androcentric classifications and forged autonomous roles, outside of male supervision and sexual ownership. Their findings indicate that "female gang members confront a tension between establishing their independence from men and toughness on one hand and negotiating and accommodating constraining norms regarding femininity of the other" (Shalet, Hunt, and Joe-Laidler 2003, 139). In her examination of young women's sexual decision making, Dunn (1998, 508) similarly concludes that "a woman is neither the product of her circumstances (a victim) nor the producer of her world (a powerful female), but rather she is both."

By simultaneously challenging and participating in aspects of sexual subjectivity and sexual objectification, polyamorous women inhabit the borderland between what Connell (1987, 183) identifies as *emphasized femininity*, or a version of womanhood that is "defined around compliance with this subordination and is oriented to accommodating the interests and desires of men" and an alternative, noncompliant form of femininity. Polyamorous women, like the majority of women currently living in the United States, face a complex set of social and sexual norms with disparate requirements. L. Rubin (1990a; see also L. Rubin 1990b) explores heterosexuality in the aftermath of the sexual revolution and declares the social landscape a tangle of contradictory meanings, especially confusing regarding women's sexual subjectivity. She concludes that while men enjoy increased sexual access to a larger variety of women, they simultaneously wish for women who are "real" in the sense of being sexually submissive and personally compliant. Women in her study recognize these divergent messages and chafe against the thinly veiled and more elaborate double standard their mothers endured a generation before:

> Men, then, still take certain prerogatives unto themselves, as if they were given in natural law, and women are left to deal with messages that are wildly mixed. Be an equal, but not wholly so. Be independent, but tread with care. Be assertive, but ready to give way. Make money, but not too much. Commit to a career, but be ready to stay home with the children. Be sexually aggressive, but don't push too hard. (L. Rubin 1990a, 146; see also L. Rubin 1990b)

L. Rubin's respondents report negotiating androcentric standards, which define sexuality as a masculine territory in which women are judged by the degree to which they meet men's needs and fulfill masculine desires rather than their own. Numerous theorists agree with L. Rubin's (1990a; see also L. Rubin 1990b) assessment that the gendered sexual double standard remains firmly entrenched (Crawford and Popp 2003; Dunn 1998; Jeffreys 1990; Martin 1996; Risman and Schwartz 2002).

If, as Lorde (1984, 55) suggests, conventional sexual arrangements are designed to silence women's authentic spirits, then an alternative erotic system could offer women a more authentic expression of sexual subjectivity from which

to "rise up empowered." Through their involvement in polyamory, the women in my sample explored new roles and avenues of sexuality while shifting the balance of power in their relationships. Polyamory, however, is a complex relationship style, and its impact on their lives is concomitantly intricate. These shifts were unable to completely obscure the patriarchal culture, which remains active in the polyamorous subculture, nor did they negate the price some women paid for the stigma of nonmonogamy. In this article, I explore the impact the alternate sexual system of polyamory exerts on some women's lives. In so doing, I detail some of the ways in which polyamorous women expand "normal" social roles, discuss their sexual lives and identities, and explore the novel and traditional forms of power polyamorous practice engenders for these women's relationships. . . .

My data for this article come from extensive participant observation, including attendance at support group meetings, workshops, and national polyamorists conferences, as well as informal conversations and forty in-depth interviews (twenty women and twenty men). Reflecting mainstream polyamorous communities in the Western United States, my respondents were in their mid-30s to late 50s and tended toward middle- and upper-middle-class socioeconomic status, usually college educated, overwhelmingly white,[2] and frequently employed as professionals in computer or counseling/therapy fields. I used semi-structured interviews that lasted from one and one half to two hours, a format that yields data suitable for answering questions about members' interpretations, actions, and interactions. . . .

Polyamorous Women, Sexual Subjectivity, and Power

While many polyamorous women reported a sense of exhilaration accompanying their liberation from traditional cultural roles they found overly constraining, some revealed a simultaneous experience of terror and anomic pain that accompanied the loss of traditionally recognized roles.

Expanded Roles

Some polyamorous women who felt constrained and disempowered by monogamy reported a sense of release upon embarking on polyamorous relationships. Departure from accepted forms of relationships required polyamorous women to form new roles or expand roles previously available to them as monogamists. The women in my sample expanded their familial, cultural, gendered, and sexual roles.

Family and monogamous culture.   Peck, a thirty-six-year-old white magazine editor and mother of three, rejected the traditional wifely role she observed in her family of origin and had originally replicated in her monogamous marriage: "Women got married, had children, raised the children and stayed in the home, that's what I was taught and brought up with. And that was the role I was following. . . . That period in my life, I was thinking and wanting things different and was starting to get my own empowerment as a woman, changing roles, and wanting more." "Wanting more" involved not only pursuing higher levels of education but also rejecting a form of sexuality and family that was not working for her and forging a polyamorous alternative. Polyamory provided the impetus for Peck to shift long-standing roles she found ill fit.

Others found participation in polyamory spurred a willingness to challenge social conventions and attendant roles. Phoenix, a fifty-three-year-old white computer programmer, saw polyamory as fundamental to her larger interrogation of social norms and values:

I have a tendency to think that somebody who is in their body, aware of what they want and don't want, making their own decisions, is much less likely to maybe go quietly off to war or send their kids off to war because that's what's supposed to be done. They're much less controllable in some ways because you're used to making your own decisions. . . . I think that my choice to be polyamorous has a lot to do with my willingness to look at how I really want to live my life . . . I think I have felt a lot

freer to do things differently than the rest of society does, in other areas of my life as well. Once you've had to think about it rather than just follow society's scripts, you may be more open to making different choices in other parts of your life as well.

Rejecting such a fundamental social tenet as monogamy often granted polyamorous women self-permission to question other norms as well.

Gender roles.   The majority of the polyamorous women in my sample reported shifting gender roles resulting from, or precipitating, participation in polyamory. Yansa, a twenty-nine-year-old African American health care provider and stepmother of one, related her reasons for agreeing to monogamous relationships even though she knew she desired multiple partners.

I didn't want to hurt my partner's feelings. I felt that I wanted to be the righteous one and do the right thing for them and for the relationship. . . . When we became committed and like kind of in a monogamous relationship I think the relationship immediately went down hill from there. And it was more of a situation where he had sown his wild oats. He was tired of playing around. I was the one, but I had just begun and it was like, quelled this desire and I was just like, this is not enough for me. And he was like, this is enough for me, and I said, we have a problem.

Yansa initially conformed to a traditionally feminine role of ignoring her own desire for multiple partners in favor of being "righteous" and engaging in the monogamy her partner desired. Eventually, she came to define their disparate needs as "a problem" and transitioned to a polyamorous relationship style and identity.

Similarly, Louise, a thirty-seven-year-old white astrologer and photographer with three children, found that her roles shifted once she engaged in polyamory:

I am more aware of what I need for myself. I'm more aware of taking care of myself and not always living for other people. Not that I don't care about people, I'm a very caring person.

The problem is that I had a bad habit of always putting everyone else first. I'm still working on that one. But it [polyamory] has made me realize how much I need to take care of me. . . . It's just being true to who I am.

Engagement in polyamory spurred Louise to reexamine her traditionally feminine focus on "living for other people" and "putting everyone else first" and transition to a more agentic life pattern of self-focus with a concomitant experience of greater authenticity.

Some polyamorous women reported distaste for dualistic gender arrangements that they found overly constraining. Emmanuella, a forty-year-old Chicana Web designer and mother of three, was uncomfortable with a bipolar gender system and sought relational styles that allowed her greater latitude. "I'm not sure it matters, gender, as regards to . . . levels of communication and respect, tolerance. I'm not sure that it matters, male or female." Emmanuella asserted that personal qualities outweighed gender as priorities for establishing sexual or affective relationships.

Sexual roles. Sexuality was one of the primary areas in which polyamorous women reported expanding their roles. Julia, a forty-one-year-old Lebanese American software consultant, found polyamory to be instrumental in redefining the cultural ideal of sex and sexuality that failed her personally:

My motive of expressing my sexuality has really changed a lot since finding polyamory. . . . On the face of it, you could just say that it's been limited a lot and the things that other people usually call sex, things that involve genital contact and bringing one another to orgasm, mostly I don't do that anymore because it's too emotionally wrought for me. It's too, I just can't do it with integrity anymore. . . . So for me, when I talk about any sexual relationships or interactions I have had they've been relationships dominated overwhelmingly by what other people might just call smooching or a lot of breathing and gazing into each other's eyes and caressing and

things where for me arousal is what's enjoyable and orgasm is not.

Some other polyamorous women eroticized gender fluidity. Nori, a forty-nine-year-old white mother of one and small business owner, described it as "gender bending":

I've got strong-ass bending desire stuff going on. . . . The person I am most attracted to on the street is someone I don't know their gender. . . . I love those girls that look like boys and those boys that look like dykes, not girly girls, but dykes. . . . I am totally eroticized by the thought of drag, not necessarily what some of those drag queens do but boys or girls bending and a handful of transgendered women or men either way that just flipped over, that didn't like the outer edges of fem or masculine.

Several other respondents expressed a similarly strong desire to date transsexuals or crossdressers. Dylan, a thirty-three-year-old white costume designer and mother of one, embraced her own transgendered tendencies:

I love playing with the transgender thing because it totally tweaks how I know myself that way and I like it. I have been involved with several transgendered people, and I like that energy where it's like I'm more unexpected or more unknown to myself and I can grow in a place where I haven't before. So as I accepted myself as being more transgendered, I found my attractions to broaden. . . . Eventually, I just got really bored with trying to pick people apart by how they're male or female, and for me, it's really part of being transgendered where I don't like doing that to myself and I don't like doing it to other people. I find it a way to separate us instead of connect us, and I'm much, much, much more juiced by the connection!

Nori, Dylan, and other polyamorous women rejected a sexual and gender system that separated people with a false emphasis on small differences between men and women. Many of these polyamorous women embraced forms of sexual subjectivity that allowed them to redefine mores and social institutions such as sexuality and monogamy to better fit their own needs. Some consciously refused the subject/object dichotomy that cast women as passive objects of men's sexual satisfaction (Sedgwick 1990). Others simply forged novel roles without theorizing a social context. Still, the loss of traditional roles could hold hidden costs, and the aftermath of reorganizing sexual roles was extremely uncomfortable for some polyamorous women. While many respondents reported exhilaration at the liberation from confining traditional roles, they also reported terror that accompanied psychic freefall with no roles to emulate.

Sexuality

Polyamorous women frequently discussed sexuality in support groups, social gatherings, and with their partners. These discussions emphasized sexuality in relation to polyamorous women's high sex drives, connections with other women, and bisexual identities.

High sex drive.   In direct opposition to cultural mandates of female sexual submission and a double standard that requires women restrain their sexual desires (L. Rubin 1990a; Tolman 2002; see also L. Rubin 1990b), a number of polyamorous women reported viewing themselves as highly sexual people. Louise asserted that

> I have such a high sex drive and literally feel I need sex on a regular basis to feel grounded, to feel clear, to feel good, and it's just, it's very, it's like exercise for me. It feels good. I enjoy it. . . . If I haven't had sex in a while, after about three to four weeks I start climbing the walls and I get very bitchy and I'm just not in a good mood and I don't feel good and I feel on edge. Whereas if I get sex on a regular basis, I'm calm, I'm fine, I'm happy.

This description of sexual appetite would be unremarkable coming from a man, but from a woman, it contrasts dominant cultural scripts mandating women's disinterest in sex except to meet masculine needs. Although images of Britney Spears, Jennifer Lopez, and Halley Barry

convey an unbridled female sexuality, ordinary women face a more mundane version of the entrenched sexual double standard. In their examination of research on the gendered implications of teenage (hetero)sexuality, Risman and Schwartz (2002, 20) found that

> girls today may be able to have sex without stigma, but only with a steady boyfriend. For girls, love justifies desire. A young woman still cannot be respected if she admits an appetite driven sexuality. If a young woman has sexual liaisons outside of publicly acknowledged "couple-dom," she is at risk of being defamed. . . . This puts her one down as a power player in her relationships, because her boyfriend does not have to worry about moving on too quickly and being stigmatized for his sexual choices.

Risking defamation by eschewing the constraints of coupledom, polyamorous women reject the power dynamic embedded in the persistent sexual double standard that continues to limit women's sexual choices and stigmatize those who refrain from living by its mandates.

Some polyamorous women spoke of their high sexual appetites in even more consciously gendered transgressive terms. Peck defied cultural conditioning that defined highly sexual women in derogatory terms and instead recast her sexual appetite as empowering:

> Women with multiple lovers are usually called sluts, bitches, very derogatory, very demeaning in sexual context. Whereas men who have multiple lovers—they're studs, they're playboys, they're glorified names where with a woman it's very demeaning. So to be a woman and have multiple partners, it's been very empowering and claiming some of that back, saying I have just as much right to be a sexual person with many lovers as men do. So that's where I see tying in without the shame and the guilt.

Similarly, Yansa redefined the meaning of multiple-partner sexuality:

> At the time, I called myself sexually liberated and, um, it was kind of a nice thing to say because it didn't have, it's better than saying I'm

a slut. I mean, it gave people an open door to ask you what you meant and it gave me the opportunity to define what I felt that meant at the time . . . It gives women power over our sexual beings, for so long women have had husbands who have cheated on them, and some haven't and hooray for them. So it gives women an opportunity to, um, expect their sexual side, which is again, I'm playing back to nature versus nurture, I think it's in every being to want to have their needs met and women as sexual beings have sexual needs that's like men.

While Yansa reported feeling empowered by her access to multiple partners and redefinition of sexuality, in another section of the interview, she lamented the impact of this redefinition on her marriage. She had discussed her discomfort with her husband regarding one of his girlfriends:

> He was like, well, you're the physical and you're caring, but she's the one I can talk to and she's the one . . . (trails off). And that's like the worst thing you can tell a woman. That some other woman has your emotional connection and you're just the physical.

While Yansa desired sexual freedom "like a man," she was offended when her husband defined her as "the physical" at the exclusion of the emotional. Sexual redefinition was enticing for many polyamorous women but could have unexpected negative consequences as well.

Connections with other women.   The majority of the women in my sample viewed sexuality as a source of unity with other women, even some who had previously experienced sexuality as divisive. Louise discussed the new sense of connection she had developed with women since finding the polyamorous community:

> One of the things that has probably been the best thing about finding the poly community is meeting women that I can relate to because I haven't had women friends before now. This is the first time in my life, with a few exceptions, that I have really had close women friends. It's

been wonderful to meet women who are highly sexual who don't feel threatened that I'm highly sexual. . . . And it's brought me a closeness with women that I thought I'd never have.

Louise found not only social connection with other women, but sexual and affective links as well. Louise discussed the additional advantages she found in her sexual relationship with her husband's girlfriend, Monique:

> Monique is beautiful, I mean gorgeous. And she is big, like me, we are both big. And that was—being able to see how amazingly beautiful she is and feel my desire for her made me realize that I am that beautiful, too. I mean, now I can see how others see me as beautiful and see myself that way too since I have seen Monique that way. It opened my eyes. It really did (laughs).

Louise found herself gaining not only friendships and sexual interactions through her associations with other polyamorous women, but a new appreciation for her body in a culture that does not generally view large women as sexy. Some women forged unanticipated bonds with kindred sisters in the polyamorous community that they had been unable to establish in monogamous society.

Other polyamorous women reported a mutual sexuality or love for the same man as a source of connection with other women. Morgan, a twenty-nine-year-old white accountant and mother of one, opined that monogamous relationships fostered competition among women and that the polyamorous relationship she had with her husband Carl, her lover Josh, Carl's lover Vicky, and Josh's wife Jessica made competition a nonentity between herself, Vicky, and Jessica.

> I fully and completely realize that Josh can love me and Jessica equally and it just doesn't take anything away from the other and same with Carl because I know I feel, I love Carl and Josh both very much in different ways. I don't love one lesser than the other, so I know that that's how they feel about me too. . . . Even if Jessica and I even weren't sexually attracted to each

other, it would be good for us to have a deep bond because we're both in love with the same man. And I love my friendship with Vicky and she loves me, too! It just works out better when we love each other, it is much easier that way. . . . And I think polyamory can help raise the status of women because it gives, it also gives women the freedom to be with who they want, power over their own bodies.

Morgan viewed her greater freedom in relationships as integrally linked with her sexual and platonic love for other women. She connected what she viewed as stronger bonds between polyamorous women not only to the potential for them to develop a sexual relationship but the shift in the balance of power generated by bisexuality and attendant increase in choice and autonomy from men.

Facile connection with other women was not universal, however, and feelings of jealousy or strife often plagued relationships among polyamorous women. The most common source of discord was difficulty sharing a lover. Dylan reported hearing from a woman who was in love with one of Dylan's lovers that she wished to "kill me off. And she was serious, the look in her eye, I mean, scary shit! There was no way I was gonna turn my back on her, ever!"

Other polyamorous women reported strife that occurred frequently at the end of relationships. Alicia, an unemployed white woman in her late thirties, discussed her rage at being disenfranchised when the quad (four-person relationship) she and her soon to be ex-husband had been involved in for eight years dissolved. A back injury had prevented Alicia from performing paid labor, but she had been able to care for the home and the biological children of the other quad members. She was extremely angry with Monique, the other woman in the quad. "Now that bitch has my husband and the kids, too! I cooked for them for eight years, did their laundry, and cleaned the damn house and now I am out cold and she—I could just kill her!" Polyamorous relationships that ended badly could lead to rancorous sentiment among ex-lovers.

Bisexuality. Bisexual women were quite numerous in polyamorous communities. In fact, bisexuality was so common among women in the polyamorous community that they had a standing joke that it allowed them to "have their Jake and Edith too!" Bisexual women were also among the highest status members of the subculture because they were most often sought as additions to existing female/male dyads to create the coveted and elusive F/M/F (female, male, female) triad. While the high status of the role might have encouraged some women to experiment with bisexuality, others had identified as bisexual long before their association with the polyamorous community. Some polyamorous women sought independent sexual relationships with other women, while others preferred group sexual encounters involving both women and men. Women in polyamorous communities interacted with varying degrees of sexuality that created social space for multiple definitions of bisexuality to coexist.

Some polyamorous women relished a specifically group-oriented bisexuality when they engaged in multiplistic relationships. Julia reported her experience of attending a polyamorous women's retreat:

Twenty-four of us went to a log cabin on the coast and spent the weekend together. And on the second evening, half of them went to bed and half of us stayed up and had this big cuddle pile kind of thing. We were all on the couch and on the floor and leaning against each other's legs or having our arms around each other. It kind of evolved in an erotic direction, some kind of smooching started to happen and then we moved to the big king sized bed and I really enjoyed that a lot. . . . It really kind of fed into a fantasy world of mine, like that network with all the interconnections. I love women. I feel safest with groups of women . . . , though in a really close intimate and possibly sexual relationship I am most comfortable with a man. . . . I tend to connect intimately with women if it's not a one-on-one thing, but we have a lover in common or we're in a group at a retreat or something like that.

Julia had not previously identified herself as bisexual prior to exploring same-sex sexuality with the large group of women.

On the other hand, some bisexual women in the polyamorous community had a multiplistic orientation toward seemingly everything *but* sexual encounters. While Nori identified as bisexual and polyamorous for her entire adult life, she felt, "As group, community, or network oriented as I am, my handful of group sexual activities hasn't been all that for me. So I really like, I am also oriented more one on one, sexually." Bisexuality did not always mean multiple simultaneous partners.

Other polyamorous women reported shifting relationships with women that came to include sexuality, even when it had not initially been the focus. Peck discussed her joy at finding another polyamorous family in the area of Ohio where she had lived:

> We had met another family in '94 that was polyamorous that lived about an hour away. They had three children and have been good friends for a long time. It was nice just to get some community and some support and another mom that was involved (in polyamory) and had kids involved. And so the mother of this family and I became really close friends and then ended up becoming lovers. And that was one of my first bisexual relationships. And that was another thing I learned from polyamory was that I was bisexual and had an opportunity to explore that within the polyamorous relationship.

Peck explicitly connected her bisexuality with her passion for polyamory and felt that the two were intertwined in a way that allowed her the greatest authenticity: "Because, being bisexual, if I was monogamous I'd have to choose to be either with a man or a woman. And this way, under a polyamorous lifestyle, I can do both, I can be with both." Peck and numerous other polyamorous women reported that they valued the range of choices that accompanied a bisexual orientation. Many women identified the relief from the necessity to choose either a male or a fe-

male partner as a primary benefit that they experienced in polyamory.

Some women in the polyamorous community identified disparate reactions in relationships with men and women. Dylan explained that

> I found myself more alive in my relationships with women than I was with men. I found them more of a celebration. I find my attractions to men and women to be different. I find fewer women really move me, but when one does, it usually cuts deeper, to the core. Where I have many more attractions to men, but I also have kind of this laissez-faire attitude towards them. It's like, oh, its another man I'm attracted to. Its like, whatever. But when a woman really moves me, then its like, YEAH!

Dylan's relationships with men and women each had distinct qualities that she felt a monosexual relationship could not hope to satisfy.

This nearly ubiquitous bisexuality among polyamorous women was so pervasive as to create an assumption of universal female bisexuality in polyamorous communities. In fact, all but one of the women I interviewed for the study identified themselves as bisexual or "biquestioning." Shelly, a white thirty-nine-year-old mother of three and legal secretary, was the sole respondent who identified herself as heterosexual, though she did so with qualification:

> I would call myself heterosexual, although I have had a couple of experiences with women. . . . I don't feel bisexual, but I don't feel adverse to it. I don't feel a yearning of, "Oh, I would really love to be with a woman," but I wouldn't rule it out if the circumstances were right. I have felt attracted to other women several times, but not necessarily acted on it.

Even those women who questioned the legitimacy of their bisexual identity because of their greater attraction for men made it clear that they had felt attractions to and engaged in sexual relationships with women as well as men. . . .

While many polyamorous women spoke of the sexual freedom and power they felt in multiple-partner relationships, they concurrently spoke of feeling objectified by men who sought simultaneous sex with multiple women. Some of the women in my sample were chagrined by the intensity of male focus on simultaneous sex or relationships with multiple women. Louise hosted a coed support group for people seeking or involved in polyamorous relationships. She related an exchange with a male newcomer who arrived early for a support group meeting. He mentioned that he was seeking a triad with two women to which she replied, "Yeah, you and every other damn guy out there!" He remarked "You seem a little upset by that," to which she responded,

> Well, it gets real old, forever dealing with the hot bi babe fantasy. I mean, I would love to be in a triad with two men devoted to me, who wouldn't? But my personal ad online as a single woman looking for two men gets only responses from f/m (female/male) couples who want a third. I am soooooo damn sick of that!

Other women shared Louise's disdain for heterosexual polyamorous men's seemingly ubiquitous obsession with "having" multiple women.

Women who joined existing female/male couples to form a triad often reported feeling that the couple retained more power than they did. Dylan related,

> I like threes a lot. I've often become involved with couples and find that [I am] the third with them being in primary partnership and that configuration makes me feel often like the disposable partner in the relationship. And it's also, by now, after many, many years of this kind of lifestyle, I'm hypersensitive when I am not being treated more as an equal. And I don't always expect equality because I know they have their primary partnership, but especially if the two of them gang up on me or try to punish me together, I'm really, really sensitive to that. . . . I think that in this [polyamorous] culture being the bodacious bi babe and that being a lot of primary partners', like their dream, that I related as a fantasy and not as a person. And I felt exploited by that.

Tina, a white thirty-six-year-old urban planner, expressed similarly negative sentiments for a couple who appeared to desire her as a sexual accessory to their relationship: "literally, the only reason they wanted me around was to have threesome sexual activities." Other polyamorous women who joined existing female/male couples objected to being related to as a "sex toy." While the majority of the polyamorous women reported seeking and often successfully creating relationships based on equality and power sharing, the objectification of the "hot bi babe" remained a source of tension and inequality in numerous polyamorous relationships.

Nothing is simple in this intricate relational style, and it is not only bisexual women who may be viewed as sexual objects by polyamorists. Dylan emphatically stated, "I have really intensely been attracted to bi boys, extremely, intensely attracted to bi boys, like in a very bad bi boy stage for a long, long time now. . . . I just can't get enough of bi boys."

Even with this intense attraction for bisexual "boys," Dylan reported, "And inside of that, I'm finding my attention is again drawn more towards women than before. And I feel like my connections there mean more to me and I'm finding that I want to play more with boys, just kind of play, casual thing." Dylan reserved her intense emotional connections for relationships with women and saw bisexual men as fodder for solely "play, casual relationships."

Clearly, the relationship between gender and bisexuality within the polyamorous community is complex. On one hand, women were sometimes sexualized as "hot bi babes" and sought to endow a new level of eroticism upon established male/female sexual relationships. On the other hand, men were sometimes objectified as sex toys but excluded from emotional relationships. In the relationally intricate world of polyamory, both scenarios operated simultaneously. Still, in patriarchal societies, men generally retain greater social and financial power on average, endowing their definitions of a given situation with greater weight (Becker 1963). Power remains a complex issue within polyamorous relationships.

Power

While both men and women involved in poly-amorous subcultures tended to view women as retaining more power in polyamorous relation-ships, women who had initiated the entree into polyamory themselves seemed more secure in their perceived enhanced power than did women who engaged in polyamory at the behest of their male partners. Yet both types of women endured stigma and the attendant loss of power that accompanies deviation from cherished social norms such as monogamy.

Women in power.   Some polyamorists perceived women to have greater power in polyamorous subcultures. Emmanuella felt women's greater control of sexuality within polyamorous com-munities endowed them with increased social power in a potentially highly sexualized setting.

> The women seem to have more of a sexual par-lance because the women decide whether sex is available and there are still some incredibly conventional notions about who approaches whom. The men seem to swing between being very sort of kid in a candy store, elated, can't believe this whole practice is happening to them, but yeah, buddy, let's get it on of thing. And the other extreme is feeling very dour about the fact that their woman is participating in this and really uncertain whether they want to have that, but are going along with it because there might be sex involved. But they are not really emanating the yeah, buddy, yippee kind of energy. So what happens is that there are a bunch of poly women who are very much drawn to that, that very dour energy because they like the wounded spirit. So you know you see this group of women who will cluck around these men, and the men start thinking this isn't so bad after all. (laughing) But in either sce-nario the women retain the power.[3]

Yansa acknowledged what she perceived to be greater sexual and relational power than that of her new husband, but she kept it in check to educate him in a form of polyamory that she found acceptable.

> My husband has actually gone out on more dates than I have. I have not gone out on one date yet since we have been married and it's not that I can't or that I won't, it's just that I wanted to give my husband the opportunity to date and have him get his feet wet and get a feel for what was ethically okay with it and what was unethi-cal and this, this when we went out with this per-son and he did that, that was not okay, but when you did this that was great. Keep doing that. Just to give him a new way of looking at poly. . . . I get invited, oftentimes, to parties alone, by myself, without him, and I have had numerous men and women who want to date. But I have turned them down for him because he wasn't comfortable with me going and so . . . (trails off).

Ostensibly, Yansa held less relational power since her husband was dating and she was not. It was clear, however, that he dated at her behest, following her guidelines, in a temporary arrange-ment she created and could end at her own dis-cretion. When the two went to sex parties together, Yansa had many more sexual encoun-ters than he, and both were aware that once she started dating again, she had far more options than he. Her husband acknowledged his position of lower power and bemoaned her greater rela-tional cache in his own interview.

Power shifts.   Other polyamorous women viewed power as more equally shared. Julia asserted,

> Equal say is such a necessary thing for me that I don't even think about it. I mean, being raised in the '70s and encouraged, I was good in school, my parents encouraged me I could do whatever I wanted to do and I was a strong woman, I was a smart woman, I was a power-ful woman. I've never, it's just kind of out of the question for me to be in a relationship where I don't have equal power, at least at the gross level. Of course, not everything is equal all the time on a finer level, but yeah, I would never even be in a romantic relationship where somebody had power over me.

Julia and other polyamorous women main-tained the ostensibly equitable balance of power via rigorous communication, an esteemed ideal of polyamorous relationships. Some discussed a division of labor with their partner(s) that included some task division but ultimately established parity, while others explained how they shared all tasks with their partners and split everything equally.

Some women asserted that polyamorous men supported and indeed sought relationships based on equality in relationship. Louise said that she found that the polyamorous men "just think differently." She explained:

They are much more nontraditional. They aren't looking, most men that I've seen that are polyamorous aren't looking for a relationship with a woman they can control or be in charge of. They like independent women who are highly sexual, who are exciting. They like that. That's why they're attracted to this kind of lifestyle is because they like strong women. And because of that, they're looking for an equal relationship in most cases.

This perception of equality stood in sharp contrast to some other polyamorous women's experiences with both polyamorous and monogamous men who became increasingly uncomfortable with multiple-partner sexuality as the relationship became more serious. Yansa discussed her experiences with men who were initially enthusiastic about polyamory and then became reluctant to participate:

Well, when we were dating, they thought it was great. They thought, what person would not want someone who is sex positive and comfortable with a stronger sense of sexuality because it gives them an opportunity to open up and try new things and see how far they can go. So while we were dating it was, they were attracted to it, they were curious. But when we initiated the relationship and it became more serious, they were very much not happy with it because they understood exactly through my actions what that meant, and they over time realized they weren't comfortable with it.

Yansa was disappointed by what she viewed as a failing on the part of the men who relished

the idea of a "sexual free for all" but balked at the emotional consequences.

Others redefined the meaning of power in a relationship. Dylan, who identified as polyamorous since she was fourteen,[4] detailed her feeling of power in polyamorous relationships:

I'm very personable and I really like people a lot and I talk big in that way and being female in the poly world, I had more opportunities for relationships than sometimes my male partners or more shy female partners. And in that way, I felt the balance of power was off because I had more possibilities and opportunities than they did. At least relationally and sexually. I think that socially we consider that ability to acquire resources and have allies as a way of being powerful and I have that. I have very close friends and sometimes a bubbly character, so I think that can create power balances. I also travel a lot and the ability to walk away from a relationship without, like, knowing full well I can take care of myself and that they can take care of themselves has created, that I have more power at times.

Dylan recast the basis of power in a relationship and came to view her gregarious style of interaction and ability to leave as sources of power within polyamorous settings.

This shifting power base may initially appear androcentric and then become gynocentric through the machinations of polyamorous relating. Some women who were previously reluctant to engage in polyamory found themselves empowered by the gender dynamics of polyamorous relationships. Dylan noted,

It is a poly phenomenon that often the woman in the couple is kind of reluctant and is dragged kicking and screaming into poly. Then when the man is done with his experimentation, the woman often finds that it suits her character and stays with it. It is almost like acquiring a skill, once she's got it, it becomes part of how she wants to live her life. It can be real confronting when the man wants to become involved in the poly lifestyle and then finds out that it is really much easier for a woman to establish relationships, and not only do they establish them easier, they tend to get more intimate and deeper faster, cause that is what women are good at. Speaking generally, women like that kind of stuff. So the men can become very uncomfortable.

While women being "dragged kicking and screaming" evinces lower relational power, the tables can turn once the previously monogamous couple engages in polyamory. Carlie, a thirty-four-year-old white educator and mother of two involved in one such relationship, related,

> Ricco (her husband and father of her children) badgered me about it for forever, like eight years or something. And it made me feel terrible, like I was not enough for him or too fat or something. Finally, I tell him just go out and get laid if it will shut you the fuck up about it already! I did not expect to get together with anyone else, much less fall in love. Now we are screwed because I am in love with someone else and Ricco does not like him, does not want me to see him. Ricco will do anything for me now, he would be monogamous and never bring it up again. But I am REALLY REALLY pissed! I totally would have left him if we did not have kids.

Carlie felt that she gained power with additional suitors and that Ricco's insistence on polyamory backfired when it did not work out as he had imagined. Increased power did not translate to increased joy for Carlie, however, since she felt trapped in a no-win situation of staying in a relationship she found distasteful or breaking up her family and subjecting her small children to the upheavals of divorce. Rather than reveling in her newfound power, she felt that "now *we* are screwed" (emphasis added) since she felt compelled to choose between her own happiness and that of her children. Even though the power base shifted in her relationship, Carlie reported few benefits from her new found relational cachet beyond the fact that a man she no longer loved would "do anything" for her.

Women disempowered. Some polyamorous relationships retained elements of a traditional power structure in which men relied on their female partners to perform a greater share of the emotional maintenance. These relationships seemed to regularly self-destruct. Louise reported encouraging Max, her husband of thirteen years and the father of two of her children, to deepen emotional intimacy with her and facilitate her attempts at friendly contact with his other lovers. Max reported feeling that these demands were excessive and refused to meet them because they "invade my privacy." Louise linked her emotional work to the balance of power in their relationship:

> I didn't want to be in control, but I couldn't get him to take any of the control. And this was a catalyst for that happening, for changing the power structure of our relationship. . . . He's taking more power in our relationship and I totally gave up power, like you can have it! And what I mean by that is simply I was taking all the emotional responsibility and he didn't have to participate in our relationship because I was doing all the emotional work. With the kids, with our lives, with our families, with everything . . . he didn't even have to participate and rarely showed up in our relationship. He would just kind of wander around the edges, not really participating in what was going on. And this forced him to participate, because he had to either participate or I would be gone.

While Louise connected her completion of the emotional work with her control in the relationship, she simultaneously implied that Max retained control through his refusal to perform emotional work. After thirteen years of marriage, Louise initiated divorce proceedings, primarily because of what she perceived as Max's reluctance to participate in the emotional work in the relationship. Louise reported that it was easier for her to leave Max since she had the emotional and sexual support of her other lovers and polyamorous friends who "understood what was going on."

Some women reported an increased sense of insecurity in their relationships with the advent of polyamory. Shelly was eloquent regarding the numerous personal costs of polyamory. She had chosen to engage in polyamory at the behest of Sven, her forty-two-year-old white bisexual husband employed as a computer consultant. Sven hoped to find another bisexual man with whom he and Shelly could establish a long-term triad. This ideal relationship proved difficult to establish, and Shelly felt some emotional pain in connection with Sven's desire for outside relationships:

> It's definitely better now than it was at first. I was much more threatened by him [Sven] being with someone else and I just didn't understand it, like I went through why can't he just be with me, why aren't I enough? Sometimes it still makes me insecure. . . . I have lost part of what I receive from Sven, although one-on-one time and attention, we are both very busy. . . . Another disadvantage is just trying to keep two people happy. It's hard to just make a marriage work, no matter who the two people are, and trying to be there emotionally and sexually and every other way with two people rather than one, trying to keep every one happy and balance I would think would be really difficult.

Shelly continued to pursue a polyamorous relationship but initially hypothesized that she would have been more comfortable in a monogamous relationship had she fallen in love with a monogamous man. Upon meeting another bisexual man with whom Shelly and Sven formed a triad, Shelly reported feeling far more optimistic about her engagement in polyamory. "This has turned out way, way better than I expected!"

Even those women who intentionally chose polyamory faced stigma and attendant loss of power in monogamous society. Peck found herself alienated from both her family of origin and a spiritual group after she initiated a triad with her husband and their good friend. During a difficult period of their triadic relationship, Peck sought emotional support from friends and instead found that

> any of our close friends that we approached with it had a lot of judgments about it and actually we got ostracized from several communities because of it. People [who] really cared about us said, "That's the wrong thing to do, we can't believe you are doing that." . . . There

was no positive information being said. It was tearing apart our family.

Regardless of potential power shifts in intimate relationships, polyamorous women retained their positions relative to the power base of monogamous society. This created some problems for them, primary among which was the anomic pain borne of failing to fit in to a monogamous society. Many discussed the social intolerance and fear of censure that sometimes accompanied their polyamorous lifestyle. Dylan described this as "being profoundly unacceptable on many levels." Peck detailed the legal difficulties that plagued her when she was married to one man but had a child with another and wanted the "real" father's name listed on the birth certificate. Ultimately she chose to divorce, partially to disentangle herself from legal issues surrounding multiple-partner relationships.[5]

While all of the polyamorous women in my sample faced the social risks of stigma, the women of color felt at greater risk of stigma and consequences for engaging in polyamory than did the white women I interviewed. Yansa detailed her reasons for remaining closeted at work:

> At the time, I was a president's assistant, and I was working for the Union Bank of Switzerland, and I was like an assistant and I was pretty high up there, and I supported eight executives who went to Wharton and Harvard and they were Republicans and assholes and their wives had nannies and they lived in like houses on hills and they were very just very closed minded. And that, but I got the impression that they were already not comfortable with me, being a person of color. To throw in the other stuff that I did may confirm their stereotypes about black people or it may have just gone, they may have just thought she's the weirdest shit on the planet, I don't trust her, I want her out of here. We don't want her in this job any more, someone may find her out.

While other women detailed reasons for remaining closeted and felt that they risked losing their jobs if they were exposed as polyamorists at work, none of the white women linked their feelings of fear or vulnerability at work with race.

Conclusions

The polyamorous women who participated in this ethnographic study related their experiences of attempting to expand their social roles, explore sexuality (especially bisexuality), and create and maintain the assorted power arrangements associated with polyamorous relationships, with varied results. Many of the women in my sample discussed feelings of power, with feelings of empowerment and disempowerment coexisting in the same relationships. While very few of the respondents explicity linked access to shifting power dynamics and social arrangements with race, the impact of race and class privilege cannot be ignored. The fact that the majority of these polyamorous women have considerable financial and cultural capital to fall back on should their nontraditional relationships fail made this complex and somewhat risky relationship style more accessible to them than it might have been to women with fewer social or personal resources. It is no coincidence, then, that women with class and race privilege reported feeling greater freedom in relationship style. The ample resources they commanded conferred increased ability to transgress social boundaries since their cultural cachet created the safety net that allowed them to challenge monogamous social norms while simultaneously weathering the storms of the complex relationship style. My findings thus support Becker's (1963) conclusion that those with power are at greater liberty to alter the social fabric around them.

The women in my sample recognized and rejected the propensity to define female sexual desire in male terms. Many were aware of their transgressions and sought the company of others who supported their efforts to reshape dominant forms of female sexuality in a way that better met their needs. They experienced some success at a gynocentric redefinition of sexuality, gaining greater social power within polyamorous communities and relationships. By rejecting conventional social mores, polyamorous women were forced to create their own roles and examine their sexual relationships. Reflexive action necessitated

greater sexual subjectivity and encouraged polyamorous women to shed a more limiting form of relationship for one that allowed greater freedom and self-expression.

Shifts in the base of relational power may have endowed polyamorous women with greater power because their ostensible greater ease in finding additional partners translated to greater capital within the relationship. Coltrane and Collins (2001, 265) discuss the relationship "market" and conclude, "Whom a person will be able to 'trade' with depends on matching up with someone of the same market value. . . . [This market value depends on the] bundle of resources each person has to offer." Increased access to other lovers amplifies the resources of the more sought-after lover. In this market-based relationship model, successful polyamorous women (and especially bisexual women) would indeed have greater power in their relationships because of their superior market worth. At least for some polyamorous women, the expanded horizons of choice conferred greater power than that which they experienced in monogamous relationships. . . .

Though numerous women in my sample reported feelings of empowerment, they simultaneously discussed experiences that left them feeling disempowered in their own relationships or larger, monogamous society through the impacts of stigma. Sexuality remains a contested region, and women who challenge it often do so at a cost. The promise of sexual freedom, which theoretically accompanied the sexual revolution beginning in the 1960s, translated into increased sexual freedom for men, but not for women. Feminist theorists hypothesize that it "released" women's sexual appetites in the service of male sexual desire and retained an androcentric focal point (Jeffreys 1990). Many polyamorous women experienced the lingering affects of this stalled sexual liberation when they felt periodically objectified as sex toys. Others grated at the assumption that they would perform the majority of emotional management in an extremely high-maintenance relational style (Hochschild 1983). While polyamorous women offered new visions of expanded sexual subjectivity and alternative roles for women, many continued to struggle under the yoke of an androcentric society that demands that women's sexuality function in the service of men. Even though they reported varying degrees of success in their attempts to create new roles and power dynamics within their own relationships, they continued to live with the impacts of stigma attributed by a monogamous society that views their actions as deviant. In both cases, they were unable to completely reform power dynamics in either their own relationships or society at large.

Lorde (1984, 53) eloquently links oppression with sexual systems designed to suppress women's erotic selves and silence women's authentic sexual spirit: "In order to perpetuate itself, every oppression must corrupt or distort those various sources of power within the culture of the oppressed that can provide energy for change. For women, this has meant suppression of the erotic as a considered source of power and information within our lives."

Erasure of women's erotic power has deleterious effects on other areas of their lives as well (Collins 1990; Tolman 2002; L. Rubin 1990a; see also L. Rubin 1990b). While polyamorous women created an incomplete and flawed liberation from androcentric definitions of sexuality, they nonetheless attempted to redefine sexuality on their own terms. Ultimately, polyamorous women's attempts at self-redefinition were active resistance to suppression. Even though their defiance was imperfect and left their emancipation unfinished, they still attempted to forge lives outside of the narrow confines allowed by heterocentric patriarchal culture. Any attempts at liberation serve to undermine the suppression of women and sexual minorities and are worthy of recognition in their myriad forms.

Notes

1. This research is part of a larger project in which I examine polyamorous subcultures in a midsized, Western college town I call Keegan and the San Francisco Bay Area. This portion addresses solely polyamorous women; other articles and my forthcoming book address community, men, family, and present a typology of those involved in polyamory.

2. Of the forty people I interviewed, two were Asian American (one woman, one man), one was a Latina, one was Latina and white, and three were African American (two men and one woman). The woman who identified as a Lebanese American did not define herself as a person of color, and I respected her self-definition. I intentionally sought out people of color to interview whenever possible, and all accepted my invitation. There was a similar racial and ethnic mix of polyamorists I interacted with at social gatherings.

3. Ricco, a white social worker in his early forties and father of two, echoed Emmanuella's opinion with his characterization of his local polyamorous community: "seems like there are lots of lonely, desperate men looking for women and the women can pick and choose."

4. The term "polyamory" had not yet been coined when Dylan was fourteen, but what she practiced and publicly claimed as her identity mirrored what was later to become known as polyamory.

5. While Peck legally divorced her husband, she remained in sexual and emotional relationships with both men in her triad. For a more detailed discussion of polyamorous divorce, please see my forthcoming article on the polyamorous family.

References

Anapol, D. 1997. *Polyamory: The new love without limits: Secrets of sustainable intimate relationships*. San Rafael, CA: IntiNet Resource Center.

Bartell, G. 1971. *Group sex: A scientist's eyewitness report on the American way of swinging*. New York: Van Rees.

Becker, H. 1963. *Outsiders: Studies in the sociology of deviance*. London: Free Press of Glencoe.

Cloud, J. 1999. Henry and Mary and Janet and . . . *Time Magazine* 154 (20): 90–91.

Collins, P. H. 1990. *Black feminist thought: Knowledge, consciousness and the politics of empowerment*. New York: Routledge, Chapman and Hall.

Coltrane, S., and R. Collins. 2001. *Sociology of marriage and the family: Gender, love and property*. Belmont, CA: Wadsworth.

Connell, R. W. 1987. *Gender and power*. Stanford, CA: Stanford University Press.

———. 1995. *Masculinities*. Berkeley: University of California Press.

Constantine, L., and J. Constantine. 1973. *Group marriage*. New York: Collier Books.

Crawford, M., and D. Popp. 2003. Sexual double standards: A review and methodological critique of

two decades of research. *Journal of Sex Research* 40 (1): 13–26.

Crawley, S., and K. Broad. 2004. Be your (real lesbian) self: Mobilizing sexual formula stories through personal (and political) storytelling. *Journal of Contemporary Ethnography* 33 (1): 39–71.

Dunn, J. 1998. Defining women: Notes toward an understanding of structure and agency in the negotiation of sex. *Journal of Contemporary Ethnography* 26 (4): 479–510.

Dworkin, A. 1979. *Pornography: Men possessing women.* New York: E. P. Dutton.

Easton, D., and C. Liszt. 1997. *The ethical slut.* San Francisco: Greenery.

Fang, B. 1976. Swinging: In retrospect. *The Journal of Sex Research* 12:220–37.

Gould, T. 1999. *The lifestyle: A look at the erotic rites of swingers.* Buffalo, NY: Firefly.

Henshel, A. 1973. Swinging: A study of decision making in marriage. *American Journal of Sociology* 4:885–91.

Hochschild, A. 1983. *The managed heart: Commercialization of human feeling.* Berkeley: University of California Press.

Hutchins, L., and L. Kaahumani, eds. 1991. *Bi any other name: Bisexual people speak out.* Los Angeles: Alyson.

Jeffreys, S. 1990. *Anticlimax: A feminist perspective on the sexual revolution.* London: Women's Press.

Jenefsky, C., and D. Miller. 1998. Girl-girl sex in penthouse. *Women's Studies International Forum* 21 (4): 375–85.

Jenks, R. 1998. Swinging: A review of the literature. *Archives of Sexual Behavior* 27(5): 507–22.

Jones, J. 1997. *Alfred C. Kinsey: A public/private life.* New York: Norton.

Kurtz, S. 2003. Heather has 3 parents. *National Review Online*, March 12. Available at http://www.nationalreview.com/kurtz/kurtz031203.asp.

Lorde, A. 1984. *Sister outsider: Essays and speeches.* Trumansburg, NY: Crossing.

MacKinnon, C. 1986. Pornography as sex discrimination. *Law and Inequality: A Journal of Theory and Practice* 38 (4): 38–39.

Martin, K. 1996. *Puberty, sexuality, and the self: Girls and boys at adolescence.* New York: Routledge.

Michael, R., J. Gagnon, E. Laumann, and G. Kolata. 1994. *Sex in America: A definitive survey.* Boston: Little, Brown.

Nearing, R. 1992. *Polyfidelity primer.* 3rd ed. Captain Cook, HI: PEP.

Ramazanoglu, C., and J. Holland. 1993. Women's sexuality and men's appropriation of desire. In *Up against Foucault,* edited by C. Ramazanoglu. New York: Routledge.

Risman, B., and P. Schwartz. 2002. After the sexual revolution: Gender politics in teen dating. *Contexts* 1 (1): 16–24.

Roof, J. 1991. *A lure of knowledge: Lesbian sexuality and theory.* New York: Columbia University Press.

Rubin, L. 1990a. *Erotic wars: What happened to the sexual revolution?* New York: Farrar, Straus, and Giroux.

——— 1990b. *Intimate strangers: Men and women together.* New York: Harper Perennial.

Rubin, R. 2001. Alternative family lifestyles revisited, or whatever happened to swingers, group marriage and communes? *Journal of Family Issues* 7(6): 711–27.

Rust, P. 1993. Coming out in the age of social constructionism: Sexual identity formation among lesbian and bisexual women. *Gender and Society* 7(1): 50–77.

Sedgwick, E. 1990. *The epistemology of the closet.* Berkeley: University of California Press.

Shalet, A., G. Hunt, and K. Joe-Laidler. 2003. Respectability and autonomy: The articulation and meaning of sexuality among the girls in the gang. *Journal of Contemporary Ethnography* 32 (1): 108–43.

Smith, J., and L. Smith, eds. 1974. *Beyond monogamy: Recent studies of sexual alternatives in marriage.* Baltimore: The Johns Hopkins University Press.

Swedberg, D. 1989. What do we see when we see woman/woman sex in pornographic movies? *NWSA Journal* 1 (4): 602–16.

Tannenbaum, L. 1999 *Slut! Growing up female with a bad reputation.* New York: Seven Stories.

Tolman, D. 2002. *Dilemmas of desire: Teenage girls talk about sexuality.* Boston: Harvard University Press.

Weinberg, M., C. Williams, and D. Pryor. 1994. *Dual attraction: Understanding bisexuality.* New York: Oxford University Press.

———. 2001. Bisexuals at midlife: Commitment, salience, and identity. *Journal of Contemporary Ethnography* 30 (2): 180–208.

West, C. 1996. *Lesbian polyfidelity.* San Francisco: Bootlegger.

Yip, A. 1997. Gay male Christian couples and sexual exclusivity. *Sociology* 31 (2): 289–306.

Mothering and the Family

The family is the primary site where gender is enacted and reproduced. Historically, within the United States, the family was considered women's appropriate domain. Essentialist ideas of women depicted their capacity and inclination to care for home and children as biologically based and natural. Over the past few decades, however, the family has undergone dramatic shifts in composition and in the ways that women and men enact their gendered roles. The male breadwinner, female housewife, nuclear family model was the dominant family form in the United States for a relatively brief period of time following World War II to the early 1960s, and for many groups it has never been the most typical model. In the early 2000s, married couples with children are only about 25 percent of all families and in the majority of these families, both mother and father are employed outside the home. There are actually more *nonfamily* households, that is people living alone or with unrelated people (31 percent), than married couples with children (Fields and Casper 2001). The family form has become more diverse but the ideolo-

gies relating to families and motherhood remain powerful forces shaping our identities, institutions, and social values.

Motherhood is one of the most highly cherished and idealized aspects of women's lives. A good mother embodies our ideals of unselfish love, care, and devotion. A bad mother, on the contrary, is reviled as perversely unfeminine, selfish, and dangerous to her children and the larger society. There have always been debates about whether stay-at-home moms or working moms were better for kids. Today's media celebrities compare alpha (super) and beta (slacker) moms. Whatever the specific terms of the debate, women seem to struggle with unrealistic expectations for performing the role of mother.

People's valuations of good and bad mothers shift across time and reflect the intersectional influences of race and class. The ability of women to choose motherhood and to care for their children is not primarily an individual decision but is shaped by social ideologies, law and policy, and the distribution of resources. Motherhood is idealized in the United States but the practicalities of mothering are left to individuals and their families. As Joan Blades and Kristin Rowe-Finkbeiner point out in their "motherhood manifesto," the United States is the only industrialized nation that does not have national childcare and paid maternal leave policies. This lack of structural support has a direct correlation with the wage gap. The gap in earnings is larger between women with children and those without than between women and men. Without structural supports, motherhood is more of a privilege enjoyed by some women than a right available to all women.

The essays in this section discuss both the practical challenges facing mothers and the symbolic power of ideal images of the family and motherhood. Patricia Hill Collins describes the ways that family serves as both an ideology and a fundamental principle of social organization (1998: 63). It is an ideology that prescribes the cultural meaning of family and an organizing principle that informs access to resources and status. She refers to the family as "a privileged exemplar of intersectionality in the United States" (1998: 63). The family, rather than being a universal form, reflects and generates unique patterns of inclusion and exclusion. Collins identifies six ways that the family ideal informs and organizes social relationships: naturalizing hierarchies, maintaining borders, segmenting society into mutually exclusive racial groups, delineating rights and responsibilities based on membership, regulating the transmission of wealth and property (omitted from this condensed version), and framing discussions of population and family planning. Her analysis illuminates the salience of race and gender for understanding how the family ideal perpetuates inequalities and exclusions. She recommends a transformation of the family ideal that rejects hierarchies and is grounded in a dedication to democratic ends.

Deborah Eicher-Catt provides a poignant description of her experience as a non-custodial mother. In trying to perform as a "competent mother" in the atypical position of not having physical custody of her kids, Eicher-Catt confronted the idealized expectations of mothers and the social approbation directed at women who violate them. Eicher-Catt employs semiotic and communications theory to illustrate how mothering in the absence of one's children is a performance accountable to multiple audiences, including herself and her children. Her performance is more visible since she violates the basic assumption that mothers live with

their children. Eicher-Catt describes her experience as a cultural paradox. She is a mother who does not conform to social expectations of mothering. Her insecurities about her adequacy as a mother and the choices she has made mirror the experiences of many women who cannot physically be with their children—immigrant women who leave their children behind in order to earn money for their survival, sick and incapacitated women, and incarcerated women. Yet she resists the position of victim and uses her situation to work toward an alternative practice of mothering that confirms her relationship with her sons and alters the meanings of motherhood. She is able to use her everyday interactions during visitations to craft an identity as a competent mother with deep emotional ties and commitments to her children while violating the dominant expectation of shared residency.

Eicher-Catt's analysis sheds light on another group of non-custodial mothers, women in jail. With Angela M. Moe, I spoke with incarcerated women about their children. For many women, their crimes were connected to their efforts to provide for their children in a context of extreme poverty. All of the women were victims of interpersonal violence, and domestic violence figured directly in several women's crimes. Women sold drugs, committed welfare fraud, or wrote bad checks as a way to pay for rent, utilities, and food. Other women who were abused lost custody of their children due to their husband's abuse and their own use of drugs or alcohol. Women with children, who made up 90 percent of our interviewees, did not receive help from the children's fathers and were solely responsible for all aspects of their care. Their mothering simultaneously reproduced the sexual division of labor and offered them pleasure, hope, and resistance to marginalization and despair. Women internalized the social condemnation directed against "crack mothers," prostitutes, and petty thieves. Two women who used crack while pregnant, one of whom lost her baby, described themselves as monsters and suffered enormous guilt and sadness. Other women who had lost custody of their children clung to the belief that they would someday be reunited. Although worry about the effects of incarceration on their children and sadness over loss of custody were the most painful aspects of imprisonment, women drew on their position as mothers to construct and sustain positive identities.

Mothering and the social ideology of good mothering may be a vector of the social control of women. It is also, however, a resource from which women draw love, pleasure, purpose, and identity. Women mother their children in many ways, some of which are more socially rewarded than others. But all women's ability to mother depends on the social policies and resources that facilitate the job that we symbolically hold in the highest regard.

References

Collins, Patricia Hill. (2001). "It's All in the Family: Intersections of Gender, Race, and Nation." *Hypatia* 13(3):62–82.

Fields, Jason, and Lynne M. Casper. (2001). *America's Families and Living Arrangements: March 2000.* Current Population Reports, P20-537. Washington, DC: US Census Bureau.

Joan Blades
Kristin Rowe-Finkbeiner

The Motherhood Manifesto

In the deep quiet of a still-dark morning, Renee reaches her arm out from under her thick flowered comforter and across the bed to hit the snooze button on her alarm clock. For a few blessed (and pre-planned) minutes she avoids the wakeful classic rock blaring into her bedroom from her alarm. Renee hits the snooze button exactly three times before finally casting off her covers. She does this each morning, and each morning she sleepily thinks the same thing: "It's too early. I was just at work two seconds ago, and I don't want to go back already."

Everything about Renee's morning is structured for speed and efficiency. At 5:45, with her young son, Wade, and husband, Alan, still sleeping, Renee drags herself out of bed and sleepwalks to the shower. She brushes her teeth while the shower is warming, making sweeping circles on the mirror with her hand so she can see her reflection. Renee's movements, though she's thoroughly tired, are crisp, hurried and automatic—she's repeated the routine daily for several years.

Renee knows exactly how long each of her morning tasks will take, to the minute. That, for instance, between 6 and 6:12 she needs to put on her makeup, get herself dressed, get her son's clothes out and ready for the day, and get downstairs to the kitchen to start breakfast.

All this is done with an eye on the clock and a subtle, yet constant, worry about time. Her mind loops over the potential delays that could be ahead: "Is there going to be traffic? Am I going to get stuck behind a school bus? Is my son going to act normal when I drop him off or is he going to be stuck to my leg? Am I going to get a parking space in the office garage or am I going to have to run five blocks through the city to get to work on time?" And if there isn't any garage parking, which happens often, then in order to be on time for work Renee has to run up six flights of stairs in heels because she doesn't have extra time to waste waiting for an elevator. She's done this climb more than once.

Why the stress? At her work, if Renee is late more than six times, she's in danger of losing her job. Like many American mothers, Renee needs her income to help provide for her family. In our modern economy, where more often than not two wage earners are needed to support a family, American women now make up 46 percent of the entire paid labor force. In fact, a study released last June found that in order to maintain income levels, parents have to work more hours—two-parent families are spending 16 percent more time at work, or 500 more hours a year, than in 1979.

Despite all the media chatter about the so-called Opt-Out Revolution—and all the hand-wringing about whether working moms are good for kids—women, and mothers, are in the workplace to stay. Yet public policy and workplace structures have yet to catch up. . . .

For example, the option of flextime would make a world of difference for Renee and her family. "Flextime would make a huge difference in my life because with my job function, there are busy days and late days. As long as I'm there forty

Source: "The Motherhood Manifesto," by Joan Blades and Kristin Rowe-Finkbeiner. Reprinted with permission from the May 22, 2006 issue of *The Nation.* For subscription information, call 1-800-333-8536. Portions of each week's Nation magazine can be accessed at http://www.thenation.com.

hours a week and get my job done, then I don't know why anyone would care. I don't understand why there's such an 8 AM to 5 PM 'law' in my workplace."

Seemingly mundane challenges like getting out the door in time for work and the morning commute, Renee tells us, become overwhelming when coupled with the financial anxieties that face so many families in America. Renee and Alan would like to have a second child, but they worry that they simply can't afford one right now. "By no means do we live, or want to live, extravagantly: We just want two cars, two kids and a vacation here and there," says Renee.

She and millions of other parents across the country are seriously struggling to meet the demands of work and parenthood. Vast numbers of women are chronically tired and drained. But the American credo teaches us to be fierce individualists, with the result that most parents toil in isolation and can't envision, or don't expect, help. It's time to recognize that our common problems can be addressed only by working together to bring about broad and meaningful change in our families, communities, workplaces and nation.

It's often said that motherhood is perhaps the most important, and most difficult, job on the planet. This cliché hits fairly close to the mark. While we raise our children out of an innate sense of love and nurturing, we also know that raising happy, healthy children who become productive adults is critical to our future well-being as a nation.

But right now, motherhood in America is at a critical juncture. As women's roles continue to evolve, more women than ever are in the workforce and most children are raised in homes without a stay-at-home parent. At the same time, public and private policies that affect parenting and the workplace remain largely unchanged. We have a twenty-first-century economy stuck with an outdated, industrial-era family support structure. The result is that parents, mothers in particular, are struggling to balance the needs of their children with the demands of the workplace.

America's mothers are working, and working hard. Almost three-quarters have jobs outside their homes. Then, too, America's mothers are working hard but for less money than men (and less money than women who are not mothers). In fact, the wage gap between mothers and nonmothers is greater than that between nonmothers and men—and it's actually getting bigger. One study found that nonmothers with an average age of 30 made 90 cents to a man's dollar, while moms made only 73 cents to the dollar, and single moms made 56 to 66 cents to a man's dollar.

"It is well-established that women with children earn less than other women in the United States," writes Jane Waldfogel of Columbia University in *The Journal of Economic Perspectives*. "Even after controlling for differences in characteristics such as education and work experience, researchers typically find a family penalty of 10–15 percent for women with children as compared to women without children."

What's more, it's still common for women and men to hold the same job and receive different pay. In fact, women lost a cent between 2002 and 2003, according to the US Census, and now make 76 cents to a man's dollar. Most of these wage hits are coming from mothers, because the lower wages they receive drag down the overall average pay for all women.

The United States has a serious mommy wage gap. Why? Because, as Waldfogel writes, "The United States does at least as well as other countries in terms of equal pay and equal opportunity legislation, but . . . the United States lags in the area of family policies such as maternity leave and childcare." Studies show that this mommy wage gap is directly correlated with our lack of family-friendly national policies like paid family leave and subsidized childcare. In countries with these family policies in place, moms don't take such big wage hits.

Consider one family-friendly policy: paid family leave. The United States is the only industrialized country that doesn't have paid leave other than Australia (which does give a full year of guaranteed unpaid leave to all women, compared with the scant twelve weeks of unpaid leave given to those who work for companies in the

United States with more than fifty employees). A full 163 countries give women paid leave with the birth of a child. Fathers as well often get paid leave in other countries—forty-five give fathers the right to paid parental leave.

By way of example, our close neighbor to the north, Canada, gives the mother fifteen weeks of partial paid parental leave for physical recovery, and then gives another thirty-five weeks of partial paid leave that has to be taken before the child turns 1. These thirty-five weeks of parental leave can be taken by the mother or the father, or can be shared between the two.

Sweden, with about a year of paid family leave and some time specifically reserved for fathers, is often held up as a model. Not surprisingly, with this support, Ann Crittenden writes in *The Price of Motherhood*, "Swedish women on average have higher incomes, vis-á-vis men, than women anywhere else in the world."

America, on the other hand, generally leaves it up to parents to patch together some type of leave on their own. Some states are starting to give more support to new parents, but only one of our fifty states, California, offers paid family leave. The federal government simply doesn't offer a paid family leave program at all. A weighty consequence emerges from this lack of family support. Research reveals that a full 25 percent of "poverty spells," or times when a family's income slips below what is needed for basic living expenses, begin with the birth of a baby.

Speak to mothers across the nation and you will hear that the vast majority of them find they hit an economic "maternal wall" after having children. By most accounts, this wall is why a large number of professional women leave the workforce, and it's a core reason so many mothers and their children live in poverty. Amy Caiazza, from the Institute for Women's Policy Research, notes, "If there wasn't a wage gap, the poverty rates for single moms would be cut in half, and the poverty rates for dual earner families would be cut by about 25 percent."

But mothers across America are not just crying out for better (or at least fair and equal) pay;

they are also yearning to live a life in which they aren't cracking under pressure, a life in which they know that their children will be well cared for, a life in which it's possible to be at home with their son or daughter even just one afternoon a week without worrying about sacrificing a disproportionate amount of their income and benefits—or losing their job altogether. Some would argue that mothers just need to find the proper balance between parenting and career. We believe there's more to it than that.

While Renee's story captures the essence of what millions of working American women face each morning, Kiki's daunting experience simply trying to find a job shows just how deeply rooted, and widely accepted, discrimination against mothers has become.

A single mother of two, Kiki moved to a one-stoplight Pennsylvania town in 1994. She was truly on her own. Her husband had left several years earlier, when her children were 2 and 4. Kiki hadn't known how she'd make it as a single parent until her mother, a petite powerhouse and survivor of a World War II Russian gulag, stepped in to help. But when Kiki's mother died, there was nothing to keep Kiki in the Long Island town where she'd been living. The rapid property-tax increases in Kiki's carefully landscaped neighborhood of gorgeous Colonial houses were quickly exceeding her economic reach as a single working mother. So Kiki left in search of a smaller town with a lower cost of living.

With this move, Kiki and the kids were alone in a new town that had just two supermarkets. Several diners served a variety of aromatically enticing pork, sauerkraut and dumpling dishes. It was just the change she wanted. Kiki was able to buy a Dutch Colonial house at the top of a small mountain in the Poconos with nearly two acres of land for a fraction of the price of her old house. It seemed ideal, until she started looking for a job to support her family.

On a hot, humid August day, at an interview for a legal secretary position in a one-story brick building, Kiki sat down in a hard wooden chair to face a middle-aged attorney ensconced behind a mahogany desk. His framed diplomas lined the walls, and legal books filled the shelves behind him. Kiki remembers the attorney clearly, even his height of 5'10" and the color of his light brown hair. The interaction was significant enough to remain seared in her mind a decade later. "The first question the attorney asked me when I came in for the interview was, Are you married? The second was, Do you have children?"

It was the eleventh job interview in which she'd been asked the very same questions. After answering eleven times that she wasn't married, and that she was the mother of two, Kiki began to understand why her job search was taking so long.

She decided to address the issue head-on this time. "I asked him how those questions were relevant to the job, and he said my hourly wage would be determined by my marital and motherhood status." What's that? "He said, If you don't have a husband and have children, then I pay less per hour because I have to pay benefits for the entire family." The attorney noted that a married woman's husband usually had health insurance to cover the kids, and since Kiki didn't have a husband, he "didn't want to get stuck with the bill for my children's health coverage."

The attorney insisted that this blatant discrimination was perfectly legal—and he was right. Pennsylvania, like scores of states, does not have employment laws that protect mothers.

Recent Cornell University research by Shelley Correll confirms what many American women are finding: Mothers are 44 percent less likely to be hired than nonmothers who have the same résumé, experience and qualifications; and mothers are offered significantly lower starting pay. Study participants offered nonmothers an average of $11,000 more than equally qualified mothers for the same high-salaried job. Correll's ground-breaking research adds to the long line of studies that explore the roots of this maternal wage gap. "We expected to find that moms were going to be discriminated against, but I was surprised by the magnitude of the gap," explains Correll. "I expected small numbers, but we found huge numbers. Another thing was that fathers were actually advantaged, and we didn't expect fathers to be offered more money or to be rated higher." But that's what happened.

The "maternal wall" is a reality we must address if we value both fair treatment in the workplace and the contributions working mothers make to our economy.

Stories like those of Renee and Kiki confirm that something just isn't right about what we're doing—or not doing—to address the needs of mothers across our nation. Some companies and states are experimenting with family-friendly programs, but such programs are not the norm. We need to open a whole new conversation about motherhood by illuminating the universal needs of America's mothers and spelling out concrete solutions that will provide families—whether working- or middle-class—with real relief.

National policies and programs with proven success in other countries—like paid family leave, flexible work options, subsidized childcare and preschool, as well as healthcare coverage for all kids—are largely lacking in America. The problems mothers face are deeply interconnected and often overlap: Without paid family leave parents often have to put their infants in extremely expensive or substandard childcare facilities; families with a sick child, inadequate healthcare coverage and no flexible work options often end up in bankruptcy.

Fixing even one of these problems often has numerous positive repercussions. Companies that embrace family-friendly workplace policies are thriving, with lower employee turnover, enhanced productivity and job commitment from employees, and consequently with lower recruiting and retraining costs. Flexible work options also allow parents to create work schedules that are well suited to raising happy, healthy children.

The good news is that more enlightened policies would provide practical benefits to the whole society. But we need a genuine motherhood revolution to achieve this sort of change. We believe the following Motherhood Manifesto points are a good place to start:

§ **M** = Maternity/Paternity Leave: Paid family leave for all parents after a new child comes into the family.

§ **O** = Open, Flexible Work: Give parents the ability to structure their work hours and careers in a way that allows them to meet both business and family needs. This includes flexible work hours and locations, part-time work options and the ability to move in and out of the labor force without penalties to raise young children.

§ **T** = TV We Choose & Other After-School Programs: Offer safe, educational opportunities for children after school doors close, including a clear and independent universal television rating system for parents along with technology that allows them to choose what is showing in their own homes; quality educational programming for kids; expanded after-school programs.

§ **H** = Healthcare for All Kids: Provide quality, universal healthcare to all children.

§ **E** = Excellent Childcare: Quality, affordable childcare should be available to all parents. Childcare providers should be paid at least a living wage and healthcare benefits.

§ **R** = Realistic and Fair Wages: Two full-time working parents should be able to earn enough to care for their family. And working mothers must receive equal pay for equal work.

By tackling these interconnected issues together, we can create a powerful system of support for families, improving the quality of our lives and making sure our children inherit a world in which they will thrive as adults and parents. The Motherhood Manifesto is a call to action, summoning all Americans—mothers, and all who have mothers—to start a revolution to make motherhood compatible with life, liberty and the pursuit of happiness.

Patricia Hill Collins

It's All In the Family: Intersections of Gender, Race, and Nation

Intersectionality has attracted substantial scholarly attention in the 1990s. Rather than examining gender, race, class, and nation as distinctive social hierarchies, intersectionality examines how they mutually construct one another. I explore how the traditional family ideal functions as a privileged exemplar of intersectionality in the United States. Each of its six dimensions demonstrates specific connections between family as a gendered system of social organization, racial ideas and practices, and constructions of U.S. national identity.

When former vice president Dan Quayle used the term *family values* near the end of a speech at a political fundraiser in 1992, he apparently touched a national nerve. Following Quayle's speech, close to three hundred articles using the term *family values* in their titles appeared in the popular press. Despite the range of political perspectives expressed on "family values," one thing remained clear—"family values," however defined, seemed central to national well-being. The term *family values* constituted a touchstone, a phrase that apparently tapped much deeper feelings about the significance of ideas of family, if not actual families themselves, in the United States.

Situated in the center of "family values" debates is an imagined traditional family ideal. Formed through a combination of marital and blood ties, ideal families consist of heterosexual couples that produce their own biological children. Such families have a specific authority

Source: "It's All in the Family: Intersections of Gender, Race, and Nation," by Patricia Hill Collins. *Hypatia*, Volume 13, Issue 3, pp. 62–82. Used by permission of the Indiana University Press.

structure; namely, a father-head earning an adequate family wage, a stay-at-home wife, and children. Those who idealize the traditional family as a private haven from a public world see family as held together by primary emotional bonds of love and caring. Assuming a relatively fixed sexual division of labor, wherein women's roles are defined as primarily in the home and men's in the public world of work, the traditional family ideal also assumes the separation of work and family. Defined as a natural or biological arrangement based on heterosexual attraction, this monolithic family type articulates with governmental structures. It is organized not around a biological core, but a state-sanctioned, heterosexual marriage that confers legitimacy not only on the family structure itself but on children born into it (Andersen 1991).[1]

The power of this traditional family ideal lies in its dual function as an ideological construction and as a fundamental principle of social organization. As ideology, rhetoric associated with the traditional family ideal provides an interpretive framework that accommodates a range of meanings. Just as reworking the rhetoric of family for their own political agendas is a common strategy for conservative movements of all types, the alleged unity and solidarity attributed to family is often invoked to symbolize the aspirations of oppressed groups. For example, the conservative right and Black nationalists alike both rely on family language to advance their political agendas.

Moreover, because family constitutes a fundamental principle of social organization, the significance of the traditional family ideal transcends ideology. In the United States, understandings of social institutions and social policies are often constructed through family rhetoric. Families constitute primary sites of belonging to various groups: to the family as an assumed biological entity; to geographically identifiable, racially segregated neighborhoods conceptualized as imagined families; to so-called racial families codified in science and law; and to the U.S. nation-state conceptualized as a national family.

The importance of family also overlaps with the emerging paradigm of intersectionality. Building on a tradition from Black Women's Studies, intersectionality has attracted substantial scholarly attention in the 1990s.[2] As opposed to examining gender, race, class, and nation, as separate systems of oppression, intersectionality explores how these systems mutually construct one another, or, in the words of Black British sociologist Stuart Hall, how they "articulate" with one another (Slack 1996). Current scholarship deploying intersectional analyses suggests that certain ideas and practices surface repeatedly across multiple systems of oppression and serve as focal points or privileged social locations for these intersecting systems.[3]

The use of the traditional family ideal in the United States may function as one such privileged exemplar of intersectionality.[4] In this paper, I explore how six dimensions of the traditional family ideal construct intersections of gender, race, and nation. Each dimension demonstrates specific connections between family as a gendered system of social organization, race as ideology and practice in the United States, and constructions of U.S. national identity. Collectively, these six dimensions illuminate specific ways that ideological constructions of family, as well as the significance of family in shaping social practices, constitute an especially rich site for intersectional analysis. . . .

Manufacturing Naturalized Hierarchy

One dimension of family as a privileged exemplar of intersectionality lies in how it reconciles the contradictory relationship between equality and hierarchy. The traditional family ideal projects a model of equality. A well-functioning family protects and balances the interests of all its members—the strong care for the weak, and everyone contributes to and benefits from family membership in proportion to his or her capacities. In contrast to this idealized version, actual families remain organized around varying patterns of hierarchy. As Ann McClintock observes, "the family image came to figure *hierarchy within unity* [emphasis in original] as an organic element of historical progress, and thus became indispensable for legitimating exclusion and hierarchy within nonfamilial social forms such as nationalism, liberal individualism and imperialism" (McClintock 1995, 45). Families are expected to socialize their members into an appropriate set of "family values" that simultaneously reinforce the hierarchy within the assumed unity of interests symbolized by the family and lay the foundation for many social hierarchies. In particular, hierarchies of gender, wealth, age, and sexuality within actual family units correlate with comparable hierarchies in U.S. society. Individuals typically learn their assigned place in hierarchies of race, gender, ethnicity, sexuality, nation, and social class in their families of origin. At the same time, they learn to view such hierarchies as natural social arrangements, as compared to socially constructed ones. Hierarchy in this sense becomes "naturalized" because it is associated with seemingly "natural" processes of the family.

The "family values" that underlie the traditional family ideal work to naturalize U.S. hierarchies of gender, age, and sexuality. For example, the traditional family ideal assumes a male headship that privileges and naturalizes masculinity as a source of authority. Similarly, parental control over dependent children reproduces age and seniority as fundamental principles of social organization. Moreover, gender and age mutually construct one another; mothers comply with fathers, sisters defer to brothers, all with the understanding that boys submit to maternal authority until they become men. Working in tandem with these mutually constructing age and gender hierarchies are comparable ideas concerning sexuality. Predicated on assumptions of heterosexism, the invisibility of gay, lesbian, and bisexual sexualities in the traditional family ideal obscures these sexualities and keeps them hidden. Regardless of how individual families grapple with these hierarchical notions, they remain the received wisdom to be confronted.

In the United States, naturalized hierarchies of gender and age are interwoven with corresponding racial hierarchies, regardless of whether racial hierarchies are justified with reference to biological, genetic differences or to immutable cultural differences (Goldberg 1993). The logic of the traditional family ideal can be used to explain race relations. One way that this occurs is when racial inequality becomes explained using family roles. For example, racial ideologies that portray people of color as intellectually underdeveloped, uncivilized children require parallel ideas that construct Whites as intellectually mature, civilized adults. When applied to race, family rhetoric that deems adults more developed than children, and thus entitled to greater power, uses naturalized ideas about age and authority to legitimate racial hierarchy. Combining age and gender hierarchies adds additional complexity. Whereas White men and White women enjoy shared racial privileges provided by Whiteness, within the racial boundary of Whiteness, women are expected to defer to men. People of color have not been immune from this same logic. Within the frame of race as family, women of subordinated racial groups defer to men of their groups, often to support men's struggles in dealing with racism.

The complexities attached to these relationships of age, gender, and race coalesce in that the so-called natural hierarchy promulgated by the traditional family ideal bears striking resemblance to social hierarchies in U.S. society overall. White men dominate in positions of power, aided by their White female helpmates, both working together to administer to allegedly less-qualified people of color who themselves struggle with the same family rhetoric. With racial ideologies and practices so reliant on family for meaning, family writ large becomes race. Within racial discourse, just as families can be seen naturally occurring, biologically linked entities who share common interests, Whites, Blacks, Native Americans, and other "races" of any given historical period can also be seen this way. The actual racial categories of any given period matter less than the persistent belief in race itself as an enduring principle of social organization that connotes family ties. Thus, hierarchies of gender, age, and sexuality that exist *within* different racial groups (whose alleged family ties lead to a commonality of interest) mirror the hierarchy characterizing relationships *among* groups. In this way, racial inequality becomes comprehensible and justified via family rhetoric.

This notion of naturalized hierarchy learned in family units frames issues of U.S. national identity in particular ways. If the nation-state is conceptualized as a national family with the traditional family ideal providing ideas about family, then the standards used to assess the contributions of family members in heterosexual, married-couple households with children become foundational for assessing group contributions to overall national well-being. Naturalized hierarchies of the traditional family ideal influence understandings of constructions of first- and second-class citizenship. For example, using a logic of birth order elevates the importance of time of arrival in the country for citizenship entitlements. Claims that early-migrating, White Anglo-Saxon Protestants are entitled to more benefits than more recent arrivals resemble beliefs that "last hired, first fired" rules fairly discriminate among workers. Similarly, notions of naturalized gender hierarchies promulgated by the traditional family ideal—the differential treatment of girls and boys regarding economic autonomy and free-access to public space—parallel practices such as the sex-typing of occupations in the paid labor market and male domination in government, professional sports, the streets, and other public spaces.

As is the case with all situations of hierarchy, actual or implicit use of force, sanctions and violence may be needed to maintain unequal power relations. However, the very pervasiveness of violence can lead to its invisibility. For example, feminist efforts to have violence against women in the home taken seriously as a bona fide form of violence and not just a private family matter have long met with resistance. In a similar fashion, the extent of the violence against Native American, Puerto Rican, Mexican-American, African-American, and other groups who were incorporated into the United States not through voluntary migration but via conquest and slavery remains routinely overlooked. Even current violence against such groups remains underreported unless captured in a dramatic fashion, such as the videotaped beating of motorist Rodney King by Los Angeles police officers. Despite their severity and recent increase, hate crimes against gays, lesbians, and bisexuals also remain largely invisible. Through these silences, these forms of violence not only are neglected, they become legitimated. Family rhetoric can also work to minimize understandings of violence in groups that self-define in family terms. In the same way that wife battering and childhood physical and sexual abuse become part of the "family secrets" of far too many families, so does the routine nature of violence targeted against women, gays, lesbians, and children within distinctive racial and ethnic groups.

Subordinated groups often face difficult contradictions in responding to such violence (Crenshaw 1991). One response consists of analyzing one or more hierarchies as being socially constructed while continuing to see others as naturalized. In African-American civil society, for example, the question of maintaining racial solidarity comes face-to-face with the question of how naturalized hierarchies construct one another. Maintaining racial solidarity at all costs often requires replicating hierarchies of gender, social class, sexuality, and nation in Black civil society. Consider, for example, typical understandings of the phrase "Black on Black violence." Stressing violence among Black men permits patterns of Black male violence targeted toward Black women—domestic abuse and sexual harassment in the workplace—to remain hidden and condoned. In the face of sexual harassment, especially at the hands of Black men, African-American women are cautioned not to "air dirty laundry" about internal family problems. The parallel with victims of domestic violence who are encouraged to keep "family secrets" is startling. In general, whether it is family as household, family as a foundation for conceptualizing race, or the national family defined through U.S. citizenship, family rhetoric that naturalizes hierarchy inside and outside the home obscures the force needed to maintain these relationships.

Looking for a Home: Place, Space, and Territory

The multiple meanings attached to the concept of "home"—home as family household, home as neighborhood, home as native country—speak to its significance within family as a privileged exemplar of intersectionality. In the United States, the traditional family ideal's ideas about place, space, and territory suggest that families, racial groups, and nation-states require their own unique places or "homes." Because "homes" provide spaces of privacy and security for families, races, and nation-states, they serve as sanctuaries for group members. Surrounded by individuals who seemingly share similar objectives, these homes represent idealized, privatized spaces where members can feel at ease.

This view of home requires certain gendered ideas about private and public space. Because women are so often associated with family, home space becomes seen as a private, feminized space that is distinct from the public, masculinized space that lies outside its borders. Family space is for members only—outsiders can be invited in only by family members or else they are intruders. Within these gendered spheres of private and public space, women and men again assume distinctive roles. Women are expected to remain in their home "place." Avoiding the dangerous space of public streets allows women to care for children, the sick, and the elderly, and other dependent family members. Men are expected to support and defend the private, feminized space that houses their families. Actual U.S. families rarely meet this ideal. For example, despite feminist analyses that discredit the home as a safe place for women, this myth seems deeply entrenched in U.S. culture (Coontz 1992).

A similar logic concerning place, space, and territory constructs racialized space in the United States.[5] Just as the value attached to actual families reflects their placement in racial and social class hierarchies, the neighborhoods housing these families demonstrate comparable inequalities. Assumptions of race- and class-segregated space mandate that U.S. families and the neighborhoods where they reside be kept separate. Just as crafting a family from individuals from diverse racial, ethnic, religious or class backgrounds is discouraged, mixing different races within one neighborhood is frowned upon. As mini-nation-states, neighborhoods allegedly operate best when racial and/or class homogeneity prevails. Assigning Whites, Blacks, and Latinos their own separate spaces reflects efforts to maintain a geographic, racial purity. As the dominant group, Whites continue to support legal and extra-legal measures that segregate African-Americans, Native Americans, Mexican-Americans, Puerto Ricans, and other similar groups, thereby perpetuating cultural norms about desirability of racial purity in schools, neighborhoods, and public facilities. For example, tactics such as the continual White flight out of inner cities, deploying restrictive zoning in suburban communities in order to restrict low-income housing, and shifting White

children into private institutions in the face of increasingly colored schools effectively maintain racially segregated home spaces for White men, women, and children. This belief in segregated physical spaces also has parallels to ideas about segregated social and symbolic spaces. For example, lucrative professional categories remain largely White and male, in part, because people of color are seen as less capable of entering these spaces. Similarly, keeping school curricula focused on the exploits of Whites represents another example of ideas about segregated spaces mapped on symbolic space. Overall, racial segregation of actual physical space fosters multiple forms of political, economic, and social segregation (Massey and Denton 1993).

Securing a people's "homeland" or national territory has long been important to nationalist aspirations (Anthias and Yuval-Davis 1992; Calhoun 1993). After its successful anticolonial struggle against England and its formation as a nation-state, the United States pursued a sustained imperialist policy in order to acquire much of the land that defines its current borders. This history of conquest illustrates the significance of property in relations of space, place, and territory. Moreover, just as households and neighborhoods are seen as needing protection from outsiders, maintaining the integrity of national borders has long formed a pillar of U.S. foreign policy. Because the United States has operated as a dominant world power since World War II, shielding its own home "soil" from warfare has been a minor theme. Instead, protecting so-called American interests has been more prominent. Individuals and businesses who occupy foreign soil represent extensions of U.S. territory, citizens of the national family who must be defended at all costs.

Overall, by relying on the belief that families have assigned places where they truly belong, images of place, space, and territory link gendered notions of family with constructs of race and nation (Jackson and Penrose 1993). In this logic that everything has its place, maintaining borders of all sorts becomes vitally important. Preserving the logic of segregated home spaces requires strict rules that distinguish insiders from outsiders. Unfortunately, far too often, these boundaries continue to be drawn along the color line.

On "Blood Ties": Family, Race, and Nation

Presumptions of "blood ties" that permeate the traditional family ideal reflect another dimension of how family operates as a privileged exemplar of intersectionality. In the United States, concepts of family and kinship draw strength from the flow of blood as a substance that regulates the spread of rights (Williams 1995). While the legal system continues to privilege heterosexual married couples as the preferred family organization, the importance given to bonds between mothers and children, brothers and sisters, grandmothers and grandchildren, illustrates the significance of biology in definitions of family. Representing the genetic links among related individuals, the belief in blood ties naturalizes the bonds among members of kinship networks. Blood, family, and kin are so closely connected that the absence of such ties can be cause for concern. As the search of adoptees for their "real" families or blood relatives suggests, blood ties remain highly significant for definitions of family.

Given the significance attached to biology, women of different racial groups have varying responsibilities in maintaining blood ties. For example, White women play a special role in keeping family bloodlines pure. Historically, creating White families required controlling White women's sexuality, largely through social norms that advocated pre-marital virginity. By marrying White men and engaging in sexual relations only with their husbands, White women ensured the racial purity of White families. Thus, through social taboos that eschewed pre-marital sexuality and interracial marriage for White women, White families could thereby avoid racial degeneration (Young 1995). When reinserted into naturalized hierarchies of gender, race, class, and nation, and institutionally enforced via mechanisms such as

segregated space and state-sanctioned violence, efforts to regulate sexuality and marriage reinforced beliefs in the sanctity of "blood ties."

Historically, definitions of race in U.S. society also emphasized the importance of blood ties.[6] Biological families and racial families both rely on similar notions. The connections between the race and blood ties were so self-evident that nineteenth-century Black nationalist thinker Alexander Crummell claimed, "races, like families, are the organisms and ordinances of God; a race feeling is of divine origin. The extinction of race feeling is just as possible as the extinction of family feeling. Indeed, a race is a family" (quoted in Appiah 1992, 17). Definitions of race as family in the United States traditionally rested on biological classifications legitimated by science and legally sanctioned by law. By grouping people through notions of physical similarity, such as skin color, facial features, or hair texture, and supported by law and custom, scientific racism defined Whites and Blacks as distinctive social groups (Gould 1981). Just as members of "real" families linked by blood were expected to resemble one another, so were members of racial groups descended from a common bloodline seen as sharing similar physical, intellectual, and moral attributes. Within this logic, those lacking biological similarities became defined as family outsiders, while racially different groups became strangers to one another.

A similar logic can be applied to understandings of nation. One definition views a nation as a group of people who share a common ethnicity grounded in blood ties. Cultural expressions of their peoplehood—their music, art, language, and customs—constitute their unique national identity. Under this ethnic nationalism model, each nation should have its own nation-state, a political entity where the ethnic group can be self-governing. While this understanding of nation has a long history in European cultures (Anthias and Yuval-Davis 1992; Yuval-Davis 1997, 26–29), it is less often applied to questions of U.S. national identity. Instead, the United States is often seen as an important expression of civic nationalism where many different ethnic groups cooperate within the boundaries of one nation-state (Calhoun 1993). In contrast to nation-states where ethnic or tribal membership confers citizenship rights, the democratic principles of the U.S. Constitution promise equality for all American citizens. Regardless of race, national origin, former condition of servitude, and color, all citizens stand equal before the law. Via these principles, the United States aims to craft one nation out of many and to transcend the limitations of ethnic nationalism. . . .

In a situation of naturalized hierarchy, conceptualizing U.S. national identity as composed of racial groups that collectively comprise a U.S. national family fosters differential patterns of enforcement of the rights and obligations of citizenship. Members of some racial families receive full benefits of membership while others encounter inferior treatment. Gender hierarchies add additional complexity. African-American women's experiences with entitlement criteria for 1930s Social Security programs, for example, illustrate how institutionalized racism and gender-specific ideology public policies shaped national public policy. Race was a factor in deciding which occupations would be covered by Social Security. Two occupational categories were expressly excluded from coverage: agricultural and domestic workers, the two categories that included most African-American women. Also, by providing differential benefits to men and women through worker's compensation (for which Black women did not qualify) and mothers's aid, from its inception, Social Security encompassed ideas about gender. Eligibility rules rewarded women who remained in marriages and were supported by their husbands but penalized women who became separated or divorced or who remained single and earned their own way. Black women who were not in stable marriages lacked access to spousal and widows benefits that routinely subsidized White women. In this case, the combination of race-targeted polices concerning occupational category and gender-targeted policies concerning applicants' marital status worked to exclude Black women from benefits (Gordon 1994). On paper, Black women may have been first-class U.S. citizens, but their experiences reveal their second-class treatment. . . .

Family Planning

The significance of the family as an exemplar of intersectionality can also be seen in one final dimension of family rhetoric. Family planning comprises a constellation of options, ranging from coercion to choice, from permanence to reversibility regarding reproduction of actual populations. In the case of individual families, decision-making lies with family members; they decide whether to have children, how many children to have, and how those children will be spaced. Feminist scholars in particular have identified how male control over women's sexual and reproductive capacities has been central to women's oppression (see, for example, Raymond 1993). However, just as women's bodies produce children who are part of a socially constructed family grounded in notions of biological kinship, women's bodies produce the population for the national "family" or nation-state, conceptualized as having some sort of biological oneness. In this sense, family planning becomes important in regulating population groups identified by race, social class, and national status (Heng and Devan 1992; Kuumba 1993).

Social policies designed to foster the health of the United States conceptualized as a national family follow a family planning logic, as demonstrated via eugenic thinking. Early twentieth century "racial hygiene" or eugenic movements compellingly illustrate the thinking that underlies population policies designed to control the motherhood of different groups of women for reasons of nationality and race (Haller 1984; Proctor 1988). Eugenic philosophies and the population policies they supported emerged in political economies with distinctive needs, and in societies with particular social class relations. Common to eugenic movements throughout the world was the view that biology was central to solving social problems. Societies that embraced eugenic philosophies typically aimed to transform social problems into technical problems amenable to biological solutions effected via social engineering. Eugenic approaches thus combined a "philosophy of biological determinism with a belief that science might provide a technical fix for social problems" (Proctor 1988, 286).

Three elements of eugenic thinking seem remarkably similar to themes in American public policy. Those embracing eugenic thinking saw "race and heredity—the birth rates of the fit and the unfit—as the forces that shape[d] . . . political and social developments" (Haller 1984, 78). First, eugenic thinking racializes segments of a given population by classifying people into mutually exclusive racial groups. Because the United States has operated as a racialized state since its inception, race remains a fundamental principle of U.S. social organization. While racial meanings change in response to political and economic conditions, the fundamental belief in race as a guiding principle of U.S. society remains remarkably hardy. Associating diverse racial groups with perceived national interests, a second element of eugenic thinking, also has a long history in the United States. The third feature of eugenic thinking, the direct control of different racial groups through various measures also is present in U.S. politics. So-called positive eugenic—efforts to increase reproduction among the better groups who allegedly carried the outstanding qualities of their group in their genes—and negative eugenic—efforts to prevent the propagation by less desirable groups—also have affected U.S. public policy.

While now seen as an embarrassment, past ideas concerning eugenics gained considerable influence in the United States. As Haller points out, Francis Galton, the founder of the eugenic movement in England, believed that "Anglo-Saxons far outranked the Negroes of Africa, who in turn outranked the Australian aborigines, who outranked nobody. Because he believed that large innate differences between races existed, Galton felt that a program to raise the inherent abilities of

mankind involved the replacement of inferior races by the superior" (Haller 1984, 11). Galton's ideas proved popular in the racially segregated United States. U.S. eugenic laws preceded by twenty years the sterilization laws of other countries, and were seen as pioneering ventures by eugenicists abroad. The U.S. Supreme Court's 1927 *Buck vs. Bell* decision held that sterilization fell within the police power of the state. Reflecting the majority opinion, Oliver Wendell Holmes wrote,

> It would be strange if it could not call upon those who already sap the strength of the state for these lesser sacrifices, often not felt to be such by those concerned, in order to prevent our being swamped by incompetence. It is better for all the world, if instead of waiting for their imbecility, society can prevent those who are manifestly unfit from continuing their kind. The principle that sustains compulsory vaccination is broad enough to cover cutting the Fallopian tubes. . . . Three generations of imbeciles is enough. (Haller 1984, 139)

Given this intellectual context, differential population policies developed for different segments of the U.S. population emerge in direct relation to any group's perceived value within the nation-state.[7] In periods of profound social change, such as the massive European migration that preceded the *Buck vs. Bell* decision, eugenic philosophies can reemerge. With the civil rights, women's, anti-war, and other social movements of the 1950s and 1960s, as well as the growing nonwhite immigrant population of the 1970s and 1980s, the United States experienced profound change. Omi and Winant (1994) interpret the expanding conservative social projects that emerged during this period as a direct response to the perceived gains of Blacks and women. One core feature characterizing the rhetoric of social projects of the Right was a return to the family values of the traditional U.S. family. By associating the ideal family with U.S. national interests, these movements linked those interests to their own political agendas concerning race and gender.

Returning to "family values" not only invoked racial and gendered meanings, it set the stage for reviving a logic of eugenics that could be applied to adolescent pregnancy, women's poverty, street crime, and other social issues.

In this context, contemporary American social policies from the 1960s through the "family values" debate of the 1990s become more comprehensible. When attached to state policy in a racialized nation-state, questions of controlling the sexuality and fertility of women from diverse race, social class, and citizenship groups become highly politicized. For example, White women, especially those of the middle class, are encouraged to reproduce. In contrast, women of color, especially those lacking economic resources or not in state sanctioned marriages, are routinely discouraged from having children (Raymond 1993). Population policies such as providing lavish services to combat infertility for White, middle class women, while offering a limited range of Norplant, Depo Provera, and sterilization to poor African-American women constitute contemporary reflections of the logic of eugenic thinking (Davis 1981; Nsiah-Jefferson 1989).

In the logic of the family as a privileged exemplar of intersectionality, viewing race- and gender-based policies as regulating different forms of social relations is fallacious. Current assumptions see African-Americans as having race, White women as having gender, Black women as experiencing both race and gender, and White men experiencing neither. These assumptions dissipate when confronted with actual population policies designed to regulate the childbearing patterns of different racial and ethnic groups generally, and the mothering experiences of different groups of women in particular.

Reclaiming Family

Family occupies such a prominent place in the language of public discourse in the United States that rejecting it outright might be counterproductive for groups aiming to challenge hierarchies. Because the family functions as a privileged ex-

emplar of intersectionality in structuring hierarchy, it potentially can serve a similar function in challenging that hierarchy. Just as the traditional family ideal provides a rich site for understanding intersectional inequalities, reclaiming notions of family that reject hierarchical thinking may provide an intriguing and important site of resistance.

Many groups aim to dismantle social hierarchy, yet use unexamined ideas about family in crafting their political programs. Consider how Black nationalist-influenced projects within African-American civil society invoke family rhetoric. Sociologist Paul Gilroy (1993) notes that the "trope of kinship" permeates Black understandings of culture and community to the point that African-Americans largely accept the notion of race as family and work within it. In Black-influenced projects, families are seen as building blocks of the nation. The Afrocentric yearning for a homeland for the Black racial family and the construction of a mythical Africa to serve this purpose speaks to the use of this construct. Family language also shapes everyday interactions: African-American strangers often refer to one another as "brother" and "sister"; some Black men refer to each other as "bloods." In hip-hop culture, "homies" are Black males from one's neighborhood, or home community. Within this political framework, Whites remain the strangers, the outsiders who are castigated in Black political thought. Ironically, though the popular press often associates the traditional family ideal with conservative political projects, this rhetoric finds a home in what many African-Americans consider to be the most radical of Black political theories (Appiah 1992; Gilroy 1993).

Feminist politics can contain similar contradictions regarding family. U.S. feminists have made important contributions in analyzing how the traditional family ideal harms women. However, feminism's longing for a sisterhood among women has proved difficult to sustain in the context of U.S. race and class politics. Assumptions of an idealized sisterhood floundered because women of color, among others, questioned their place in the feminist family. Even more significant is the U.S. media's routine characterization of feminism as anti-family. Although much of the backlash against feminism claims that U.S. feminists are anti-family, many women who are not part of this backlash probably remain suspicious of any political movement that questions such an important social institution by appearing to dismiss it. This is unfortunate, because family rhetoric often forms a powerful language to organize people for a variety of ends.

Given the power of family as ideological construction and principle of social organization, Black nationalist, feminist, and other political movements in the United States dedicated to challenging social inequality might consider recasting intersectional understandings of family in ways that do not reproduce inequality. Instead of engaging in endless criticism, reclaiming the language of family for democratic ends and transforming the very conception of family itself might provide a more useful approach.

Notes

1. By dislodging beliefs in the naturalness or normality of any one family form, feminist scholarship analyzes the significance of specific notions of family to gender oppression (Thorne 1992). As Stephanie Coontz (1992) reports, this traditional family ideal never existed, even during the 1950s, a decade that is often assumed to be the era of its realization. Feminist anthropologists also challenge the traditional family ideal by demonstrating that the heterosexual, married couple form in the United States is neither "natural," universal, nor cross-culturally normative (Collier et al. 1992). Recent family scholarship suggests that large numbers of U.S. families never experienced the traditional family ideal, and those who may have once achieved this form are now abandoning it (Coontz 1992; Stacey 1992).

2. In the early 1980s, several African-American women scholar-activists called for a new approach to analyzing Black women's lives. They claimed that African-American women's experiences were shaped not just by race but also by gender, social class, and sexuality. In this tradition, works such as *Women, Race, and Class* by Angela Davis (1981), "A Black Feminist Statement" drafted by the Combahee River Collective

(1982), and Audre Lorde's (1984) classic volume *Sister Outsider* stand as groundbreaking works that explore interconnections among systems of oppression. Subsequent work aimed to name this interconnected relationship with terms such as *matrix of domination* (Collins 1990), and *intersectionality* (Crenshaw 1991). Because Black lesbians were at the forefront in raising the issue of intersectionality, sexuality was one of the emphases in early work by African-American women. However, pervasive homophobia in African-American communities, as evidenced by the reaction to the works of Alice Walker, Ntosake Shange, Michele Wallace and other early modern Black feminists, diverted attention from intersectional analyses that emphasized sexuality. The absence of a developed tradition of queer theory in the academy also worked against more comprehensive intersectional analyses. For early intersectional analyses that included sexuality, see the essays in Barbara Smith's (1983) edited volume *Home Girls: A Black Feminist Anthology.*

3. A wide range of topics, such as the significance of primatology in framing gendered, raced views of nature in modern science (Haraway 1989); the social construction of Whiteness among White women in the United States (Frankenberg 1993); race, gender, and sexuality in the colonial conquest (McClintock 1995); and the interplay of race, class, and gender in welfare state policies in the United States (Brewer 1994; Quadagno 1994) have all received an intersectional treatment. Moreover, the initial emphasis on race, social class, and gender has expanded to include intersections involving sexuality, ethnicity, and nationalism (Anthias and Yuval-Davis 1992; Parker et al. 1992; Daniels 1997).

4. Theoretical and empirical work on women of color's location in work and family not only challenges the traditional family ideal, but paves the way for the more general question of family as a privileged site of intersectionality. For work in this tradition, see Dill 1988, Zinn 1989, and Glenn 1992.

5. In this section, I emphasize land as literal space. However, symbolic space, or the terrain of ideas, is organized via similar principles. Foucault's (1979) idea of disciplinary power in which people are classified and located on a knowledge grid, parallels my discussion of the mapping of symbolic space.

6. By tracing the changing meaning of race in the sixteenth-century *Oxford English Dictionary,* David Goldberg identifies the foundational meanings that

subsequently link race with family. Goldberg notes, "in general, 'race' has been used to signify a 'breed or stock of animals' (1580), a 'genus, species or kind of animal' (1605), or a 'variety of plant' (1605). It refers at this time also to 'the great divisions of mankind' (1580) and especially to 'a limited group of persons descended from a common ancestor' (1581), while only slightly later to a 'tribe, nation or people considered of common stock' " (1600) (Goldberg 1993, 63). Note the connections between animals, nature, family, tribe, and nation.

7. For extended discussions of this concept, see the essays in Bridenthal et al. (1984) *When Biology Became Destiny: Women in Weimar and Nazi Germany.* This volume contains one of the best discussions I have encountered of the links between gender, social class, race, and nation, when policies were actually implemented in one nation state.

References

Andersen, Margaret L. 1991. Feminism and the American family ideal. *Journal of Comparative Family Studies* 22(2)(Summer): 235–46.

Anthias, Floya, and Nira Yuval-Davis. 1992. *Racialized boundaries: Race, nation, gender, colour and class in the anti-racist struggle.* New York: Routledge.

Appiah, Kwame Anthony. 1992. *In my father's house: Africa in the philosophy of culture.* New York: Oxford University Press.

Brewer, Rose. 1994. Race, gender and US state welfare policy: The nexus of inequality for African American families. In *Color, class and country: Experiences of gender,* ed. Gay Young and Bette Dickerson. London: Zed Books.

Bridenthal, Renate, Atina Grossmann, and Marion Kaplan, eds. 1984. *When biology became destiny: Women in Weimar and Nazi Germany.* New York: Monthly Review Press.

Calhoun, Craig. 1993. Nationalism and ethnicity. *Annual Review of Sociology* 19: 211–39.

Collier, Jane, Michelle Z. Rosaldo, and Sylvia Yanagisako. 1992. Is there a family?: New anthropological views. In *Rethinking the family.* See Thorne and Yalom 1992.

Collins, Patricia Hill. 1990. *Black feminist thought: Knowledge, consciousness, and the politics of empowerment.* New York: Routledge, Chapman and Hall.

Combahee River Collective. 1982. A Black feminist statement. In *But some of us are brave,* ed. Gloria T. Hull, Patricia Bell Scott, and Barbara Smith. Old Westbury, NY: Feminist Press.

Coontz, Stephanie. 1992. *The way we never were: American families and the nostalgia trap.* New York: Basic Books.

Crenshaw, Kimberle. 1991. Mapping the margins: Intersectionality, identity politics, and violence against women of color. *Stanford Law Review* 43(6): 1241–99.

Daniels, Jessie. 1997. *White lies.* New York: Routledge.

Davis, Angela Y. 1981. *Women, race, and class.* New York: Random House.

Dill, Bonnie Thornton. 1988. Our mothers' grief: Racial ethnic women and the maintenance of families. *Journal of Family History* 13(4): 415–31.

Foucault, Michel. 1979. *Discipline and punish: The birth of the prison.* New York: Schocken.

Frankenberg, Ruth. 1993. *The social construction of whiteness: White women, race matters.* Minneapolis: University of Minnesota Press.

Gilroy, Paul. 1993. It's a family affair: Black culture and the trope of kinship. In *Small acts: Thoughts on the politics of Black cultures.* New York: Serpent's Tail.

Glenn, Evelyn Nakano. 1992. From servitude to service work: Historical continuities in the racial division of paid reproductive labor. *Signs* 18(1): 1–43.

Goldberg, David Theo. 1993. *Racist culture: Philosophy and the politics of meaning.* Cambridge, MA: Blackwell.

Gordon, Linda. 1994. *Pitied but not entitled: Single mothers and the history of welfare.* Cambridge: Harvard University Press.

Gould, Stephen Jay. 1981. *The mismeasure of man.* New York: W. W. Norton.

Haller, Mark H. 1984 [1963]. *Eugenics: Hereditarian attitudes in American thought.* New Brunswick: Rutgers University Press.

Haraway, Donna. 1989. *Primate visions: Gender, race, and nature in the world of modern science.* New York: Routledge, Chapman and Hall.

Heng, Geraldine, and Janadas Devan. 1992. State fatherhood: The politics of nationalism, sexuality and race in Singapore. In *Nationalisms and sexualities,* ed. Andrew Parker, Mary Russo, Doris Sommer and Patricia Yaeger. New York: Routledge.

Jackson, Peter, and Jan Penrose. 1993. Introduction: Placing "race" and nation. In *Constructions of race, place and nation*, ed. P. Jackson and J. Penrose. Minneapolis: University of Minnesota Press.

Kuumba, Monica Bahati. 1993. Perpetuating neo-colonialism through population control: South Africa and the United States. *Africa Today* 40(3): 79–85.

Lorde, Audre. 1984. *Sister outsider.* Trumansberg, NY: Crossing Press.

Massey, Douglas S., and Nancy A. Denton. 1993. *American apartheid: Segregation and the making of the underclass.* Cambridge: Harvard University Press.

McClintock, Anne. 1995. *Imperial leather.* New York: Routledge.

Nsiah-Jefferson, Laurie. 1989. Reproductive laws, women of color, and low-income women. In *Reproductive laws for the 1990s*, ed. Sherrill Cohen and Nadine Taub. Clifton, NJ: Humana Press.

Oliver, Melvin L., and Thomas M. Shapiro. 1995. *Black wealth/White wealth: A new perspective on racial inequality.* New York: Routledge.

Omi, Michael, and Howard Winant. 1994. *Racial formation in the United States: From the 1960s to the 1990s.* New York: Routledge.

Parker, Andrew, Mary Russo, Doris Sommer, and Patricia Yaeger, eds. 1992. *Nationalisms and sexualities.* New York: Routledge.

Proctor, Robert N. 1988. *Racial hygiene: Medicine under the Nazis.* Cambridge: Harvard University Press.

Quadagno, Jill. 1994. *The color of welfare: How racism undermined the war on poverty.* New York: Oxford University Press.

Raymond, Janice. 1993. *Women as wombs: Reproductive technologies and the battle over women's freedom.* San Francisco: Harper San Francisco.

Slack, Jennifer Daryl. 1996. The theory and method of articulation in cultural studies. In *Stuart Hall: Critical dialogues in cultural studies*, ed. David Morley and Kuan-Hsing Chen. New York: Routledge.

Smith, Barbara, ed. 1983. *Home girls: A Black feminist anthology.* New York: Kitchen Table Press.

Stacey, Judith. 1992. Backward toward the postmodern family: Reflections on gender, kinship, and class in the Silicon Valley. In *Rethinking the family.* See Thorne and Yalom 1992.

Takaki, Ronald. 1993. *A different mirror: A history of multicultural America.* Boston: Little Brown.

Thorne, Barrie. 1992. Feminism and the family: Two decades of thought. In *Rethinking the family: Some feminist questions.* See Thorne and Yalom 1992.

Thorne, Barrie, and Marilyn Yalom, eds. 1992. *Rethinking the family: Some feminist questions.* Boston: Northeastern University Press.

Williams, Brackette F. 1995. Classification systems revisited: Kinship, caste, race, and nationality as the flow of blood and the spread of rights. In *Naturalizing power: Essays in feminist cultural analysis*, ed. Sylvia Yanagisako and Carol Delaney. New York: Routledge.

Young, Robert J. C. 1995. *Colonial desire: Hybridity in theory, culture and race.* New York: Routledge.

Yuval-Davis, Nira. 1997. *Gender and nation.* Thousand Oaks, CA: Sage.

Zinn, Maxine Baca. 1989. Family, race, and poverty in the eighties. *Signs* 14(4):875–84.

Deborah Eicher-Catt

Noncustodial Mothering: A Cultural Paradox of Competent Performance–Performative Competence

This article interrogates the cultural experience of being a noncustodial mother. Framed by the discrete event of child visitation, the author provides a personal account of her struggles to perform successfully in such a constraining context of discourse. Employing a dramatistic metaphor, she extends the praxis of autoethnography by critically exploring the semiotic and phenomenological nature of this communicative experience. She reveals that noncustodial mothering presents a cultural paradox that foregrounds the dialectical movement between a competent performance and a performative competence of mothering. She discusses the implications of this cultural phenomenon in light of the concepts of performativity and la parole that deepens our appreciation of the communicative praxis of ethnography.

As I fold the last batch of warm clothes from the dryer, I glance over at the kitchen clock on the far wall. Oh, dear . . . it's almost four thirty in the afternoon. It's Sunday and I need to get the boys ready to go home to their dad's. If I'm going to get them back on time, we need to leave here no later than 5 p.m. Yes, I remember now their father mentioned on Friday when I picked them up that he had dinner plans for them tonight. Surely he's not cooking. He probably has a church dinner to attend. It still amazes me that he has returned to the church as a practicing Catholic. I would not have predicted that when we got married some fourteen years ago. I never saw it coming.

Of course, I never saw a lot of things coming. The course of my life has changed rather dramatically. I'm divorced, in graduate school, and living without my sons. Most of my possessions and traces of my former life have disappeared.

The signifiers of my past femininity as a homemaker have faded. Things as common as my own dishes, prized linens, and pots and pans have long since been discarded. I always thought that when I had children I'd be the "Kool-Aid, mom," as one of my coparticipants in this study put it. In other words, I'd provide a stable, caring environment that would act as an emotional magnet for not only my own children but the neighborhood children as well. I'd bake my own bread, can fruits and vegetables, be the dutiful wife, and even homeschool my children, perhaps. Like many mothers before me, I fully adopted the cultural definition for what constitutes a "good mother" (Thurer 1994), an intersubjectively constructed but nonetheless powerful system of signification that serves to uphold the dominant discourse of traditional motherhood (Glenn, Chang, and Forcey 1994). Running deep within my psyche, I now understand how this social construction forms an overriding fantasy theme (Bormann 1972) from which all mothers judge their competency, regardless of custodial status. My dilemma is that such a fantasy theme sharply contradicts my present reality.

Nowadays, I live in someone else's house, see my kids every other weekend, and pay child support. How can I continue to call myself a mother when I no longer provide their regular care and nurturance? Unlike some mothers, though, who lose custody of their children during divorce or separation, I voluntarily chose my status. I have no one to blame but myself. With little money coming in as a full-time student, I am unable to provide adequately for them. Like other mothers I've interviewed, making the difficult decision to leave the care of my children to someone else because I deemed it "in their best interest" is not a decision reached lightly. There is the risk I could somehow lose my children as a result. Not that my ex-husband would literally take them from me, although that is a common occurrence for some mothers with whom I've spoken. Rather, I could fail to find an operative communicative ground from which to competently negotiate or enact my new role as *visiting mother*. I could fail in my attempts to construct a new rhetorical vision (Bormann 1972) of motherhood that would sustain my efforts to perform my ambiguous role. For, unlike traditional motherhood, there is no social stock of knowledge from which to draw insights (Schutz 1970). Indeed, failing to competently handle this situation could be a death sentence for my future relationship with my children. I know that is not a drama I want to live.

No time to dwell on the complexities of this turn of events now. I close the dryer door and drop the folded clothes in the basket. In my ruminations, I typically get the "short end of the stick," on this subject anyway. Right now, my task is to round up the boys and make sure they are cleaned up before we leave. Their dad's expecting them.

* * *

My status as a *visiting mother* brings to the fore two key aspects of my experience that simultaneously shape my past, present, and future understandings of my relationship with my absent children and my designation as a *mother*. One aspect is my continuing "performance" as a mother, a role that typically is highly scripted or codified,

semiotically speaking. The other is my communication "competency" as I attempt to perform in my capacity as *mother yet not mother*. Now, more than ever before, I understand my activities, communication processes, and everyday events of which I am involved as performances or as social actions performed within a complex matrix of signifying systems (Anderson and Meyer 1988). Because all of my interactions with my children are now framed by the unique context (or stage) known as *child visitation*, they are performances. That is, they are "aesthetically marked and heightened mode[s] of communication, framed in a special way and put on display for an audience" (Bauman 1992, 44). This is so even though my display of motherhood is not always an action consciously chosen. Because noncustodial motherhood transgresses the typical assumptions and highly codified role of traditional motherhood, my existence necessarily represents to others around me a "lost absoluteness" for what a mother should be (Miller 1998, 319). Unlike fathers who become noncustodial, my context of mothering includes no parameters that would serve to make possible, codify, and therefore legitimize my existence within the wider network of social relations. I am simply perceived (by myself as well as others) as an anomaly (Jackson 1994). If anything, I reinstantiate the norm of good, traditional mothering by serving to fulfill a sociocultural desire for its negative representation.

As "any doing of an act of communication," my performance of noncustodial motherhood highlights the interrelationship between myself and the myriad of audiences that serve as sign systems to me (Bauman 1992, 44). As I have discovered, my new-found status invokes the powerful presence of many audiences whether real, imaginary, or symbolic, as psychoanalyst Jacque Lacan would have us understand (Wilden 1987). Whether contiguous or remote, my engagement with these audiences holds us both "communicatively accountable; [for] it assigns to an audience the responsibility for evaluating the relative skills and effectiveness of the performer's accomplishment" (Bauman 1992, 44). These audiences witness and scrutinize my competency and shape my perceptions of myself as a cast member enacting the "play" we call mothering. As time passes, I become more aware that any sociocultural context like child visitation "is not a neutral or stable 'frame,' 'schema,' or 'speech event'; but the ordering of power relations in discourse that establishes conditions" from which I speak as a woman *and* mother, either legitimately or illegitimately (Linstrom 1992, 103-4). Therefore, in my continuing efforts to perform my role as mother, I have to ask myself, at any given moment, "What audiences am I addressing and under what conditions do I speak? What kind of role is demanded of me? What do my communicative actions of mothering represent to others and myself?" Even though I remain highly vigilant to my task of deconstructing the sign systems these roles and social situations represent, I easily become "tangled in the [cultural] rules" (Bateson 1972) for assessing what performance role is currently applicable and demonstrating its corresponding rules of competency. I am, after all, a *visiting mother*, and I soon find that the paradoxical implications of that cultural designation are enormous to my ongoing sense of well-being.

In what follows, I continue my personal narrative or confessional tale (Van Maanen 1988) of my experiences as a noncustodial mother. As a narrative performance, it represents how my sense of mothering is rhetorically constituted through my communicative actions, that is, how my expressions and perceptions of the unique context of *child visitation* shape my ongoing lived experiences and identification with the sign of motherhood. I must acknowledge at the outset that my narrative offering, while written by a white, middle-class, Protestant academic, also reflects a polyphony of stories I have collected from other noncustodial mothers. Following Bakhtin, their voices are now interwoven with mine, producing the following intersubjective, heteroglossic account of this cultural experience (Holquist 1981). Even though this ethnographic approach resembles a critical autoethnography as described and espoused by contemporary theorists (see, for example, Conquergood 1991; Crawford 1996;

Denzin 1997; Bochner 1997; Ellis 1999), I attempt to expand beyond a descriptive level of analysis that autoethnographies typically provide. To turn "the ethnographic gaze inward on the self (auto), while . . . looking at the larger context wherein self experiences occur" (Denzin 1997, 227), I blend the cultural theory of signs, that is, semiotics (Peirce 1955; Jakobson 1971), with a radical, empirical interrogation supplied through phenomenological reflection (Merleau-Ponty 1962; Jackson 1989). This theoretical lens helps me reveal the lived embodiment of what Pierce would describe as discursive thirdness, that is, the semiotic and phenomenological mediation that occurs when persons interact with the sign systems that produce cultural experience. Taking my narrative of noncustodial mothering as an existential sign condition, I pragmatically explore its communicative dimensions. This entails explication of the dynamic interactions among a cultural text/context of discourse, performer, and audience. As Riessman (1993) explained, such a pragmatic focus on narrative "gives prominence to human agency and imagination [and] is well suited to studies of subjectivity and identity" (p. 5). It reflects a cultural exemplar of the struggle we all face as we attempt to embody a *meaningful* subjectivity.

Such a theoretical stance provides me a means by which to "highlight the social, cultural, and aesthetic dimensions of the communicative process" (Turner 1986, 24). It also demonstrates how performances become privileged spaces of social reflexivity and occasions ripe for intense critical scrutiny and evaluation (Strine 1998, 313). Although the lived-body experience of noncustodial mothering feels anything but a "privileged space," it is an example of socialized discourse that provides an occasion for intense social *and* personal scrutiny. My story continues as our weekend visit comes to a close.

* * *

I suddenly realize that it's awfully quiet in the house. "Ty . . . Zachary," I call out, with the basket of clothes now resting on one hip. No response. All I hear is the low drone of a televised basketball game coming from the sunken living room. That's odd. I wonder where they could be, looking into the dining room. I'm sure they were just here a minute ago, playing with my landlord's son, Alex, also visiting his dad for the weekend. Have I been too involved in cleaning up our breakfast mess or doing laundry to notice that they'd disappeared? It is a rarity that my boys, Ty, age ten, and Zac, age six, would be unaccounted for during a weekend visit. After all, I consider our time together precious time, although very much punctuated and measured according to planned activities and events. Granted, I have been daydreaming about how good this weekend with them has been. I think I've managed to keep them sufficiently "entertained," consciously acknowledging my role as performer. I know that's not my only goal while they're with me, but I do want them to enjoy coming to see me. Yes, let's see. Friday night we went to the movies. Yesterday afternoon, I took them roller skating. They still can't believe I skated all the time when I was their age. Alex and his dad, Doug, my landlord, met us for pizza afterwards. We all stayed up late last night and watched a rented movie. Dare I say it felt like "family time," if only temporarily? This morning our time together was more improvised as needs and issues arose. Zac talked me into making waffles for breakfast. How long has it been since I did that? Seldom do I cook anymore. Since breakfast, our time together has taken on a carefree tone. I helped Ty finish some homework and talked with him about dealing with his math teacher whom he hates. I must admit the "down time" with them has been nice. After all, we don't always have to be doing planned activities, I remind myself. Any sense of normalcy with them is a welcome gift given how difficult it is to achieve these days. (Most noncustodial mothers with whom I've talked echo these sentiments. It's the routine patterns of being together, the sense of everydayness that we miss the most. Saying prayers or tucking them into bed every night was always as comforting to me as it was for them, I'm sure.)

But where could they have gone? I quickly move through the spacious house to the small room that I rent at one end. Perhaps I just can't hear them behind my closed door. I open the door and drop the basket on the bed. I am immediately engulfed by a sea of pink filtered light provided by the pink curtains, bedspread, bed ruffle, throw rugs, and other accessories I use to decorate my personal space. It's probably no coincidence that my décor reflects my continuing need to affirm a femininity I think I've long since lost. I do know that its warm glow soothes my spirit and offers a welcome respite when I enter.

They aren't there, but evidence of their occupation immediately captures my attention. I see GI Joes, jeeps, tanks, and small rifles scattered across my floor. My shoes are being used as bunkers for their "men" to hide in, and my academic books seem to be arranged as a fort. How many times have I told them not to leave all this stuff lying around? I can't help but smile, though. The apposition of our worlds—the budding masculine and affirmed feminine—humors me. At least I see evidence of our existential juxtaposition. That's a rarity, these days. I rather enjoy seeing any presence of them in my otherwise solitary life. That wasn't always the case, though. I remember when they first went to live with their dad. I had to put their school pictures in a drawer for a while. It was too painful. Their photographs on my window ledge haunted me. Their smiling faces suggested a betrayal for leaving them and served as testimonials that I was, indeed, a bad mother.

Muffled voices outside my window bring me back from my thoughts. They must be outside, I conclude, as I make my way back through the living room and kitchen to the patio doors. I see Doug coming down from upstairs. "Have you seen the boys?" I ask, noticing a slight nervousness in my voice.

"I think they're out in the side yard," he replies, as he opens the refrigerator door. He takes out a hunk of raw cabbage for a snack. We all are entitled to our idiosyncrasies, I think to myself. Doug and I get along well, actually. We have from the beginning. I think it's because we give one another a lot of psychological space. His divorce is almost final, I think. I don't intrude in his life and he, refreshingly, has never asked questions about mine. I hope the boys haven't gotten dirty playing in the mud, I think to myself as I make my way toward the back kitchen door. Did it rain last night or the night before? Do I have extra clothes, just in case, or did I send those back with them the last time they were here? What will their dad say if I have to take them home dirty? Have I been irresponsible?

"Mom, come here, quick!" Ty yells excitedly as I walk toward them in the side area of the spacious yard. I look over and see all three boys scurrying rapidly in and out of a couple of run-down storage sheds constructed from what looks like leftover building materials. The roofs are filled with gaping holes, and I see that birds have nested in the eves. Piles of old lumber, scrap metal, and concrete blocks are scattered about, and I worry how soon they will encounter the many protruding nails I already see. There's a feeling of urgency in the air.

"Ty and Zac, what are you doing in that mess? You'll get hurt. Didn't I tell you not to play there?" I speak more harshly than I intend, making my way closer.

"But Mom," Zachary protests, "we're building a fort! Alex says it's OK. Come see!"

I look over at Alex who is busy moving a long, splintered piece of wood. "Alex, did you ask your dad if you guys could play in here?" I ask.

Alex looks up, "Yeah, he said we could as long as we cleaned up the mess while we're at it."

"Yeah, Mom, come see the space we cleared," Ty chimed. I peer through a large crack in the side of the closest shed. I see only a shadowed but cluttered interior. "We've got these tree stumps to use as chairs. Alex's dad is even going to pay us for helping organize this stuff," he continues.

"Well, that sounds pretty good guys, but it's almost time to go and you still haven't packed up yet. Your dad's expecting you for dinner, remember?"

"Ah, Mom, can't we stay a little longer," Ty insists, "we just got started."

"I know, honey, but this project will be here when you come to visit next time. You can finish it then," I hear myself reluctantly saying.

"Ah, come on, Zac. We've gotta go," Ty says defeatedly. "Don't clean this up by yourself, Alex, before we get back, OK?" Ty prods, wanting to make sure his chance for making some money doesn't slip by.

"Ok," we hear Alex say as we work our way back to the house. "Bye."

"See ya," echo Ty and Zac.

I'm immediately filled with mixed emotions. Although I'm happy to see them finally comfortable enough to make some aspect of this experience their own, I have to begin the departure process. I've learned that it's not emotionally productive for any of us to quickly take our leaves with one another. Our times together already feel laced with abrupt meetings, exchanges, and departures. If I don't get them moving now, I won't keep my agreed-on visitation schedule with their dad. I don't want to make him angry about any aspect of our visitation arrangement. We're on good terms, now, and I want to keep it that way. And yet, if I had my way, I'd let them play out here until dark, if only to see them create a space here at Doug's that they could look forward to visiting. I've always worried that it's not enough for them that they are coming to see me. What do I have to offer? What kinds of things can they do here? What's in it for them? I'm fully aware that on successful completion, however insignificant it might appear to outsiders, their "fort" would signify that we *shared* space together, like we did when we were living with one another. As it is now, they merely enter, visit, and exit my limited space for a prescribed time. Taking turns sleeping on the floor in my room or on the futon couch in the living room, throwing their things wherever, and dressing in a cold bathroom are not the best of circumstances. (They are, however, better than some visiting arrangements I've heard about. For example, Ann, another noncustodial mother, "lives out of a suitcase," as she puts it. She's relegated to visits with her three-year-old daughter at public places. They celebrated Christmas one year in the lobby of the university's student union, next to "the biggest tree" her daughter had ever seen.)

As we walk back to the house, I'm fully aware of the weight these unusual circumstances of visitation have on our relationship. Sensing a greater consequence to this seemingly mundane exchange than merely stopping an activity they were excitedly doing, I realize that we've just enacted the epitome of our circumstances of visitation. "It will have to wait 'til next time," is a theme played over and over again, with every visit, with every departure. Do they feel the existential angst this produces as much as I do, I wonder? If so, I must try to spare them.

Quickly refocusing, "You guys don't look too dirty," I say with a strained smile. Just the thought of leaving them begins to upset me. It's been so good to see them this time. I know visits can be extremely rocky, so much so that other mothers have admitted welcoming their end, if only to stop the emotional roller-coaster rides they evoke. I reassure myself that this time I've succeeded in countering the entropic forces that seem to work against our relationship. I brush some smudges from Zac's jacket and turn Ty's face toward me to get a good look. "You'll want to wash up a bit and don't forget to pack up the GI Joes. They're all over my floor. You know where your bags are guys? And don't forget your homework, Ty. It's on the coffee table, I think. We've got fifteen minutes before we need to leave." We've entered the kitchen and the door slams behind us, as if to punctuate my words and mark the beginning of our "departure routine." The three of us take the cue and scatter to make preparations. This is such an atypical context or stage from which to perform motherhood. I'm never really sure how well I'm doing.

* * *

As seen in the narrative above, our experiences together are shaped by unique temporal and spatial parameters within which our communication transpires and on which my performance of mothering is to be judged. All of our communication is shaped by an interplay of varying audiences (the imaginary, the real, and the symbolic) that works semiotically to influence my expressions and my perceived competence as a mother (Wilden 1987). I am often left wondering if it is even possible to construct a meaningful subjectivity of motherhood that will satisfy these audiences, whose narrative representations and expectations continually frame my own, too much so if I am not careful. Although often confused, it *is* clear to me that *my perceptions* of my sit-

uation do, indeed, heavily influence how I think, feel, and express myself to others (Merleau-Ponty 1964; Lanigan 1988, 1992). Theoretically, I am aware of the fact that my predicament is an existential product of my interaction with these various objects, people, and events (signs) that I encounter in the world and the subsequent interpretations I make (Jakobson 1960, 353). Ultimately, I know that these perceptions will prove to be the key to understanding and possibly transforming the way I approach my difficult and ambiguous circumstances. Part of my challenge is not only the shifting nature of my embodiment as *visiting mother* but also the changing status of the audiences before whom I enact my part. Which audience is more present or absent to my experience will depend, of course, on the communicative event we are enacting at any given moment.

When I am with my children, they are the real audience before whom I am performing non-custodial mothering. They are, after all, the actual persons who are immediately present to my experience. I find that typically, as my real audience, they provide the least amount of direct criticism concerning my performance as a mother, (although, as we shall see below, this does not mean that challenges to my authority as a parental figure do not sometimes surface). Understood as a code condition, my children as the real audience give me a certain degree of parental latitude, freedom, and power to just *be* with them as I see fit. We can, therefore, improvise new familial role enactments, such as our activities on Saturday (mentioned above) and our Sunday morning time together. Rather than appealing to restrictive cultural codes already in place, our exchange of various messages helps to create new mother-to-son relations. . . .

At the same time, however, an imaginary audience is present to my experience every time I attempt to instantiate the sociocultural discourse of conventional motherhood while I am with my sons. This discourse, as we know, both illusory as a rhetorical vision *and* real in its many written and oral manifestations in the popular media, serves to construct mother love as an all-encompassing, self-sacrificing, and unconditional feminine performance (Thurer 1994). In addition, this discourse demands "typical" parental enactment routines, such as reprimanding them for playing unsafely in a potentially harmful area or making sure they are clean and "presentable" before returning to their father's house. I do this as a way to regulate my perceived fledgling performance of mothering and to reinstill a competency as "parent" I so earnestly desire. Consequently, I appeal to familiar *regulative* rules found in traditional mothering discourse as I attempt to enact my role (Searle 1969). The standards for judging my performance by this imaginary audience are especially restrictive, if not harsh, given the fact that two hours from now I will have no direct authority to intervene in their play whatsoever. Every time I think about how I should really be with my children regularly and not merely visiting (e.g., when I'm folding my clothes or when I'm packing them up to "deliver" them to their father), this audience is prominent in my consciousness. My children also conjure this audience for me when they question why they have to "go home" or when we are going to see one another again.

Unfortunately, when I appeal to these implicit scripts (dictated by this sociocultural discourse), my speech acts function to merely operationalize predetermined code conditions that do not match my situation of noncustody. I often feel as though I mistakenly walked through the wrong stage door for my performance. I am quickly reminded that most mothers do not send their children "home" on Sunday afternoons. My timing may be appropriate but my embodiment of space is definitely not. I keep trying, however, to demonstrate a competent performance. I eventually find that enacting these scripts under such atypical circumstances is a difficult performance to maintain. Ultimately, appealing to such code conditions only acts as a strong message to me that I might, in the end, fail miserably. My enactment of these scripts, unfortunately, prohibits more spontaneous interactions with my children that might prove more productive.

Given these circumstances, I am quickly reminded that any performance on my part necessarily drifts between past conceptions of mothering and present misgivings and that "every performance marks out a unique temporal space that nevertheless contains traces of other now-absent performances" (Diamond 1996, 1). I cannot seem to escape these traces as I interact with these contradictory sign systems and embody the existential confusion and disequilibrium they create. . . .

The time we spend apart from one another is difficult to handle as well, in part because the designations for what constitutes the imaginary and the real audiences become existentially and semiotically reversed, as do my appeals to constitutive and regulative rules for social enactments. Being absent, my children now serve as my imaginary audience, while other social contexts and relationships that are typically less intimate in nature assume the qualities and evaluative functions of the real audience. I easily get "tangled in the [cultural] rules" (Bateson 1972) for assessing what performance role is relevant. . . .

When a relative stranger hears of my custody situation and responds with a hesitant, monotone "oh," or an equally inquisitive but telling look, it seems as though I am suddenly performing on stage before a full house. I immediately become an object of reflection and speculation. How do I respond without being perceived as defensive, without a definite admission of wrongdoing or guilt that significantly places my social status as a mother and a woman in immediate jeopardy? As I have heard many times from other noncustodial mothers, it is precisely these kinds of situations that accentuate the lived reality of existing in the contradictory space between social identification and marginalization. Our angst is prompted by the fact that we immediately become a sign of social deviance as an existential boundary is immediately drawn that signifies us as now "other" and "different." Because of the emotional negativity these social situations produce, many noncustodial mothers simply choose to avoid the justification performance by not admitting they have children when confronted with the question by relative strangers. In my case, the degree of justification is relative to the value I place on my audience's approval. . . .

I am slowly learning that to negotiate the cultural paradox, I need to change my concept of the mothering performance. I must cease telling *another's* story, as an accomplishment of some codified role for what mothers should be. I need to accept the possibility that the unique text/context of visitation presents a constitutive space from which *my story* of noncustody *and* motherhood might unfold (Butler 1990). Rather than viewing my circumstances as dictated by my ambiguous text/context of visitation, I must embody my subject position as *mother yet noncustodial* through a *performativity* produced by my continual interpersonal engagement with my sons and others. Such an existential orientation keeps me focused on the immediacy of our engagement and, consequently, makes my embodiment of noncustodial motherhood more meaningful. Resisting the initial feelings of estrangement from Ty that surface on my arrival at their house, for example, I perform greeting practices that seek to establish a better communicative ground for us to relate as mother and son. I have learned, in other words, a valuable "tactic," as described by de Certeau, that offers an intangible means of seizing opportunities to mother my children "on the wing," so to speak (quoted in Carlson 1996, 172). Rather than succumbing to the psychological pressure I feel as an outsider in my boys' home (especially when I view their daily surroundings that exclude me entirely) and the memories of our past life together, I seize the opportunity to create alternative means of relating with them as we begin our journey back to where I live. I realize that to be successful at mothering them under these circumstances, I should not try to reinstantiate these former contexts of relating but reposition us within a new context of discourse that has yet to be narrated. This requires me to shift my focus from mothering as a scripted performance to the performativity of mothering, as an ongoing process and event of the speaking/listening per-

son. I leave their house thinking, for example, that I *do* have ongoing opportunities to create the degrees of mutual intimacy and care that I desire.

Unlike the previous stories or themes of mothering I performed, the emerging narrative that I subsequently spin serves political functions (Langellier 1989, 271). As Langellier (1999) contends, this new-found tactic or "performativity articulates and situates [me] . . . within the forces of discourse, the institutionalized networks of power relations, such as medicine, the law, the media, and the family, which constitute subject positions and *order* context" (p. 129, italics mine). Importantly, someone who lives outside the temporal and spatial boundaries of "normalized" motherhood discourse realizes that the notion of performativity "assert[s] the possibility of materializing something that exceeds our knowledge, that alters the shape of sites and imagines other as yet unsuspected modes of being" (Diamond 1996, 2). In contrast to "identity thinking" that attempts to deny or limit the slippage to maintain a total congruity between concept and experience (Carlson 1996, 171), I am learning to appreciate the slippage, and the corresponding ambiguity it produces, for what it portends that I may become. As Carlson (1996) reminds me, "the possibility of innovative agency is always present" in the slippage (p. 171). Thus, I know my hope for creating a meaningful noncustodial subjectivity resides in the fact that all performances contain this emergent dimension, a "radically contextual, improvisational, and transformational character" (Bauman 1992, 42). Only when I keep focused on this idea in my praxis of mothering am I able to enact a performative competence of mothering. Although I still exist outside the acceptable grammar for typical motherhood relations, I gain the ability to better position myself within a context of discourse. At times I am able, however temporarily, to feel personally empowered in my situation. . . .

Ironically, it appears that my continued willingness to engage my children, in spite of the negativity that surrounds the discursive structure of visitation, may actually bring me closer to actualizing the idealized and highly rhetorical visions of motherhood our culture so ardently endorses. For the lived value I now place on the precious time and space I share with my children becomes an all-encompassing and often self-deprecating raison d'être. No longer taking my relationship with them for granted gives me a renewed perspective on what it truly means to mother and to love my children no matter what conditions. Through many eyes, I know that I may not competently perform motherhood anymore. Even when I lived with them regularly, I am sure I did not measure up to the rhetorical ideal. But now, at least, I can embody a performative competence, a self-motivated ability to continue to actively engage with them through discursive and nondiscursive means, to continue to make the effort to connect and reconnect, and to never take that connection for granted. I begin to appreciate that it is precisely "at these [semiotic and phenomenological] borders [i.e., boundaries of conscious experience] that meaning is continually being created and negotiated" (Carlson 1996, 188).

* * *

Within American culture, the drama that unfolds for many noncustodial mothers is one that is particularly difficult to manage. Often isolated and socially marginalized (Eicher-Catt 1997), these women no longer support the rhetorical vision provided by the cultural codes of traditional motherhood—a vision, I might add, that often requires women to don a superwoman role. Regardless of their social positioning in terms of age, class, race, ethnicity, and so forth, these women typically lack the necessary political means by which to effect widespread social change. Existing outside the boundaries of normalized discourse, these women have few rhetorical opportunities to collectively advance an alternative and more conducive rhetorical vision by which to live as competent mothers *yet* noncustodial. For the noncustodial mothers who continue the struggle to care for their absent children despite the constraints of visitation, their lived experiences of negativity attest to the powerful cultural expectations the sign of motherhood still imposes on all of us. Even in our contemporary culture that repeatedly espouses women's rights and freedoms, the presence of noncustodial mothers causes awkward social uneasiness. And yet, for the many mothers who do continue to care and nurture their children successfully, their performative competence testifies to the individual potential we have to transform the implications of discursive practices. For all women who, in whatever measure or degree, choose to blur the boundaries between personal and cultural visions of motherhood, the dialectical tension that exists between their performance and performativity provides hope in their fledgling relationships with their children. Such a theoretical turn offers renewed appreciation for the dynamic palpability within every interpersonal engagement. It reminds us that our transformative power resides in everyday events of speaking and listening, in which the contests of discourse and culture play out.

References

Anderson, J. A., and T. P. Meyer. 1988. *Mediated communication: A social action perspective*. Newbury Park, CA: Sage.

Bateson, G. 1972. *Steps to an ecology of mind*. New York: Ballantine.

Bauman, R. 1992. Performance. In *Folklore, cultural performances, and popular entertainments: A communication-centered handbook*, edited by R. Bauman, 41–49. New York: Oxford University Press.

Bochner, A. 1997. It's about time: Narrative and the divided self. *Qualitative Inquiry* 3 (4): 418–38.

Bormann, E. G. 1972. Fantasy and rhetorical vision: The rhetorical criticism of social reality. *Quarterly Journal of Speech* 58:396–407.

Carlson, M. 1996. *Performance: A critical introduction*. London: Routledge.

Conquergood, D. 1991. Rethinking ethnography: Towards a critical cultural politics. *Communication Monographs* 58:179–94.

Crawford, L. 1996. Personal ethnography. *Communication Monographs* 63:158–70.

Denzin, N. K. 1997. *Interpretive ethnography: Ethnographic practices for the 21st century*. Thousand Oaks. CA: Sage.

Diamond, E. 1996. Introduction. In *Performance and cultural politics*, edited by E. Diamond, 1–12. New York: Routledge.

Eicher-Catt, D. 1997. Mobilizing motherhood: Women's experiences of visiting their children. In *Courage of conviction: Women's words, women's wisdom*, edited by L. A. M. Perry and P. Geist, 201–19. Mountain View. CA: Mayfield.

Ellis, C. 1999. Heartful autoethnography: Keynote addresses from the first annual advances in qualitative methods conference. *Qualitative Health Research* 9 (5): 669–83.

Glenn, E. N., G. Chang, and L. R. Forcey, eds. 1994. *Mothering: Ideology, experience, and agency*. New York: Routledge.

Holquist, M., ed. 1981. *The dialogic imagination: Four essays by M. M. Bakhtin*. Austin: University of Texas Press.

Jackson, M. 1989. *Paths toward a clearing: Radical empiricism and ethnographic inquiry*. Bloomington: Indiana University Press.

Jackson, R. 1994. *Mothers who leave: Behind the myth of women without their children*. London: Pandora.

Jakobson, R. 1960. Closing statement: Linguistics and poetics. In *Style in language*, edited by T. A. Sebeok, 350–77. New York: John Wiley.

———. 1971. Linguistics and communication theory. In *Selected writings*, vol. 2, 570–79. The Hague, the Netherlands: Mouton.

Langellier, K. 1989. Personal narratives: Perspectives on theory and research. *Text and Performance Quarterly* 9:243–76.

———. 1999. Personal narrative, performance, performativity: Two or three things I know for sure. *Text and Performance Quarterly* 19:125–44.

Lanigan, R. 1988. *Phenomenology of communication: Merleau-Ponty's thematics in communicology and semiology*. Pittsburgh, PA: Duquesne University Press.

———. 1992. *The human science of communicology: A phenomenology of discourse in Foucault and Merleau-Ponty*. Pittsburgh, PA: Duquesne University Press.

Linstrom. L. 1992. Context contests: Debatable truth statements on Tanna (Vanuaru). In *Rethinking context: Language as an interactive phenomenon*, edited by A. Duranti and C. Goodwin, 101–24. Cambridge, UK: Cambridge University Press.

Merleau-Ponty, M. 1962. Freedom. In *Phenomenology of perception*, translated by Colin Smith, 434–56. New York: Humanities Press.

———. 1964. The primacy of perception and its philosophical consequences. In *The primacy of perception*, translated by J. Edie, 12–42. Evanston, IL: Northwestern University Press.

Miller, L. C. 1998. Witness to the self: The autobiographical impulse in performance studies. In *Communication: Views from the helm for the 21st century*, edited by J. Trent, 318–22. Boston: Allyn & Bacon.

Peirce, C. S. 1955. Logic as semiotic: The theory of signs. In *The philosophical writings of Peirce*, edited by J. Buchler, 98–119. New York: Dover.

Riessman, C. K. 1993. *Narrative analysis*. Newbury Park, CA: Sage.

Schutz, A. 1970. *On phenomenology and social relations*. Edited by H. Wagner. Chicago: University of Chicago Press.

Searle, J. R. 1969. *Speech acts: An essay in the philosophy of language*. Cambridge, UK: Cambridge University Press.

Strine, M. 1998. Articulating performance/performativity: Disciplinary tasks and the contingencies of practice. In *Communication: Views from the helm for the 21st century*, edited by J. Trent, 312–17. Boston: Allyn & Bacon.

Thurer, S. L. 1994. *The myths of motherhood: How culture reinvents the good mother*. Boston: Houghton Mifflin.

———. 1986. *The anthropology of performance*. New York: PAJ Publications.

Van Maanen, J. 1988. *Tales of the field: On writing ethnography*. Chicago: University of Chicago Press.

Wilden, A. 1987. *The rules are no game: The strategy of communication*. New York: Routledge Kegan Paul.

ARTICLE 36

Kathleen J. Ferraro
Angela M. Moe

Mothering, Crime, and Incarceration

This article examines the relationships between mothering, crime, and incarceration through the narratives of thirty women incarcerated in a southwestern county jail. The responsibilities of child care, combined with the burdens of economic marginality and domestic violence, led some women to choose economic crimes or drug dealing as an alternative to hunger and homelessness. Other women, arrested for drug- or alcohol-related crimes, related their offenses to the psychological pain and despair resulting from loss of custody of their children. Many women were incarcerated for minor probation violations that often related to the conflict between work, child care, and probation requirements. For all women with children, mothering represented both the burdens of an unequal sexual division of labor and opportunities for resistance to marginalization and hopelessness.

The dramatic increase in the incarceration of women in recent years has stimulated renewed discussion of child care and mothering responsibilities of women in prisons and jails. Although prisons in the United States and Great Britain originally permitted children to accompany mothers, this practice changed during the Progressive Era with the belief that the prison was a corrupting influence on children (Dobash, Dobash, and Gutteridge 1986). Today, in the United States, there are very few correctional facilities that provide the opportunity for children to reside with incarcerated mothers. A survey conducted by the National Institute of Corrections found that eleven state department of corrections provided at least one facility for newborns, infants, and babies up to eighteen months of age to accompany their mothers; the vast majority provide none (National Institute of Corrections 2002). Internationally, the manner in which mothers and young children are treated

within the correctional system varies from no accommodation (New Zealand) to accommodation up to six years of age (Spain) (Caddle 1998). Russia recently took the most dramatic action to address the problem of mothering by incarcerated women by passing legislation that pardons and releases all female inmates with children in prison nurseries, approximately five hundred women, regardless of their crimes (Karush 2002). . . .

This article focuses on women's experiences with mothering, crime, and incarceration. Each of these socially constructed categories reflects and reinforces gendered expectations for women's performance, as well as race and class hierarchies. Some research has suggested that the legal system tends to de-emphasize, excuse, justify, and downplay women's crimes, even those that are targeted at or incidentally harm their children (Allen 1987; Daly 1994). According to such reports, women are portrayed within the legal system in ways that are consistent with paternalistic hegemonic standards of passivity and weakness and, as such, are unable to be held fully accountable for their criminal activities. Such research, supportive of the chivalry thesis in criminology

Source: "Mothering, Crime, and Incarceration," by Kathleen J. Ferraro and Angela M. Moe. 2003. *Journal of Contemporary Ethnography 32*(1):9–40. Used by permission.

(see Pollak 1950), contrasts with other studies that find that women are processed through the criminal justice system in misogynist ways, demonized and vilified for countering hegemonic womanhood and motherhood vis-à-vis their criminal offenses (Chesney-Lind 1997; Gilbert 1999; Nagel and Hagan 1983; Young 1986). The women most likely to benefit from hegemonic notions of womanhood and motherhood within the criminal justice system are those that fit the ideal image within society at large, namely white, middle to upper class, heterosexual women (Belknap 2001). Much current research suggests that the disproportionate rate of incarceration of women of color is a reflection of racist perceptions, policing, and sentencing policies (Belknap 2001; Gilbert 1999; Richie 2001).

While women are capable of and certainly do commit many forms of crime, including interpersonal violent crimes that in some cases harm their children, they also commit their crimes from gendered, as well as raced and classed, positions that are politically, economically, and historically rooted (Allen 1987; Humphries 1999). Despite instances in which the contexts of women's crimes resemble those of men's (see as examples Miller 1998; Sommers, Baskin, and Fagan 2000), overall, women are more likely to commit minor property offenses than serious or violent offenses as compared to men and are less likely to recidivate than men (Smart 1995). The crimes for which they are most often arrested and incarcerated are suggestive of their gendered and raced social positioning (Richie 2001; Ross 1998). Such crimes include nonviolent and minor property crimes such as prostitution, larceny, shoplifting, check or credit card fraud, forgery/counterfeiting, and drug possession (Immarigeon and Chesney-Lind 1992; Bloom, Chesney-Lind, and Owen 1994; Chesney-Lind 1997; Chesney-Lind, Harris, and deGroot 1998; Greenfield and Snell 1999; Watterson 1996). The growth in the number of incarcerated women between 1990 and 2000 is composed largely of drug offenders (Harrison and Beck 2002). . . .

The vast majority of prisons and jails have not developed the most rudimentary resources for women inmates (Morash 1998; U.S. General Accounting Office 1999). Women are assessed and classified using instruments designed for males, and programming is designed without consideration of the differing needs of women. Although at least 70 percent of women in jail have minor children, few jails have programs that foster parenting skills or contact between mothers and children, and there are virtually no programs designed to assist children with problems related to the incarceration of their mothers (Greenfield and Snell 1999).

There have been several studies of mothering from inside prisons and jails over the past twenty-five years, including Bloom (1992), Bloom and Steinhart (1993), Watterson (1996), Henriques (1982), Snell (1994), Enos (2001), Baunach (1985), Stanton (1980), Zalba (1964), and Glick and Neto (1977). The existing literature indicates that mothering is a central concern of incarcerated women and that correctional facilities have failed to respond adequately to this concern. Studies on incarceration and mothering report that many women commit minor property crimes to provide for their children, although there is no systematic data on the prevalence of this influence on women's crimes (Henriques 1982; Watterson 1996). Previous research has documented that women's concerns about their children's well-being, as well as their distress at separation, are the most salient features of incarceration for women with children (Boudin 1998; Enos 2001; Henriques 1982; Watterson 1996). Comparison of incarcerated mothers and fathers indicates that women are more likely to have custody of children prior to incarceration and that men are much more likely to have female partners to care for children during their incarceration (Mumola 2000; Schafer and Dellinger 1999). Women most commonly use female relatives rather than male partners to care for children in their absence. This suggests that women's incarceration creates unique concerns about the welfare of their children from which most men are protected by the presence of a female partner who attends to their children.

Social Constructions of Good Mothers

Mothering is simultaneously a positive source of pleasure and identity formation and a vector for the social control of women. For women with children, mothering is a central component of identity, daily activity, and life plans. At the same time, the burdens and social expectations of mothering reinforce oppressive notions of femininity including self-sacrifice and subordination of personal goals to the needs of "the family." Naturalized assumptions regarding masculinity and femininity and raced and classed standards of gender performance saturate and reinforce constructions of mothering (Smart 1998). The ability to mother one's children according to social expectations and personal desires depends ultimately on one's access to the resources of time, money, health, and social support. A significant proportion of mothers negotiates their child rearing through obstacles that undermine their efforts to be "good mothers," both on their own terms and in the eyes of the state.

Kline (1995) described the dominant ideology of motherhood as "the constellation of ideas and images in Western capitalist societies that constitute the dominant ideals of motherhood against which women's lives are judged" (p. 119). The ideology is composed of historically constituted conceptions of maternal fitness that reflect race and class biases, as well as heterosexist and patriarchal notions of the family (Fineman 1995; Hill Collins 2000; Kline 1995). Women who are deemed "bad" or "unfit" mothers are often those who deviate from this ideology. Ikemoto (1997) outlined the stereotypes that are applied to women classified as "bad" or "unfit" mothers:

> She has little education. . . . She is unsophisticated, easily influenced by simple religious

dogma. She is pregnant because of promiscuity and irresponsibility. She is hostile to authority even though the state has good intentions. She is unreliable. She is ignorant and foreign. She does not know what is best. . . . These assumed characteristics are particular to stereotypes of poor women of color. So . . . she is Black; she is Hispanic; she is Asian; and she is poor. (p. 140)

The dominant ideology of motherhood reflects essentialist conceptions of women as inherently caring and self-sacrificing and simultaneously enforces distinctions among women based on race and class prejudices. While the dominant ideology of motherhood may distort the experiences and aspirations of all women, white, heterosexual, married, middle-class women continue to represent the most desired mothers in popular culture and social policy in the United States (Roberts 1995). Women who are identified as inadequate mothers are especially susceptible to social and legal regulation of their maternal rights (Kline 1995). Thus, motherhood resembles more of a privilege for some women rather than a right for all women (Molloy 1992). As such, it may be withheld from women who are not members of dominant social groups and women deemed unfit by social and legal standards (Kline 1995).

Despite rhetoric of a robust economy and envious standard of living, approximately 40 percent of all single mothers in the United States in 2000 lived at or below poverty level (Caiazza 2000). Women at the lower end of the economic spectrum work tedious, unstable jobs; negotiate the rough terrain of "dating" or maintaining intimate relationships; transport children to less than optimal "child care" arrangements; cook; clean; shop; wash; attend whatever classes may lead to better jobs or are required by caseworkers or probation officers; and provide the hugs, stories, conflict resolution, and moral guidance that help their children grow. Their identities and choices may revolve around their children, but the conditions in which they labor to nurture, protect, and educate their children are determined by others in increasingly miserly ways.

Method and Sample Characteristics

Our study was formulated to examine the relationships between women's experiences of violent victimization and incarceration. We developed a semistructured interview schedule designed to elicit topical life-history narratives. Such an approach has become a preferred means of data collection among those working with incarcerated and otherwise marginalized populations whose experiences are not easily predetermined or quantifiable (see as examples Arnold 1990; Gilfus 1992; Richie 1996). This methodology allowed us to center our analysis on the specific vantage points of the jailed women and to honor their location for developing understanding of mothering and incarceration (Hill Collins 1989, 2000; Elliott 1994; Hartsock 1987; Narayan 1988; Smith 1987). Assuming that members of marginalized groups can offer meaningful accounts of the ways in which the world is organized according to the oppressions they experience, we felt it appropriate to center our data collection and analysis on the direct accounts provided by the women about their life experiences (Sandoval 2000). In analyzing these accounts, we do not assume that they represent the objective truth of women's mothering any more than probation and court records represent such truth. Incarcerated women may have a unique stake in constructing accounts of mothering that emphasize their conformity to social expectations to counterbalance the stigma attached to criminalization (see Orbuch 1997). While strategies of self-presentation are always a concern in conducting interviews, we did not find that women portrayed their mothering in a particularly positive light. Rather, women were very emotional, often crying and on one occasion ending the interview, and expressed remorse and guilt over the impact of their crimes on their children. . . .

Our success in obtaining such rich narratives was due in no small part to the access and accommodations accorded us by the administrators and staff at the Pima County Adult Detention Facility (PCAD) in southern Arizona. Access was granted to the inmates at the facility during the spring of 2000. Approximately two hundred women were incarcerated in the detention center at this time, with roughly sixty-five volunteering to be interviewed. . . . Our only constraint on the number of women who could participate was funding as we were only able to pay thirty interviewees a ten- to twenty-dollar stipend. . . .

The women ranged in age from twenty-one years to fifty years, with an average of thirty-four years. Fifteen (50 percent) women identified as white, seven (23 percent) as Black, three (10 percent) as Latina, three (10 percent) as American Indian, and two (6 percent) as biracial. This distribution was comparable to the proportions of women in each racial/ethnic group in the jail at the time of our interviews in which 53 percent were white, 24 percent Latina, 13 percent Black, and 9 percent American Indian. Few of the women had stable or sustainable employment prior to their incarceration and generally identified themselves as lower to working middle class. Twenty-seven (90 percent) of the women had children, with an average of three children each. Two of these women were also pregnant at the time of their interviews.

Impact of the Role of Mothering on Criminal Offending

Arizona, like most states in the United States, provides a very low level of financial and social support for mothering. Overall, 16.5 percent of Arizona women live in poverty, with the proportion rising to 22.3 percent in rural counties bordering Mexico and 53.3 percent on American Indian reservations (Caiazza 2000). Throughout the state, approximately one-third of Latina and African American women and one-half of American Indian women live in poverty. Poverty data by race and family composition are not available, but overall, 41.5 percent of single women with children live in poverty, which is comparable to the national rate of 41 percent (Caiazza 2000). Nearly 25 percent of Arizona women do not have health insurance (compared with a national rate of 18.5 percent), and the average annual cash benefit provided to single mothers through Temporary Assistance for Needy Families in Arizona, $3,345, is considerably lower than the U.S. average of $4,297. Child support is awarded in about 30 percent of mother-headed households, but only 43.6 percent of orders for collection result in actual collections. Single mothers, especially those with less than a high school education and women of color, face harsh economic constraints and a lack of low-cost housing, child care, and medical services.

Some of the mothers interviewed correlated this economic situation directly with their participation in criminal activity. Women with children in their custody conceptualized crime as an alternative to hunger and homelessness. Women without dependent children did not discuss the relationship between economic survival and economic crimes and most often referenced drugs and alcohol as the basis for their offenses. Several women linked their financial difficulties, and the crimes they committed to obtain money, to efforts to escape from or cope with violent men while providing for their children. These women articulated the structural barriers to successful mothering and viewed nonviolent crime as a rational, responsible action taken to meet their children's needs. This interpretation of the reasonableness of crimes contrasted with individualistic and self-blaming views expressed by most women incarcerated for drug and prostitution crimes committed to support addictions. In this way, the role of mothering served as catalyst and a rationale for crime that was not available to women without children in their custody.

Racial differences were apparent in the accounts of women, as African American women were more fully cognizant of the ways in which race, gender, and poverty were intertwined through institutionalized patterns of exclusion. All the African American women in our sample had been battered, and they were the most realistic about economic exclusions and their sole responsibility for meeting the economic needs of their children. American Indian women also dis-

cussed their experiences with racism but linked them more to addictions than to poverty. Latina women most often described their offending in terms of individual deficiencies and/or victimizations rather than structural economic constraints.

Alicia, a twenty-one-year-old biracial (African American/white) woman with two children, ages three and five, reported that she had been on her own since she was seventeen, having left the abusive father of her children. She completed a training program as a nursing assistant and had been working as well as selling crack. She was in jail for possession of crack, powder cocaine, and paraphernalia. The "paraphernalia" was the cigarette case she used to transport the drugs for sale. Although she thought that selling was wrong "because crack destroys people's lives," she felt her actions were "right at the time" because they allowed her to support her children:

I don't regret it because without the extra income, my kids wouldn't be fed every day. Even though I do have a good job when I work and stuff like that, it's hard raising two kids by yourself. . . . You get used to having money every day and you don't have to worry about the electric being off or the rent being paid. Your check is like your hard earned money; you're not going to spend it ridiculously like, "Oh, let's go buy a hundred-dollar pair of shoes with it." You know what I'm saying? You budget it because it's the only thing you look forward to for paying your bills. . . . But with that other money [paycheck] it goes so fast. As soon as you get it, the kids need new clothes or spend twenty dollars at the Circle K for candy. . . . We may not have chosen the right paths to go along in life, but I'm not a dummy. . . . They get mad at you if you can't get a job in two weeks. Who in the hell is going to employ you? I'm not going to McDonald's. McDonald's is not going to pay my rent. That's what they want you to do, lower your self-esteem to where you will take anything. I'm sorry, I have never worked for a five dollar an hour job, not since I was a teenager. I'm not going to now. I have two kids to support. Where am I going to live with them? In a shelter, making five dollars an hour. I'm not going to subject my kids to something like that. I'd rather just do my prison time if I have to do it and get rid of all of this.

Although she was one of the youngest women in the sample, Alicia rejected total, individual responsibility for her crime. Her explanation for selling crack reflects some of the aspects of individual worth in the African American community described by Gilbert (1999, 239): self-help, competence, confidence, and consciousness. She understood that the options available to her as a single mother were limited and that she was "a grain of sand" in the underground economy that would grind on with or without her participation. Her "good job" as a nursing assistant was sporadic and unreliable and paid about ten dollars an hour. She made a decision to sell crack to support her family and preferred going to jail to working at a minimum wage, dead-end job and living in a shelter with her children. She had a boyfriend who was also in jail, but she had no expectation that he would support her or her children.

Angel also committed crimes to support her seven children. A forty-one-year-old African American woman who grew up in an extremely abusive and violent environment, Angel disclosed that her father was a pimp and that she grew up in a house full of people who "used drugs twenty-four/seven." She moved out and lived on her own at age seventeen and put herself through two and a half years of college. She had been working at a well-paying sales job when her violent husband tracked her down and began to harass her. She quit her job and moved her family to Phoenix but was unable to find a job that would pay her bills. She began writing bad checks as a way of making ends meet. When asked if she was receiving any benefits while she was writing checks, she responded,

Sometimes yes, as the check writing went off and on for a period, for a number of years, so yes. Sometimes I was getting benefits; sometimes I wasn't. I would have to supplement my income writing the checks, buying the gro-

ceries, stealing money from the bank to pay for rent or to pay for a car repair. You know, it was always something. [Question: How much is your restitution?] Six thousand dollars, which isn't that bad, because most of it I was buying was just stuff for the kids: groceries, and clothing for the children, toys for the kids, just basic stuff, and my rent. There were a couple of times I went to the bank and wrote checks for cash and made it out for one thousand dollars cash that was for covering things, bills, stuff like that. There's a lot of girls in here that have restitution much greater than mine.

Restitution was one of the burdens women faced as they left jail, which added to their already precarious economic situations. The other significant burden was the terms of probation. Eight women (27 percent) had been incarcerated because of minor probation violations, such as failing to inform a probation officer of one's whereabouts or missing an appointment because of work, sickness, or lack of transportation. Complying with probation requirements, or drug court requirements, places tremendous demands on the resources of single mothers, which are already strained. Alicia explained the difficulties of parenting and following the guidelines of intensive probation services (IPS):

This is my probation's terms. Three to four times a week, counseling, but you have to pay for it. One girl said she was paying like sixty dollars a week just for three counseling sessions. Every time it was twenty bucks, bang. . . . They expect us to have a full-time job, which is fine, counseling four times a week, on top of community service two hours a day; so that's ten hours a week, so where is the time for your kids? And they know some people have kids, but they don't care. You mess up any step of the law and they're violating you and putting you in prison. That's a lot of things to look forward to. That's a lot of stuff. And if you don't go to counseling when they say to go, you're violated even if you drop clean every day. If you mess up in any of those areas. Say the traffic is bad, or say my daughter is asthmatic. She goes into an asthma attack in the middle of the night, I have to make sure I page my IPS worker and make sure he calls me back in time before I go to the doctor. My daughter could be suffocating in this time while he's taking his time calling me back and they don't care. You leave without them knowing, you're violated. They don't care if you're dying or your kids are dying. Good thing my daughter hasn't been in the hospital. She has a heart murmur. Anything can happen to her, and I don't feel like that's right for them to violate if I am at the hospital with my child. Even if I get there right away and I page them, they say, "Well, too bad. You're prison bound." That's what IPS stands for: in prison soon. A lot of people say that.

One other African American woman's original crime, welfare fraud, was obviously related to providing for her three children. She was not incarcerated for welfare fraud, however, but for violating the probation she received for that original offense by smoking marijuana. Her "dirty" urine analysis prompted the judge to revoke her probation and give her a felony conviction plus 120 days in jail. She felt this was unfair, created additional problems for her children, and limited her opportunities for employment. Patrice explained that at the time she "signed the welfare check," her baby's father was in prison, and she had no source of funds:

I wanted my baby a baby bed and wanted her this and I wanted her that, and he wasn't there. I didn't know where he was. Just one day he disappeared and I didn't know where he was. When I went for my sentencing, I thought he was going to let me go because I paid for all of my restitution for the welfare check and everything. My lawyer's like, "We think she should be released." And the judge goes, "No, I'm going to give her about 121 days." I said, "Why?" He goes, "'Cause you shouldn't have smoked that joint."

Patrice had recently obtained work release status and was trying to find a job. She wanted to get her three children back from her sister and move into a house but was worried about finances. Her story reflects the spiraling effects of getting caught up in the criminal justice system while trying to make ends meet:

Is there anything preventing me from getting a job? Yes, the felony that he gave me because of a little joint. I don't think he was very fair at all. I think that a felony is for somebody who did something really actually bad or something like that. I ain't sayin' what I did wasn't a crime. I know it was a crime. I just can't imagine why he would give me a felony because I broke probation and smoked a joint. I write down "felony" on my applications and everybody goes, "Oh no, we can't hire you." . . . A lot of us are in here for probation violations. The judge didn't care that we had kids or care that we lost our house or anything.

Lonna, a thirty-one-year-old biracial (Latina/white) woman with three children, was also in jail for violating probation after arrest for welfare fraud. She blamed her abusive husband for taking her money and creating an economic situation in which she felt compelled to commit welfare fraud:

I don't want to make it sound like it was all his fault, but it is. I've been married since 1986. There came a time, about 1995, when there was sometimes no water in the house, no electric, no food. So while I was working I collected welfare. Not only that, sometimes he would take my money anyway no matter if he was working or not. It didn't matter. Sometimes he'd just take my money anyway, so I would go and get extra checks.

Lonna was sentenced to probation and was able to maintain a good job. After she was switched to a new probation officer, however, she had trouble maintaining contact, was arrested, and was jailed for four months.

While these women's initial crimes were motivated by a desire to provide for their children, it was minor violations of probation terms that caused the greatest problems for them. Women attempted to manage the demands of motherhood, interlaced with traditional prescriptions for femininity, while providing income and dealing with prior and ongoing victimization. Scripted notions of successful mothering and of femininity made compliance with elaborate probation terms difficult as the women's lives were filled with expectations of caring for others while under the gaze of the state.

Jail as a Retreat

For many women, life was so arduous and precarious that incarceration was actually perceived as an improvement. This was particularly true for women who had lived in extreme battering situations, who felt protected from their abusers while in jail (although some women continued to be terrorized through prison and jail networks and threats to their children). Jail and prison are also dangerous for women, as abuse by correctional staff, neglect of health, and overuse of medications are common (see Human Rights Watch Women's Rights Project 1996; Amnesty International 1999, 2001; Moe and Ferraro 2002). The women in PCAD described many problems with the care and level of safety they experienced, but some also commented on the jail as a break from the demands of mothering, street life, and male violence. Angel, for example, was passionate about literature and was using her time to read and write. She said she had read more than fifty books since she had been in jail and was writing a novel called *My Sister's Wedding* in longhand. She also had plans for another book designed to help women find jobs after getting out of prison. She planned to write at least three books if she received the longest prison term possible. With six young children at home and her oldest son in prison, she viewed her time in jail as a "vacation":

> Yeah, this has really been like a vacation for me in a way, 'cause I get a chance to, when I was at home with the kids, I never got a chance to sit down and read books. It's impos-
sible to find the time to write when you have to work and you have to get the kids off to school or you have to do all of the things. I want to try to take this time and use it the best that I can to prepare myself for a career as a writer. If I'm paid to write and that's all I have to do, well then I can do that at home when my kids are at school. I don't have to get up and go to work.

Angel had a positive outlook on life. "You have to try to find the goodness in all the bad things that happen to us in life, and there's plenty if you look." She placed all six of her little girls with her mother in Florida when she was arrested. Although she was in a good relationship with a man at the time of her arrest, "he wasn't able to handle all six of the girls 'cause they're all girls." She discussed working with this man as photographers in a restaurant, but she had no expectation that he would share in parenting activities. The children's biological fathers were abusive or had abandoned them, and thus Angel took full responsibility for their care and delayed her personal goals. This was true for all women, none of whom had male partners on whom they could rely for child care.

Other women viewed the minimal health and nutrition services as a respite from street life. Boo was pregnant with her fourth child, and she felt the care she received in jail was positive. She had been incarcerated so many times that she knew the guards like family:

> To me this is my home away from home 'cuz I don't have nobody on the outside. So it's kind of hard for me but then at the same time I like it in here 'cuz I get that special attention that I crave. . . . I know all of the COs [correctional officers] here. They're like my uncles and aunts in my way, you know what I'm saying. They're real good people to me. I like them. . . . I get taken care of in here very well. They give us three pregnancy bags a day which contain two cartons of milk, two orange juices, and two fruits, and you get three pills three times a day during breakfast, lunch, and dinner, so you have your little snack bag.

Although most women complained about the food and health care available in the jail, for Boo, who lived on the streets, the jail provided a relatively healthy environment for her pregnancy.

Other women viewed their incarceration as a way to get away from an abusive husband. Lonna, quoted earlier, who was jailed for violating her probation for welfare fraud, explained that her jail time allowed her to break from her husband and that she would not return home. Her children were having problems while she was in jail, but she felt a divorce would benefit them eventually:

> They don't have a mom or a dad. My mother-in-law asked my son, "Why are you acting this way?" He says, "Why do I have to come home? I don't have a family." I hear in the background my older daughter says, "It's true. My mom's in jail and my dad's out partying." Damn. Anyway, I think it's a good thing that I came to jail. . . . I'm not going back home. I'm getting a divorce when I leave here. I'm just going to take the kids and leave. That's my plan when I leave here. . . . It's a good thing I'm here I guess. Not for the kids but it will be better in the long run.

Lonna had tried for fifteen years to make her marriage work, keep her family together, and have their bills paid. She assumed all the responsibility for her three children while her husband used her paycheck to buy drugs and liquor. She was attending classes in jail, which she believed were helping her to break free of that relationship and to help her children.

Similar to the women in Bosworth's (1999) study of women prisoners in England, femininity established the burdens and constraints women at PCAD faced as well as provided a grounds for resistance. The socially structured mandate for maternal responsibility for children's well-being and the failure of fathers and other men to provide support for parenting create a situation in which low-income women must struggle for money while providing care and denying their own dreams and interests. The state's interven-

tion creates additional burdens through incarceration and terms of probation that further complicate the already overwhelming demands on mothers. Jobs and wages are lost due to violent husbands, women are arrested for crimes of economic survival, and criminal records make it more difficult to find good jobs. At the same time, the care of children provided a grounds on which women could focus on future goals and improvements: a career in writing, a healthy pregnancy, and divorcing an abusive husband. While some women could embrace the role of mothering as an opportunity for personal growth and social acceptance, for others, that opportunity had already been lost through state intervention in custody.

Addictions and Child Protective Services

The majority (80 percent) of women interviewed were addicted to illegal drugs or alcohol. Crack cocaine was the most common drug, followed by heroin and crystal methamphetamine. Both crack and crystal were cheap and easily available in southern Arizona. A small "rock" of crack could be purchased for five dollars on the street. Heroin from Mexico was also quite easy to obtain. Thirteen women (43 percent) indicated that they were addicted to crack, with several of these women also using heroin, powder cocaine, or alcohol. Three women were alcoholics, and two women used crystal methamphetamine. Three of the six women who were not addicted to any substance were in jail because of their sale of crack or crystal. As Chesney-Lind (1997) and others have noted, the war on drugs clearly translates into a war on women.

Many women had lost custody of their children because of their addictions. Twelve women had children removed by CPS because of their alcohol or drug use. Ten had their parental rights severed and could not see their children until they turned eighteen, and two were still actively trying to have their children returned. The other twelve women with addictions had placed their children with relatives prior to incarceration. Several women indicated that the final severance decision was what pushed them into resumption of drug or alcohol use or into more serious addiction.

Theresa, a thirty-nine-year-old white woman with four children younger than sixteen and a twenty-two-year-old son, had much difficulty during her interview because of her extreme sadness and pain over the loss of her children. She showed no expression and spoke in a monotone. She was not pressed to elaborate on answers as it was obviously hard for her to remember and talk about her life. She was in jail because of a second driving under the influence charge that occurred when she resumed drinking after being sober for three and a half years. Her parental rights were severed because she reunited, briefly, with her abusive husband:

> I quit for three years, three and a half years, since 1995, and then when they said severance and adoption, I slightly fell off the wagon. [Question: You actually quit for three years and they still?] Yeah, they just brought up so many different things. They said we caused problems for the kids because of our arguments and our fighting and this and that. They bring up so many different things. [Question: Don't they have a plan, though, that you follow? And if you follow the plan then you get your kids back?] Yeah, I followed the plan. But then I got back with their dad, and he messed up and so then CPS said because it was my choice to get back with him that it ruined both of our chances of getting the kids back. And I told them, "I don't see how." That's when I lost it. The hardest I've ever drank in my life was last year. They were doing random drug testing and I was dropping clean. And I was doing all of their parenting classes and all their going to their psychiatrists plus going to my own psychiatrist plus doing my groups and doing AAs [Alcoholics Anonymous] and still, it didn't matter.

According to Theresa, her husband had received a two-and-a-half-year prison sentence for "trying to kill us." As she explained, "He beat me

up severely so where one eye, this whole side of my face was just black and blue and swollen shut for like a whole month, and he cut me, stabbed me, three times." Although her husband was out of the situation because of his incarceration, CPS severed Theresa's rights and placed her children up for adoption. As Theresa phrased it, "Until they're eighteen they've been sentenced to adoption." Her plans focused on the day of their reunification: "What are my plans? To stay sober. I want to finish my education, get on with my life. Hopefully it will go a little faster so I can see my kids when they're eighteen."

Theresa's case illustrates the importance of children to women's recovery from alcohol and drugs and the despair that emerges when rights are severed. Her case also reflects the ways in which CPS agencies fail to respond appropriately to domestic violence by removing children from women who are abused. The district court ruling in *Nicholson v. Scoppetta* found that New York City's Administration for Children's Services had demonstrated "benign indifference, bureaucratic inefficiency and outmoded institutional biases" in removing children from the custody of women who had been beaten by their abusers (Friedlin 2002). . . .

Gillian, a thirty-six-year-old white woman, began using crack after CPS severed her rights to her daughter. Her only child was removed from the home after reporting to her grandmother that her father had sexually molested her. Gillian and her daughter moved in with Gillian's mother after her husband assaulted and threatened to kill her. Her daughter was nine at the time and intellectually gifted, while Gillian had a learning disability and had not graduated from high school. Although she was following all the guidelines set by CPS, her rights were severed and she felt as if she had lost everything:

> She [her daughter] had been sexually molested when she was younger than that. I didn't know it. I had been going through the courts doing everything they asked me to, and they lied to

me. [Question: Child protective services?]
Yeah, CPS lied to me. [Question: What did
they lie to you about?] Saying that if I did
everything they told me to I would get her back.
They lied to her too saying that she was going
to be moving back in with me. They lied to both
of us. We went to court. I didn't have a GED
[general equivalency diploma]. I have dyslexia.
I have a learning disability. They said her intelligence would be wasted if they gave her back
to me because I couldn't afford her education
and I couldn't teach her how to read as she got
older. I have dyslexia and I see words backward
sometimes if I'm not careful. They used her IQ.
It was 121 at the age of seven. She could not
read. They figured her being with me would be
a waste of time because I couldn't give her the
education she needed. I didn't know that education was more important than love. I guess it
is in their eyes. . . . I was like, "They've been
lying to me all this time." Finally we went to
court and they tried to say I had a drug and
alcohol problem. I didn't even do drugs back
then. I smoked pot, but since I've been in Tuc-
son, I haven't smoked no weed. I did drink.
They said I had a drug problem, and I don't
even know where they got that. I wasn't even
doing drugs. I did start drugs after I lost her.
About two to three months later, I did it. I was
like, "Hell, they said I did it." I didn't have
nothing to lose then. I had already lost her, so
that's when I started doing drugs.

Certainly, there is a possibility that women
misunderstood or misrepresented the severance
process that resulted in the loss of their children.
The important point that can be drawn from these
narratives, however, is that women's use of drugs
or alcohol was often related in their own minds to
the loss of their children. With "nothing to lose,"
and easy access to crack and alcohol, these
women were drawn into usage that eventually resulted in their incarceration.

For some addicted women, use of crack cocaine preceded state intervention; however, they
felt it was impossible to stop using. The threat of
losing their children, or even damaging their children, could not overcome their dependence on

crack. All the women indicated their sincere desire to stop using crack and their belief that crack
had "taken everything." Many were awaiting limited bed space in residential treatment centers. All
were attending Narcotics Anonymous and AA
groups, and most felt that God was helping them
get off drugs by sending them to jail. Women addicted to crack indicated that it was not possible
for them to stop using while they lived in the
neighborhoods where crack was easily available
and all their acquaintances were using.

Two women had used crack while they were
pregnant and felt enormous grief and guilt about
endangering their babies. Peaches, a thirty-two-
year-old African American woman, gave birth to
a stillborn baby because of her use of crack. In
jail for prostitution, she described a horrendous
history of childhood sexual abuse. Peaches was
the youngest of thirteen children, and her mother
forced her to have sex with all of her siblings, as
well as herself and her boyfriend. Her father took
her away from this situation when she was six,
but he also sexually abused her. She had a seven-
teen-year-old daughter and fourteen-, thirteen-,
twelve-, and nine-year-old sons and had lost custody of all of them. Of all of the traumas she had
experienced, however, she described the death of
her baby as the worst:

I have six kids. I have four boys, and I have a
daughter, and then I have a little boy who
passed away. [Question: Oh, I'm sorry. When
did that happen?] In 1990. He was a crack baby.
He was stillborn. I carried him for the whole
nine months. I felt his last kick. That was the
hardest thing I had to go through in my life. I
don't think all the molestation and everything
that I've been through has been worse than having a stillborn. I carried that baby for nine
months. I don't think none of that that I've
been through can top that day. I think that's the
biggest problem that I'm having. I can't forgive
myself for that. That's my biggest problem.
[Question: You think the drugs did it?] Oh yes.
There's no doubt in my mind that the drugs did
it. I was doin' drugs as I was in labor. [Ques-
tion: Did the doctors actually say that it was

because of the drugs?] No, they didn't exactly say it was because of the drugs, but deep down inside, I know that was what it was. They wanted to go before a judge and get court orders to do autopsies. At that time, they had just passed a law that if a woman has a baby that's dead or something's wrong with the baby . . . like, my baby was dead so they could have charged me for murder on that child because I had been smokin' drugs. I didn't want that to happen so I did not give them permission to do an autopsy on my baby. The judge wouldn't give them permission because at the time that I was going for prenatal care, they were tellin' me that the baby was fine.

Peaches could not forgive herself and had little hope of ever seeing her children again. She had decided, however, that she was at the end of the line with crack and had to give it up or die:

When I leave, I'm leaving here with nothing. No probation. When I do go to rehab, it's because I want to. . . . Matter of fact, I think it is the only option for me because there's only two lives. If we choose drugs, that's death. That's the way I feel. If you choose to not do drugs, that's life. I don't want to die doin' drugs. I don't want to die and have to be put in a cardboard box and buried in a cemetery because nobody claims me. That's the only option for me.

Tina's baby did not die, and she had not yet lost custody of her two children who were living with her parents. A twenty-seven-year-old Latina, Tina had been taken directly to jail after giving birth. She was arrested for violating probation, which she had received for drug trafficking and racketeering. During her interview, she lifted her T-shirt to show forty to fifty small, round burn scars on her stomach that had been caused by hiding her hot crack pipe in the waistband of her maternity pants. Tina had also been molested as a child, raped at age twelve, and stabbed and beaten by a group of girls who attacked her for her jewelry. At the time of the interview, her baby was a month old and Tina had been in jail for three

weeks and four days. She had stopped using crack for six months during her pregnancy and was living far from town with a friend. There was no public transportation available, and she did not have a car, so her probation officer issued a violation for missed appointments. Tina knew she was facing IPS anyway, so she decided to attend a party with her friend and succumbed to the offer of crack. She cried heavily as she explained:

I did it; and I was laughing; and I remember hitting it and then feeling her move inside of me, like right after I hit the crack; and I still didn't stop; and then the fourth time I hit it, my plug broke and then my water broke. They wanted to go get more drugs and I was there by myself, and I called my dad and I told him. I was scared, you know? What if she died? They could at least treat her for the cocaine. They didn't violate me for probation for it or anything. I figured I couldn't stop; I mean, I stopped because I was away from it. But I couldn't stop when I was around it. So that's why I needed the help. And after seeing her go through the IV, you know, they were testing her, making sure. . . . It threw her complete blood count off. It was real bad; it was real off. But she's healthy now, but to see her hooked up to all them things and bruised up from them. She's just a little baby. It's awful, just seeing her. . . . She's a little angel from God. For me to just imagine one hit . . . what it does to me. Imagine what it did to her little brain. . . . Looking at her little eyes, her little smiles, thinking every little thing, "Is that because I did crack?" You know? "Is that because I had smoked when she had first developed?" I was scared, 'cuz I didn't know I was pregnant. But every little thing that I saw, I was just paranoid. Excuse me [crying hard], I'm like, just like for me to hurt her, just horrible. . . . CPS got involved; I mean, I don't blame them, the hospital called them, and you know, they treated me like a monster, and I felt like a monster; I *knew* I was a monster. But the remorse I feel, the hurt. . . . My dad gets mad when I tell him I love my kids and I'm gonna change. He says, "Don't tell me you love them; every time you tell me, that makes me sick after what you did."

Tina and Peaches expressed a desire to stop using crack and bore tremendous sadness and guilt about the harm caused to their babies and their families. They shared the hegemonic public view of crack mothers as evil baby killers who deserve nothing but contempt, and they felt self-contempt as "monsters." They desperately wanted help and had long histories of abuse in addition to their addictions. The intensive assistance required to help them recover from their addictions and return to a mothering role was not available to them. Instead, the only motivation for recovery, their children, had been taken away, and they have nothing to look forward to except guilt and regret. These data suggest that decisions about child custody play a central role in women's resistance to the psychological anesthesia offered by drugs and alcohol. Balancing the need to protect children and promote women's health and well-being requires programs that are attuned to both mothers and children and flexible in their ability to provide support to both.

Mothering and Identity from Inside

The majority of women in jail had identities that reflected some of the social approbation that their incarceration signified. Like Tina and Patrice, cited earlier, the linkage of their drug usage with harm to their children contributed to self-images as "monsters," and they were unable to forgive themselves. Women who had prostituted for drugs or lost custody because of drugs also had negative judgments about those aspects of their identities. Other women resisted stigmatization by contextualizing their offenses within the realities of economic marginalization and violent victimization. As Alicia pointed out, "We're not all bad people."

In struggling to develop positive identities, mothering was critical in sustaining perceptions of value and goodness. In the abstract, motherhood is a highly valued status, and women viewed the facts of their motherhood as a potential source of social acceptance. At a deeper level, however, many women indicated that their links

to their children were central to their selfhood. Children were extensions of their own identities, separate yet constitutive of women's subjectivity. In one case in which it was physically possible, a woman returned to one of us with pictures of her children after her own interview ended. Other women indicated regret that they did not have photographs available to show us and spoke of how beautiful and cute their children were.

India, a thirty-one-year-old American Indian woman with six children, illustrated the importance of children to women's identities most graphically. She had tattoos for each child's name on various parts of her body. A heart with flowers around a blank space on her right breast was reserved for her youngest child whose name she had not yet had tattooed. She had lost her children to CPS at one point but regained custody after following their requirements. Her children were with their father's sister, and she planned to reunite with them after completing her sentence.

Even women whose rights had been terminated and who were prohibited from interacting with their children believed that they would be reunited one day. Julianna had lost custody of her four children but believed that some day they would be together again:

I believe in my heart of hearts, once you birth a child, they can take your child from you for so long, but that child will come back. Listen to a lot of these talk shows on how families are starting to reunite. Just look at the awesome power of God to bring families back together that haven't been together for fourteen, twenty, thirty years. I have a dream that one day my two children that is within the state, I will see them. We will reunite and be together. With my other children in Nebraska, I have no doubt that I will see them. They'll be family. God will show me the way for us to reunite and be together again. That's my strong belief.

The likelihood of Julianna reuniting her family was small, but focusing on this dream gave her the hope and strength to go on living. Like many jailed women, she believed that God was guiding her life and would ultimately return her children to her. She described what she believed to be direct communication with God:

> That's when He spoke to me, sternly this time. "I'm gonna pick you up, and I will turn your life around, and I will make you want success and great things. Most of all, I will make you a great woman of God and you will be a great woman. I'm gonna bring you back to your children again." That, right there, is enough for me to hold on, to walk through the storm and the rain, and move on with my life.

Linda, who lost custody of three children because of her crack and heroin addictions, also believed that God would return her children to her:

> I ask God to give me my life back, give me my children back. And so now, this is a start. I'm okay with where I'm at because I know when I leave here it won't be long before I can reunite with my children. Not right away, but eventually it's goin' to come together. I know God is gonna give them back to me. I know I'm goin' to see them real soon. Without them, I'm nothin'. I just thank God.

Even women whose children had died carried their memories and the grief over their loss as a central aspect of their identities. Buckwheat's son had been killed in a drive-by shooting five years before we met her. She said that she went into a "blackout" for eight days and was finally awakened by the boy's father. He told her, "You didn't do nothin'. I had to go up to you and put the mirror to your face to see if you were alive." She described how a recent Valentine's Day visit at the jail had confirmed her son's eternal life and continued relationship to her:

> This past Valentine's, they had these Christian women come out here for a Valentine's thing in here. They gave out these little heart-shaped doilies and they had a little prayer on them, and they said to all of us, "These are special gifts

that we're goin' to give you and hopefully the right one is goin' to reach you." Well, it surprised me about the one that they gave me because it said, "I gave my son to the Lord and for. . . ." I can't think of all of it but that he would live forever. I said, "Oh my God." And He told me to let it go. To let him go.

The continued importance of children to women's identities, despite severance or even death, was clear in all the women's narratives. This connection helped women to survive and look forward to the future with hope. It also made incarceration and separation from children more painful and worrisome due to the impact on children and the difficulties of mothering from inside the detention facility.

Conclusion

Mothering in an environment of scarce resources places women in a web of demands and constraints that may lead to incarceration. Selling drugs or cashing bad checks to meet bills and turning to drugs and alcohol as a way of coping with the psychological pain of childhood sexual abuse or the ongoing pain of domestic violence are the primary pathways that lead women to jail (Daly 1994; Henriques and Manatu 2001; Katz 2000). Incarceration then creates greater burdens for maintaining positive relationships with children and for managing the demands of probation once released. Women interviewed at the PCAD had survived horrendous abuse and poverty yet maintained hope for a positive future and eventual reunion with their children.

Mothering simultaneously reproduces the unequal sexual division of labor and provides possibilities for resistance to marginalization and despair. The assumption that women will be primary caretakers and will provide resources and love for children when men do not demands that women obtain money and dispense care without much assistance. The possibility that women will become involved in crime as a result of trying to meet these demands is exacerbated by race and class hierarchies that restrict access to incomes adequate to support children.

The chaotic and demanding community contexts that lead women to view jail as a "vacation" suggest that there are complex problems facing low-income mothers that cannot be resolved either through programs for the children of incarcerated mothers or through revisions in sentencing policies. Reversing the trend of incarceration of minor drug and property offenders would ameliorate some of the harsh circumstances for both mothers and children created by incarceration. However, the violence, poverty, drug abuse, and mental health problems that women face outside of jail can only be addressed through systematic attention to the sources of these problems for women. Recent social policy trends exacerbate the obstacles facing many women. Exclusion of convicted drug offenders from social welfare programs, zero-tolerance housing policies that evict battered women from public housing, punitive and restrictive Temporary Assistant to Needy Families guidelines, and programs that encourage women to marry as a solution to poverty make it more difficult for low-income single mothers to survive in the United States than at any time since the Great Depression. The narratives of jailed women reflect this difficulty and the failure of social policies to remedy the cumulative effects of violent victimization, poverty, racism, drug addictions, and mental health problems on women's abilities to mother their children.

While mothering complicates women's abilities to negotiate marginalized existence, it also provides a resource for hope and positive identity. The dominant ideology of motherhood is reflected in women's accounts of their inadequacies and failures but also in their insistence on fighting against addictions, male violence, and poverty. Although the desire to be a "good mother," and the dimensions of that construct, may be a vector of the social control of women, it is simultaneously a grounds from which women challenge structural and individual sources of oppression.

References

Allen, Hilary. 1987. Rendering them harmless: The professional portrayal of women charged with serious violent crimes. In *Gender, crime and justice*, edited by Pat Carlen and Anne Worrall, 81–94. Philadelphia: Open University Press.

Amnesty International. 1999. *"Not part of my sentence": Violations of the human rights of women in custody*. Available from http://web.amnesty.org.

———. 2001. *New reports of children and women abused in correctional institutions. Findings from Amnesty International research trip*. Available from http://webamnesty.org.

Arnold, Regina. 1990. Processes of victimization and criminalization of black women. *Social Justice* 17: 153–66.

Baunach, Phyllis Jo. 1985. *Mothers in prison*. New Brunswick, NJ: Transaction Publishing.

Belknap, Joanne. 2001. *The invisible woman: Gender, crime, and justice*. 2d ed. Belmont, CA: Wadsworth.

Bloom, Barbara. 1992. Incarcerated mothers and their children: Maintaining family ties. In *Female offenders: Meeting the needs of a neglected population*. Laurel, MD: American Correctional Association.

Bloom, Barbara, Meda Chesney-Lind, and Barbara Owen. 1994. *Women in California prisons: Hidden victims of the war on drugs*. San Francisco: Center on Juvenile and Criminal Justice.

Bloom, Barbara, and David Steinhart. 1993. *Why punish the children? A reappraisal of the children of incarcerated mothers in America*. San Francisco: National Council on Crime and Delinquency.

Bosworth, Mary. 1999. *Engendering resistance: Agency and power in women's prisons*. Aldershot, UK: Ashgate.

Boudin, Kathy. 1998. Lessons from a mother's program in prison: A psychosocial approach supports women and their children. In *Breaking the rules: Women in prison and feminist therapy*, edited by Judy Harden and Marcia Hill, 103–125. New York: Haworth.

Caddle, Diane. 1998. *Age limits for babies in prison: Some lessons from abroad*. London: Home Office Research, Development and Statistics Directorate.

Caiazza, Amy B. 2000. *The status of women in Arizona*. Washington, DC: Institute for Women's Policy Research.

Chesney-Lind, Meda. 1997. *The female offender: Girls, women, and crime.* Thousand Oaks, CA: Sage.

Chesney-Lind, Meda, Mary Kay Harris, and Gabrielle deGroot. 1998. Female offenders. *Corrections Today* 60(7): 66–144.

Daly, Kathleen. 1994. *Gender, crime and punishment.* New Haven, CT: Yale University Press.

Dobash, Russell P., R. Emerson Dobash, and Sue Gutteridge. 1986. *The imprisonment of women.* London: Basil Blackwell.

Elliott, Terri. 1994. Making strange what had appeared familiar. *Monist* 77: 424–33.

Enos, Sandra. 2001. *Mothering from the inside: Parenting in a women's prison.* New York: State University of New York Press.

Fineman, Martha A. 1995. Images of mothers in poverty discourse. In *Mothers in law: Feminist theory and the legal regulation of motherhood,* edited by Martha A. Fineman and Isabel Karpin, 205–23. New York: Columbia University Press.

Friedlin, Jennifer. 2002. Judge exposes agency harm to battered mothers, kids. *Women's E News,* April 28.

Gilbert, Evelyn. 1999. Crime, sex, and justice: African American women in U.S. prisons. In *Harsh punishment: International experiences of women's imprisonment,* edited by Sandy Cook and Suzanne Davies, 230–49. Boston: Northeastern University Press.

Gilfus, Mary E. 1992. From victims to survivors to offenders: Women's routes of entry and immersion into street crime. *Women and Criminal Justice* 4:63–90.

Glick, Ruth M., and Virginia V. Neto. 1977. *National study of women's correctional programs.* Washington, DC: U.S. Department of Justice.

Greenfield, Lawrence A., and Tracy L. Snell. 1999. *Bureau of Justice Statistics special report: Women offenders* (NCJ 175688). Washington, DC: U.S. Department of Justice.

Harrison, Paige M., and Allen J. Beck. 2002. *Bureau of Justice Statistics bulletin: Prisoners in 2001* (NCJ 195189). Washington, DC: U.S. Department of Justice.

Hartsock, Nancy. 1987. The feminist standpoint: Developing a ground for a specifically feminist historical materialism. In *Feminism and methodology,* edited by Sandra Harding, 157–76. Milton Keynes, UK: Open University Press.

Henriques, Zelma W. 1982. *Imprisoned mothers and their children.* Lanham, MD: University Press of America.

Henriques, Zelma W., and Rupert N. Manatu. 2001. Living on the outside: African American women before, during, and after imprisonment. *The Prison Journal* 81 (1): 6–19.

Hill Collins, Patricia. 1989. The social construction of black feminist thought. *Signs* 14:745–73.

———. 2000. *Black feminist thought: Knowledge, consciousness, and the politics of empowerment.* New York: Routledge.

Human Rights Watch Women's Rights Project. 1996. *All too familiar: Sexual abuse of women in U.S. state prisons.* New York: Human Rights Watch.

Humphries, Drew. 1999. *Crack mothers.* Columbus: Ohio State University Press.

Ikemoto, L. C. 1997. Furthering the inquiry: Race, class, and culture in the forced medical treatment of pregnant women. In *Critical race feminism: A reader,* edited by Adrien K. Wing, 136–143. New York: New York University Press.

Immarigeon, Russ, and Meda Chesney-Lind. 1992. *Women's prisons: Overcrowded and overused.* San Francisco: National Council on Crime and Delinquency.

Karush, Sarah. 2002. Kremlin pardons imprisoned mothers. *The Globe and Mail,* March 20, p. A16.

Katz, Rebecca S. 2000. Explaining girls' and women's crime and desistance in the context of their victimization experiences: A developmental test of revised strain. *Violence Against Women* 6 (6): 633–60.

Kline, Marlee. 1995. Complicating the ideology of motherhood: Child welfare law and First Nation women. In *Mothers in law: Feminist theory and the legal regulation of motherhood,* edited by Martha A. Fineman and Isable Karpin, 118–41. New York: Columbia University Press.

Miller, Jody. 1998. Up it up: Gender and the accomplishment of street robbery. *Criminology* 36:37–65.

Moe, Angela M., and Kathleen J. Ferraro. 2002. Malign neglect or benign respect: Women's health care in a carceral setting. Paper presented at the annual meetings of the Academy of Criminal Justice Sciences, March 5–9, Anaheim, CA.

Molloy, Maureen. 1992. Citizenship, property, and bodies: Discourses on gender and the inter-war labor government in New Zealand. *Gender and History* 4:293–304.

Morash, Merry. 1998. *Women offenders: Programming needs and promising approaches*. Washington, DC: U.S. Department of Justice.

Mumola, Cristopher J. 2000. *Incarcerated parents and their children*. Bureau of Justice Statistics special report. Washington, DC: U.S. Department of Justice.

Nagel, Irene H., and John Hagan. 1983. Gender and crime: Offense patterns and criminal court sanctions. In *Crime and justice*, vol. 4, edited by Michael Tonry and Norval Morris, 91–144. Chicago: University of Chicago Press.

Narayan, Uma. 1988. Working together across difference: Some considerations on emotions and political practice. *Hypatia* 3 (2): 31–47.

National Institute of Corrections. 2002. *Services for families of prison inmates*. Longmont, CO: National Institute of Corrections Information Center.

Orbuch, Terri L. 1997. People's accounts count: The sociology of accounts. *Annual Review of Sociology* 23:455–78.

Richie, Beth E. 1996. *Compelled to crime: The gender entrapment of battered black women*. New York: Routledge.

———. 2001. Challenges incarcerated women face as they return to their communities: Findings from life history interviews. *Crime & Delinquency* 47:368–89.

Roberts, Dorothy E. 1995. Racism and patriarchy in the meaning of motherhood. In *Mothers in law: Feminist theory and the legal regulation of motherhood*, edited by Martha A. Fineman and Isabel Karpin, 224–49. New York: Columbia University Press.

Ross, Luana. 1998. *Inventing the savage*. Austin: University of Texas Press.

Sandoval, Chela. 2000. *Methodology of the oppressed*. Minneapolis: University of Minnesota Press.

Schafer, N. E., and A. B. Dellinger. 1999. Jailed parents: An assessment. *Women and Criminal Justice* 10 (4): 73–118.

Smart, Carol. 1995. Criminological theory: Its ideology and implications concerning women. In *Law, crime and sexuality: Essays in feminism*, edited by Carol Smart, 16–31. London: Sage.

———. 1998. The woman of legal discourse. In *Criminology at the crossroads: Feminist readings in crime and justice*, edited by Kathleen Daly and Lisa Maher, 21–36. New York: Oxford University Press.

Smith, Dorothy. 1987. *The everyday world as problematic: A feminist sociology*. Toronto, Canada: University of Toronto Press.

Snell, Tracy L. 1994. *Women in prison: Survey of state prison inmates*, 1991. Washington, DC: U.S. Department of Justice.

Sommers, Ira B., Deborah Baskin, and Jeffrey Fagan. 2000. *Workin' hard for the money: The social and economic lives of women drug sellers*. Huntington, NY: Nova Science Publishers.

Stanton, Ann M. 1980. *When mothers go to jail*. Lexington, MA: D. C. Health.

U.S. General Accounting Office. 1999. *Women in prison: Issues and challenges confronting U.S. correctional systems*. Washington, DC: U.S. General Accounting Office.

Watterson, Kathryn. 1996. *Women in prison: Inside the concrete womb*. Rev. ed. Boston: Northeastern University Press.

Young, Vernetta D. 1986. Gender expectations and their impact on black female offenders and victims. *Justice Quarterly* 3:305–27.

Zalba, Serapio R. 1964. *Women prisoners and their families*. Albany, NY: Delmar.

PART EIGHT

Resistance and Social Change

Resistance to social injustice takes many forms. Previous chapters have described the ways that women assert their subjectivity against dehumanizing work, relationships, sexual practices, and cultural scripts that restrict their desires and aspirations. Women's personal strategies of resistance provide the foundation for organizing with others for collective goals. Without a sense of agency and efficacy, women may not feel they can change the world around them. Social change begins at the personal level and gains power and momentum as people join together to address social and political problems.

People are often paralyzed by the complexity and scope of the problems facing contemporary society. When the entire planet seems on the brink of a meltdown, people may feel that there is little that one individual can do. People may also view social activism as something in which only devoted purists can participate. All people living in the United States in the twenty-first century face contradictions and compromises between their beliefs and actions. If only ideological purists participated in activism, there would be no activism. As Winona

LaDuke writes, "You don't have to be Superwoman to change the world. You just have to take responsibility for your life and your community—and realize that you have the power to do so, even from your own sticky kitchen table" (quoted in Baumgardner and Richards, 2005: xv).

The arenas in which women participate in social activism are not limited to "women's issues," as women's lives are connected to every aspect of their communities. In this section, women describe their participation in environmental, anti-war, anti-racist, and labor issues. Barbara Schulman describes the value of a human rights framework for representing political claims. Her article outlines some of the gains of the global women's human rights movement and ways the human rights model can be applied to local issues in the United States. People in the United States often assume that "human rights" are already guaranteed at home and are only an issue in the developing world. Schulman demonstrates the utility of adopting the international treaties, the Convention on the Elimination of All Forms of Discrimination Against Women (CEDAW) and the Convention on the Elimination of All Forms of Racial Discrimination (CERD) to address discrimination against women of color in the United States. Although the United States has not ratified CEDAW (the only industrialized country that has failed to do so), individual cities have passed ordinances that endorse the principles of CEDAW. This allows cities to use international treaties to develop mechanisms for monitoring and enforcing the guarantees of basic human rights to all people. Schulman notes this strategy is particularly effective at embracing an intersectional approach to social change, an approach that has proven difficult to implement with existing U.S. law. While Schulman defines our current global situation as a "terrible time," she finds significant hope in the human rights model of social change.

While some women have the luxury of choosing which issues they'll address, at what time and in what manner, other women become involved in activism as a matter of survival. Janet McCloud (1934–2003), for example, became involved in Native activism when her community's livelihood was threatened. In the early 1960s, Washington state agents violated treaty rights by cordoning off ancient fishing areas on the Nisqually River to secure dwindling catches for commercial and tourist fishing. Without an advanced university degree, a grant, or specific training, McCloud organized her community in the "fishing wars" that led to a district court ruling upholding the treaty rights entitling indigenous tribes to half of all the salmon and steelhead catch in Washington. Her work on the issue of fishing rights led her to join with indigenous activists around the world who work to protect their lands. Like most indigenous activists, McCloud did not consider herself exceptional or separate from the community. She devoted much of her life to reinvigorating Native traditions, producing food on her ten-acre homestead with her husband and eight children. In her later years, she opened her home to children, helping them connect with Native traditions and practices. Her collectivist orientation differs from some activists in the non-Native world, suggesting one of the dimensions of difference that may stymy social movements.

Chrystos's poetry often addresses the ways that non-Natives, whites in particular, fail to see the women of color around them. In "Maybe We Shouldn't Meet if There Are No Third World Women Here," Chrystos expresses her rage at the "familiar shock" of racism that causes white women to be oblivious to the ways they exclude women of color and then wonder why they are absent. Even when women of color attend meetings, they seem to be invisible to the white leadership, both in terms of their physical presence and their ideas. The bitterness engendered by white privilege and exclusionary practices renders the white women invisible to Chrystos and the possibilities for coalition are deferred until the time that white women take full responsibility for their racism. If you are a white woman and Chrystos's poem makes you feel defensive, try reversing the scenario. How would you feel at a meeting where you were the only white woman in attendance and a speaker announced, "There are no white women here"? Remember that Chrystos wrote and published her poem, baring her pain and disillusionment, to bring this issue into the open. We certainly cannot move forward together without acknowledging the problems that keep us apart.

You will also read about eighteen-year-old Lila Zucker of the Radical Cheerleaders and sixteen-year-old Ava Lowery who created a website and video pieces against the Iraq War. These young women illustrate that age is no barrier to social activism. Lowery's work makes use of the new internet technologies that allow global activism from the comfort of your home, and Zucker's work demonstrates that activism can be fun and humorous. Finally, the Madres de Este Los Angeles-Santa Isabel (MELASI) and Detroiters Working for Environmental Justice (DWEJ) are examples of successful grassroots organizing against the harmful actions of large corporations. The MELASI motto is: "Not economically rich, but culturally wealthy. Not politically powerful, but socially conscious. Not mainstream educated, but armed with the knowledge, commitment, and determination that only a mother can possess." Elsa Lopez, a project director for MELASI, found that her social invisibility at meetings actually helped achieve her goals. The lawyers and corporate executives did not recognize her as a political activist and so spoke freely about their plans, arming her with the information to challenge their proposed impact on her community.

What would you like to change in your own community, and what prevents you from taking the first step? The essays in this section are a tiny sampling of the work women are doing to create social change. You may find that you are already an activist, or that there are ways to become an agent of change that do not require you to relinquish the things you enjoy but to simply be more conscious of your everyday choices and their consequences.

Reference

Baumgardner, Jennifer, and Amy Richards. (2005). *Grassroots: A Field Guide for Feminist Activism*. New York: Farrar, Straus and Giroux.

Chrystos

Maybe We Shouldn't Meet if There Are No Third World Women Here

My mouth cracks in familiar shock   my eyes flee
to the other faces where my rage desperation fear pain ricochet
a thin red scream   How can you miss our brown & golden
in this sea of pink   We're not as many as you
But we're here   You're the ones who called a community
meeting & didn't contact the Black Lesbians or G.A.L.A. or
Gay American Indians or the Disabled Women's Coalition or
Gay Asians or anyone I know
You're the ones who don't print your signs in Spanish or Chinese
or any way but how you talk   You're the ones standing three
feet away from a Black woman saying
There are no Third World women here
Do you think we are Martians
All those workshops on racism won't help you open your eyes & see
how you don't even see us
How can we come to your meetings if we are invisible
Don't look at me with guilt   Don't apologize   Don't struggle
with the problem of racism like algebra
Don't write a paper on it for me to read or hold a meeting in
which you discuss what to do to get us to come to your
time & your place
We're not your problems to understand & trivialize
We don't line up in your filing cabinets under "R" for rights
Don't make the racist assumption that the issue of racism
between us
is yours   at me
Bitter boiling I can't see you

ARTICLE 38

Barbara Schulman

Effective Organizing in Terrible Times: The Strategic Value of Human Rights for Transnational Anti-Racist Feminisms

These are terrible times, and terrible times require those committed to social change to rethink our approaches—not only to ensure that we remain relevant but also to help sustain hope, both in ourselves and in others.

Recently, I've encountered hope in an unexpected place. After twenty years of activism, writing and teaching under a variety of mantles —primarily feminism and anti-racism, but also anti-militarism, anti-imperialism, and queer liberation—I've become immersed in the world of human rights. My turn to the human rights framework is certainly contextual: it is a response to the current political climate, as well as to the expansion and radicalization of the global human rights movement, both of which I will address below. But more fundamentally, it is a strategic turn, one that engages issues of naming and movement-building. While I passionately subscribe to the multiracial and transnational feminist vision articulated by radical women of color, indigenous and "two-thirds world" women, this is a difficult politic to package accessibly. Moreover, representing oneself as a feminist of any kind can trigger knee-jerk antipathy from a variety of quarters, even before one has a chance to begin the conversation. In the face of the intense and

rapid consolidation of repressive forces globally since 9/11, it is obvious that if those seeking to upend the existing social order can't work together across issues and identity groups or make our messages meaningful to broader sectors of the disenfranchised and disenchanted, we simply can't be effective. The question of how we represent our politics is therefore more urgent than ever.

In light of these challenges, one of the most important strategic advantages of the term "human rights" for proponents of social change in the United States is its ubiquity. Barring religious extremists, there are few who do not profess support for human rights—at least in the abstract. Both government officials and their most radical critics are equally comfortable claiming the term, often, of course, to advance disparate agendas. But the overall goodwill that attaches to human rights only runs skin deep, since few are actually acquainted with either its specific principles or formal mechanisms. Despite the best efforts of human rights advocates, the vast majority of U.S. Americans remain unaware that every human being is entitled to a comprehensive and internationally accepted slate of rights, regardless of gender, race, nationality (or lack thereof), citizenship status, political or religious affiliation, or any other identity; that this slate includes the rights to an adequate standard of living, affordable healthcare, a life free from violence and discrimination, a culture, and even adequate time for rest; or that an increasingly elaborate system of legal tools and monitoring bodies has been designed to

Source: "Effective Organizing in Terrible Times: The Strategic Value of Human Rights for Transnational Anti-Racist Feminisms," by Barbara Shulman. 2004. Meridians, Volume 4, Issue 2, pp. 102–108. Used by permission of Indiana University Press.

enable ordinary people to hold our government accountable for respecting, protecting and fulfilling these rights.

This disparity between the general favor directed toward human rights and the lack of concrete knowledge about it actually creates a raft of opportunities for activists working within a variety of liberatory traditions, because the relatively non-threatening language of human rights can function as the opening wedge in conversations with those who may be resistant to more pointed critiques. Re-framing issues through the lens of human rights can help garner support for all manner of progressive agendas. But this is not a politics of mirage, since all manner of progressive agendas legitimately fall within the domain of human rights. The drafters of the Universal Declaration of Human Rights or UDHR—the originary statement of principles adopted by the United Nations in 1948 from which all formal human rights instruments flow—sought to identify the conditions necessary for every human being to live a safe, fulfilled, and dignified life. This aim required a vision and a system flexible enough to address unforeseen abuses, to be extended to newly disenfranchised groups, and to accommodate new rights claims as they might arise. It is this adaptability and comprehensiveness, all wrapped in a broadly palatable package, that makes human rights a radical model in liberal clothing.

I was not always a proponent of human rights. For many years I was extremely resistant to the model, in large part because its ostensibly "universal" standards obscured an analysis of the global imbalance of power. In the context of accelerating inequalities between nations and peoples, human rights has frequently been wielded as an ideological club by wealthy and powerful nations—such as our own—against those they seek to keep in line. Similarly, the language of human rights has provided yet another rhetorical means for globally dominant cultures to demonize cultural and ethnic groups already ravaged by centuries of colonialism, racism, and, now, neoliberalism.

So what accounts for my conversion? I want to identify a few of the factors that pushed me to rethink my resistance to the human rights model, because I believe they help point to some of its advantages, especially for feminists working from anti-racist and transnational perspectives. First, as I alluded to earlier, I was increasingly concerned about the disconnect between various progressive movements at a time when broadening our base of action was critical. Like many before me, I recognized in human rights a vehicle for grass-roots multi-issue organizing across communities of comfort, identity, and interest. Second, in this era of globalization, many of the problems facing individuals in our communities are directly linked to the same international economic, social, and political forces affecting others around the world. Yet we often are mired in domestic myopia, working with limited international consciousness, and in structural isolation from opposition movements elsewhere. Since the human rights framework is transnational not only in concept but in formal structure, engaging the model positions us as part of a global movement, and provides forums, tools, resources, and a common language that facilitate conversations and strategic networking across national and cultural boundaries.

Third, much has transpired over the last decade to dramatically alter the face of the human rights movement, and these factors play a role in enhancing both the appeal and the relevance of human rights in the current moment. One important shift has been in the area of economic, social, and cultural rights, which are theoretically considered to be indivisible from civil and political rights, but which have remained virtually ignored by both Western governments and large human rights organizations alike. In recent years, activists in the Global South have been especially successful in getting these rights—which pertain to the provision of food, housing, healthcare, and education—onto the movement's agenda, and more and more organizations are integrating this perspective into their work at both international and domestic levels.

On a related plane, here in the United States—where most people think we already have all the human rights we need—social justice advocates increasingly have been "bringing human rights home" by integrating the model's rubric and tools into their work. When U.S. activists identify and confront human rights abuses here in the United States, we challenge the imbalance of power within the global human rights movement by disrupting the master script of cultural superiority that legitimates the "rescue" of others ostensibly victimized by their own (presumably inferior) cultures. We also undermine our government's self-righteous posturing in the international arena by forcing recognition that it, too, is a human rights violator.

Another important shift in the human rights landscape over the past decade has been the emergence of a vibrant and remarkably effective global women's human rights movement. Using human rights principles and tools, and supported by a series of formal international conferences and forums held under the auspices of the United Nations—including the 1995 Fourth World Conference on Women held in Beijing—advocacy networks representing women from every corner of the globe have, in a very short period of time, succeeded in redefining the terrain of human rights to address the specific conditions, experiences, and vulnerabilities of women. Similarly, activists have secured recognition within the human rights framework of the particular abuses directed at members of lesbian, gay, bisexual and transgendered communities, and along with proponents of women's human rights are developing new standards for a sexual rights agenda.

Yet another area of expansion related to identity-based discrimination is transpiring among racial justice activists, including those from indigenous communities, both in the U.S. and internationally. Renewed focus on race and human rights—a prominent feature in the development of the human rights system, birthed, as it was, amidst a landscape of anti-colonialist and national independence movements—led to coordination of the 2001 World Conference Against Racism (WCAR). For many U.S. civil rights activists who participated, the experience of addressing racism from a transnational perspective and an international base generated new interest in the possibilities of the human rights model.

To illustrate how some of the advantages of human rights can be put to work on the ground, I turn now to a local campaign that I'm currently involved in: the New York City Human Rights Initiative. Amnesty International USA's Women's Human Rights Program, where I am working as a consultant on this project, is one of five organizations currently coordinating a campaign to pass a NYC law that will locally implement two important international human rights treaties—the Convention on the Elimination of All Forms of Discrimination Against Women, or CEDAW, and the Convention on the Elimination of All Forms of Racial Discrimination, also known as CERD. The four other coordinating organizations are the Urban Justice Center Human Rights Project, the Women of Color Policy Network at NYU's Wagner School, NOW Legal Defense and Education Fund, and the American Civil Liberties Union Women's Rights Project.

The vision of human rights articulated in the UDHR is formally brought into law through a series of international treaties that governments can choose to ratify, but the United States has an abysmal record when it comes to treaty adoption. While our government has ratified the Covenant on Civil and Political Rights (ICCPR), the Convention Against Torture (CAT), and the Convention on the Elimination of All Forms of Racial Discrimination (CERD), it has done little to implement many of these treaties' standards. And, thus far, the U.S. has failed to ratify CEDAW, the Covenant on Economic, Social and Cultural Rights (ICESCR), and a number of other important international agreements.

One of the most transformative aspects of international human rights treaties is that they obligate governments to *pro-actively* identify discrimination, and to implement remedies that fulfill the promise of human rights and prevent future violations. This aspect of treaty adoption is what makes it so appealing as a local, grass-roots informed, bottom-up human rights strategy. The precedent for the New York City campaign was a successful San Francisco mobilization of women's human rights advocates and local feminist activists led by the Women's Institute for Leadership Development (WILD) for Human Rights.[1] This coalition secured passage of a city ordinance in 1998 that endorsed the principles of CEDAW and created a framework for integrating them into municipal governance. A task force comprised of community representatives and public officials has since been overseeing gender analyses of the employment practices, budget allocations, and service provision of various city departments. Each of the six departments that has completed a review thus far has come up with an action plan, and has begun implementing concrete changes that redress inequities.

Inspired by the San Francisco success, the New York City Human Rights Initiative was launched in 2002. While the San Francisco law focused exclusively on CEDAW, the New York campaign will break new ground by integrating the principles of the "women's convention" *and* the convention on racial discrimination. Combining these two treaties addresses the problems facing a broader cross-section of New Yorkers and counters discrimination against one of the most marginalized populations in the city: women of color. One of the most exciting aspects of this campaign—and there are many—is that integrating the principles of two international anti-discrimination treaties may enable us to encode intersectionality into law, a strategy that has proven rather elusive within existing U.S. jurisprudence. The New York City Human Rights Initiative is working with members of the New York City Council to introduce the legislation sometime in the next year. The Initiative is also conducting workshops and presentations to educate local grass-roots and advocacy organizations about the campaign and about the value of bringing human rights frameworks and tools to their work, as well as soliciting input from these groups as to what they would like this legislation to achieve.

Local treaty implementation is an innovative strategy that enables activists to bypass federal resistance to international human rights standards and instead focus on putting these standards to work right where we live. Mobilizing communities to hold their *local* governments accountable to international human rights law, especially in the current political climate, offers an important new avenue for improving the lives of women and their families. But this local strategy also points to the broader advantages of the human rights model for feminists seeking to advance complex agendas in terrible times. In addition to the generally benevolent feelings it inspires, human rights offers a comprehensive range of rights covering every area of life and addressing multiple forms of discrimination, and thus a natural platform for broad-based multi-issue organizing; obligations to which governments can be held accountable and pro-active mechanisms to make accountability meaningful; opportunities for public participation at local, national, and international levels; and both a connection to global women's movements and a structure for participating in them. Finally, like transnational anti-racist feminism, it offers the vision of a world in which every one of us is fed, housed, clothed, educated, and secure from discrimination, dislocation or abuse.

Note

1. A Guide to replicating the San Francisco initiative is available from WILD for Human Rights, http://www.wildforhumanrights.org.

Lila Zucker

"My Age Has No Impact on How Much I Care"

In 1999, when I was 11, my parents took me to the Seattle protests of the World Trade Organization. I remember seeing the turtles and the Teamsters marching together, representing the unity that environmentalists and union activists felt in fighting the WTO.

The energy at the WTO protests and hearing about the Radical Cheerleaders—a group of young activists who cheer at rallies and protests—made me want to get involved on my own. My grandma is a proud member of the Seattle Raging Grannies, so I guess activism has always been in my blood.

The Radical Cheerleaders seemed so cool because they were inspiring change and having fun at the same time. Through the Cheerleaders, I found the group Portland Peaceful Response Coalition (PPRC), which is a progressive social justice group that helps to organize many events in the Portland area. They became my second family.

In PPRC, I was treated as an equal, not as a child. At all the meetings I started going to, people were so excited to see "new blood." The adults treated me, and the handful of other students who were there, as though we would one day save the world. Everyone was excited to have students speak at large marches and participate in planning—people were there to listen and did not care that I couldn't vote or even drive. The entire group became my mentors, pushing me to contribute even more by being a labor reporter for a local progressive newspaper and working with the Cascadia Network for Peace & Justice, which organized the mass demonstrations in Portland before and during the wars in Afghanistan and Iraq. There were always opportunities to contribute, and I was able to do things I never thought I would do and which led me to my passion—social justice and union organizing.

Still, we student activists often get the feeling that, in the minds of other activists, we are somehow less capable of doing certain things. Want to get young people involved? Listen to us

Source: This article originally appeared in the Fall, 2006 issue of *Peace and Freedom*, the magazine of the Women's International League for Peace and Freedom.

because of our ideas, not our age, and encourage us to take leadership roles. For example, we can do things usually reserved only for "seasoned" activists, like getting march permits, planning actions, and acting as police liaisons.

Being a beat reporter and working with the labor group Jobs with Justice has helped me show others that being a student activist does not mean that I care only about "youth" issues such as military recruitment or education. Breaking everyone's stereotypes of lazy, apathetic, trouble-making teenagers makes it fun to do the work I do.

Joining the Radical Cheerleaders showed me that you can always make someone's day by trying to change the world, even one pom-pom-filled cheer at a time. I am just as excited to become a Raging Granny as I was to become a Radical Cheerleader, because my age has no impact on how much I care.

Ava Lowery: Teen Activist Making a Difference in the Iraq War

Sixteen-year-old Ava Lowery has been making political statements with video since March 2005. Her videos and website (peacetakescourage.com) have caught the eye of many people—some in a positive way and some . . . not so much. Despite the death threats and insulting responses, Ava continues to express her opposition to the Iraq War and encourages other teens to "Speak out!" Teen Editors Shaquana Nedd, Chavonne Dunbar, Amber McConnico, all 17, interviewed Ava this spring about the way she chooses to get her opinions out into the world.

TEEN VOICES: What inspired you to make your website and video pieces against the Iraq War?

AVA LOWERY: I wanted a way to speak out. I thought the internet was a great way because it reaches out to so many people, and me being in a small town, and a teenager it's very hard for me to do that in another way.

TEEN VOICES: What is your goal in putting together your webpage and your animations?

AVA: My goal is to warn people about the Iraq War and change people's minds about war and think about the issues some more.

TEEN VOICES: How do you feel about the Iraq War?

AVA: I feel that the Iraq War is wrong. In the very beginning I gave the president the benefit of the doubt and supported the war. That's something I regret, and after doing a

lot of research online I found several reasons to really dislike the war. For example, there were no weapons of mass destruction to begin with.

TEEN VOICES: What are some tips you can give us to speak out to the public about a world issue?

AVA: I'd suggest to anyone who wants to speak out to start up a blog or make videos of your own. Youtube's a great site to upload any videos because anyone can upload anything and get their message across.

TEEN VOICES: How do you choose the songs for the videos?

AVA: Well, usually I choose the songs before I actually make the video. I would hear a song, it would inspire me to make a video, and that's how I chose the song.

TEEN VOICES: Which video are you most proud of?

AVA: That's a hard one to answer because there are so many that are very different. For example, I am really proud of, "What Would Jesus Do?" because it focuses on Iraqi civilians, and on Christianity, two things that are important to me. Also I really like the video I did on, "How This Must End" and its specific emphasis on the soldiers. I have two uncles who have been to Iraq and they are important to me.

TEEN VOICES: We saw the video, "What Would Jesus Do" too and it was very powerful.

AVA: Thank you.

Source: Teen Voices is a nonprofit organization dedicated to changing the world for girls through media. Call 1-888-882-TEEN or visit www.TeenVoices.com.

TEEN VOICES: I understand you have received many death threats and vicious responses to your work. How has this affected you?

AVA: Well, when I first got the first few death threats my immediate response—well, my mom's immediate response—was to shutdown the website. We ended up not doing that because we knew that if we had done that then it would have just been backing down to what had happened, proving that sending death threats works. That is something that I don't believe in and, after all, the name of the website is "Peace Takes Courage" and I think I am proving that with the death threats. I haven't gotten death threats in a long time. I still get hate mail, but the death threats have stopped. That is something that I am really glad about.

TEEN VOICES: How did you deal with the death threats?

AVA: I dealt with the death threats by not responding to the actual death threats. I put them out there for other people to see along with the videos that caused the death threats. That's the best thing to do—put it out there for people to see.

TEEN VOICES: Does your family support your work?

AVA: My family does support my work. I am very lucky to have such a supportive family. They think it is great that I am so involved because I am learning a lot through the website.

TEEN VOICES: Many people are impressed with the quality and honesty of your pieces, even when they don't know you are only 16 years old. Do you think your age affects how people react to your work? Do you think it helps or hinders you or both?

AVA: I think my age does help me and it also discredits me because a lot of adults at times don't want to listen to young people. The thing is, we young people are the ones whose futures are being decided right now. I think it

is important for us to speak up and voice our opinions.

TEEN VOICES: What kind of reaction has your work received from people in the military?

AVA: I have gotten a lot of really nice and positive responses from the military. Very rarely do I get a response from the military that is disagreeing with me. And it has been great through my website to hear from some soldiers who have been to Iraq and say they agree. A lot of times soldiers can't speak if they are active duty soldiers.

TEEN VOICES: Do you ever read the critical comments about your videos?

AVA: I have actually made videos out of the critical comments before and a lot of them are really nasty and not very nice at all. But by putting the attention on them I think it shows the hypocrisy of people sitting next to you.

TEEN VOICES: Do you think the people who make those comments about you know you are 16?

AVA: I hope they don't, and I give them the benefit of the doubt that they don't. But a lot of them do because a lot of them specifically target that in the e-mail. I think it is sad that anyone would send that to someone, regardless of their age, but the fact that they are sending them to a 16-year-old is completely sad.

TEEN VOICES: What do you hope to accomplish next?

AVA: Well, I am working on my first documentary now and that is something I am hoping to do great things with by focusing on the soldiers who have come back from Iraq. I think that is something people should focus more on, that there are soldiers who are returning or who have returned home.

TEEN VOICES: To other teens looking for a way to fight against the war, or for any cause they are passionate about, what would your advice be to them?

AVA: Get out there and speak out! The most important thing to do is engage others in discussion about things you think are important because staying silent isn't going to accomplish anything.

TEEN VOICES: Do you think you are an activist?

AVA: I definitely think I am an activist! I am proud to call myself an activist. Everyone should be an activist about one thing or another and it doesn't require devoting your whole life to be an activist. It just requires devoting some of your time to an issue you think is important.

TEEN VOICES: How long do you think this war will go on?

AVA: Hopefully, it won't go on for much longer. Bush himself said that he is not going to end this war while he is in office, and that is something that is terribly upsetting, but

hopefully our new Congress will do something soon about this war. It is important for citizens to send a message that they need to do something.

TEEN VOICES: Have you written anything to Bush or talked to him in person?

AVA: No, I have not. I have directed my videos at Bush several times, but I have not actually spoken with him. I don't think he has seen my videos. Maybe the secret service has.

TEEN VOICES: If you had a chance to talk to him, what would you say?

AVA: I would tell him to bring our troops home. I'd tell him he needs to start listening. There are many people around him telling him that this war is a disaster and it is time to admit mistakes and bring our troops home. This war started on lies, has continued based on ego, and it is something that is scary and frightening.

Tracy Rysavy

Mothers for Eco-Justice

Mothers in East Los Angeles, Detroit, and other communities started out saying "no" to toxic neighbors. Now they are also building a future for their cities.

An East L. A. family has a metal recycling plant where their back yard used to be; in Niagara Falls, a school finds barrels of toxic waste erupting on the playground; a line of black communities stretching from several miles north of Baton Rouge, Louisiana to the Mississippi border is dubbed "Cancer Alley" because of the abundance of toxic waste dumps and chemical plants. Across the US, low-income and minority communities find themselves the unwitting neighbors of toxic waste dumps, chemical plants, and incinerators.

National statistics paint a grim picture of what many call "environmental racism," the deliberate targeting of minority communities for hazardous facility sites: the US has performed nearly all of its nuclear weapons testing on Native American lands; when income is held constant, African-American children are two to three times more likely to suffer from lead poisoning than their Anglo counterparts; the portion of minori-ties living in communities with incinerators is 89 percent higher than the national average.

Coincidence? Not likely, says Grace Boggs, a longtime environmental and civil rights activist from Detroit, Michigan. "These companies move into low-income neighborhoods that are hungry for jobs. They say things like, 'We need to put a medical waste incinerator here, and we can supply you with 80 jobs.' And they think of the people there as passive and unable to resist."

Evidence points to the fact that communities are chosen for a waste-disposal facility or an industrial plant based on demographics. In her book, *Love Canal: The Story Continues*, Lois Gibbs, founder of the Center for Health, Environment, and Justice (CHEJ), cites two reports that give some insight into the mentality behind this practice of siting polluting facilities near and in communities of color—one completed by Cerrell Associates, Inc. for the State of California Solid Waste Division and the other report prepared by Epley Associates, a public relations firm hired by Chem Nuclear Systems, Inc. Both outline criteria for "communities least likely to resist" the placement of toxic facilities. The criteria include: "Southern, Midwestern, or rural communities that demonstrate openness to the promise of economic benefits in exchange for allowing the facilities into their areas; residents who are, on the average, older than middle age, have a high school education or less, and who are not involved in social issues." The Epley report used the term "shack" to describe living conditions in targeted communities that fit the criteria, and "black population" to describe the race of the residents.

Source: Reprinted from "RX for the Earth," the Summer 1998 *YES! Magazine*, PO Box 10818, Bainbridge Island, WA 98110. Subscriptions: 800-937-4451. Used by permission.

The Mothers of East L.A.

The good news is that some minority communities are fighting these toxic intrusions and winning. One organization with a particularly impressive track record is the Madres de Este Los Angeles—Santa Isabel, or Mothers of East L.A. (MELASI).

In the late 1950s, many Latin-Americans who lived in Los Angeles were forced out of their homes to make way for the East L.A. freeway interchange. Juana Gutierrez, her husband Ricardo, and her children were uprooted during the highway construction and again in the 1960s to make way for the construction of Dodger Stadium. Despite the intrusions, Gutierrez kept to her role as mother, homemaker, and Neighborhood Watch Program organizer until 1984, when a California State assembly woman told her that a proposed prison was to be built near her third home.

Then she became an activist.

Gutierrez knocked on doors around her neighborhood, asking people to help her block the prison. She called a May 24, 1984 meeting at her home and invited fellow Neighborhood Watch captains who were concerned about the deterioration a prison might bring to their neighborhood and fearful of the dangers a breakout could mean for their families. At that meeting, Madres de Este Los Angeles was formed.

MELASI eventually fulfilled its main goal—it defeated the prison and saw a bill passed that declared no state prisons could be built in Los Angeles County. However, no sooner was that mission accomplished than MELASI discovered that East L.A. was being targeted for a municipal waste incinerator and an oil pipeline. (The pipeline was being routed 20 extra miles through East L.A. so as to miss the affluent beach communities.) In the next few years, MELASI would successfully fight off both facilities, plus a chemical treatment plant, two more incinerators, a dump site, malathion spraying, and more.

Before MELASI was formed, corporations found it easy to get rid of their wastes in the Latino community by using smoke-and-mirrors tactics, says Elsa Lopez, MELASI project director: "These companies had always come into East L.A. and dumped their toxins. No one ever confronted them; they would have hearings, and no one from the communities would show up." To further complicate matters, says Lopez, the corporations would often pay people to sit in on the hearings and support the company's agenda. "These people would ask questions about whatever toxic facility was coming into East L.A., and then say, 'I'm from the community. I'm all for it.'"

Members say that MELASI got its name because the at-home mothers were the only ones available to be the voice of East L.A. residents at the hearings, which were held during the day when others were at work. MELASI appeals directly to mothers as part of their outreach strategy. "We ask them, 'Are you ready to defend and protect your family?'" says Lopez. MELASI eventually summed up the power of the maternal protective instinct in their motto: "Not economically rich, but culturally wealthy. Not politically powerful, but socially conscious. Not mainstream educated, but armed with the knowledge, commitment, and determination that only a mother can possess."

Celene Krauss, assistant professor of sociology at Kean College in New Jersey, says that it's not uncommon for mothers to take the lead in keeping toxic substances out of their communities. "By and large, it is women in their traditional roles as mothers who make the link between toxic wastes and their children's ill health. They discover the hazards of toxic contamination: multiple miscarriages, birth defects, cancer deaths, and so on."

Armed with thorough research, alliances with other organizations, including the Audubon Society and Communities for a Better Environment, and a relentless attitude, MELASI members have educated themselves and minority communities throughout California on environmental issues, empowering the residents to join them as they work for environmental justice. They've lobbied city and state governments, held candlelight vigils, networked with other organizations and churches, gone door-to-door in neighborhoods, and mounted large media campaigns, all in the name of making East L.A. cleaner and safer. Their reputation as a group that wins its battles has grown to the point where their mere presence at a meeting can signify a battle won or lost to a corporation.

"When I first started working with MELASI," remembers Lopez, "they sent me alone to a town meeting. I was behind a bunch of lawyers and corporate types, and they kept saying, 'I don't see the president of MELASI, so they didn't get wind of what we're doing. We've got it made.' When I had a chance to speak, I said I was from MELASI and listed the concerns I had brought with me, and then I added a few more based on what I had heard the lawyers say. They looked so disappointed. I think I ruined their day."

Environmental Justice

Although effective minority activist groups like MELASI have existed for years, it wasn't until 1991 that the Environmental Justice Movement truly came into its own. In October of that year, the First National People of Color Environmental Leadership Summit was held in Washington, DC. Says Grace Boggs, "Three hundred African-American, Native American, Latino, and Asian-Pacific Islander grassroots activists from all over the country gave a new definition to 'the environment.' This definition went beyond land, air, and water to include all the conditions that affect our quality of life, including crime, unemployment, failing schools, dangerous working conditions, and pesticide-filled foods."

The most significant outcome of the summit was the formulation of 17 Principles of Environmental Justice, which immediately took the fledgling movement beyond the "Not In My Back Yard" mentality.

After attending the second summit in 1994, Boggs and others founded Detroiters Working for Environmental Justice (DWEJ), taking much of their inspiration from the 17 principles. "They're

extraordinary and very visionary principles," she says. "For example, Principle 12 affirms the need 'to clean up and rebuild our cities and rural areas in balance with nature, honoring the cultural integrity of all our communities, and providing fair access for all to the full range of resources.'" Boggs and DWEJ members referred to Principle 12 when a company threatened to build an incinerator in their neighborhood, which was to burn wood from demolished houses—despite the fact that much of the wood was coated with lead-based paint. "People resisted the factory, even though it would create new jobs, and then the whole question of what kind of economic development we did want in our neighborhood entered in," says Boggs.

DWEJ has a dual purpose that Boggs feels is the key to their success: "Our mission on the one hand is to challenge the threats to our daily lives. But we also want to rebuild Detroit safer, cleaner, and more self-reliant." DWEJ and other environmental justice organizations around the country have introduced community gardening programs, neighborhood clean-ups, and youth programs that help young people get in touch with and learn to value their communities. "Inner city kids need to be related to the land and to their elders. All people have is the image of inner city kids smoking dope or something. They don't know this is a hunger among the kids," says Boggs.

Two thousand miles to the west, the Mothers of East L.A. have discovered the same hunger among their youth. After they defeated the prison, MELASI made the natural progression to thinking about how to improve East L.A. as well as protect it.

"We were very surprised at how many young people wanted to participate," says Elsa Lopez. Inner city youth help clean up graffiti and litter in the business district. By means of a scholarship fund, a community youth garden, a week-long camp at Mono Lake, and a tobacco prevention program, MELASI members educate young people about environmental issues and keep them connected to the community.

In addition, MELASI has developed a Water Conservation Program, which has been emulated in 17 US cities and in South Africa. Through this program, MELASI gives free ultra low-flush toilets, each one of which saves up to 5,000 gallons of water a year, to customers of local water utilities. MELASI gets a rebate from the utility for each toilet they help install, and the money is used to fund other projects.

As the environmental justice movement continues to grow, it is evolving into an international network of communities working not just for a higher standard of living, but for a whole new way of living. As the last of the 17 Principles states, "Environmental justice requires that we make personal choices to consume as little of Mother Earth's resources and to produce as little waste as possible, and that we make the conscious decision to challenge and reprioritize our lifestyles to ensure the health of the natural world for present and future generations."

Agnes Williams

The Great Janet McCloud

Janet McCloud traveled the continent like her ancestor Chief Seattle with salmon, dentalium, abalone, dried huckleberries and meat. She shared the traditions in the great wealth of the Northwest (United States) bestowed upon her Tulalip and Nisqually peoples by the Great Mystery, the Creator. Janet always said that our aboriginal rights were given to us by the Creator and could not be taken away by other men (or women.) It is Native North Americans who gave rights to non-Natives by making treaties. Janet represented the Northwest fishing rights struggle as no one has since. After police raids in 1961 and 1965 Janet, her husband Don and their family became a target of the fishing rights struggle. "We were just fishing people. We didn't have any councils, we didn't have any lawyers, we didn't have any money, and we just saw ourselves as kamikazes. All we had was us, so we'd go out there and they'd beat us up, they'd mace us, they'd throw us in jail, terrorize our kids and come and harass us at our homes, terrorize our kids in school. . . . We were the front line" (Turtle Quarterly, Niagara Falls, NY Summer 1990). In 1964 Janet led the organization of the Survival of American Indian's Association in the Seattle/Tacoma area and interacted with other political movements, like the civil rights movement. "You know because Dick Gregory came to support us and all the racism would come out . . . (people would say) you had our moral support and sympathy until you brought that so-and-so." (IBID) Janet McCloud was a political force not to be ignored,

as she defined an American Indian political agenda that addressed police brutality, race, economics and gender in the *Last Indian Wars*, Part I by Yet Si Blue. Janet's down home political correctness flushed out many a want-to-be Native activist and put us all on a path of self-discovery and honesty. For these reasons, it was not always easy or popular to follow her lead. Janet wrote about the fishing struggle and first identified October 13, 1965, at Franks Landing, as a National Fish In Day. Later, she instigated an IWN campaign to make October 13, UNPLUG America Day to focus consumers on our need and greed for Native Peoples' natural resources, using the Northwest fishing struggle as her point in her attack.

The Elders Circle's traditional teachings inspired Janet to garden and be a steward for her ten acres of land in her husband's Nisqually reservation border town of Yelm, WA. Walking their talk, Janet and Don taught their children and grandchildren to fish, smoke and can foods, garden and care for others in need. They opened their hearts and opened their home to traditional ceremonials and provided a place to challenge modern thinking and life ways. Constantly aware of the poverty that surrounded them, Janet, Don and their children blazed a trail in the Northwest to re-traditionalize Indian people. Recognized as a mother to all, Janet was named by her Indian peoples, Yet Si Blue placing her in a mother clan where only mothers belong. Janet recalled, "I have heard there was up to ten maybe more from different nations around here" (Northwest, Yelm WA.) It also means one who speaks her mind. (IBID) Janet's mentors were the Elders Circle, the Haudenosaunee (Iroquois) in the

Source: "The Great Janet McCloud," by Agnes Williams. *Indigenous Women's Network*, April 19, 2007. Used by permission.

Northeast and the Hopi in the Southwest and the traditional peoples from the Plains in addition to her Northwest Elders. It was at annual Elder Circle gatherings and during international travels together that Janet's talents as a writer and spokesperson found another source of inspiration. Janet stirred the pot of traditional teachings and contemporary politics in her writings and speeches. It was here, a political analysis with the intersections of economic and cultural class, race, gender and the environment was fine-tuned within a spiritual context of traditional philosophy and religion. Janet collaborated with Elders such as Thomas Banyaca and Oren Lyons to produce written Communiques, traditional messages to the Peoples. With each Elders Circle trip abroad, Janet incorporated a traditional world view that empowered her to speak to larger and larger audiences about North American Indians, and ultimately the survival of the planet. Janet was an advocate for the Hopi Prophesy and wrote, A Warning Message to All Indian Nations and our Friends and Supporters, a second 20 page treatise dated January of 1978.

That was the year of the Longest Walk from San Francisco to Washington, DC where 30,000 people demonstrated and successfully defeated eleven pieces of anti-Indian legislation. When the Black Bass Act came out, along with other anti-Indian federal legislation that surfaced in Congress; and later, David So Happy was put in jail for fishing on the Columbia River, Janet continued to campaign for our basic right to have food and clean water. On the Longest Walk, Janet lectured on the Forced Sterilization of Indian women by the US Indian Health Services estimating that 70% of US Native women were forcibly sterilized. After the Walk, Janet, Pine

Ridge South Dakota's Lorelie Means, Madonna Gilbert and others started the Women of All Red Nations, WARN, as a women's component of AIM. Janet said we needed to give more attention to our internal sovereignty, what is happening in the homes with families and the children (Article, The Backbone of Everything by Crystal Mountain in *Indigenous Woman* 15th Anniversary Edition, Austin TX). Each founder made a commitment to go back home and start a chapter of WARN. Janet's grassroots organizing for WARN resulted in the Northwest Indian Women's Circle. Janet sought and received the blessings of the Elders of Assumption, Canada to do this work. Janet instituted the spiritual sanctioning of community organizing as a model for Native activism. The Elders left Janet with only one reservation, don't become sexist and get involved in the separation of the sexes. (IBID) By this time Janet had met with and counseled many leaders of the American Indian Movement. Janet felt a kinship with Dennis Banks and shared a collegial relationship with Russell Means. She encouraged Bill Wahpepah s organizing in the San Francisco International Indian Treaty Council office, visiting us frequently. Janet was respected for her intellect, outspokenness and counsel to women in the American Indian Movement who she gathered up in SF, White Earth and NY to convene in her back yard at Yelm WA the first Indigenous Women's Network (IWN) Gathering in August of 1985 only a few months after her beloved husband's passing in April 1985.

To hear Janet speak at the founding of IWN, she was a passive supporter of women, but to have seen and heard her in action, she continues to be a role model and inspiration to us today.

PART NINE

Culture and Creativity

For many people, culture and creativity are the foundation for living a rich and joyful life. "I live in music; is this where you live?" asks ntozake shange in her poem expressing the centrality of music to her existence. We may weep or laugh, feel exalted or depressed in reaction to music, art, literature, theater, film, and dance but people everywhere seek out these art forms to deepen their understanding of and connection to life. The most enduring and influential cultural products transcend specific locations and speak to the general human condition. People recognize their own emotions and psychic struggles in the creations of artists and are assured that others share the confusing, joyful, frustrating, depressing, and exhilarating feelings that are part of human existence. As Daphne Harrison wrote about the blues, art "speaks directly of and to the folk who have suffered pain and assures them that they are not alone" (Harrison 1988: 8). People's identities, their sense of self and belonging, are shaped in part by their reception of cultural products. Culture can act as a progressive force that links individual problems to larger social forces and provides people a political context for understanding their lives.

Culture also has a conservative aspect that can reinforce and legitimate existing relations of power and domination. Until the civil rights movement and women's liberation movement of the 1960s and 1970s, the worlds of culture and fine arts in the United States revolved around the work of white male artists. This work often reproduced negative, demeaning images of women and people of color or simply reinforced their exclusion. Television programs in the 1950s and early 1960s, for example, depicted stereotypical gender roles in middle-class, white, suburban families in programs like *Ozzie and Harriet, Father Knows Best, Donna Reed*, and *Leave It to Beaver*. These programs now have kitsch value in the rerun market where they are a humorous and nostalgic reminder of outmoded gender, race, and class relations.

Today, the conservative elements of culture are more subtle and also are intertwined with corporate power. Popular media, like television and radio, are increasingly owned and controlled by a small group of corporate interests, such as Disney, AOL-Time Warner, Viacom, and General Electric. The news, information, and entertainment produced through this corporate funding tends to represent the financial and political interests of their sponsors and to narrow the range of perspectives presented. As women and people of color have emerged as significant market sectors, the media has responded and offered more programming that is directed at these markets. So there are now more culturally diverse images, including the lesbian and gay community, in the mainstream culture. Yet these images continue to draw on and reinforce historically developed "controlling images" (Collins 2000) that normalize and naturalize the oppression of people based on their gender, race, ethnicity, sexuality, and nation. For example, Chrystos's poem "I Am Not Your Princess" addresses the stultifying mythic images of Native women as a homogeneous group with mystical powers. She admonishes non-Natives to "Look at my heart not your fantasies" to see the real woman and the painfully real struggles of Native peoples. Her poetry highlights the tensions between a hegemonic culture and a culture produced by people at the margins of society.

Cultural production by marginalized people has often been invisible to the mainstream or devalued. In 1971, Linda Nochlin published her article, "Why Have There Been No Great Women Artists?" in *ARTnews*. This article tackled a question often raised about the absence of great women painters, sculptors, musicians, composers, and film directors. The question has also been asked about people of color in the United States. If there are no gender, race, or ethnic differences in creative abilities, where is the female equivalent of Shakespeare, the Latina Michelangelo, the American Indian Beethoven? Of course these examples reflect Eurocentric standards of aesthetic genius. White Americans often assume, incorrectly, that their cultural icons represent universal standards of excellence. Nochlin, however, was not concerned with the accuracy of the observation of lack but rather with how the question was framed. She argued that the question is premised on an individualistic understanding of how art is produced as well as the nature of genius. Geniuses of the art world, like Vincent van Gogh, Raphael Sanzio, and Jackson Pollock, are often described by art historians as possessing an "atemporal and mysterious power" that flows from the artist to the canvas untouched by spe-

cific material circumstances. Nochlin describes the naiveté of this conception of how art is produced. She suggests that all art, including great art, is linked to a specific situation that includes the process of obtaining education, access to resources, and the assessment of artistic work. Her analysis shifted the discussion of women's art from questions of essential gender qualities to a sociological investigation of the conditions under which all art is created.

Carly Berwick's 2005 article, "Why Have There Been No Great Women Comic-Book Artists?" parodies Nochlin's work and addresses a contemporary expression of the ongoing exclusion of women from this popular genre. She describes the elevation of comics to fine art via an exhibition at the Museum of Contemporary Art and the University of California's Hammer Museum. Featuring the work of fifteen "masters," the show did not include any female artists. Berwick attributes this neglect, in part, to the male-dominated themes of early comics, such as the SPLAT-BOOM-POW action sequences and science-fiction heroes. She also notes the explicit discrimination against female cartoonists in the early years of the twentieth century. Despite exclusion from the first major comics exhibit, women are creating new comics that appeal to everyone and were featured in their own exhibition at the Museum of Comic and Cartoon Art in New York in 2006. Within the upper echelons of institutionalized visual art, women and people of color are still underrepresented (see the Guerilla Girls website: http://www.guerrillagirls. com/).

Nochlin also raised the issue of the "woman problem" in her article and argued that "problems" are often formulated by those in power in order to rationalize their own behavior. She echoed W. E. B. DuBois's analysis of the "race problem" and the double-consciousness required of African Americans who must always view themselves through the veil of racism as they are viewed by white Americans (DuBois 1903). Marcyliena Morgan and DoVeanna S. Fulton address women artists' negotiations of this double-consciousness.

Morgan and Fulton both argue that black women in the United States today live with multiple consciousness (King 1988) "in a state of schizophrenia where there are multiple voices and messages about what it means to be a woman and what it means to be black in relation to men" (Morgan 2005:425). Women artists, and especially women artists of color, negotiate cultural prescriptions for "good women" and "real women." As Morgan notes, African American women were excluded from these categories through the ideologies and material deprivations of slavery and Jim Crowism. Whites jusitifed these systems of inhuman abuse by defining African American women as less than "real women" and as inherently flawed. Similar arguments are made about Native women (Smith 2003). During slavery, African American women were prohibited by law from gaining fundamental literacy skills. During most of the twentieth century, the demands for their manual labor in the segregated market left little time for artistic and intellectual expression for most African American women. It is in this historical context that music plays a vital role in creative expression.

It has often been said that blues and jazz are uniquely American musical forms. The African American roots of American popular music are often buried in the celebrity-focused media. But today's popular music is indebted to early twentieth century blues, and women played a central role in the creation of both blues and jazz. The blues were created and performed by African American people during the post-emancipation period in the South. They captured the experiences and feelings of a group who had endured horrific suffering and repression and who faced an uncertain, dubious freedom. The blues were a vehicle for sharing information and developing a critical consciousness about the place of black people in the U.S. social hierarchy. As Josh Kun writes, the blues marked "the emergent, audible site of identity as a matrix—a 'blues matrix'—of racial and sexual intersectionality that maps out new and quite different 'blues geographies'" (Kun 1999, quoted in Braziel 2004:15). The transgressive, in-

tersectional nature of the blues offered African American women an art form that challenged dominant images and provided a creative structure for forging an African American woman's identity. The blues also opened the doors to travel and sexuality in an era when women, African American women especially, were restricted in movement and conduct.

Bessie Smith was one of the founding artists of the blues. Known as the Empress of the Blues, Bessie Smith violated all the boundaries defining "good women" and was regarded by many as "vulgar, crude, lewd, common, rough, raucous, lowlife" (Kay 1997, quoted in Braziel 2004: 5). She had many lovers, both male and female, drank whiskey, swore, and dressed in outlandish costumes. She had her own bright yellow railway car that allowed her to travel freely to performances, since railways were segregated during her lifetime. Her life of excess came to an abrupt end in a car accident when she bled to death after being denied treatment at a white hospital. Her music lives on, forming the basis for much jazz of the 1930s and 1940s and the rock and roll of the 1950s and onward. As Braziel notes, Janis Joplin was one of Smith's biggest fans and modeled her music and her lifestyle after Smith's. Joplin did not face the racist bigotry that was central to Smith's experiences. She did, however, develop a similar raucous persona that challenged dominant assumptions of hetero- and homosexuality as well as images of white femininity. Her "sex, drugs, and rock-n-roll" lifestyle also led to her untimely death by a heroin overdose at the age of twenty-seven.

Jennie Ruby describes the male-dominated realm of hard rock music and the ways that women are gaining access to rock audiences. A handful of women rock artists have achieved mainstream success (Grace Slick, Joan Jett, Heart, Stevie Nicks) but few have gained fame as instrumentalists. The electric guitar has been closely associated with masculine sexuality and women who wanted to play electric guitar have faced discouragement in ways similar to the barriers encountered by Nochlin's and Berwick's women artists.

Although they remain on the margins of the hard rock scene, Ruby documents the relative success of all-girl cover bands like Lez Zeppelin and Cheap Chick who pay tribute to the icons of heavy metal rock music.

While white women artists are drawn to electric guitars and rock, African American women are challenging male dominance within hip-hop music. Marcyliena Morgan describes hip-hop as a musical descendent of the blues. Hip-hop women claim an identity that contests both white notions of "real" women and black male misogyny and combativeness. Hip-hop, like the blues, draws on African American communicative and musical traditions and helps to define a space where women can represent all their experiences without censorship. Hip-hop women directly confront sexist male artists through their own rhymes. In Morgan's words, "they construct knowledge, intelligence, and emotion as connected and demand that they be heard."

This section concludes with a discussion of women's comedy. Women have always used laughter and humor to subvert male authority and provide relief and support to one another. DoVeanna Fulton also links black comediennes to blues performers and pioneering comics like Jackie "Moms" Mabley who adopted the nonthreatening image of a matronly woman to deliver forthright critiques of white racism. Contemporary black comediennes also subvert notions of "real women," as in Adele Givens's notoriously confrontational one-liner, "I'm such a fucking lady." Fulton describes a "postsoul aesthetic" that involves a "willingness to undermine or deconstruct the most negative symbols and stereotypes of Black life via the use and distribution of those very same symbols and stereotypes" (Neal 2002, quoted in Fulton 2004: 93). Rather than attempt to dispel these negative symbols by embodying their opposites, black comediennes appropriate them for comic relief. When they use the word "bitch," like their hip-hop sisters, they redefine the negative connotations of "aggressive women" to embrace a strong, assertive woman who stands up for herself and her sisters. Like other historically derogatory terms,

the use of "bitch" in stand-up routines and hip-hop music must be understood within a historical and cultural context as a parody of white male disdain.

Roseanne Barr has also used comedy, in her television show and her stand-up routines, to skewer white middle-class images of "real women." Barr was one of the first women to challenge the passive, submissive housewife image depicted on most television sitcoms. She yelled at her kids, complained about housework, and was insistent on her own sexual satisfaction while being overweight. Barr's television show was a huge success, running from 1988 to 1997 and winning an Emmy, a Peabody, and a Golden Globe award. But Roseanne Barr was also vilified as an abrasive, overweight bully in the press. How often have male comics been criticized for being abrasive or overweight? Barr, like other female performers, confronts a double standard in media evaluations of both her humor and personal conduct. In 1990, when Roseanne concluded her off-key rendition of the national anthem at a San Diego Padres' game, she mimicked male baseball players by spitting and scratching her crotch. She was pilloried by the press, and even President George H. W. Bush commented that her performance was "disgraceful." Since then, other comedians, including Sasha Baron Cohen (Borat) and Maya Rudolph of Saturday Night Live, have lampooned the Star Spangled Banner. These comics poke fun at American icons of patriotism and masculinity and expose the human frailties behind the facades of power. This is insulting and threatening to some, but one purpose of humor is to subvert hubris and remind people of the complicated messiness of real life. If you invite a comic to perform an important ritual, you should expect some creative twists on hallowed traditions.

Creativity allows us to explore novel ways of viewing the world and ourselves. Women's creative contributions to the arts, music, and comedy are often oppositional challenges to the status quo. Like Bessie Smith's blues, the best creative acts create a bridge between the artist and the audience that sheds new light on old "metaphysical dilemmas" and assures people that they are not alone.

References

Braziel, Jana Evans. (2004). "'Bye, Bye Baby': Race, Bisexuality, and the Blues in the Music of Bessie Smith and Janis Joplin." *Popular Music and Society* 27(1):3–26.

Collins, Patricia Hill. (2000). *Black Feminist Thought: Knowledge, Consciousness and the Politics of Empowerment.* 2nd ed. London: Routledge.

DuBois, W. E. B. (1903). *The Souls of Black Folk.* Chicago: A.C. McClurg.

Fulton, DeVeanna S. (2004). "Comic Views and Metaphysical Dilemmas: Shattering Cultural Images through Self-Definition and Representation by Black Comediennes." *Journal of American Folklore* 117(462):81–96.

Harrison, Daphne Duval. (1988). *Black Pearls: Blues Queens of the 1920s.* New Brunswick, NJ: Rutgers University Press.

King, Deborah K. (1988). "Multiple Jeopardy, Multiple Consciousness: The Context of a Black Feminist Ideology." *Signs* 14(1):42–72.

Morgan, Marcyliena. (2005). "Hip-Hop Women Shredding the Veil: Race and Class in Popular Feminist Identity." *South Atlantic Quarterly* 104(3): 425–444.

Smith, Andrea. (2003). "Not an Indian Tradition: The Sexual Colonization of Native Peoples." *Hypatia* 18(2):70–85.

Chrystos

I Am Not Your Princess

Sandpaper between two cultures which tear
one another apart I'm not
a means by which you can reach spiritual understanding or even
learn to do beadwork
I'm only willing to tell you how to make fry bread
1 cup flour, spoon of salt, spoon of baking powder
Stir   Add milk or water or beer until it holds together
Slap each piece into rounds   Let rest
Fry in hot grease until golden
This is Indian food
only if you know that Indian is a government word
which has nothing to do with our names for ourselves
I won't chant for you
I admit no spirituality to you
I will not sweat with you or ease your guilt with fine turtle tales
I will not wear dancing clothes to read poetry or
explain hardly anything at all
I don't think your attempts to understand us are going to work so
I'd rather you left us in whatever peace we can still
scramble up   after all you continue to do
If you send me one more damn flyer about how to heal myself
for $300 with special feminist counseling
I'll probably set fire to something
If you tell me one more time that I'm wise I'll throw up on you
Look at me
See my confusion   loneliness   fear   worrying about all our
struggles to keep   what little is left for us
Look at my heart   not your fantasies   Please don't ever
again tell me about your Cherokee great-great grandmother
Don't assume I know every other Native Activist

Source: "I Am Not Your Princess," by Chrystos. Pages 66–67 in *Not Vanishing*.
© 1988. Vancouver: Press Gang Publishers.

in the world personally   That I even know names of all the tribes
or can pronounce names I've never heard
or that I'm expert at the peyote stitch
If   you ever
again tell me
how strong I am
I'll lay down on the ground & moan so you'll see
at last   my human weakness   like your own
I'm not strong   I'm scraped
I'm blessed with life while so many I've known are dead
I have work to do   dishes to wash   a house to clean
There is no magic
See my simple cracked hands which have washed the same things
you wash   See my eyes dark with fear in a house by myself
late at night   See that to pity me or to adore me
are the same
1 cup flour, spoon of salt, spoon of baking powder, liquid to hold
Remember this is only my recipe   There are many others
Let me rest
here
at least

Linda Nochlin

Why Have There Been No Great Women Artists?

"Why have there been no great women artists?" The question tolls reproachfully in the background of most discussions of the so-called woman problem. But like so many other so-called questions involved in the feminist "controversy," it falsifies the nature of the issue at the same time that it insidiously supplies its own answer: "There are no great women artists because women are incapable of greatness."

The assumptions behind such a question are varied in range and sophistication, running anywhere from "scientifically proven" demonstrations of the inability of human beings with wombs rather than penises to create anything significant, to relatively open minded wonderment that women, despite so many years of near equality and after all, a lot of men have had their disadvantages too have still not achieved anything of exceptional significance in the visual arts.

The feminist's first reaction is to swallow the bait, hook, line and sinker, and to attempt to answer the question as it is put: that is, to dig up examples of worthy or insufficiently appreciated women artists throughout history; to rehabilitate rather modest, if interesting and productive careers; to "rediscover" forgotten flower painters or David followers and make out a case for them; to demonstrate that Berthe Morisot was really less dependent upon Manet than one had been led to think—in other words, to engage in the normal

activity of the specialist scholar who makes a case for the importance of his very own neglected or minor master. Such attempts, whether undertaken from a feminist point of view, like the ambitious article on women artists which appeared in the 1858 Westminster Review, or more recent scholarly studies on such artists as Angelica Kauffmann and Artemisia Gentileschi, are certainly worth the effort, both in adding to our knowledge of women's achievement and of art history generally. But they do nothing to question the assumptions lying behind the question "Why have there been no great women artists?" On the contrary, by attempting to answer it, they tacitly reinforce its negative implications.

Another attempt to answer the question involves shifting the ground slightly and asserting, as some contemporary feminists do, that there is a different kind of "greatness" for women's art than for men's, thereby postulating the existence of a distinctive and recognizable feminine style, different both in its formal and its expressive qualities and based on the special character of women's situation and experience.

This, on the surface of it, seems reasonable enough: in general, women's experience and situation in society, and hence as artists, is different from men's, and certainly the art produced by a group of consciously united and purposefully articulate women intent on bodying forth a group consciousness of feminine experience might indeed be stylistically identifiable as feminist, if not feminine, art. Unfortunately, though this remains within the realm of possibility it has so far not occurred. While the members of the Danube School, the followers of Caravaggio, the painters

Source: "Why Have There Been No Great Women Artists?" by Linda Nochlin. *ARTnews* January, 1971. Used by permission.

gathered around Gauguin at Pont-Aven, the Blue Rider, or the Cubists may be recognized by certain clearly defined stylistic or expressive qualities, no such common qualities of "femininity" would seem to link the styles of women artists generally, any more than such qualities can be said to link women writers, a case brilliantly argued, against the most devastating, and mutually contradictory, masculine critical cliches, by Mary Ellmann in her *Thinking about Women*. No subtle essence of femininity would seem to link the work of Artemesia Gentileschi, Mine Vigee-Lebrun, Angelica Kauffmann, Rosa Bonheur, Berthe Morlsot, Suzanne Valadon, Kathe Kollwitz, Barbara Hepworth, Georgia O'Keeffe, Sophie Taeuber-Arp, Helen Frankenthaler, Bridget Riley, Lee Bontecou, or Louise Nevelson, any more than that of Sappho, Marie de France, Jane Austen, Emily Bronte, George Sand, George Eliot, Virginia Woolf, Gertrude Stein, Anais Nin, Emily Dickinson, Sylvia Plath, and Susan Sontag. In every instance, women artists and writers would seem to be closer to other artists and writers of their own period and outlook than they are to each other.

Women artists are more inward-looking, more delicate and nuanced in their treatment of their medium, it may be asserted. But which of the women artists cited above is more inward-turning than Redon, more subtle and nuanced in the handling of pigment than Corot? Is Fragonard more or less feminine than Mme. Vigee-Lebrun? Or is it not more a question of the whole Rococo style of eighteenth-century France being "feminine," if judged in terms of a binary scale of "masculinity" versus "femininity"? Certainly, if daintiness, delicacy, and preciousness are to be counted as earmarks of a feminine style, there is nothing fragile about Rosa Bonheur's Horse Fair, nor dainty and introverted about Helen Frankenthaler's giant canvases. If women have turned to scenes of domestic life, or of children, so did Jan Steen, Chardin, and the Impressionists Renoir and Monet as well as Morisot and Cassatt. In any case, the mere choice of a certain realm of subject matter, or the restriction to certain subjects, is not

to be equated with a style, much less with some sort of quintessentially feminine style.

The problem lies not so much with some feminists' concept of what femininity is, but rather with their misconception—shared with the public at large—of what art is: with the naive idea that art is the direct, personal expression of individual emotional experience, a translation of personal life into visual terms. Art is almost never that, great art never is. The making of art involves a self-consistent language of form, more or less dependent upon, or free from, given temporally defined conventions, schemata, or systems of notation, which have to be learned or worked out, either through teaching, apprenticeship, or a long period of individual experimentation. The language of art is, more materially, embodied in paint and line on canvas or paper, in stone or clay or plastic or metal. It is neither a sob story nor a confidential whisper.

The fact of the matter is that there have been no supremely great women artists, as far as we know, although there have been many interesting and very good ones who remain insufficiently investigated or appreciated; nor have there been any great Lithuanian jazz pianists, nor Eskimo tennis players, no matter how much we might wish there had been. That this should be the case is regrettable, but no amount of manipulating the historical or critical evidence will alter the situation; nor will accusations of male-chauvinist distortion of history. There are no women equivalents for Michelangelo or Rembrandt, Delacroix or Cezanne, Picasso or Matisse, or even, in very recent times, for de Kooning or Warhol, any more than there are black American equivalents for the same. If there actually were large numbers of "hidden" great women artists, or if there really, should be different standards for women's art as opposed to men's—and one can't have it both ways—then what are feminists fighting for? If women have in fact achieved the same status as men in the arts, then the status quo is fine as it is.

But in actuality, as we all know, things as they are and as they have been, in the arts as in a hundred other areas, are stultifying, oppressive, and discouraging to all those, women among them, who did not have the good fortune to be born white, preferably middle class and, above all, male. The fault lies not in our stars, our hormones, our menstrual cycles, or our empty internal spaces, but in our institutions and our education—education understood to include everything that happens to us from the moment we enter this world of meaningful symbols, signs, and signals. The miracle is, in fact, that given the overwhelming odds against women, or blacks, that so many of both have managed to achieve so much sheer excellence, in those bailiwicks of white masculine prerogative like science, politics, or the arts.

It is when one really starts thinking about the implications of "Why have there been no great women artists?" that one begins to realize to what extent our consciousness of how things are in the world has been conditioned—and often falsified—by the way the most important questions are posed. We tend to take it for granted that there really is an East Asian Problem, a Poverty Problem, a Black Problem and a Woman Problem. But first we must ask ourselves who is formulating these "questions," and then, what purposes such formulations may serve. (We may, of course, refresh our memories with the connotations of the Nazis' "Jewish Problem.") Indeed, in our time of instant communication, "problems" are rapidly formulated to rationalize the bad conscience of those with power: thus the problem posed by Americans in Vietnam and Cambodia is referred to by Americans as the "East Asian Problem," whereas East Asians may view it, more realistically, as the "American Problem"; the so-called Poverty Problem might more directly be viewed as the "Wealth Problem" by denizens of urban ghettos or rural wastelands; the same irony twists the White Problem into its opposite, a Black Problem; and the same inverse logic turns up in the formulation of our own present state of affairs as the "Woman Problem."

Now the "Woman Problem," like all human problems, so-called (and the very idea of calling anything to do with human beings a "problem"

is, of course, a fairly recent one) is not amenable to "solution" at all, since what human problems involve is reinterpretation of the nature of the situation, or a radical alteration of stance or program on the part of the "problems" themselves. Thus women and their situation in the arts, as in other realms of endeavor, are not a "problem" to be viewed through the eyes of the dominant male power elite. Instead, women must conceive of themselves as potentially, if not actually, equal subjects, and must be willing to look the facts of their situation full in the face, without self-pity, or cop-outs; at the same time they must view their situation with that high degree of emotional and intellectual commitment necessary to create a world in which equal achievement will be not only made possible but actively encouraged by social institutions.

It is certainly not realistic to hope that a majority of men, in the arts or in any other field, will soon see the light and find that it is in their own self-interest to grant complete equality to women, as some feminists optimistically assert, or to maintain that men themselves will soon realize that they are diminished by denying themselves access to traditionally "feminine" realms and emotional reactions. After all, there are few areas that are really "denied" to men, if the level of operations demanded be transcendent, responsible, or rewarding enough: men who have a need for "feminine" involvement with babies or children gain status as pediatricians or child psychologists, with a nurse (female) to do the more routine work; those who feel the urge for kitchen creativity may gain fame as master chefs; and, of course, men who yearn to fulfill themselves through what are often termed "feminine" artistic interests can find themselves as painters or sculptors, rather than as volunteer museum aides or part-time ceramists, as their female counterparts so often end up doing; as far as scholarship is concerned, how many men would be willing to change their jobs as teachers and researchers for those of unpaid, part-time research assistants and typists as well as full-time nannies and domestic workers?

Those who have privileges inevitably hold on to them, and hold tight, no matter how marginal the advantage involved, until compelled to bow to superior power of one sort or another.

Thus the question of women's equality—in art as in any other realm—devolves not upon the relative benevolence or ill-will of individual men, nor the self-confidence or abjectness of individual women, but rather on the very nature of our institutional structures themselves and the view of reality which they impose on the human beings who are part of them. As John Stuart Mill pointed out more than a century ago: "Everything which is usual appears natural. The subjection of women to men being a universal custom, any departure from it quite naturally appears unnatural." Most men, despite lip service to equality, are reluctant to give up this "natural" order of things in which their advantages are so great; for women, the case is further complicated by the fact that, as Mill astutely pointed out, unlike other oppressed groups or castes, men demand of them not only submission but unqualified affection as well; thus women are often weakened by the internalized demands of the male-dominated society itself, as well as by a plethora of material goods and comforts: the middle-class woman has a great deal more to lose than her chains.

The question "Why have there been no great women artists?" is simply the top tenth of an iceberg of misinterpretation and misconception; beneath lies a vast dark bulk of shaky ideas recues about the nature of art and its situational concomitants, about the nature of human abilities in general and of human excellence in particular, and the role that the social order plays in all of this. While the "woman problem" as such may be a pseudo-issue, the misconceptions involved in the question "Why have there been no great women artists?" points to major areas of intellectual obfuscation beyond the specific political and ideological issues involved in the subjection of women. Basic to the question are many naive, distorted, uncritical assumptions about the making of art in general, as well as the making of great art. These assumptions, conscious or unconscious, link together such unlikely superstars as Michelangelo and van Gogh, Raphael and Jackson Pollock under the rubric of "Great"—an honorific attested to by the number of scholarly monographs devoted to the artist in question—and the Great Artist is, of course, conceived of as one who has "Genius"; Genius, in turn, is thought of as an atemporal and mysterious power somehow embedded in the person of the Great Artist. Such ideas are related to unquestioned, often unconscious, meta-historical premises that make Hippolyte Taine's race-milieu-moment formulation of the dimensions of historical thought seem a model of sophistication. But these assumptions are intrinsic to a great deal of art-historical writing. It is no accident that the crucial question of the conditions generally productive of great art has so rarely been investigated, or that attempts to investigate such general problems have, until fairly recently, been dismissed as unscholarly, too broad, or the province of some other discipline, like sociology. To encourage a dispassionate, impersonal, sociological, and institutionally oriented approach would reveal the entire romantic, elitist, individual-glorifying, and monograph-producing substructure upon which the profession of art history is based, and which has only recently been called into question by a group of younger dissidents.

Underlying the question about woman as artist, then, we find the myth of the Great Artist—subject of a hundred monographs, unique, godlike-bearing within his person since birth a mysterious essence, rather like the golden nugget in Mrs. Grass's chicken soup, called Genius or Talent, which, like murder, must always out, no matter how unlikely or unpromising the circumstances.

The magical aura surrounding the representational arts and their creators has, of course, given birth to myths since the earliest times. Interestingly enough, the same magical abilities attributed by Pliny to the Greek sculptor Lysippos in antiquity—the mysterious inner call in early youth, the lack of any teacher but Nature herself—is repeated as late as the nineteenth century by Max Buchon in his biography of Courbet. The supernatural powers of the artist as imitator, his control of strong, possibly dangerous powers, have functioned historically to set him off from others as a godlike creator, one who creates Being out of nothing. The fairy tale of the discovery by an older artist or discerning patron of the Boy Wonder, usually in the guise of a lowly shepherd boy, has been a stock-in-trade of artistic mythology ever since Vasari immortalized the young Giotto, discovered by the great Cimabue while the lad was guarding his flocks, drawing sheep on a stone; Cimabue, overcome with admiration for the realism of the drawing, immediately invited the humble youth to be his pupil. Through some mysterious coincidence, later artists including Beccafumi, Andrea Sansovino, Andrea del Castagno, Mantegna, Zurbardn, and Goya were all discovered in similar pastoral circumstances. Even when the young Great Artist was not fortunate enough to come equipped with a flock of sheep, his talent always seems to have manifested itself very early, and independent of any external encouragement: Filippo Lippi and Poussin, Courbet and Monet are all reported to have drawn caricatures in the margins of their schoolbooks instead of studying the required subjects— we never, of course, hear about the youths who neglected their studies and scribbled in the margins of their notebooks without ever becoming anything more elevated than department-store clerks or shoe salesmen. The great Michelangelo himself, according to his biographer and pupil, Vasari, did more drawing than studying as a child. So pronounced was his talent, reports Vasari, that when his master, Ghirlandalo, absented himself momentarily from his work in Santa Maria Novella, and the young art student took the opportunity to draw "the scaffolding, trestles, pots of paint, brushes and the apprentices at their tasks" in this brief absence, he did it so skillfully that upon his return the master exclaimed: "This boy knows more than I do."

As is so often the case, such stories, which probably have some truth in them, tend both to reflect and perpetuate the attitudes they subsume.

Even when based on fact, these myths about the early manifestations of genius are misleading. It is no doubt true, for example, that the young Picasso passed all the examinations for entrance to the Barcelona, and later to the Madrid, Academy of Art at the age of fifteen in but a single day, a feat of such difficulty that most candidates required a month of preparation. But one would like to find out more about similar precocious qualifiers for art academies who then went on to achieve nothing but mediocrity or failure—in whom, of course, art historians are uninterested—or to study in greater detail the role played by Picasso's art-professor father in the pictorial precocity of his son. What if Picasso had been born a girl? Would Senor Ruiz have paid as much attention or stimulated as much ambition for achievement in a little Pablita?

What is stressed in all these stories is the apparently miraculous, nondetermined, and asocial nature of artistic achievement; this semireligious conception of the artist's role is elevated to hagiography in the nineteenth century, when art historians, critics, and, not least, some of the artists themselves tended to elevate the making of art into a substitute religion, the last bulwark of higher values in a materialistic world. The artist, in the nineteenth-century Saints' Legend, struggles against the most determined parental and social opposition, suffering the slings and arrows of social opprobrium like any Christian martyr, and ultimately succeeds against all odds generally, alas, after his death—because from deep within himself radiates that mysterious, holy effulgence: Genius. Here we have the mad van Gogh, spinning out sunflowers despite epileptic seizures and near-starvation; Cezanne, braving paternal rejection and public scorn in order to revolutionize painting; Gauguin throwing away respectability and financial security with a single existential gesture to pursue his calling in the tropics; or Toulouse-Lautrec, dwarfed, crippled, and alcoholic, sacrificing his aristocratic birthright in favor of the squalid surroundings that provided him with inspiration.

Now no serious contemporary art historian takes such obvious fairy tales at their face value.

Yet it is this sort of mythology about artistic achievement and its concomitants which forms the unconscious or unquestioned assumptions of scholars, no matter how many crumbs are thrown to social influences, ideas of the times, economic crises, and so on. Behind the most sophisticated investigations of great artists—more specifically, the art-historical monograph, which accepts the notion of the great artist as primary, and the social and institutional structures within which he lived and worked as mere secondary "influences" or "background"—lurks the golden-nugget theory of genius and the free-enterprise conception of individual achievement. On this basis, women's lack of major achievement in art may be formulated as a syllogism: If women had the golden nugget of artistic genius then it would reveal itself. But it has never revealed itself. Q.E.D. Women do not have the golden nugget theory of artistic genius. If Giotto, the obscure shepherd boy, and van Gogh with his fits could make it, why not women?

Yet as soon as one leaves behind the world of fairy tale and self-fulfilling prophecy and, instead, casts a dispassionate eye on the actual situations in which important art production has existed, in the total range of its social and institutional structures throughout history, one finds that the very questions which are fruitful or relevant for the historian to ask shape up rather differently. One would like to ask, for instance, from what social classes artists were most likely to come at different periods of art history, from what castes and subgroup. What proportion of painters and sculptors, or more specifically, of major painters and sculptors, came from families in which their fathers or other close relatives were painters and sculptors or engaged in related professions? As Nikolaus Pevsner points out in his discussion of the French Academy in the seventeenth and eighteenth centuries, the transmission of the artistic profession from father to son was considered a matter of course (as it was with the Coypels, the Coustous, the Van Loos, etc.); indeed, sons of academicians were exempted from the customary fees for lessons. Despite the noteworthy and dra-

matically satisfying cases of the great father-rejecting revolts of the nineteenth century, one might be forced to admit that a large proportion of artists, great and not-so-great, in the days when it was normal for sons to follow in their fathers' footsteps, had artist fathers. In the rank of major artists, the names of Holbein and Durer, Raphael and Bernim, immediately spring to mind; even in our own times, one can cite the names of Picasso, Calder, Giacometti, and Wyeth as members of artist-families.

As far as the relationship of artistic occupation and social class is concerned, an interesting paradigm for the question "Why have there been no great women artists?" might well be provided by trying to answer the question "Why have there been no great artists from the aristocracy?" One can scarcely think, before the anti traditional nineteenth century at least, of any artist who sprang from the ranks of any more elevated class than the upper bourgeoisie; even in the nineteenth century, Degas came from the lower nobility more like the haute bourgeoisie, in fact—and only Toulouse-Lautrec, metamorphosed into the ranks of the marginal by accidental deformity, could be said to have come from the loftier reaches of the upper classes. While the aristocracy has always provided the lion's share of the patronage and the audience for art—as, indeed, the aristocracy of wealth does even in our more democratic days— it has contributed little beyond amateurish efforts to the creation of art itself, despite the fact that aristocrats (like many women) have had more than their share of educational advantages, plenty of leisure and, indeed, like women, were often encouraged to dabble in the arts and even develop into respectable amateurs, like Napoleon III's cousin, the Princess Mathilde, who exhibited at the official Salons, or Queen Victoria, who, with Prince Albert, studied art with no less a figure than Landseer himself. Could it be that the little golden nugget—genius—is missing from the aristocratic makeup in the same way that it is from the feminine psyche? Or rather, is it not that the kinds of demands and expectations placed before both aristocrats and women—the amount of time necessarily devoted to social functions, the very kinds of activities demanded—simply made total devotion to professional art production out of the question, indeed unthinkable, both for upper-class males and for women generally, rather than its being a question of genius and talent?

When the right questions are asked about the conditions for producing art, of which the production of great art is a subtopic, there will no doubt have to be some discussion of the situational concomitants of intelligence and talent generally, not merely of artistic genius. Piaget and others have stressed in their genetic epistemology that in the development of reason and in the unfolding of imagination in young children, intelligence—or, by implication, what we choose to call genius—is a dynamic activity rather than a static essence, and an activity of a subject in a situation. As further investigations in the field of child development imply, these abilities, or this intelligence, are built up minutely, step by step, from infancy onward, and the patterns of adaptation-accommodation may be established so early

within the subject-in-an-environment that they may indeed appear to be innate to the unsophisticated observer. Such investigations imply that, even aside from meta-historical reasons, scholars will have to abandon the notion, consciously articulated or not, of individual genius as innate, and as primary to the creation of art.

The question "Why have there been no great women artists?" has led us to the conclusion, so far, that art is not a free, autonomous activity of a super-endowed individual, "influenced" by previous artists, and, more vaguely and superficially, by "social forces," but rather, that the total situation of art making, both in terms of the development of the art maker and in the nature and quality of the work of art itself, occur in a social situation, are integral elements of this social structure, and are mediated and determined by specific and definable social institutions, be they art academies, systems of patronage, mythologies of the divine creator, artist as he-man or social outcast.

Carly Berwick

Why Have There Been No Great Women Comic-Book Artists?*

With a dual-venue exhibition in Los Angeles, comics by masters such as Winsor McCay, Chris Ware, and Charles Schulz have been elevated from pop culture to fine art. But as these artists receive their due, the show has sparked debate over the rightful place of women in the comic canon.

In case anyone still doubted it, comics are now officially an art form, with the opening this month of "Masters of American Comics" in Los Angeles. The first exhibition in an American art museum to set forth a canon of graphic masters, it is on display at the Museum of Contemporary Art and the University of California's Hammer Museum from the 20th of this month to March 12, 2006. The 15 masters, selected by independent curators John Carlin and Brian Walker with input from Art Spiegelman, include Lyonel Feininger ("The Kin-der-Kids"), George Herriman ("Krazy Kat"), Winsor McCay ("Little Nemo"), Milton Caniff ("Steve Canyon"), Charles Schulz ("Peanuts"), Jack Kirby ("Fantastic Four," "X-Men"), Harvey Kurtzman (*MAD*), R. Crumb, Spiegelman (*Maus*), Chris Ware (*Jimmy Corrigan: The Smartest Kid on Earth*), and Gary Panter ("Jimbo").

Fans may note the exclusion of a favorite or two. But how about half the population? There are no women in the show. With apologies to Linda Nochlin, why have there been no great women comic-book artists? Nochlin wrote in her famous essay "Why Have There Been No Great Women Artists?" published in this magazine in

*With apologies to Linda Nochlin

Source: "Why Have There Been No Great Women Comic-Book Artists?" by Carly Berwick. *ARTnews*, November, 2005. Used by permission of the author.

January 1971, that in fact there are no woman Michelangelos or Warhols, and that elevating "forgotten flower painters" didn't make those artists any better. True female genius, Nochlin noted, had been curtailed by social conditions—the "overwhelming odds" against it—for want, as Virginia Woolf so succinctly put it, of a room of one's own: a studio, some time, a helpmate, some ready admiration, all the factors that helped Pollock be Pollock and Picasso be Picasso.

The curators of "Masters of American Comics" have provided plenty of grist for querulous feminists. "These are 15 artists who used comics to express themselves," says curator Carlin, who explains that selections were based on the criteria of craft and formal innovation. Of the marquee catalogue essayists who give personal glosses on the artists, the only women are *New Yorker* art editor Françoise Mouly (who also happens to be Spiegelman's wife), who provides an informative take on Crumb, and art historian Karal Ann Marling, who writes on Frank King ("Gasoline Alley"). "These artists are mostly white, middle-class, male," acknowledges Carlin, who readily admits that women artists got cut as the list narrowed from 40 to 15 artists. "But I felt a canon needed to be there, in order to be challenged." (Notably, Herriman is African American; however, Stanley Crouch notes in his catalogue essay that "most of us were introduced

A panel from "Brenda Starr," 1960, by Dale Messick, who changed her name from Dalia so she could get more jobs.

Source: © Trbune Media Services, Inc. All rights reserved. Reprinted by permission.

to George Herriman's ethnicity" only when Ishmael Reed dedicated his 1972 novel *Mumbo Jumbo* to him.)

Back when comics were a newsman's game in the first two decades of the 20th century, few women became comic-strippers. But Trina Robbins, a cartoonist and independent comic-art historian, points to some pre-women's-lib comic artists who drew and thrived. There was Nell Brinkley, who contributed "The Brinkley Girl" to Hearst papers before World War II; Grace Drayton, who created the Campbell Kids in the 1930s; and Dale Messick, whose Brenda Starr, globe-trotting girl reporter, inspired legions of preteen investigators in the 1940s and '50s. Brinkley girls, says Robbins, were "romantic, beautifully dressed girls, not naked babes," who took off on adventures and even went surfing. Many of the extant Brinkley drawings have been found in scrapbooks made by young girls. But she and other early women comic artists "have been lost in the semi-official history," says Robbins, because of a prevailing esthetic mindset that values explosive drawing—SPLAT, BOOM, POW—and adventure stories over more girlish themes and styles. The exhibition doesn't emphasize superhero comics, but the style, picked up so forcefully by Roy Lichtenstein, arguably casts a shadow over the entire field. Female comic artists also faced overt discrimination: Messick, the first woman to have a syndicated comic strip, changed her name from Dalia to get more jobs.

Still, not everyone agrees that the contributions of these women were as critical to the development of the genre as those of their contemporaries Herriman, Caniff, and Will Eisner ("The Spirit"). "There were women comics artists, but they were not as important," says "Artbabe" and "La Perdida" creator Jessica Abel. "I love Dale Messick, but was she on that level? No."

Comics may not be altogether different from other pop-culture forms, such as film or jazz, in which prominent women creators have gone missing. This absence reflects "the overall role of women in culture" in the past, Abel adds. "How many women writers, painters, and more important, filmmakers were there?" Exhibition cocurator Walker says that since the 1970s, however, comic artists once outside the mainstream, including women, have gained wider acceptance. "Underground comics have had tremendous success," says Walker, and they have brought in different voices. "Crumb's work, which is raw and uncensored and disturbing, was noncommercial and very different."

It took the advent of Crumb and his *Zap Comix* in the late 1960s to show *New Yorker* cartoonist Roz Chast "that comics could be about what you personally thought was funny, that it didn't have to conform to a particular style," she says. The superhero and fantasy genres that dominated comics before Kurtzman's and Crumb's more personal styles tend to bore many women, says Chast. "I think women—in general—like comics that are more verbal and personal and are perhaps more based in everyday experience." Roberta Gregory, for instance, has drawn strips where a character named Bitchy Bitch grouses about such realities as sex, abortions, and coffeehouse collectives.

Abel says that being a female cartoonist in the early 1990s garnered her attention, in part because it was seen as unusual. She is in growing company these days, however, as the stylistic innovations of "literary comics," such as Ware's *Jimmy Corrigan: The Smartest Kid on Earth*, and *manga* (Japanese comics) are drawing in ever more women as readers and artists. "*Shoju*, girls' *manga*, is structured like sitcoms," says Abel. "It's funny, light, and really appealing to a 12-year-old girl. That's all anybody was trying to get across all those years when people were discussing why girls weren't reading comics."

The appeal of "male" comics to women— and of "women's" comics to male readers—was limited until the genre began to evolve beyond such distinctions, becoming more narrative and more focused on recognizable realities and emotions than on fantasies about spaceships and superheroes. It is a nice irony that Crumb, whose pneumatic women and lascivious hippies have been called misogynistic, may have inspired more women to enter the field. The ranks of well-known comic artists now include such women as Lynda Barry (*One Hundred Demons* and other graphic novels), Gregory ("Naughty Bits"), Marisa Acocella ("Cancer Vixen"), Sue Coe (a former contributor to Spiegelman's *RAW*) and Aline Kominsky-Crumb, who coauthored, with her husband R. Crumb, *Dirty Laundry*, about the travails of modern cohabitation.

There are so many women now in the field that the Museum of Comic and Cartoon Art (MOCCA) in New York will mount an all-female exhibition called "She Draws Comics," running from May through September 2006. The show will feature the work of early women artists, with special attention paid to Messick, who died this year at 99, as well as a section on contemporary woman cartoonists.

"Great women comics artists emerged in the 1960s," says Laura Hoptman, who curated the 2004 Carnegie International, as well as R. Crumb's recent show there. She notes Aline Kominsky-Crumb in particular. "The argument could be made that there's a female Chris Ware, but up until recently it was a guy's thing," says Hoptman. But if there were a female Ware, would we know her if we saw her? Robbins thinks that a pervasive esthetic mindset still, however unconsciously, relegates comics by women to the category of "draws like a girl." For whatever reasons, women's comics may be messier and less minimal than the elegant remove conveyed by artists from Feininger to Ware: the lines marking out the characters in works by Chast or Coe, for example, are often wobbly and slightly harried.

Carlin, the "Masters" cocurator, says that he has wondered whether there might be an inherently female way of "organizing space" and whether there is indeed a "male bias that makes it even harder for female artists to break through." The first part of that question may never have a satisfactory answer. But in a way, this first important show of "masters" already answers the second question in the affirmative. Women comic artists may not have contributed as much as men in the art's first century, but their continued omission today looks to some critics like a bias against supposedly "feminine" subject matter and wavering, equivocal lines. As Nochlin observed 34 years ago, greatness can depend on all the little things going right—including, say, having someone else do the laundry. Today, Aline and Robert Crumb show that an argument about the laundry can make for a pretty good comic book.

Jennie Ruby

Women's "Cock Rock" Goes Mainstream

What does it mean when women get up on stage wearing pants and slinging guitars and doing the rockstar thing like men? Is it a drag show? Is it lesbian? Is it transgender? Is it—gasp—feminist? These questions rolled around in my brain as I got my tickets to see Lez Zeppelin at a medium-sized venue in suburban Virginia.

Some years ago, say in the late 1980s, I would have known what to expect when attending a concert by a band with the word "lez" in its name. I would have been among mostly women, recognizing each other on the street approaching the venue in a secret-handshake kind of way, by the short hair, the Birkenstocks, the hermaphroditic clothing, the pairings of women, the absence of boyfriends. I would have felt the thrill of recognition of political bumper stickers on cars parked in the vicinity. I would have resisted the impulse to hold my girlfriend's hand until we were safely inside the concert hall, and then relaxed into the safety of a, for the moment, lesbian space.

But this concert experience was quite different. The concert was advertised, not through home-made looking flyers posted in a women's bookstore, but through email advertising, with tickets available through a popular ticket outlet. The line to get into the concert was disconcertingly full of straight white men. And the band was not exactly what you might call "out." Or even particularly lesbian, for that matter. In fact the only clear allusion to "lesbian" I saw was on a tee shirt stretched over a decidedly masculine

beer belly: "I'm a lesbian trapped in a fat, ugly biker's body."

What has changed in the meantime? The mainstreaming of "lesbian" started in the early 1990s. k.d. lang appeared with Cindy Crawford on the cover of Vanity Fair, Melissa Etheridge came out and my sister figured out I was a lesbian when some TV news show covered the Michigan Womyn's Music Festival she knew I attended. With the gay rights movement kicking into full swing with the massive 1993 March on Washington, and the idea that lesbians existed slowly creeping into the public consciousness, it had suddenly become harder, and also less necessary, to stay in the closet. About the same time, postmodernism took the academy by storm, and clear, singular meanings—such as lesbian concerts meant for lesbians—faded before the onslaught of multi-culti, LGTBQ, you-can't-know-another-person's-experience, everything-is-relative–ism.

So now we have *Spin* magazine's writer Chuck Klosterman (in *Spin*'s June issue) covering a party celebrating "The L-Word" and struggling to understand the current phenomenon of all-girl tribute bands. Chuck seems troubled by the possibility that women playing men's music might be political—returning to that worry throughout his article in between trying to find ways where it is just about the music, or about fun, or about sex, or about something else, anything else but "political" (read feminist).

But as a woman who grew up in the 60s and 70s. I can tell you it is political. The degree to which women were excluded as performers from mainstream rock music in the 1970s—Joan Jett,

Source: "Women's 'Cock Rock' Goes Mainstream," by Jennie Ruby. *Off Our Backs*, Vol. 35, No. 7/8. © 2005. Used by permission.

Heart, and Stevie Nicks are the exceptions everyone can name—means that women playing men's rock music is asserting women's ability, in yet another area, to prove they can do anything men can do. And that is feminist, at least in one small way. As Lisa Brigantino of Lez Zeppelin told *Spin*: "Historically, women in rock are rarely seen as instrumentalists, and that is what we're trying to achieve. These songs are intricate and heavy and wonderful to play. As someone who grew up playing a lot of different instruments, I caught a lot of flak from guys and always felt this pressure to prove myself, simply because I was a woman and no one expected me to be any good."

One requisite of male-centric/male-dominant culture is that there are areas restricted only to men, where men attend to and recognize and respect only other men. It is always feminist for women to enter those areas and debunk the myth of male ascendancy. And that debunking is a project that has to be done over and over again. It's been over thirty years since Billy Jean King beat Bobby Riggs in a famous tennis match, yet it is still news when, for example, golfer Annika Sorenstam or Michelle Wie goes head to head with men in the professional golf tour. And women have rocked for just about as long as men, but it has to be proved, over and over, that women can actually play musical instruments. Remember what a big deal it was when the Dixie Chicks first stood up holding guitars and mandolins?

So, 30-some years after a kind of invisible force field made of peer, parental and cultural pressure prevented me from taking up electric guitar in high school, I went to see Lez Zeppelin to have it confirmed, irrefutably, once and for all, that women can rock.

And Lez Zeppelin certainly proved that. Guitarist Steph Paynes' playing was awesome—true to the original, and demonstrating way past mastery of the instrument. Especially memorable was her playing the guitar with a bow. The music was heavy, rocking. She had the full attention of everyone in the house.

Singer Brooke Gengras proved just how much the music of Led Zeppelin really lends itself to a woman's singing voice—in fact, I would have to say that Gengras is a major improvement over Robert Plant.

And yet . . . there was something missing, something a little odd about this performance. There was extreme musical competence, certainly. Wildly excellent entertainment, yes. But with a predominantly male audience, what did it all mean?

Singer Gengras sometimes bounced around obviously in her own right enjoying the music, feeling it. At other times she lapsed into the kind of pornographic, undulating movements that are allowed to women rockers these days. Somehow there is something different about a woman's hip-thrusting with the microphone stand than a man making virtually those same moves. And when the performers threw in a little lezzie action—as when the singer began touching the guitarist's hair seductively—how much was that pandering to the male audience, as opposed to being a self-motivated move of self-expression?

Women playing up to the male gaze is not the same as women's self-actualization as artists. And what do female artists have to do to get audience respect? Since the days of George Elliot and George Sand, women have taken on a male persona to this end. And to some degree, female tribute bands are making this move.

Emily Landes for *Wave* magazine, reports that [Paulette] "Kasal, vocalist for Mistress of Reality, had been trying to break into the heavy metal scene for years and never felt any acceptance until she took on a male persona. She says it's frustrating to know that her true personality and musical skills get more credibility when she plays a man. 'I've always acted this way. All the girls in my band are very masculine women who never wanted to play with other women,' she says. 'So, even though I'm impersonating a man, it's already me anyway. That's why I can be accepted now. But if it was just me in a regular band, it's like, "Oh, what's that?"'"

And women are finding larger, more reliable audience pull with tributes to male bands than with their own work: Pam Utterback, bassist with

A Sampling of All-Girl Cover Bands

Lez Zeppelin (Led Zeppelin)

Cheap Chick (Cheap Trick)

AC/DShe (AC/DC)

Hell's Belles (AC/DC)

Whole Lotta Rosies (AC/DC)

ThundHerStruck (AC/DC)

Black Diamond (Kiss)

The Ramonas (The Ramones)

Ms. Fits (The Misfits)

Iron Maidens (Iron Maiden)

Mistress of Reality (Black Sabbath)

Cheap Chick, told *Los Angeles Magazine* (Sept. 03) that when she saw Whole Lotta Rosies play to a large crowd: "I'm like, 'What the heck am I doing in an original band playing for 20 people?' Now I'm just. 'You know what? I want to play for a lot of people, have a good time, make money and have fun.'"

All-girl tribute bands can automatically draw a crowd, because men and women will come to see a performance of men's music. But women doing men's music to get some respect is not the same thing as women's music getting respect.

Ultimately, seeing Lez Zeppelin perform for a crowd of mostly men left me wanting something just a little more radical; something a little more woman-centric, something a little less mainstreamed—like, say, Tribe 8 at the Michigan Womyn's Music Festival: women performing their original material as themselves. Lynn Breedlove of Tribe 8 has no trouble expressing her own masculine personality while performing original material, and her mostly lesbian/bi/trans audience does not have to bother to ask "Oh, what's that?" We know what that is. That is broadening the category of "woman" and freeing women to express masculinity in their own right. That is not playing gender in a way that has mainstream acceptability. That is pushing the goddam envelope.

Nevertheless, all-girl tribute bands to the male rock gods of the 1970s do have their small place in chipping away at the relentless male dominance of our social system, if only in the "once again we prove we can do anything men do" category. They are doing a bit of feminist work, whether they acknowledge it or not.

Marcyliena Morgan

Hip-Hop Women Shredding the Veil: Race and Class in Popular Feminist Identity

Until the late 1950s, one of America's worst-kept secrets was its repression of blacks, other non-whites, the working class, and women. African American communities lived behind a veil that hid their complex and personal struggle to define manhood and womanhood within an ideological system that denied them social, cultural, and moral citizenship.[1] One result of this veiling has been contempt toward African American women in the United States and the world. If W. E. B. Du Bois's notion of double consciousness represents two voices, two worlds, and the "real" black soul,[2] then black women live in a state of schizophrenia where there are multiple voices and messages about what it means to be a woman and what it means to be black in relation to men. Nearly a century ago, Du Bois foresaw this complex state of affairs when he wrote: "So some few women are born free, and some within insult and scarlet letters achieve freedom; but our women in black had freedom thrust contemptuously upon them. With that freedom they are buying an untrammeled independence and dear as the price they pay for it, it in the end will be worth every taunt and groan."[3]

While feminists today find problematic the sort of society that Du Bois describes—one that requires patriarchal protection—the notion that women should be protected nevertheless provided some form of safety and propriety. It also was the basis of American cultural views of "the good woman" and the cult of true womanhood.[4] The good woman needs and gets protection and is provided for. Yet this ideology does not include and was never intended to include black women. Not only was the black female slave denied protection from assault; she was also forced to perform physical labor under harsh circumstances while under constant surveillance.[5] Following slavery, black women had to engage in paid labor to support themselves and their families. Consequently, since they did not benefit from a white patriarchy that could or would provide for and protect them, they experienced limited freedom to control economic aspects of their lives. However, as Mullings warns, "this window of freedom, narrow and equivocal as it is, poses a problem, a threat to the dominant society's rationalizations of gender hierarchy."[6] The price was "special" treatment for surviving their collective ordeal and emerging with a defiant sense of the self that embodies an unspoken critique of America and what it calls a "good woman." They were labeled with and routinely worked within the limitations of contested notions of mammy, matriarch, castrator, manipulator, and whore. Today, the situation for the black woman remains one where she is routinely derided for her sexuality, social class, determination, commitment to family, passion, and public displays of womanhood. She must deal with confrontations similar to the one canonically described by Du Bois in 1902—confrontations predicated on cloaked interrogations from white Americans about what it must feel like to be a racial problem. However, unlike Du Bois, instead of responding with "seldom a

Source: Marcyliena Morgan, "Hip-Hop Women Shredding the Veil: Race and Class in Popular Feminist Identity," in *South Atlantic Quarterly,* Volume 104, no. 3 (Summer), pp. 425–444. Copyright © 2005, Duke University Press. Used by permission of the publisher.

word" to the question "How does it feel to be a problem?" young urban black women respond with actions that suggest their answers come with an open palm in the interrogator's face and the response: "You're the one with the problem!" This article will examine the moves that hip-hop women make to eradicate "the problem" and shred the veil of racism, sexism, and classism within African American communities and America in general. It focuses on how hip-hop performers use discursive strategies to transform the notion of "real" American womanhood through public performances that become resources for racial and feminist identity—and for ongoing political contestation.[7]

Do Right Woman

In the midst of hip-hop's rise into America's consciousness, concern over both the representation and involvement of women often has been in the form of scandal, moral panic, and cultural and political hysteria. Since the mid-1990s, politicians and public figures such as C. Delores Tucker, as well as respected musicians like Dionne Warwick, have publicly derided hip-hop artists for what they deem to be widespread misogyny and violence in lyrics, videos, and staged performances.[8] In contrast, scholars and many feminists, while highly critical of sexism and violence in hip-hop, argue that it is a product and representation of male-dominated culture and should be criticized within American culture and media representation.[9] While well intentioned, this public debate does not improve the day-to-day life of the young women hip-hop fans and artists. Their reality is fraught with numerous physical threats and stereotypical media images of young urban women who are frequently cast in sexist, racist, paternalistic, contested, and convoluted notions of the strong, angry, promiscuous, childbearing, wild black woman. Moreover, the representations of these notions of young urban women occur within a panoply of discursive practices and symbols of womanhood, motherhood, sexuality, class, authority, race, influence, and desire: It

should come as no surprise that hip-hop women are not only aware of representations of their generation but are also invested in understanding the musical, social, political, and cultural history of black women that led to these representations. Female MCs use hip-hop to develop and display their lyrical skills as well as present and challenge what it means to be a young black woman in America and the world. They do not use their musical and verbal genre to destroy the veil of race, gender, and class discrimination. They prefer to render it diaphanous, so that it can be seen and manipulated as symbol, warning, and memory of what it meant to live under its tyranny and the dangers of underestimating dominant society's desire to erect it once again.

African American musical traditions often connect younger generations to mothers, women, workers, singers, activists, and organizers who have struggled to place the lives and values of black working-class women within general American and African American culture. Musical forms have a central role in African American culture as a major source of socialization, social change, political thought, and expression of desire, religious belief, and love.[10] The music, history, and memories of past generations are the seeds of the hip-hop generation, and the women prepare to both run with them and use them to incinerate race and gender stereotypes—if necessary. The history that these musicians deliver to the hip-hop generation includes details of how black women were treated as property under slavery and denied rights to their bodies and any argument of femininity, family, and motherhood. Evidence of a sense of connectedness to their female predecessors often appears as responsibility and entitlement in the practiced lyrics of artists. One strategy is the performance of racially marked and "strong woman/sister" authenticity that challenges pernicious stereotypes and uses figures such as Angela Davis (e.g., the artist Medusa) to represent uncompromising revolutionary commitment and spirit. Others look to Mother Africa (embodied in, say, Queen Latifah), explicitly promote self-respect, and engage in educational dialogue with men and women who lack knowledge of their history and culture. Still others offer a variety of street-smart perspectives (e.g., Eve, Rah Digga, Missy Elliott) and that of the down-to-earth, thoughtful, and conscious woman (e.g., Lauryn Hill, Mystic).

Irrespective of style, hip-hop women share the same value of performance: hard, skillful, provocative, and intelligent rhyming. They are skilled MCs, and they represent the lives of women in hip-hop and the world. Medusa, a prominent underground MC, describes herself as "One Bad Sista" who speaks with her ancestors by her side and contemplates their sacrifices and triumphs through the power ("gangsta") and wisdom of her womb and vagina as she croons, "This pussy gangsta."[11] This explicit reference is simultaneously sexual and nonsexual, defiant and compliant. It is the unambiguous telling of the black woman's story as she carries, produces, and attempts to protect that which she holds dear.

Ain't No Way

Female MCs devour and set to rhyme black women's history, social life, and dreams of being treated with respect as women in America. Virtually every female rapper has "shouted out" the names of strong, talented women who were symbols of excellence and leadership. These names include Angela Davis, Harriet Tubman, Sojourner Truth, Rosa Parks, Nina Simone, Bessie Smith, Billie Holiday, Aretha Franklin, and more.[12] Though not all female MCs are versed on the details of the treatment of black women in the United States, they are well aware that black women had to struggle to be valued as both women and black people in American history. For many black women, a claim to womanhood has been a matter not only of social practice but also of the courts.

The tragic 1855 case *State of Missouri v. Celia* set the stage for how black women would be treated and viewed by society for decades to come. After attempting to resist repeated rapes by her master that left her pregnant and sick, Celia

struck and killed him and then tried to destroy the evidence. During her trial for murder, the defense's argument was that in the state of Missouri, women are protected from rape and therefore Celia should be subject to a lesser sentence. The court ruled that the assault did not constitute rape, since she was a slave rather than a woman, and thus could not be adjudicated under laws that protect women.[13] The precedent had been set. Because she was a slave, Celia was not a woman. Later, because black women worked to support their families, unlike many white women, their claims to womanhood were treated as dubious. As Evelyn Higginbotham argues, "Gender, so colored by race, remained from birth until death inextricably linked to one's personal identity and social status. For black and white women, gendered identity was reconstructed and represented in very different, indeed antagonistic, racialized contexts."[14]

This racialized context was also one that regulated the public attitude and behavior of blacks. During U.S. slavery and until the 1960s in the South, blacks could not exhibit linguistic agency, nor could they initiate verbal interactions with whites under the threat of death.[15] Submission to white supremacy demanded nonverbal communication as well. Thus, while the place of black women in the legal history concerning women's rights is truly disturbing, control and surveillance were relentless and occurred within all aspects of black life, especially in terms of day-to-day interactions. Since discursive practices of all black people were regulated by white supremacists, all black communication with whites in general was performed as powerless, agentless, childlike, and thus feminine. Interaction styles included nearly every conservative, overly polite verbal and nonverbal expectation of women's speech, such as: use formal address when speaking to a white person, do not speak unless spoken to, do not speak assuredly (use hedges), do not make statements (overuse tag questions), and so on. The discursive requirements also included nonverbal rules such as stepping aside when a white person approaches, keeping one's head lowered, and not looking someone directly in the eye. Thus linguistic and conversational cues of subservience and dependence were necessary as performatives to corroborate the defense for slavery, and later Jim Crow segregation.

While the speech of all blacks was monitored to address the needs and demands of white patriarchy, this was true for white women's speech as well. White women's speech has historically been relegated to subservient status in the role of servant or sex object.[16] The "normal" woman's speech was thus described as less informal and more standard and conservative than men's. This designation did not result in equality in conversation. Instead, white women were treated to more interruptions from males and the frequent use of back channels (urging others to continue). Rather than initiating conversations on their own, they focused on helping others keep their turn at talk. In contrast to stereotypes of the dominant, subversive, emasculating, uncaring black woman, feminist psychology and linguistic theory portrayed middle-class white women as indiscriminate "people pleasers," concerned with harmony and with being accepted in life and in conversation. Signifying, loud-talking black women simply didn't stand a chance.[17] Rejecting the cult of the good woman who speaks without agency, hip-hop women have chosen a discourse style that is not only independent of patriarchal censorship and control but also freely critiques the loss of power and responsibility of the good woman.

I Say a Little Prayer

The power of women to discursively claim a space and challenge both patriarchy and feminism was born during the discursive struggles of the black power movement. While many identify the black power movement as the beginning of collective black pride, it was also the end of discursive compliance with white supremacy. The civil rights movement employed the polite and nonconfrontational discursive style of the middle class in order to construct the image of the equal,

worthy, intelligent citizen. Once the black power movement reframed the struggle for civil rights as one that demanded the same entitlements as whites, a discourse style was ushered in that did not simply address, confront, and resist compliant African American discourse. The new discourse annihilated the old and considered it a symbol of a slave and self-hate mentality. Suddenly, to speak in a deferential manner marked one as a lackey of white supremacists (an Uncle Tom). The new discourse style confronted white supremacy and neither complied nor demanded rights within it. Instead, the discourse style asserted a black presence on its terms, one that reflected a different consciousness and a sense of entitlement. As a result, African American speech in white-dominated contexts went from childlike, feminine, overly polite, and self-effacing to aggressive, impolite, direct, and in-your-face threatening.

Black women found themselves caught in the crevices of the movement from powerless and feminine discourse to a powerful one symbolizing not simply masculinity but a powerful black masculinity that challenges, threatens, and competes with white masculinity. To assert equal entitlements meant negotiating both feminine and masculine discourses, with racist and sexist baggage embedded in both. Thus, while this discursive space is potentially a powerful one, it is also one of unending contestation and mediation. This space was occupied not only by black women after slavery but also by the women of the blues, who in singing about women's realities introduced their strategies and methods for change and representation. Their only alternatives were to portray or defend cultural values about accurately describing people and treating them fairly and equally. It is not surprising that at the core of black communities are women who were prepared and compelled to confront racial, class, and gender injustice. There are rewards for women who are adept at handling discourse concerning these subjects, and there is punishment for those who are naive and fail to recognize the power they and those in power have over their words.

As a result, there are two intertwined themes throughout African American women's discourse. One is associated with representing individual and group identity and the other with representing racial, gender, and class injustice. Consequently, any critique of gender hegemony is also a critique of race.

Respect

Your revolution will not happen between
  these thighs
Will not happen between these thighs
Will not be you shaking
And me [sigh] faking between these thighs

Because the real revolution
That's right, I said the real revolution
You know, I'm talking about the revolution
When it comes
It's gonna be real
It's gonna be real
It's gonna be real
When it finally comes
It's gonna be real.[18]

While hip-hop women are committed to representing their lives and compete equally with men, their quest is not without peril and retaliation. On October 1999, Sarah Jones's recording of "Your Revolution" was played on public radio station KBOO-FM, in Portland, Oregon. Before that date, it was considered by college radio to be a creative and important response to misogynistic representations of women in male-MC popular hip-hop lyrics. Soon after the program aired, the FCC informed the station that it had broken decency laws and would be fined. On May 17, 2001, the FCC penalized KBOO for playing the recording, fining them $7,000 for indecent language. The FCC's ruling states: "The rap song 'Your Revolution' contains unmistakable patently offensive sexual references. We have considered the KBOO Foundation's arguments concerning the context of this material. Specifically, the KBOO Foundation asserts that the rap song 'Your Revolution' cannot be separated from its contempo-

rary cultural context . . . [and] is 'a feminist attack on male attempts to equate political "revolution" with promiscuous sex' and as such, is not indecent."[19]

Both Sarah Jones and the station argued that not only was the feminist perspective necessary to respond to misogyny in some male performer's lyrics, it is appropriate within hip-hop's tradition of lyrical battle. They also argued that the FCC had lost previous rulings regarding hip-hop radio play.[20] Though the FCC eventually reversed its ruling, it remains disturbing that they focused on a female spoken-word and hip-hop artist who defended herself in male terms. Moreover, their malfeasance not only exposed the nature of patriarchal control; it also educated many women on inequities in the application of power and authority.

While the FCC may protect America from women speaking their minds, the agency also expects black women to fend for themselves against unfetered misogyny. For example, some students at Spelman College, a prominent black women's college in Atlanta, successfully pressured the rapper Nelly to cancel an appearance at their school because they found his song "Tip Drill" and its accompanying video offensive.[21] Their protest resulted in a public dialogue that highlights many of the vexing issues that complicate hip-hop's interpretive framework. The dialogue occurred within a complex contestation of realities. First, the "Tip Drill" video played late night on BET, the only national cable station in the United States with a format directed toward African Americans.[22] Second, Nelly's music, as well as that of other artists who use misogynist lyrics, is regularly played at dance clubs frequented by students from the area, including the Spelman women. Some of the women in the video are purported to be students at colleges in Atlanta. Not only did the incident involve a black performer and business, but Nelly was visiting the campus in order to educate African Americans about the need for marrow and blood-stem-cell donors among minorities! All of these facts are significant in terms of the specificities of hip-hop as both an African American and popular product. By rejecting Nelly's appearance, the women of Spelman also argued that though they regularly participate in all forms of hip-hop music, and though they watch and support the only major black-themed cable station, and though they consider the bone marrow drive important to the health of their community, these were not sufficient reasons to accept the offensive representation of black women.

The contestation, with its multiple twists and entanglements in terms of race, gender, and sexuality, are common for women in hip-hop culture.[23] Women have consistently protested and complained about sexual exploitation in lyrics and videos—though they dance to many of these same songs in clubs. Hip-hop artists both dance and protest as cultural participants and innovators. They use their skills and constantly embody and reframe feminist identity. They do so within a move to incorporate the range of emotions that they encounter within hip-hop. They do not leave the game; rather, they play and critique it as members while constantly raising the stakes on race and gender.

Call Me

As discussed earlier, music is part of the fabric of African American culture and serves as the backdrop for virtually every ordinary and important event. It is constantly played and heard. It often serves as a call to home where African traditions (and tales of African traditions) provide a strategy for how to deal with family, ancestors, threats, culture, and power.[24] Works detailing the use of song to inform slaves of locations of the Underground Railroad are legend, as are songs that signify on white supremacy and act as a way to exercise some sense of agency during Jim Crow.[25] African American music provides information and knowledge by telling indirect and embedded stories about life and injustice in America. Early blues and jazz artists performed during periods of rampant white supremacy. The mere existence of these performers, as well as their performances and recordings, provided lessons and confirma-

tion of a black reality for those who wanted to hear the truth. Daphne Harrison describes the importance of these musicians' roles: "The blues artist speaks directly of and to the folk who have suffered pain and assures them that they are not alone." They present a story that says, "We have been through that too."[26]

While there are many writings on the women who developed both jazz and the blues in America, the women of the blues have received most of the academic attention. This is largely due to their role in presenting an identity that included working-class realities as well as one that suggested agency regarding sex, knowledge of both the white and black world's attitude and treatment of women, and complicity as well as critique of life for a black woman. The lives of these artists provided essential information about the world and black life that was not available to most of the black population until the late 1960s. They were living proof that bad luck and trouble could be survived if you were Ma Rainey, Dinah Washington, and Bessie Smith. It could also take you down if you were Billie Holiday. These performers' mere existence was witness not to what *could* happen to you if you were a black woman, but what *did* happen to you with regularity. Blues singers took the old saying "All you have to do is stay black and die" and provided the deeply layered meanings and webs of irony, betrayal, bitterness, and longing that comprised staying black in America.

Thanks to their bawdy and brilliant language use and perspective, blues women were able to engage in romantic, sexual, and political rhetoric. As Angela Davis writes, "That their aesthetic representations of the politics of gender and sexuality are informed by and interwoven with their representations of race and class makes their work all the more provocative."[27] The blues emerged from ex-slaves who participated in and experienced the slave spiritual as the religious symbol for freedom, representing the collective need and desires of the enslaved. The end of slavery was also the beginning of the expression of individual and emotional needs and desires of

African Americans. As Davis argues, "The birth of the blues was aesthetic evidence of new psychological realities within the black population" (5). The blues performance world was a man's world, and they sang of loss, injustice, irony, power, heartbreak, and the need to keep moving away from their bad, hard luck and trouble. They sang about being a black man in a white man's world—and it was a man's world, indeed. Women blues singers, and later jazz singers, sang about a man's world where they tried to please their men who were subjugated and who also left them regularly. They knew their men's notion of a better world did not include women's equality. Blues women chronicled the evidence of patriarchal ideology with accounts of physical and sexual abuse and financial ruin. They were often audacious in their depictions of a woman's life, where romantic love was the equivalent of abuse and heartbreak and the only happy ending was getting out with a little dignity and "some of what you came with."

Hip-hop performers took their cues from the blues and jazz women who preceded them. As black people began to exercise their voice, the blues represented the "real" world of hardworking black people who knew their only chance to succeed (make it) was to work and try to protect oneself from the uncontrolled power of white supremacy. The often-heard refrain "If it wasn't for bad luck, I wouldn't have no luck at all" is part of the irony of being black in the land of the free. It is not surprising, then, that the discourse of women in hip-hop includes a critique of the clueless and naive woman who lacks agency; does not speak up or examine patriarchy or respect her own sexuality; does not recognize patriarchy; and does not value class, race, or culture. Hip-hop artists build from the blues and then broaden their notion of womanhood to incorporate hip-hop's female science. While both the blues and jazz have been dominated by men, the women performers have not only demonstrated remarkable talent but also negotiated womanhood in a man's world. Likewise, hip-hop artists value lyrical skill and make a conscious effort to provide a full as-

sessment and critique of racism and sexism, while offering alternatives that explicitly explore social class as well as desire, emotion, power, and patriarchy. Blues women often focused on cheating lovers, relationships, domestic violence, and what Davis calls the "ephemerality of many sexual partners" (3). While women of hip-hop focus on similar topics, they also articulate a position that is both individual and related to the collective good.[28] Talented hip-hop women toil alongside men when they want or need to—whether the men like it or not—and challenge both patriarchy and prescribed notions of feminism. Medusa proudly and brazenly demonstrates that she has the skill and power of the word: "I'm the mouth almighty, I got tongue everlasting. . . . Rhymes like these invented the phrase 'next level.'"[29] Hip-hop women represent the spiritual, the blues song, and the drum. They construct knowledge, intelligence, and emotion as connected and demand that they be heard.

Chain of Fools

The right to talk and represent oneself and one's community is a fundamental aspect of citizenship. Black women in particular have worked to reframe family, womanhood, relationship, and sexuality to guarantee their right to represent women within the American life. Yet no matter what image or ideology a hip-hop woman represents, she operates within an adolescent world where identities, roles, and status are constantly being explored and where participants are convinced that everything is at stake and everything is about them. The hip-hop nation's insistence on noncensorship and representation of frank honesty and realism means that virtually any activity or opinion that exists can be reflected and/or critiqued. Within this system, silencing is an unacceptable practice, since ideological censorship is viewed as the work of hegemonic forces attempting to co-opt and corrupt hip-hop. But the hip-hop community does not provide a platform for all views, since it can be fanatically heterosexist. This is exacerbated by the conflicts and excesses that result from negotiating adolescent desire (and rejection), emerging and conflicting gender identities and roles, and racism in a society that produces, avoids, and silences public discourse on sex and sexuality and the objectification of women in general. The misogynist representations of male desire—where any woman who does not support or like a man who likes her is by definition dishonest, scheming, unfaithful, or a lesbian—is one outcome of this situation. It is within this fully charged context that women in hip-hop forge an identity and presence that is consistently feminist, progressive, passionate, and sexual.

Considering the powerful language of male discourse and the overall protection that it receives, it is not surprising that research on teenage girls' identity finds that adolescent girls unselfconsciously rejected constructs of feminism in favor of "benign versions of masculinity that allowed them to be 'one of the guys.'"[30] It is also predictable that they are conflicted regarding the expression of sexuality that is not exclusively dependent on men and society's notion of the good woman. As Audre Lorde explains, "The erotic is a measure of our sense of self and the chaos of our strongest feelings."[31] At the same time that the erotic may represent power and joy, it can also be objectified and represent a loss of power through voyeuristic fantastic reinterpretations. The tension created by unbridled male adolescent sexual exploration and the desire of young women to represent themselves honestly and unashamedly creates an energizing space for young women, one where all hip-hop artists gain membership through artistic skills and where audiences and crews insist that their lives—including contradictions—be represented.

Baby, I Love You

It is common for hip-hop women to say that they support men and at the same time want to be respected and in control of their bodies. Supporting men recognizes race and class hypocrisy and does not mean that men make decisions for women. Rather, irrespective of who is leading, women and men support their relationship, critique racism and classism, and respect each other. For example, the ultimate queen of hip-hop, Queen Latifah, began her recording career as an alternative to the male construction of the scheming, disloyal woman by situating herself as a woman of royalty who chooses her sex partners, is not interested in a man who needs to control her, has superb rap skills, and is committed to educating her community. Her proclamation not only claims her personal identity but reconfigures the black nationalist notion of the man-dependent Queen Mother to one who is independent of men for her identity.

> You asked, I came
> So behold the Queen
> Let's add a little sense to the scene . . .
> From Latifah with the Queen in front of it
> Droppin' bombs, you're up in arms and
>   puzzled
> The lines will flow like fluid while you
>   guzzle . . .
> 'Cause it's knowledge I'm seekin'
> Enough about myself, I think it's time that I
>   tell you
> About the evil that men do.[32]

Though artists like Queen Latifah can proclaim a strong identity as a woman of power, that is not to say that hip-hop operates with fairness regarding gender. Successful female MCs are constantly besieged with gossip regarding their sexuality, a form of gossip not summarily directed toward men. Mainly because they insist on respect for and the safety of women, they are often rumored to be lesbian and bisexual. Women MCs often address their own sexuality in reference to their own desire and knowledge of society's desire for them—whether male or female. Some women are openly bisexual, simultaneously lesbian and intensely heterosexual. While some artists consider it important to talk about their sexual preference, overwhelmingly they argue that feminism and sexuality do not determine their skill as artists and their determination to say it the way they see it. They insist on performing with their sexuality intact and want to be judged by their skills and ability to represent all aspects of their lives. Consequently, while men's lyrics often reflect male adolescent desire, women MCs reflect a multiplicity of perspectives and discourses about relationship, sex, desire, and friendship—the issues facing young women.[33]

The method for supporting and critiquing sexually assertive female rappers was established in the early 1990s with two female rap groups: Hoes wit Attitude (HWA) and Bytches with Problems (BWP). HWA considered their group a copy of gangsta and sex-obsessed groups like NWA and 2 Live Crew, but absent of lyrical skills. They presented themselves as sexual objects from a gangsta's perspective and were never seriously considered true hip-hop. Their performances were sexually explicit.[34] BWP, on the other hand, argued that they were a progressive and educational response to the misogyny that persisted in hip-hop in the early 1990s.

> You finally reach a point when you say, "It's not working. Let me just come down to your level for a minute." I know how to go back up when I want to . . . the music women have been doing is, "Oh, my man cheated on me, and he left me. But I'll be strong. I'll love him, and he'll come back." I want to hear, "Fuck you, muthafucka! I don't need you!" That's why we came up with this concept. It's time for raw music like that.[35]

BWP insisted that they sold reality and not sex and cited seven problems that concerned them: men who cheat on their girlfriends and wives; men who preach positive messages and then leave their families and don't pay child support; men who beat women; men who talk about how great they are in bed but can't live up to it, even for two minutes; date rape; women who get their period and take it out on everyone else; and female rappers who get ahead by putting down other female rappers.[36] When hip-hop women address explicit concerns of young women, they consistently construct a fully developed context

that includes working-class realities, relationship issues, and a variety of women's issues. Another instance of this is artists' attempts to use the word *bitch* to discuss issues of physical and sexual abuse, jealousy, power, and the reality of life for strong young women. In "U.N.I.T.Y.," Queen Latifah spells the word and contrasts a community need to act as one unified group against racism and sexism by considering the disrespect of women as a factor that renders the black community less powerful. She both asks for romantic and platonic love from men and criticizes them for disrespecting women. In turn she asks for sisterhood from women and criticizes those who don't respect themselves and their families and do not critique misogyny.

> U.N.I.T.Y.
> U.N.I.T.Y., that's a unity
> U.N.I.T.Y.
> U.N.I.T.Y., that's a unity
> U.N.I.T.Y., love a black man from infinity
>   to infinity
> Who you callin' a bitch?
> Here we go. We got to let them know.
> U.N.I.T.Y., love a black woman from
>   infinity to infinity
> You ain't a bitch or a ho

Similarly, early in her career, MC Lyte considered herself hard-core and argued that any viewpoint that exists in the community should be allowed in hip-hop. In her work she introduced prochoice themes, AIDS awareness, and antidrug messages consistently in a style that was unsentimental and powerful. Even though she supported positions often viewed as feminist, she was not comfortable with the label.[37] When asked if the term *bitch* should be used toward women in general, she responded: "I've been called a bitch. And I have no problem with being called a bitch if you know me. If you don't know me then no! You don't have the right to call me that."[38] Years later, women are still being called "bitch," and Missy Elliott explains exactly what MC Lyte meant by "if you know me." For Missy Elliott, *bitch* indicates that the speaker, the one who uses that name, is a loser who can only resort to name-calling as a sign of loss of social face.[39] She extends this meaning to include the notion of the proud woman with skills who cannot be stopped.

"She's a bitch"
When you say my name
Talk mo' junk but won't look my way
"She's a bitch"
See I got more cheese
So back on up while I roll up my sleeves
"She's a bitch"
You can't see me, Joe
Get on down while I shoot my flow
"She's a bitch"
When I do my thing
Got the place on fire, burn it down to flame.[40]

This is also true for Rah Digga, whose *Dirty Harriet* release is introduced with the acknowledgment that she is a strong, bad bitch:

Rah Digga, the Harriet Tubman of hip-hop, has returned, baby!
C'mon!
I be that bitch niggas wantin' in the lab
Rhymes comin', rhymes goin' like I was a dollar cab
Fingerin' the man tryin' to tap into his feelings
A misguided soul so ain't checkin' for the lyrics
Many different players, only one hold the ball
Ghetto-fabulous chick, go against the protocol
With the grittiest lingo, still such a little sweetheart
Book-educated with a whole lotta street smarts
Follow me now, as I build my fan base.[41]

Think

The passion in hip-hop for a "fresh" representation of womanhood is not focused exclusively on the inclusion of young African American women. It is part of the "world economy of passion"[42] and proposes to reframe feminism to acknowledge and incorporate aspects of all women's lives. Yet this passion is about not only emotion and desire but also the emotional connection that one has to aesthetics, culture, memory, and others.[43] Hip-hop women argue that the desire to be included as a woman in society is the passion to be accepted as a product of all of their experiences. Furthermore, as Bennett argues, this desire and passion has political implications in that it makes "the most private of interactions culturally and socially meaningful."[44]

Hip-hop women practice and perform desire: the desire for love; the desire for revolution, for respect, for fulfillment, for politics; the desire for a feminist ideology that includes all women and privileges none. Desire is a powerful, deep, unending force that exists through reason, war, love, and pain. Desire shreds the veil. Instead of hip-hop aggressively putting "bass in your face," it places race and class in your face—as well as the womb, the clitoris, the family, the ancestors, and Bessie Smith. Because they focus on women's responsibility for their own lives and bodies, women in hiphop consistently explore feminism, the intersections of race and class, and gender marginalization and oppression. They also express their support of African American men, the male friends and family members who are routinely targeted by the state. As Gwendolyn Pough explains: "When you call someone your sister or brother, or comrade in the struggle against racism, a bond is created. In that bond there is love. Rap music therefore offers space for public dialogues about love, romance and struggle in a variety of combinations."[45]

Most successful female MCs are building bridges and shredding veils and refashioning them to wear in their hair and around their waists. They recognize that for them there are more than two worlds, and the only place where they can negotiate race, class, gender, and sexuality with relative freedom is the hip-hop world. It is not an ideal space, but it is one populated by those searching for discourse that confronts power. Everyone in that world expects to be respected. Young feminists are watching as hiphop women develop their skills, represent their communities, and demand respect from and for their brothers who, along with the rest of society, are slowly and reluctantly losing their hostility and ambivalence about showing solid respect for them. They accept their turn at being "the problem" with a refreshing, kick-ass fierceness that encourages women everywhere to discuss their lives openly.

Notes

1. See Paula Giddings, *When and Where I Enter: The Impact of Black Women on Race and Sex in America* (New York: William Morrow, 1984); Hazel Carby, *Reconstructing Womanhood: The Emergence of the Afro-American Woman Novelist* (Oxford: Oxford University Press, 1987); Barbara Smith, ed., *Home Girls: A Black Feminist Anthology* (New York: Kitchen Table/Women of Color, 1983); Smith, "Toward a Black Feminist Criticism," in *The New Feminist Criticism: Essays on Women, Literature, and Theory*, ed. Elaine Showalter (New York: Pantheon, 1985), 168–85; and Leith Mullings, "Images, Ideology, and Women of Color," in *Women of Color in U.S. Society*, ed. Maxine Baca Zinn and Bonnie Thornton Dill (Philadelphia: Temple University Press, 1994), 265–89.

2. W. E. B. Du Bois, *The Souls of Black Folk* (1903; Chicago: A. C. McClurg, 1990).

3. W. E. B. Du Bois, *Dark Water: Voices from within the Veil* (1920; Millwood, NY: Krauss International, 1975), 172. I would like to thank Leith Mullings for first introducing me to this quote.

4. See Angela Davis, *Women, Race, and Class* (New York: Vintage Books, 1981); Giddings, *When and Where I Enter*; and Patricia Hill Collins, *Black Feminist Thought: Knowledge, Consciousness, and the Politics of Empowerment* (New York: Routledge, 1990).

5. See Bonnie Thornton Dill, "Fictive Kin, Paper Sons, and Compradrazgo: Women of Color and the Struggle for Family Survival," in *Women of Color in U.S. Society*, ed. Maxine Baca Zinn and Bonnie Thornton Dill (Philadelphia: Temple University Press, 1994), 149–69.

6. See Mullings, "Images, Ideology, and Women of Color," 265.

7. The phrase *hip-hop women* refers to those who assert that they grew up in hip-hop culture and are a product of it. Though misogyny in hip-hop continues to be a major issue, the focus of this article is women's voices and their agency within the male-dominated genre of hip-hop. This article is also an attempt to participate in what Marta Savigliano, in *Tango and the Political Economy of Passion* (Boulder, CO: Westview, 1995), calls the "world economy of passion." She uses passion to analyze the contestations around race, class, sexuality, nation, and the tango.

8. C. Delores Tucker was chair of the National Political Congress of Black Women and Chair of the Democratic National Committee Black Caucus. In the 1990s, she participated in a national campaign against violent lyrics in rap music. In 1997, she and her husband sued the estate of Tupac Shakur for $10 million over lyrics in which Shakur rhymed her name with an obscenity. Her lawsuit alleged, among other things, that her husband, William Tucker, had suffered loss of "consortium."

9. See, for instance, bell hooks, *Outlaw Culture: Resisting Representations* (New York: Routledge, 1994).

10. Angela Davis, *Blues Legacies and Black Feminism: Gertrude "Ma" Rainey, Bessie Smith and Billie Holiday* (New York: Pantheon, 1998); Michael C. Dawson, *Black Visions: The Roots of Contemporary African-American Political Ideologies* (Chicago: University of Chicago Press, 2001); Tricia Rose, *Black Noise: Rap Music and Black Culture in Contemporary America* (Hanover, NH: Wesleyan University Press, 1994); Dionne Bennett, "The Love Difference Makes: Intersubjectivity and the Emotional Politics of African American Romantic Ritual" (PhD diss., University of California, Los Angeles, 2003).

11. Medusa, "My Pussy's Gangsta."

12. The performers invoking these names include Medusa, Lauryn Hill, Lil' Kim, MC Lyte, Rah Digga, and more.

13. See Evelyn Brooks Higginbotham, "African-American Women's History and the Meta-language of Race," *Signs 17* (1992): 251–74.

14. Ibid., 8. Thus while Butler (1990) interrogates the meaning of women within historical and political contexts regarding sexuality, Harris (1996) is concerned with when the legal status of black women moved from "property" to "woman." Judith Butler, *Gender Trouble: Feminism and the Subversion of Identity*

(London and New York: Routledge, 1990); Cheryl L. Harris, "Finding Sojourner's Truth: Race, Gender, and the Institution of Property," *Cardozo Law Review* 18 (1996): 306–409.

15. Marcyliena Morgan, *Language, Discourse, and Power in African American Culture* (Cambridge: Cambridge University Press, 2002).

16. Robin Lakoff, *Language and Woman's Place* (New York: Harper & Row, 1975).

17. These, of course, are references to African American verbal genres. See Morgan, *Language, Discourse, and Power in African American Culture*; Claudia Mitchell-Kernan, *Language Behavior in a Black Urban Community* (Berkeley, CA: Language Behavior Research Laboratory, 1971); Geneva Smitherman, *Talkin That Talk: Language, Culture and Education in African America* (London: Routledge, 2000).

18. Sarah Jones, "Your Revolution," 1999.

19. According to the FCC, "The KBOO Foundation cites a case decided under Florida's criminal obscenity statute as support for its argument that material with artistic merit is not indecent. The court's determination that a lower court had not properly applied the tripartite obscenity standard of *Miller v. California*, 413 U.S. 15 (1973), does not control our indecency analysis here." *Luke Records, Inc. v. Navarro*, 960 F.2d 134 (11th Cir. 1992), *cert. denied, Navarro v. Luke Records, Inc.*, 506 U.S. 1022 (1992).

20. Ibid., 3, n. 2.

21. In a tip drill, basketball players line up and throw the ball against the backboard. The exercise is designed to develop timing and jumping ability for rebounding. In hip-hop, *tip drill* refers to a woman with a beautiful body and an unattractive face. In the music video, various strippers in thongs are filmed from the back as they gyrate their buttocks and simulate sex. The final shot is of Nelly swiping a credit card down the buttocks of a gyrating woman.

22. According to its corporate statement, BET was founded by Robert L. Johnson, chairman and chief executive officer, in 1980. A subsidiary of Viacom, it is the leading African American-owned and -operated media and entertainment company in the United States. BET runs twenty-four-hour programming that targets African American consumers, reaching more than 65 million U.S. homes and more than 90 percent of all black cable households.

23. See Gwendolyn Pough, *Check It While I Wreck It: Black Womanhood, Hip-Hop Culture, and the Public Sphere* (Boston: Northeastern University Press, 2004); Cheryl L. Keyes, *Rap Music and Street Consciousness* (Urbana: University of Illinois Press, 2002); Joan Morgan, *When Chickenheads Come Home to Roost: My Life as a Hip-Hop Feminist* (New York: Simon & Schuster, 1999).

24. See Lawrence Levine, *Black Culture and Black Consciousness: Afro-American Folk Thought from Slavery to Freedom* (Oxford: Oxford University Press, 1977); and Roger Abrahams and John Szwed, *After Africa: Extracts from the British Travel Accounts and Journals of the Seventeenth, Eighteenth, and Nineteenth Centuries Concerning the Slaves, Their Manners and Customs in the British West Indies* (New Haven, CT: Yale University Press, 1983).

25. See, for example, Levine, *Black Culture and Black Consciousness*.

26. Daphne Duval Harrison, *Black Pearls: Blues Queens of the 1920s* (New Brunswick, NJ: Rutgers University Press, 1988), 8.

27. Davis, *Blues Legacies and Black Feminism*, xv.

28. See Rose, *Black Noise*.

29. Medusa performs this song at concerts but has not yet recorded it.

30. For studies of teenage girls' identity, see Michelle Fine and Pat Macpherson, "Over Dinner: Feminism and Adolescent Female Bodies," in *Gender and Education*, ed. Sari Knopp Biklen and Diane Pollard (Chicago: University of Chicago Press, 1993), 126–54; Bonnie J. Ross Leadbeater and Niobe Way, eds., *Urban Girls: Resisting Stereotypes, Creating Identities* (New York: New York University Press, 1996); Deborah Tolman, *Dilemmas of Desire: Teenage Girls Talk about Sexuality* (Cambridge, MA: Harvard University Press, 2002).

31. Audre Lorde, "Uses of the Erotic: The Erotic as Power," in *Writing on the Body: Female Embodiment and Feminist Theory*, ed. Katie Conboy, Nadia Medina, and Sarah Stanbury (New York: Columbia University Press, 1997), 277–82.

32. Queen Latifah, "The Evil That Men Do," 1989.

33. These two approaches parallel the typical discourse styles of teenagers, where males often play verbal games focused exclusively on skill and women focus on verbal practices that require both skill and determining the nature of friendship (see Morgan, *Language, Discourse, and Power in African American Culture*).

34. The women were similar to the professional strippers that appear with some of the acts from the "dirty South" (e.g., 2 Live Crew and Luther Campbell).

35. Michael Small, *Break It Down: The Inside Story from the New Leaders of Rap* (New York: Citadel, 1992), 51–53.

36. Ibid.

37. See Rose, *Black Noise*.

38. MC Lyte, 1991.

39. A hater who has lost social standing by not demonstrating (Goffman).

40. Missy Elliott, "She's a Bitch" (Background Records, 1999).

41. Rah Digga, "Dirty Harriet" (Elektra Records, 1999).

42. Savigliano, *Tango and the Political Economy of Passion*. See also Dorinne Kondo, *About Face: Performing Race in Fashion and Theater* (London: Routledge, 1997).

43. See Zora Neale Hurston, *I Love Myself When I Am Laughing . . . and Then Again When I Am Looking Mean and Impressive: A Zora Neale Hurston Reader*, ed. Alice Walker (New York: Feminist Press, 1979).

44. Bennett, "The Love Difference Makes," 14.

45. Pough, *Check It While I Wreck It*, 86.

DoVeanna S. Fulton

Comic Views and Metaphysical Dilemmas: Shattering Cultural Images through Self-Definition and Representation by Black Comediennes[1]

Using the paradigm of Gary Alan Fine's "folklore diamond," this essay analyzes comedic material of contemporary African American women comics. This comedic material conveys the uniqueness of African American women's position at the intersections of race, gender, and class dynamics, thereby marking the performers as not only Black, not only female, but as Black women entertainers who are changing the face of Black women's comedy.

"Being able to laugh about one's tragedies presupposes the formation of a pretty solid identity."—Michele Najlis, *Sandino's Daughters Revisited*[2]

Historically, African American Women have used humor to assuage painful experience. "If there is any one thing," folklorist Daryl Cumber Dance insists, "that has brought African American women whole through the horrors of the middle passage, slavery, Jim Crow, Aunt Jemima, the welfare system, integration, the O.J. Simpson trial, and Newt Gingrich, it is our humor. If there is any one thing that has helped us to survive the broken promises, lies, betrayals, contempt, humiliations and dehumanization that have been our lot in this nation and often in our families, it is our humor" (1998:xxi). This legacy of humor in the face of pain lives in the texts of contemporary Black comediennes, many of whom first gained a national audience on "Russell Simmons'

Def Comedy Jam," telecast by Home Box Office (HBO) and are featured on the recently released *Queens of Comedy* video production (Latham and Purcell 2000). This comedic material conveys the uniqueness of African American women's position at the intersections of race, gender, and class dynamics, thereby marking the performers as not only Black, not only female, but as Black women entertainers who follow in the tradition of predecessors like Jackie "Moms" Mabley, who Trudier Harris has said, "urged people to laugh with rather than at her" (1988:766).

Gary Alan Fine's "folklore diamond" is a useful paradigm to determine the strategies these women employ to both distinguish themselves from Black male and White female comics, and his approach offers possibilities for representations of African American women that contradict dominant ideologies of the inferiority of Blacks, women, and Black women in particular. Fine's model, as described in his book,

Manufacturing Tales: Sex and Money in Contemporary Legends, consists of four main points—social structure, personal imperatives, performance dynamics, and narrative content—that demonstrate how "the external world" is linked "to the content of the text, through the mediation of the person and the situation," illuminating the narrator and audience's involvement and connection in the performance and perpetuation of folklore (1992:5). Although Fine uses this model to examine urban legends, I posit that these elements are present in African American women's comic performances as well.

I choose to analyze the women on the "Def Comedy Jam" circuit as opposed to Black comediennes on either another program or in a different media because "Def Comedy Jam" allows them to present their material in a manner that parallels that of a live performance, which is important for understanding the overall function and context in which the humor is actuated. These women performers have changed the face of stand-up comedy and because the "Def Comedy Jam" audiences reflect the hip-hop scene, the comediennes articulate the experiences of many young African American women. Furthermore, through the mass media of home video and cable television, the audience for the "Def Comedy Jam" circuit is enlarged from that of a relatively insular, mostly young, Black audience to a wider mainstream American audience. Because of the voicelessness many Black women have experienced and because of the historical and cultural complexity of degrading images of Black women, resistance inherent in this humor demands explication for audiences who either are not cognizant of the history and pervasiveness of these images and their effects on Black women's lives or for those who may be aware but will use these performances as confirmation of racist and sexist ideologies.

Social structure, the first element in Fine's model, explores the impact and influence of the larger social and cultural structures that surround the narrator, audience, and thus the text. These structures include class structure, demographic divisions (race, gender, ethnicity, age, and other factors), institutional structures (state, economic, religious, educational, and familial), and the organization of social networks. All of these components form the larger setting in which the narrative is performed. The American social structure of race and gender divisions is fundamental to cultural impositions that make up the landscape in which African American women's humor resides. The documentary *Ethnic Notions* (1987), produced and directed by filmmaker Marlon Riggs, reveals the history of destructive racist images and representations of African Americans that permeate American popular culture. These images became stereotypes that African American performers were forced to adopt, modify, or challenge on the American stage. As a result of the continued representations of African American women as large, domineering, emasculating women who fail to conform to essentialized notions of womanhood, Black women comic performers consistently focus on the thematic issues of body image, male-female relationships, and racial and gender authenticity.

The innovative female comics of the "Def Comedy Jam" are a result of and react against the history of constraints forced on Black comediennes to tailor and modify performances according to societal expectations, while simultaneously presenting narratives in a manner understood and appreciated by African American communities. The social constructs of race that influence these performances echo W.E.B. Du Bois's concept of double consciousness ([1903] 1994:2–3). Yet, whereas Du Bois's trope of the veil signifies the duality of race consciousness, Black feminist theorists articulate the "brave" standpoint that African American women must contend with the complexity of self-representations.[3] We are faced with the "multiple jeopardy, multiple consciousness" of society's images as Blacks and as women (King 1988). In addition, I would add that we must contend with a third facet—our own consciousness as selves that are sometimes all, or none of, but always wading through, such representations.[4]

Thus, we develop—what I see as—triple consciousness that calls for struggle and laughter.

From Josephine Baker (who refused to accept abuse and discrimination from American audiences), to actresses such as Hattie McDaniel, Louise Beavers, and Butterfly McQueen (who were forced to continually portray servants on stage and screen), the history of Black comediennes is filled with resistance. These women understood the social structure that surrounded them and worked within and against it. In an interview regarding thesse performers, veteran actress Della Reese maintains, "The people of the era understood what was going on at that time. There was no need for Louise Beavers or Hattie McDaniel to think that they were ever going to be the ingénue. They understood that so they took what they had and worked it, and turned it into something magnanimous. They took that that was supposed to be a slur or a put down and turned it into a wonderfulness" (Smith 1993). Like their foremothers, contemporary Black women performers are cognizant of the dominant society's standards of beauty that, for the most part, exclude Black women. In fact, they appreciate the Black female body in relation to and in spite of these standards. In her analysis of Black female rappers, folklorist Cheryl Keyes (2000) identifies four personae ("Queen Mother," "Fly Girl," "Sista with Attitude," and "Lesbian") that many female hip-hop performers adopt.[5] These performers "portray via performance the fly girl as a party-goer, an independent woman, but, additionally, an erotic subject rather than an objectified one" (Keyes 2000:260). "Def Comedy Jam" comedienne Mo'Nique adopts the "fly girl" persona as a consciously erotic woman who is appreciated without being objectified. A full-figured woman, Mo'Nique dresses in the latest fashions and celebrates her position as the primary wage-earner in her marriage. According to Mo'Nique, rather than perceiving her as threatening to men or an undesirable wife, her husband finds her attractive and sexually appealing. Mo'Nique's "fly girl" image encourages women viewers to reject destructive objectifications in favor of a self-de-fined sexuality that is uncommon in mainstream American culture. For instance, throughout her routine, Mo'Nique praises the virtues of large women: She exhorts the large women in the audience to stand up and take a bow, insisting they are attractive and sexy to men and threatening to slimmer women because "Once you go fat you never go back" (Latham and Purcell 2000). This position flies in the face of the stereotype perpetuated in American popular culture of the Black mammy who is maternal, asexual, and nonthreatening. The mammy is a controlling image, maintains Patricia Hill Collins, that sustains "interlocking systems of race, gender, and class oppression," through the figure of "an asexual woman, a surrogate mother in Blackface devoted to the development of a white family" (1990:71–2). Instead of adopting and reinscribing the stereotype, Mo'Nique inverts it to disempower the destructive force of the racial construct.

Other gender constructs influence these women's performances. Critic June Sochen recognizes the constraints women have traditionally encountered when attempting to enter the profession of comic performance. "Men could be satirists and physical comics," she writes, and "Preferably, women were neither, but if they ventured into this culturally forbidden land, they should only display restrained wit—sly humor, perhaps, but not raucous, screaming, demonstrative stuff" (1991:13). Black comediennes also faced these constraints. For Black comediennes in the early twentieth century, audience acceptance and performance opportunities were, respectively, difficult and rare. Mel Watkins explains, "Some of the earliest Black comediennes were blues singers who expanded their roles and became regulars in the comedy bits" (1994:390). In the first half of the twentieth century, like their male counterparts, Black comediennes performed in tent shows, on minstrel and vaudeville stages, and on the "chitlin' circuit"—the stage circuit comprised of cabarets, nightclubs, and theatres that featured Black artists performing, almost exclusively, for Black audiences—with the rare performance opportunity in Broadway musical

comedies such as Eubie Blake and Noble Sissle's *Shuffle Along*.

Although the history of early African American women comics has been largely ignored, comedienne Jackie "Moms" Mabley's work has received critical attention.[6] Born in 1897 in North Carolina, Mabley became a dancer and singer by the time she was sixteen but quickly turned to comedy in traveling tent shows. Early in her career Mabley "assumed the character of an elderly earth mother. The guise provided the buffer or intermediary necessary to quell resistance to a woman doing a single comic routine" (Watkins 1994:391). Adopting the styles of monologues and stand-up routines that her contemporaries eschewed, Mabley constructed her material and persona in a manner that fostered a familiar relationship with the audience, and thus, detracted from any perceived threat her texts might have engendered. According to Lawrence W. Levine, "The appeal of Mabley's humor was precisely its degree of folkishness. . . . Her antique clothing, her easy manner, her sense of kinship with her audiences—marked by her references to them as her 'children'—her lack of pretentiousness, the easy familiarity of her language, her movements, her dialogue, were at the core of her vast popularity" (1977:362–3). Clearly "Moms" Mabley situated herself in the position as mother, a safe and accepted role for women; however, her material dealt with sexual and political issues—issues unacceptable for women to discuss publicly. By creating a character that appeared nonthreatening, Mabley was able to subvert the gender constructs of the day.

Following in this tradition, Black comediennes on the "Def Comedy Jam" confront traditional gender constructs. Adele Givens, one of the most popular women to appear on the show, uses what has become her signature line, "I'm such a fucking lady," in direct opposition to societal norms of what a lady does and does not say. She dismisses negative responses to her use of expletives and contends that her attitude is inherited, "Grandma told me that it's not what comes out of your mouth that makes it filthy, it's what you put in it" (Latham and Purcell 2000). Indeed, Givens's signature line reminds the audience to resist societal markers and, as Dance asserts, "[love] (or at least not [hate]) themselves as Black-brownbeigecreamdamnnear-whitewomen with straightcurlybushykinkylongdamnneardowntothewaistmediumshorthair and breasts and hips of varied and sundry descriptions" (1998:xxvi). In her *Queens* routine, Givens declares:

> Know that you are beautiful. Understand that. You know what happened, we started getting tricked by these magazines and these televisions. These bitches is tricking you. You think you can live up to the celebrity bitches, don't you? Well, it can't happen 'cause the hoes ain't real. You know they build them bitches, you know that? . . . Ladies these hoes are not made out of the same stuff you made out of. You a real woman, them bitches are not. They there to entertain yo' ass. You know they ain't made out of the same thing 'cause you read about them going to the hospital for shit like exhaustion and dehydration. Now, what bitch you know so tired she got to go to the hospital? I know some exhausted bitches. I know some women who got two jobs, six kids, no man. The bitch got things to do. (Latham and Purcell 2000)

With this declaration, Givens undermines media representations of women with "perfect" figures. She privileges the lives of working-class, "ordinary" women—who survive alone in spite of enormous economic and familial pressures—as true reflections of beauty and human substance.

Givens's declaration exemplifies Fine's second point on the folklore diamond; it directly reflects the narrator and consists of factors such as the personal self, unconscious motives, mood states, and rational choice. The importance of the performer's mood state is highlighted in the context of these recorded live performances. Featuring comedians who, for the most part, honed their performance skills and developed routines in venues that traditionally cater to Black audiences, "Russell Simmons' Def Comedy Jam" recreates the atmosphere of insulation and intraracial interaction that African Americans often exhibit outside the presence of Whites. The comedians exhibit forms of Black oral traditions of call and response, signifying, the dozens, and Black vernacular speech.[7] In addition, the "Def Comedy Jam" contains all the elements of the hip-hop scene of young African Americans, chiefly reflected by the music featuring the latest in hip-hop and rap and clothes fashion. The show is performed before a live audience at New York City's Academy Theater.[8] The mood is always upbeat and boisterous. Comediennes usually come onto the stage while dancing or in a similar lively state. They may first inquire about the audience's mood with a question such as "How y'all doin' out there?" Certainly, the comic's mood influences the performance; however, the audience's initial mood state determines the receptivity of the material as well. The audience's response, which is an aspect of performance dynamics, clearly affects the mood states of both the audience and performer. Recognizing the matrix produced by the interaction of each of these elements illuminates the significance of "Def Comedy Jam" comediennes' humor to contemporary Black women's self-definition and struggle.

The performer's personality and the rational choices the comedienne exhibits in her material are further aspects of personal imperatives. Fine discusses the personality as part of the "personal self" that is a "nexus between social forces and individual principles. . . . Instead of conceiving of personality as something that is mystifyingly internal, we can understand personality traits as situated modes of responding to external stimuli" (1992:15). Comediennes usually present themselves as gregarious and sociable. Although they do not adopt the maternal figure as their comedic foremother "Moms" Mabley did, these comediennes demonstrate a direct relation to Mabley by presenting themselves as nonthreatening and familiar beings with whom the audience feels comfortable even as they are far more risqué and explicit than Mabley. One of the more notorious "Def Comedy Jam" comediennes, Cheryl Underwood, represents herself as—in her vernacular—an "easy bitch." Her text centers on her sexual promiscuity, friendships with other women, and their subsequent betrayal. Discussing why she slept with her friend's boyfriend, she says, "Bitch goin' have nerve enough to get mad at me. Talkin' 'bout, 'Cheryl, what you doin'?' I say, 'Bitch, I'm tryin' to help you. Nigger say if he don't get no pussy soon, he goin' leave yo' ass.' Cause I'm a friend to the end" (Underwood 1994). Her personality, as she represents it, is one of "sluttish" girl next door. If the personality is a combination of "social forces and individual principles" (Fine 1992), Underwood's character's personality is informed by the cultural definition of friendship and the character's individual principles of sexual promiscuity that respond to the external stimulus of the boyfriend's sexual objectification of women. The incongruity of these values combines to present a humorous situation. Moreover, Underwood's material displays her rational choice in presenting such a character. The use of expletives is a deliberate choice that illustrates Joan Radner and Susan Lanser's concept of appropriation of "coding strategies that involve adapting to feminist purposes forms or materials normally associated with male culture or androcentric images of the feminine" (1993:10). Not only does Underwood—indeed, all of the "Def Comedy Jam" comediennes—appropriate the language commonly judged unacceptable for women, the absurdity of her braggadocio attitude about promiscuity and betrayal highlights the detrimental effects of objectification of women on romance and friendship. With this appropriation, Underwood claims her sexuality while simultaneously critiquing sexist gender reductions and definitions.

This appropriation parallels Keyes's discussion of women rappers. Keyes suggests, "Women artists appropriate male performance behavior and use performance as a vehicle to express their responses to stereotypes and male standards, while simultaneously achieving recognition and success in the male-dominated tradition" (1993:204). Underwood's rational choice in appropriating these characteristics shows her response to male-defined objectifications of women as sexual entities. In the same way, the use of the word "bitch" is appropriated by many of these comediennes. The word seems to function similarly to the word "nigger" in the African American community.[9] Like "nigger," "bitch" is used with pride, derision, or simply as a common name. Keyes demonstrates the term varies in definition and acceptance among female rap artists (2000:262–3). Although for many this word is offensive and degrading, the flagrancy with which these comediennes toss the term about suggests an attempt to dispel the offensive connotations. Comedienne Mo'Nique scoffs at the affront of the term and claims, "We give that word so much . . . power . . . and if it's used at the right time, at the proper time, oh, it's a wonderful word" (Latham and Purcell 2000). Describing the "Sista with Attitude" persona affected by some female hip-hop performers, Keyes notes, "Female MCs revise the standard definition of bitch, from an 'aggressive woman who challenges male authority' to an aggressive or assertive female who subverts patriarchal rule" (2000:263). The term is an appropriation of misogynist discourse traditionally used to deride and insult women, but it now has a multivalent quality dependent upon use.

According to Fine, another factor of personal imperatives is unconscious motive. Although this factor involves psychoanalytic theorizing, which can be unduly steeped in Freudian patriarchal concepts, it is helpful to study the performer's text for displays of unconscious motives. Zita Dresner suggests that women's humor tends to be more humane and compassionate than male humor (1991:180). She discusses Whoopi Goldberg and Lily Tomlin's respective one-woman shows and asserts "the 'humanity' of the humor ascribed to these two performers derives from the form and content of their work. For one thing, both women insist on defining themselves as actresses rather than comediennes, because neither is interested in simply standing up and telling jokes or performing a comic routine as herself or

in the persona of herself as jokester" (1991:181). The expression of human characters that are derived from Goldberg's and Tomlin's personal ideals concerning their profession demonstrates an unconscious motive of attempting to change the concept of what constitutes a comedian and how a comedian performs. The women of "Def Comedy Jam" exhibit the unconscious motive of distinguishing themselves—and by implication, African American women in general—from Black males and White females alike. The material, language, and overall performance of Black comediennes illustrate this motive. Although these women performers often appropriate male characteristics, their texts, for the most part, center on a kind of parody of females and feminine concerns. Furthermore, although feminine issues are privileged, the female performers are also able to explicitly discuss issues that are of significance to African American women. They distance and distinguish themselves from other comedians, resulting in a celebration of Black womanhood, another unconscious motive.

The performance dynamics involved in the production of "Def Comedy Jam" illustrate the communication paths between the performer and audience. More than any other point, performance dynamics highlight the connection and collaboration of the narrator and audience. This element includes the setting (spatial and temporal) in which the folklore takes place, style and texture of how it is performed, interactional purpose, and audience response. As previously mentioned, "Def Comedy Jam" is an extraction of the hip-hop scene: its setting, music, performers, and audience are all part of the contemporary rap arena. The stage is set very close to the audience so that comics are neither at a distance from nor at an exaggerated level above them. This setting engenders a sense of community and familiarity. Indeed, instead of the usual monologue that comedians normally present in stand-up comic situations, this setting allows for the comics to carry on a dialogue with the audience. Comedians often ask questions of the audience, and the answers are heard by nearly everyone. This dialogue is a form of the African American oral tradition of call and response, which is quite different from the hecklers mainstream comedians may encounter. Although hecklers are generally an undesirable, but often expected, aspect of stand-up comic routines, the call and response of "Def Comedy Jam" is an essential element of African American dialogic performances. Similarly, the audience's response to the performance illustrates the connection between them and the performer. The "Def Comedy Jam" audience is made up largely of young African Americans; the laughter is animated and boisterous. Many male audience members jump out of their seats, stand up, shout, and "high five" one another—or even the comic—when they find an anecdote, joke, or situation particularly amusing. Laughter is an unapologetic expression. Although Blacks, and particularly Black women, have had to be conscious of offensive representations by Whites, the familiarity between audience members and performers is positive in this context. Past association and familiarity greatly influence audience response. . . .

The style and texture of the performance influences its reception. Fine suggests, "The first thing that most audiences—academic and folk—listen for in a text is its content; yet the aesthetic qualities of how the narrative is performed are crucial to analysis" (1992:23). The style these comediennes exhibit necessarily conforms to hip-hop, or "old school," style, as in the case of Miss Laura Hayes, who is clearly older and not of the hip-hop generation. Because much of rap and hip-hop music has been criticized for its misogynist themes and lyrics, many comediennes present themselves with dignity and integrity—in direct opposition to the images characterized by much of the music. Jeff Niesel reasons, "It is important, however, to ensure that rap music on the whole is not equated with misogyny, an assumption that supports the stereotype that Black males are unrestrained sexual animals" (1997:242). "Def Comedy Jam" comediennes destabilize the equation of hip-hop and misogyny with material that examines sexism, racism, and parody of the

self, rarely making humorous remarks at someone's expense except, obviously, the pointed critique of men and sex. Their style adds to their strength and integrity as comic performers and Black women.

All of the aforementioned points on Fine's folklore diamond impact the final point, narrative content. Narrative content comprises the details of the narrative, the themes it advances, its moral structure, and the function of the narrative in contemporary society. Fine asserts, "Content is the product; the other issues represent the conditions and process of narration. No matter how much folklorists wish to examine the conditions or process of production, we cannot escape the necessity of confronting the text" (1992:27). Although I have given examples of the material the comediennes use to illustrate the significance of social structure, personal imperatives, and performance dynamics in a substantive challenge to cultural race and gender ideologies, detailed attention to the material reveals resistance to dominant ideas *and* self-definition without essentializing Black women and our experiences. Although the texts might seem antithetical to feminist values, when read in the context of parody, they often critique patriarchal objectification of women and, in doing so, claim a space for Black womanhood that defines it against patriarchy and outside of mainstream feminism.

The details and themes of the material often center on sex and gender constructs. These comediennes often celebrate sexuality while simultaneously denouncing sexism and male sexual domination. Far from reinscribing the stereotype of Black women as hypersexual and emasculating, they personify Toni Morrison's alternative interpretation of the stereotyped aggressive Black woman as "sexually at home in [their] bod[ies]" and "self-sufficient and tough" (Williams 1991:72). They do not mind discussing women's healthcare and sexual satisfaction, or lack thereof. Exploring the conditions of single life, Givens says,

I watch Oprah 'cause I ain't got a man. But that's alright 'cause between Oprah and my gynecologist, I'm satisfied. That's right, I learned to appreciate that fucking pap smear. Talkin' about once a year, bullshit, I'll see you tomorrow motherfucker. Shit, ten inches of iron, hard, safe shit. When he's finished, I smoke a fucking cigarette and ask him, "Was it good for you too?" And some women like foreplay. If you creative enough, you can get foreplay with that fucking pap smear. Oh yeah, all I got to do is say something like, "Doc, could I get a breast exam before the pap smear?" (1992)

This narrative parodies the pseudointimacy offered by the Oprah Winfrey talk show through the discursive acts of self-disclosure and the impersonal—and for many women, highly uncomfortable—nature of gynecological exams.[10] Claiming fulfillment through these activities, which are generally recognized as nonintimate, unsatisfying encounters, speaks to the lack of satisfaction sexual relationships can offer.

Other female performers describe situations in which men attempt to dominate, coerce, or otherwise exploit women; in doing so, they condemn the trivialization of women as sexual commodities. Melanie Comacho expresses this attitude:

All they think about is sex, sex, sex, sex. We can't even go to the movies with the brothers no more. I'm mean, there's so much sex in the movies that by the time the movie is over, the brother talkin' that same old drag, "Well baby, how come we don't never do that what they was doin' in the movies?" I was like, "Well baby, they paid her $450,000 to jump on that table like that. Now exactly how much money you talkin' about? I mean what you think you goin' get for a Pepsi and some goddamn popcorn? Not a goddamn thing here." (1994)

This scenario critiques the complex system of sexual commodification, for not only does Hollywood's portrayal of women as sexual objects color the male gaze, but by pointing to the irony of selling herself, Comacho demonstrates that the commodification of the female body de-

creases the value and substance of heterosexual relationships.

Infidelity and domestic abuse are other topics these comediennes are not ashamed to expose. Using her age to claim the position as older, wiser advisor to her audience (the "Queen Mother" image, as identified by Keyes [2000]), Miss Laura Hayes describes the unity and support she and her many sisters provide one another that also provides the privilege to criticize self-destructive behaviors, such as ignoring their male partners' infidelity and lies. Hayes narrates, "You know how your sisters and your girlfriends won't tell you when your man is fooling around? Oh, we tell, baby. Go right to the phone, "Eh sis, yeah motherfucker down at the mall. Oh, you right, that's disrespectful. *Mr. Motherfucker* down at the mall" (Latham and Purcell 2000). The absurdity of including the appellation "Mr." with the expletive "motherfucker" enhances the parody without dismissing the man's culpability. The sister fails to identify the respect Hayes shows her by calling, but she demands respect for someone disrespecting her man. This situation displays the skewed sense of self some women hold. Domestic violence situations also occasion sisterly support, as Hayes narrates:

You marry one of us, you marry all of us. Okay. And when there's some problems we'll get together, baby,' cause moms is the dispatcher. Aw, my little sister got in trouble. She had to call mamma. "Mamma, this, this nigger hit me." Woo, mamma was cool, though. She was like, "Don't worry about it, baby." Moms hung up the phone, dialed one number, all our phones rang: "Bertha, Laura, Eulah, Ruthie, get on over to Alice's house. That nigger done gone crazy." That's all we needed. We jumped in the car. We rollin'. We slappin' five over the seat. . . . Get to the house, screech up real fast, walk in the door, the nigger just 'bout to hit my sister. We go, "Aw naw, not tonight." (Latham and Purcell 2000)

Hayes removes her wig and makes a motion to fight, and the audience erupts into gales of laughter. She demonstrates the tradition of support structures in her family that has been passed from mother to daughters. Yet, rather than the stereotype of the Black matriarchal family, á la Moynihan,[11] part of Hayes's narrative (not included above) begins with a description of her father's insistence that she and her sisters deprecate Barbie doll play for pursuits that require strength and physical skills. Therefore, that Hayes and her sisters physically defend their sister is not attributable to some faulty notion of "strong Black women," but is a result of parental guidance by mother *and* father to support and defend one another.

In a similar way, Givens critiques the lack of consciousness many woman possess in the face of exploitation by men. According to Givens, "real" women are conscious and independent as opposed to her sister, whom she describes as a "fake bitch":

> My sister, fake bitch. I'm not lying, thirty-five years old and fake than a motherfucker. She think she know all there is about a man just' cause she's been married for fifteen years. Give the bitch a few drinks and she gives you advice. . . . "Baby sister, come on let me tell you something. You know big sister ain't gone tell you nothing wrong. Let me tell you something. If my husband come home, on payday, it's late, and he's broke, he ain't getting no pussy." Fake bitch, bless her heart. She don't know. I say, "Let me tell you something, sister. If your husband come home, on payday, it's late, and he's broke, he done *had* some pussy." (1992)

Instead of the passive aggressive resistance her sister suggests, Givens urges further critique of the situation and recognition of the signs of infidelity, which is a far more substantive action. She refutes the implication that marriage bestows wisdom and consciousness and that her sister's sexual withholding is an effective tool to combat unfaithfulness.

The concept of a "real woman" is in direct opposition to "normalized" gender constructs in American culture. The term "real woman" echoes notions of "true womanhood"—which in-

cluded ideals of piety, domesticity, purity, and submission—that were propagated in the nineteenth century and still reside in contemporary culture; however, the tenets of the "cult of true womanhood" were essentialist and excluded African American women. Nineteenth-century race ideology viewed people of African descent as excessively sexual and deviant. Hazel Carby shows how this racial ideology marked Black women as overly sexual and precluded recognition of their chastity (1987:27). Therefore, Black women were not considered virtuous enough to exhibit purity. Following this rationale, Black women's immorality made their ability to maintain the concomitant values (piety, domesticity, and submissiveness) of the "cult of true womanhood" suspect. Yet, African American women adopted the values of "true womanhood" in what Evelyn Brooks Higginbotham calls "the politics of respectability," which included a discourse that "emphasized manners and morals while simultaneously asserting traditional forms of protest, such as petitions, boycotts, and verbal appeals to justice" (1993:187). This ideology was problematic because of an inherent contradiction—it paralleled White middle-class values and held African Americans responsible for adopting and representing these ideals; however, although Givens's term "real women" echoes the past by evoking a concept of "authenticity," her text typifies the three central aspects of Black feminist thought that Patricia Hill Collins identifies: African American women's self-definition and self-evaluation, the interlocking nature of oppression, and the importance of African American women's culture (Bell et al. 2000:42). Givens's narrative of communication within the sisterly relationship signifies African American women's culture of communication, particularly that of advising and tutoring one another based on personal experience. Although the sister's self-definition and evaluation are problematic, the situation and Givens's response illustrate the intersection of sex and class domination. Givens suggests— instead of the illusion of power her sister thinks she has—women who are economically dependent on males are disempowered sexually and economically. Givens's critique of the sister centralizes African American women's experiences without reducing us to an undifferentiated whole. These comediennes do not present themselves as feminist, although some of the material could be termed feminist. Their work can be more accurately described as womanist. The outrageous, audacious, willful character of the texts and performers exemplify the womanist concept first articulated by Alice Walker in her pioneering work on Black women writers (Walker 1983).

Representations of African American women offered by African American female comics have been received by a growing audience of Americans through mass media, which becomes an additional factor in analysis of these performances. Charles S. Dutton asserts, "The crossover success of 'Russell Simmons' Def Comedy Jam' signals the dominance of urban Black youth on American culture" (Smith 1993). This dominance suggests that mainstream America is absorbing these images of Black women. Although some of us are able to analyze these images and understand them for their value, I worry about how these representations affect the overall perception of African American women by American society. On the one hand, although these comediennes celebrate Black culture and womanhood and confront gender constructs, the methods they employ may not be understood by viewers who lack historical and cultural knowledge. This concern is compounded by the fact that these performances are viewed by large audiences through television and video recordings. The sheer magnitude of viewers exponentially increases the chances of misinterpreting contemporary Black women's humor. On the other hand, these performances function as a vehicle for changing the ideals and conceptualizations of Black women. Michael Omi and Howard Winant's discussion of Black nationalism and its use as a vehicle for change parallels the potential significance of "Def Comedy Jam" comediennes. They write, "Painting, theater, dance, music, language, even cars and clothes, all became media

through which a new style could be developed, and through which 'genuine' oppositional culture could be distinguished from assimilationist practices" (1994:109). In short, these comediennes are "soul babies."[12] In order to foster this transition, however, mainstream culture must be willing to both accept change and understand African American culture, looking beyond the appropriation of expletives and "hard-core" styles to discern the messages that are being advanced—for the trajectory the material and performances have taken since the early days of Black comic performance has continually moved away from the center of mainstream society. Comedian-turned-activist Dick Gregory expresses his view that "these Black comics [are] out there. They can never come back to our level. They're out there for good and all we can do is document the metamorphosis" (Smith 1993).

Even though contemporary Black comediennes diverge from Black comics of the past, their work is grounded in African American oral traditions using common themes and motifs that are passed on generationally. For example, comedienne Sommore uses material derived from "tales and stories that are almost exclusively the property of Afro-Americans, including ones that focus on heaven and hell, as well as those that treat the relationships between blacks and whites" (Harris 1988:772). Compare the following two narratives that employ the heaven and hell motif. The first text was related by "Moms" Mabley in the 1960s.

> Colored fellow down home died. Pulled up to the gate. St. Peter look at him, say, "What do you want?" "Hey, man, you know me. Hey, Jack, you know me. I'm old Sam Jones. Old Sam Jones, man, you know me. Used to be with the NAACP, you know, CORE and all that stuff, man, marches, remember me? Oh, man, you know me." He just broke down there, "You know me." He looked in his book. "Sam Jones," he say, "no, no, you ain't here, no Sam Jones." He said, "Oh, man, yes, I am; look there. You know me. I'm the cat that married that white girl on the capital steps of Jackson, Mississippi." He said, "How long ago has that

been?" He said, "About five minutes ago." (Harris 1988:772)

In her *Queens* routine, Sommore relates the following:

I had a dream that I was standin' at the gates of heaven and got into a fight. It wasn't my fault, they was fuckin' with me in line. Let me tell you. Now, I'm standin' in line at the gates of heaven. Foxy Brown, the rapper, is standin' in front of me. Monica Lewinsky is standin' in back of me. So Foxy Brown gets up to the gate, she say, "How you doin', St. Peter? My name is Foxy Brown, I'm a rapper. I've done some sins in my life but I'm still a good person." He say, "Foxy Brown, my child, what part of your body have you sinned with?" She said, "my hands." He said, "Go over there and rinse your hands out in the faucet and you may enter the gates of heaven." Next, it was my turn. I went up to the gate. I said, "How you doin', St. Peter? My name is Sommore. I'm a stand-up comedian. I've done some sins in my life but I'm still a good person." He said, "Sommore, my child, what part of your body have you sinned with?" Before I can say any fucking thing, Monica Lewinsky pushed me out the way and said, "Excuse me, but can I rinse my mouth out in the faucet before this bitch put her ass in the water?" "You don't know me. You, do not know me." (Latham and Purcell 2000)

As Harris points out, "Part of the [jokes center] upon the fact that death, the usual entry to heaven, frequently does not suffice for Black people. They must pass another test with St. Peter, the traditional keeper of the gate comparable to Legba in African folklore" (1988:772). Mabley's text humorizes the notions that racism kills Blacks faster than good deeds can be recorded and that the civil disobedience used by major civil rights organizations is less risky than violating southern dictates against interracial marriage. The amusing element of Sommore's narrative combines media awareness and parody of the self. The humor derives from the public's knowledge of the sexual activities of Foxy Brown—whose sexually explicit lyrics are infamous—and

Monica Lewinsky—whose sexual relationship with the president gained worldwide attention—and Sommore's sex life. That Brown and Lewinsky can enter heaven before Sommore can speaks to the notoriety of her life. While Mabley's protagonist's assertion that St. Peter knows him is meant to vouch for his character, Sommore's insistence that Lewinsky is not acquainted with her points to Sommore's blatant sexuality. By claiming a sexuality that is equal to these very public figures, she locates herself in the entertainment and political arenas where women have been publicly castigated for explicit or revealed sexuality. Sommore suggests that spiritual cleansing for private acts is a private matter and anyone who gainsays that is presumptuous. Mabley's narrative is a political joke that turns on the sexual, while Sommore's is a sexual joke that turns on a political situation. Harris's assessment of Mabley is equally true of Sommore. Harris contends, "Moms's awareness of those traditional encounters in the lore, along with her incorporation of the topical focus, makes the humor a unique blend of the old and the new, doubly recognizable, and double funny" (1988:772).

While I agree with Gregory that these comics cannot return to the level of comedy performed by Mabley, Gregory, and their contemporaries, we can do more than document the change in performance, language, and acceptable comedic subjects as he suggests. Ultimately, the characteristics of performance style and subject matter contemporary Black women comics display reflect the social changes brought about by the activism of civil rights advocates such as Gregory. Using the term "postsoul" to delineate the period of social, political, and aesthetic experiences in African American communities since the Civil Rights and Black Power movements, Mark Anthony Neal recognizes that individuals and cultural products of this era have "been fueled by three distinct critical desires, namely, the reconstitution of community, particularly one that is critically engaged with the cultural and political output of Black communities; a rigorous form of self and communal critique; and the willingness to undermine or deconstruct the most negative symbols and stereotypes of Black life via the use and distribution of those very same symbols and stereotypes" (2002:120).

But the repertoires of Black comediennes reflect an even deeper acknowledgment of the difficult lives of Black women. The comedic performances of African American female comics illustrate this postsoul aesthetic. As scholars and critics, it is imperative that we analyze these texts and facilitate understanding by different audience communities. Analysis and understanding may not be simple or readily apparent, in view of Alan Dundes's (1973) claim that the study of folk humor has been long neglected because the various nuances and subtleties can be lost even on the researcher, regardless of whether she is a member of the community. Nevertheless, we must endeavor in our study of African American humor to understand the historical and cultural factors underlying the humor in hopes of rendering credible and satisfactory analyses. This article is presented in that spirit.

Notes

1. My title comes in part from a line in Ntozake Shange's choreopoem, *for colored girls who have considered suicide when the rainbow is enuf:* "but bein alive and bein a woman and bein colored is a metaphysical dilemma/I havent conquered yet" (1977:45). This line reflects the difficulties Black women have regarding both self-definition and self-representation, which point to inner conflicts about the self. The epigraph from Najlis, however, suggests this metaphysical dilemma is conquerable and that the expression of humor demonstrates a medium through which to triumph over the dilemma.

2. From an interview with Najlis titled "Women's Solidarity Has Given Our Lives a New Dimension: Laughter," see Margaret Randall (1994).

3. I am echoing the title of the pioneering anthology of Black women's studies criticism, *All the Women Are White, All the Men Are Black, But Some of Us Are Brave* (Hull, Scott, and Smith 1982).

4. In an effort to disrupt the academic writing/African American discourse distinction, I often use

"our" and "we" pronouns throughout this essay when referring to African American women to reflect my subject position in connection with the texts and my analysis.

5. Keyes defines the characteristics of each of these categories as follows: "Queen Mother," an African-centered, wise, regal, self-assured woman; "Fly Girl," a highly fashionable, independent, flamboyant woman with an explicit sexuality; "Sista with Attitude," an aggressive, assertive, self-empowered woman; and "Lesbian," an openly lesbian woman who explores the dynamics of race and role play that concern the Black lesbian community (2000). Keyes points out that, because the categories are fluid, performers can shift and occupy multiple categories simultaneously.

6. Although Watkins produces an invaluable history of Black comedic performance, his work barely highlights the experiences and work of Black women comics (1994). According to Dance, in her introduction to *Hush Honey*, "African American women have been pretty much ignored in every kind of study of humor—American humor, women's humor, African American humor" (1998:xxix).

7. The practice of "signifying" in African American culture is thoroughly explored in Henry Louis Gates's *The Signifying Monkey* (1988). Signifying is an African American oral tradition that is a discursive strategy in which the meaning of words or actions is determined by the situation or identities of both speaker and listener and is generally used to subvert or triumph over an adversary. With this practice, one can signify to, about, or upon someone or something. Signifying takes multiple forms but consistently "entails formal revision and an intertextual relation" (1988:51). See Gates for a discussion of signifying as a literary technique. The "dozens" is a verbal contest of mockery in which contestants ridicule their opponents or their relatives with verbal wit. These oral traditions can be found in similar forms and are rooted in West African cultures from which many of the Africanist aspects of African American culture derive. See Watkins (1994) and Abrahams (1985) for more detailed discussion of these verbal traditions.

8. This information comes from a press release that HBO distributed to print media, dated June 22, 1994.

9. The term "nigger" "ranges in connotations from a term of endearment to a vilification, and it is used

freely in conversation among many African Americans. Among upper-class Blacks, it tends more toward the pejorative. Blacks almost always consider 'nigger' an offensive term when it is used by whites" (Dance 1998:xxv). Randall Kennedy extensively probes the history of the use of "nigger" in his book *Nigger: The Strange Career of a Troublesome Word* (2002).

10. See Laurie L. Haag (1993) for a discussion of the constructed intimacy of the Oprah Winfrey show.

11. The "pathology" of African American family structures has been the foundation of many sociological studies of Black culture and is exemplified in Daniel Patrick Moynihan's 1965 study *The Negro Family*. Moynihan concludes that the reason Blacks do not succeed in America is because Black families are often headed by women "matriarchs" and that this structure is so different from mainstream White families that Blacks are ill equipped to integrate into American society. Moynihan's report was based on the work of E. Franklin Frazier and suffered not only from a lack of understanding of race, gender, and class issues, but also a disregard of African survivals in African American culture, thereby producing a study that held African Americans—particularly African American women—responsible for our own oppression. Unfortunately, Moynihan's report determined public policy with respect to African Americans for more than two decades.

12. Neal (2002) uses this term to describe African Americans who came of age in the period following the cultural and social changes resulting from the Civil Rights and Black Power movements, what he defines as the "postsoul" era.

References Cited

Abrahams, Roger D. 1985. *Afro-American Folktales: Stories from Black Traditions in the New World*. New York: Pantheon Books.

Bell, Katrina E., Mark P. Orbe, Darlene K. Drummond, and Sakile Kai Carmara. 2000. Accepting the Challenge of Centralizing without Essentializing: Black Feminist Thought and African-American Women's Communication Experiences. *Women's Studies in Communication* 23:41–62.

Carby, Hazel. 1987. *Reconstructing Womanhood: The Emergence of the Afro-American Woman Novelist*. New York: Oxford University Press.

Collins, Patricia Hill. 1990. *Black Feminist Thought: Knowledge, Consciousness, and the Politics of Empowerment*. New York: Routledge.

Comacho, Melanie. 1994. Stand-up Comic Performance. *Russell Simmon's Def Comedy Jam*, dir. Stan Lathan. Home Box Office. July.

Dance, Daryl Cumber. 1998. Introduction. In *Honey, Hush!: An Anthology of African American Women's Humor*, pp. xxi-xxxv. New York: W. W. Norton.

Dresner, Zita. 1991. Whoopi Goldberg and Lily Tomlin: Black and White Women's Humor. In *Women's Comic Visions*, ed. June Sochen, pp. 179–92. Detroit: Wayne State University Press.

Du Bois, W. E. B. [1903] 1994. *The Souls of Black Folk*. New York: Dover.

Dundes, Alan. 1973. *Mother Wit from the Laughing Barrel: Readings in the Interpretation of Afro-American Folklore*. Englewood Cliffs, N.J.: Prentice-Hall.

Fine, Gary Alan. 1992. *Manufacturing Tales: Sex and Money in Contemporary Legends*. Knoxville: University of Tennessee Press.

Gates, Henry Louis, Jr. 1988. *The Signifying Monkey: A Theory of African-American Literary Criticism*. New York: Oxford University Press.

Givens, Adele. 1992. Stand-up Comic Performance. *Russell Simmons' Def Comedy Jam*, dir. Stan Lathan. Home Box Office. September.

Haag, Laurie L. 1993. Oprah Winfrey: the Construction of Intimacy in the Talk Show Setting. *Journal of Popular Culture* 26:115–21.

Harris, Trudier. 1988. Moms Mabley: A Study in Humor, Role Playing, and the Violation of Taboo. *Southern Review* 24:765–76.

Higginbotham, Evelyn Brooks. 1993. *Righteous Discontent: The Women's Movement in the Black Baptist Church, 1880–1920*. Cambridge, Mass.: Harvard University Press.

Hull, Gloria, Patricia Bell Scott, and Barbara Smith. 1982. *All the Women Are White, All the Men Are Black, But Some of Us Are Brave: Black Women's Studies*. New York: Feminist Press.

Kennedy, Randall. 2002. *Nigger: The Strange Career of a Troublesome Word*. New York: Pantheon Books.

Keyes, Cheryl. 1993. "We're More than a Novelty Boys:" Strategies of Female Rappers in the Rap Music Tradition. In *Feminist Messages: Coding in Women's Folk Culture*, ed. Joan Radner, pp. 203–20. Urbana: University of Illinois Press.

———. 2000. Empowering Self, Making Choices, Creating Spaces: Black Female Identity via Rap

Music Performance. *Journal of American Folklore* 113:255–69.

King, Deborah. 1988. Multiple Jeopardy, Multiple Consciousness: The Context of a Black Feminist Ideology. *Signs* 14:42–72.

Latham, Walter, and Steve Purcell, prod. 2000. *Queens of Comedy*, perf. Adele Givens, Miss Laura Hayes, Sommore, and Mo'Nique. DVD. Paramount Pictures and Latham Entertainment.

Levine, Lawrence W. 1977. *Black Culture and Black Consciousness: Afro-American Folk Thought From Slavery to Freedom*. New York: Oxford University Press.

Moynihan, Daniel Patrick. 1965. *The Negro Family— The Case for National Action*. Washington, D.C.: Office of Policy Planning and Research, U.S. Department of Labor.

Neal, Mark Anthony. 2002. *Soul Babies: Black Popular Culture and the Post-Soul Aesthetic*. New York: Routledge.

Niesel, Jeff. 1997. Hip-Hop Matters: Rewriting the Sexual Politics of Rap Music. In *Third Wave Agenda: Being Feminist, Doing Feminism*, ed. Leslie Heywood and Jennifer Drake, pp. 239–53. Minneapolis: University of Minnesota Press.

Omi, Michael, and Howard Winant. 1994. *Racial Formation in the United States: From the 1960s to the 1990s*. New York: Routledge.

Radner, Joan, and Susan Lanser. 1993. Strategies of Coding in Women's Cultures. In *Feminist Messages: Coding in Women's Folk Culture*, ed. Joan Radner, pp. 1–29. Urbana: University of Illinois Press.

Randall, Margaret. 1994. *Sandino's Daughters Revisited: Feminism in Nicaragua*. New Brunswick: Rutgers University Press.

Riggs, Marlon, prod. and dir. 1987. *Ethnic Notions: Black People in White Minds*. California Newsreel. VHS.

Shange, Ntozake. 1977. *for colored girls who have considered suicide when the rainbow is enuf*. New York: Collier Books.

Smith, Yvonne, dir. 1993. *Mo' Funny: Black Comedy in America*. Narrated by Charles S. Dutton. Home Box Office. February.

Sochen, June. 1991. *Women's Comic Visions*. Detroit: Wayne State University Press.

Underwood, Cheryl. 1994. Stand-up Comic Performance. *Russell Simmons' Def Comedy Jam*, dir. Stan Lathan. Home Box Office. July.

Walker, Alice. 1983. *In Search of Our Mother's Gardens*. New York: Harcourt Brace Jovanovich.

Watkins, Mel. 1994. *On the Real Side: Laughing, Lying, and Signifying—The Underground Tradition of African American Humor that Transformed American Culture, from Slavery to Richard Pryor*. New York: Simon & Schuster.

Williams, Elsie A. 1991. Moms Mabley and the Afro-American Comic Performance. In *Women's Comic Visions*, ed. June Sochen, pp. 158–78. Detroit: Wayne State University Press.

Zita Z. Dresner

Roseanne Barr: Goddess or She-Devil

From the stand-up routines, which utilized the *persona* of a disgruntled housewife who insisted upon being called "domestic goddess," to her top-rated domestic sit-com, to her film debut in and as "She Devil," to her appearance as an interpreter of the "The Star-Spangled Banner," Roseanne Barr has been surrounded with controversy, most of it created and exacerbated by the media. While she has been chastised publicly for her rebelliousness, privately—as the high ratings of her sit-com suggest—many American males, as well as females, enjoy her outrageousness and identify with the outsider images that she embodies. In fact, I would argue that much of both the negative publicity and the success that has accompanied Barr's career has been due to her rebelliousness. As a stand-up comic, a television personality, an actress and a "performance artist," Barr has presented the public with images that overtly and covertly subvert traditional ideas about women and challenge the status quo: the housewife who eschews doing housework: the fat female who is not embarrassed by being what social propaganda describes as physically unacceptable and, even more disconcerting, who flaunts her sexuality; the working mother who is not ashamed of being working-class or afraid of disciplining her kids or confronting her husband; the Hollywood personality who does not hide from or allow herself to be intimidated by the media's exposure of what the tabloids promote as "shocking" revelations about her private life; the feminist who dares to poke fun at the machismo of American politics and sports. These rebellious personae that Barr creates are es-

pecially powerful. I believe, because they evoke deep-seated, conflicting, often subconscious feelings in both men and women about women's proper roles, nature, image and status. . . .

While very little has actually been written (since the initial review of *Roseanne* appeared) about the show itself, which has retained high audience ratings, much has been written about the various controversies and personal problems surrounding Barr. Unlike *All in the Family*, which received numerous complaints from viewers about its controversial content without Carroll O'Connor being personally attacked for the views of Archie Bunker, there is little or no indication of viewer complaint about the content of *Roseanne*. In fact, Walter Goodman asks about *Roseanne* in a *New York Times* article looking back at the Fall 1988 television season, "What's to offend?" "Here we are, a television generation after *All in the Family*, and the Connor household is wondrously free of bigotry," Goodman contends, going on to suggest that the show has no religious or political content and that even the one-liners "are unprovocatively domestic . . . soft-core humor, redeemed by a hug" (11, 29). So, what is all the fuss about?

I believe that the fuss is and always has been about Barr's desire, as stated in the interview reported by Horowitz, to have creative control of *Roseanne* in order to use the show to tell "the truth" about people's lives, to reflect "how people really live" in the 1990s and what a "real woman-mother" is like (10). Concurrently, it has been about what Horowitz labels Barr's "darker side," the "she-devil" side—the ways in which she has expressed her anger and frustration at the manipulations of the entertainment industry and media establishment to thwart and impugn this

Source: "Roseanne Barr: Goddess or She-Devil," by Zita Z. Dresner. *Journal of American Culture*. Summer, 1993, pp. 37–43. Used by permission of Blackwell Publishing.

desire—so "unbecoming to a woman: that it threatens both the white male/Jewish male power structure and the women seeking approval and advancement within that structure. Finally, it has been about her weight and her refusal to apologize for it, make fun of it, or allow it to erase her sexuality—which is a very revolutionary stance because it challenges the entertainment industry's and the media's propaganda that a woman's ability to be desired, loved and valued depends upon how thin and self-effacing she is. As Barr asserted in an interview with Elaine Dutka in *Time* magazine, "To me, being fat isn't a negative. Being fat is a response. If you eat, you're choosing to be fat. . . . [She gives some reasons for choosing, including that fat is sexy]. Being fat, for a woman, also means you take up more space, so you're seen—and probably heard—more easily. It's real ironic. At the same time that women were encouraged to be politically active and speak out, we unconsciously started to starve ourselves skinny, which is what *men* want us to do" (83).

To punish Barr for her refusal to bow to the conventional and stereotypical, critics have tried to undermine her success and diminish her power to attract audiences. Critics use the press to report (and the tabloids to further exaggerate) every conflict she has had with producers, directors and writers on the show—from their point of view— in order to make her appear (as women have always been made to appear) the unreasonable, intractable, destructive party—the bitch who always has to have her way, not knowing or appreciating what's good for her. In addition, she has been (and continues to be) hounded by the tabloids more persistently and shamelessly, it seems to me, than most Hollywood personalities. Not only have the tabloids intruded upon and published the most intimate details of her private life—her marital problems, her children's alcohol and addiction problems, and her relationship with Tom Arnold—but they also dug up and, despite her pleadings, exposed the fact that she had a baby when she was eighteen whom she gave up for adoption—something that neither the adopted daughter nor Barr's own family had even known.

No one protected her from these invasions of her privacy, as, for example, Hollywood's homosexual actors have been protected from exposure. Moreover, her justifiably angry responses to this media mistreatment—mooning the press, having an especially obnoxious photographer beaten up, putting on the kinds of exhibits of outrageous behavior for publicity purposes that the media crave—have been judged not as self-protective devices but only as further evidence of her being out of control, of her need to be slapped down and reined in—a ploy that has consistently been used to disempower women as Gilman's *The Yellow Wallpaper* so graphically illustrated over 100 years ago.

Another way in which critics have sought to minimize Barr's popularity, and thus remove from her the only weapon she has to fight for control of her show, is by attacking her weight, by suggesting that while she may have power as a comedian, she has no value as a woman because she is unappealing to men. That a woman's value resides in her attractiveness to men is, of course, (as Barr has noted and Naomi Wolf's *The Beauty Myth: How Images of Beauty Are Used Against Women* recently demonstrated) the message that men continue to transmit through their control of the media. It is also the message that the movie version of *She-Devil* conveyed. Moreover, attractiveness in American culture, as its females of all ages know, is, above all, thinness. . . .

Most male critics define these aspects of her persona as abrasive or offensive. An especially virulent instance of this attitude appears in Peter Freundlich's *Esquire* article "Roseanne, Nay!" which focuses almost entirely on her size, suggesting that men pretend to tolerate Barr only because they feel guilty about admitting that they are repelled by her in an era that admonishes us to accept the diseased and afflicted (99). However, women like Young and Horowitz have shown themselves to be a bit touchy as well about these aspects of Barr's persona because, I believe, women are afraid of being rejected by men by association, and Barr personifies everything about women that women have been told is unacceptable to men and that women, therefore, are afraid to own or applaud in themselves or in other women.

Nowhere is this anxiety more evident than in two articles written in 1990—one by Anne Taylor Fleming in the *New York Times* and one by Barbara Grizzuti Harrison in *Mademoiselle*. While Fleming's thesis is that Roseanne's "tough act . . . is too harsh," she provides little or no specific detail to support her conclusion other than her personal response to Barr: "There's something about Roseanne Barr that hits a real visceral nerve with people, certainly with men, but with women, too." Fleming goes on to say that, although she's tried to like Barr, she just doesn't—that although she knows that Peter Rainer, *Los Angeles Times* movie critic, "is right" when "he said he thinks a lot of the heat [Barr] generates has an anti-female edge," she still finds Barr's act "irritating." While Fleming admits that her response to Barr, while unanalyzed, may be due to the fact that she was "just being squeamish, a goody-two-shoes suburban feminist who was used to her icons being chic and sugar-coated," Harrison admits of no ambivalence in her dismissal of Barr as an "obsessively self-indulgent" person who "sees crudeness as a virtue," and who calls her "outrageous conduct" art or revolution or both. Apparently basing her assessment of Barr on her book, *Roseanne: My Life as a Woman*, because, she declares, "her show makes me cranky," Harrison concludes that "it's [Barr's] calculated, arrogant 'nuttiness'—so unlike the sweet nuttiness of dear Mary Tyler Moore—that makes me so dislike Barr. . . . I think it's unwholesome." Why it's unwholesome, Harrison implies, is because Barr reminds her of the militants of the 1960s, whom she castigates en masse "rebels without a cause." Perhaps a deeper reason, however, is that Harrison and *Mademoiselle* fear Barr as an inappropriate role model for America's young women, the antithesis of sweet, thin, Mary Tyler Moore—a career girl, but a properly feminine, demure and self-effacing one, who dressed in heels and hose, deferred to men, and attracted attention by her cuteness and perkiness.

The "crankiness" of Harrison's tone, which seems to stem from resentment that the 1950s models of womanhood have been displaced, is in direct contradiction to the feminist view of Roseanne articulated in Dworkin's and Schine's discussions—a view reformulated more extensively and incisively in Barbara Ehrenreich's analysis of Barr in *The New Republic*. Early in the article, Ehrenreich accounts in part for the fact that, despite all the negative publicity and criticism Barr has received in the media, her show has remained at or near number one in the ratings for the two years of its run because everyday American people apparently enjoy it. As Ehrenreich says, "Since the entertainment media do not normally cast about for fat, loud-mouthed feminists to promote to superstardom, we must assume that Roseanne has something to say that many millions of people have been waiting to hear," (28). That "something" is connected for Ehrenreich to her theory that Roseanne represents two seemingly contradictory types. On the one hand, she "is the neglected underside of the eighties, bringing together its great themes of poverty, obesity, and defiance . . . portraying the hopeless underclass of the female sex: polyester-clad, overweight occupants of the slow track; fast-food waitresses, factory workers, housewives, members of the invisible pink-collar army; the despised, the jilted, the underpaid." But Barr, on the other hand— "and this may be her most appealing feature—is never a victim" (28). Ehrenreich goes on to give numerous examples from the episodes to support her contention that "in the work-place as well as in the kitchen, Roseanne knows how to dish it out," that her "radicalism is distributed over the two axes of class and gender," enabling her to give voice not only to problems women confront at home but to class conflicts as well (28–29). And it is this "dialectical vision," I believe, as well as the authenticity she brings to her portrayal of the non-professional working wife and mother, that keeps those who watch her, rather than write about her, literally and figuratively tuned in to her.

Although Ehrenreich's article was published months before Barr's infamous performance of

"The Star Spangled Banner" before a crowd of nearly 30,000, as part of the San Diego Padres' Working Women's Night baseball game, Ehrenreich may have been prophetic in concluding her piece with a slap at middle-class feminism (and perhaps at women like Fleming and Harrison) for having become "too dainty for its own good" and with a reminder to readers that "we have a long tradition of tough-talking females behind us, after all, including that other great working-class spokes-person, Mary 'Mother' Jones, who once advised the troops, 'Whatever you do, *don't* be ladylike' " (31). Indeed, it is difficult to think of any non-news story that received so much media publicity and commentary, even by the President of the United States, as Barr's "unladylike" behavior of reaching for her crotch and spitting on the ground in a parody of the average baseball player's response to a bad call, a poor performance, or boos like those Barr received for her off-key rendition of the National Anthem. While dire effects were being predicted in the press about the effect Barr's latest outrage would have on her show's ratings and on her future as the show's star, the ratings continued to soar, even in re-runs, apparently because those who watch the show viewed the incident either as a tempest in a teapot or as simply comical.

Despite comments of "disgraceful" from Mr. Bush and "disgusting" from Secretary of State Baker, and complaints from more than 2,000 irate fans who called the stadium (*People Weekly* 13 Aug. 1990, 44). Cynthia Janovy, in a *New York Times* op-ed column, suggests that Barr's rendition was no more than "a profoundly funny statement about the average American, who can't sing the tune and doesn't know the words" to the anthem and that her scratching/spitting finale was simply her way of parodying a staple of American culture. That a group of veterans could get a lot of laughs on "America's Funniest Home Videos" the following Sunday night for singing the anthem as off-key as Barr did, Janovy continues, and that "Americans are not disgusted by regular TV images of professional athletes grabbing their crotches and spitting," simply illustrates

"that men just aren't ready for women to be making fun of them on national TV" and that Barr's humor is acceptable "as long as she stays in her rightful place—the home" (A21).

Where is Roseanne now and where is she heading on the goddess/she-devil scale? As the lead-in to her interview with Barr in *Penthouse*, Varian notes that "Roseanne-bashing is raised to new heights as the woman we love for being funny and honest and a little bit rude is chastised for being funny and honest and a little bit rude. The Designated Heathen is propped up and struck down and propped up again" (82). While it seems to me that the needle has swung as far as possible in the press to the negative without destroying Roseanne and may therefore begin moving back to a more balanced view, Barr will probably always evoke conflicting responses in the public. In earlier articles and interviews, Barr attributed the ambivalence she provokes to her position as an outsider—an overweight, working-class woman in a culture that worships thinness and wealth. To Varian, Barr offers another reason why she has been "put down on an almost daily basis" in the press even though she is "the star of America's favorite TV show": "Maybe the press does represent a part of the mass unconscious that finds me, and other women with some kind of power, largely frightening," she suggests. "So . . . everything that the press ever attaches to me has a lot of fear and loathing in it, because they don't get what I'm about" (84). At the same time, however, and despite the attacks on her by the media, Barr has been successful in the past and, as she has wrested more control over the show and begun to develop the more vulnerable side of her character, will probably continue to attract new viewers to *Roseanne* because of what she is "trying to get across." As she expressed it to Dutka, "I want to be a voice for working women, to get the same kind of roar from them that Lenny Bruce and Richard Pryor did from their subgroups. I see myself as a role model for people left of normal, a three-dimensional woman, not a token, not a supermom. I'm trying to show that there's more to being a woman than being a mother, but there's a hell of a lot more to being a mother than most people suspect" (83). And, I would add, to being Roseanne Barr.

Works Cited

Dutka, Elaine. "Slightly to the Left of Normal." *Time* 8 May 1989: 82–3.

Ehrenreich, Barbara. "The Wretched of the Hearth." *The New Republic* 2 April 1990: 28–31.

Fleming, Anne Taylor. "Roseanne's Tough Act: Is It Too Harsh?" *The New York Times* 1 Jan. 1990: C10.

Freundlich, Peter. "Roseanne, Nay!" *Esquire* Aug. 1989: 99.

Givens, Ron. "A Real Stand-Up Mom." *Newsweek* 31 Oct. 1988: 62–3.

Goodman, Walter. "Roseanne Is No Cousin to Archie Bunker." *The New York Times* 1 Jan. 1989: II, 29.

Harrison, Barbara Grizzuti. "Roseanne TV gets real . . . or just rude?" *Mademoiselle* March 1990: 135.

Horowitz, Joy. "June Cleaver Without Pearls." *The New York Times* 16 Oct. 1988: II, 1 & 10.

Janovy, Cynthia. "Roseanne Barr's High Art." *The New York Times* 1 Aug. 1990: A21.

Varian, Nanette. "Roseanne Barr." *Penthouse* Jan. 1991: 81–4, 177–86.

Young, Tracy. "Roseanne Barr: Domestic Goddess." *Vogue* April 1987: 335–6.

PART TEN

Migration and Globalization

As evidence of the reality and consequences of global warming becomes undeniable, people are beginning to realize that the notion of separate, competing national interests is obsolete. The ozone layer is not marked by national boundaries; a hole in this protective layer of the atmosphere affects everyone. Human practices that contribute to global warming in one part of the globe can have direct, often devastating, consequences for people on the other side of the planet. If people have been reluctant to accept responsibility for the impact of their actions, the environment is providing dramatic object lessons in the form of droughts, hurricanes, tsunamis, and floods. In the twenty-first century, we cannot avoid the fact that the local and the global are intimately intertwined. It is impossible for us to understand the lives of women anywhere in the world without considering the processes of globalization.

Globalization is an umbrella term that describes the ways that countries have become increasingly interconnected at the economic and cultural levels. There are undeniable benefits of globalization in terms of communication, cultural exchange, and economic development. At the same time, these benefits are not shared equally. Economic globalization has increased through the implementation of free trade agreements, such as GATT (General Agreement on Tariffs and Trade) and NAFTA (North American Free Trade Agreement), resulting in huge corporate benefits and increased standards of living for many people working in the developing world (Stiglitz 2002). The wealth gap between rich and poor individuals and between First and Third World countries, however, has continued to expand. Although wealth comparisons are not simple to calculate, a general estimate by the World Institute for Development Economics Research is that in 2000, the top 1 percent of the world's population accounted for 40 percent of the world's total net worth while the bottom half owned 1.1 percent of the world's wealth. Put another way, the top 1 percent of the population owns almost forty times as much as the bottom 50 percent (Davies et al. 2006: 26). The United States is the wealthiest nation in the world, but there is also a large wealth gap within the United States. In 2001, 20 percent of the population owned 84 percent of the wealth, and the top 1 percent owned 33.4 percent (Domhoff 2006). Wealth disparities have been aggravated through globalization, and certain sectors of the human population, notably women and people of color, have borne the brunt of these disparities and the consequent social problems they exaggerate.

Although globalization is often portrayed as transcending physical space, the people who perform the labor and live the realities of poverty and inequality do so in real, material communities. Saskia Sassen refers to these communities as the "countergeographies of globalization." The high-tech, mobile industries characteristic of the global economy depend on local infrastructures created and maintained by low-income, unskilled and semi-skilled workers. These workers often perform the labor that was once performed by housewives, such as cleaning, food preparation, and childcare. As First World, educated women move into professional careers, they and their male counterparts create a demand for low-waged work within their homes and the businesses they frequent. This demand is met increasingly through immigrant labor moving from impoverished countries to what Sassen calls "global cities" of the north, including New York, Berlin, London, and Paris. Global economics depends on migration of people, goods, and capital. In the United States, immigration is a major source of population growth that is shaping the demographic and cultural composition of the country. Some immigrants to the United States are highly educated professionals who work in the high-tech industries, but the majority are low-skilled workers. These immigrant workers, along with native-born people with limited educational and cultural capital, perform the hidden labor that sustains the upper levels of global capitalism. According to Sassen, 30 to 50 percent of workers in the leading economic sectors are low-wage workers.

A great deal of this labor has been shifted to the informal economy. That is, rather than being organized in factories or unionized workforces, the labor is performed within households, sweatshops, or illegal domains such as brothels. The informal economy has a double-edged impact on women. On the one hand, it offers opportunities for independence and thus empowerment within their families and communities. The downside is that the informal nature leaves women vulnerable to abuse and exploitation. As Helen Zia points out in "Made in the U.S.A.," the garment industry depends on sweatshop workers who earn a tiny fraction of the retail price of the clothing they produce. For example, Zia describes a sweatshop in Queens, New York, where workers earned 15 cents for each outfit that retailed for $60 in stores. Workers also labor in unsafe, unsanitary conditions with no labor law protections for 14 to 16 hours a day, seven days a week. Outside of sweatshops, in individual homes, women who work as domestic servants are subject to sexual and physical abuse and the whims of their employers (as discussed in Chisun Lee's "The Heart of the Work"). Yet these workers are a primary source of income for their home countries. In 1998, migrant workers globally sent over $70 billion home.

Immigration provides much of the labor force for the low-waged infrastructure of the global economy. The people who migrate in search of better lives, however, are subject to multiple disruptions and discontinuities in their own and their children's lives. Pat Mora's poem, "Legal Alien," describes her hyphenated life as a Mexican American who is not fully accepted by either group. The current debates and controversies over Mexican immigration reflect the ongoing discrimination faced by people who have recently migrated from Mexico as well as by those whose families have lived in what is now the United States for centuries. Yolanda Chavez Leyva provides a personal narrative of the historical trauma inflicted on her family through immigration practices and attempts to assimilate Mexicans to Anglo American customs and language. She describes the deaths of her twin sister in Juarez, Mexico, and grandmother and infant uncle in El Paso, Texas, linking these deaths to poverty, overwork, and the loneliness and alienation of immigration. She also describes the indignities suffered by her father, children beaten for speaking Spanish in U.S. schools, and racist slurs that punctuate anti-immigrant discourse. The work performed by Mexican immigrants, however, is required by the globalized economy, and she notes how immigration policies reflect the shifting needs for Mexicans' low-waged labor. Chavez Leyva's work illuminates the personal, familial, and historic experience of immigration that is hidden in debates and statistics on immigration.

Dramatic differences in wealth among countries—especially between developed and developing nations—have been exacerbated by the economic policies of international financial organizations. As Bharati Sadasivam argues, these policies have had a disproportionate impact on women around the globe. The World Bank and International Monetary Fund are the principle sources of loans to developing countries. In order to obtain loans, countries must adhere to the economic reforms known as structural adjustment and stabilization policies (SAPS). These policies are based on neo-liberal economic principles that advocate free market strategies for development. The deregulation of markets, removal of trade barriers, elimination of subsidies and cut-backs on state-supported public services are designed to stimulate profit and thus reduce debt. However, the level of external debt in many developing countries is so great that it is impossible for governments to make economic progress. For example, Sassen notes that highly indebted poor and middle-income countries pay $3 in debt service for every $1 they receive in development assistance. Some countries pay more than 50 percent of their revenues toward debt service. The combination of high debt payments and the cut-back or elimination of government programs leaves large segments of the population in dire poverty and without basic essentials like clean water, shelter, and education. As women have traditionally provided care to children, the elderly, and the infirm, they are especially burdened by these hardships. Women are also more likely to be affected in their occupational lives as the public enterprises, state sectors and traditional industries most likely to employ women are downsized or closed. The impact on women is seen most starkly in child and maternal death rates. Women in developing countries accounted for 99 percent of global maternal deaths in 2005. One in 26 women die of childbirth complications in Africa, compared to one in 7,300 in the developed world and one in 48,000 in Ireland (World Health Organization 2007). Reduction of child and maternal deaths are two of the eight Millennium Development Goals set for 2015.

These goals are an international agreement and commitment to reduce some of the preventable problems facing humankind. Although the most recent report indicates a reduction in both child and maternal mortality, in 2005 about 10.1 million children died before their fifth birthday and more than 500,000 women died from pregnancy-related causes. Most of the deaths occurred in sub-Saharan Africa and could have been prevented through basic medical and pre- and post-natal care (United Nations 2007).

Women in low-income and developing countries have become part of the survival circuits created as alternatives to traditional economies. These circuits include illegal human trafficking for various forms of labor and for the sex industry. The sex trade has become a "development strategy" in some countries where tourism and entertainment have emerged as significant sources of revenue. The United Nations estimates that sex trafficking is at least a $7 billion a year business, right behind drug trafficking and about equal with illegal arms dealing. Young women, some as young as thirteen, are kidnapped, sold by impoverished parents, or tricked into sexual servitude by criminal gangs. They are transported across borders and held captive in squalid conditions where they are beaten, raped, and required to service twenty to thirty men each day. Women are also trafficked for agricultural and sweatshop labor as modern-day slaves and as mail-order brides. Growing international awareness of human trafficking has led to the passage of the Victims of Trafficking and Violence Protection Act in the United States as well as a United Nations protocol on trafficking and a Council of Europe Convention on Action Against Trafficking in Human Beings. These positive legal steps establish resources and policies for combating trafficking. But as long as extreme poverty exists with customer demand for young women's bodies, this alternative survival strategy will be difficult to eliminate.

Finally, Rosalind Petchesky addresses the roles of militarism and fundamentalism in structuring globalization. She notes that the struggle for land, water, and oil has always shaped global relationships and continues to do so today. As money and resources are channeled into military conflicts, they are diverted from fundamental human needs and efforts to achieve social justice. Petchesky asks, with Martin Luther King, whether perpetual war can be compatible with the goal of assuring equity, justice, and a healthy life for all. According to a report by Amy Belasco, prepared through the Congressional Research Service for members of Congress, between 2001 and May 25, 2007, a total of $610 billion was spent on the war on terror (Belasco 2007). Compare this to the $40 billion Congress allocated for the SCHIP program, designed to provide health care to low-income children for ten years, between 1997 and 2007. This effective program was allowed to die in 2007 due to claims that it was encouraging a socialist view of health care in the United States.

Petchesky paints a realistically grim portrait of the potential for redirecting militarism to the peaceful pursuit of social justice. She does not conclude this section with pessimism, however. The women of the world have begun to reshape unequal relationships in their homes, communities, and governments. For all of the negative results of globalization, it has also provided women with new access to income, communication, knowledge, and activism. Transnational feminist movements have played a leading role in organizing for human rights against the dictates of fundamentalists and repressive governments. People, both women and men, are organizing at the grassroots levels and across national boundaries to demand an end to militarism and insist on global governance that is founded on human dignity rather than corporate profits.

References

Belasco, Amy. (2007). "The Cost of Iraq, Afghanistan, and Other Global War on Terror Operations Since 9/11." Washington, DC: Library of Congress, Congressional Research Service. Retrieved from http://www.comw.org/warreport/fulltext/0703CRSRL33110.pdf November 5, 2007.

Davies, James B., Susanna Sandstrom, Anthony Shorrocks, and Edward N. Wolff. (2006). *The World Distribution of Household Wealth.* World Institute for Development Economics Research. Retrieved from http://www.wider.unu.edu/research/2006-2007/2006-2007-1/wider-wdhw-launch-5-12-2006/wider-wdhw-report-5-12-2006.pdf November 5, 2007.

Domhoff, William. (2006). "Who Rules America: Wealth, Income, and Power." Retrieved from http://sociology.ucsc.edu/whorulesamerica/power/wealth.html November 5, 2007.

Stiglitz, Joseph E. (2002). *Globalization and Its Discontents.* New York: W.W. Norton.

United Nations. (2007). *The Millennium Development Goals Report.* Retrieved from http://mdgs.un.org/unsd/mdg/Resources/Static/Products/Progress2007/UNSD_MDG_Report_2007e.pdf November 5, 2007.

World Health Organization. (2007). *Maternal Mortality in 2005.* Retrieved from http://www.who.int/reproductive-health/publications/maternal_mortality_2005/mme_2005.pdf November 5, 2007.

Pat Mora

Legal Alien

Bi-lingual, Bi-cultural,
able to slip from "How's life?"
to "*Me'stan volviendo loca*,"
able to sit in a paneled office
drafting memos in smooth English,
able to order in fluent Spanish
at a Mexican restaurant,
American but hyphenated,
viewed by Anglos as perhaps exotic,
perhaps inferior, definitely different,
viewed by Mexicans as alien,
(their eyes say, "You may speak
Spanish but you're not like me")
and American to Mexicans
a Mexican to Americans
a handy token
sliding back and forth
between the fringes of both worlds
by smiling
by masking the discomfort
of being pre-judged
Bi-laterally.

Source: "Legal Aliens," by Pat Mora. *Chants.* © 1984 by Arte Publico Press. Used by permission.

Yolanda Chávez Leyva

"There is great good in returning": A *Testimonio* from the Borderlands

> There is a great good in returning to a landscape that has had extraordinary meaning in one's life. It happens that we return to such places in our minds irresistibly. There are certain villages and towns, mountains and plains that, having seen them walked in them lived in them even for a day, we keep forever in the mind's eye. They become indispensable to our well-being; they define us, and we say, I am who I am because I have been there, or there.
>
> N. Scott Momaday, "Revisiting Sacred Ground," in *The Man Made of Words*

I moved back home to *la frontera* between Texas and Chihuahua in the summer of 2001, back into the little *casita de piedra* where I had grown up. It had been vacant since the deaths of my parents years ago. I knew living back on the border, where the divisions are so great and painful and the people so resilient and persistent, would be exciting and challenging. Returning to the place where I could say, in the most profound way, "I am who I am because I have been there," meant that I would be confronting an often painful history— my own and, in a myriad of ways, that of my people—on a daily basis. It meant that, for my own survival, I had to continue my efforts to make sense of the painful stories and to find ways to create a healing history.

I had been imagining a healing history for several years, inspired in part by historian, poet, and activist Aurora Levins Morales's essay, "The Historian as Curandera." Her advice to "make absences visible," to "identify strategic pieces of misinformation and contradict them," and to "tell untold or under-told stories" spoke to my own sensibilities as a historian who consciously cultivated ties to my communities of origin.[1]

On my first night back in my childhood home, I stood on the porch and looked south toward the greenish-hued lights of Ciudad Juárez, and I felt my sister Elisa near me. Identical twins, we were born to Guadalupe in the spring of 1956 in a small *clínica* near downtown Ciudad Juárez. Unmarried, impoverished, and just nineteen years old, our mother, Lupe, was frightened to keep us. My great aunt and uncle, Esther and Gerónimo Leyva, took me across the border to EI Paso where they adopted me and raised me as their daughter in a lower-middle-class/upper-working-class neighborhood in central EI Paso.

My sister Elisa stayed in Juárez with Lupe and died several weeks later of an intestinal disease, still the predominant killer of babies in Juárez. She was buried in the *panteón municipal* in an unmarked grave that I have never seen. Yet, because her bones lie in this earth just south of the Rio Grande/Rio Bravo, I know that I belong here on the border, too. Because generations of my people's bones lie buried in this earth, I am grounded to this place, the border, as a *fronteriza*, and I grew up to be a Chicana lesbian historian.

I left home at nineteen to attend the University of Texas at Austin. My journey was a winding road that led me to a degree in business administration, a decade spent as a social worker in the Chicano and African American neighborhoods of East Austin, and finally back to graduate school in my thirties. In my forties, I earned a Ph.D. in history and began teaching in San Antonio.

From elementary school through high school, history bored me. Yet, at home the *historias* of my family riveted me. Historian Vicki Ruiz has written, "When I was a child, I learned two types of history—the one at home and the one at school. . . . Bridging the memories told at the table with printed historical narratives fueled my decision to become a historian."[2] This is my story as well. At school I learned about the Puritans, George Washington, and what was presented as the inevitable westward movement of Manifest Destiny and "progress." I also noted the invisibility of anything that felt familiar to me.

Around the kitchen table at home, listening to my mother as she cooked *albóndigas* or spaghetti while we waited for my father to come home from his civil service job, I learned another history. Here I learned of what it was like to be a girl child during the Mexican Revolution, taken from a comfortable home in Chihuahua and relocated to a place where nothing seemed recognizable. She cried remembering that her mother had died within six years of immigrating—the result of an increasingly hard life. She sighed as she explained that her baby brother had died shortly thereafter—of a broken heart, missing his mother. Watching her cook, I learned of her work as a nanny to the babies of upper-class families who complimented her for her cleanliness. Here I listened to stories of how she fought to protect her sisters from abusive husbands and insincere suitors. She laughed as she told me about her arrest in the early 1940s. She hit a border patrolman with her purse because he was being disrespectful to my father who was in military uniform at the time. I learned from her what it is to be a strong woman.

Sitting outside in the yard with my father as he carefully tended his beloved lawn, I learned another history. Here I listened to what it was like to be born on a hacienda just as the Mexican Revolution tore the nation apart. I paid close attention as he spoke of his love for his grandmother who was *pura indita*. From his stories I learned to think of *puro indio* as an endearment rather than the shame that the phrase often evokes.[3] I learned to be proud of hard work and to believe that we belonged here, for this was our land. These were my childhood *historias* of common people, faced with small and momentous challenges, struggling to make a good life. I had not yet made the connection between *historias*/stories and histories.

In the mid-1970s I began taking Chicano studies courses. I finally began to see my/our reflection in the mirrors of history. Chicana and Chicano professors taught us about the U.S.-Mexican War, the Mexican Revolution of 1910, and shifting immigration policies, which allowed *Mexicanos* to cross over easily when we were needed as cheap labor, but that pushed us back to Mexico during times of economic crisis. Finally, the *historias* of my family and our neighbors made sense in the larger socioeconomic-cultural context. I remember the anger that burned inside of me when I learned that history is so full of injustices and pain.

There was another anger, another pain, that I carried inside. I had come out at eighteen, and my university years were marked with political activity as a Chicana and as a lesbian. I was often the only Chicana in lesbian spaces and the only out lesbian in Chicana spaces. Those were difficult years. On campus, much of the leadership in Chicana/o organizations was queer, yet that queerness was largely invisible. When several of us challenged that invisibility in the Mexican American Youth Organization (MAYO), the group splintered under the weight of the controversy.

In 1977, Chicano movement activists organized the First National Chicano/Latino Conference on Immigration and Public Policy. The conference, held in San Antonio, drew over two thousand participants with political views ranging from radical to moderate.[4] In the weeks preceding the conference, a group of gay and lesbian Chicanos and Chicanas—mostly students—had drafted a statement to take before the gathering. We asked that one of the resolutions call for an end to homophobic immigration policies that denied entry to homosexual immigrants. I remember standing at the back of the great hall as the conference proceeded, wondering who would take our proposal forward. We believed that it would have more credibility if it was taken forward by a professor and looked to our allies at the university for help. After several professors declined, one agreed to carry the proposal to the front of the room. As our resolution was read, there were snickers in the audience. When the person reading the proposal did an on-the-spot translation, he used the word *joto* rather than homosexual, and the audience burst into laughter. My memories of this great event in *Movimiento* history are collapsed into that one humiliating and painful moment when my own people dismissed the treatment of gay and lesbian Mexican immigrants with laughter and scorn. For years I tried to forget that day in San Antonio.[5]

Twenty years later, I accepted a job on the faculty at the University of Texas at San Antonio. It was during my time in San Antonio that I began the healing process that eventually led me back home to the border. Soon after I arrived in San Antonio in 1997, I began working with the Esperanza Peace and Justice Center, a cultural arts organization with a national reputation for their multi-issue organizing and progressive politics. For a year I met with a small group of women—Chicana, African American, Anglo, heterosexual and queer—to think about ways to create what would become the Esperanza's Community School *Puentes de Poder*/Bridges of Power Program.

Weekly for two months each one of us would tell "our story." We brought photographs and looked into the faces of each other's ancestors; we made time lines showing how our family histories fit into the context of larger local, regional, national, and international histories; we wrote about our experiences and read them out loud. We remembered the painful stories we often kept hidden deep inside our beings. We cried and laughed. And most importantly, we listened, attentively and respectfully, to each other's words.

In *The Decolonial Imaginary: Writing Chicanas into History*, Emma Pérez writes:

> Voices of women from the past, voices of Chicanas, Mexicanas, and Indias, are utterances which are still minimized, spurned, even scorned. And time, in all its dialectical invention and promise, its so-called inherent progress, has not granted Chicanas, Mexicanas or Indias much of a voice at all. We are spoken about, spoken for, and ultimately encoded as whining, hysterical, irrational, or passive women who cannot know what is good for us, who cannot know how to impress or authorize our own narratives.[6]

Over the course of that year we healed by speaking ourselves into being as women who had survived the traumas inflicted upon us as women and people of color.

One particularly powerful interaction occurred when our facilitator asked the white women in the group to actively listen to what we women of color wanted them to know. The white women would listen, but they could not speak. It was a compelling and emotional moment for all of us. It was our chance to be heard as women of color. For a moment in time we said things we had never said aloud before. That year of listening to and telling stories began my healing from the trauma of history that I had carried inside of me, as had my parents, and their parents, and their parents before them.

Healing from the trauma of history is a process that is ongoing, complex, and felt physically, intellectually, and spiritually. In recent years, for example, when someone makes a racist comment about Mexicans being lazy or about sending "Mexicans back where they came from on a burro," I experience the comment as an overwhelming, almost suffocating, pain in my chest.

While working with traditional Chicana and Native American healers, I learned that I carry my own traumas in my heart area. I have begun to understand why the ancient Nahuas attributed not just life, but also emotion, memory, and knowledge to the heart.[7] My heart is responding not just to the comment as it is being said but to the memory of similar slurs against my people over the course of the past one hundred and fifty years. The insults and affronts against Chicanos that I read regularly on right-wing electronic discussion lists are the same ones hurled at us during the Texas Revolution of the 1830s, the U.S.-Mexican War of the 1840s, and the immigration debates of the 1920s onward.

The effects of historical trauma are insidious. Native American scholars Bonnie Duran, Eduardo Duran, and Maria Yellow Horse Brave Heart have explored the effects of historical trauma on contemporary Native peoples. They assert:

> Historical trauma and its effects are complex, multigenerational, and cumulative. A constellation of features that occur in reaction to multigenerational, collective, historical, and cumulative psychic wounding over time—over the lifespan and across generations—historical trauma is characterized as incomplete mourning and the resulting depression absorbed by children from birth onward.[8]

Historical trauma, or soul wound, is a result of colonization. It is a wound we experience in our spirits, our minds, and our bodies.

The forms of colonialism that Duran, Duran, and Brave Heart identify, including the loss of physical territory through military means, ongoing attacks on identity and culture, overwhelming changes in economic and social systems, coerced efforts at assimilation, and sterilization of women, resonate deeply for Chicana and Chicano history.[9] These acts of colonization have deeply affected us, and I see it every day in my family, in my students, and in my community.

My generation and the generation before me have personal memories of the forced steriliza-tions of poor women of color, of educational policies that mandated corporal punishment for the speaking of Spanish on school grounds, of segregated schools, of forced repatriations, and police brutality. As I teach, I see the effects of these traumas working in the lives of the younger generation even when they cannot yet name the trauma. My Chicana-Kikapu friend and teacher Patrisia Gonzáles writes, "Trauma takes away language. If we can't put language to our experience, either through journaling, therapy, or talking circles, it burrows further inside our beings."[10] Putting language to that pain is one of my responsibilities as a historian.

For example, while speaking to a class recently as a guest lecturer, I casually mentioned that many parents who were born in the 1930s, 1940s, and 1950s had not taught Spanish to their children, and that those children should not be ashamed. In passing, without thinking consciously about it, I had touched upon a historically based trauma that immediately affected two young women in the class. Both were ashamed and angry that they did not speak Spanish. Other Chicanos and Mexicanos criticized them for it. On the border there are tremendous pressures to be an "authentic" Mexican, and these young women felt inadequate as individuals. Their comments opened a space in the class to talk about how Spanish had been taken forcibly from us. I encouraged them not to blame their parents. Their parents, too, had been made to feel ashamed and inadequate by an educational system intent on erasing our Mexican-ness. I related how Americanization programs from the early part of the twentieth century had instilled English as a form of social control. Even in the 1960s, schools in the El Paso area paddled students who spoke Spanish on campus. The pattern was repeated throughout the Southwest to the detriment of children's psychological and physical health. The young women spoke of their desire to learn Spanish and showed relief when I told them I knew other people who had learned Spanish as adults.

The discussion touched me as well in ways I did not expect. As I listened to the pain expressed by the women in class, I thought back to my own childhood pain when, entering catechism, my parents told me to pray only in English. My cousins, a few years older than I was, had entered school knowing only Spanish. As a result they were constantly punished and ridiculed by their teachers. My parents did not want me to suffer what my cousins had suffered and started by taking away my *rezos*, my nightly prayers. I forgot how to pray in Spanish for many years. As part of my own healing and reclaiming, I now pray in Spanish, and I learn prayers in Indigenous languages that tie me spiritually to our ancient roots on this continent. Historical trauma wounds our spirits as well as our minds and bodies.

In the last year of my mother's life, when time was no longer linear and the past and present existed simultaneously, historical trauma came unexpectedly to the surface of her day-to-day existence. Fragile, emotionally and physically vulnerable, she returned to the landscape that had made her who she was. She relived crossing the border as a child almost eighty years earlier. Looking at me and seeing her sister instead, she worried about the move. What would it be like "over there"? Would there be problems for her parents? For days she experienced anxiety. Frequently she asked me if we were still in Juárez, wanting some assurance that we were still on familiar ground. Having learned from the geriatric nurses not to contradict her, I reassured her that we were still in México.

Suddenly one day my mother's mood changed dramatically. The worry was replaced with relief and even self-assurance. "*Ellos saben que somos gente buena*," she announced. I asked why. "They didn't make us take a bath when we crossed." The words shocked me. As a border historian I knew of the various quarantines, health inspections, and baths that had been imposed on Mexicans crossing into the United States during the time period my family had crossed. In a 1974 interview, longtime El Paso resident José Cruz Burci-

aga remembered the kerosene baths and the shaving of heads forced on many working-class immigrants in the early part of the century.[11] I had read of the disinfection plant built literally under the bridge connecting El Paso and Ciudad Juarez in 1910 and of the continuing and degrading inspections and disinfections that continued into the 1920s.[12] What I had never considered was that my mother, her mother, and her brothers and sisters had experienced an inspection themselves. That evening, sitting by her bed as she slept, I wondered what other fears and anxieties about crossing the border her child self held inside. Her joy and relief at not having to be disinfected only revealed how fearful the prospect had been to her nine-year-old self. I wondered how much fear and trauma had been instilled in the thousands of women, children, and men who crossed daily.[13]

In *Native American Postcolonial Psychology*, Eduardo Duran and Bonnie Duran argue that the practice of psychology must be historicized. They urge their colleagues to understand the history behind the pain. Only by understanding history will psychologists be able to effectively work with Native Americans and other colonized peoples.[14] As a historian, I would urge my colleagues to acknowledge the pain behind the history.

I am not advocating a history of victimization. Much of the historiography in Chicano studies over the past two decades has consciously steered away from such a model. Historically, people of color have demonstrated their agency and their resistance to oppression in multiple and ingenious ways. I look forward to a growing body of literature documenting this fact. However, I support our commitment to look at the ways in which we carry the traumas of history inside our spirits, our bodies, and our minds. Historians can be healers, as Levins Morales asserts. Living on the border, where the landscape itself holds so much pain, I will continue to look for ways to create a history that heals.

Notes

1. Aurora Levins Morales, "The Historian as Curandera," in *Medicine Stories: History, Culture and the Politics of Integrity* (Cambridge, Mass.: South End Press, 1998), 23–38.

2. Vicki L. Ruiz, *From Out of the Shadows: Mexican Women in Twentieth-Century America* (New York: Oxford University Press, 1998), xiii.

3. Inés Hernández-Ávila, "An Open Letter to Chicanas: On the Power and Politics of Origin," in *Reinventing the Enemy's Language: Contemporary Native Women's Writings of North America*, ed. Joy Harjo and Gloria Bird (New York: W.W. Norton and Company, 1997), 240.

4. David G. Gutiérrez cites this conference as a landmark in Mexican American politics in his book, *Walls and Mirrors: Mexican Americans, Mexican Immigrants, and the Politics of Ethnicity* (Berkeley: University of California Press, 1995), 201–2.

5. Gutiérrez, *Walls and Mirrors*, 202. Ironically, Gutiérrez quotes one participant as saying that unity had been possible at the conference because, "When they come to deport us, we're all in the same boat." For lesbian and gay Chicanas and Chicanos, we were left to drown when the boat came.

6. Emma Pérez, *The Decolonial Imaginary: Writing Chicanas into History* (Bloomington: Indiana University Press, 1999), xv.

7. Alfredo Lopez Austin, *The Human Body and Ideology: Concepts of the Ancient Nahuas*, vol. 2, trans. Thelma Ortiz de Montellano and Bernard Ortiz de Montellano (Salt Lake City: University of Utah Press, 1988), 244–49.

8. Bonnie Duran, Eduardo Duran, and Maria Yellow Horse Brave Heart, "Native Americans and the Trauma of History," in *Studying Native America: Problems and Prospects*, ed. Russell Thornton (Madison: University of Wisconsin Press, 1998), 64.

9. Duran, Duran, and Brave Heart, *Studying Native America*, 62–63.

10. Patrisia Gonzáles, "Grieving and Transforming Rape," *Column of the Americas* (March 9, 2001), http://www.uexpress.com/columnoftheamericas.

11. Quoted in Raul R. Reyes, "'Gringos' and 'Greasers' and the Rio Grande Border: Race Resentment in the Mexican Revolutionary Era in El Paso, 1914–1916" (master's thesis, University of Texas at El Paso, 1997), 80.

12. Alexandra Minna Stern, "Buildings, Boundaries, and Blood: Medicalization and Nation-Building on the U.S.-Mexico Border, 1910–1930," *Hispanic American Historical Review* 79:1 (1999): 41–81.

13. Stern, "Buildings, Boundaries," 44–45. Stern provides a dismal description of the inspection and disinfection process. Individuals were forced to strip naked and their clothes were taken from them for laundering. The heads of the men and boys were shaved while women's hair was washed with a mixture of water, soap, and kerosene. They were then bathed with the same mixture. An attendant watched the entire process.

14. Eduardo Duran and Bonnie Duran, *Native American Postcolonial Psychology* (Albany: State University of New York Press, 1995).

Saskia Sassen

Global Cities and Survival Circuits

When today's media, policy, and economic analysts define globalization, they emphasize hypermobility, international communication, and the neutralization of distance and place. This account of globalization is by far the dominant one. Central to it are the global information economy, instant communication, and electronic markets—all realms within which place no longer makes a difference, and where the only type of worker who matters is the highly educated professional. Globalization thus conceived privileges global transmission over the material infrastructure that makes it possible; information over the workers who produce it, whether these be specialists or secretaries; and the new transnational corporate culture over the other jobs upon which it rests, including many of those held by immigrants. In brief, the dominant narrative of globalization concerns itself with the upper circuits of global capital, not the lower ones, and with the hypermobility of capital rather than with capital that is bound to place.

The migration of maids, nannies, nurses, sex workers, and contract brides has little to do with globalization by these lights. Migrant women are just individuals making a go of it, after all, and the migration of workers from poor countries to wealthier ones long predates the current phase of economic globalization. And yet it seems reasonable to assume that there are significant links between globalization and women's migration, whether voluntary or forced, for jobs that used to be part of the First World woman's domestic role.

Source: "Global Cities and Survival Circuits," by Saskia Sassen, as seen in Barbara Ehrenreich and Arlie Russell Hochschild, eds., *Global Woman*. New York: Henry Holt & Co. © 2002. Used by permission of Saskia Sassen.

Might the dynamics of globalization alter the course or even reinscribe the history of the migration and exploitation of Third World laborers? There are two distinct issues here. One is whether globalization has enabled formerly national or regional processes to go global. The other is whether globalization has produced a new kind of migration, with new conditions and dynamics of its own. . . .

Toward an Alternative Narrative About Globalization

The spatial dispersal of economic activities and the neutralization of place constitute half of the globalization story. The other half involves the territorial centralization of top-level management, control operations, and the most advanced specialized services. Markets, whether national or global, and companies, many of which have gone global, require central locations where their most complex tasks are accomplished. Furthermore, the information industry rests on a vast physical infrastructure, which includes strategic nodes where facilities are densely concentrated. Even the most advanced sectors of the information industry employ many different types of workplaces and workers.

If we expand our analysis of globalization to include this production process, we can see that secretaries belong to the global economy, as do the people who clean professionals' offices and homes. An economic configuration very different from the one suggested by the concept of an "information economy" emerges—and it is one that includes material conditions, production sites, and activities bounded by place.

The mainstream account of globalization tends to take for granted the existence of a global economic system, viewing it as a function of the power of transnational corporations and communications. But if the new information technologies and transnational corporations can be operated, coordinated, and controlled globally, it's because that capacity has been produced. By focusing on its production, we shift our emphasis to the *practices* that constitute economic globalization: the work of producing and reproducing the organization and management of a global production system and a global marketplace for finance.

This focus on practices draws the categories of place and work process into the analysis of economic globalization. In so broadening our analysis, we do not deny the importance of hypermobility and power. Rather, we acknowledge that many of the resources necessary for global economic activities are not hypermobile and are, on the contrary, deeply embedded in place, including such sites as global cities and export processing zones. Global processes are structured by local constraints, including the work culture, political culture, and composition of the workforce within a particular nation state.[1]

If we recapture the geography behind globalization, we might also recapture its workers, communities, and work cultures (not just the corporate ones). By focusing on the global city, for instance, we can study how global processes become localized in specific arrangements, from the high-income gentrified urban neighborhoods of the transnational professional class to the work lives of the foreign nannies and maids in those same neighborhoods.

Women in the Global City

Globalization has greatly increased the demand in global cities for low-wage workers to fill jobs that offer few advancement possibilities. The same cities have seen an explosion of wealth and power, as high-income jobs and high-priced urban space have noticeably expanded. How, then, can

workers be hired at low wages and with few benefits even when there is high demand and the jobs belong to high-growth sectors? The answer, it seems, has involved tapping into a growing new labor supply—women and immigrants—and in so doing, breaking the historical nexus that would have empowered workers under these conditions. The fact that these workers tend to be women and immigrants also lends cultural legitimacy to their non-empowerment. In global cities, then, a majority of today's resident workers are women, and many of these are women of color, both native and immigrant.

At the same time, global cities have seen a gathering trend toward the informalization of an expanding range of activities, as low-profit employers attempt to escape the costs and constraints of the formal economy's regulatory apparatus. They do so by locating commercial or manufacturing operations in areas zoned exclusively for residential use, for example, or in buildings that violate fire and health standards; they also do so by assigning individual workers industrial homework. This allows them to remain in these cities. At its best, informalization reintroduces the community and the household as important economic spaces in global cities. It is in many ways a low-cost (and often feminized) equivalent to deregulation at the top of the system. As with deregulation (for example, financial deregulation), informalization introduces flexibility, reduces the "burdens" of regulation, and lowers costs, in this case of labor. In the cities of the global north—including New York, London, Paris, and Berlin—informalization serves to downgrade a variety of activities for which there is often a growing local demand. Immigrant women, in the end, bear some of the costs.

As the demand for high-level professional workers has skyrocketed, more and more women have found work in corporate professional jobs.[2] These jobs place heavy demands on women's time, requiring long work hours and intense engagement. Single professionals and two-career households therefore tend to prefer urban to suburban residence. The result is an expansion of high-income residential areas in global cities and a return of family life to urban centers. Urban professionals want it all, including dogs and children, whether or not they have the time to care for them. The usual modes of handling household tasks often prove inadequate. We can call this type of household a "professional household without a 'wife,'" regardless of whether its adult couple consists of a man and a woman, two men, or two women. A growing share of its domestic tasks are relocated to the market: they are bought directly as goods and services or indirectly through hired labor. As a consequence, we see the return of the so-called serving classes in all of the world's global cities, and these classes are largely made up of immigrant and migrant women.

This dynamic produces a sort of double movement: a shift to the labor market of functions that used to be part of household work, but also a shift of what used to be labor market functions in standardized workplaces to the household and, in the case of informalization, to the immigrant community.[3] This reconfiguration of economic spaces has had different impacts on women and men, on male-typed and female-typed work cultures, and on male- and female-centered forms of power and empowerment.

For women, such transformations contain the potential, however limited, for autonomy and empowerment. Might informalization, for example, reconfigure certain economic relationships between men and women? With informalization, the neighborhood and the household reemerge as sites for economic activity, creating "opportunities" for low-income women and thereby reordering some of the hierarchies in which women find themselves. This becomes particularly clear in the case of immigrant women, who often come from countries with traditionally male-centered cultures.

A substantial number of studies now show that regular wage work and improved access to other public realms has an impact on gender relations in the lives of immigrant women. Women gain greater personal autonomy and independence, while men lose ground. More control over budgeting and other domestic decisions devolves to women, and they have greater leverage in requesting help from men in domestic chores. Access to public services and other public resources also allows women to incorporate themselves into the mainstream society; in fact, women often mediate this process for their households. Some women likely benefit more than others from these circumstances, and with more research we could establish the impact of class, education, and income. But even aside from relative empowerment in the household, paid work holds out another significant possibility for women: their greater participation in the public sphere and their emergence as public actors.

Immigrant women tend to be active in two arenas: institutions for public and private assistance, and the immigrant or ethnic community. The more women are involved with the migration process, the more likely it is that migrants will settle in their new residences and participate in their communities. And when immigrant women assume active public and social roles, they further reinforce their status in the household and the settlement process.[4] Positioned differently from men in relation to the economy and state, women tend to be more involved in community building and community activism. They are the ones who will likely handle their families' legal vulnerabilities as they seek public and social services. These trends suggest that women may emerge as more forceful and visible actors in the labor market as well.

And so two distinct dynamics converge in the lives of immigrant women in global cities. On the one hand, these women make up an invisible and disempowered class of workers in the service of the global economy's strategic sectors. Their invisibility keeps immigrant women from emerging as the strong proletariat that followed earlier forms of economic organization, when workers' positions in leading sectors had the effect of empowering them. On the other hand, the access to wages and salaries, however low; the growing feminization of the job supply; and the growing feminization of business opportunities thanks to informalization, all alter the gender hierarchies in which these women find themselves.

New Employment Regimes in Cities

Most analysts of postindustrial society and advanced economies report a massive growth in the need for highly educated workers but little demand for the type of labor that a majority of immigrants, perhaps especially immigrant women, have tended to supply over the last two or three decades. But detailed empirical studies of major cities in highly developed countries contradict this conventional view of the postindustrial economy. Instead, they show an ongoing demand for immigrant workers and a significant supply of old and new low-wage jobs that require little education.[5]

Three processes of change in economic and spatial organization help explain the ongoing, indeed growing, demand for immigrant workers, especially immigrant women. One is the consolidation of advanced services and corporate headquarters in the urban economic core, especially in global cities. While the corporate headquarters-and-services complex may not account for the majority of jobs in these cities, it establishes a new regime of economic activity, which in turn produces the spatial and social transformations evident in major cities. Another relevant process is the downgrading of the manufacturing sector, as some manufacturing industries become incorporated into the postindustrial economy. Downgrading is a response to competition from cheap imports, and to the modest profit potential of manufacturing compared to telecommunications, finance, and other corporate services.[6] The third process is informalization, a notable example of which is the rise of the sweatshop. Firms often take recourse to informalized arrangements when they have an effective local demand for their goods and services but they cannot compete with cheap imports, or cannot compete for space and other business needs with the new high-profit firms of the advanced corporate service economy.

In brief, that major cities have seen changes in their job supplies can be chalked up both to the emergence of new sectors and to the reorganization of work in sectors new and old. The shift from a manufacturing to a service-dominated economy, particularly evident in cities, destabilizes older relationships between jobs and economic sectors. Today, much more than twenty years ago, we see an expansion of low-wage jobs associated with growing sectors rather than with declining ones. At the same time, a vast array of activities that once took place under standardized work arrangements have become increasingly informalized, as some manufacturing relocates from unionized factories to sweatshops and private homes. If we distinguish the characteristics of jobs from those of the sectors in which they are located, we can see that highly dynamic, technologically advanced growth sectors may well contain low-wage, dead-end jobs. Similarly, backward sectors like downgraded manufacturing can reflect the major growth trends in a highly developed economy.

It seems, then, that we need to rethink two assumptions: that the postindustrial economy primarily requires highly educated workers, and that informalization and downgrading are just Third World imports or anachronistic holdovers. Service-dominated urban economies do indeed create low-wage jobs with minimal education requirements, few advancement opportunities, and low pay for demanding work. For workers raised in an ideological context that emphasizes success, wealth, and career, these are not attractive positions; hence the growing demand for immigrant workers. But given the provenance of the jobs these immigrant workers take, we must resist assuming that they are located in the backward sectors of the economy.

The Other Workers in the Advanced Corporate Economy

Low-wage workers accomplish a sizable portion of the day-to-day work in global cities' leading sectors. After all, advanced professionals require clerical, cleaning, and repair workers for their state-of-the-art offices, and they require truckers to bring them their software and their toilet paper. In my research on New York and other cities, I have found that between 30 and 50 percent of workers in the leading sectors are actually low-wage workers.[7]

The similarly state-of-the-art lifestyles of professionals in these sectors have created a whole new demand for household workers, particularly maids and nannies, as well as for service workers to cater to their high-income consumption habits.[8] Expensive restaurants, luxury housing, luxury hotels, gourmet shops, boutiques, French hand laundries, and special cleaning services, for example, are more labor-intensive than their lower-priced equivalents. To an extent not seen in a very long time, we are witnessing the reemergence of a "serving class" in contemporary high-income households and neighborhoods. The image of the immigrant woman serving the white middle-class professional woman has replaced that of the black female servant working for the white master in centuries past. The result is a sharp tendency toward social polarization in today's global cities.

We are beginning to see how the global labor markets at the top and at the bottom of the economic system are formed. The bottom is mostly staffed through the efforts of individual workers, though an expanding network of organizations has begun to get involved. (So have illegal traffickers, as we'll see later.) Kelly Services, a Fortune 500 global staffing company that operates in twenty-five countries, recently added a home-care division that is geared toward people who need assistance with daily living but that also offers services that in the past would have been taken care of by the mother or wife figure in a household. A growing range of smaller global staffing organizations offer day care, including dropping off and picking up school-children, as well as completion of in-house tasks from child care to cleaning and cooking.[9] One international agency for nannies and au pairs (EF Au Pair Corporate Program) advertises directly to corporations, urging them to include the service in their offers to potential hires.

Meanwhile, at the top of the system, several global Fortune 500 staffing companies help firms fill high-level professional and technical jobs. In 2001, the largest of these was the Swiss multinational Adecco, with offices in fifty-eight countries; in 2000 it provided firms worldwide with 3 million workers. Manpower, with offices in fifty-nine different countries, provided 2 million workers. Kelly Services provided 750,000 employees in 2000.

The top and the bottom of the occupational distribution are becoming internationalized and so are their labor suppliers. Although midlevel occupations are increasingly staffed through temporary employment agencies, these companies have not internationalized their efforts. Occupations at the top and at the bottom are, in very different but parallel ways, sensitive. Firms need reliable and hopefully talented professionals, and they need them specialized but standardized so that they can use them globally. Professionals seek the same qualities in the workers they employ in their homes. The fact that staffing organizations have moved into providing domestic services signals both that a global labor market has emerged in this area and that there is an effort afoot to standardize the services maids, nannies, and home-care nurses deliver.

Producing a Global Supply of the New Caretakers: The Feminization of Survival

The immigrant women described in the first half of this chapter enter the migration process in many different ways. Some migrate in order to reunite their families; others migrate alone. Many of their initial movements have little to do with globalization. Here I am concerned with a different kind of migration experience, and it is one that is deeply linked to economic globalization: migrations organized by third parties, typically governments or illegal traffickers. Women who enter the migration stream this way often (though not always) end up in different sorts of jobs than those described above. What they share with the women described earlier in this chapter is that they, too, take over tasks previously associated with housewives.

The last decade has seen a growing presence of women in a variety of cross-border circuits. These circuits are enormously diverse, but they share one feature: they produce revenue on the backs of the truly disadvantaged. One such circuit consists in the illegal trafficking in people for the sex industry and for various types of labor. Another circuit has developed around cross-border migrations, both documented and not, which have become an important source of hard currency for the migrants' home governments. Broader structural conditions are largely responsible for forming and strengthening circuits like these. Three major actors emerge from those conditions, however: women in search of work, illegal traffickers, and the governments of the home countries.

These circuits make up, as it were, counter-geographies of globalization. They are deeply imbricated with some of globalization's major constitutive dynamics: the formation of global markets, the intensifying of transnational and translocal networks, and the development of communication technologies that easily escape conventional surveillance. The global economic system's institutional support for cross-border markets and money flows has contributed greatly to the formation and strengthening of these circuits.[10] The countergeographies are dynamic and mobile; to some extent, they belong to the shadow economy, but they also make use of the regular economy's institutional infrastructure.[11]

Such alternative circuits for survival, profit, and hard currency have grown at least partly in response to the effects of economic globalization on developing countries. Unemployment is on the rise in much of the developing world; small and medium-sized enterprises oriented to the national, rather than the export, market have closed; and government debt, already large, is in many cases rising. The economies frequently grouped under the label "developing" are often struggling, stagnant, or even shrinking. These conditions have pressed additional responsibilities onto women, as men have lost job opportunities and governments have cut back on social services.[12] In other words, it has become increasingly important to find alternative ways of making a living, producing profits, and generating government revenues, as developing countries have faced the following concurrent trends: diminishing job prospects for men, a falloff in traditional business opportunities as foreign firms and export industries displace previous economic mainstays, and a concomitant decrease in government revenues, due both to the new conditions of globalization and to the burden of servicing debts.[13]

The major dynamics linked to economic globalization have significantly affected developing economies, including the so-called middle-income countries of the global south. These countries have had not only to accommodate new conditions but to implement a bundle of new policies, including structural adjustment programs, which require that countries open up to foreign firms and eliminate state subsidies. Almost inevitably, these economies fall into crisis; they then implement the International Monetary Fund's programmatic solutions. It is now clear that in most of the countries involved, including Mexico, South Korea, Ghana, and Thailand, these solutions have cost certain sectors of the economy and population enormously, and they have not fundamentally reduced government debt.

Certainly, these economic problems have affected the lives of women from developing countries. Prostitution and migrant labor are increasingly popular ways to make a living; illegal trafficking in women and children for the sex industry, and in all kinds of people as laborers, is an increasingly popular way to make a profit; and remittances, as well as the organized export of workers, have become increasingly popular ways for governments to bring in revenue. Women are by far the majority group in prostitution and in trafficking for the sex industry, and they are becoming a majority group in migration for labor.

Such circuits, realized more and more frequently on the backs of women, can be considered a (partial) feminization of survival. Not only are households, indeed whole communities, increasingly dependent on women for their survival, but so too are governments, along with enterprises that function on the margins of the legal economy. As the term *circuits* indicates, there is a degree of institutionalization in these dynamics; that is to say, they are not simply aggregates of individual actions.

Government Debt: Shifting Resources from Women to Foreign Banks

Debt and debt-servicing problems have been endemic in the developing world since the 1980s. They are also, I believe, crucial to producing the new countergeographies of globalization. But debt's impact on women, and on the feminization of survival, has more to do with particular features of debt than with debt *tout court*.

A considerable amount of research indicates that debt has a detrimental effect on government programs for women and children, notably education and health care. Further, austerity and adjustment programs, which are usually implemented in order to redress government debt, produce unemployment, which also adversely affects women[14] by adding to the pressure on them to ensure household survival. In order to do so, many women have turned to subsistence food production, informal work, emigration, and prostitution.[15]

Most of the countries that fell into debt in the 1980s have found themselves unable to climb out of it. In the 1990s, a whole new set of countries joined the first group in this morass. The IMF and the World Bank responded with their structural adjustment program and structural adjustment loans, respectively. The latter tied loans to economic policy reform rather than to particular projects. The idea was to make these states more "competitive," which typically meant inducing sharp cuts in various social programs.

Rather than becoming "competitive," the countries subjected to structural adjustment have remained deeply indebted, with about fifty of them now categorized as "highly indebted poor countries." Moreover, a growing number of middle-income countries are also caught in this debt trap. Argentina became the most dramatic example when it defaulted on $140 billion in debt in December 2001—the largest ever sovereign default. Given the structure and servicing of these debts, as well as their weight in debtor countries' economies, it is not likely that many of these countries will ever be able to pay off their debts in full. Structural adjustment programs seem to have made this even less likely; the economic reforms these programs demanded have added to unemployment and the bankruptcy of many small, nationally oriented firms.

It has been widely recognized that the south has already paid its debt several times over. According to some estimates, from 1982 to 1998, indebted countries paid four times their original debts, and at the same time their debt increased four times.[16] Nonetheless, these countries continue to pay a significant share of their total revenue to service their debt. Thirty-three of the officially named forty-one highly indebted poor countries paid $3 in debt service to the north for every $1 they received in development assistance. Many of these countries pay more than 50 percent of their government revenues toward debt service, or 20 to 25 percent of their export earnings.

The ratios of debt to GNP in many of the highly indebted poor countries exceed sustainable limits; many are far more extreme than the levels considered unmanageable during the Latin American debt crisis of the 1980s. Such ratios are especially high in Africa, where they stand at 123 percent, compared with 42 percent in Latin America and 28 percent in Asia.[17] Such figures suggest that most of these countries will not get out of their indebtedness through structural adjustment programs. Indeed, it would seem that in many cases the latter have had the effect of intensifying debt dependence. Furthermore, together with various other factors, structural adjustment programs have contributed to an increase in unemployment and in poverty.

Alternative Survival Circuits

It is in this context—marked by unemployment, poverty, bankruptcies of large numbers of firms, and shrinking state resources to meet social needs—that alternative circuits of survival emerge, and it is to these conditions that such circuits are articulated. Here I want to focus on the growing salience of the trafficking of women as a profit-making option and on the growing importance of the emigrants' remittances to the bottom lines of the sending states.

Trafficking, or the forced recruitment and transportation of people for work, is a violation of human, civil, and political rights. Much legislative effort has gone into addressing trafficking: international treaties and charters, U.N. resolutions, and various bodies and commissions have all attempted to put a stop to this practice.[18] Nongovernmental organizations have also formed around this issue.[19]

Trafficking in women for the sex industry is highly profitable for those running the trade. The United Nations estimates that 4 million people were trafficked in 1998, producing a profit of $7 billion for criminal groups.[20] These funds include remittances from prostitutes' earnings as well as payments to organizers and facilitators. In Poland, police estimate that for each woman delivered, the trafficker receives about $700. Ukrainian and Russian women, highly prized in the sex market, earn traffickers $500 to $1,000 per woman delivered. These women can be expected to service fifteen clients a day on average, and each can be expected to make about $215,000 per month for the criminal gang that trafficked her.[21]

It is estimated that in recent years, several million women and girls have been trafficked from and within Asia and the former Soviet Union, both of which are major trafficking areas. The growing frequency of trafficking in these two regions can be linked to increases in poverty, which may lead some parents to sell their daugh-

ters to brokers. In the former Soviet republics and Eastern Europe, unemployment has helped promote the growth of criminal gangs, some of which traffic women. Unemployment rates hit 70 percent among women in Armenia, Russia, Bulgaria, and Croatia after the implementation of market policies; in Ukraine, the rate was 80 percent. Some research indicates that need is the major motivation for entry into prostitution.[22]

The sex industry is not the only trafficking circuit: migrant workers of both sexes can also be profitably trafficked across borders. According to a U.N. report, criminal organizations in the 1990s generated an estimated $3.5 billion per year in profits from trafficking migrants. Organized crime has only recently entered this business; in the past, trafficking was mostly the province of petty criminals. Some recent reports indicate that organized-crime groups are creating strategic intercontinental alliances through networks of co-ethnics in various countries; this facilitates transport, local distribution, provision of false documents, and the like. These international networks also allow traffickers to circulate women and other migrants among third countries; they may move women from Burma, Laos, Vietnam, and China to Thailand, while moving Thai women to Japan and the United States.[23] The Global Survival Network reported on these practices after it conducted a two-year investigation, establishing a dummy company in order to enter the illegal trade.[24]

Once trafficked women reach their destination countries, some features of immigration policy and its enforcement may well make them even more vulnerable. Such women usually have little recourse to the law. If they are undocumented, which they are likely to be, they will not be treated as victims of abuse but as violators of entry, residence, and work laws. As countries of the global north attempt to address undocumented immigration and trafficking by clamping down on entry at their borders, more women are likely to turn to traffickers to help them get across. These traffickers may turn out to belong to criminal organizations linked to the sex industry.

Moreover, many countries forbid foreign women to work as prostitutes, and this provides criminal gangs with even more power over the women they traffic. It also eliminates one survival option for foreign women who may have limited access to jobs. Some countries, notably the Netherlands and Switzerland, are far more tolerant of foreign women working as prostitutes than as regular laborers. According to International Organization for Migration data, in the European Union, a majority of prostitutes are migrant women: 75 percent in Germany and 80 percent in the Italian city of Milan.

Some women know that they are being trafficked for prostitution, but for many the conditions of their recruitment and the extent of the abuse and bondage they will suffer only become evident after they arrive in the receiving country.[25] Their confinement is often extreme—akin to slavery—and so is their abuse, including rape, other forms of sexual violence, and physical punishment. Their meager wages are often withheld. They are frequently forbidden to protect themselves against AIDS, and they are routinely denied medical care. If they seek help from the police, they may be taken into detention for violating immigration laws; if they have been provided with false documents, there will be criminal charges.

With the sharp growth of tourism over the last decade, the entertainment sector has also grown, becoming increasingly important in countries that have adopted tourism as a strategy for development.[26] In many places, the sex trade is part of the entertainment industry, and the two have grown in tandem. Indeed, the sex trade itself has become a development strategy in some areas where unemployment and poverty are widespread, and where governments are desperate for revenue and hard currency. When local manufacturing and agriculture no longer provide jobs, profits, or government revenue, a once marginal economic wellspring becomes a far more important one. The IMF and the World Bank sometimes recommend tourism as a solution to the troubles of poor countries, but when they provide loans for its development or expansion, they may well inadvertently contribute to the expansion of the entertainment industry and, indirectly, of the sex trade. Because it is linked to development strategies in this way, the trafficking of women may continue to expand in these countries.

Indeed, the global sex industry is likely to expand in any case, given the involvement of organized crime in the sex trade, the formation of cross-border ethnic networks, and the growing transnationalization of tourism. These factors may well lead to a sex trade that reaches out to more and more "markets." It's a worrisome possibility, especially as growing numbers of women face few if any employment options. Prostitution becomes—in certain kinds of economies—crucial to expanding the entertainment industry, and thereby to tourism as a development strategy that will in turn lead to increased government revenue. These links are structural; the significance of the sex industry to any given economy rises in the absence of other sources of jobs, profits, and revenues.

Women, and migrants generally, are crucial to another development strategy as well: the remittances migrant workers send home are a major source of hard-currency reserves for the migrant's home country. While remittances may seem minor compared to the financial markets' massive daily flow of capital, they are often very significant for struggling economies. In 1998, the latest year for which we have data, the remittances migrants sent home topped $70 billion globally. To understand the significance of this figure, compare it to the GDP and foreign currency reserves in the affected countries, rather than to the global flow of capital. For instance, in the Philippines, a major sender of migrants generally and of women for the entertainment industry in particular, remittances were the third largest source of foreign currency over the last several years. In Bangladesh, which sends significant numbers of workers to the Middle East, Japan, and several European countries, remittances totaled about a third of foreign-currency transactions.

Exporting workers is one means by which governments cope with unemployment and foreign debt. The benefits of this strategy come through two channels, one of which is highly formalized and the other a simple by-product of the migration process. South Korea and the Philippines both furnish good examples of formal labor-export programs. In the 1970s, South Korea developed extensive programs to promote the export of workers, initially to the Middle Eastern OPEC countries and then worldwide, as an integral part of its growing overseas construction industry. When South Korea's economy boomed, exporting workers became a less necessary and less attractive strategy. The Philippine government, by contrast, expanded and diversified its labor exports in order to deal with unemployment and to secure needed foreign-currency reserves through remittances.

The Philippines Overseas Employment Administration (POEA) has played an important role in the emigration of Filipina women to the United States, the Middle East, and Japan. Established by the Filipino government in 1982, POEA organized and supervised the export of nurses and maids to high-demand areas. Foreign debt and unemployment combined to make the export of labor an attractive option. Filipino workers overseas send home an average of almost $1 billion a year. For their parts, labor-importing countries had their own reasons to welcome the Filipino government's policy. The OPEC countries of the Middle East saw in the Filipina migrants an answer to their growing demand for domestic workers following the 1973 oil boom. Confronted with an acute shortage of nurses, a profession that demanded years of training yet garnered low wages and little prestige, the United States passed the Immigration Nursing Relief Act of 1989, which allowed for the importation of nurses.[27] And in booming 1980s Japan, which witnessed rising expendable incomes but marked labor shortages, the government passed legislation permitting the entry of "entertainment workers."[28]

The largest number of migrant Filipinas work overseas as maids, particularly in other Asian countries.[29] The second largest group, and the fastest growing, consists of entertainers, who migrate mostly to Japan. The rapid increase in the number of women migrating as entertainers can be traced to the more than five hundred "entertainment brokers" that now operate in the Philippines outside the state umbrella. These brokers provide women for the Japanese sex industry, which is basically controlled by organized gangs rather than through the government-sponsored program for the entry of entertainers. Recruited for singing and entertaining, these women are frequently forced into prostitution as well.[30]

The Filipino government, meanwhile, has also passed regulations that permit mail-order-bride agencies to recruit young Filipinas to marry foreign men. This trade rapidly picked up pace thanks to the government's organized support. The United States and Japan are two of the most common destinations for mail-order brides. Demand was especially high in Japan's agricultural communities in the 1980s, given that country's severe shortage of people in general and of young women in particular, as the demand for labor boomed in the large metropolitan areas. Municipal governments in Japanese towns made it a policy to accept Filipina brides.

A growing body of evidence indicates that mail-order brides frequently suffer physical abuse. In the United States, the Immigration and Naturalization Service has recently reported acute domestic violence against mail-order wives. Again, the law discourages these women from seeking recourse, as they are liable to be detained if they do so before they have been married for two years. In Japan, foreign mail-order wives are not granted full legal status, and considerable evidence indicates that many are subject to abuse not only by their husbands but by their husbands' extended families as well. The Philippine government approved most mail-order-bride brokers before 1989, but during Corazon Aquino's presidency, the stories of abuse by foreign husbands led the Philippine government to ban the mail-order-bride business. Nonetheless, such organizations are almost impossible to eliminate, and they continue to operate in violation of the law.

The Philippines may have the most developed programs for the export of its women, but it is not the only country to have explored similar strategies. After its 1997–1998 financial crisis, Thailand started a campaign to promote migration for work and to encourage overseas firms to recruit Thai workers. Sri Lanka's government has tried to export another 200,000 workers in addition to the 1 million it already has overseas; Sri Lankan women remitted $880 million in 1998, mostly from their earnings as maids in the Middle East and Far East. Bangladesh organized extensive labor-export programs to the OPEC countries of the Middle East in the 1970s. These programs have continued, becoming a significant source of foreign currency along with individual migrations to these and other countries, notably the United States and Great Britain. Bangladesh's workers remitted $1.4 billion in each of the last few years.[31]

Conclusion

Globalization is not only about the hypermobility of capital and the ascendance of information economies. It is also about specific types of places and work processes. In order to understand how economic globalization relates to the extraction of services from the Third World to fulfill what was once the First World woman's domestic role, we must look at globalization in a way that emphasizes some of these concrete conditions.

The growing immiserization of governments and economies in the global south is one such condition, insofar as it enables and even promotes the migration and trafficking of women as a strategy for survival. The same infrastructure designed to facilitate cross-border flows of capital, information, and trade also makes possible a range of unintended cross-border flows, as growing numbers of traffickers, smugglers, and even governments now make money off the backs of women.

Through their work and remittances, women infuse cash into the economies of deeply indebted countries, and into the pockets of "entrepreneurs" who have seen other opportunities vanish. These survival circuits are often complex, involving multiple locations and sets of actors, which altogether constitute increasingly global chains of traders and "workers."

But globalization has also produced new labor demand dynamics that center on the global cities of the north. From these places, global economic processes are managed and coordinated by increasing numbers of highly paid professionals. Both the firms and the lifestyles of these professionals are maintained by low-paid service workers, who are in growing demand. Large numbers of low-wage women and immigrants thus find themselves incorporated into strategic economic sectors in global cities. This incorporation happens directly, as in the case of low-wage clerical and blue collar workers, such as janitors and repair workers. And it happens indirectly, through the consumption practices of high-income professionals, which generate a demand for maids and nannies as well as low-wage workers in expensive restaurants and shops. Low-wage workers are then incorporated into the leading sectors, but under conditions that render them invisible.

Both in global cities and in survival circuits, women emerge as crucial economic actors. It is partly through them that key components of new economies have been built. Globalization allows links to be forged between countries that send migrants and countries that receive them; it also enables local and regional practices to go global. The dynamics that come together in the global city produce a strong demand for migrant workers, while the dynamics that mobilize women into survival circuits produce an expanding supply of workers who can be pushed or sold into those types of jobs. The technical infrastructure and transnationalism that underlie the key globalized industries also allow other types of activities, including money-laundering and trafficking, to assume a global scale.

Notes

1. By emphasizing that global processes are at least partly embedded in national territories, such a focus introduces new variables into current conceptions of economic globalization and the shrinking regulatory role of the state. That is to say, new transnational economic processes do not necessarily occur within the global/national spatial duality that many analysts of the global economy presuppose. That duality suggests two mutually exclusive spaces, one beginning where the other ends. National states play a role in the implementation of global economic systems, and this role can assume different forms, depending on the level of development, political culture, and mode of articulation with global processes. By reintroducing the state into our analysis of globalization, we open the way toward examining how this transformed state articulates the gender question. One way in which states have been reconfigured is through the political ascendance of ministries of finance and the decline of departments dealing with social concerns, including housing, health, and welfare.

2. Indeed, women in many of these settings are seen, rightly or wrongly, as better cultural brokers, and these skills matter to global firms. In the financial-services industry, women are considered crucial to interfacing with consumers, because they are believed to inspire more trust and thereby to make it easier for individual investors to put their money in what are often known to be highly speculative endeavors. See Melissa Fisher, "Wall Street Women's 'Herstories' in Late Financial Corporate Capitalism," in *Constructing Corporate America: History, Politics, Culture*, ed. Kenneth Lipartito and David B. Sicilia (New York: Oxford University Press, 2002).

3. I have developed this at length in *Globalization and Its Discontents*.

4. Pierrette Hondagneu-Sotelo, *Gendered Transitions: Mexican Experiences of Immigration* (Berkeley: University of California Press, 1994); Sarah Mahler, *American Dreaming: Immigrant Life on the Margins* (Princeton, N. J.: Princeton University Press, 1995).

5. Frank Munger, ed., *Laboring Under the Line* (New York: Russell Sage Foundation, 2002); Laurance Roulleau-Berger, ed., *Youth and Work in the Postindustrial City of North America and Europe* (Leiden and New York: Brill, 2002); Hector R. Cordero-Guzman,

Robert C. Smith, and Ramon Grosfoguel, eds., *Migration, Transnationalization, and Race in a Changing New York* (Philadelphia: Temple University Press, 2001); see generally for data and sources, Saskia Sassen, *The Global City* (Princeton, N.J.: Princeton University Press, 2001), chapters 8 and 9.

6. At issue here is a type of manufacturing that requires an urban location because it is geared toward urban markets and belongs to a fairly developed network of contractors and subcontractors. We have called this type of manufacturing "urban manufacturing" to distinguish it from sectors that respond to very different constraints and advantages. It generally consists of design-linked manufacturing done on contract: jewelry making, woodwork and metalwork for architecture and real estate firms, the production of fashion, furniture, lamps, and so on. Many components of urban manufacturing are not downgraded, or at least not yet. One major policy implication is that city governments should support this type of manufacturing and cease to subsidize the kind that will leave the city sooner or later anyhow (see Matthew T. Mitchell, "Urban Manufacturing in New York City" [Master's thesis, Department of Urban Planning, Columbia University, 1996]). Women, especially immigrant women, are the key labor force in urban manufacturing.

7. For evidence and multiple sources, see Sassen, 2001, chapters 8 and 9.

8. The consumption needs of the growing low-income population in large cities are also increasingly often met through labor-intensive, rather than standardized and unionized, forms of producing goods and services: manufacturing and retail establishments that are small, rely on family labor, and often fall below minimum safety and health standards. Cheap, locally produced sweatshop garments and bedding, for example, can compete with low-cost Asian imports. A growing range of products and services, from low-cost furniture made in basements to "gypsy cabs" and family day care, are available to meet the demands of the growing low-income population in these cities. Inequality reshapes the consumption structure of cities in innumerable ways, and this in turn has feedback effects on the organization of work, in both the formal and the informal economy.

9. Very prominent in this market are the International Nanny and Au Pair Agency, headquartered in Britain;

Nannies Incorporated, based in London and Paris; and the International Au Pair Association (IAPA) based in Canada.

10. I have argued this for the case of international labor migrations (e.g., Saskia Sassen, *Guests and Aliens* [New York: The New Press, 1999]). See also Max Castro, ed., *Free Markets, Open Societies, Closed Borders?* (Berkeley: University of California Press, 2000); and Frank Bonilla, Edwin Melendez, Rebecca Morales, and Maria de los Angeles Torres, eds., *Borderless Borders* (Philadelphia: Temple University Press, 1998).

11. Once there is an institutional infrastructure for globalization, processes that have previously operated at the national level can scale up to the global level, even when they do not need to. This phenomenon contrasts with processes that are by their very nature global, such as the network of financial centers underlying the formation of a global capital market.

12. An older literature on women and debt links the implementation of a first generation of structural adjustment programs to the growth of government debt in the 1980s; this literature documents the disproportionate burden these programs put on women. It is a large literature in many different languages, and including a vast number of limited-circulation items produced by various activist and support organizations. For overviews, see Kathryn Ward, *Women Workers and Global Restructuring* (Ithaca, N.Y.: School of Industrial and Labor Relations Press, 1990); Kathryn Ward and Jean Pyle, "Gender, Industrialization and Development," in *Women in the Latin American Development Process: From Structural Subordination to Empowerment*, ed. Christine E. Bose and Edna Acosta-Belen (Philadelphia: Temple University Press, 1995), pp. 37–64; Christine E. Bose and Edna Acosta-Belen, eds., *Women in the Latin American Development Process* (Philadelphia: Temple University Press, 1995); Lourdes Beneria and Shelley Feldman, eds., *Unequal Burden: Economic Crises, Persistent Poverty, and Women's Work* (Boulder, Colo.: Westview Press, 1992); York Bradshaw, Rita Noonan, Laura Gash, and Claudia Buchmann, "Borrowing Against the Future: Children and Third World Indebtness," *Social Forces*, vol. 71, no. 3 (1993), pp. 629–656; Irene Tinker, ed., *Persistent Inequalities: Women and World Development* (New York: Oxford University Press, 1990); and Carolyn Moser, "The Impact of Recession and Structural Adjustment Policies at the Micro-Level: Low-Income Women and Their Households in Guayaquil, Ecuador," *Invisible*

Adjustment, UNICEF, vol. 2 (1989). Now there is also a new literature on structural adjustment's second generation. These studies are more directly linked to globalization; I will cite them later in this article.

13. In many of these countries, a large number of firms in traditional sectors oriented to the local or national market have closed, and export-oriented cash crops have increasingly often replaced survival agriculture and food production for local or national markets.

14. See Michel Chossudovsky, *The Globalisation of Poverty* (London: Zed/TWN, 1997); Guy Standing, "Global Feminization Through Flexible Labor: A Theme Revisited," *World Development*, vol. 27, no. 3 (1999), pp. 583–602; Aminur Rahman, "Micro-credit Initiatives for Equitable and Sustainable Development: Who Pays?" *World Development*, vol. 27, no. 1 (1999), pp. 67–82; Diane Elson, *Male Bias in Development*, 2nd ed. (Manchester, 1995). For an excellent overview of the literature on the impact of the debt on women, see Kathryn Ward, "Women and the Debt," paper presented at the Colloquium on Globalization and the Debt, Emory University, Atlanta (1999). On file with author at kbward@siu.edu.

15. On these various issues, see Diana Alarcon-Gonzalez and Terry McKinley, "The Adverse Effects of Structural Adjustment on Working Women in Mexico," *Latin American Perspectives*, vol. 26, no. 3 (1999), 103–17; Claudia Buchmann, "The Debt Crisis, Structural Adjustment and Women's Education," *International Journal of Comparative Studies*, vol. 37, nos. 1–2 (1996), pp. 5–30; Helen I. Safa, *The Myth of the Male Breadwinner: Women and Industrialization in the Caribbean* (Boulder, Colo.: Westview Press, 1995); Nilufer Cagatay and Sule Ozler, "Feminization of the Labor Force: The Effects of Long-term Development and Structural Adjustment," *World Development*, vol. 23, no. 11 (1995), pp. 1883–94; Erika Jones, "The Gendered Toll of Global Debt Crisis," *Sojourner*, vol. 25, no. 3, pp. 20–38; and several of the references cited in the preceding footnotes.

16. Eric Toussaint, "Poor Countries Pay More Under Debt Reduction Scheme?" (July 1999), www.twnside. org.sg/souths/twn/title/1921-cn.htm. According to Susan George, the south has paid back the equivalent of six Marshall Plans to the north (Asoka Bandarage, *Women, Population, and Crisis* [London: Zed, 1997]).

17. The IMF asks HIPCs to pay 20 to 25 percent of their export earnings toward debt service. In contrast,

in 1953 the Allies canceled 80 percent of Germany's war debt and only insisted on 3 to 5 percent of export-earnings debt service. These general terms were also evident as Central Europe emerged from communism. For one of the best critical examinations of globalization, see Richard C. Longworth, *Global Squeeze: The Coming Crisis for First World Nations* (Chicago: Contemporary Books, 1998).

18. See Janie Chuang, "Redirecting the Debate over Trafficking in Women: Definitions, Paradigms, and Contexts," *Harvard Human Rights Journal*, vol. 10 (winter 1998). Trafficking has become sufficiently recognized as an issue that it was addressed in the G8 meeting in Birmingham in May 1998, a first for the G8 (*Trafficking in Migrants*, International Office of Migration quarterly bulletin, Geneva: IOM, 1998). The heads of the eight major industrialized countries stressed the importance of cooperating against international organized crime and people trafficking. President Clinton issued a set of directives to his administration in order to strengthen efforts against trafficking in women and girls. This in turn generated a legislative initiative by Senator Paul Wellstone, which led to a Senate bill in 1999. (For a good critical analysis, see Dayan, "Policy Initiatives in the U.S. against the Illegal Trafficking of Women for the Sex Industry," Department of Sociology, University of Chicago, 1999, on file with the author).

19. The Coalition Against Trafficking in Women has centers and representatives in Australia, Bangladesh, Europe, Latin America, North America, Africa, and Asia Pacific. The Women's Rights Advocacy Program has established the Initiative Against Trafficking in Persons to combat the global trade in persons. Other organizations are referred to throughout this article.

20. See, generally, the Foundation Against Trafficking in Women (STV) and the Global Alliance Against Traffic in Women (GAATW). For regularly updated sources of information on trafficking, see http://www.hrlawgroup.org/site/programs/traffic.html. See also Sietske Altink, *Stolen Lives: Trading Women into Sex and Slavery* (New York: Harrington Park Press, 1995); Kamala Kempadoo and Jo Doezema, *Global Sex Workers: Rights, Resistance, and Redefinition* (London: Routledge, 1998); Susan Shannon, "The Global Sex Trade: Humans as the Ultimate Commodity," *Crime and Justice International* (May 1999), pp. 5–25; Lap-Chew Lin and Wijers Marjan, *Trafficking in Women, Forced Labour and Slavery-like Practices in Mar-*

riage, Domestic Labour and Prostitution (Utrecht: Foundation Against Trafficking in Women [STV], and Bangkok: Global Alliance Against Traffic in Women [GAATW], 1997); Lin Lim, *The Sex Sector: The Economic and Social Bases of Prostitution in Southeast Asia* (Geneva: International Labor Office, 1998).

21. For more detailed information, see the STV-GAATW reports; IOM 1996; CIA, "International Trafficking in Women to the United States: A Contemporary Manifestation of Salvery and Organized Crime," prepared by Amy O'Neill Richard (Washington, D.C.: Center for the Study of Intelligence, 2000). www.cia.gov/csi/monograph/women/trafficking.pdf

22. There is also a growing trade in children for the sex industry. This has long been the case in Thailand, but it is now present in several other Asian countries, eastern Europe, and Latin America.

23. There are various reports on trafficking routes. Malay brokers sell Malay women into prostitution in Australia. Women from Albania and Kosovo have been trafficked by gangs into prostitution in London. Teens from Paris and other European cities have been sold to Arab and African customers; see Susan Shannon, "The Global Sex Trade: Humans as the Ultimate Commodity," *Crime and Justice International* (May 1999), pp. 5–25. In the United States, the police broke up an international Asian ring that imported women from China, Thailand, Korea, Malaysia, and Vietnam; see William Booth, "Thirteen Charged in Gang Importing Prostitutes," *Washington Post*, August 21, 1999. The women were charged between $30,000 and $40,000 in contracts to be paid through their work in the sex trade or the garment industry. The women in the sex trade were shuttled around several states in the United States in order to bring continuing variety to the clients.

24. See Global Survival Network, "Crime and Servitude: An Expose of the Traffic in Women for Prostitution from the Newly Independent States," at www.globalsurvival.net/femaletrade.html, November 1997.

25. A fact sheet by the Coalition to Abolish Slavery and Trafficking reports that one survey of Asian sex workers found that rape often preceded their being sold into prostitution and that about one-third had been falsely led into prostitution.

26. Nancy A. Wonders and Raymond Michalowski, "Bodies, Borders, and Sex Tourism in a Globalized

World: A Tale of Two Cities—Amsterdam and Havana," *Social Problems*, vol. 48, no. 4 (2001), pp. 545–71. See also Dennis Judd and Susan Fainstein, *The Tourist City* (New Haven: Yale University Press, 1999).

27. About 80 percent of the nurses imported under the new act were from the Philippines. See generally, Satomi Yamamoto, "The Incorporation of Women Workers into a Global City: A Case Study of Filipina Nurses in the Metropolitan New York Area," (2000). On file with the author at syamamot@uiuc.edu.

28. Japan passed a new immigration law—strictly speaking, an amendment of an older law—that radically redrew the conditions for entry of foreign workers. It allowed professionals linked to the new service economy—specialists in Western-style finance, accounting, law, et cetera—but made the entry of what is termed "simple labor" illegal. The latter provision generated a rapid increase in the entry of undocumented workers for low-wage jobs. But the new law did make special provisions for the entry of "entertainers."

29. Brenda Yeoh, Shirlena Huang, and Joaquin Gonzalez III, "Migrant Female Domestic Workers: Debating the Economic, Social and Political Impacts in Singapore," *International Migration Review*, vol. 33, no. 1 (1999), pp. 114–136; Christine Chin, "Walls of Silence and Late 20th-Century Representations of Foreign Female Domestic Workers: The Case of Filipina and Indonesian Houseservants in Malaysia," *International Migration Review*, vol. 31, no. 1 (1997), pp. 353–85; Noeleen Heyzer, *The Trade in Domestic Workers* (London: Zed Books, 1994).

30. These women are recruited and transported both through formal legal channels and through informal or illegal ones. Either way, they have little power to resist. Even as they are paid below minimum wage, they produce significant profits for their brokers and employers. There has been an enormous increase in so-called entertainment businesses in Japan.

31. Natacha David, "Migrants Made the Scapegoats of the Crisis," *ICFTU Online* (International Confederation of Free Trade Unions, 1999). www.hartford-hwp.com/archives/50/012.html

Helen Zia

Made in the U.S.A.

This is not the usual shopping tour of fashionable San Francisco. The small band of women dodge cable cars in the city's tiny Union Square district, home to chic designer boutiques. They proceed along the bustling sidewalks with their hand-held bullhorn, exhorting shoppers to boycott the high-end, high-frill dresses made by Jessica McClintock, a designer who, until recently, maintained her flagship store in the area.

"Jessica McClintock says 'Let them eat lace,'" proclaim their flyers, which move like hot sale items. Near Macy's, a crowd of high school students gathers around. "I just bought one of her dresses," laments a teenager. "You'll just have to return it," says her friend.

The demonstrators are activists from Asian Immigrant Women's Advocates (AIWA). McClintock first came to AIWA's attention when a manufacturer of her clothing closed shop, owing more than $15,000 in back wages to 12 seamstresses. The workers turned to AIWA, which came up with something unusual in the garment industry: a highly visible consumer campaign directed not at the contracted manufacturer, but at a company that had hired it to make the clothes. Of all the companies AIWA looked into, Jessica McClintock had the best-known label.

As a point of fact, McClintock had paid for the dresses and had no legal responsibility for a contractor's failing—a point that AIWA readily concedes. But in an industry rife with labor abuses, AIWA reasoned, the responsibility for violations against garment workers goes beyond that of the direct employer. "Jessica McClintock is one of many clothing manufacturers who abdicate responsibility for their workers' health, safety, and just compensation," says Young Shin, executive director of AIWA. "Their sweat and blood made her $145 million in gross sales. She must be accountable to the women who make her clothes."

It's hard to imagine that a parent wants the cute outfits she buys for her child to be made by exhausted women with children of their own whom they rarely see because they're putting in 16-hour days. Despite a campaign to "Buy American," most consumers don't realize that much of the clothing bearing the proud label "Made in the U.S.A." has been produced by women who work for pennies a garment in conditions that rival turn-of-the-century sweatshops. The U.S. General Accounting Office (GAO) defines a sweatshop as a business that regularly violates wage, child labor, health and/or safety laws. The clothing brands found in sweatshops include some of the United States' best known labels: Esprit, The Gap, The Limited, Liz Claiborne, Patagonia, and Ralph Lauren.

The garment industry is like a pyramid, with retailers—department stores like Bloomingdale's, Macy's, Sears, and others—at the top. They buy their fashions from companies like Liz Claiborne and Guess?, who are known as manufacturers although they rarely make their own clothes. The majority farm out their work to thousands of factory owners—the contractors whose factories are

Source: "Made in the U.S.A.," by Helen Zia. Reprinted by permission of *Ms.* Magazine, © 1996. This article also appeared in Bill Bigelow and Bob Peterson, eds., *Rethinking Globalization: Teaching for Justice in an Unjust World.* Rethinking Schools Press. Milwaukee: 2002.

often sweatshops. Contractors are the small fry in the pyramid: They are often former garment workers themselves, who can't afford to spend much on equipment or rent, taking in a small profit per garment.

At the bottom of the pyramid is the worker, generally a woman (and sometimes her child) who is paid 50¢ or $1 for a dress that costs $120 at retail. As a general rule, prices within the pyramid follow a doubling effect at each tier. The contractors double their labor costs and overhead when quoting a price to the garment companies, which, in turn, calculate their overhead and double that to arrive at a price to charge the retailer. The retailer then doubles this price, and sometimes adds still more, to assure a profit even after two or three markdowns.

According to a 1994 GAO report, the number of U.S. sweatshops is increasing. Los Angeles and New York City are the largest apparel centers and home to the most sweatshops. San Francisco, Miami, New Jersey, and Texas are not far behind. Most sweatshops are hidden away where inspectors never find them, but about 22,000 contract shops around the country do business openly, sewing clothing for approximately 1,000 manufacturers. Even among these seemingly legal shops, many operate in near-sweatshop conditions.

Working in these contract shops are some 800,000 employees; about 650,000 are women. Latina and Asian immigrants, both documented and undocumented, are thought to be the most heavily represented in the shops.

The Sweatshop

The sweatshop is just off one of the busiest streets in New York City's borough of Queens, near Shea Stadium and the tennis courts of the U.S. Open. To enter, you walk up a trash-strewn parking lot into a gray building, up two flights of cement stairs, down a cold, dimly lit hall to a double set of heavy steel doors and chain-link gates.

Beyond piles of pastel clothes in various stages of completion are two long rows of women, each hunched over a droning sewing machine. They have the dazed look of people who have been performing the same task far too long. It's Saturday night, and most of them have been working since morning.

Rising above the piles of clothes are tangled wires that power the sewing machines and steam presses. A single spark could turn the whole place, crammed with flammable fabric and lint, into a blazing inferno. No one seems concerned; in one section of the crowded room a few workers sit under the "No Smoking" sign, cutting loose threads and puffing away on cigarettes. The only open window in the hot, stuffy room is by the huge steam press that fuses interfacings to fabric.

From out of the stacks of clothes, a smiling, gap-toothed woman appears. Bibi (these are not real names), perspiring and disheveled, steps gingerly over the ladies' blouses she has neatly folded and stuffed into plastic bags, now strewn in slippery piles on the floor. She is 56, but looks much older. Her husband, 65-year-old Kailung, works nearby, putting tags on the blouses. They greet me and introduce me to a few of the other workers, none of whom seem the least surprised to see me —an obviously Chinese woman—show up, ostensibly to help Bibi and Kailung, and perhaps fall into a job for myself. The two are among the shop's few older employees—the sewing jobs are filled by young women, some in their teens. All of them have been working 14 to 16 hours a day, seven days a week, for the last three months. They put in the time because there is no guarantee of more work once the current job is done. And because, with their limited English, they have few choices. "I'm so tired," says Bibi to no one in particular, "This job is going to kill me."

Overtime pay is unheard of. Everyone is paid a piece rate, determined by the garment and the task. A collar is worth more than a straight seam, for instance. In theory, piece rates are not meant to circumvent minimum wage and overtime laws, but to provide an incentive for more productive workers. In practice, however, low piece rates force everyone to work as hard, fast, and as long as they can to make the pennies add up. But no matter how hard they work, the pay almost never reaches minimum wage—a direct violation of federal labor laws.

For her 16 hours on this day, Bibi will take home about $50. In a good year, she may earn $13,000—about the norm among sweatshop workers. Some like Kailung, who brings home about $8,000 a year, earn much less because they can't work very fast. Good years have been few and far between for Bibi and Kailung—who often end up out of work for long stretches. Since they never know if they will have work—and money for the rent—from month to month, they live in substandard housing, putting dollars aside for the lean times. Bibi's only consolation is that she gets to keep everything she earns—no deduction for Social Security, unemployment insurance, or taxes. Bibi shrugs at the suggestion that the deductions could benefit her. "I need the money more," she says simply.

When they finally leave the factory after midnight, Bibi and Kailung are so tired that they take a bus home. More often, they walk two miles in order to save the $2.50 fare. Home is in the basement of a three-story house. The crudely furnished space has been subdivided into a maze of three bedrooms, a kitchen, and a bathroom. Each of the rooms rents for $250 a month. Bibi and Kailung's home, a 12-by-12-foot cubicle with dark wood paneling that makes it seem even smaller, is filled with broken-down furniture. The old bureau has several missing drawers; no matter, the couple use the space as shelves to store plastic bags, screwdrivers, and an ancient radio. Bibi hurriedly heats up a dinner of Chinese dumplings and soup while Kailung washes their clothes in the bathtub and hangs them by the water heater. After they gulp down their soup, the first meal they've had since lunch, they collapse on the tattered sofa bed.

At 7:30 on Sunday morning, Bibi and Kailung get ready to go back to work. Their bodies stiff with fatigue, they move slowly about the kitchen area. Kailung's face is swollen from a toothache that is so painful he can't eat. Instead, he prepares an herbal concoction in a glass jar to take to work. As Bibi packs a lunch of leftover rice, vegetables, and hard-boiled eggs, she complains about her living quarters. "This place is very dirty. My home in China was much nicer," she says. "In winter there's no heat. But it's all we can pay."

A permanent resident, Bibi emigrated from Shanghai in 1992; Kailung came in 1995. In China, Bibi would soon be retiring from her office job, while Kailung had already retired. They came to the United States in hopes of saving enough money to bring their grandchildren over. Despite their own working conditions, they believe the children will have a better life here. But if the job runs out, they'll soon be on the street. Bibi doesn't speak English well enough to find work as a cleaning woman or in a fast-food restaurant. Even with her green card, she can't quit.

By 9 a.m. they're at the shop. As the workers filter in, Bibi and Kailung sweep up piles of trash and debris from around the work stations. The floor looks as if an explosion dumped pink, yellow, green, and blue fabric everywhere. Most of the seamstresses are from a rural area of China's Guangdong province. Since Bibi and Kailung's Shanghai dialect is quite different from theirs, they can't talk with their co-workers. The shop owner, a fortyish man also from Guangdong, speaks some Mandarin, as do Bibi and Kailung. In any case, language ability is not critical to the functioning of a garment shop, where tasks can be readily taught nonverbally.

Conversation lulls as the cadence picks up. The pressers start feeding hundreds of skirts to Bibi, who dispatches them to hangers and the proper rack, sized from 8 to 14. Kailung is supposed to be hanging skirts too, but his tooth hurts so much that he is sitting at an unoccupied sewing machine with his head down while Bibi tries—with my inexperienced help—to keep up with his work as well as hers. While the pressers steam their way through bundles of skirts, the seamstresses work on the matching jackets. Because fabrics are pliant and are stitched into curved shapes, the work must be done by hand, ensuring that the sewing process remains labor-intensive.

At the sweatshop, everyone is busy except the boss, who is eating a bowl of noodles. At 11:30, a small entourage arrives: the owner's wife, son, daughter-in-law, and infant grandson. The son, a cheerful-looking twentysomething, with gold chains on his neck and wrists, starts working a steam press. His wife sits at a sewing machine and also begins working. Holding the baby, the boss's wife strolls into a side room where the time clock sits unused, surrounded by posters on state and federal labor laws—all printed in English. She turns on a radio that's piped into the shop: music with a loud disco beat that gets the machines humming faster than ever.

As the jackets are pressed, Bibi and Kailung pair them with skirts, then button on a satiny front panel. They attach tags, then bag the complete ensemble. They'll be paid 15¢ for each outfit. In 12 hours, and with my help, they'll do 400 sets—for a total of $60 between the two of them. The pressers and the seamstresses get about 25¢ for each outfit they work on. The total labor cost for assembling the Sunday suit: under $3. Each will retail for about $60.

The aroma of rice and Chinese turnips in oyster sauce begins to waft through the shop—the boss has been cooking at a hot-plate in the back. At noon he clears off one of the worktables. "Eat, eat!" he says. The workers walk over, then return quickly to their workstations to eat in silence. "The boss is cooking lunch for us because it's a Sunday," says Bibi. Nevertheless, it's not a regular Sunday event. Within 15 minutes everyone is finished eating, except the boss and his family, who hover like hosts proud to have treated their guests to a fine meal.

The temperature in the shop is rising as the afternoon sun hits the windows. Bibi takes advantage of a break in the pressers' work to rush to the bathroom. First she reaches into the cardboard box near her work area, where she hides her lunch and the house slippers she wears at work. She pulls out a roll of toilet paper. "You have to bring your own," she whispers. We go through the steel doors that are the shop's sole entrance and exit, back into the dark hallway strewn with refuse. To get to the women's room, we walk down several corridors, past other garment shops. "That one is owned by Americans," she says, meaning Caucasians. "Americans work for them," by which she means non-Asians. All the factories in the building share the women's room. The doors on the two grimy wooden stalls don't shut. There is neither toilet paper nor paper towels, not even a trash can, so used paper products, including sanitary napkins, line the floor. The sinks are encrusted with food waste, dirt, and grease. Bibi just shakes her head and leaves as fast as she can.

Back in the shop, the boss's son is picking up the bagged blouses that Bibi folded yesterday, and packing them in boxes. He looks furtively at boxes near Bibi that hold neatly stacked plastic hangers. When he thinks she isn't looking, he dumps out her hangers and takes the box. Bibi starts yelling

Li Sung Feng, 70, takes part in an anti-sweatshop rally with other garment workers in New York's Chinatown in 1998.

at him. The son ignores her, until his father makes him put the hangers back.

Late in the evening, Bibi goes to an area piled high with linen vests. Each one has six tiny buttons. Her job is to button and sort them, for which she gets 3¢ per vest. The buttons are so small that it's hard to work them through the button-holes. After doing several hundred buttons, Bibi's fingers are stiff and sore. Bibi and Kailung are expected to stay until all the vests are buttoned, pressed, hung, tagged, and bagged. But Bibi is so tired she's thinking of quitting. "I don't want to die in this job," she says. Kailung, whose jaw has been aching all day, is also eager to leave. The boss talks them into staying by offering to drive them home when they're done. Reluctantly, they agree. Bibi returns to the vests that bear two labels—one, the name of a popular mall retailer; the other, "Made in the U.S.A."

Who Has the Power?

Growing consumer concern over the social cost of clothing has spurred a number of recent developments. A women's group called Common Threads, based in Los Angeles, is linking middle-class and working-class women through consumer campaigns to support workplace organizing. "Two-thirds of the clothing purchases are made by women, who are manipulated a million ways as fashion consumers," says sociologist Edna Bonacich of University of California at Riverside, one of the organizers of Common Threads.

Another group, Sweatshop Watch, a coalition of workers' and immigrants' advocates, women's organizations, and legal and civil rights groups across California, is starting a newsletter to inform consumers about the clothes they purchase, providing "Buy" and "Don't Buy" lists. "Our approach is three-pronged," says attorney Lora Jo Foo, an organizer of Sweatshop Watch: "making manufacturers liable through legislative change and legal action, empowering workers through workplace organizing, and enlisting consumer support."

Around the country, workers' centers like Fuerza Unida, La Mujer Obrera, and AIWA joined recently in a national consortium to build a community-based workers' movement.

Consumer consciousness has caused some manufacturers and retailers to develop guidelines, which often set forth high-sounding principles that support fair wages and environmentally sound practices. Yet even these companies continue to get caught in sweatshop violations. And ethics codes rarely cover the new and creative ways that employers come up with to transfer costs to workers. Recently a California contractor was found to be charging seamstresses $126.75 plus tax, each month, for the needles and bobbins they used at work.

According to AIWA's Young Shin, "U.S. consumers have the bargaining power to tell the multinationals what their concerns are, to rid the garment industry of inhuman practices, and make it a humane place to work."

Bharati Sadasivam

The Impact of Structural Adjustment on Women: A Governance and Human Rights Agenda

Introduction

It is now well-established that structural adjustment and stabilization policies (SAPs) undertaken in developing countries to receive condition-based loans from the World Bank and the International Monetary Fund (IMF) have exacerbated conditions of poverty and deprivation for large sections of the population.[1] Several commentators have also shown that these macroeconomic policies are not class-neutral or gender-neutral. The World Bank's emphasis on "safety nets" to cushion the poor from the impact of orthodox stabilization and adjustment policies is an admission that these policies do not affect all sections of the population equally.

The human and social costs of adjustment have evoked growing concern and unease at the United Nations, among governments, and among some donors. These concerns arise out of the institutionalization of the market model of economic growth that has made such growth synonymous with the dominant view of "development," although it does not favor equity, sustainability, or redistribution of wealth and resources.[2] Recent UN conferences, most notably the World Summit for Social Development in Copenhagen in March 1995 and the Fourth World Conference on Women in Beijing in Sep-

tember 1995, have highlighted the ways in which such economic policies have focused on debt repayment by developing countries at the cost of human development.[3] Specialized UN agencies, such as the United Nations Children's Fund (UNICEF), the United Nations Development Programme (UNDP), and the United Nations Development Fund for Women (UNIFEM), have also pointed to the growing human and economic inequalities caused by market driven growth and stressed the need to protect the vulnerable, women in particular, from marginalization.[4]

These criticisms and the deterioration in economic and social conditions in the majority of adjusting countries during the "lost decade" of the 1980s have occasioned much introspection at the international financial institutions. In fact, recent World Bank evaluations of the results of SAPs acknowledge that while macroeconomic stabilization policies are necessary for growth, they are not sufficient in reducing poverty or income inequality in all countries.[5]

In recent years, gender analysis and feminist economics have provided a conceptual framework for understanding the differential impact of macroeconomic policies such as structural adjustment on men and women. There is now a vast and growing volume of literature that not only shows how the gender bias in neoclassical economic theory renders the effects of SAPs on women invisible in any standard measures of policy evaluation, but that also provides empirical evidence of the heavy transitional costs of adjustment on women.[6]

Source: Sadasivam, Bharati. The Impact of Structural Adjustment on Women: A Governance and Human Rights Agenda. *Human Rights Quarterly* 19:3 (1997), 630–665.

In fact, recent poverty assessments by the World Bank show that women respond differently to the opportunities afforded by economic growth due to constraints on the access to productive resources such as land and credit.[7] Some of these findings demonstrate that extreme poverty affects women differently and often more severely than men. While the gender impact of SAPs is not uniformly negative throughout the reform process and across countries and economies, it is clear that it is women who, as workers, producers, consumers, wives, and mothers, are the shock absorbers of adjustment efforts at immense cost to their well-being.[8] There is now growing awareness of these effects of adjustment within the Bank.

These findings, along with the emphasis on sustainability and equity in recent UN conferences, have led the World Bank to recognize the relevance of gender issues to poverty alleviation and economic growth. The Bank approved an operational policy on gender in 1994.[9] It also set up an external gender consultative group (EGCG) composed of fourteen members who are selected for their wide-ranging policy and research experience in gender issues and familiarity with international development.[10] Taken together, these initiatives provide a promising basis for an assessment of the gender impact of adjustment policies from the economic and human development perspectives. They also lay the groundwork for closer and concerted interaction between those who design and execute SAPs and the advocates for human development. . . .

Feminist Critiques of SAPs

Direct and Indirect Effects of SAPs on Women

It is widely documented that adjustment policies such as currency devaluation, price deregulation, privatization, export-led growth strategies, and the removal of subsidies on food and health services leave large sections of the poor in adjusting countries poorer in the short run.[11] It follows that

women, who form the great majority of the world's one billion absolute poor,[12] are overwhelmingly affected by these policies. Some features of orthodox reform packages, such as the shrinking of public enterprises, state sectors, and traditional industries that employ large numbers of women, affect women wage earners directly. Other aspects, like cutbacks in public health care, food subsidies, and social security programs, affect women indirectly.[13] Given their inferior standing in the home and family in many societies, women have even less access to these services when they are reduced.

The distress signals resulting from the "invisible" impact of adjustment policies can be acute, especially in the area of health and reproduction. SAPs worsen the conditions in which women have to perform their family and community tasks. In many countries, they have led to a crisis in human reproduction, made worse by shrinking public health sector spending. In Tanzania, for example, seventy-one mothers died in the first thirteen weeks of 1988, when economic reforms were in force—four times the maternal death rate of previous years.[14] The deaths were attributed to poor hospital conditions as well as a shortage of blood, drugs, and transport facilities; more tellingly, they were an indication of the deteriorating physical conditions in which women carried out their reproductive roles.[15] These indirect effects of SAPs pose the greater challenge because they are not easily measured and cannot be analyzed in purely economic terms and are therefore harder to resolve politically. . . .

Conclusions

The experiences of women as producers and reproducers, workers in industry and agriculture, wives, consumers, mothers, and crisis managers during adjustment programs show the unequal distribution of costs and benefits of SAPs. The gender-blind nature of neoclassical economic theory and gender biases inherent in societies and cultures have served to obscure the increased burdens imposed on women, which manifest themselves as deteriorating health and well-being in adjusting economies.

The differential impact of structural adjustment on women has just started to come to the attention of those who design and implement economic reform programs. This awareness is due in large part to the sustained work of feminist economists at both theoretical and empirical levels over the last two decades. Together with the focus on issues of gender and development in the international women's movement since the 1980s, this has led to a greater visibility accorded to these subjects in international forums, especially at the United Nations.

As a result, references to gender bias, gender neutrality, and gender responsiveness are now commonplace in Bank parlance and government statements on structural adjustment. However, there is still a tendency to conflate "gender" with "women," to view gender analysis as the categorizing of society into men and women. This limited understanding, combined with the pervasive faith in market driven growth as a solution to all inequities, has led to a set of add-on responses such as safety nets and poverty alleviation schemes.

While such measures are clearly necessary to offset the devastating impact of SAPs on the poor and women in the short term, they do not go to the root of the problem. The goal of gender advocacy is therefore to transform economic policymaking so that the human rights dimensions of SAPs are considered at the design stage of the programs and not as a postscript. Insofar as economic reform policies change the rights of women, the international financial institutions and governments are accountable to the human rights standards enshrined in various international and domestic covenants. As feminist economists and rights advocates have shown, SAPs do this by transferring burdens from the paid economy to the unpaid economy, exacerbating existing gender inequities in the household and the workplace, and worsening conditions of poverty and deprivation for women.

Gender advocacy in structural adjustment emphasizes that both human rights and sustainability are at stake in the economic reform process, which must aim not only at economic efficiency but economic justice. The overall negative social impact of adjustment in most countries is proof that policies that work to disenfranchise and marginalize one half of humanity cannot be sustainable in the long run. Having laid the ground for such debate, women's advocates must now build on the recent willingness shown by international financial institutions and some governments to address the gender dimensions of structural adjustment through greater involvement of women's representatives and other concerned sections of civil society. The emerging governance and human rights approaches at the lending institutions present real opportunities for policy reform and democratization of development through the principles of transparency, accountability, and participation. Today, there is a rhetorical consensus in all of these institutions about the need for equitable and gender-aware policies. The challenge lies in putting these principles into practice in order to realize the possibility of shared economic development for all.

In the final analysis, it is women's collective strength and creativity that remains the basis for transformative politics and development. Despite the severe setbacks and crises of the 1980s, women the world over have demonstrated their resilience and resourcefulness through a myriad of networks of grassroots movements as well as formal and informal lobbies. The emergence of this global coalition of women's NGOs who have created a significant political space and voice for themselves has been a positive outcome of the Women's Decade. Together and individually, these groups constitute a vibrant force that has grown in strength and sophistication during the 1990s. Through sustained feminist scholarship and unflagging activism, women's advocates have gained the authority and credibility to influence UN documents, and thereby some national governments and international financial institutions, to reflect gender and poverty concerns in economic policymaking. For the choice can no longer be between the state and the market: women have to organize to transform both patriarchal entities to be responsive to their needs.

Notes

1. In this paper, the term structural adjustment refers to the economic reform policies promoted by the Bretton Woods and other financial institutions in developing countries since the 1980s. In exchange for structural adjustment loans (SALs), recipient countries are expected to restructure their economies, chiefly by dismantling protectionist structures such as tariffs, controls, and subsidies for local capitalism. The basic assumption of this reorientation is that an economy's health, efficiency, and productivity will improve if market forces are allowed to operate, without outcomes being influenced by government policies of protection, subsidization, and regulation. *See generally* Walden Bello, *Dark Victory: The United States, Structural Adjustment and Global Poverty* (1994); *Fifty Years Is Enough: The Case Against the World Bank and the International Monetary Fund* (Kevin Danaher ed., 1994); Cheryl Payer, *The World Bank: A Critical Analysis* (1982); Cheryl Payer, *The Debt Trap: The IMF and the Third World* (1974).

2. *See* George Martine & Marcela Villareal, *Gender, Population and Sustainability: Critical Problems and Unresolved Issues*, consultants' paper submitted to the United Nations Expert Group Meeting on Women, Population and Sustainable Development: The Road from Rio, Cairo and Beijing, Santo Domingo, 18–22 Nov. 1996 (copy on file with author).

3. Chapter 2.27a of the Copenhagen Declaration and Programme of Action of the World Summit for Social Development urges governments to combat poverty by:

Analysing policies and programmes, including those relating to macroeconomic stability, structural adjustment programmes . . . markets and all relevant sectors of the economy, with respect to their impact on poverty and inequality, assessing their impact on family well-being and conditions, as well as their gender implications, and adjusting them, as appropriate, to promote a

more equitable distribution of productive assets, wealth, opportunities, income and services.

United Nations, The Copenhagen Declaration and Programme of Action: World Summit for Social Development 57, 61, U.N. Doc. A/Conf. 166/9 (1995). Paragraph 20 of the Beijing Declaration and Platform for Action of the Fourth World Conference on Women states:

Macro and micro-economic policies and programmes, including structural adjustment, have not always been designed to take account of their impact on women and girl children, especially those living in poverty. Poverty has increased in both absolute and relative terms, and the number of women living in poverty has increased in most regions.

Beijing Declaration and Platform for Action, *adopted by* the Fourth World Conference on Women, U.N. Doc. A/Conf.177/20 (1995) [hereinafter Beijing Platform for Action].

4. An early and exhaustive critique of structural adjustment came from UNICEF's *Adjustment with a Human Face*, which called for a more "people-sensitive approach to adjustment." Giovanni Andrea Cornia et al., *Introduction*, in *Adjustment with a Human Face* 1, 3 (Giovanni Andrea Cornia et al., eds., 1987). In a follow-up assessment, *Development with a Human Face* (Santosh Mehrotra & Richard Jolly eds., forthcoming) (manuscript on file with the author), UNICEF documents the advances in human development that have occurred in ten developing countries since the latter half of the 1980s due to *inter alia* "greater attention given by the Bretton Woods institutions to education, health and human concerns, active engagement of NGOs and donors in this field and crucial low-cost, high-impact interventions." *Id.* The UNDP's Human Development Reports were conceived to highlight the need for indicators other than economic growth to measure human welfare. For example, the 1996 report characterizes the current model of market-driven growth as "jobless, ruthless, voiceless, rootless and futureless" and one that does not favor equity or redistribution, both between and within countries. UNDP, *Human Development Report 2–4* (1996). It shows that the globalized market economy has, over the last fifteen years, deepened the economic polarization between developed and developing nations. *Id.* at 2. Only fifteen countries registered

improved growth and income during this period, while nearly 100 have shown negative rates of economic growth and per capita income. *Id.* at 1. In seventy of these countries, average income was lower than it had been in 1980 and in forty-three countries, lower than in 1970. *Id.* The difference in income between the developing and industrialized world tripled from $5,700 in 1970 to $15,400 in 1993. *Id.* at 2. The United Nations Development Fund for Women, in preparation for the Beijing Women's Conference, stressed the need for a forceful call to action by the world's governments and international institutions to address gender inequity and women's advancement. *See* Noeleen Heyzer, *A Women's Development Agenda for the 21st Century, in A Commitment to the World's Women: Perspectives on Development for Beijing and Beyond* 1, 1 (Noeleen Heyzer ed., with Sushma Kapoor & Joanne Sandler, 1995).

5. *See Social Dimensions of Adjustment: World Bank Experience, 1980–93* at 2, 54 (A World Bank Operations Evaluation Study, 1996) [hereinafter *Social Dimensions*]. The study tracks poverty and income distribution in fifty-three adjusting countries during the period 1980–1993. *Id.* at xi. Only 60 percent of the adjusting countries that adopted the right policies and reduced poverty also reduced inequality. *Id.* at 1. The Bank, however, refutes charges that the 1980s were a decade of deteriorating human welfare, pointing out that poverty declined in twenty-three out of thirty-three countries and increased in ten. *Id.* at 54.

6. *See generally The IMF, the World Bank and the African Debt, Volume 2: The Social and Political Impact* (Bade Onimode ed., 1989); *Engendering Adjustment for the 1990s: Report of a Commonwealth Expert Group on Women and Structural Adjustment* (Commonwealth Secretariat, London, 1989) [hereinafter *Engendering Adjustment*]; *Women and Adjustment Policies in the Third World* (Haleh Afshar & Carolyne Dennis eds., 1992); *Unequal Burden: Economic Crises, Persistent Poverty, and Women's Work* (Lourdes Beneria & Shelley Feldman eds., 1992) [hereinafter *Unequal Burden*]; *Male Bias in the Development Process* (Diane Elson ed., 1991); *The Strategic Silence: Gender and Economic Policy* (Isabella Bakker ed., 1994) [hereinafter *The Strategic Silence*]; *Women Pay the Price: Structural Adjustment in Africa and the Caribbean* (Gloria Thomas-Emeagwali ed., 1995); *Mortgaging Women's Lives: Feminist Critiques of Structural Adjustment* (Pamela Sparr ed., 1994) [hereinafter *Mortgaging Women's Lives*].

7. *See The World Bank, Implementing the World Bank's Gender Policies, Progress Report No. 1* at 5 (Mar. 1996) [hereinafter *Bank Progress Report*]. However, the Bank maintains that very little quantitative data is currently available on differences between the impact of economic reform on men and women. In two countries where statistical data is available, Peru and the Philippines, the Bank cites studies that show that in the former, "female-headed households appear to have fared better on average than male-headed households during the economic reform of the 1990s," while in the latter, "welfare indicators for women during periods of economic reform seem to be at least as favorable as for men." *Id.*

8. In 1989, a Commonwealth Expert Group summarized the impact of adjustment on women as follows:

> Women are at the epicentre of the crisis and bear the brunt of the adjustment efforts: it is women who have been most severely affected by the deteriorating balance between incomes and prices, and who have desperately sought means for their families to survive. It is women who have had to find extra work to supplement family income; it is women who have rearranged family budgets . . . and it is women who have been most immediately affected by cuts in health and educational facilities, and by the rising morbidity and deaths among their children. Women are at the frontline of the crisis in the developing world— and it is they who have been most severely affected and have had the greatest responsibility for adjusting their lives to ensure survival.

Engendering Adjustment, supra note 7, at 31–32.

9. *See* Josette L. Murphy, *Gender Issues in World Bank Lending* 21 (A World Bank Operations Evaluation Study, 1995) [hereinafter *Gender Issues*]. Although Bank strategies to include gender issues were formulated as early as 1967, management began to take a proactive stance only in the latter half of 1986. *Id.* at 22. The visibility of gender issues during the UN Decade for Women (1975–1985) helped in part to raise their profile in the Bank. Since 1991, more than a third of all investment projects include measures dealing with gender-related issues, although these still do not include structural adjustment and debt reduction lending. *Id.* at 21.

10. Set up by the Bank in April 1996 in response to demands made by women's organizations during the

Beijing women's conference, the EGCG aims *inter alia* to provide a mechanism for implementing the Bank's gender policies, responding to the Beijing Platform for Action and providing a forum for discussing public concerns about the Bank's approaches to gender. *The World Bank, External Gender Consultative Group: A Report on the First Annual Meeting, April 29–30, 1996* at 1 (1997) [hereinafter *Bank Gender Group Report*].

11. *See, e.g.*, Madhura Swaminathan, *The Impact of Policies of Orthodox Stabilization and Structural Adjustment on Women: Some Evidence from India* (paper presented at the annual summer conference of the International Association of Feminist Economists, Tours, France, 5–7 July 1995) (on file with the author). Income, poverty, and inequality worsened in India between 1991, when structural adjustment reforms were introduced, and 1994. *Id.* The proportion of households below the official poverty line rose from 39.3 percent in 1987–1988 to 40.7 percent in 1992–1993. *Id.*

12. Beijing Platform for Action, *supra* note 4, ¶ 47.

13. See *Adjustment with a Human Face*, *supra* note 5, at 76 for a list of twenty-two adjusting countries which suffered the most severe cuts in health and education expenditure in the 1980s. Of these, Bolivia, regarded by the World Bank as a success in structural adjustment, peaked with an annual percentage cut of 77.7 percent between 1980 and 1982, followed by Guatemala (58.3 percent) between 1980 and 1984 and the Dominican Republic (46.5 percent) between 1980 and 1984. *Id.* These were also countries with high rates of decline in GDP, demonstrating the link between GDP per capita and expenditure on social sector per capita. *Id.* For the effects on child welfare of government cuts in real expenditure per capita on social services, see Giovanni Andrea Cornia, *Economic Decline and Human Welfare in the First Half of the 1980s*, in *Adjustment with a Human Face*, 11, 21–47. Expenditure on food subsidies declined in four countries studied by UNICEF: Sri Lanka, Chile, Peru, and Zimbabwe. *Id.* at 28.

14. *See* Ulla Vuorela, *The Informal Sector, Social Reproduction and the Impact of the Economic Crisis on Women, in Tanzania and the IMF: The Dynamics of Liberalization* 109 (Horace Campbell & Howard Stein eds., 1992).

15. *See id.*

Rosalind Pollack Petchesky

Reflections on Global Governance and Transnational Feminist Movements in an Era of Infinite War

> A few years ago . . . it seemed as if there was a real promise of hope for the poor—both black and white—through the Poverty Program. There were experiments, hopes, new beginnings. Then came the buildup in Vietnam and I watched the program broken and eviscerated as if it were some idle political plaything of a society gone mad on war, and I knew that America would never invest the necessary funds or energies in rehabilitation of its poor so long as adventures like Vietnam continued to draw men and skills and money like some demonic destructive suction tube. So I was increasingly compelled to see the war as an enemy of the poor and to attack it as such.
>
> Rev. Martin Luther King, Jr., 1967

> What is emerging is the need for globalization as an economic process to be subject to moral and ethical considerations and to respect international legal standards and principles.
>
> Mary Robinson, 2002

Prologue

My purpose . . . has been twofold: first, to explore the manifold ways in which reproductive and sexual rights intersect with, and are embraced within, a wide range of health, human rights, human development and social and gender justice issues; and, second, to use this inquiry to rethink the complex political dynamics in which transnational women's NGOs [non-governmental organizations] find themselves, as they manoeuvre within a globalizing yet deeply divided and grossly inequitable world. In the 1990s and early 2000s, transnational women's NGOs continued to play a central role in the creation and implementation of international norms and agreements related to reproductive and sexual rights. Feminist groups in the 1990s had a major impact at both international and national levels in shifting dominant discourses about reproduction, population and sexuality in a direction that puts the ends of women's health and empowerment above that of reducing population growth and that links sexual and reproductive rights to macroeconomic transformation and human development. This is a major historical achievement and a mark of the power of transnational women's NGOs and feminist ideas.

Yet in the new millennium an increasingly hostile economic, cultural and political climate has severely limited the translation of this discursive shift into effective policies and programmes. In the circumscribed world of UN conferences, women's groups have found themselves on the defensive even to retain the language achieved in the 1990s regarding sexual and reproductive health rights, much less to obtain the necessary accountability mechanisms and resources to make good on the promises. At the UN Special Session on Children in 2002, they managed—with extraordinary difficulty and skill—to defeat the agenda of conservative religious groups, led by the Bush administration, for "abstinence-only" sex education, reproductive health services that explicitly preclude abortion, family planning without contraceptives, and a definition of "the family" solely as marriage between a man and a woman. But the result was a mere two paragraphs on "sexual and reproductive health" that basically cross-reference the previous conference documents and give most emphasis to the important but uncontroversial goal of reducing maternal and neonatal morbidity and mortality (Girard 2002). At the Millennium Summit in 2000 and the Financing for Development Conference in 2002 women's health groups were powerless to prevent the holistic vision of Cairo and Beijing being replaced by a handful of "feasible," quantifiable, and presumably cost-effective targets. And in Johannesburg, at the World Summit on Sustainable Development in September 2002, the US-led conservative faction once again tried to subvert health as a human right by making it conditional upon "national laws and cultural and religious values" and replacing every reference to human rights in the final Declaration with the nebulous phrase "human dignity."[1]

Meanwhile, women's and all progressive social justice groups have watched the UN itself—a political arena where it seemed to matter in the 1990s that we make "women's voices" heard—become increasingly ineffectual and subservient to global corporate, military and fundamentalist forces. These forces, despite their patent moral and ethical corruption, wield institutional and material power far greater than any that feminist groups could possibly attain at this moment—especially after 11 September 2001.

Shortly after the horrific attacks on the World Trade Center and the Pentagon, George W. Bush launched a "war against terrorism" that would have no end in time or space. Deploying a classic imperialist manipulation of feminism, its rationale was not only to avenge and protect America but also to "rescue" the women of Afghanistan, if not the entire Gulf and Central Asian regions. As I was revising this manuscript for publication, the US government was spending $2 billion a month to wage its "war against terrorism"—a total of $37 billion one year after the 11 September attacks and projected to multiply by tenfold over the ensuing decade (Stevenson 2002). Its search-and-destroy missions in the mountains of Afghanistan, its relentless bombings there that killed more innocent civilians than all those lost in the World Trade Center, and its efforts to fortify "homeland security" within the US had not succeeded in capturing Osama bin Laden or destroying the Al Qaeda network or making Afghanistan and Afghan women more secure or free from warlord violence.[2] Yet the Bush administration was proposing a $48 billion increase in its military spending for 2003, the largest increase in a generation (Dao 2002). It concluded a treaty on nuclear weapons with Russia that essentially abandoned the mutual protections of the old ABM treaty and preserved thousands of nuclear missiles for imminent use (Plesch 2002; Arkin 2002). And it proclaimed a new strategic doctrine of unprecedented bellicosity that would give the Imperial United States a unilateral right of pre-emptive attack and "permanent military supremacy" over "*any* imaginable adversary at *any* point in time" (Klare 2002: 12; Sanger 2002).[3] It thus prepared the way for a preemptive invasion of Iraq—against the opposition of the United Nations and most of the world, with only a single ally-in-arms, Britain—and the perpetuation of the bloody mimetic saga of Jihad vs. Crusade.

Why was this happening? What was it all about? Some astute observers of US foreign policy surmised that the Great Game this time—the ultimate stakes over which some lives become valued much more than others—is not very different from what it was through most of the last two centuries: land, water and, above all, oil. A former member of Tony Blair's Cabinet writes in the *Guardian* that the movement of massive numbers of US troops, tanks and fighter planes back into the Gulf region under cover of ousting the evil Saddam Hussein has more to do with instability in neighbouring Saudi Arabia and the goal of seizing control over "the world's largest oil reserves" before they fall "into the hands of an anti-American, militant Islamist government" than it does with "fighting the war on terrorism." With an overwhelming military presence in the region, "no longer would the US have to depend on [and protect] a corrupt and unpopular royal family to keep it supplied with cheap oil" (Mowlam 2002). *Corporate tribalism*—the allegiance to the oil, gas and military hardware industries based in the south-western and western US states—bears certain resemblances to ethnic and warlord tribalism. The Bush government, mirroring its jihadist enemies, thrives on war, a permanent state of war. But the war it seeks is not only against terrorism but for Unocal, the Carlyle Group, Aramco, Halliburton, cheap crude, unimpeded pipelines, unlimited SUVs, and a President whose image is manly (see Petchesky 2001/2002).

Amidst this grotesque explosion of masculinist militarism, feminist visions for social and gender justice embodied in UN documents come to seem utopian and futile, and the regime of international law and the UN agencies responsible for global health and conflict resolution are consigned to irrelevance. Human rights, multilateralism and international cooperation get buried beneath the wings of the phoenix superpower that issues ultimatums in return for rubber-stamp approvals. And lesser powers (Israel, India, Russia, China, Zimbabwe) follow the lead, declaring their own "wars against terrorism" to justify repressive policies. In such a climate, ideas like "health security," "human security" and "social security" become shadowy relics in the face of the prerogatives of "national security" (or oil security); the welfare state and the democratic state become ghosts in the citadel of the total security state. Of course, the US, which can boast 40 per cent of the world's military spending, already has sufficient high-tech military power to overwhelm any and all countries (if not terrorists with box-cutters). But its unrivalled imperial might is not gaining Americans more actual security in everyday life, any more than it is Afghanis or Israelis or Europeans. The world has never been more dangerous.

Women's human rights groups have been at the forefront of efforts to seek non-violent, multilateral solutions to conflicts through international law. The new International Criminal Court's founding statute makes rape, sexual slavery, enforced pregnancy and other forms of sexual violence war crimes and crimes against humanity. Resolution 1325, adopted unanimously by the UN Security Council in October 2000, calls attention to the gender dimensions of armed conflict and ensures women's equal participation in peacekeeping and peace-building efforts (Rome Statute 1998; Hague Appeal *et al.* 2000). These are historic achievements that women's peace groups can claim: without their efforts none would have come about. But the US, having "unsigned" the ICC treaty, threatens to subvert it; and Resolution 1325 remains a noble sentiment, unenforced in Afghanistan, the Middle East or anywhere else. "National sovereignty," now enfolded within a US imperial order, is alive and well, as much a patriarchal construct as ever. The "war against terror" becomes a pretext for power that claims immunity from international accountability, democracy and human rights.

A year before the fatal 11 September, leaders of 191 nations, including the US under Bush's watch, agreed to the following targets to be reached by 2015, as part of the Millennium Development Goals (MDGs): cut in half the proportion of people living in poverty and suffering from hunger; reduce by two-thirds the under-five mortality rate; reduce by three-quarters the maternal mortality ratio; halt and begin to reverse the spread of HIV/AIDS as well as the incidence of malaria and other major diseases; cut in half the proportion of people in the world without access to sustainable drinking water (then numbering over 1 billion but expected to reach 3 billion, or 40 per cent of the world's population, by 2015).[4] How sobering that only a year and a half later—in the shadow of the "war on terrorism" and the perpetual security state—this agenda, which seemed paltry and reductive to many of us at the time, now seems a veritable utopia.

Even Americans, in the heartland of imperial power, suffer a social and health toll exacted by militarism and the boundless "war on terrorism." Ironically, the anthrax scare and the perceived threat of bioterrorism that rattled the United States in the fall and winter of 2001 exposed the gaping inadequacies in the US public health system, after 15 years of budgetary cutbacks and privatization. For a brief moment, US health advocates thought the bioterrorism threat might be a wake-up call that would result in restoring decent funding for public health in the US. Yet the $11 billion the Bush administration budgeted to defend America against bioterrorism turned out to be for expanded stockpiles of vaccines and antibiotics, construction of containment laboratories, research into new drugs and biodetectors—in other words, a new bioterrorism industry, not more public hospitals, clinics or sexual and reproductive health or primary health care services for the poor (Stolberg 2001, 2002). In fact, Bush's budget would *reduce* Medicaid payments to public hospitals in at least 31 states and clamp down on other mechanisms states have found to finance health care for the poor and disabled (Pear 2002a). It would do little or nothing to address the escalating costs of prescription drugs for the elderly—far be it from the capital of global capitalism to regulate drug prices as most European countries and Canada do. And it would do absolutely nothing for the 41.2 million men, women and children without health insurance in the country—unless they happen to be victims of a bioterrorist attack, or foetuses. The Bush administration cynically offers pre-natal care to "unborn children," not to pregnant women, under the Children's Health Insurance Program—a cheap toss to right-wing anti-abortionists in the US but degrading to low-income women (Toner 2002; Pear 2002b). Losing one's job in America means losing health insurance; being uninsured in America is a low-grade, daily kind of terror.

This grim scenario brought me to a pessimistic train of questions that recalled Martin Luther King's ominous words in the midst of the Vietnam War, over thirty-five years ago. Can war—particularly a globalized state of permanent war and ubiquitous police surveillance—ever be compatible with the goal of assuring equity and justice in access to health care and a healthy life for all? Is the "war against terrorism" ultimately a war against health and all forms of social justice—an "enemy of the poor" and especially women? Will we allow human rights and women's empowerment to get buried in the ashes of 11 September? I believe a worse danger than terrorism now is that all the resources that might have been channeled toward reducing misery; eliminating maternal mortality; treating, preventing and curing AIDS; and promoting equality will be diverted into the waging and deflecting of violence. As the US military-corporate establishment careens from Iraq towards new adventures in North Korea, Syria, the Philippines, Uzbekistan, Kyrgyzstan, Yemen and Iran; as our borders become more patrolled and fortified and Muslim, Arab and South Asian immigrants increasingly become the targets of unconstitutional detentions and racist harassment, I have to wonder whether this endless war and all its ancillary security production will sap the energies and budgets for health, education, and racial and gender justice for years to come—meanwhile inflaming the global hostility and terror it was supposed to curtail.[5]

And yet . . . never was the need greater for those "international legal standards and principles" Mary Robinson calls for, to challenge the violence of global capitalism and global militarism and subject them to an effective system of democratic and participatory governance.

* * *

At the end of this project, the state of the world leaves me teetering between pessimism of the intellect and optimism of the will. Earlier in my thinking I had reservations about the fitness of the language of empire, yet today I find myself unavoidably reverting to it all the time. The Bush government's designs on the Middle East, Central Asia and Africa, on the replacement of regimes and the redrawing of maps; its pronouncements of not only manifest destiny but also absolute, uncontestable dominion over all other countries and international organizations, have all the markings of classic imperialist behaviour (Armstrong 2002; Hardt and Negri 2000). As a citizen of this country, I will now have to work with many others to mobilize a huge mass movement at home to oppose this juggernaut that our government has become, and this will consume much of our energies and many (how many?) years, as it did in the days of Vietnam. We'll put on hold the battles for health, gender equality, racial equality and human rights.

Earlier I thought it accurate to designate only certain governments in the rest of the world as imperial lackeys and copycats, assuming that some would still exercise their veto in the Security Council and their power in other UN forums to counter US domination and hubris. Today I wonder if there will be any objectors left (besides Cuba, and perhaps Brazil under the new government of Lula) after all fall in line behind the scramble for markets and investments and the relentless march towards armaments and war in Iraq and beyond. Will this become a failed test of the UN's "relevance" as the Bush administration clearly wants? A whole world of lackeys and copycats.

Another scenario: on the last day of writing this book, there was a bomb scare in the famous Jewish delicatessen on the ground floor of the building where I live—where I have lived for the past eighteen years. As I left the building, suspended between fear and disbelief (probably it's all just a hoax), I remembered one thing I knew on 11 September a year ago: "As an American, a woman, a feminist and a Jew, I have to recognize that the bin Ladens of the world hate me and would like me dead" (Petchesky 2001/2002). But I also remembered what every moment since that day has confirmed: Bush's America not only will not but cannot "rescue" me, since its wealth and power and the hubris they generate do so much to foment the angers and hatreds that terrorists thrive upon. Why should I or any Americans have a privileged haven from the dangers and risks that menace the daily lives of so many others elsewhere?

Yet scattered among the grim and militaristic features of the post-9/11 world are also some hopeful signs, nourishing my optimism. In the wake of the corporate corruption scandals and the church paedophilia and sexual abuse scandals that crowded the headlines in 2001–2, these centres of power have lost some of their veneer of invincibility and holiness. Perhaps many more people will join the popular uprisings in Latin America, the women protesters who shut down the oil companies in Nigeria, and gay and lesbian, feminist and social justice groups everywhere in voicing their doubts about global capitalism and global fundamentalism.

In China a catastrophic HIV/AIDS epidemic has prompted a new social movement, including a petition from rural patients demanding "that the government provide free medicine, or medicine we can afford, and [that it] . . . produce copies of Western medicines as quickly as possible." Although the Chinese government jailed the principal organizer of the Chinese AIDS Action Project for nearly a month, it released him to continue his work after an international outcry and in order to pursue a desperately needed grant from the Global Fund to Fight AIDS. And, notwithstanding its eagerness to join the WTO, it promised to "manufacture a full complement of AIDS drugs if Western patent holders did not lower prices within the next few months." A not insignificant aspect of this story is that the activist in question, Dr. Wan Yanhai, has been organizing around AIDS and gay and lesbian rights since the mid-1990s and is linked through the Internet and direct connections to gay and lesbian and treatment access groups in the US and around the world (Rosenthal 2002a, 2000b, 2000c).

This recent development in China represents yet another eruption of global movements and coalitions for health as a human right, in a society that has had little affinity with human rights strategies and concepts. It is one more among many, many indicators that transnational movements for social justice, health rights and gender and sexual equality are growing stronger and more effective all the time and will be the force that democratizes global governance and transforms global capitalism through local democratic participation. Inevitably, women's movements are playing a leading role in this transformative process. As Eisenstein (2004) writes, "although global capital, as such, is no friend to women and girls, it unsettles existing gender relations in ways it cannot simply control."[6] Likewise, fundamentalisms have spawned resistance, however quiet, among women and girls in Iran, Afghanistan, India, and Israel and within the Catholic Church. And global militarism too will create its own backlash, as resentment builds against US bullying and women's and peace and human rights groups throughout the world demand that the UN uphold the principles written in its own Charter.

I see this vision of global governance through civil society representation, women's empowerment and local participatory democracy. I see it in my mind's eye, though I hear, more loudly than ever, the drums of war.

Notes

1. See United Nations, World Summit on Sustainable Development (WSSD), Plan of Implementation (September 2002), Chapter VI ("Health and Sustainable Development"), paragraph 47; and United Nations, WSSD, "The Johannesburg Declaration on Sustainable Development," A/conf.199/L.6/Rev.2 (4 September 2002). Many thanks to Joan Ross Frankson and June Zeitlin for information on the outcomes at WSSD.

2. At this writing, rival groups still contended for power in most of the country; only the capital city of Kabul was considered stable; a car bomb had killed 28 bystanders in Kandahar; an assassination attempt on the US-backed president, Hamid Karzai, had come within inches of succeeding; and the Bush administration was still hesitating to join the International Security Force set up to help stabilize the country.

3. President Bush signalled this new doctrine in the same State of the Union address of January 2002 in which he called Iraq, Iran, and North Korea an "axis of evil," when he announced: "America will do what is necessary to ensure our nation's security. . . . I will not wait on events while dangers gather. I will not stand by as peril draws closer and closer. The United States of America will not permit the world's most dangerous regimes to threaten us with the world's most destructive weapons" (*New York Times*, 30 January 2002, p. A22). For further background to the doctrine, see the excellent article by Armstrong (2002).

4. The World Summit on Sustainable Development in 2001 added to this list the goal of cutting in half by 2015 the number of people in the world without access to sanitation.

5. Klare (2002), in an excellent overview of "The New Bush Doctrine," makes a similar point.

6. Quoting Lisa Lowe, Naples (2002) makes a very similar point: "Ironically 'the very processes that produce a racialized feminized proletariat . . . displace traditional and national patriarchies,' thus generating 'new possibilities precisely because they have led to a breakdown and a reformulation of the categories of nation, race, class, and gender'" (p. 9).

References

Arkin, W. (2002) "Secret Plan Outlines the Unthinkable," *Los Angeles Times*, 10 March.

Armstrong, D. (2002) "Dick Cheney's Song of America," *Harper's Magazine*, October.

Dao, J. (2002) "Bush Sees Big Rise in Military Budget for Next 5 Years," *New York Times*, 2 February.

Eisenstein, Z. (2004) *Feminisms Against Empire* (forthcoming), Zed Books, London.

Girard, F. (2002) "UN Special Session on Children: Bush Administration Continues Its Attacks on Sexual and Reproductive Health," *Reproductive Health Matters*, Vol. 10, No. 20, November.

Hague Appeal *et al.* (2000) *Women Count, At Last!* Hague Appeal for Peace, The Hague, Netherlands.

Hardt, M. and A. Negri (2000) *Empire*, Harvard University Press, Cambridge, MA.

King, Jr., M. L. (2000/1967) "To Atone for Our Sins and Errors in Vietnam," in M. Marable and L. Mullings (eds.), *Let Nobody Turn Us Around: Voices of Resistance, Reform, and Renewal*, Rowman and Littlefield Publishers, Lanham, MD.

Klare, M. (2002) "Endless Military Superiority," *The Nation*, 15 July.

Mowlam, M. (2002) "Comment," *Guardian*, 5 September.

Pear, R. (2002a) "Budget Would Cut Medicaid Payments," *New York Times*, 1 February.

———. (2002b) "After Decline, the Number of Uninsured Rose in 2001," *New York Times*, 30 September.

Pear, R. and R. Toner (2002) "Amid Fiscal Crisis, Medicaid Is Facing Cuts from States," *New York Times*, 13 January.

Petchesky, R. (2001/2002) "Phantom Towers: Feminist Reflections on the Battle between Global Capitalism and Fundamentalist Terrorism," *The Women's Review of Books*, November 2001; *Economic and Political Weekly*, Vol. 36, No. 43, 27 October-2 November 2001; *Ms. Magazine*, December 2001. Reprinted in: S. Hawthorne and B. Winter (eds.), *September 11, 2001: Feminist Perspectives*, Spinifex Press, Australia (2002); K. Pollitt and B. Reed (eds.), *Nothing Sacred: Women Respond to Religious Fundamentalism and Terror*, Nation Books, New York (2002); R. Menon (ed.), *Feminist Perspectives on Peace and Terror*, Kali for Women, New Delhi (2002).

Plesch, D. (2002) "Why Bush's Deal with Putin Doesn't Make the World a Safer Place," *Observer* (London), 26 May.

Robinson, M. (2002) "Globalization Has to Take Human Rights into Account," *The Irish Times*, 22 January.

Rome Statute/United Nations (1998) *Rome Statute of the International Criminal Court*, adopted by the United Nations Diplomatic Conference of Plenipotentiaries on the Establishment of an International Criminal Court, A/CONF.183/9, 17 July (http://www.un.org/icc/part1.htm).

Rosenthal, E. (2002a) "China Now Set to Make Copies of AIDS Drugs," *New York Times*, 7 September.

———. (2002b) "China Frees AIDS Activist After Month of Outcry," *New York Times*, 20 September.

———. (2002c) "AIDS Scourge in Rural China Leaves Villages of Orphans," *New York Times*, 25 August.

Sanger, D. (2002) "Bush to Outline Doctrine of Striking Foes First," *New York Times*, 20 September.

Stevenson, R. (2002) "New Study on Antiwar Spending Is Fodder for Rival Camps," *New York Times*, 6 September.

Stolberg, S. (2001) "Some Experts Say US Is Vulnerable to a Germ Attack," *New York Times*, 29 September.

———. (2002) "Buckets for Bioterrorism, but Less for Catalog of Ills," *New York Times*, 4 February.

Toner, R. (2002) "Administration Plans Care of Fetuses in Health Plan," *New York Times*, 31 January.

PART ELEVEN

Spirituality and Religion

Women's connection to the realm of the sacred is a source of energy, meaning, and comfort. Women experience the sacred in deeply personal ways and often enact their beliefs and feelings through organized communities of faith. Organized religions are one avenue for connecting to the sacred that provides a spiritual home for millions of women. Yet most formal religions contain doctrines that restrict women's roles and power within the religion and the larger society. Many women today negotiate spiritual traditions that simultaneously empower and subordinate them to male authority. From Southern Baptists to Muslims, women challenge the notion that their religions are inherently misogynistic, incompatible with women's emancipation, and they balance their faith with their personal and political beliefs.

Some women have chosen to abandon mainstream religions and develop woman-centered spiritualities, such as Wicca and Goddess Worship, which draw on ancient traditions. These traditions differ from most of the major world religions in their emphasis on the magical qualities of the natural world and the Goddess in Her many manifestations. Both individual and collective practices are available to women and men who adopt these belief systems, but they are still marginalized in a culture that often equates witches, as practitioners of Wicca are known, with evil. For other women, their family religion is a central component of their identities and they work within their traditions to help reform and develop practices that resonate with their desires for inclusion and equality. The very concept of religion as a distinct realm is foreign to Native women who view all life as sacred, although many Native women combine traditional beliefs and practices with membership in organized religions. As the United States becomes a more diverse country, and as globalization links our fates more closely, the range of religious and spiritual beliefs multiplies and the need for mutual understanding and respect increases.

Across the diverse range of religious and spiritual beliefs, what threads traverse women's experiences of the sacred? Feminist theologians have worked to articulate the principles of an approach to the sacred that is consistent with a commitment to social justice for all women. The critique of essentialist ideas of women applies to much feminist theology as well. Some of the early, radical feminist critiques of patriarchal religion, such as Mary Daly's *Beyond God the Father*, did not distinguish the varieties of women's experiences and failed to incorporate a political analysis of race, class, and colonialism. The articles in this section discuss the importance of linking spirituality and activism. This activism is informed by awareness of the ways in which some groups have been and continue to be oppressed by others and how some women benefit from this oppression. One common thread in feminist theology is an awareness of the matrix of domination and the hypocrisy that can arise when religiosity and spirituality are divorced from an ongoing commitment to social justice. In other words, the sacred is not separated from the material world.

A second, related thread is the relational aspect of women's religious and spiritual lives. Catherine A. Faver's research on Episcopal laywomen found that women describe a sense of relatedness to four entities: their work of service to others, God, supportive communities, and clients or recipients of service. The women Faver interviewed described the joy and vitality produced by these relationships that sustained their dedication to activism. They also emphasized "the holy in the ordinary," or the ways in which they felt an ongoing sacred presence in other people and nature. Andrea Smith (Cherokee) also describes this sense of connectedness in the lives of Native women. Discussing the spirituality-liberation praxis of Native women, Smith contrasts relational spirituality that seeks an increase in well-being for all (including nonhuman nature) with individualistic ideals of personal enlightenment. In Native spirituality, it is not possible to consider individual spirituality apart from the well-being of the entire community. The Lakota begin and end prayers and ceremonies with "Mitakuye Oyasin," meaning "all my relations" to signify that spiritual communication is made for the benefit of all people, animals, plants, and rocks rather than the lone individual. As Smith notes, this commitment to the community does not end with prayers and rituals, but extends to social and political action. In this vein, she quotes Mililani Trask (Native Hawai'ian), "We cannot stand by the stream and say our chants and beat the drum and pray that the river people will survive . . . Prayers are the foundation, but . . . [we need] to seize control and political power. We cannot go out and fight America with the spear and a prayer; we need to do more" (Smith 1998: 193). Unlike many spiritual tradi-

tions in the United Sates, Native spirituality is linked closely to the land. Sacred sites, such as the Black Hills in South Dakota, the San Francisco Peaks in Arizona, and Blue Lake in New Mexico are essential to ceremonial practice and cannot be substituted with another location.[1] Thus, Smith argues that "Native women's spirituality/liberation praxis is centered in a national land-based struggle" (Smith 1998: 190).

In a consumer-based culture like that of the United States, people may view spirituality as a commodity that can be purchased. As Smith notes, American Indians are engaged not only in a battle for land and resources, but also in a battle over cultural appropriation. She uses the terms "spiritual racism" and "theological vandalism" to describe the appropriation of indigenous spiritual traditions. Spirituality that is grounded in place and culture cannot be transmitted outside of that context. It is deeply disturbing and disrespectful when ancient ceremonial objects and practices are turned into commodities for tourists with no understanding of or connection to their cultural contexts.

Spirituality that is based in oral traditions, such as American Indian and Afro-Carribean spiritualities, has a built-in capacity for flexibility. A third theme that runs through women's approach to the sacred is the priority given to lived experience over doctrinal orthodoxy. Even Jewish, Christian, and Muslim women, whose religions are based in the written word, are more concerned with developing an ethical approach to life than with adherence to orthodoxy. Spiritualities and religions shift and adapt to changing social circumstances, and today those conditions include globalization and the widening gulf between rich and poor, as discussed in the previous section. As Nami Kim writes in her piece "'My/Our' Comfort *Not* at the Expense of 'Somebody Else's,'" "the central concern is not so much about how one can believe in God in the midst of rampant 'secularism' as about how one can live as a *human being* in the midst of prevalent injustice" (Kim 2005: 91).

Kim brings the issues of globalization to bear on questions of spirituality. She reminds us that not all Asian women, nor all Third World women, are sewing jeans or doing domestic labor; some are buying products and services produced by low-waged workers. Kim deconstructs identity politics that are divorced from global and historical contexts, including histories of colonialism, racism, and sexism. Simple dichotomies, such as East and West, First World and Third World, reify categories that conceal complex relationships of power and domination. Her analysis focuses on the importance of interrogating the ways religion can be used to legitimate inequality and exploitation. For example, she refers to transnational Pax Americana Christianity, the foreign policy of the George W. Bush administration, that justifies pre-emptive wars on the basis of a belief in the global superiority of the United States linked to putative directives from a Christian god. Many religious critics, including Kim and many Christians, argue that when governments use religion to instigate and legitimate violence, they distort basic beliefs and adopt a fundamentalist stance. In Kim's view, it is possible to construct a critical global feminist theology that confronts differences across borders yet also builds alliances based on critique of the various forms of violence and oppression that are endorsed by religions.

Jennie Ruby describes the problems of fundamentalisms, particularly for women. She intentionally pluralizes the term to underscore the fact that it is not a single religion that is fundamentalist, but rather fundamentalist movements that utilize religions to enforce their narrow and rigid beliefs on people. Ruby lists the ways that fundamentalist religions are problematic for women, as well as the characteristics of fundamentalist movements. Women often lose control over their reproductive lives as well as freedom of movement under fundamentalist regimes. In the United States, the media has emphasized the harm to women's rights resulting from Islamic fundamentalists in Afghanistan, Iran, and Iraq. But as you read Ruby's list of common rhetoric and beliefs, you may recognize many that are obvious within the United States. Neil MacFarquhar's article on Ingrid Mattson, the president of the Islamic Society of North America (ISNA), describes the misconceptions many westerners hold about Islam. Like the Christian Bible, the Isalmic Koran can be interpreted to mean that women should be excluded from public life. Matson, both a leader in ISNA and a religious scholar, is a role model demonstrating that Islam does accommodate women's equality. She works to make Islamic law relevant to people's lives and to dispel myths about Islam that fuel fear and misunderstanding among people in the United States.

The articles in this section describe women's spiritual and religious lives as vibrant, living, and changing phenomena. All authors point to the links between spirituality and political activism and commitment as well as the dangers of mixing government and religion. Religion may provide the energy and personal fulfillment required to sustain work toward social justice. But when specific religious ideologies are used to impose one group's beliefs on another, civil and religious repression and persecution follow. The success of a religion, or a spiritual practice, is not measured by the number of adherents or the money in its coffers, but by how well it helps each member live "as a *human being* in the midst of prevalent injustice" (Kim 2005:91).

Note

1. These names, of course, are English names for sacred sites that have ancient names in indigenous languages. There are hundreds of such sites throughout the world, most lacking protection from "development."

References

Kim, Nami. (2005). " 'My/Our Comfort' *Not* at the Expense of 'Somebody Else's' " Toward a Critical Global Feminist Theology." *Journal of Feminist Studies in Religion* 21(2): 75–94.

Smith, Andrea. (1998). "Walking in Balance: The Spirituality-Liberation Praxis of Native American Women." Pp. 178–98 in J. Weaver, ed., *Native American Religious Identity*. Maryknoll, NY: Orbis Books.

Catherine A. Faver

To Run and Not Be Weary: Spirituality and Women's Activism

Through narrative analysis of interviews with fifty Episcopal laywomen, this study examines how spirituality supports and sustains women's involvement in social service and social reform. Assuming that moral and spiritual development are essentially relational in nature, philosophers Nel Noddings (1984) and Carol Ochs (1983, 1986) suggest that the mode of consciousness associated with recognizing and strengthening one's relatedness (to other people, to the natural world, to ideas and projects) produces joy, or vitality, which sustains a commitment to caring. Accordingly, the findings of this study indicate that the factors that sustain the respondents in their work reflect a sense of relatedness or connection to four entities: the work itself, God, supportive communities such as other parishioners or co-workers, and clients or recipients of service.

The past decade has seen a revival of interest in the role of religion as a "disruptive force" that can mobilize social change (Smith 1996, 1991; Spickard 1998; McGuire 1997). Moreover, recent studies suggest that women often use the resources of religious institutions to work for social justice (Winter, Lummis, and Stokes 1994; Plaskow and Christ 1989; Eck and Jain 1987). However, relatively little is known about the role of spirituality in women's activism. This study addresses this question by considering how spirituality sustains women's work in social service and social reform.

This study stands at the intersection of research on (1) women and religion, (2) women and social protest, and (3) religion and social protest. The relevant contributions and limitations of literature in each area will be reviewed briefly, before the study's conceptual framework is introduced.

Source: "To Run and Not Be Weary: Spirituality and Women's Activism," by Catherine A. Faver. *Review of Religious Research 2000,* 42 (1):61–78. © Religious Research Association, Inc. All rights reserved.

Women, Religion and Social Protest

Women and Religion

In recent decades feminist scholars and women of faith have analyzed the patriarchal dimensions of institutional religion. Indeed, the disparity between religion's moral imperatives for justice and women's lower status in religious ritual, doctrine and organizational structure is well documented (e.g., Sharma 1987; King 1993; Nesbitt 1997). While some women have responded to this disparity by abandoning religious institutions, others have worked from within to reform and restructure their religious traditions (Christ and Plaskow 1979; Plaskow and Christ 1989; Eck and Jain 1987; Winter et al. 1994; Nesbitt 1997).

In light of the tension in women's relationship to institutional religion, some scholars have sought to understand how women express their spirituality outside, as well as within, the boundaries of religious organizations. In a recent study of Christian feminist women (Winter et al. 1994), the researchers found that many women who rejected the church's patriarchal authority nevertheless remained in the church ("defected in place") because they found "continuity, . . . community, and connection" (p. 196) through congregational participation. However, many respondents in this study were also members of women's spirituality groups, where they found spiritual support, alternative forms of worship, and opportunities to work for social change. Other scholars (e.g., Eck and Jain 1987; Plaskow and Christ 1989; Farmer 1992; King 1993; Cannon 1994; Gillespie 1995) also suggest that the ideal of social justice and the opportunity to work for social change are important to many women of faith. However, we know little about how spirituality motivates and sustains women's activism.

The recent investigations of women and spirituality have been especially attentive to the *diversity* among women of different racial and ethnic groups, nationalities, and religious traditions (Eck and Jain 1987; Plaskow and Christ 1989; King 1993; Winter et al. 1994). Nevertheless, from within this diversity several common themes emerge, including non-dualism (nonseparation of the sacred and secular) and the significance of relationships and community in women's lives. Accordingly, feminist scholars have constructed models of psychological, moral, and spiritual development which make relationships, rather than lone individuals, the central focus (Gilligan 1982; Noddings 1984; Ochs 1983). However, most theorists do not assume that a relational focus is either exclusive to women or universal among women. To the extent that women share common features of their spirituality, moral reasoning, or identity development, these commonalities are usually believed to be a consequence of women's social roles or social status rather than a reflection of inherent capacities or propensities (Eck and Jain 1987; Plaskow and Christ 1989; Ochs 1983).

Women and Social Protest

For many years, theories of social protest defined political activism primarily in terms of participation in electoral politics or public leadership in formally recognized mass social movements. Recently, however, feminist scholars have argued that such male-biased definitions ignore many common forms of social protest and especially underestimate women's protest activities, most of which have been "lost in history" (West and Blumberg 1990:9; see also Bookman and Morgen 1988).

A new, broader definition of social protest includes a wider range of behaviors aimed at challenging existing power relations and changing the status quo (West and Blumberg 1990; Morgen and Bookman 1988). This definition recognizes that "protest politics is an everyday experience" occurring "within the polity *and* other institutions in society" (West and Blumberg 1990:6). Specifically, scholars "acknowledge that women participate politically in ways that are rarely recognized or documented as political behavior or social protest—for example, by engaging in action through churches, clubs, and other organizations" (West and Blumberg 1990:9).

Historical studies indicate that religion has provided ideological and organizational resources for women's participation in major social movements including abolitionist, anti-lynching, civil rights, welfare rights, anti-poverty, labor and peace (Blumberg 1990; West 1981; Giddings 1984; Payne 1990; West and Blumberg 1990; Sklar 1999). Using a broader definition of protest politics, recent studies affirm that women's activism emerges from their roles as family members, workers, and volunteers (Morgen and Bookman 1988; West and Blumberg 1990; Faver 1994). Moreover, women's activism often crosses the boundary between social service and social reform. For example, Susser (1988) studied a multi-racial coalition of women who organized to provide a social service in a Brooklyn neighborhood, and Gilkes (1988) documented Black women's agitation for agency accountability from within their roles as social service providers. . . .

In short, women are in the forefront of providing services through paid employment and volunteer work in social agencies, churches, and other organizations. When service providers engage in advocacy, organizing, and empowerment of clients, their work can be considered activism because it challenges the status quo. An important question is how spirituality sustains women in these activities which can empower themselves, as well as those they serve.

One study in particular points to a need for research on the forms of activism which are predominant among women. In a sample of peace activists including both men and women, Downton and Wehr (1997) found that persistence in activism was related to both structural factors, such as proximity to targets of peace action, and social psychological variables, including a sense of responsibility for action. Moreover, the "persisters" developed an activist identity by integrating peace action into daily life. As noted above, much of women's work for social change through their roles as employees, family members and volunteers has not been designated as "activism" by society, scholars, or even the women themselves. This raises a question about the nature of the relationship between women's sense of identity and their activism.

Religion and Social Protest

Although religion is often used to legitimate existing power arrangements, scholars of religion emphasize that "religion can serve not only to support and justify, but also to critique and disrupt the social status quo" (Smith 1996:7). Moreover, Smith (1996:11) contends that social movements cannot be sustained by "the simple motive of obtaining an end-goal benefit" but instead require "symbolic and emotional resources" which religion can provide (see also Spickard 1998). For example, religiously-grounded moral imperatives for love, justice, peace, or equity can motivate activism by judging the status quo as unjust and unacceptable. Similarly, religious rituals, symbols and narratives can be used by social movements "to draw inspiration and strength in difficult times" (Smith 1996:11).

Theory suggests, and research affirms, that religion supports social protest by providing both ideological and organizational resources (e.g., Smith 1996; Harris 1994; Calhoun-Brown 1999; Billings and Scott 1994). For example, religious

organizations can provide leadership and an institutional base for movement activity (Morris 1996), enhance collective identity through rituals and narratives (Nash 1996; Smith 1996), and empower their members through opportunities for democratic participation in an egalitarian community (Nepstad 1996).

However, no simple generalizations can be made about the impact of religion on social activism because "differing components of religion have different effects" (Calhoun-Brown 1994: 208). Overall, the research suggests that the way in which religion supports activism depends on the characteristics of the particular religious meaning system. Indeed, scholars of religion make an important distinction between formal and informal religion, that is, between the ideology of religious institutions and the interpretations and practices of individual members (McGuire 1997; see also Williams and Blackburn 1996). This distinction is important because as we have seen, many women have replaced religious orthodoxy with alternative forms of spiritual expression (Winter et al. 1994). Thus, to understand the impact of spirituality on women's activism, we must ask how particular groups of women experience and express their spirituality in everyday life. Moreover, we must acknowledge that women's work for social justice is channeled not only through social movements, but also through women's roles as workers and volunteers in church and community agencies and organizations. . . .

Summary of Conceptual Framework

The question of this study is how spirituality sustains the work of justice and service. The ideas of Noddings (1984) and Ochs (1983, 1986) suggest an answer to this question. Assuming that moral and spiritual development are essentially relational, they argue that joy is induced by particular forms of consciousness and behavioral practices associated with recognizing and strengthening relationships. Joy, in turn, is a form of vitality and strength which sustains commitment to the work of caring for others and for the world.

Method

The Sample

The respondents in this study are fifty Episcopal laywomen involved in work related to peace, justice or social service as volunteers or paid employees. The researcher recruited the women through contacts with clergy and lay leaders in one diocese of a southeastern state.[1] Three respondents are African-American; the others are white. All respondents are middle or upper-middle class and well-educated (many have graduate degrees). Approximately two-thirds of the women are in their 40s or 50s, and about a third are over 60. Over half (56%) are single (divorced, widowed, or never married), and about two-thirds are currently employed.

Episcopal women are not representative of all Christian women, thus limiting the generalizability of this study. However, the interview data do provide information on potentially relevant differences between the women in this sample and women of other denominations. In fact, only ten percent of the respondents are lifelong Episcopalians. A few respondents were formerly Roman Catholics; the others had been affiliated with various Protestant denominations. In describing what attracted them to the Episcopal Church, the respondents mentioned the church's liturgical style of worship, its intellectual openness, and its social liberalism.

The respondents are involved in diverse forms of peace, justice, and social service activities. As an overview, each respondent's work involves some combination of social action, advocacy or service related to one or more *issues* or *population groups*. The issues include poverty and economic inequality, the environment, community development, anti-racism and civil rights for minorities, world peace, mental and physical health, and education. The population groups include low-income and homeless people, racial and ethnic minorities, people who are mentally or physically ill, senior adults, women, children, people with disabilities, and immigrants and refugees.

The respondents' work for social change occurs in various institutional contexts, including community- or church-based organizations and social service agencies, in which they work as employees, employers, or volunteers. Often their work for social change combines advocacy or organizing with the provision of basic social services. Because the respondents seek to empower vulnerable groups and challenge social inequality, their work is consistent with a broad definition of social protest as described in a previous section of this paper. . . .

Results

To reiterate, Ochs and Noddings argue that the mode of consciousness associated with recognizing and experiencing relationships (or relatedness) produces joy (or vitality) which strengthens and sustains caring. This perspective serves as a useful interpretive framework for the respondents' descriptions of what sustains them in their work. To be sure, none of the respondents explicitly stated that she is "sustained by joy." Clearly, however, the respondents indicate that their energy, strength and ability to persist (to "keep going") emerges from their connections to their work, to God, to supportive communities, and to the recipients of their service.

Relationship to Work

The respondents' connection to their work was reflected in a sense of *calling*, a sense of *responsibility*, and a sense of *efficacy*.

Responding to a call. According to Ochs (1986:107), "relatedness to our work can be found in moments when we recall that this work is what we were meant to do, or at least that it is a context in which we can do what seems most important." Both themes—a sense of doing what one was meant to do and a conviction that one's work is important—were found in the respondents' narratives about what sustained them. As an example of the first theme, a respondent working in parish-based neighborhood ministry said she is sustained by "having the feeling that I'm in the right place, and I'm doing what I'm supposed to be doing . . . just knowing that I'm supposed to be here."

Calling was experienced by some respondents as a sense of inner urgency. A peace activist whose attempts to organize in her community were met with apathy and opposition said she continually asked herself, "Why am I doing this?" From deep within her the answer came: "It's the truth; I *have* to do it."

For others, calling was experienced as "finding one's niche," that is, discovering the areas in which one serves best. A respondent who works in an urban ministry center and in a hospice program described the process of discovering her own particular gifts for ministry:

> "It took me till I was almost fifty years old to believe that, in God's wisdom, we all have different gifts, and that when I'm doing something because I think I should, or that society in some way tells me that I should . . . and it's not what God's created for me, then I'm really taking a place of somebody else that ought to be there, and the people there, as well as myself, don't get the best they can get. And so I have felt that I've really found my niche in a few things that I do."

The second theme emphasizes the significance of the work itself; the work is perceived as so essential or important that it compels commitment. For example, a white civil rights activist and children's advocate recalled an experience from the 1960s, when she suddenly realized that her African-American male co-workers were afraid of being observed traveling with a white woman. Their fear was an awakening for her:

> "That kind of awareness continually hits you and wakes you up and says to you that what you're doing's important. It makes a difference to make a change in this society, where grown men have to be afraid for their lives. That's . . . the kind of thing that keeps you going."

The daily drive into work renews the commitment of an environmental activist. She explained why:

> "It's beautiful. There's horses and sunrise. And again, that's a motivating factor, just how beautiful it is, and things can get changed and done. Just the beauty of the earth, you know, reminds me that this is something important, and this is what I want to do."

The two themes—a sense of calling to the work and a belief that the work is important—converged in the respondents' conviction that they could make a particular contribution to an important cause. An AIDS activist, for example, explained that for many years she had volunteered on behalf of a variety of social causes. Then during a period in which she was trying to decide what she really wanted in life, she began a practice of intentional reflection and meditation. Through this process she finally narrowed her focus to AIDS because, as she said, "I really think I can make a difference where this disease is concerned."

Fulfilling responsibility. Some respondents persist because of a strong, spiritually based sense of responsibility to act in accordance with their convictions about social justice. A respondent who provides services for low-income women workers was emphatic on this point:

> "Well, I don't think you can separate spirituality from social justice. You know, I think if you are spiritual that you have a quest to make life different and more just, and trying to say I could have one without the other, I couldn't."

The creator of an innovative social program also emphasized her belief in the necessity of taking ameliorative action regarding one's concerns:

> "I've always believed, I've been taught, and experienced, that if there is something that needs to be corrected, you don't just sit and

complain and worry about it. You'd go out and you'd act. And action can have positive effects."

Her conviction about the importance of acting on one's beliefs had been shaped in part by her experiences in a Jesuit college in another country. Those experiences, she said,

> "forever . . . heightened my social consciousness to the need to act rather than just study or ponder. I mean, those things are good and very needed, but that if you don't put your concerns into action, then you're no better than someone that isn't even concerned, because you're not having an impact."

A sense of efficacy. Some respondents are also sustained by evidence of success or effectiveness, even if modest, in the work they are doing. To some respondents, "success" in their work means that other people have been helped in some direct, tangible way. This type of "success" illustrates Noddings' (1984) concept of "reciprocity" in which the "one-caring" is rewarded by the growth and well-being of the "cared-for." For example, a respondent working in an urban ministry center commented:

> "I think one of the things that is most satisfying is when someone comes in and can work out their problems, and if we assist them a little bit, that's what it's about."

For other respondents, success means that the overall community has benefited from their work. The director of a recycling agency is gratified and energized as she recalls the history of her organization's work for change:

> "I guess what keeps me going is that I see things changing. To think that this tiny organization, ten years ago, came in, and put in a recycling center by themselves, and paid for it, and did it with volunteers . . . They just did it, because it was important."

Finally, to some respondents success means that the message of justice has been heard. For example, a journalist explained that she had writ-

ten articles about a particular social issue for many years with no apparent effect. Then unexpectedly someone commented on what she had written, and she realized that her efforts had made a difference. "So I guess that's what keeps me going," she said.

The director of an organization to encourage parental involvement in public schools is encouraged and sustained by two of these forms of success. First, she is gratified by the results of direct service to individuals:

> *"What sustains me in my work is the belief that we are making a difference. We're helping one person at a time. One student at a time."*

In addition, she is encouraged by changes in public attitudes about the possibility of meeting the educational needs of all children:

> *"It's very fulfilling, knowing that we are changing attitudes, not wholesale, but gradually changing attitudes and making people believe that our public schools can be fixed."*

In sum, to the respondents in this study success or effectiveness means that (1) direct service results in improved life situations for individuals, (2) a community problem is addressed to make life better for many people, such as when the environment is made cleaner or more sustainable, or (3) a message of social justice is heard and received, creating positive changes for vulnerable groups. To be sure, in each case the respondents achieved a goal, which reflects a form of instrumental (or means–end) success. However, a relational perspective offers an alternative interpretation. The common thread in all three meanings of "success" is that the respondents *connected* with those they were trying to reach and received a response, which constitutes a form of reciprocity.

Relationship with God

Most respondents feel sustained and supported by their relationship with God, reflected in their spiritual *experiences* and spiritual *practices*.

Spiritual experiences: The holy in the ordinary.
For many respondents, a major source of support and strength is a pervasive sense of sacred companionship in their lives. Perceiving "the holy in the ordinary" (Ochs 1986: 109), the respondents sense the presence of the sacred in other people and in the natural world. This comment by an assistant director of an urban ministry center was typical:

> *"I see God in people, in nature, and I know that he's always there. I know he's surrounding us. I feel that very strongly. He's just walking beside me. He's woven into the texture of my life."*

Specifically, perceiving "the holy in the ordinary" sustains the respondents by helping them not to feel isolated or alone in their work. Moreover, if God resides in other people, including those least valued by society, then reaching out to others is a way of seeking God. Thus, the respondents' comments allude to the gospel teaching that the quality of a person's relationship with God is revealed in her relationships with poor and vulnerable people (see Gospel of Matthew 25:40). As a parish outreach leader explained: "The connection we make with one another—this is how we recognize God in each other."

Indeed, recognizing the "presence of the sacred" in others is easily translated into an emphasis on "the sacredness of personhood," that is, the worth of every person beyond his or her "utility" in society. Thus, a reformer of public education emphasized the need to perceive the whole child, not just one aspect of a child, such as his or her talent or learning style. As she advocates for disadvantaged children, she is attempting to convince the school and community "that every person has worth, and that every child can learn, if you just give them the opportunity to." Her view of personhood is related to her experience of sacred presence: "God is everywhere with me. Absolutely everywhere. And I think that that kind of feeling of the wholeness of a person comes from my image of God as just omnipresent."

Perceiving the sacred in nature was also a common theme. Recalling a hike in the mountains, one respondent described an array of wildflowers as "a gorgeous altar." Another respondent who enjoys flowers and gardening spoke of "the spiritual aspect" of gardening: "I find great peace and strength in weeding, not having to think about meetings, deadlines, writing, phone calls, dinner, just weeding. That's a very spiritual moment for me." In Noddings' (1984) terms, this respondent's engrossment with the natural world was rewarded with receptive joy.

In sum, the respondents attest to their experience of sacred presence "in and through [their] everyday, ordinary, . . . mundane concerns" (Ochs 1986: 123). Because they perceive the holy in the ordinary, they feel connected to God, other people, and the natural world. Their sense of God's presence infuses everyday encounters with sacred meaning and sustains their desire to honor the sacred presence in others by seeking social justice.

Spiritual practices: Rituals of relatedness. As we have seen, the respondents believe they experience God's presence through the ordinary events of daily life. Their spiritual practices serve as *reminders* of their relationship to God. Ochs (1986: 104) refers to such reminders as *rituals of relatedness*, for they "help us hold in effective memory the experience of presence." Without effective reminders of our connectedness, we lose a sense of meaning:

> *"Rituals of relatedness . . . constantly reconnect us to our own basic commitments. When we strengthen the relatedness we experience joy: when we loosen the relatedness, we find the world growing stale"* (Ochs 1986:107).

The respondents' spiritual practices include various forms of meditation and prayer, reading of sacred texts and other literature, attendance at worship services, and spending time in the natural world. Their "rituals of relatedness" sustain their commitment to activism by serving three functions.

First, spiritual practices remind them that they are connected and loved, which gives them the strength to pursue courses of action for which there is little external support. In fact, the respondents often described their spiritual practices in relational terms. A number of respondents echoed a civil rights activist's description of prayer as "an ongoing conversation with God, just like I'd have with my husband or best friend." Similarly, another anti-racism activist described a week-long spiritual retreat as an "opportunity to reconnect" during which she "really got some messages about being loved" through meditative Bible reading. Meditating on these biblical messages is now a regular part of her spiritual practice: "There's some verses in Isaiah that say, you know, I called and you are mine and you are loved . . . That's something that I fall back on."

A second important function of spiritual practices is to reassure the respondents that their connection to the sacred cannot be broken. For example, a community organizer in a low-income community often turns for support to biblical texts "where God never leaves us, and God strengthens us, and God loves us no matter what we do." Similarly, the director of an advocacy organization frequently reflects on a poem by Francis Thompson ("The Hound of Heaven") whose "powerful, powerful" message to her is "you cannot hide from the grace of God."

Finally, the respondents' spiritual practices help them to discover or reconnect with "who they really are" on a deep level, enabling them to base their "unique contribution" on their "unique identity" (Ochs 1986:29). A journalist who covers social issues such as racism and domestic violence for a church publication made this point quite succinctly: "As I become more aware of who I really am, I know that the kinds of things that I do to nurture my spirituality are the kinds of things that keep me who I am." As Ochs (1986:73) explains, "rituals act as devices for remembering who we are."

This particular journalist had occasionally felt a desire "to do hands on helping ministry. Be at the soup kitchen, handing out food, rather than writing about the people at the soup kitchen." Over the years, however, her personal experiences and her spiritual practices, which include "a way of reading the Bible and journaling and praying all together," have facilitated the "ongoing process" of clarifying and accepting her gifts and limitations. Now she believes that she is most effective as a writer, informing people about issues and needs, facilitating the development of new projects, and recruiting others into service. She concluded: "So you know, while I'm not actually out there in the field doing hands on stuff, I'm getting the word out there, probably affecting more people."

The process of clarifying one's unique "call," or most effective contribution, based on one's unique identity is especially challenging for women because many are socialized to meet others' needs, to feel responsible for others' well-being, and to desire outside affirmation of their inner worth. Thus they may become overburdened with responsibilities and feel guilty about the many needs they cannot possibly meet. As an antidote to this syndrome of burden and guilt, spiritual practices help the respondents to identify their particular contribution to society based on their unique gifts and skills. This enables them to respond to their own "call to service" and decline the requests that are not theirs to answer. In short, spiritual practice is not a "turning inward" that stops with the self: instead, it is self-care that leads to more authentic, useful service to and connections with others.

In sum, spiritual practices can be conceptualized as rituals of relatedness which remind the respondents of their basic commitment and connection to God and the world. The respondents' reliance on their spiritual practices supports Ochs' (1986:121) assessment of the sustaining power of such rituals:

> *"Our rituals of relatedness will sharpen our awareness of our interconnectedness, sustain the connection, and remind us of being connected when it feels as though all our supports have been knocked out from under us"* (Ochs 1986:128).

Relationships with Supportive Communities

The respondents often reported that they were sustained by supportive communities within the workplace or church. Within the context of work (i.e., within the organization or agency), the respondents' colleagues and co-workers provided both moral support and task assistance. For example, an African American respondent who initiated a career development program for minority youth spoke of her co-workers as "a saving grace" who believe that "together we can do anything." Indeed, having a common goal helps to create a "collective identity" among colleagues that makes it possible to transcend ideological differences. Thus, a respondent who directs employee assistance programs for low-income women is energized and sustained by a diverse group of co-workers:

> "I get my energy from the people I work with. You know when you get a group of people together, that are all interested [in helping], I don't care how diverse your belief systems are, and they often are very diverse, but it's still people who want to help other people. So they're a big support."

The church typically provides somewhat different forms of support. In many cases, the respondents are more socially concerned and committed than many of their fellow parishioners. Thus, what the respondents value in their church relationships is not necessarily a shared ideology about social issues, but rather, a strong connection to a caring community. For example, an advocate for the rights of gays and lesbians spoke of her connection to her parish as a "family relationship" and added: "If I'm not there I know I'm missed. So that's about support and strength." Similarly, an advocate for senior citizens often shares a "brown-bag lunch" with seven other women in her parish. They meet at one another's homes, and "talk about everything under the sun, and just really support each other."

Moreover, despite ideological differences about political and social issues, the respondents believe that the church affirms and supports them in their social ministries. Thus, a respondent who works with homeless people commented: "I think you have to have some kind of support group, and the church itself, as a community and as clergy, can be wonderfully supportive."

Finally, regardless of differences in political perspectives, the respondents share with other parishioners a commitment to serving God. This shared commitment creates security and strength in community membership, as a public school reformer explained:

> "I've always felt . . . that the church is always there for me . . . I feel like, when I'm in church, it's almost like it's a safe place, I mean, you're a part of a larger group. I think it's a feeling of the community. It's being one with them in the service of God."

* * *

Discussion

As in Downton and Wehr's (1997) study of peace activists, the respondents in this study are sustained by a sense of responsibility to act, a belief that action can be effective, and successful outcomes from their efforts. In addition, however, our respondents are sustained by a sense of calling characterized by a conviction that they can make a particular contribution to an important cause.

Downton and Wehr (1997) also found that bonding to the activist community helped to sustain activism. Similarly, the respondents in this study seem to draw strength from a "collective identity" shared by co-workers with a commitment to a common project. The church helps to sustain the respondents as well, but in different ways. What the respondents find in their parish communities is a shared commitment to the service of God, affirmation for their ministries, and a concern for their well-being regardless of ideological differences about political and social issues.

The respondents' perception of "the holy in the ordinary," including their sense of God's presence in those they serve, infuses their work with transcendent meaning. In addition, because they are open to being challenged and changed by their clients' perspectives and insights, their activism is an arena for their own spiritual transformation. As a result, they are more likely to be renewed, rather than "burned out," through their service.

The respondents' spiritual practices serve as "rituals of relatedness" that sustain their activism by reminding them of their connection to a God who loves and strengthens them. Moreover, spiritual practices reconnect the respondents with "who they really are," enabling them to discern their specific calling and base their "unique contribution" on their "unique identity" (Ochs 1986:29).

In Downton and Wehr's (1997) study, the persistent peace activists had built an "activist identity" by integrating peace action into daily life and by bonding to the peace community. Because they identified so strongly with their activism, leaving the peace movement would have been costly to their sense of identity; thus the probability of persistence was increased. By comparison, the respondents in this study did not build their identity around their activism; instead, they discovered the cause that allowed them to express their identity. In short, their work is not burdensome because through it they are fulfilling what they perceive as a unique call. They had internalized the conviction that "we have all been called . . . We are uniquely able to contribute something" (Ochs 1986: 102–103).

Conclusion

Previous research suggests that building relationships and working for social justice are important values to many women of faith (Winter et al. 1994; Eck and Jain 1987). This study explored the possibility that "relatedness" itself is a source of energy and strength for the work of social justice. Clearly, the activists in our study experience connectedness through a sense of calling to their work; through a perception of sacred presence in other people and in the natural world; through spiritual practices which remind them that they are loved and called as unique individuals; through reliance on co-workers and communities of faith; and through a willingness to be challenged and changed in relationships with those they serve. Although we lack direct evidence that connectedness produces joy in their lives, the respondents' narratives do indicate that they are energized and sustained by these connections. Overall, the findings suggest that the "relational self," that is, a sense of identity grounded in relationship, is a model of moral and spiritual development in which individual fulfillment and responsibility for others are inextricably linked.

Note

1. To identify appropriate respondents for the study, the researcher distributed copies of a "Call for Participation" to clergy and lay leaders throughout the diocese. The "Call for Participation" sought Episcopal laywomen in the diocese "who have been involved in some form of work for justice or peace" such as work "related to civil rights, women's rights, anti-poverty, peace, human rights, and environmental protection." Recruitment efforts continued until a sample of fifty was obtained. Of the women nominated for participation by clergy or lay leaders, only two declined the invitation to participate, and logistical difficulties prevented scheduling an interview with a third potential respondent.

It should be noted that the method of recruiting respondents may have introduced a selection bias. Specifically, clergy and lay leaders may have been more likely to nominate for the study women who were not only social activists but also leaders in their parish. If so, social activists who were less involved in parish life would have been excluded from consideration for the study. Indeed, most (but not all) respondents were frequent attenders of worship services and were active participants in parish activities.

References

Billings, Dwight B. and Shaunna L. Scott. 1994. "Religion and Political Legitimation." *Annual Review of Sociology.* 20: 173–201.

Blumberg, Rhoda L. 1990. "White Mothers As Civil Rights Activists: The Interweave of Family and Movement Roles." In Guida West and Rhoda L. Blumberg (eds.) *Women and Social Protest*. Pp. 166–179. New York: Oxford University Press.

Bookman, Ann and Sandra Morgen, eds. 1988. *Women and the Politics of Empowerment*. Philadelphia: Temple University Press.

Calhoun-Brown, Allison. 1999. "The Image of God: Black Theology and Racial Empowerment in the African American Community." *Review of Religious Research*. 40:197–212.

Cannon, Katie G. 1994. "The Positionality of Women in the African American Church Community." In Miriam T. Winter, Adair Lummis, and Allison Stokes (eds.) *Defecting in Place*. Pp. 210–216. New York: Crossroad.

Christ, Carol P. and Judith Plaskow. 1979. *Womanspirit Rising: A Feminist Reader in Religion*. New York: Harper & Row.

Downton, James, Jr. and Paul Wehr. 1997. *The Persistent Activist: How Peace Commitment Develops and Survives*. Boulder: Westview Press.

Eck, Diana L. and Devaki Jain, eds. 1987. *Speaking of Faith: Global Perspectives on Women, Religion and Social Change*. Philadelphia: New Society Publishers.

Farmer, Marjorie N. 1992. "Different Voices: African American Women in the Episcopal Church." In Catherine M. Prelinger (ed.) *Episcopal Women: Gender, Spirituality and Commitment in an American Mainline Denomination*. Pp. 222–238. Oxford: Oxford University Press.

Faver, Catherine A. 1994. "Feminist Ideology and Strategies for Social Change: An Analysis of Social Movements." *Journal of Applied Social Sciences*. 18:123–134.

Giddings, Paula. 1984. When and Where I Enter: The Impact of Black Women on Race and Sex in America. New York: Morrow.

Gilkes, Cheryl T. 1988. "Building in Many Places: Multiple Commitments and Ideologies in Black Women's Community Work." In Ann Bookman and Sandra Morgen (eds.) *Women and the Politics of Empowerment*. Pp. 53–76. Philadelphia: Temple University Press.

Gillespie, Joanna B. 1995. *Women Speak of God, Congregations and Change*. Valley Forge: Trinity Press International.

Gilligan, Carol. 1982. *In a Different Voice*. Cambridge: Harvard University Press.

Harris, Frederick C. 1994. "Something Within: Religion as a Mobilizer of African-American Political Activism." *The Journal of Politics*. 56: 42–68.

King, Ursula. 1993. *Women and Spirituality: Voices of Protest & Promise*. Second edition. University Park: Pennsylvania State University Press.

McGuire, Meredith B. 1997. *Religion: The Social Context*. Fourth edition. Belmont, CA: Wadsworth.

Morgen, Sandra and Ann Bookman 1988. "Rethinking Women and Politics: An Introductory Essay." In Ann Bookman and Sandra Morgen (eds.) *Women and the Politics of Empowerment*. Pp. 3–32. Philadelphia: Temple University Press.

Morris, Aldon. 1996. "The Black Church in the Civil Rights Movement: The SCLC as the Decentralized, Radical Arm of the Black Church." In Christian Smith (ed.) *Disruptive Religion: The Force of Faith in Social Movement Activism*. Pp. 29–46. New York: Routledge.

Nash, June. 1996. "Religious Rituals of Resistance and Class Consciousness in Bolivian Tin-Mining Communities." In Christian Smith (ed.) *Disruptive Religion: The Force of Faith in Social Movement Activism*. Pp. 87–102. New York: Routledge.

Nepstad, Sharon E. 1996. "Popular Religion, Protest, and Revolt: The Emergence of Political Insurgency in the Nicaraguan and Salvadoran Churches of the 1960s–90s." In Christian Smith (ed.) *Disruptive Religion: The Force of Faith in Social Movement Activism*. Pp. 105–124. New York: Routledge.

Nesbitt, Paula D. 1997. *Feminization of the Clergy: Occupational and Organizational Perspectives*. New York: Oxford University Press.

Noddings, Nel. 1984. *Caring: A Feminine Approach to Ethics and Moral Education*. Berkeley: University of California Press.

Ochs, Carol. 1983. *Women and Spirituality*. Totowa, NJ: Rowman & Allanheld.

———. 1986. *An Ascent to Joy: Transforming Deadness of Spirit*. Notre Dame: University of Notre Dame Press.

Payne, Charles. 1990. "'Men Led, But Women Organized': Movement Participation of Women in the Mississippi Delta." In Guida West and Rhoda L. Blumberg (eds.) *Women and Social*

Protest. Pp. 156–165. New York: Oxford University Press.

Plaskow, Judith and Carol P. Christ. 1989. *Weaving the Visions: New Patterns in Feminist Spirituality*. San Francisco: Harper & Row.

Sharma, Arvind, ed. 1987. *Women in World Religions*. Albany: State University of New York Press.

Sklar, Katherine K. 1999. "Beyond Maternalism: Protestant Women & Social Justice Activism, 1890–1920." *Women and Twentieth Century Protestantism*. 3:2–7.

Smith, Christian. 1991. *The Emergence of Liberation Theology: Radical Religion and Social Movement Theory*. Chicago: University of Chicago Press.

———. 1996. "Correcting a Curious Neglect, or Bringing Religion Back In." In Christian Smith (ed.) *Disruptive Religion: The Force of Faith in Social Movement Activism*. Pp. 1–25. New York: Routledge.

Spickard, James V. 1998. "Rethinking Religious Social Action: What is 'Rational' About Rational-Choice Theory?" *Sociology of Religion*. 59:99–115.

Susser, Ida. 1988. "Working-Class Women, Social Protest, and Changing Ideologies." In Ann Bookman and Sandra Morgen (eds.) *Women and the Politics of Empowerment*. Pp. 257–271. Philadelphia: Temple University Press.

Thompson, Francis. 1922. *The Hound of Heaven*. New York: Dodd, Mead and Company.

West, Guida. 1981. *The National Welfare Rights Movement: The Social Protest of Poor Women*. New York: Praeger.

West, Guida and Rhoda L. Blumberg. 1990. "Reconstructing Social Protest from a Feminist Perspective." In Guida West and Rhoda L. Blumberg (eds.) *Women and Social Protest*. Pp. 3–35. New York: Oxford University Press.

Williams, Rhys H. and Jeffrey Blackburn. 1996. "Many Are Called But Few Obey: Ideological Commitment and Activism in Operation Rescue." In Christian Smith (ed.) *Disruptive Religion: The Force of Faith in Social Movement Activism*. Pp. 167–185. New York: Routledge.

Winter, Miriam T., Adair Lummis, and Allison Stokes. 1994. *Defecting in Place: Women Claiming Responsibility for Their Own Spiritual Lives*. New York: Crossroad.

Andrea Smith

Walking in Balance: The Spirituality-Liberation Praxis of Native Women

This essay is not meant to be a definitive account of Native women's spirituality and political activism. It reflects my particular perspective as an urban-based activist, but there are certainly diverse experiences among Native women, depending on tribe, geographic location, age, whether one is urban- or reservation-based, and so forth. Rather, this chapter is meant to be suggestive of what Native women might contribute to theological conversations about liberation, particularly among women-of-color theologians. More extensive and thorough research among the diverse forms of Native women's organizing is necessary for a more exhaustive account.

Before continuing, however, I should make two interpretive points that are not, properly speaking, questions of methodology, but which will frame the rest of this discussion. First, because Native religions, like Native cultures in general, are orally based, they are quite flexible. Indians tend to give less weight to an orthodoxy of religious belief than to spiritual centeredness and ethical behavior—what Native people call "walking in balance."[1] Second, Indian spiritualities tend to be more practice-centered than belief-centered; that is, what makes one Indian is not simply holding the proper set of core beliefs but behaving like an Indian. Vine Deloria, Jr. (Standing Rock Sioux), notes that, in a Native context, religion is "a way of life" rather than "a matter of the proper exposition of doctrines."[2] Of course,

this should not be taken to mean either that Indian religions have no content or that anyone gets to be Indian who "decides" to "behave like one." Rather, these points suggest that, in looking at Native women's activism as a source for spirituality/liberation praxis, standard theological categories do not have much relevance. New categories come to the fore. As Chung argues, "Doctrinal purity or religious boundaries [are] not of concern. . . . What matter[s is] the life-giving power of justice in whatever form it comes.[3] The "meanings" of Native political and spiritual practices refract through culturally specific lenses, and in the sections that follow I will discuss a few of them.

Relationship to Tradition

Aloysius Pieris calls upon the Asian church to lose itself in "the *non-Christian experiences* of liberation."[4] Native liberation also requires a de-centered Christianity. This post-Christian approach is not a wholesale rejection of Christianity, although some do reject it entirely and try to reclaim the traditions of their particular nations. Haunani Kay Trask (Native Hawai'ian), for example, calls Christianity "the most vicious religion in the world."[5] Since many Native people can trace the abuse in their families to within a generation or two of mission boarding schools, they have had to reject Christianity to heal their trauma. Some indigenous women also reject Christianity to recover their more woman-centered indigenous traditions. In some respects, however, the neo-traditional rejection of Christianity is a legacy of Christian dualistic thinking.

Source: "Walking in Balance: The Spirituality-Liberation Praxis of Native American Women." by Andrea Smith, in *Native American Religious Identity*, Jace Weaver, ed. © 1998 by Orbis Books. Used by permission.

Vine Deloria notes that neo-traditionalist attempts to reclaim Native spirituality occur within an either/or logic system foreign to Native cultures. Ironically, however, Deloria himself maintains an either/or stance, writing, "We cannot reject the Christian religion piecemeal. . . . The whole religion has been misdirected from its inception."[6]

It is possible to critique the oppressive practices of the Christian church without wholly rejecting Christianity itself. Belief systems that seem mutually inconsistent to the dominant culture, like Christianity and indigenous religions, can coexist in indigenous cultures. To illustrate with a real-life example: At a conference several years ago I heard a story about an Indian man who gave a speech in which he claimed that the next speaker was going to say things that were completely wrong. When his turn came, the next speaker, also Indian, began, not by attacking the preceding speaker, but by announcing that everything he said was completely true. He then went on with his talk. The event is notable because it struck no one present—not the speakers, not the Indian audience—as odd.

Consequently, even Natives raised with a more traditional worldview do not always feel the need to reject Christianity outright, even as they criticize its abuses. Many Indians tend to relate to both Christianity and to their Native traditions along a continuum. (Of course, there are Native women who choose to embrace a variety of other foreign traditions, from Judaism to Zen Buddhism, but Christianity has long been the colonizing religion of Native women.) Some define themselves as wholly Christian, others as wholly traditional, but probably most relate to both in some degree or fashion. For instance, someone who is primarily traditional may occasionally attend church. This flexibility can lessen the need for many Native Christians to "reinterpret" Christian concepts that they find oppressive; they simply may ignore what they find inadequate or offensive in Christianity and look elsewhere, usually to Native traditions, for what they need. For example, in contrast to White Christian feminists

like Elisabeth Schüssler Fiorenza, it has been my experience that Indian people generally do not try to "re-envision" scripture because they often do not read it in the first place. At one sermon at an Indian church I attended, for example, the pastor noted, "Obviously reading the Bible is not necessary for salvation, because otherwise no Indians would be saved." When Native people do grapple with the biblical text, as Robert Warrior does in "Canaanites, Cowboys, and Indians," they tend to produce critiques directed toward non-Indians and their oppressive approaches to the Bible. Indians who are not theologically trained generally do not concern themselves with the Canaanites. In fact, at one gathering of Native seminarians that I attended, one pastor challenged us to find out who in our communities knew what seminary was. Thus, attempts to "re-envision" scripture in response, for instance, to Warrior's work may be evidence of what Isasi-Díaz describes as an academic theologian's impulse to answer questions that those at the grassroots are not asking.[7] . . .

Change is an issue that Native women also have been forced, albeit in different ways and for different reasons, to contend with. Patriarchy is now firmly entrenched within most Native societies, although nonpatriarchal worldviews on gender relations still persist. Consequently, women (like former Principal Chief of the Cherokee Nation Wilma Mankiller) who strive for political leadership are accused, ironically, of not being traditional. Rayna Green (Cherokee) tells the story of an Indian conference on development at which a man gave a speech condemning the breakdown of traditional Indian values. He attributed this to the increasing number of Native women leaving home and assuming leadership positions. An elderly woman responded, "You know, I'm very interested in speech about the old days—your old days must have been really different from our old days, because in our old days, women were at the seat of power. . . . In our old days, women were at the center of knowledge and understanding about leadership, about distribution of power, about the distribution of goods and about the allotments of roles and power. . . . Let's talk about the old days; I say, 'Bring on the old days.'"[8] . . .

Native cultures have always changed to meet current needs. As Marilou Awiakta (Cherokee) notes, one attribute of an oral culture is the ability to adapt rather than to try to maintain itself against a written, fixed set of principles.[9] The only cultures that *never* change are the dead and petrified kind; however, after the damaging transitions forced upon Native cultures by colonization, now virtually all change is regarded with suspicion. The challenge, then, is to find a way of welcoming change that may be helpful but to root it firmly within tradition. As Leslie Silko (Laguna Pueblo) writes in her novel *Ceremony:*

> "There are some things I have to tell you," Betonie began softly. "The people nowadays have an idea about the ceremonies. They think the ceremonies must be performed exactly as they have always, maybe because one slip or mistake and the whole ceremony must be stopped. . . . That much is true. . . . But long ago when the people were given these ceremonies, the changing began . . . if only in the different voices from generation to generation. . . . You see, in many ways, the ceremonies have always been changing. . . .
>
> "Things which don't shift and grow are dead things. . . . That's what the witchery is counting on: that we will cling to the ceremonies the way they were, and then their power will triumph, and the people will be no more."[10]

Spiritual/Cultural Appropriation

Native women also practice a version of what Chung calls a "survival-liberation centered syncretism" (though this may not always be the appropriate term in that they might also practice multiple traditions without blending them, as in syncretism). Unlike Korean Chung, however, Native women are concerned more centrally with issues of cultural/spiritual appropriation, and, as a result, are reticent about sharing this process of "syncretism" with outsiders. In fact, Indian spiritual and cultural appropriation—a form of thievery that activist Justine Smith (Cherokee) calls "spiritual racism"—has become so pervasive that indigenous people are declaring war against it. Most Indian activist groups have written position papers condemning the use of their cultural traditions by outsiders. Hopi and Lakota elders have issued similar statements.[11] One Oakland-based group known as SPIRIT exists only to expose such theft. Indian nations are even using the legal theories of intellectual property rights to file lawsuits against those who make a profit by stealing their culture. Natives who write openly about Indian spirituality are generally viewed with suspicion, and many are exposed as "plastic medicine people."[12]

Even Native theologians like Steven Charleston (Choctaw) and George Tinker (Osage), who write defenses of Native spiritual practices in the interest of showing that they are not "satanic," risk encouraging the long-standing propensity of non-Natives to commit what Pieris calls "theological vandalism"—that is, the adoption of "exotic" foreign practices in isolation from the culture to which they rightfully belong.[13] The issue of appropriation calls into question the value of writing defenses of Indian spirituality for non-Indians. Fumitaka Matsuoka sheds some light on this problem. He notes that the important battle to be fought is not for cultural validation. The dominant culture is prepared to accommodate a little "multiculturalism"—a pow wow here, a pipe ceremony there—as long as the structures of power are not challenged. As he states, "The central problems . . . have to do, ultimately, not with ethnic groupings or the distinctness of our cultural heritages as such, but with racism and its manifestations in American economic policy, social rule and class relations."[14]

During my four years in Chicago I found that whenever Native people agitated for something big, like restoring "minority" status to American Indians for affirmative action purposes or eradicating the Columbus Day parade, the powers that be invariably said, "No, but why don't you hold a pow wow, or come in regalia to this or that public event?" At one session on

Native women at the 1995 annual meeting of the American Academy of Religion, an audience participant suggested that future panels on Native issues include singing, dancing, and other forms of cultural "sharing." Inés Hernandez-Avila (Colville/Nez Perce) responded that she is reluctant to do so because providing entertainment would contribute to the stereotype that Indians are not capable of critical intellectual activity.

It is unquestionably true that there is much intolerance toward, and ignorance about, Native religions and cultures in the United States. We still do not even have freedom to practice our traditional religions. But as activist/scholar Gabrielle Tayac (Piscataway) notes, intolerance toward Indian religions cannot be addressed by educating White people about our spiritual beliefs, because our religious oppression is not based on ignorance but on the seizure of Indian lands upon which Indian spiritualities are based.[15] It is not an accident that Congress allows the use of peyote by the Native American Church but will not pass a law protecting Indian sacred sites, since the latter would entail a threat to U.S. government corporate control over Native lands. Writing defenses of Indian spirituality outside of a discussion of land claims not only leaves us open to cultural appropriation but diverts attention from the central issues of sovereignty over our lands and resources. Thus many Natives have joined with Chrystos in declaring to non-Indians: "While I am deeply spiritual, to share this with strangers would be a violation. Our rituals, stories, and religious practices have been stolen and abused, as has our land. I don't publish work which would encourage this. . . . My purpose is to make it as clear & as inescapable as possible, what the actual material conditions of our lives are."[16]

In response to the problem of spiritual appropriation, the Traditional Elders Circle has issued a communique on what is appropriate to share with non-Indians. The simple message is that all of creation is connected; people must live in balance with each other and with the earth to ensure our collective survival; abuse, repression, and exploitation of the earth's resources are not part of "the natural law."[17] These values are probably common to all indigenous cultures. Gay and lesbian theologians also seem to have adopted some version of them, although they do not stress the need for a balanced relationship between humans and the earth. Carter Heyward, for example, calls God "our relational power"; Gary Comstock likewise refers to God as "mutuality-in-relationship" and describes sin as "the violation of mutuality and reciprocity."[18] Spirituality, then, is not something to be purchased by paying $300 for a pipe ceremony. Instead, it is a way of living in "right relation" with the awareness that everything one does affects everything else. As Chrystos writes in her poem "Shame On":

> We've been polite for five hundred years
> & you still don't get it
> Take nothing you cannot return
> Give to others, give more
> Walk quietly
> Do what needs to be done
> Give thanks for your life
> Respect all beings
> simple
> and it doesn't cost a penny.[19]

*　*　*

At the United Nations Conference in Beijing, the indigenous women's caucus began formulating a statement criticizing the struggle for gender equality as oppressive to indigenous women. Winona LaDuke explained that attempting to be "equal" with men under the current capitalist and imperialist world order will do nothing to liberate most women. "It is not, frankly, that women of the dominant society in so-called first world countries should have equal pay and equal status, if that pay and status continue to be based on a consumption model which is not only unsustainable, but causes constant violation of the human rights of women and nations elsewhere in the world."[20] The statement, still in process, does denounce sexism but calls for its eradication *within* the context of self-determination for all peoples.

Spirituality is integral to this anti-colonial struggle because Native spiritualities depend upon the land base that gave rise to them; they cannot easily be transplanted to another geographic area. Many ceremonies must be performed at specific locations. As Vine Deloria states:

> The structures of their traditions is taken directly from the world around them, from their relationships with other forms of life. Context is therefore all-important for both practice and understanding of reality. The places where revelations were experienced were remembered and set aside as locations where, through rituals and ceremonials, the people could once again communicate with spirits. . . . The sacred lands remain as permanent fixtures in their cultural or religious understanding.[21]

This close relationship with the land makes environmental issues central to indigenous liberation struggles. Like Rosemary Radford Ruether, Sallie McFague, and other ecofeminist theologians, Indians "envision a healed society, in the sense of nondominating relations between human beings in interrelation with the rest of nature."[22] Both Ruether and McFague, however, only peripherally analyze environmentalism in relation to colonialism, imperialism, and capitalism. McFague states, "The nuclear issue and issues of political and social oppression are intrinsically related, for at the heart of all these issues is the question of power: who wields it and what sort it is." She, however, seems startlingly unaware of environmental racism when she says that "as a threat rather than a reality, nuclear doom requires an act of imagination if it is to become part of our reality, part of our "world."[23] Native people require no such act. They are living currently with the "reality" of "nuclear doom" because *all* uranium mining and nuclear testing take place on or near Indian land. Consequently, Native communities face 60 percent birth defect rates in some areas, 80 percent cancer rates in others.

Ruether similarly states, "The issue of poverty, of the growing division between misery and affluence, will thread through this whole account [of environmental destruction]." But then she writes, "The challenge that humans face . . . is whether they will be able to visualize and organize their own reproduction, production, and consumption in such a way as to stabilize their relationship to the rest of the ecosphere and so avert massive social and planetary ecocide." She seems to assume that all contribute equally to ecological disaster, that all are equally affected by population policies, that all have the same power to organize their production and consumption.[24] Native activists more precisely locate the environmental crisis in the question, "Who controls the land?" The majority of energy resources in the United States are on Indian land, and thus Indian people are generally the first to be affected by the destruction caused by resource extraction. Their lands also are targeted for dumping of toxic waste. Many Indian activists believe that treaty rights are the best protection against environmental devastation wrought by rampant capitalism.[25] Multinational corporations believe it, too. That is why they fund anti-Indian hate groups to fight treaty enforcement. "Naming reality" in light of the ecological crisis we face, as McFague argues, is important.[26] Changing personal consumption patterns, as Ruether suggests, is also important. Native women activists recognize, however, that the struggle to protect the earth entails a long, hard battle against the United States government and multinationals. As Mililani Trask (Native Hawai'ian) argues, "We cannot stand by the stream and say our chants and beat the drum and pray that the river people will survive. . . . Natural resource management is a tool, a skill, and a weapon that the women warriors of today need to attire themselves with if they are going to be prepared for battle. Prayers are the foundation, but . . . [we need] to seize control and political power. We cannot go out and fight America with the spear and a prayer; we need to do more."[27] Native women are prominent in these struggles. . . .

Conclusion

I have attempted to echo the spirituality/liberation praxis of Native women who fight for Indian sovereignty. One pitfall for theologians who attempt to "reproduce" the voices of their community, however, is that they inadvertently appoint themselves community spokespersons. Particularly in the celebrity-driven culture of the United States, the predominantly non-Indian readers of theological texts inevitably fixate on the author rather than the Native communities the author is discussing. Clearly, good intentions are no substitute for a strategy. Perhaps theologians can stop signing their own names to their books, or use their clout to push through collaborative, community-based publications. Further discussion on such strategies is a pressing need for Native people, as well as all liberation theologians in academic circles. Because Native women are constantly battling the forces of genocide, they cannot afford to waste time on academic efforts that have no real relevance for the community. The challenge liberation theologians face today is not just to devise sophisticated theological analyses that reflect the needs of our communities but actively to be part of a grassroots-based movement for social transformation. Our job is to be engaged in the task of eliminating the oppression our communities face, not making a living from it.

Notes

1. This is one reason why Native people in an urban setting are more likely to attend an Indian church regardless of denomination than to go to a predominantly non-Indian church of their own denomination. Native people are also notorious for not attending church regularly. Consequently, Indian ministries generally focus on community action.

2. Vine Deloria, Jr., "A Native American Perspective on Liberation," *Occasional Bulletin of Missionary Research* 1 (July 1977), p. 16.

3. Chung, p. 95.

4. Aloysius Pieris, *An Asian Theology of Liberation* (Edinburgh: T & T Clark, 1988), p. 86 (emphasis added).

5. Haunani Kay Trask, speech, Sisters of Color International, 5th Annual Conference, Hamilton College, Clinton, N.Y., April 21–23, 1996.

6. See Paula Gunn Allen, *The Sacred Hoop* (Boston: Beacon Press, 1986); Deloria, p. 17; Vine Deloria, Jr., *God Is Red,* 2d ed. (Golden, Colo.: Fulcrum, 1992), p. 265.

7. Robert Allen Warrior, "A Native Perspective: Canaanites, Cowboys, and Indians," in *Voices from the Margin*, ed. R. S. Sugirtharajah (Maryknoll, N.Y.: Orbis Books, 1991), pp. 294–95; Isasi-Díaz, p. 63.

8. Rayna Green, "American Indian Women: Diverse Leadership for Social Change," in *Bridges of Power: Women's Multicultural Alliances*, ed. Lisa Albrecht and Rose Brewer (Philadelphia: New Society Publishers, 1990), p. 63.

9. Marilou Awiakta, *Selu: Seeking Corn-Mother's Wisdom* (Golden, Colo.: Fulcrum, 1993), p. 16.

10. Leslie Marmon Silko, *Ceremony* (New York: Penguin, 1986), p. 126.

11. See Marilyn Masayevsa, "Cultural Appropriation: A Hopi Response," *Indigenous Woman* 2 (1995), pp. 35–36.

12. See Traditional Elders Circle, *Communique No. 9* (June 21, 1986).

13. Steven Charleston, "The Old Testament of Native America," in *Life Every Voice: Constructing Christian Theologies from the Underside*, ed. Susan Brooks Thistlethwaite and Mary Potter Engel (San Francisco: Harper & Row, 1990), pp. 49–61; George Tinker, "Spirituality, Native American Personhood, Sovereignty, and Solidarity," in *Native and Christian*, ed. James Treat (New York: Routledge, 1996), pp. 115–31.

14. Fumitaka Matsuoka, *Out of Silence* (Cleveland: United Church Press, 1995), p. 93.

15. Gabrielle Tayac, "Native Struggles for Freedom under the Law," respondent, American Academy of Religion, Philadelphia, Penn., November 1995.

16. Chrystos, *Not Vanishing* (Vancouver: Press Gang, 1988), preface.

17. Traditional Circle of Indian Elders and Youth, *Communique No. 12* (June 14, 1989).

18. Carter Heyward, *Touching Our Strength* (San Francisco: Harper & Row, 1989), p. 24; Gary Comstock, *Gay Theology without Apology* (Cleveland: Pilgrim Press, 1993), pp. 28, 30.

19. Chrystos, *Dream On* (Vancouver: Press Gang, 1991), p. 101.

20. Winona LaDuke, keynote address, UN Conference on Women, Beijing, China; reprinted in *The Circle* 16 (October 1995), p. 8.

21. Deloria, *God Is Red*, p. 67.

22. Rosemary Radford Ruether, *Gaia and God* (San Francisco: Harper & Row, 1992), p. 9.

23. Sallie McFague, *Models of God* (Philadelphia: Fortress Press, 1987), p. 15.

24. Ruether, pp. 87, 47.

25. See Rudolph C. Ryser, "Anti-Indian Movement on the Tribal Frontier," Occasional Paper #16, Center for World Indigenous Studies, April 1991.

26. McFague, p. 3.

27. Mililani Trask, "Indigenous Women Are the Mothers of Their Nations," *Indigenous Woman* 2 (1995), p. 26.

Neil MacFarquhar

Putting a Different Face on Islam in America

Professor Ingrid Mattson, a 43-year-old convert, was elected president of the Islamic Society of North America, the largest umbrella organization for Muslim groups in the United States and Canada. She is both the first woman and, as a Canadian, the first non-immigrant to hold the post.

In a class on Islamic history at the Hartford Seminary some years back, the students were discussing a saying ascribed to the Prophet Muhammad that translates roughly as, "Whenever God wants the destruction of a people, he makes a woman their leader."

The professor, Ingrid Mattson, suggested that the phrase should be analyzed in its historical context when Islamic societies consisted largely of tribal raiding parties. A male Saudi student contended that all such sayings were sacred and not to be challenged, the argument growing so heated that he stormed out of the classroom. Professor Mattson stood her ground, as was her style.

Now she is challenging convention again. In September 2006, Professor Mattson, a 43-year-old convert, was elected president of the Islamic Society of North America, the largest umbrella organization for Muslim groups in the United States and Canada, making her a prominent voice for a faith ever more under assault by critics who paint it as the main font of terrorism. She is both the first woman and, as a Canadian, the first non-immigrant to hold the post.

To her supporters, Professor Mattson's selection comes as a significant breakthrough, a chance for North American Muslims to show that they are a diverse, enlightened community with real roots here—and not alien, sexist extremists bent on the destruction of Western civilization. Some naysayers grumble that a woman should not head any Muslim organization because the faith bars women from leading men in congregational prayers, but they are a distinct minority.

"The more Americans see Muslims who speak English with a North American accent, Muslims who were born and raised here, who understand this culture, the more it will cease to be a foreign phenomenon but something local and indigenous," said Mahan Mirza, a Yale doctoral candidate in Islamic studies who recalled the classroom scene above from the master's program at the Hartford Seminary in Connecticut.

At the annual Islamic Society conference in Chicago where her election was officially announced to the thousands of Muslims in attendance, women rushed to have snapshots taken at her side.

"When I see her, I just feel that there is this beam of light on her," said Reem Hassaballa, 30, of Chicago, a teacher and a mother of three. "She is a very good role model. If it can happen in a little convention like this, hopefully it could happen in the whole Muslim world. She could be the start of something bigger." Ms. Mattson sees both pluses and minuses in the fact that her election is being viewed as a watershed. The Islamic Society of North America is a 20,000-member group representing all manner of organizations, from student clubs to professional associations for doctors and lawyers to mosque boards to political activists. Her immediate predecessor was a religious scholar who often wore the flowing white robes and stacked turban of his native Sudan.

"Somehow there is the feeling that someone who is white is safer and less scary," Professor Mattson said. "But I am who I am. So if there is some social capital that I can use to counteract some of the negative perception and open ears to what we have to say as a community, then that is a benefit."

A short, trim woman with a quiet manner that belies her authority, Ms. Mattson grew up, by her own description, as a good, middle-class Roman Catholic school girl in Kitchener, Canada, a suburban community about 60 miles southwest of Toronto. She attended a Catholic girls high school and took piano lessons at the convent, spending hours in church praying or contemplating the art. It was a peaceful asylum removed from the raucous household where she was the sixth of seven children.

At 16, though, she stopped attending Mass. "I believe I made a very serious attempt to understand my faith," she said, repeatedly sitting with her religion teacher to ask questions about Catholicism and spirituality. She found the answers wanting, she said, less and less relevant to her teenage life.

Ms. Mattson enrolled in the nearby University of Waterloo to study philosophy and fine arts, a determined agnostic. In 1986, while studying in Paris, she met her first Muslims, mostly West African students, and was struck by their warmth, dignity and generosity.

Back home, she started to read more books about Islam and took classes in Arabic, which she now speaks fluently. When first delving into the Koran, its explanations of the presence of the creator in the natural world struck a chord. That echoed her own spiritual sentiments developed during summers spent at the family's 200-year-old cottage on an island in a Canadian lake without running water or a telephone.

In 1987, as a college senior, she converted. "This religious community was giving me the framework for my spiritual experience, and so I entered into it," she said in an interview.

At first she told only her mother, whom Ms. Mattson describes as a strong, flexible, understanding woman. Her father, a criminal lawyer, had died when she was 12 and her mother had worked in a factory to support the family.

"My mother was confused at first and did not understand it," she said. The change was eased somewhat by the fact that her oldest sister, Peggy Smith, had converted to Judaism before her marriage.

But her brothers and sisters only found out months later, when she wrote them a letter from overseas. They were mostly concerned, she said, that she had not joined some cult, and vaguely dismayed that her bar-hopping days with them had ended because Islam demands temperance.

Now, Ms. Mattson and Ms. Smith share certain common concerns—like keeping pork off the table at family gatherings.

"Sometimes it's only the Muslim and the Jew who are eating Christmas dinner with my mother," Professor Mattson said with a laugh, explaining that her siblings are off with their spouses. Conversation tends to run around family issues rather than comparative religion, she said.

Ms. Mattson's first exposure to the larger Muslim world came after she graduated from college, when childhood lessons about missionary work inspired her to volunteer to teach Afghan women in a sprawling refugee camp of about 100,000 people in Peshawar, Pakistan. There, in what might be called the wild Muslim east, the group later known as the Taliban barred their women from attending her classes.

"I remember clearly someone pointing a man out to me and saying 'That's the brother of the man who killed Anwar Sadat."' she recalled. "That was freaky. I was thinking, what is going on here, and who are these people?"

But the most important person she met was Amer Aatek, an Egyptian engineer working to install a water system in the camp and playing uncle to numerous orphans. Not long afterward, they were quietly married in her house in Peshawar. When the destitute refugee women learned that there had been neither trousseau nor a banquet, they gave her a party and presented her with a wedding outfit: a red velveteen top and billowing blue silk pants dotted with multicolored pompoms. It was not exactly her style. She is given to headscarves in dark blue or brown with long matching skirts and long-sleeved jackets.

In 1989, she enrolled in the University of Chicago as a Ph.D. student in early Islamic history. Her husband played the main role in raising their daughter and son during much of the 10 years it took to complete her dissertation, which was based on a line from the Koran that translates as, "A believing slave is better than a nonbelieving free man."

The idea behind the revelation is that the faithful should ignore social status. Ms. Mattson said she wanted to know why slavery continued although the holy texts discouraged it, ultimately deciding that it was because religious scholars ignored political issues.

"She is one of those people who constantly strives for social justice," said Wadad Kadi, one of her University of Chicago professors. "She recognized the importance of fundamentally understanding Islamic law and making it relevant to people's lives."

In addition to being a professor of Islamic studies at the Hartford Seminary, she directs the program that trains Muslim chaplains for hospitals, universities or the military.

Since her time as a student in Chicago, Professor Mattson has worked with the Islamic Society, which was founded in 1963. She had served as vice president for the past five years, so her election was both anticipated and unopposed. (Not only is the post unpaid, but she also is expected to donate 1 percent of the salary from her paid job to the organization.)

American Muslims generally put their numbers around 6 million but some demographers suggest it might be as little as half that.

Ms. Mattson hopes to focus on Muslim women's rights and on how the current negative image of Islam will affect the young generation. She is also concerned that the "terrorist" label is being abused—extended too widely against Muslim groups doing charitable work among the Palestinians and elsewhere.

Like other mainstream Muslims, she struggles with how best to convince people that the faith does not condone terrorist violence. She detects what she calls "Muslim fatigue" among North Americans weary both of the extremists who use the religion to justify their attacks and of the moderates who seem powerless to influence them.

"The sense I have from Americans is that they don't want to hear Muslims talking about Islam anymore," she said. "They just want us to do something to stop causing all these problems in their lives."

Jennie Ruby

Fundamentalisms on the Rise

Whether it is Hindu fundamentalism fueling violence against Muslims and others in India, Muslim fundamentalism taking away women's rights in Afghanistan, Algeria or Iran, Catholic fundamentalism in Austria, or fundamentalist Christians unduly influencing the federal government in the United States, fundamentalist movements worldwide are an active and imminent threat to women's rights—and women's lives—right now.

There are two levels at which fundamentalist religions are a problem for women:

1. Fundamentalist religions are patriarchal and so codify social systems in which men generally dominate women and control reproductive decisions.
2. When a religion is taken up as a fundamental identity for a group or state, issues of women's rights and position in society become the battlefield on which power struggles over national or cultural identity are played out—to the extreme detriment of women's rights and lives.

Of these two levels, it is the fundamentalist movements—not the religions themselves—that are the primary threat.

While it is true that many religions reify male domination and the subordination of women in their founding documents and in their historic traditions, many women are working within religions to liberalize male-female relations in practice while salvaging the spiritual and uplifting messages that religions also contain. In

practice, religions can and do change to reflect the society they are embedded in, and feminist advances in society are often reflected in religion. Furthermore, religions have often been key factors in progressives struggles such as the U.S. Civil Rights movement and other liberation struggles and are thus not always conservative.

What is a problem for women is the rise of fundamentalisms worldwide. What makes the fundamentalist versions of religions so dangerous is that they are being used as a means of reasserting male dominance and evolving into tools for civic repression, suite control and violence.

What is fundamentalism? It can be defined as a religious movement that demands a strict adherence to a set of basic principles. Amrita Chhachhil says that "fundamentalism constructs a particular version of Islam/Hinduism/Shiksm/Christianity as the only valid representation of that religion."

For feminists, it is important to see that repressive fundamentalist movements exist in many different cultures using many different religions—and/or ethnicities—as their base. In their introduction to *Warning Signs of Fundamentalisms*, Ayesha Imam and Nira Uval-Davis emphasize the importance of recognizing "fundamentalisms" rather than just one kind of fundamentalism.

What is important to watch out for in fundamentalist movements is when they begin to gain power to enforce adherence to their strictly interpreted version of a religion. What begins as social pressure graduates into attempts to influence or control media and education, violent coercion and, ultimately, legal sanctions through control of the government.

Source: "Fundamentalisms on the Rise," by Jennie Ruby. *Off Our Backs* 36(3): 11–13. © 2006. Used by permission.

For example, in *Baghdad Burning*, Riverbend describes the social pressure of receiving "critical stares" when she went to a shopping area in central Baghdad and found herself one of the few women not wearing a hijab (headscarf). At the more extreme end, in Algeria numbers of women have been killed for refusing to wear the hijab. The establishment of hudud laws in two states in Malaysia means, for example, that women who report rapes must prove the charge through the testimony of four male Muslim eyewitnesses or face 80 lashes. The institution of shari'a law in Nigeria and other countries severely restricts women's rights.

In the United States, right-wing fundamentalist groups have harassed, threatened, bombed, and murdered abortion providers; used their media ownership and influence to forward spurious claims such as "postabortion syndrome"; limited the teaching of evolution in science classrooms and pushed the fundamentalist-backed notion of "intelligent design" or creationism; and pressured legislators and rallied voters to institute state constitutional amendments to prevent gay and lesbian citizens from gaining marriage rights.

Across religions and across ethnicities, fundamentalist movements re-assert male dominance in the family and put control of women's bodies, sexuality and reproductive choices into the hands of men. In the process, they restrict women's freedom of movement, access to resources and civil rights. In their more extreme forms, they deliberately perpetrate violence against women. Repression of women is one of the key characteristics of fundamentalist movements, and it is the reason feminists must counter these movements at all costs.

What Fundamentalist Movements Do to Women

Although any given fundamentalist movement may not result in all of these effects, fundamentalist movements are characterized by these kinds of efforts to control women and worsen the conditions of women's lives:

- Deny women freedom of movement [e.g., by forcing women to be accompanied by a man]
- Restrict women to the household by denying women free access to public space
- Prevent women from being able to earn a living independent from a man
- Deny women full access to education
- Deny women political positions and power
- Pressure women to have lots of children
- Deny women access to abortion and birth control
- Expect or require girls to marry at an extremely young age
- Expect abstinence/virginity until marriage
- Deliver severe punishment to women who violate sexual norms/laws
- Restrict women's clothing choices more than men's
- Verbally or physically attack women not dressed in required attire
- Inflict female genital mutilation on girls, causing women severe health issues throughout their lives
- Rape and kill women in episodes of genocidal violence

How to Recognize a Fundamentalist Movement

In order to fight the rise of fundamentalisms, feminists must be able to recognize the signs when a religion is taking a dangerous fundamentalist turn—and when a fundamentalist movement is attempting to gain political power. The following signs may be present, in whole or in part.

Obsession with Sexual "Morality"

Because a key component of fundamentalist movements is control over women's reproductive choices, a near obsession with sexual "morality" is frequently present. Often fundamentalist religions prescribe strict sexual observances—the Christian "missionary position," the Unification

Church's prescribed sexual positions, the Mormon demand for a specific type of restrictive underwear. Many of the clothing requirements for women stem from efforts to control sexuality. Other efforts include violent repression of gay and lesbian behavior; oppression and violence toward people who identify as gay, lesbian, bisexual, or transgender; and attempts to codify sexual morality into law. Perhaps the most extreme effort at control is the horrendous practice of female genital mutilation.

Characteristic Rhetoric and Beliefs

Here are some typical beliefs and types of arguments used by fundamentalist groups.

- Asserting that the fundamentalist view is the only true one
- Creating an impression of returning to an (illusory) older time when things were better
- Creating a homogenous identity—erasing or glossing over differences within a religious or ethnic group [e.g., Hindu fundamentalists in India assert a particular brand of Brahminical Hinduism, denying the history of the Shramanic tradition; Islamists during the Iranian revolution put down and attempted to erase the existence of an active feminist movement]
- Defining the cultural identity through strict interpretations of ancient or revered texts
- Seeing the fundamentalist group as embattled by opposing forces—which in reality are oppressed minorities [e.g., Hindu fundamentalists in Gujarat in India cultivated fear of the Muslim minority]
- Denouncing opponents as evil or immoral (rather than arguing the points or using logic) [e.g., Bush labeling countries an "axis of evil."]
- Believing in authoritarianism/obedience to one leader
- Pillorying critics—by exaggerating, repeating and magnifying their critical statements against the fundamentalist group and expressing outrage that they said them [e.g.,

treatment of Taslima Nasreen in Bangladesh for her comments critical of Islamic fundamentalism; treatment of Rosie O'Donnell in U.S. press when she remarked that "radical Christianity is just as threatening as radical Islam in a country like America."]
- Cracking down on individual criminals rather than focus on social justice
- Emphasizing faith over facts
- Obsessing over sexual "morality" while ignoring killing, lying, unjust war, and torture [religious right in the United States]

Methods Fundamentalist Movements Use to Gain Power

Education

- Destruction of knowledge by, for example, banning books
- Insisting that scientific findings be in accord with religious texts
- Denial of education to women [e.g., Taliban in Afghanistan]
- Control of educational materials by fundamentalist groups
- Erosion of secular schooling
- Funding/enabling/establishment by law of religious schools

Media

- Undue influence over media by religious right
- Control of media by religious right groups
- Restricted access to all women and to minority religious or ethnic groups

Political Power

- Establishment of a state religion
- Adoption of religious laws
- Legislating a restrictive and repressive version of sexual "morality" [e.g., outlawing adultery and imposing severe penalties; passing constitutional amendments against gay rights]
- Undue effect on government by fundamentalist groups

- Increased membership in fundamentalist religious organizations
- The accrual of massive wealth by fundamentalist religious groups
- Control of government by fundamentalist organizations/groups

Antidotes to Fundamentalisms

Three important principles for working against fundamentalist movements are separation of church and state; secular, social justice values; and feminism.

Keeping the civil state or government separate from religion is key. Allowing a religion to dominate a government means religious oppression for the diverse members of today's societies. The law must remain secular—and take precedence over any lesser authority religions have over their members. The government should also ensure that people's participation in any religion is strictly voluntary—not coerced. Without this key separation, human freedoms—and women's rights and lives—are severely threatened.

Governments must remain secular. A government's legitimacy must come from people's collective consent, not from any kind of supposed divine right. The government should be responsive to people's material needs, not focus on the precepts of a god or religion. Since fundamentalism often arises in response to social and economic crises, governments should work to ensure that human needs are met and that such crises do not disrupt people's lives.

Feminism is the final key principle for countering fundamentalist movements. In order to stave off fundamentalist takeovers, civil government must be dedicated to the concept of women's equality. Women's civil rights under government must be strongly defended against the precepts of patriarchal religions. When women participate in religion, that participation must be freely chosen, not coerced.

Commitment to these three principles is the only way to guarantee that women's human rights are not curtailed by religious and cultural traditions that have a history of controlling, oppressing and even physically harming women.

References

Chhachhi, Amrita. "Religious Fundamentalism and Women" Dossier 4, September 1988. Combaillaux, France: Women Living Under Muslim Laws. Reprinted online at http://waf.gn.apc.org

Imam, Ayesha, Jenny Morgan & Nira Yuval-Davis (eds.). *Warning Signs of Fundamentalisms*. UK: Women Living Under Muslim Laws. December 2004. Available online at www.whrnet.org/fundamentalisms/docs/doc-wsfmeeting-2002.html

Morgan, Robin. *Fighting Words*. New York: Nation Books, 2006.

Riverbend, *Baghdad Burning*. New York: The Feminist Press, 2005.

Nami Kim

"My/Our" Comfort *Not* at the Expense of "Somebody Else's"

Toward a Critical Global Feminist Theology

Asking what it means to do theology in "my" or "our" context when we find that wo/men's lives are closely interrelated to one another across national borders through the process of globalization, this article attempts to reconsider both critical and global characteristics of Asian feminist theology rather than maintaining it as a theology that speaks only for or to "Asian women" from the "Asian women's perspective" in the "Asian" context.[1] Although the use of the unitary category "Asian women" was indispensable to a certain extent in the earlier processes of formulating Asian women's/feminist theology, it has since rendered wo/men in and from Asias a monolithic group irrespective of varied sociocultural, religious, political, and economic differences among them.[2] As Asian American theorist Laura Hyun Yi Kang puts it, both "the shifting geographical terrain of transnational sex work in Asia" and that of transnational labor migration in Asia as well as across the Asian Pacific demand a critical reconsideration of the category "Asian women."[3] Feminist theologians Wai-Ching Angela Wong and Namsoon Kang have also criticized the unexamined use of the homogeneous category "Asian women."[4] Current transnational market economies, cultural exchanges, political interventions, and military expansions also illustrate how difficult it is to retain a unifying category "Asian" along with the category "Asian women."

Challenging the unexamined use of the homogeneous category "Asian women" and the unifying category "Asian," this article aims to articulate Asian feminist theology as a critical global feminist theology. A critical global feminist theology is an attempt to respond to the increasing forces of globalization under which "my/our comfort" is often maintained at the expense of "somebody else's" and vice versa. It is also an effort to form global resistance against ongoing injustice and global solidarity among wo/men in and across national borders. Building on a critical feminist theory that stresses the importance of a systemic social analysis to explicate how social differences have been systematically produced and continue to operate within the social structures, a critical global feminist theology seeks to investigate how differences among wo/men are produced across the different socioeconomic and religio-cultural locations.[5] Calling attention to the limits of identity politics, a critical global feminist theology claims that feminist theologies cannot and should not be ghettoized as if they were relevant only to "their" own context, when "my" or "our" context is inextricably interconnected with "other" contexts under global capitalism and the military hegemony that underpins it.

However, articulating Asian feminist theology as a critical global feminist theology does not

Source: The article first appeared in *The Journal of Feminist Studies in Religion*, Vol. 21, Issue 2 (Fall 2005), p. 75–94. Used by permission.

mean discrediting or discarding the prior theological works and struggles made by Asian feminist theologians. Nor does it mean developing another "megafeminist" theological discourse that conflates "wo/men's experience" with the experience of a certain privileged group of wo/men. Rather, the articulation of a critical global feminist theology should be done through the ongoing dialogue between and interaction with existing Asian feminist theological works, the legacies of which should not be underestimated. In this sense, this article is only a first step in rethinking some of the challenges feminist theologians face in this era of globalization, thus opening the floor to discuss concerned issues among feminist theologians, especially among those who are from/in Asias.

Although this article addresses some methodological and theological issues that feminist theology needs to reconsider, it also reflects a personal and political concern that has led me to question identity politics. My "outsider within" position in the United States—first as an "international student" and later as a "resident alien" who had become part of the "Asian Pacific North American community"—pressed me to look critically at how the category "Asian women" has been constructed as a homogeneous group irrespective of differences among wo/men in and from Asias by the dominant group in the United States. Also, a critical investigation of Japan's military sexual slavery during World War II, as well as the recent transnational labor migration of wo/men in and across the Asian Pacific, has pressed me to question the unexamined categories "Asian women" and "Asia."[6] All these factors have compelled me to question the construction of identity and the theological discourses that are based on the limited notions of identity.

In the remainder of the article, I will suggest five points that need to be taken into account in articulating Asian feminist theology as a critical global feminist theology. Each point will help explain why such an articulation is necessary and important.

Challenging the Categories "Asian Women" and "Asian"

Asian feminist theology, as a critical global feminist theology, should continue to investigate how certain "Asian women's experience" is constructed, articulated, and shaped, and to further examine the sociopolitical and religio-cultural structures of domination—that is, the systemic arrangements of power in society along the axes of race/ethnicity, class, gender, nationality, sexuality, and so on—that have created such experience by analyzing how, when, by whom, and for what purposes the category "Asian women" is used without taking it for granted. In doing so, Asian feminist theology, as a critical global feminist theology, can further name structures of domination that have created such experience and at the same time provide theological visions that can dismantle those structures and empower wo/men who continue to struggle so that they may survive and flourish. Such a critical global feminist theology can articulate how wo/men not only are affected by the structures of domination but also willingly or unwillingly participate in them, sometimes taking advantage of or benefiting from them in return for disadvantaging other wo/men.

This necessitates a shift from doing theology for, to, and/or by "Asian women"—or any group of women defined by a limited notion of identity—with the "Asian women's perspective." Setting forth a new direction by engaging in methodological discussion with feminist theory concerning the homogeneous category "Asian women," Asian feminist theology, as a critical global feminist theology, no longer grounds itself on identity—that is, "Asian women"—whether singular or multiple, moving beyond what June Jordan calls "the paralysis of identity politics."[7] . . .

A critical examination of the homogeneous category "Asian women" does not necessarily imply the abandonment of it, however. It is not a kind of category that can be simply discarded or abandoned. Rather, it is crucial to continue to investigate how the category "Asian women" has been discursively constructed and used by dominant discourses *and* how it continues to be used under the increasing forces of globalization in and across the Asian Pacific without taking it for granted as a "natural" category. In other words, what Gayatri Spivak calls a "persistent critique" is necessary with the acknowledgment of "the unavoidable usefulness of something that is very dangerous" and the awareness of "the dangerousness of what one must use."[8]

Asian feminist theology, as a critical global feminist theology, then, can be claimed and articulated by one who wants to participate in an "imagined community" of struggle not because she or he is "Asian" through her or his country of origin or through racial/ethnic affiliation but because she or he is willing to engage in a critical theological discourse that unceasingly challenges the dominant racist, orientalist, and colonial discourses and that simultaneously can provide a theological vision for a better and more just world.[9] There is no automatic connection between being an "Asian woman" and doing Asian feminist theology. Claiming oneself as an Asian feminist theologian is not based on one's being a "woman" or being "Asian." Rather, identifying oneself as an Asian feminist theologian means that one is willing to engage in a "strategic use" of the term "Asian" while simultaneously developing a theology from a feminist perspective.[10]

In this sense it is problematic to categorize one's theological work as "Asian" only because she or he can be categorized as "Asian" by the standard of the dominant group. Instead, Asian feminist theologians are those who constantly question and examine the term "Asian" and the ways in which it is used, and who redefine how it should be used. This entails an ongoing critical examination of *both* how the term has been used by the dominant discourses, such as Western colonial discourse and Christian missionary discourse, in the history of multicolonialism—that is, Western colonialism and Japanese colonial-

ism—*and* how the use of the term is changing under the continuing legacy of multicolonialism imbued with the growing forces of globalization in and across the Asian Pacific.[11]. . .

Philosopher Yoko Arisaka points out the complex historical situation in East Asia when she writes, "In East Asia . . . the historical situation was complicated by the fact that the history of colonialism did not neatly fit into the Europe vs. Asia paradigm because Japan was itself a colonial power over Korea, China, the Philippines and parts of Indonesia."[12] Having affected and still affecting the lives of hundreds of thousands of people in many parts of East and Southeast Asia, the legacy of Japan's colonialism cannot be omitted or disregarded as simply a regional problem. The legacy of Japan's colonialism, as part of the legacy of multicolonialism, is inextricably connected to the problems of the capitalist global economic system and the military hegemony that sustains it. It is this complex context within which "hierarchically structured differences" among wo/men continue to be created in the midst of ongoing global exploitation.

Although increasing numbers of wo/men in and from Asias enjoy freely traveling across national borders, quite a number of women from Sri Lanka are compelled to do so in their work as domestic maids in Kuwait, Saudi Arabia, Singapore, Hong Kong, and South Korea.[13] Thousands of Chinese and Filipina women often pay high fees to work under South Korean managerial supervision in garment factories on the Pacific island of Saipan, which is the only U.S. territory exempt from federal minimum-wage and immigration laws. The clothing they make, bearing the "Made in the USA" label, is shipped duty- and quota-free to the United States and sold by some of the popular retailers.[14] The experience of lower-working-class women who work in a Nike factory making seventy-five cents a day in Thailand[15] is vastly different from that of upper-middle-class women who work as CEOs in transnational corporations in Singapore. In other words, not all wo/men in and from Asias work as domestic maids or garment workers with nimble fingers. There are those who hire domestic maids and buy clothes from the transnational clothing companies.

As Cynthia Enloe points out, we often underestimate the complex relationships it takes to sustain the current international econo-political system by picturing all wo/men in third-world societies as "sewing jeans, not buying jeans";[16] as protecting nature, not destroying nature; as fighting against neocolonialism, not being co-opted by it. Not only the difference of labor among wo/men but also caste, religious, ethnic, economic, and political differences, as feminist theologians such as Gabriele Dietrich and Aruna Gnanadason have shown, have created division, friction, and animosity among wo/men, especially in Indian and Southeast Asian contexts.[17] Difference as inequality, as Chris Weedon argues in her *Feminism, Theory, and the Politics of Difference*, is produced by economic, political, social, and cultural factors, as well as "class, caste, colonial and racist practices, and heterosexism."[18] As Weedon accurately puts it, "[H]ierarchically structured differences remain a central challenge for feminists."[19] . . .

It is crucial for feminist theologians to recognize difference as a powerful resource to dismantle the status quo, envisioning a world where difference is valued and celebrated free from the hierarchical structures of class exploitation, racism, heterosexism, and neocolonialism.[20] At the same time, feminist theologians constantly need to challenge and expose late capitalism's celebration of difference, or what Donna Haraway calls "normalization of heterogeneity," which often misleads people into believing that everybody has the same resources and equal access to power.[21] Feminist theologians should demand the end of difference as a mark of oppression. The recognition of difference requires "the ability to acknowledge privileges which come from the structural power relations within which individuals are located, something that privileged women are rarely keen to do."[22] As Chris Weedon puts

it, "[T]hinking difference differently is one of the key objectives of Third World feminism both in the West and in the Third World."[23] . . .

Envisioning Global Resistance

Asian feminist theology, as a critical global feminist theology, needs to continue to stress that "my/our" lives are inextricably connected with "your/their" lives across geographical boundaries. Asian feminist theology, as a critical global feminist theology, can become more *relevant* by construing context not just locally but also as historically situated in a particular social arrangement without forfeiting its connection to the larger social structures. Understanding context in terms of interaction between local and global helps to see how the lives of wo/men in and from Asias are interconnected not only with one another but also with wo/men in and from other parts of the world, because the current economic, political, military, and cultural globalization affects and shapes people's lives beyond national borders. This will further help to understand how "my/our" own comfort has often been maintained at the expense of "somebody else's," and vice versa, without recognizing the impact or cost of keeping one's own comfort.

Asian feminist theology, as a critical global feminist theology, should always be attentive to two different faces of globalization, as Seyla Benhabib, in *The Claims of Culture*, discusses: one that is incompatible with democratic citizenship and the other that is compatible with it. On the one hand, the trajectory of globalization that is incompatible with democratic citizenship, according to Benhabib, is still from the center to the periphery. This globalization runs through transnational and global corporations and diminishes the nation-state system. The major concern with what Benhabib calls "global.com civilization" is the lack of commitments that require "accountability and a deepening of attachment." On the other hand, there is another face of globalization that is compatible with democratic citizenship, which suggests that democratic citizenship can be "exercised across national boundaries and in transnational contexts."[24]

Being aware of these two different, conflicting aspects of globalization, Asian feminist theology, as a critical global feminist theology, should challenge and critique exploitative and oppressive systems, such as the global market economy, transnational sex trade, military expansion, various religious fundamentalisms, and institutionalized racism and heterosexism. It is necessary to vigilantly investigate the changing economic, political, cultural, and religious dynamics in and across Asias in relation to the larger global context. For instance, the transnational sex trade of women and girls, which is one of the major patterns of migratory labor not only in Asias but also in other parts of the world, challenges an analysis that frames sex trade simply as a symptom of patriarchy in a local context without making connections to the larger global economic system.[25] As Beverly Harrison has stated, we "live in a world historical situation where one geopolitical economy controls all people. . . . [S]ince the global capitalist mode of production pervades and controls all our social relations, we can no longer afford to analyze any of the patterns of exploitation shaping our own community's reality in discrete isolation."[26]

Hence, Asian feminist theology, as a critical global feminist theology, should accompany analyses of the global context in relation to the local context,[27] and vice versa, while continuing to critique the current economic structure that exacerbates the economic gap between the haves and the have-nots and that further deepens environmental problems. Instead of searching for "authentic" Asians or Asianness, Asian feminist theology, as a critical global feminist theology, needs to examine what is going on in and across Asias in relation to other contexts, because one context no longer exists unaffected by other contexts under the increasing forces of globalization. For instance, noticing the changing and multiple Asias, Kwok Pui-lan pays attention to the growing uneven economic development in Asia and the subsequent disparity among wo/men in Asias,

thereby alluding to a possibility of conceptualizing "Asian" not in terms of binary opposition to another monolithic category, "Western," but in terms of the complex interactions within, between, and across national borders under a transnational capitalist market economy.[28]

In relation to this, what feminist theologians need to do is not so much to "speak for" exploited, voiceless, and nameless wo/men as to speak for justice, liberation, equality, and well-being, condemning the structures of domination that produce hierarchies in wo/men's lives and divide wo/men from one another.[29] At the same time, feminist theologians should continue to articulate various visions for a better world in which no wo/men remain nameless, exploited, or oppressed based on their differences.

Along with the awareness of the conflicting aspects of globalization, Asian feminist theology, as a critical global feminist theology, should make a commitment to global resistance, which is multiple and creative. In the face of increasing global violence against wo/men and other marginalized people caused by voluntary or involuntary labor migration under the transnational market economy, military clashes, ethnic/racial conflicts, and religious disputes, Asian feminist theology, as a critical global feminist theology, seeks to engage in multiple ways of resisting various forms of violence through the ongoing critique of social practices of violence as well as of religious and theological discourses that reinscribe and even justify violence in the name of the Divine, scripture, tradition, and/or community. As forms of violence are multiple and dynamic, struggle must be pluralized and contextualized in ways that account for the multiplicative aspects and intersections of oppressions and resistance.

Laying Out a Theological Task

For Asian feminist theology, as a critical global feminist theology, the central concern is not so much about how one can believe in God in the midst of rampant "secularism" as about how one can live as a *human being* in the midst of prevalent injustice. Instead of asking whether or not one can have faith in God, it asks what kind of God one should proclaim. It does not stress the relationship with the Divine through fervent prayer and meditation only. Instead, such a theology empowers wo/men so that they can challenge and transform the age-old hierarchical, social, and ecclesial structures that have perpetuated systems of oppression in the name of the Divine and/or faith. It also encourages wo/men to participate in global struggles for justice and liberation, facing challenges from the "prosperity gospel" and the expansion of transnational Pax Americana Christianity that underpins U.S. imperialism and sanctions transnational capitalist patriarchal exploitation that shows the "preferential option for the rich."

Asian feminist theology, as a critical global feminist theology, strives for both personal and structural transformation. Its theological understanding of liberation no longer should be grounded on a limited notion of liberation that is often related to a limited understanding of oppression, but rather needs to be articulated in multiple ways, as oppressions are complex and multiplicative. Unless we realize that "my/our" liberation is inextricably connected with "your/their" liberation in this intricate web of economic, political, military, cultural, and religious globalization, structures of domination will not be dismantled. Asian feminist theology, as a critical global feminist theology, seeks to provide theological visions for multiplicative liberations, not for one at the expense of another.[30]

Moving Toward "Spiritual Solidarity"

As Patricia Hill Collins claims, the word "move" refers to the "power of deep feelings." Collins states, "This type of passionate rationality flies in the face of Western epistemology that sees emotions and rationality as different and competing concerns."[31] Asian feminist theology, as a critical global feminist theology, needs to move, or *gahm-dong*, people rather than simply to help people

"comprehend."[32] It should be able to affect people to the extent that it moves them to participate in the struggle for justice and liberation. Collins further maintains that spirituality, when it is fully realized, is a "passionate, deeply felt affair."[33] A theology that moves or *gahm-dongs* people to participate in struggle testifies to the power of spirituality that bears social witness. Spirituality that bears social witness is different from the popular spiritualities or various forms of self-help that tend to believe that an individual person can be free from structures of domination without being affected by them.[34] Instead, it encourages and sustains wo/men in their struggle for justice and liberation.

Arguing that Sojourner Truth's spirituality served as a "vehicle that clearly moved her struggle for justice," Collins asserts that spirituality comprises "articles of faith that provide a conceptual framework for living everyday life," rather than being merely a "system of religious beliefs similar to logical systems of ideas."[35] Spirituality defined as such revolutionizes the myopic understanding of spirituality as individualistic, dualistic, esoteric, and otherworldly. Quoting Gustavo Gutiérrez, Aruna Gnanadason captures this point: "[W]hen one is concerned with one's own stomach, it is materialism, but when one is concerned with other people's stomach, it is spirituality."[36] It is in using this understanding of spirituality that we can develop a "spiritual solidarity" among wo/men who continue to struggle against the structures of domination in the twenty-first century.

We live in a world in which developing spiritual solidarity among wo/men is ever more urgent, because the current global market system requires and promotes individualistic and commercialized spiritualities that deflect people from engaging in the active transformation of a world that values property over life. Sustaining spiritual solidarity is not about trying to understand different faith traditions in the name of tolerance but, rather, about participating in global struggles for justice and peace. Like political solidarity that has been advocated by various groups of feminists who reject the "sentimental" brand of sisterhood, spiritual solidarity begins with "women's confronting and combating each other's differences and ends with their using these very same differences to 'accelerate their positive advance' toward the goals they share in common."[37] Instead of working to eradicate difference in order to have solidarity, wo/men of different faiths can be united, in bell hooks's words, "by shared interests and beliefs, united in our appreciation for diversity, united in our struggle to end sexist oppression, united in political solidarity."[38] Such spiritual solidarity does not suggest an uncritical engagement with all faith traditions but entails "mutual criticism and openness to the critique of women of other faith traditions."[39] This is closely related to the theological question, What kind of God should one proclaim in the midst of ongoing injustice and suffering? Further, it raises the question of the relationship among different religions in a changing religious landscape along with transnational migration, both voluntary and involuntary, across the world. It is necessary to ask the place of Christianity among other religions, and the same question in regard to those other religions. As Kwok Pui-lan puts it, "[S]uch critical engagement with one another is necessary if women of all faith traditions are to work together for the liberation and well-being of all women."[40] In spiritual solidarity, wo/men of all faiths can work collectively to change the world. Asian feminist theology, as a critical global feminist theology, is committed to such spiritual solidarity.

Notes

1. The word "wo/men," Elisabeth Schüssler Fiorenza's neologism, indicates that women are not a unitary social group but are fragmented by structures of race, class, ethnicity, religion, sexuality, colonialism, and age. Schüssler Fiorenza maintains that this destabilization underscores the differences between wo/men and within individual wo/men. "Wo/men," according to her, is also inclusive and functions as a linguistic corrective to androcentric language use. See her *Jesus: Miriam's Child, Sophia's Prophet* (New York: Contin-

uum, 1994); and *Wisdom Ways: Introducing Feminist Biblical Interpretation* (Maryknoll, NY: Orbis, 2001).

Globalization includes, but is not limited to, a transnational labor market; voluntary or involuntary migration due to political and/or religious disputes and racial/ethnic or military conflicts; a transnational sex industry; and movement of commodities, money, media, and information technology. I discuss two aspects of globalization later in this article. Also see John E. Wills Jr., *1688: A Global History* (New York: Norton, 2001); Sarah Anderson and John Cavanagh with Thea Lee, and the Institute for Policy Studies, *Field Guide to the Global Economy*, rev. ed. (New York: New Press, 2005); Christa Wichterich, *The Globalized Woman: Reports from a Future of Inequality*, trans. Patrick Camiller (North Melbourne, Australia: Spinifex; London: Zed, 2000); and Cynthia D. Moe-Lobeda, *Healing a Broken World: Globalization and God* (Minneapolis: Fortress, 2002).

I will place "Asian women" and related terms in quotation marks throughout this article in order to indicate the questionableness of these terms as categories.

2. By "Asian women's/feminist theology" I refer to an already-existing Christian women's/feminist theological corpus and movement in and from Asias. However, over the years the term "Asian women's theology" has been used interchangeably with "Asian feminist theology." Kwok Pui-lan uses the term "Asian feminist theology" in her *Introducing Asian Feminist Theology* (Cleveland: Pilgrim, 2000), although most earlier works by women theologians used the term "Asian women's theology." Asian women's/feminist theology grew out of the urgent need for a relevant and liberative theology for women who live in the vast continent called Asia during a time of a growing awareness of women's oppression and the forming of progressive women's organizations. The need for taking into account a group called "Asian women" as a subject of theology was one of the major grounds for building Asian women's theology when various marginalized groups began to actively engage in theological discussions.

I am using the term "wo/men in and from Asias" to indicate that wo/men who have been living in Asias and migrating from and across Asias are not a unitary social group but are fragmented by structures of race, class, ethnicity, religion, sexuality, colonialism, and age. The term also indicates a direct and an indirect relationship with the struggle of Asian

Pacific Americans, whose history is closely related to the history of multicolonialism through U.S. foreign and economic policies. Whereas Laura Hyun Yi Kang argues for the breakdown of "Asia" into the multiple specifications of "South," "East," and "Southeast" Asias, I will use the term "Asias" to indicate such multiplicity. See Laura Hyun Yi Kang, *Compositional Subjects: Enfiguring Asian/American Women* (Durham: Duke University Press, 2002), 185.

3. Kang, *Compositional Subjects*, 185. Kang also casts doubt on the so-called shared Asian designation, saying that "the growing numbers of male tourists from South Korea, Taiwan, Singapore, and Hong Kong attest to how the contours of transnational sex tourism unsettle any sense of their shared 'Asian' designation with the Thai and Filipina sex workers" (185).

4. See Namsoon Kang, "Creating 'Dangerous Memory': Challenges for Asian and Korean Feminist Theology," *Ecumenical Review* 47 (January 1995): 21–31; and Wai-Ching Angela Wong, " 'The Poor Woman': A Critical Analysis of Asian Theology and Contemporary Chinese Fiction by Women" (PhD diss., University of Chicago, 1997). Kwok Pui-lan also warns that we must guard against a "generalized, monolithic and ahistorical image of the 'Asian woman' since the Asian societies are so diverse" (*Introducing Asian Feminist Theology*, 13).

5. Feminists who employ a critical feminist theory include Chandra Mohanty, Uma Narayan, Rosemary Hennessy, Patricia Hill Collins, and Elisabeth Schüssler Fiorenza.

6. I discuss Japan's military sexual slavery in detail in my dissertation, "Constructing 'Asian Women': A Critical Examination of Cultural-Theological Rhetoric" (ThD diss., Harvard University, 2004).

7. June Jordan, *Technical Difficulties: African-American Notes on the State of the Union* (New York: Pantheon, 1992), 168, quoted in Patricia Hill Collins, *Fighting Words: Black Women and the Search for Justice* (Minneapolis: University of Minnesota Press, 1998), 250.

8. Gayatri Spivak with Ellen Rooney, "In a Word," *Differences: A Journal of Feminist Cultural Studies*, no. 2 (Summer 1989): 129.

9. In her keynote speech at the Consultation on Asian Pacific North American Theologies at the annual meeting of the American Academy of Religion held in Toronto, Ontario, in November 2002, Kwok Pui-lan mentioned that "Asian" signified an "imagined community." Chandra Mohanty also articulates what she means by an "imagined community" of third-world oppositional struggles. It is "imagined," according to Mohanty, "not because it is not 'real' but because it suggests potential alliances and collaborations across divisive boundaries, and [it is] 'community' because in spite of internal hierarchies within third world contexts, it nevertheless suggests a significant, deep commitment to what Benedict Anderson, in referring to the idea of the nation, calls 'horizontal comradeship.' " Chandra Talpade Mohanty, "Cartographies of Struggle: Third World Women and the Politics of Feminism," introduction to *Third World Women and the Politics of Feminism*, ed. Chandra Talpade Mohanty, Ann Russo, and Lourdes Torres (Bloomington: Indiana University Press, 1991), 4, quoting Benedict Anderson, *Imagined Communities: Reflections on the Origin and Spread of Nationalism* (New York: Verso, 1983), esp. 11–16. Mohanty argues that "[t]he idea of imagined community is useful because it leads us away from essentialist notions of third world feminist struggles, suggesting political rather than biological or cultural bases for alliance. Thus, it is not color or sex which constructs the ground for these struggles," but rather "the *way* we think about race, class, and gender—the political links we choose to make among and between struggles" (4; Mohanty's emphasis).

10. One of the notable examples of the strategic use of the term "Asian" is its political use by Asian Pacific North Americans within the context of the struggle against racist oppression and against the dominant usage of "Asian" as a cultural and racial/ethnic category. Though distinctive, the history of Asian Pacific North Americans—particularly racism and the ongoing racist (orientalist) construction of people from Asia—is inextricably interconnected with the history of multicolonialisms in Asia and, further, with the transnational capitalist market economy that is underpinned by the U.S. military hegemony. The term "Asian Pacific Americans" ("APA") came into use with the development of movements for racial justice in the North American context in the 1960s and with the struggle against the Vietnam War, whereas before the 1960s, those of Asian and Pacific Island ancestries commonly identified themselves by their country of origin or ethnicity. See Rita Nakashima Brock and Nami Kim, "Asian American Protestant Women: Roles and Contributions in Religion," in *Encyclopedia of Women and Religion in North America*, ed. Rosemary

R. Ruether and Rosemary Keller (Bloomington: Indiana University Press, forthcoming). Asian Pacific American theorists and activists in the United States have attempted to conceptualize "Asian" not as an already constituted racial/ethnic entity but as a political denominator that binds a group of people together based on the common history of oppression and struggle in the United States. In spite of her awareness of the racist use of the category "Asian" and the homogeneous tendency of the category, Lisa Lowe argues for the necessity of maintaining the category "Asian American," not as an essentialized category but as a political and social category. See Lisa Lowe, "Heterogeneity, Hybridity, Multiplicity: Making Asian American Differences," *Diaspora* 1, no. 1 (Spring 1991): 24–44. Yen Le Espiritu, like Lowe, also tries to conceptualize the panethnic Asian American identity as a political construct. See Yen Le Espiritu, *Asian American Panethnicity: Bridging Institutions and Identities* (Philadelphia: Temple University Press, 1992), 2. Laura Hyun Yi Kang joins Lowe and Espiritu, stating, "The designation 'Asian American' was composed through conjoined political mobilizations *for* civil rights in the United States and *against* American imperialism in Asia, most pointedly through the Vietnam War" (*Compositional Subjects*, 5; Kang's emphasis).

11. A genealogical study of the term "Asian" shows that, as a unifying term, it first emerged within the context of Japan's nationalism and colonialism in the late nineteenth and early twentieth centuries. Specifically, Japan used the rhetoric of "pan-Asianism" as an ideological means to rally people against Western imperial power, emphasizing racial and cultural affinities as "Asian." What was often not addressed or problematized was that Japan's "pan-Asianism" was used for the purpose of expanding and increasing Japan's colonial power in Asia rather than for bringing justice and peace to people and to the region that had been devastated by Western colonial exploitation.

12. Yoko Arisaka, "Asian Women: Invisibility, Location, and Claim to Philosophy," in *Women of Color and Philosophy: A Critical Reader*, ed. Naomi Zack (Malden, MA: Blackwell, 2000), 219. Korean American feminists Elaine Kim and Chungmoo Choi argue that most postcolonial studies have focused almost exclusively on European colonialism and that hardly any work has been produced on multicolonialisms in East Asia. They claim that the work on colonialism and

gender could be enriched and diversified by critically examining the colonial challenges Korean and diasporic Korean women face. However, they insist that the discussion of these challenges should not be ghettoized as being merely country-specific or exclusively the subject of area studies. Rather, colonial and neocolonial challenges are inextricably connected to problems of the capitalistic global world system and the military hegemony that upholds it. See Elaine H. Kim and Chungmoo Choi, *Dangerous Women: Gender and Korean Nationalism* (New York: Routledge, 1998).

13. Sri Lankan migrants number more than 1 million, or "roughly 1 in every 19 citizens," 600,000 of whom are housemaids. See Amy Waldman, "Sri Lankan Maids' High Price for Foreign Jobs," *New York Times*, May 8, 2005. About 60 percent, or 153,000, of Hong Kong's foreign domestic workers are Filipinos, and about 75,000 Indonesians and 7,000 Thais also work as domestic assistants, with smaller numbers from Nepal and Bangladesh. See Agence France-Presse, "Philippines Seek Neighbors' Help against HK Maid Tax," November 24, 2002, found on Inq7.net, at http://www.inq7.net/.

14. *Behind the Labels: Garment Workers on U.S. Saipan*, directed by Tia Lessin (Brooklyn: Witness, in association with Oxygen Media, 2001).

15. Holly Sklar, *Chaos or Community? Seeking Solutions, Not Scapegoats for Bad Economics* (Boston: South End, 1995), 40–41.

16. Cynthia Enloe, *Bananas, Beaches, and Bases: Making Feminist Sense of International Politics* (London: Pandora, 1989), 196–98. Enloe argues that international debt may affect all women in Mexico, but not to the same degree or in the same ways: "Sexuality may also divide women in a Third World country" (199). Her point, as well as mine, is not just to emphasize the divisiveness or differences among third-world (or Asian) women but also to point out the necessity for a more nuanced analysis of the current complex international econo-political system.

17. Teresa Ebert argues that difference of labor—particularly the exploitation of surplus labor and thus the difference of profit—among women needs to be resolved in order to talk about "real difference." See her *Ludic Feminism and After: Postmodernism, Desire, and Labor in Late Capitalism* (Ann Arbor: University of Michigan Press, 1996), 156. Also see Gabriele Dietrich, "South Asian Feminist Theory and Its Significance

for Feminist Theology," *Concilium*, no. 1 (1996): 101–15; and Gnanadason, "Towards an Indian Feminist Theology."

18. Weedon, *Feminism*, 181.

19. Ibid., 183.

20. Weedon, *Feminism*, 195.

21. Donna Haraway, "A Manifesto for Cyborgs: Science, Technology, and Socialist Feminism in the 1980s," in Meyers, *Feminist Social Thought*, 505.

22. Weedon, *Feminism*, 185.

23. Ibid., 196.

24. See Seyla Benhabib, *The Claims of Culture: Equality and Diversity in the Global Era* (Princeton: Princeton University Press, 2002), 182–83. Among theologians, Felix Wilfred, who currently teaches at University of Madras, addresses the threat that free-market globalization poses to "the poor." See Felix Wilfred, "Religions Face to Face with Globalization," in *Globalization and Its Victims*, ed. Jon Sobrino and Felix Wilfred (London: SCM, 2001).

25. Rita Nakashima Brock and Susan Thistlethwaite demonstrate that the current pattern of migratory labor by improverished people is so widespread that "such movement renders the 'nation state' concept meaningless." See Rita Nakashima Brock and Susan Thistlethwaite, *Casting Stones: Prostitution and Liberation in Asia and the United States* (Minneapolis: Fortress, 1996), 123.

26. Beverly W. Harrison, "Theological Reflection in the Struggle for Liberation," in *Making the Connections: Essays in Feminist Social Ethics* (Boston: Beacon, 1985), 245–46, quoted in ibid., 108.

27. Emily Askew challenged the binary system of global and local in "Challenging the Globe: Theological Spatiality and Space Theory," a presentation on the theme "Religion and Globalization I," for the Theology and Religious Reflection Section of the annual meeting of the American Academy of Religion, Atlanta, GA, November 22, 2003.

28. See Kwok, *Introducing Asian Feminist Theology*.

29. For the problems of "speaking for others," see Linda Alcoff, "The Problem of Speaking for Others," in *Who Can Speak? Authority and Critical Identity*, ed.

Judith Roof and Robyn Wiegman (Urbana: University of Illinois Press, 1995).

30. Because of space limits, I am not able to fully develop this aspect of a critical global feminist theology in this article.

31. Collins, *Fighting Words*, 243. Collins paraphrases Alison M. Jaggar, "Love and Knowledge: Emotion in Feminist Epistemology," in *Gender/Body/Knowledge: Feminist Reconstructions of Being and Knowing*, ed. Alison M. Jaggar and Susan R. Bordo (New Brunswick, NJ: Rutgers University Press, 1989), 145–71.

32. The word *gahm-dong* in Korean precisely conveys Collins's meaning of the word "move." The word *gahm-dong* is made with two Chinese characters that have their own meanings respectively: *gahm* means "emotion," and *dong* refers to moving or movement. *Gahm-dong*, then, indicates the state of being affected (to be able to move).

33. Collins, *Fighting Words*, 243.

34. See Nami Kim, " Wo/men, the Ba-ram Bearers: Asian Feminist Spiritualities," *Concilium*, no. 5 (May 2000): 13–22.

35. Collins, *Fighting Words*, 245.

36. Gustavo Gutiérrez, quoted in Aruna Gnanadason, "Women and Spirituality in Asia," in *Feminist Theology from the Third World: A Reader*, ed. Ursula King (Maryknoll, NY: Orbis, 1994), 354.

37. Rosemary Putnam Tong, *Feminist Thought: A More Comprehensive Introduction*, 2nd ed. (Boulder, CO: Westview, 1998), 244.

38. bell hooks, *Feminist Theory from Margin to Center* (Boston: South End, 1984), 65.

39. Kwok, *Introducing Asian Feminist Theology*, 50. Although it is a complicated issue that needs to be carefully approached in order not to reinscribe Christian imperialist attitudes toward other faith traditions, spiritual solidarity among various faith traditions is as important as other forms of solidarity (e.g., political solidarity) in this rapidly changing global context.

40. Ibid. Given the history of Christian missionary movement in relation to Western imperialism in Asia, Christian theologians need to be cautious of what Kwok calls "indiscriminate appropriation and mindless borrowing" from "Asian" religious traditions (50).

Contributors

Sandra D. Alvarez is an Assistant Professor of Sociology at Shippensburg University in Pennsylvania. Her current research focuses on Latinas and immigration.

Margaret Andersen is a Professor of Sociology and Women's Studies at the University of Delaware. She is past president of the Eastern Sociological Society and Sociologists for Women in Society and is the 2008–09 Vice President of the American Sociological Association. She is the author of several important textbooks, including *Thinking About Women, Race, Class, and Gender: An Anthology* and *Social Problems* as well as numerous articles on women's lives.

Joanne Belknap is a Professor of Sociology at the University of Colorado, Boulder. She is the author of *The Invisible Woman: Gender, Crime, and Justice* (3rd edition in 2007) and numerous articles addressing women, crime, and victimization.

Carly Berwick writes widely about art and culture and is a contributing editor to ARTnews.

Joan Blades is co-founder of MoveOn.org and Berkeley Systems with her husband, Wes Boyd. She is also co-founder and President of MomsRising.org. She is on the steering committee of Reuniting America: A Transpartisan Campaign of Political Reconciliation (ReunitingAmerica .org), and author of *Mediate Your Divorce* (1985).

Sarah Blustain is a senior editor at *The New Republic*, Deputy Editor of the *American Prospect*, and author of numerous articles on women's lives.

Christine Braumberger is an Associate Professor of English at Onondaga Community College in Syracuse, New York.

Karen Brodine (1947–1987) was a poet and a feminist activist who lived in San Francisco until her death from cancer in 1987. Her books include, among others, *Woman Sitting at the Machine, Thinking*; *Illegal Assembly*; and *Slow Juggling*.

Deborah Carr is an Associate Professor of Sociology at Rutgers University. She is the coeditor of *Spousal Bereavement in Late Life* (forthcoming) and numerous articles on the life course, gender, and the family.

Meda Chesney-Lind is a Professor of Women's Studies at the University of Hawaii at Manoa. She is the author of *Girls, Delinquency and Juvenile Justice* (3rd edition in 2003), which was awarded the American Society of Criminology's Michael J. Hindelang Award in 1992; *The Female Offender: Girls, Women and Crime* (1997); and *Female Gangs in America* (1999). She has been recognized with numerous honors, including the Donald Cressey Award from the National Council on Crime and Delinquency for "her outstanding academic contribution to the field of criminology."

LeeAnn Christian is the Director of Organizational Effectiveness at the Orange County Regional Center in California.

Chrystos (Menominee) is a poet and activist. She was the winner of the Audre Lorde International Poetry Competition in 1994 and of the Sappho Award of Distinction from the Astraea National Lesbian Action Foundation in 1995. Her books include *Not Vanishing* (1988), *Dream On* (1991), *In Her I Am* (1993), *Fugitive Colors* (1995), and *Fire Power* (1995).

Patricia Hill Collins is a Distinguished University Professor at the University of Maryland and the Charles Phelps Taft Distinguished Emeritus Professor of Sociology at the University of Cincinnati. She is the 2008–09 President of the American Sociological Association. Her book *Black Feminist Thought: Knowledge, Consciousness and the Politics of Empowerment* (1990), won the ASA Jessie Bernard Award for significant scholarship on gender and the C. Wright Mills Award from the Society for the Study of Social Problems. Her other books include *Black Sexual Politics: African Americans, Gender and the New Racism; Fighting Words: Black Women and the Search for Justice; From Black Power to Hip Hop: Racism, Nationalism, and Feminism*; and, with Margaret Andersen, *Race, Class, and Gender: An Anthology.*

Heather Dillaway is an Assistant Professor of Sociology at Wayne State University. She is the coeditor of *Understanding Race, Class, Gender, and Sexuality: Case Studies* (2001) and author of several articles addressing women's experiences of menopause. She received the Wayne State President's Award for Excellence in Teaching in 2007.

Lori Ann Dotson is the Director of IABA-North at the Institute for Applied Behavior Analysis and a doctoral candidate at the Fielding Institute.

Zita Z. Dresner is a scholar of American women's humor and the co-author (with Nancy A. Walker) of *Redressing the Balance: American Women's Literary Humour from Colonial Times to the 1980s* (1988).

Gillian Dunne is a Lecturer in Sociology, Law and Social Science at the University of Plymouth in Devon, England. Her books include *Living Difference: Lesbian Perspectives on Work and Family Life* (1998) and *Lesbian Lifestyles: Women's Work and the Politics of Sexuality* (1997).

R. Danielle Egan is an Associate Professor of Gender Studies at St. Lawrence University in Canton, New York. She is the author of *Dancing for Dollars and Paying for Love: The Relationship between Exotic Dancers and Their Customers* (2006) and an editor of *Flesh for Fantasy: Producing and Consuming Exotic Dance* (2006).

Deborah Eicher-Catt is an Assistant Professor of Communication Arts and Sciences at Pennsylvania State University, York. Her research on family communication crosses several methodological boundaries, exploring the intersection of communication theory with semiotics, phenomenology, ethnography, narrative, and feminism. She recently founded the Community-University Partnership at Pennsylvania State University, York, an interdisciplinary research-based initiative composed of faculty interested in improving services and programming for children, youth, and families in the greater York area.

Cynthia Enloe is a Research Professor of International Development and Women's Studies at Clark University. Among her nine books are: *The Morning After: Sexual Politics at the End of the Cold War* (1993); *Bananas, Beaches and Bases: Making Feminist Sense of International Politics* (2000); *Maneuvers: The International Politics of Militarizing Women's Lives* (2000); and *The Curious Feminist: Searching for Women in a New Age of Empire* (2004).

Cynthia Fuchs Epstein is a Distinguished Professor of Sociology at The Graduate Center of the City University of New York. She was honored in 2004 with the ASA Jessie Bernard award for her pioneering work exploring women's exclusion from the professions. She was President of the American Sociological Association in 2005–2006. Among her books are *Woman's Place* (1970), *Women in Law* (1981), and her landmark theoretical work *Deceptive Distinctions* (1988).

Catherine A. Faver is a Professor of Social Work at the University of Texas-Pan American. In addition to her work on relational spirituality, her current research focuses on the links between animal abuse and domestic violence.

William Finlay is a Professor of Sociology and department head at the University of Georgia. He is the coauthor (with James E. Coverdill) of *Headhunters: Matchmaking in the Labor Market*. His current research is on the training and professional socialization of surgeons.

DoVeanna S. Fulton is an Associate Professor of English at Arizona State University, Tempe. She is the author of *Speaking Power: Black Feminist Orality in Women's Narratives of Slavery* (2006), as well as numerous articles on African American literature and manifestations of oral traditions by Black women. Her current research project, *Radical Prohibition: African Americans Writing Race and the Anti-Drink Movement, 1860–1919*, is on African American activism in the Temperance Movement.

J. Hall (Julia Hall) is an Associate Professor of Sociology at D'Youville College in Buffalo, New York. Her work considers youth culture and the cultural production of identity within the context of neoliberal policies and agendas. Human rights concerns and debates are at the core of her research.

Anita Harris is a Lecturer in Sociology at Monash University in Victoria, Australia. She was formerly a Visiting Scholar at the City University of New York. She is the author of *Future Girl: Young Women in the 21st Century* (2003); *All About the Girl: Culture, Power, and Identity* (2004); and coeditor of *Young Femininity: Girlhood, Power, and Social Change* (2005).

Kevin S. Andrade Hauck completed a Fulbright Fellowship in Tijuana, Mexico, and has since worked in the San Diego area as a community organizer and governmental liaison. Located in the heart of a predominantly Hispanic and East African community, his work has led to public policy development and implementation of issues from Housing and Redevelopment to Public Health and Safety. He is currently an Alcohol and Drug Program Specialist with the County of San Diego Health and Human Services Agency.

Sharon Hays is the Barbara Streisand Professor of Contemporary Gender Studies and Professor of Women's Studies at the University of Southern California. She is the author of *Flat Broke with Children: Women in the Age of Welfare Reform* (2004), which won the C. Wright Mills Award from the Society for the Study of Social Problems, and *Cultural Contradictions of Motherhood* (1998).

April Herndon is an Assistant Professor of English and Women's and Gender Studies at Winona State University in Minnesota. She is the author of *Baby Fat: Mothers, Children, and the American War on Obesity* (forthcoming) and numerous articles on women's bodies and intersex rights.

Shere Hite is a Visiting Professor of Gender and Culture at Nihon University in Japan and Director of Hite Research International. Among her eleven books are *The Hite Report on Female Sexuality* (1976); *The Hite Report on Men and Male Sexuality* (1981); *Women and Love: A Cultural Revolution in Progress* (1987); and *The Hite Report on the Family: Growing Up Under Patriarchy* (1994).

Alex Jabs graduated from Ohio State University and is currently a manager at Steak n' Shake in Columbus Ohio. She would like readers to know that she no longer feels ostracized by her family. They have become very supportive and love her for all that she is. Her possible futures include becoming an EMT, an English teacher in a high school, and/or an outspoken and witty public commentator.

June Jordan (1935–2002) was a poet, activist, teacher, essayist, scholar, and tireless fighter for social justice. Her books include *Some of Us Did Not Die* (2002); *Kissing God Goodbye: New Poems* (1997); *Technical Difficulties: New Political Essays* (1992); and *Things That I Do in the Dark* (1977) among many others.

Nami Kim is an Assistant Professor of Religion at Spelman College. Her current research interests include the megachurch phenomenon on college campuses and a critical global feminist theology as a resisting voice to the transnational alliance of the Religious Right. Her articles on women and religion appear in the *Journal of Feminist Studies in Religion* and *Concilium*.

Chisun Lee is an attorney in the Democracy Program of the Brennan Center at New York University, focusing on campaign finance reform and other means of achieving and protecting broader participation in the political process. Prior to joining the Brennan Center, she served as law clerk to the Hon. Gerard E. Lynch of the U.S. District Court in the Southern District of New York. She previously covered the law, politics, and public policy as a print journalist, chiefly as a staff writer at the *Village Voice*, and earned numerous awards and honors for her work.

Yolanda Chávez Leyva is an Associate Professor of History at the University of Texas, El Paso. She is the author of numerous articles and book chapters on the lives of Latina women and children. Her current projects include *Cruzando la Linea: Mexican Children along the Texas-Mexican Border, 1880–1940*, a study that explores the critical role that Mexican and Mexican American children played in the economic and social development of the border region, and *Heart Knowledge: Chicana/o History, Memory, and Pedagogy*, an investigation of the interconnection of Chicana/o history, memory, public presentations of history, and pedagogy. She directs the public history program at the university, is a published poet, and works as a traditional healer.

Audre Lorde (1934–1992) was a feminist poet and activist for justice. Her inspiring work was internationally recognized and honored. She was New York State's poet laureate in 1991–1993. She published many volumes of her poetry, which have become central to our understanding of women's lives. They include, *Zami: A New Spelling of My Name* (1983); *Sister Outsider* (1984); *A Burst of Light* (1989); and *The Cancer Journals* (1980).

Neil MacFarquhar is a national correspondent, based in San Francisco, for the *New York Times*. In addition to his journalistic coverage of Muslim issues, he is the author of a novel, *The Sand Café* (2006).

PJ McGann is a Lecturer in Sociology and Women's Studies at the University of Michigan specializing in gender, sexualities, deviance, and qualitative methods. She is the Vice-President of the Society for the Study of Social Problems (2009–2010) and is currently completing a monograph on tomboys.

Ashley Mears is a doctoral candidate in Sociology at New York University. She was a co-recipient of the Rose Laub Coser Dissertation Award from the Eastern Sociological Association in 2008. Her dissertation is an ethnography of the modeling industries in New York and London. She traces the backstage work that goes into producing and packaging models as "looks" for fashion clients to purchase, and shows how gender and race shape every model's success or failure. In 2006, she was a Mainzer Fellow to the Center for Gender Studies at Cambridge University.

Angela M. Moe is an Associate Professor of Sociology and Criminal Justice, with affiliation with Gender and Women's Studies, at Western Michigan University. Her research interests include violence against women, gender and justice, and sociology of the body. Her work may be found in *Violence Against Women; Criminal Justice Studies; Women and Therapy; Women's Studies Quarterly; Journal of Contemporary Ethnography; Women and Criminal Justice*; and *Journal of Interpersonal Violence*. She is currently earning a graduate certificate in holistic health care, with the aim of developing a line of action-based research in third-wave feminist movement therapy.

Susan Moon is a writer living in Berkeley, California. She's the author of *The Life and Letters of Tufo Roshi* and numerous stories and articles that have appeared in *Ms., Mother Jones, Ploughshares, American Short Fiction*, and *The Sun*. She won a Pushcart prize in 1992 and a National Endowment for the Arts grant in 1993. She's the editor of *Turning Wheel*, the quarterly magazine of the Buddhist Peace Fellowship.

Pat Mora received Honorary Doctorates in Letters from North Carolina State University and SUNY Buffalo and is an Honorary Member of the American Library Association. Among her other awards are the 2006 National Hispanic Cultural Center Literary Award and a 2003 Civitella Ranieri Fellowship to write in Umbria, Italy. She was a Visiting Carruthers Chair at the University of New Mexico, a recipient and judge of the Poetry Fellowships from the National Endowment for the Arts, and a recipient and advisor of the Kellogg National Leadership Fellowships. She is the author of many books, including *Chants* (1984), *House of Houses* (1997), *Nepantlta* (1993), and *Aqua Santa: Holy Water* (1995) as well as many award-winning children's books.

Marcyliena Morgan is Professor of African and African American Studies at Harvard University and the Executive Director of the Hiphop Archive. She is the author of *Language, Discourse and Power in African American Culture* (2002); *The Real Hiphop—Battling for Knowledge, Power, and Respect in the Underground* (forthcoming); and editor of *Language and the Social Construction of Identity in Creole Situations* (1994). Her other publications include articles and chapters on gender and women's speech, language ideology, discourse and interaction among Caribbean women in London and Jamaica, urban youth language and interaction, hiphop culture, and language education planning and policy.

Linda Nochlin is the Lila Acheson Wallace Professor of Modern Art at New York University Institute of Fine Arts. She holds an honorary doctorate from Harvard University and was named Scholar of the Year by the New York State Council for the Humanities. She is considered a leader in feminist art history and is the author of *Women, Art and Power: And Other Essays* (1988), *Realism* (1993), and *Representing Women* (1999) among other books and articles.

Rosalind Pollack Petchesky is a Distinguished Professor of Political Science and Women's Studies at Hunter College. She is the author of *Global Prescriptions: Gendering Health and Human Rights* (2003) and coauthor (with Karen Judd) of *Negotiating Reproductive Rights: Women's Perspectives Across Countries and Cultures* (1998) as well as numerous articles on women and political and human rights. She is the founder and past international coordinator of the International Reproductive Rights Research Action Group (IRRRAG) and a MacArthur Fellow.

Kristin Rowe-Finkbeiner is an author, freelance journalist, and consultant in the field of environmental policy and political strategy. She is the Executive Director of MomsRising.org and author of the award-winning book, *The F-Word: Feminism in Jeopardy—Women, Politics, and the Future* (2004).

Jennie Ruby is a member of the *off our backs* collective and has published numerous articles on a range of feminist issues.

Tracy Rysavy was the associate editor with *Yes! Magazine*.

Bharati Sadasivam is a policy advisor with the Civil Society Organizations Division at the United Nations Development Programme in New York. She has published numerous reports and articles concerning the impact of development on women.

Saskia Sassen is the Robert S. Lynd Professor of Sociology at Columbia University. She is the author of *The Mobility of Labor and Capital* (1988); *The Global City* (1991, 2002); *Territory, Authority, and Rights: From Medieval to Global Assemblages* (2006); and *A Sociology of Globalization* (2007) among numerous other publications. Through UNESCO, she set up a network of researchers and activists in thirty countries to address the issue of sustainable human settlement.

Barbara Schulman is a long-time feminist activist who has worked with the New York City Human Rights Initiative.

Elisabeth Sheff is an Assistant Professor of Sociology at Georgia State University. Her areas of research include gender, sexuality, family, and deviance, and her publications include an examination of polyamorous men's relationships with masculinity in "Polyhegemonic Masculinities" (2006) and ethnographic research methods in "The Reluctant Polyamorist: Autoethnographic Research in a Sexualized Setting" (2007). She is currently editing a volume of interdisciplinary research on polyamory and conducting longitudinal research on polyamorous families.

Andrea Smith (Cherokee) is the author of *Conquest: Sexual Violence and American Indian Genocide* (2005), winner of the Gustavas Myers Outstanding Book Award, and *Native Americans and the Christian Right: The Gendered Politics of Unlikely Alliances* (2008) as well as numerous articles. She is the co-founder of INCITE! Women of Color Against Violence and the Boarding School Healing Project.

Jennifer Stinson is a practicing psychologist at Pacific Clinics in Pasadena, California.

Andrea Townsend was an 11th grade student at Franklin High School in Portland, Oregon, when she wrote the poem "Woman."

Agnes Williams (Seneca) is a mother of three daughters, grandmother of four; daughter, sister, and auntie living in the occupied territory of Western New York State on the Cattaraugus Indian Reservation near Irving. Agnes's daughter Josie contributed the title to the article, "The Great Janet McCloud." Agnes is a founding mother and on the Advisory Board of the Indigenous Women's Network, a Women of All Red Nations central committee member, and currently organizes for the Indigenous Women's Initiatives of Buffalo, New York, a project of the Grand Island, NY-Riverside Salem United Church of Christ. The IWI empowers indigenous women, their families, communities, and nations by applying indigenous values to contemporary settings supporting projects that encourage sustainable life ways by recognizing and strengthening leadership capacities across generations. Agnes is a licensed Master in Social Work consulting with the Native American Community Services, also of Buffalo.

L. Susan Williams is an Associate Professor of Sociology at Kansas State University who specializes in gender and inequality. Dr. Williams's studies of adolescent girls in Connecticut and Kansas document the effect of local milieus on life decisions of individual girls, examining ways in which various groups "try on gender." More recently, Dr. Williams's research focused on youth and gendered violence, resulting in a comprehensive study of incarcerated girls and boys.

Cathy Winkler is an anthropologist and rape-survivor activist in Virginia. She is the author of *One Night: Realities of Rape*.

Nellie Wong is a poet and feminist activist who lives in San Francisco. Her books include *Dreams in Harrison Railroad Park; The Death of Long Steam Lady; Stolen Moments*; with Merle Woo and Mitsuye Yamada, *Three Asian American Women Speak Out on Feminism*; and with Yolanda Allinez, *Voices of Color*.

Helen Zia is an award-winning journalist and activist. She is the former Executive Editor for *Ms.* and the author of *Asian American Dreams: The Emergence of a People* (2001) and coauthor (with Wen Ho Li) of *My Country Versus Me* (2003). She holds an honorary Doctor of Laws degree from the Law School of the City University of New York and was named one of the most influential Asian Americans of the decade by *A. Magazine*.

Lila Zucker is a sociology major at the University of Washington, Seattle. She is actively involved with Jobs with Justice in Portland, Oregon, and Seattle, Washington. She is dedicated to social justice and activism, especially the labor movement. She began organizing at age 14 when she became involved with the anti-war movement. She has also been involved with labor, economic, and global justice issues and has written as the labor beat reporter for a local newspaper.